KT-463-111

# MARITIME LAW

## FIFTH EDITION

**LLOYD'S PRACTICAL SHIPPING GUIDES**

Other titles in this series are:

*Chartering Documents*
3rd edition
by Harvey Williams

*The Hague and Hague-Visby Rules*
4th edition
by John Richardson

*Introduction to P&I*
2nd edition
by Chris Hill,
Bill Robertson
and Steven Hazelwood

*Laytime and Demurrage in the Oil Industry*
by Malcolm Edkins and Ray Dunkley

*Marine Claims*
2nd edition
by Christof Luddeke

*Maritime Law*
5th edition
by Chris Hill

*Multimodal Transport: Avoiding Legal Problems*
edited by Diana Faber

*Neil Cockett on Bunkers*
by Neil Cockett

# MARITIME LAW

BY

CHRISTOPHER HILL

MA(Oxon) FICS

FIFTH EDITION

LONDON HONG KONG
1998

LLP Reference Publishing
69–77 Paul Street
London EC2A 4LQ
Great Britain

EAST ASIA
LLP Asia
Sixth Floor, Hollywood Centre
233 Hollywood Road
Hong Kong

First published in Great Britain 1981
Revised reprint 1984
Second edition 1985
Third edition 1989
Fourth edition 1995
Fifth edition 1998


*British Library Cataloguing in Publication Data*
A catalogue record
for this book is available
from the British Library.

ISBN 1–85978–836–X



Text set in 10/11 Plantin by
Interactive Sciences Ltd
Gloucester
Printed in Great Britain by
MPG Books,
Bodmin, Cornwall

# PREFACE

A customary gap of approximately five years between editions has been shortened this time to roughly two years which should logically mean that there should be only two fifths of the customary volume of updating to weave into this latest edition. However, it is not that simple and the amount of work which my two self-sacrificing and devoted helpers (Alison Shaw-Lloyd, a solicitor and partner of Lewis Moore & Co., and Lewis Moore himself) and I have had to put into this revision has been as great as for the previous edition.

In attending to the chapter on charterparties which is under my personal care, I have accounted for the latest (1996) version of the Inter-Club Agreement and have extended the commentary on maritime arbitration particularly to include a summary of the more significant provisions of the 1996 Arbitration Act. Recent pertinent cases have been woven into the text throughout the chapter and a fresh commentary made upon the subject of repudiation of a charterparty contract. Another fresh feature is a description of trip charters which can be found at the beginning of the chapter.

The Merchant Shipping Act 1995, which has taken effect in England since the previous edition was printed, has been introduced into those chapters to which it relates. Being a consolidating Act, it casts its net widely over various subjects dealt with in this book, e.g. Chapter 1 (ownership/registration), Chapter 7 and Chapter 10. The chapter on salvage has been updated by the addition of the latest case law (in particular the *Nagasaki Spirit*) and by a mention of the latest version (1995) of LOF. Collisions similarly has been enlarged by recent and relevant case law.

The chapter to receive probably the most attention in the updating process is Chapter 4 (Admiralty Jurisdiction etc.) where recent cases have been added and the increasing interrelation of European Community Law and English Admiralty Law has necessitated an enlargement of the chapter with greater attention to detail.

The chapter on pollution has been updated by introducing a commentary on the 1992 Convention (which, in many countries, has replaced the 1969 Civil Liability Convention) and also the 1992 Fund Convention which has replaced the 1971 Convention. TOVALOP and CRISTAL have been relegated to recent past history as both those industrial schemes came to an end in February 1997.

The chapter on Harbour and Docks which has had a place in the book since it was first written has in this edition been dropped. I felt that it had little interest for the vast majority of readers since the very nature of its subject-matter was that it was only concerned with domestic English law and the reality of this book is that over the years it has gradually transformed from being very largely an English maritime law text into a text which incorporates and comments as much upon International Conventions and internationally flavoured agreements as on pure English law.

The law in this edition is as stated at 1 October 1997.

To conclude, I acknowledge, as in previous editions, with gratitude the valuable work done by my secretary, Mrs Irene Edwards, in the preparation of this edition. She has done it with her characteristic good humour. Alison would like to express her sincere gratitude to her secretary, Mrs Vi Rayment, particularly when faced with typing additions/amendments after some weekend work.

My thanks are also due to Matthew Vafidis of Haight Gardner Holland and Knight, San Francisco and Charles Whited of Murphy Rogers and Sloss, New Orleans, both of whom have given me useful hints and suggestions for updating and improving the American law section of the Pollution chapter.

CHRISTOPHER HILL

# CONTENTS

## Contents

# ABBREVIATIONS

| | | |
|---|---|---|
| AC | Appeal Cases (3rd series) | 1891–Current |
| All ER | All England Reports | 1936–Current |
| AMC | American Maritime Cases | Current |
| App Cas | Appeal Cases (2nd series) | 1875–1890 |
| Asp MLC | Aspinall's Maritime Law Cases | 1871–1940 |
| B & Ald | Barnewall and Alderson | 1817–1822 |
| Bos & P | Bosanquet and Puller | 1796–1804 |
| CA | Court of Appeal | |
| Ch | Chancery Division | |
| Ch Rob | Christopher Robinson (Admiralty) | 1799–1808 |
| CPD | Common Pleas Division | 1875–1880 |
| De G & J | De Gex and Jones | 1857–1860 |
| E & B | Ellis and Blackburn | 1851–1858 |
| ELD | Italian Law Reports | Current |
| Ex | Exchequer Reports | 1847–1856 |
| H & C | Hurlstone & Coltman | 1862–1866 |
| Hag Adm | Haggard (Admiralty) | 1822–1838 |
| HL | House of Lords | |
| IMO | International Maritime Organizations (formerly IMCO) | |
| KB | King's Bench | 1901–1952 |
| LJ | Law Journal Reports | 1831–1949 |
| LJCP | Law Journal Reports (Common Pleas) | 1831–1880 |
| LJP | Law Journal Reports (Probate, Divorce and Admiralty) | 1831–1949 |
| Ll.L.Rep | Lloyd's List Law Reports | 1919–1950 |
| Lloyd's Rep | Lloyd's Law Reports | 1950–Current |
| LR A & E | Admiralty and Ecclesiastical Cases | 1865–1875 |
| LR CP | Common Pleas Cases | 1865–1875 |
| LR HL | English and Irish Appeals | 1866–1875 |
| LR QB | Queen's Bench | 1865–1875 |
| LR Eq | Equity Cases | 1866–1875 |
| LT | Law Times Reports | 1859–1947 |
| Lush | Lushington (Admiralty) | 1859–1862 |
| M & W | Meeson & Welsby | 1836–1847 |
| Moo PC | E. F. Moore | 1836–1862 |

## Abbreviations

| | | |
|---|---|---|
| P | Probate Division (3rd series) | 1891–Current |
| PC | Privy Council | |
| PD | Probate Division (2nd series) | 1875–1890 |
| QB | Queen's Bench | 1891–Current |
| QBD | Queen's Bench Division | 1875–1890 |
| RSC | Rules of the Supreme Court | |
| SI | Statutory Instrument | |
| S & S | *Schip en Schade* (Dutch Law Reports) | Current |
| TLR | Times Law Reports | 1884–1952 |
| WLR | Weekly Law Reports | 1953–Current |

# TABLE OF CASES

[Page numbers printed in **bold** indicate *either* where text from a case is quoted *or* where the facts of a particular case are set out]

# TABLE OF LEGISLATION

[Page numbers printed in **bold** indicate where text is set out]

# TABLE OF INTERNATIONAL CONVENTIONS

[Page numbers printed in **bold** indicate where text is set out]

CHAPTER 1

# OWNERSHIP AND REGISTRATION

## OWNERSHIP

What constitutes absolute ownership of the thing, whether it be goods or a ship, has been the subject of much discussion since the beginning of time. Some define ownership simply as the possession of the absolute right to sell the thing, the right to enjoy quiet and uninterrupted possession of it. These are certainly facets of true ownership and indeed are reflected in the historical legal maxim, nemo dat quod non habet, a free translation of which could be 'no one can pass to another a title which is not his to give'. Clearly the vendor of anything, be it goods or a ship or land, can only effectively pass to another person the rights which he himself possesses. With land it is all-important that the title should be traced back as far and as carefully as possible so that the purchaser can satisfy himself as far as is humanly possible that his title is as unshakable as it can be made. Even freeholders of real property can never be absolutely sure that their title is good as against 'all the world'. When property passes from hand to hand it is usually, but not always, as the result of a commercial agreement supported by consideration to bind the exchange of promises into a contract enforceable at law. A total failure of consideration on either side will abort the contract and prevent the passing of property.

Evidence of ownership must necessarily largely rest on documents and, in the case of vessels, regard will be had to relevant entries in the port of registry or to executed bills of sale but this must nevertheless be necessarily prima facie evidence only, displaceable by more positive proof to the contrary. (The bill of sale under which the ownership of British ships is transferred is in no way connected with or affected by the Bills of Sale Acts.)

*The Horlock* (1877) 2 PD 243
In an action re co-ownership, it was alleged that A by process of bill of sale was registered as sole owner of the ship and that subsequently another bill of sale was executed to B, the plaintiff, who acquired the same property for value. A denied that he had signed the bill of sale and contended that if any such bill of sale was registered it was done so fraudulently.

*Held:* that as legal ownership had passed to B for valuable consideration by the execution and registration of a bill of sale without notice of fraud, B had acquired a good title.

A total failure of consideration in a commercial transaction can render a prospective new shipowner powerless to become effectively the true new owner no matter how strenuous and meticulous his efforts in completing the formal re-registration and allied statutory documentation required of a shipowner on his own behalf. How the shipping laws of the United Kingdom can in certain circumstances complicate such situations will be seen later when sale of ships is discussed.

### *Co-ownership*

Co-owners are of two classes. (1) *Joint owners*, in whom are vested the property in a ship or a share therein jointly with unity of title and no distinction of interest. (2) *Part owners* or *co-owners* properly so-called, in whom is vested severally distinct shares in the ship, but with an undivided interest in the whole.

The former are *joint tenants* of the property held, the latter are *tenants in common* with each other of their respective shares. Normally the relations of the co-owners inter se are regulated by express agreement; the management of the ship being delegated to a ship's manager or husband who may or may not be a part owner. Where, however, there is no agreement, their rights inter se are governed, at any rate in English law, by the principle that the will of the majority must prevail, provided that the interests of the dissenting minority can be properly protected. The power of sale will be exercised, though with reluctance, even on the application of a minority of part owners.

Since very early days, a ship has been notionally divided into 64 parts. Nobody really knows the reason, except possibly the obvious and practical one that dealings in and transfers of ships are simplified.

A person, or corporation, may own more than one part, but it is not practical (though perfectly possible) for more than one person to own one part. If more persons than one do own a single part, they must be regarded as joint owners in the undivided part and not as several owners of separate fractions.

A corporation may be registered as owner under its corporate name and the formation of a limited liability company is common practice in the ship-owning business. Where a ship's owner is such a corporate entity, she is registered under its corporate name and not under the names of each individual shareholder in the company.

*Part owners* are not necessarily partners in a business in the legal sense. They will almost certainly be partners in individual ventures in which the ship may be engaged from time to time, share in profits and losses, and be mutually obliged to honour liabilities incurred by the ship's manager, who may or may not be a servant or employee of the owner. Although the name of such a manager must be registered, the registration does not have the drastic effect per se of making the 64 part owners fully responsible for the mass of obligations which a vessel finds herself facing in the course of her working career. The authority extended to the manager must exist independently of the formal register. Whereas he will almost certainly have implied authority to arrange employment for the ship by way of charter or other form of contract, his authority will not extend to altering or cancelling them. For reasons of seizing profitable opportunities for the timely employment of the ship at short notice it may not always be possible for the prior consent of all part owners to be obtained before a contract needs to be concluded. A dissentient minority's rights can be protected by bond under the provisions of section 20(2)(b) of the Supreme Court Act 1981 (see further page 117 *et seq, post*).

### *Ownership and registration*

The notion of 64 shares is expressed in the Merchant Shipping (Registration of Ships) Regulations 1993 which came into force on 21 March 1994. Regulation 2(5) states that entries in the Register are made in accordance with the following provisions, which are summarised:

(a) the property in a ship shall be divided into 64 shares;
(b) not more than 64 persons shall be entitled to be registered at the same time as owners of any one ship;
(c) a person shall not be entitled to be registered as owner of a part of a share; but any number of persons not exceeding five may be registered as joint owners of a ship or of any share or shares in a ship;
(d) joint owners shall be considered as constituting one person only as regards the persons entitled to be registered and shall not be entitled to dispose in severalty of any interest in a ship or in any share in a ship in respect of which they are registered.

The Merchant Shipping Acts 1894 to 1994 have been consolidated by the Merchant Shipping Act 1995 (which came into force on 1 January 1996). By virtue of the Interpretation Act 1978, s.17(2)(b) regulations made under the repealed legislation are continued in force unless otherwise stated. By virtue of the Merchant Shipping Act 1995, s.314 and Sched. 14, para. 2 any references in any other Act (not amended by the 1995 Act, Sched. 13), or in any instrument made under any other Act to the registration of a ship or a fishing vessel under certain enactments is construed, unless the context otherwise requires, as, or as including, a reference to registration under the 1995 Act, Pt. II (ss.8–23). Sections 9 and 10 provide for registration regulations for and in connection with the registration of ships as British ships. No regulations pursuant to this Act have been made and the 1993 Regulations are still in force, although the 1993 Act (below) has been repealed. Minor amendments and corrections were made to those regulations by the Merchant Shipping (Registration of Ships) (Amendment) Regulations 1994 (SI 1994 No 541).

### *Who can own a British ship?*

Ships are potentially the means by which their owners can incur liabilities to third parties—sometimes of catastrophic proportions. It is, therefore, logical that ships should be given a nationality so that their owners' obligations, duties, rights, liabilities, immunities etc, can the more easily be regulated and recognized. In short, ships should and do fly a national flag.

The qualifications for ownership of a British-registered ship were set out in section 1 of the Merchant Shipping Act 1894. The prerequisites for the registration of a British ship then underwent a change due to the coming into effect of Part I of the Merchant Shipping Act 1988 on 1 April 1989. The Merchant Shipping (Registration, etc) Act 1993 received the Royal Assent on

1 July 1993 ('1993' Act). The Act arose from the report by the General Council of British Shipping and the Department of Transport Joint Working Party entitled *British Shipping: Challenges and Opportunities.*

The 1993 Act came into force on 21 March 1994 (The Merchant Shipping (Registration, etc) Act 1993 (Commencement No 1 and Transitional Provisions) Order 1993—1993 No 3137). There was a saving in respect of vessels currently registered which might otherwise cease to be eligible to be registered by reason of any change in qualification for ownership. Detailed provisions relating to ship registration are contained in the Merchant Shipping (Registration of Ships) Regulations 1993 which also came into force on 21 March 1994 ('1993 Regulations').

The 1993 Act and 1993 Regulations principally came about due to the impact of the EC and the Factortame litigation (see below) and replaced the law relating to ship registration contained in the 1894 and 1988 Acts. The Merchant Shipping (Registration etc) Act 1993 was, however, repealed in its entirety by the Merchant Shipping Act 1995. The previous position leading up to these recent developments is quite important at least to show the gradual evolution away from the idea of the British Empire. The European Community is very important and has brought about many changes to English law.

### *Historical development*

In the old 1894 statute (s.1), it was provided that in the case of corporations or duly registered companies owning ships (this method of ownership is these days by far the most common) these must have their principal place of business in Her Majesty's dominions.

*The Polzeath* [1916] P 241, CA
A ship was owned by a company which was registered in the UK that was in fact controlled from Hamburg by the Chairman of Directors, who held the majority of shares and resided there. Proceedings were instituted for forfeiture of the ship.

*Held*: that the principal place of business was not in His Majesty's Dominion and, therefore, the ship was forfeit to the Crown.

*The Polzeath* ruling appears then to have interpreted 'principal place of business' as meaning that place from where the *effective* control was maintained. A 'British' ship would seem, therefore, to have been one owned by British interests with the 'double' requirement that, if owned by a company, the company should not only be registered within Her Majesty's Dominions, but also have its principal place of business there. Unless the ship was thus a 'British' ship, she could not fly the British flag. There has, nevertheless, been nothing to prevent British shipowners taking advantage of the flag of convenience system described later in this chapter.

The Victorian-origin section 1 of the 1894 Act was replaced by the Merchant Shipping Act 1988. The purpose was to dissolve the imperial concept which had lingered on in the 1894 Act. That part of the 1988 Act which dealt with registration of ocean vessels became effective in the UK on 1 April 1989 and in many of the dependent territories even sooner than that. It should be borne in mind that the 1894 and 1988 Acts have been consolidated with consequential repeals by the Merchant Shipping Act 1995. The 1988 Act brought about the following fundamental changes:

(1) Under the old Victorian legislation the UK was capable of forcing its maritime law on dependent territories. In other words, whether it liked it or not and whether it had the administrative capability or not, a colony was obliged to register a British ship. The 1988 Act prevented this by bringing about the complete domestication of the 1894 Act and confining its effects to the mainland UK. This makes sound sense in the modern world where the dominions such as Canada, Australia or New Zealand are totally independent with an absolute right to 'shut the door' on British shipowners. The same may be said of some colonial territories.

(2) Under the old 1988 Act, there was no longer an obligation to register. It was an entitlement. The 1988 Act removed the compulsory nature of registration and thus also the exempted categories and it made registration an entitlement providing that the person applying for it can exhibit the required qualifications. This gave recognition to what is already the custom that British owners are not barred from seeking other registries, i.e. 'flagging out'. Thus a definition of a British ship changed from being one which, owned by British subjects or corporate persons, is *obliged* to be registered, to one of which the majority interest is owned by persons qualified to own a British ship and is *actually* so registered.

One of the prerequisites of the entitlement to register under the 1988 Act was that the majority interest in the ship shall be owned by a qualified person or persons and if those persons are not UK residents, then a representative person must be appointed who, if an individual person, must be a UK resident, if a corporate body, must be incorporated in the UK and have its principal place of business there—a double 'prerequisite'. The above requirements seem to be directed towards ships over 24 metres in length (as defined by the 1894 tonnage rules) and although this is not entirely clear, it would seem that ships of a lesser length than 24 metres may qualify in their own right as British ships, providing they are not fishing vessels, are not registered under the Merchant Shipping Act 1983 and are *wholly* owned by qualified persons.

There was a minor distinction between the prerequisite for entitlement to register where the applicant is within categories (see below) 1–4 inclusive and where he is within 5–7 inclusive. For those in categories 1–4 their entitlement is absolute with the only proviso being that if the vessel is more than 24 metres long and *none* of those qualified to own shares is a UK resident, a 'representative' person must be appointed. Under categories 5–7 the entitlement is also absolute, but with a somewhat more onerous proviso that if none of the qualified owners is resident in the UK, the Secretary of State's consent must be obtained *and* a representative person appointed. Where the ownership is spread between *both* categories but neither has an overall majority shareholding, entitlement is absolute with the proviso that if none are resident, a representative person must be appointed.

## Ownership and registration

Under the 1988 regime there are seven categories of persons who are entitled to register a British ship, six of them individual persons and one a corporate person. These were:

(1) A British citizen;
(2) citizens of British dependent territories which include Isle of Man, Guernsey, Jersey, Hong Kong, Gibraltar, Bermuda, Cayman Islands, St. Helena, the Falkland Islands, the British Virgin Islands, Montserrat, Anguilla, the Turks and Caicos Islands;
(3) persons who under the Hong Kong (British Nationality) Order 1986 are classed as British Nationals (Overseas);
(4) corporate persons incorporated in the UK or in any relevant overseas territory (these are the Isle of Man, any Channel Island and any British Colony) which have their principal place of business in the UK or any such territory (principal place of business being determined as before by applying *The Polzeath* doctrine); and/or
(5) British overseas citizens;
(6) persons who under the British Nationality Act 1981 are British subjects; and
(7) citizens of the Irish Republic.

A representative person is either an individual or corporate entity. If the latter, it must have the dual feature of being incorporated and having its principal place of business in the UK. If the former, the person must be resident in the UK. The definition of an individual resident is that he is living and sleeping in the UK for a major part of the year, or, if he is a resident in the UK for tax purposes, he will be deemed as being resident for the purpose of the application of the Merchant Shipping Act 1988. These are the basic requirements and the Secretary of State has power to impose additional requirements if he thinks fit.

As an example, a ship's manager registered under section 59(2) of the Merchant Shipping Act 1894 should satisfy the requirement. A 'representative' person once appointed does not automatically become redundant if one of the qualified owners subsequently becomes a UK resident and therefore capable of taking on that role himself, the role being mainly that of a person within the jurisdiction upon whom legal papers in connection with criminal proceedings may be served. Such substitution would need to be positively done. In the reverse, i.e. where owners who previously were residents cease to be resident, the entitlement to register would be undermined as the ship at the time registered would be exposed to become removed from the registry unless a representative person satisfying the requirement was appointed.

Part II of the 1988 Act was concerned with the registration of British fishing vessels which are defined (s.12) as 'vessels for the time being used or in the context of an application for registration intended to be used for fishing otherwise than for profit'. Thus a yacht does not become a fishing vessel merely because its owner spends an afternoon lazily fishing for mackerel off the British south coast. The 1988 Act and the Merchant Shipping (Registration of Fishing Vessels) Regulations 1988 established a new register of all British fishing vessels including those registered in the old register maintained under the 1894 Act. Only fishing vessels fulfilling the conditions laid down in section 14 of the 1988 Act could be registered in the register.

A fishing vessel was eligible to be registered only if the vessel was British owned, the vessel was managed and its operations were directed and controlled from within the UK and any charterer, manager or operator of the vessel was a qualified person or company, i.e. a British citizen resident and domiciled in the UK or a company incorporated in the UK and having its principal place of business there. The 1988 Act and the 1988 Regulations came into force on 1 December 1988 but the validity of registrations effected under the previous Act were extended for a transitional period until 31 March 1989. These provisions gave rise to the complex *Factortame* litigation in which various questions were referred by the High Court to the European Court of Justice.

*R.* v *Secretary of State for Transport, ex parte Factortame Limited and Others (No 3)* European Court of Justice [1991] 2 Lloyd's Rep. 648.

A number of companies including Factortame Limited were incorporated under the laws of the UK and the directors and shareholders of those companies were mostly Spanish nationals. The companies owned or operated 95 fishing vessels which until 31 March 1989 were registered as British fishing vessels under the Merchant Shipping Act 1894. These vessels failed to satisfy one or more of the conditions for registration under the 1988 Act and the 1988 Regulations and failed to qualify as British fishing vessels. The plaintiffs sought a declaration that Part II of the 1988 Act should not apply to them on the grounds that such application would be contrary to Community law in particular Articles 7, 52, 58 and 221 of the EEC Treaty. They sought an order prohibiting the Secretary of State from treating the existing registration of their vessels (under the 1894 Act) as having ceased from 1 April 1989 and damages.

*Held*: (inter alia) that as Community law stood at present it was for the Member State to determine in accordance with the general rules of international law, the conditions which had to be fulfilled in order for a vessel to be registered in their registers and granted the right to fly their flag but in exercising that power the Member State had to comply with the rules of Community law. The fact that a competent minister of a Member State had the power to dispense with the nationality requirement in respect of an individual in view of the length of time such individual had resided in that Member State and had been involved in the fishing industry of that Member State could not justify in regard to Community law the rule under which registration of a fishing vessel was subject to a nationality requirement and a requirement as to residence and domicile. It is contrary to the provisions of Community law and, in particular, to Article 52 of the EEC Treaty for a Member State to stipulate conditions as to the nationality, residence and domicile for registration of a fishing vessel.

The *Factortame* litigation meant that the general entitlement to registration on the British register had to be reformulated and gave rise to the 1993 Act (since repealed) and 1993 Regulations.

### *The Merchant Shipping (Registration etc) Act 1993*

This Act received the Royal Assent on 1 July 1993 and most of the provisions came into force on 21 March 1994 (SI 1993 No 3137). There was a saving in respect of vessels currently registered which might otherwise cease to be eligible to be registered by reason of any change in qualifications for ownership. As the Merchant Shipping (Registration etc) Act 1993 was wholly repealed by the

Merchant Shipping Act 1995, reference below to its provisions are of historical interest. Detailed provisions relating to registration are contained in the Merchant Shipping (Registration of Ships) Regulations 1993 which also came into force on 21 March 1994.

Registration was still an entitlement not an obligation. There was a fixed five-year period of registration which was renewable. Section 2 of the 1993 Act and Part III of the 1993 Regulations set out the qualification and entitlement for registration of British vessels on Part I of the register (i.e. not small ships, fishing vessels or bareboat chartered ships).

The following persons are qualified to be the owners of ships registered on Part I of the register (Reg. 7):

- (a) British citizens or persons who are nationals of a Member State other than the UK and are established (within the meaning of Article 52 of the EEC Treaty) in the UK;
- (b) British dependent territories citizens;
- (c) British overseas citizens;
- (d) Persons who under the British Nationality Act 1981(a) are British subjects:
- (e) Persons who under the Hong Kong (British Nationality) Order 1986(a) are British nationals (overseas);
- (f) Bodies corporate incorporated in a Member State;
- (g) Bodies corporate incorporated in any relevant British possession and having their principal place of business in the UK or in any such possession; and
- (h) European economic interest groupings being groupings formed in pursuance of Article 1 of Council Regulation (EEC) No. 2137/85(b) and registered in the UK.

A ship is entitled to be registered if the majority interest in the ship is owned by one or more persons qualified to be owners of British ships unless the Registrar refused registration (Reg. 36(4)). One or more persons shall be treated as owning a majority interest in a ship if there is vested in that person or in those persons, taken together, the legal title to 33 or more shares in the ship (there being left out of account for this purpose any share in which any beneficial interest is owned by a person who is not entitled to be an owner of a British ship). The person or persons holding the majority interest must be resident in the UK (if (a), (b), (e), (f) or (h) above applies). Where this condition is not satisfied then a representative person must be appointed under Part V. If the majority interest is owned by persons in categories (c) and (d) above the ship shall be registered only if the person is resident in the UK or if the Secretary of State furnishes a declaration that he consents to the ship being registered and in addition a representative person is appointed in relation to the ship. A representative person is either an individual resident in the UK or a body corporate incorporated in a Member State and having a place of business in the UK (Part V). With regard to a majority interest owned by a company ((g) above) the ship shall be registered only if the body corporate has a place of business in the UK or where that condition is not satisfied, if a representative person is appointed in relation to the ship. A body corporate shall be treated as resident in the UK if, being a body incorporated in a Member State, it has a place of business in the UK (Regs. 8 and 9). Government ships are excluded from these regulations and a fishing vessel cannot be registered on Part I of the register.

Part IV of the 1993 Regulations deals with the qualification and entitlement of British fishing vessels to be registered on Part II of the register. The following persons are qualified to be owners of fishing vessels (Reg. 12):

(a) British citizens or persons who are nationals of a Member State other than the UK and are established (within the meaning of Article 52 of the EEC Treaty) in the UK;
(b) Bodies corporate incorporated in a Member State with a place of business in the UK;
(c) European economic interest groupings being groupings formed in pursuance of Article 1 of Council Regulation (EEC) No. 2137/85 and registered in the UK; and
(d) A local authority in the UK.

Normally eligibility for registration depends upon the whole legal and beneficial title being vested in qualified owners listed above who, if non-resident, must appoint a representative person (see Part V of the 1993 Regulations). A fishing vessel cannot be registered unless it is managed and its operations controlled and directed from within the UK and any charterer, manager or operator of the vessel is a qualified owner. Therefore, these Regulations only followed the parts of section 14(1) of the 1988 Act which were not ruled invalid by the European Court of Justice decision in the *Factortame* case. If a false statement is given to the Registrar regarding any matter relevant to British connection then an offence is committed (1993 Act, s.7).

### *Merchant Shipping Act 1995*

This statute contains the current British law on, inter alia:

(1) Entitlement to register.
(2) Qualifications and pre-conditions for a ship to gain British registration.
(3) Machinery for registration.

### *Entitlement*

Registration of a British ship is still an entitlement and not an obligation.

Section 1(1) provides, inter alia, that a ship is a British ship if:

(a) the ship is registered in the United Kingdom under Part II; or
(c) the ship is registered under the law of a relevant British possession; or
(d) the ship is a small ship other than a fishing vessel and certain conditions in s.1(1)(i)–(iii) are complied with.

Section 9(1) provides that a ship is entitled to be registered and an application for registration is duly made if:

(a) it is owned, to the prescribed extent, by persons qualified to own British ships; and
(b) such other conditions are satisfied as are prescribed under s.9(2)(b) below.

Section 9(2) provides that it shall be for registration regulations:

(a) to determine the persons who are qualified to be owners of British ships of any class or description, and to prescribe the extent of the ownership required for compliance with subsection (1)(a) above;
(b) to prescribe other requirements designed to secure that, taken in conjunction with the requisite ownership, only ships having a British connection are registered.

Section 10(1) provides that the Secretary of State shall, by registration regulations, make provision for and in connection with the registration of ships as British ships. Such regulations, by virtue of s.10(2), may make provision, in particular, for

(b) the information and evidence (including declarations of British connection) to be provided on such application;
(c) the shares and the property in, and the numbers of owners (including joint owners) of, a ship permitted for the purposes of registration. . .;
(g) the period for which registration is to remain effective without renewal.

Reference is also made to the other subsections of section 10(2) and these are set out in full in the Appendix to this chapter. No regulations have been made following the 1995 Act and the 1993 Regulations (as amended in 1994) are still in force.

### *Port of registry*

Until the 1993 Act followed by the Merchant Shipping Act 1995 and the 1993 Regulations the owners had freedom to choose the port of registry. All information relating to the ship was entered in the register at the port selected. Where a share (or shares) in a ship was owned by more than one person (or a corporation) and that share (or shares) has more than five legal owners, only five names of such owners could appear in the register as the owners of such share (or shares). Under the old Merchant Shipping Act 1988 (Schedule 1) any officer appointed by the Commissioner of Customs and Excise for that purpose in any UK port could act as registrar. The registrar was not liable in damages or for any loss accruing to any person by reason of any act done or default made by him in his character as registrar unless this happened through his neglect or wilful act.

### *Central register of British ships*

A major administrative change was brought about by the 1993 Act and Regulations in that a central register for ships in the UK was established under the control of the Registrar General of Shipping and Seamen. This computerized central registry is maintained by the Registrar General of Shipping and Seamen and the traditional ports of registry around the country no longer have any administration purpose.

However, the person applying for registration can specify one port as their port of choice as listed in Schedule 2, Part I of the 1993 Regulations and this chosen port will appear on the vessel's stern. All existing registrations have been transferred to the central register which is divided into four parts, Part I (British ships which are not fishing vessels or small ships), Part II (fishing vessels), Part III (small ships) and Part IV (bareboat charter ships registered under section 7 of the Act). No ship may be registered on more than one part of the register at any one time (Reg. 5), including a small ship.

Section 8 of the Merchant Shipping Act of 1995 provides that there shall continue to be a Register of British Ships in the United Kingdom maintained by the Registrar General of Shipping and Seamen as Registrar. The register is divided into Part I for ships (owned by qualified persons) which are not fishing vessels or registered on that part which is restricted to small ships; Part II for fishing vessels; Part III for small ships, and Part IV for bareboat charter ships. The register shall be maintained in accordance with registration regulations, private provisions for registered ships and any directions given by the Secretary of State. Section 8 of the 1995 Act is to be found in the Appendix to this chapter.

Section 1(2) of the Merchant Shipping Act 1995 defines a 'small ship' as a ship less than 24 metres in length ('length' having the same meaning as in the tonnage regulations). Section 23 of the 1995 Act (interpretation section) states: 'The Registrar means the Registrar General of Shipping and Seamen in his capacity as Registrar or, as respects functions of his being discharged by another authority or person, that authority or person'.

Section 313 of the 1995 Act (definitions) provides 'fishing vessel' means 'a vessel for the time being used (or, in the context of an application for registration, intended to be used) for, or in connection with fishing for sea fish other than a vessel used (or intended to be used) for fishing otherwise than for profit'. No ship, including a small ship may be registered on more than one part of the register at any one time.

Every application for registration must be made to the Registrar of the General Registry of Shipping and Seamen although applications in respect of fishing vessels may also be made through a local office.

Part VI of the 1993 Regulations details the documents needed and the form of application for registration. Regulation 22 states that every application must be supported by a declaration of eligibility in a form approved by the Secretary of State and must include:

(a) a declaration of British connection;
(b) a declaration of ownership by every owner setting out his qualification to own a British ship;
(c) a statement of the number of shares in the ship the legal title of which is vested in each owner whether alone or jointly with any other person or persons; and

(d) in respect of an application to register a fishing vessel, a statement of the beneficial ownership of any share which is not beneficially owned by its legal owner.

An application by a body corporate must be accompanied by documents such as a certificate of incorporation (Reg. 24). Regulation 28 states that an application to register a ship for the first time other than an application in respect of a fishing vessel requiring simple registration must be supported by the following evidence of title:

(a) In the case of a new ship, the builder's certificate.
(b) In the case of a ship which is not new, either
 (i) in respect of a ship other than a fishing vessel
  (a) a previous bill or bills of sale showing the ownership of the ship for at least five years before the application is made, or
  (b) if the ship has been registered with a full registration at any time within the last five years, a bill or bills of sale evidencing all transfers of ownership during the period since it was so registered, or
 (ii) in respect of a fishing vessel
  (a) a previous bill or bills of sale showing the ownership of the vessel for at least three years before the application is made, or
  (b) if the ship has been registered with a full registration at any time within the last three years, a bill or bills of sale evidencing all transfers of ownership during the period since it was so registered, or
  (c) evidence that the vessel has been for at least three years continuously registered as a British fishing vessel with simple registration in the names of the owners applying to be registered and remains so registered.
(c) Where the evidence required by (a) or (b) above is not available, other evidence of title satisfactory to the Registrar.

Under Part II of the 1993 Regulations the Registrar is entitled, not obliged, to amend the register where either (a) a clerical error has occurred, or (b) sufficient evidence is produced to satisfy him that the entry is incorrect, and on making the amendment he shall issue a new certificate of registry if necessary. There is no provision by which the Registrar is obliged to pay any losses suffered by a person due to his rectification or refusal to rectify the register.

### *Marking requirements*

The 1993 Regulations provide detailed rules as to the marking of the vessels, particularly her name, official number, tonnage, port of choice and draught. Under Part XIII of the 1993 Regulations it is an offence on the part of the owner or master of a registered ship if any of the marks required by the Regulations to be marked on a ship is effaced, altered, allowed to become illegible, covered or concealed. The person charged with such offence will have a defence if he proves that (a) he took all reasonable precautions and exercised all due diligence to avoid the commission of the offence, or (b) that the effacing, alteration, covering or concealing of the marking was for the purpose of escaping capture by an enemy.

Under the 1993 Regulations the applicant has to obtain the Registrar's approval of a proposed name which basically should not be already the name of a registered British ship or so similar to that of a registered British ship as to be calculated to deceive or likely to confuse (or a vessel in the same port of choice for a fishing vessel). The name must not be confused with a distress signal and any prefix to the name must not cause confusion. The name must not cause offence or embarrassment and must not have a clear and direct connexion with the royal family. The ship must not be described by any name other than its registered name and a change shall not be made in a registered ship's name without the prior written permission of the Registrar (Reg. 30 and Schedule 1).

### *Refusal to register*

Under the 1988 Act (s.6) the Secretary of State was given powers to deny registration, even if the ship for the basic reasons is entitled, because of a discrepant condition which might adversely affect the safety of it and those on board or increase the chances of the ship causing pollution. It must be emphasized that there is no statutory compulsion to register.

Section 2(3) of the 1993 Act provided that the Registrar may, if registration regulations so provide, refuse to register a ship or terminate the registration of a ship if, having regard to any relevant requirement of the Merchant Shipping Acts, he considers it would be inappropriate for the ship to be or, as the case may be, to remain registered. The 1993 Regulations (Reg. 36 which is still in force) provide that if the Registrar is satisfied in respect of an application that:

(a) the ship is eligible to be registered as a British ship, and
(b) the ship has been duly carved and marked and that the appropriate survey or measuring certificate has been provided, and
(c) the particulars of the ship furnished to him are correct, and
(d) title to the ship has been adequately proved (where necessary), and
(e) the relevant requirements of these Regulations have been complied with,

he shall register the ship subject to his limited powers to refuse such registration. For instance, under Regulation 36(5) the Registrar, notwithstanding that a ship is otherwise entitled to be registered, may refuse to register it if, taking into account any requirement of the Merchant Shipping Acts (including any instrument made under them) relating to the condition of the ship or its equipment so far as it is relevant to its safety or to any risk of pollution or to the safety, health and welfare of persons employed or engaged in any capacity on board the ship, he considers that it would be inappropriate for the ship to be registered. Provision is made under section 14 of the Merchant Shipping Act 1995 for offences relating to the furnishing of information in connection with the decision whether to refuse registration or remove the ship from the register.

### *The certificate of registry*

The certificate of registry is sent to the owner of the ship on registration. Its main uses or purposes are:

(1) It is used in navigation and must be produced by the ship's Master on demand of, for example, an officer of Customs or an officer of Her Majesty's Navy; in fact section 13 of the Merchant Shipping Act 1995 provides: 'The certificate of registration of a British ship shall be used only for the lawful navigation of the ship, and shall not be subject to detention to secure any private right or claim';
(2) It is instrumental in helping to establish the identity of the shipowner;
(3) It is prima facie evidence that the vessel is British and can claim the privileges and be subject to the resulting obligation. N.B. It is no longer required that the certificate should contain the name of the Master.

The certificate must be surrendered if the ship is either actually or constructively lost, or is sold to a foreign person, or captured. Generally speaking, it should at all times be kept on board ship and may under no circumstances be used as security or to support a lien or claim. It may be used as prima facie evidence of ownership (see *Hibbs* v *Ross*, below), nationality (see *R* v *Bjornsen*, below) and tonnage (see *The Franconia*, below).

*Hibbs* v *Ross* (1866) LR 1 QB 534
A vessel was laid up in dock under the care of a custodian. A person was injured on board due to the custodian's negligence. The injured man instituted an action, naming as defendant the party whose name appeared in the Register as the ship's owner.

*Held*: that, in the absence of any positive evidence that the defendant appointed the custodian to guard the ship, the court was entitled to presume the custodian was employed by the defendant, thus establishing the defendant's vicarious liability.

*R* v *Bjornsen* (1865) 12 LT 473 CCR
A murder took place in a ship on the high seas. The ship flew the British flag, and the man accused of the crime was later taken to England and put on trial. In order to establish jurisdiction, evidence was put forward to prove the ship was British, including documents showing that the port of registration was London and that London was the place of business of the owner. However, overriding proof was produced that the owner was an alien (non-British), that the ship was foreign-built and that the officers and crew, including the accused man, were aliens.

*Held*: that although the registration was British, as shown in the registration certificate, this was prima facie evidence only of the ship's nationality and of the apparent British nationality of the owner. This presumption could be displaced by admissible evidence showing that the owner was in fact a foreigner.

*The Franconia* (1878) 3 PD 164, CA
The owners of a German ship commenced legal action under the provisions of the Merchant Shipping (Amendment) Act 1862 to limit their liability for damages resulting from a collision. The vessel was ordered to be measured and the tonnage entered in the register in the same fashion as British ships are required to record their tonnage with the crew space deducted.

*Held*: that the certificate was prima facie evidence of the ship's tonnage.

Any changes in the details given in the certificate must be promptly notified to the Registrar. Regulation 37 of the 1993 Regulations stipulates that upon registering a ship the Registrar shall issue and send to the owner a certificate of registry containing the particulars set out in Schedule 5 (see also s.10(2)(d) of the 1995 Act). These particulars include the full name and address of the owner, detailed information about the ship such as her name, IMO number, radio call sign, port of choice, official number, year of build, length, type of ship, gross net and registered tonnage, the date when the certificate is issued and when it expires.

A major change brought about by the 1993 Act (now repealed) and Regulations is that the registration of a ship shall, unless terminated under these Regulations, be valid for only five years beginning with the date of registration specified in the certificate of registry (Reg. 39). The 1995 Act provides that the Secretary of State shall by registration regulations, inter alia, make provision for the period for which registration is to remain effective without renewal. It will then expire unless it is renewed in accordance with Regulation 42. Registration is still an entitlement not an obligation (see the reference to entitlement in section 9 of the 1995 Act). This enables the Registrar to keep track of eligibility and other details. Three months before the expiry of the registration period the Registrar has to issue the owner with a renewal notice. An application for renewal by the owner during the last three calendar months of the current registration period must be accompanied by a declaration of eligibility and a declaration that there have been no changes to any registered details of the ship that have not been notified to the Registrar. Where no application for renewal is made the Registrar has to notify each and every mortgagee of the expiration of the ship's registration. Regulation 63 of the 1993 Regulations provides that a termination of registration 'shall not affect any entry in the register of any undischarged registered mortgage of that ship or of any share in it'. This does not apply to unregistered mortgages.

### *Transmission of ownership*

Apart from a commercial sale, a ship may change ownership by operation of law. In other words, a person may just suddenly find himself (or herself) owner of a ship.

Schedule 1 of the 1995 Act is headed 'Private Law Provisions for Registered Ships'. These are in force since 1 January 1996 by virtue of section 16 of the 1995 Act (previously the 1993 Act). It deals with proprietary rights in registered ships (which were previously contained in sections 24–38, 56–60 of the 1894 Act). These are supplemented by the 1993 Regulations. Section 16(2) of the 1995 Act provides that Schedule 1 does not apply in relation to ships which are excluded from its application by registration regulations under section 10(4)(a) of the 1995 Act. The 1993 Regulations have excluded these private law provisions in relation to small ships and to fishing vessels which opt for 'simple registration' as opposed to 'full registration'. 'Simple registration' is full registration but without the benefit of the private law provisions.

Paragraph 3(1) of Schedule 1 to the 1995 Act provides that where a registered ship or a share in a registered ship is transmitted to any person by any lawful means other than a transfer (mentioned below) and the ship continues to have a

British connection that person shall not be registered as owner of the ship or share unless (a) he has made the prescribed application to the Registrar and (b) the Registrar is satisfied that the ship retains a British connexion and that he would not refuse to register the ship.

If the application is granted the Registrar will enter the applicant's name as registered owner of the ship or share in the register. Regulation 46 of the 1993 Regulations provide that evidence shall be produced to the Registrar on an application for a registration of a transmission of a registered ship or share in a registered ship, as follows:

(a) if the transmission was consequent on death, the grant of representation or an office copy thereof or an extract therefrom;
(b) if the transmission was consequent on bankruptcy such evidence as is for the time being receivable in the courts of justice as proof of title of persons claiming under bankruptcy;
(c) if the transmission was consequent on an order of a court, a copy of the order or judgment of that court.

Regulation 47 provides that every application for the registration of a transfer or transmission of a registered ship or share therein shall be accompanied by a declaration of eligibility and if a body corporate is involved then various documents such as the certificate of incorporation are required (see Reg. 24). If on an application for transfer or transmission of a ship or shares in a ship the registrar is not satisfied that the ship is eligible to be registered, he must serve a notice on the owner of the ship, and the ship's registration will terminate at the end of the period of 14 days beginning with the date of the service of that notice (see Regulation 48).

Paragraph 4 of Schedule 1 to the 1995 Act provides that where the property in a registered ship or share therein is transmitted to any person by any lawful means other than a transfer but as a result the ship no longer has a British connection the High Court or the Court of Session may on application order a sale of the property so transmitted and direct that the proceeds of sale, after deducting the sale expenses shall be paid to the applicant or otherwise as the court directs. There are provisions regarding evidence in support of such application and time limits. If the court makes any order of sale then it shall contain a declaration vesting in the person the right to transfer the ship or share which has the same effect as if this person were the registered owner. The court can also make an order prohibiting for a specified time any dealing with the registered ship or share in a registered ship. Any order made by the court is binding on the Registrar once he has been served with a copy of any order (see also paragraphs 5 and 6 of Schedule 1 to the 1995 Act).

### *Transfer of ownership*

Paragraph 2(1) of Schedule 1 to the 1995 Act provides that any transfer of a registered ship, or a share in such a ship, shall be effected by a bill of sale satisfying the prescribed requirements, unless the transfer will result in the ship ceasing to have a British connexion. Even if a ship or share has been transferred in this manner, the transferee shall not be registered as owner of the ship or share unless he has made the prescribed application to the Registrar and the Registrar is satisfied that the ship retains a British connexion and he would not refuse to register the ship. If his application is granted the Registrar shall register the bill of sale and bills of sale are registered in the order in which they are produced to the Registrar for the purposes of registration (ss.2(2)(3) and (4)).

Regulations 43 and 44 of the 1993 Regulations provide that on application for registration of a transfer of a registered ship (or share) a bill of sale shall be produced to the Registrar although this is not necessary for registration of a transfer of a fishing vessel registered with simple registration, evidence of the transfer satisfactory to the Registrar being sufficient. The bill of sale must be in a form approved by the Secretary of State with appropriate attestation which contains a description of the ship sufficient to identify it. Under Regulation 45 the Registrar, if he grants the application for registration of transfer of a ship, shall (a) register the bill of sale by entering the name of the new owner in the register as owner of the ship or share in question, and (b) endorse on the bill of sale the fact that the entry has been made together with the date and time when it was made. The Registrar if he is satisfied with the evidence (of title on registration of transfer of ship) that the ship or share in a ship has been transferred will enter the name of the new owner in the Register and issue a new certificate which is valid for a period of five years.

The 1993 Regulations also deal with other matters such as refusal of registration of transfer or transmission, notification of changes of ownership, change in registered particulars of ship, change of name, transfer of port of choice, remarking of ship, and registration of changes of name or port of choice.

### *Removal from the register*

Under section 7 of the 1988 Act the Secretary of State had power to order the removal of a ship from the register either because of some default in its entitlement to register (e.g. all qualified owners moving their residence out of the UK), or because of some adverse physical condition of the ship perhaps prejudicing the safety of those on board. Other reasons for ordering removal are given in sub-section (3), (e.g. a penalty which may have been imposed remaining unpaid for over three months). The 1988 Act gave no protection to a mortgagee by way of notifying him of the intention to remove a ship from the register or of actual removal. A British register could be closed if the owner gave notice to the Registrar at the port of registry that he desired to terminate the ship's registry (Schedule 1, paragraph 12(c)).

Regulation 56 of the 1993 Regulations provides that the Registrar may, subject to appropriate notices being served under Regulation 101, terminate a ship's registration in various circumstances including (a) on application by the owner, (b) on the ship no longer being eligible to be registered, (c) on the ship being destroyed, (d) on his deciding that it would be inappropriate taking into account any requirements of the Merchant Shipping Acts for the ship to remain registered bearing in mind her condition so far as relevant to the ship's safety or the crew on board or to any risk of pollution, or (g) when any penalty imposed on the owner in respect of a contravention of the Merchant Shipping Acts has remained unpaid for a period of more than three months. When the Registrar terminates registration under (a) or (c) he shall issue forthwith a closure transcript to the owner of the ship and notify any mortgagees of the closure of the registration. The owner then has to immediately surrender the ship's certificate of registry to the Registrar for cancellation. Section 16(4) of the 1995 Act provides 'where the registration of any ship terminates by virtue of any provision of registration regulations, the termination of that registration shall not affect any entry made in the register so far as relating to any undischarged registered mortgage of that ship, or of any share in it'.

### *Registration in overseas territories*

Section 11 of Part I of the 1988 Act dealt with registration in overseas territories. The aim of the provision contained in this section is to try and keep control over the capability of each individual territory to provide proper supervision of registration. The statute provided by way of Order in Council different categories of registries classified by reference to ship tonnages, types or 'any other specified matter'. Each relevant overseas territory may then be assigned one of these categories 'as appears appropriate to the British Sovereign'. No territory would then have power to register any ship outside the category assigned to it. The 1995 Act covers ships registered under the law of a relevant British possession, which is defined in section 313 as including (a) the Isle of Man, (b) the Channel Islands, and (c) any colony.

Regulation 71 (Part IX) of the 1993 Regulations provides that a ship registered in Part I may be transferred to the register of a port in a relevant British possession provided that the Registrar is satisfied that registration of the ship at the intended port of registration is not precluded by any Order in Council in force under section 11 of the Merchant Shipping Act 1988 (now repealed) or any provision of the law in force in the possession in question. Any certificate signed by the Registrar of the intended port of registration and stating that any such provision is in force is conclusive evidence for these purposes. When the Registrar of the intended port of registration issues a certificate of registry and upon notification of transfer the Registrar terminates the registration of the ship.

### *Bareboat charter*

The 1993 Act and Regulations introduced for the first time registration of foreign vessels under the British flag which are bareboat chartered to British charterers. This is now embodied in section 17 of the 1995 Act as well as in the Regulations. The aim is that shipowners can retain tax advantages of being registered in a foreign country but can also fly the British flag. Only the procedural rules apply to bareboat chartered-in vessels and substantive law provisions governing mortgages, ownership, priorities, safety, etc will be governed by the law of the country of original registration. In fact, section 17(7) of the 1995 Act provides that 'private law provisions for registered ships' (which basically deals with bills of sale and mortgages) do not apply to bareboat chartered-in ships. The qualification of bareboat charterers is the same as the qualification to be owners of British ships (and the same applies to fishing vessels).

Section 17 of the 1995 Act and the 1993 Regulations 73–87 deal with bareboat chartered-in vessels. The persons qualified to be owners of British ships who charter a ship on bareboat charter terms are qualified to register a bareboat charter ship. If the charterer is not resident in the UK he has to appoint a representative person. The function of a representative person is to accept service of various documents. The period of registration will end on the expiry of the charter period or at the end of a period of five years beginning with the date of registration specified in the certificate of bareboat charter whichever is the earlier (unless there is a renewal application) (Reg. 83). Such registered bareboat chartered-in ship is entitled to fly the British flag and all merchant shipping legislation and other enactments (excluding the private law provisions for registered ships) apply to it, subject to any necessary modifications or disapplications by Order in Council. 'Bareboat charter terms' is defined as meaning 'the hiring of a ship for a stipulated period on terms which give the charterer possession and control of the ship, including the right to appoint the master and crew' (see section 17(11) of the 1995 Act). Any reference to the owner of a bareboat charter ship means the person registered as the charterer (Merchant Shipping (Modification of Enactments) (Bareboat Charter) Ships Order 1994 (SI 1994 No. 1774). An application for registration of a bareboat charter ship must be made to the Registrar at the General Registry of Shipping and Seamen. The applicant applies as if he were the owner and the application for registration must be accompanied by a declaration of eligibility, a copy of the charterparty, the certificate of registry and if the charterer is a body corporate details as to incorporation (Reg. 77). If at any time there occurs in relation to a bareboat charter ship any change affecting the eligibility of the ship to be registered, the charterer of the ship shall, as soon as practicable after the change occurs, notify the Registrar. If he fails to do so then he shall be guilty of an offence (Reg. 84). The Registrar is obliged to notify the foreign registry, where the ship is primarily registered, when a ship has been registered as a bareboat charter ship on the British register or when the ship's registration has been closed either by reason of the expiry of the certificate of registry or by reason of Regulation 87. Under Regulation 87 the Registrar can close the registration of a bareboat charter ship in the following circumstances:

(a) on application by the charterer;
(b) on the ship no longer being eligible to be registered;
(c) on the ship being destroyed;
(d) if he considers that it would be inappropriate for the ship to remain registered taking account of the requirements of the Merchant Shipping Acts relating to the condition of the ship, its safety and the safety of the crew and any risk of pollution.

On the closure of the ship's registration the charterer has to surrender to the Registrar the certificate of bareboat charter for cancellation.

### *Small ships register*

This register was originally introduced by virtue of section 5(1) of the Merchant Shipping Act 1983. It covers ships which are small—and 'small' was defined by section 10(2) of the Act to mean a ship of less than 24 metres in length, the length itself being defined as in the tonnage regulations prescribed in the 1894 Act—and which are:

(a) owned wholly by persons qualified to be owners of British ships;
(b) not fishing vessels;
(c) if registered under Part I of the 1894 Act, so registered in the UK.

The 1988 Act inter-related to the 1983 Act by providing (in section 3(3)) that for the purposes of the application of section 5 of the 1983 Act the following persons are qualified to be owners of British ships:

(1) British citizens;
(2) Persons who, under the Hong Kong (British Nationality) Order 1986, are British Nationals (Overseas);
(3) Citizens of the Republic of Ireland

and Commonwealth citizens not falling within any one of the above three categories are also qualified. Thus it would still be allowed for Commonwealth citizens *resident in the UK* to enter ships less than 24 metres in length on the Small Ships Register run for the Secretary of State for Transport by the Royal Yachting Association.

The 1993 Act and Regulations introduced a central register for small ships (Part III). Existing registrations under the 1983 Act were transferred to this register. To be eligible to be registered on Part III the ship must be a small ship other than a fishing vessel or submersible vessel. Under Regulation 89 the following persons are entitled to be the owners of a small ship registered on Part III:

(a) British citizens or persons who are nationals of a Member State other than the UK and are established (within the meaning of Article 52 of the EEC Treaty) in the UK;
(b) British Dependent Territories citizens;
(c) British Overseas Citizens;
(d) Persons who, under the British Nationality Act 1981, are British subjects;
(e) Persons who, under the Hong Kong (British Nationality) Order 1986, are British Nationals (Overseas); and
(f) Commonwealth citizens not falling within these paragraphs.

The owner must have a British connection, namely being ordinarily resident in the UK. The registration is valid for five years unless terminated. A representative person does not have to be appointed for small ships registered before 21 March 1994 (s.5, SI 1993 No 3137).

Whilst the 1993 Act has been repealed the 1995 Act deals with small ships, other than fishing vessels. A small ship is defined as a ship less than 24 metres in length ('length' having the same meaning as in the tonnage regulations).

Under the 1995 Act any ship which is a small ship other than a fishing vessel or a submersible vessel is eligible to be registered on Part III of the central register of British ships. The 1993 Regulations still apply.

This commentary is not intended to give in-depth assistance to the owners of small ships and any reader who has a specific interest in such a vessel and possible registration of it should study the relevant Acts and Regulations.

### *Open registries*

'Flags of Convenience' is a phrase which has fallen into disrepute politically. It has been used to describe the registering of ships under the flag of certain States when they are in fact beneficially owned and controlled by nationals of other countries, manned by foreign crews and seldom, if ever, enter the jurisdiction or ports of their country of registry. However, for the sake of 'convenience' the phrase will continue to be used throughout the section which follows. The registries of those countries who offer such facilities are known as 'open registries'. Shipping registration laws of such 'convenience' countries ignore the requirement of national ownership.

In the highly competitive world, after the Second World War, because of high operating costs unsubsidized US shipowners transferred their ships to flags of convenience for reasons of tax immunity to gain economic advantages over European competitors. The Greeks similarly transferred ships to avoid heavy taxation, but also to avoid inconvenient governmental regulations.

The cost of crewing, always a major expense for owners, could cripple the financial capabilities of an average shipowner if he were forced, by the domestic law of his own country of residence, to crew his ship exclusively with seafarers of his own nationality. Some countries, e.g. Portugal, still insist on this high degree of nationalism. The UK takes a 'middle of the road' view and has not obliged British nationals to fly the British flag. Indeed, as has been seen, registration is no longer a duty, but an entitlement under the latest Merchant Shipping statutory provisions. The 'totally relaxed' countries which offer their registration openly to shipowner nationals of any other nation are, to mention a few, Panama, Liberia, Honduras, Costa Rica, Somalia, Hong Kong, Cayman Islands. Also the growth of Cyprus-registered tonnage has continued.

There are no requirements for a genuine link to exist between the State and the ship which looks for registration under its flag. The rationale was originally one purely and simply of tax immunity. The problem is at present one of economic competition between developing maritime States, the flag of convenience States and the traditional maritime States.

A conflict is bound to arise when a ship is linked with several States, viz. the nationality of the crew, the place of building, the beneficial ownership, etc. It is a matter of public policy that, if possible, any State which grants its nationality and flag to a ship should be able to have effective jurisdiction over and to control in technical and social matters (cf. the Law of the Sea Conference at Geneva, 1958). The 'genuine link' policy is difficult to apply and to enforce amongst sovereign States, however, because there is no system of effective sanctions.

The provisions in the Merchant Shipping Act relating to the registration of a British ship do not prevent British owners from taking advantage of a flag of convenience. All they need to do is to form a company in a flag of convenience State and to direct it from a place within the UK. The ship must be *owned* by the company. The company's vessel then may be registered in and fly the flag of that

State. The vessel is not then a British ship since the company was not established under the laws of the UK.

It should be noted that in times of war, *actual* ownership is one of the main tests of enemy character, and thus flag-of-convenience-registered ships, when the State of *actual* ownership is a belligerent, would be regarded as enemy ships by the other belligerents. Thus, the international rule that the country of registration has the right to protect by controlling or requisitioning its registered vessels could be, and is, varied by such rights of protection being exercised not by the flag State but by the State of real, effective ownership/control.

Flags of convenience will survive so long as international law recognizes the right of each individual State to determine the terms and conditions under which it will grant its nationality to merchant ships. As registration, under international law, is also recognized as the ultimate 'root' test of a ship's nationality, the international legal position of flag of convenience countries is enhanced.

International opinion exerts great pressure on flag of convenience States to enforce effective jurisdiction and control over ships flying their flags, and particularly to maintain reasonably high standards in the safety regulations etc. to be observed by such ships.

In the late 1980s the traditional open registries are being challenged by the emergence of other categories of ship registry, one example of which is the offshore flag of which the obvious illustration geographically adjacent to the UK is the Isle of Man. By offering owners the employment of crews at rates ruling in their countries of origin and by also offering a tax concession to national crew, they aim to entice foreign-registered British tonnage away from their foreign registries, thus presenting a threat to traditional and newly emerging independent registries.

### *The International Transport Workers Federation*

The International Transport Workers Federation (ITF) has for many years been militant in its attitude towards flags of convenience. The affair of the *Globtik Venus* at Le Havre in 1976 was an example. With its Filipino crew and Bahamas flag it became the symbol for the ITF to challenge shipowners flying convenience flags to provide better pay and conditions for their seamen. The crew refused to sail her from Le Havre and her owner took drastic measures to evict them forcibly from the ship. Later a compromise was reached but threats to black-list flags of convenience generally remained.

The 'phenomenon', as it used to be called, of flags of convenience has indeed become the subject of growing international concern and the ITF are in the forefront of the campaign. Although ITF agreements may only apply to possibly one-sixth of all ships flying convenience flags, they feel they have effectively exposed a problem which, if allowed to remain unremedied, will escalate to irremediable proportions.

That the flag of convenience system has greatly outgrown its defined origin and purpose much in the same way as trade unions have become a Frankenstein creation far removed from their general purpose in the early years of their formation is illustrated most aptly by a case of real significance which became a leading case in the contemplation of Britain's Prime Minister in pursuance of her avowed intention of reforming the UK industrial relation laws. Hong Kong is one place where 'convenience companies' are formed (and indeed the list still steadily grows—the Cayman Islands is another example). This particular case concerned the vessel *Nawala* which used to trade under the Norwegian flag and ownership and was crewed by highly paid Norwegians. Owing to a freight market slump her owners were faced with financial ruin but a Swedish banking concern which had a small interest in the vessel acquired her by paying off the mortgage. Finding themselves with a 'white elephant' in Sweden her new owners were advised that one practical way of trading her profitably would be to engage an Asian crew. The Swedish company immediately established a company in Hong Kong especially to own the vessel, all the shares in which were beneficially owned by the Swedish parent company. Thus the Hong Kong 'veil', if swept aside, would reveal a Swedish 'face'. In view of Hong Kong registry the owners employed a Hong Kong Chinese crew and things went well until July 1978 when the ITF attempted to black the vessel at the British port of Redcar but were ironically thwarted by the refusal of the Transport and General Workers Union to assist the ITF by requesting its members to black the vessel. Nevertheless the incident became the subject of litigation because the *Nawala's* owners had, despite last-minute events, applied to the courts for an injunction to restrain the ITF from their intended action. The ITF who, on the face of it, were interfering ostensibly to protect the interests of allegedly exploited Asian seamen were in fact reckoned to be pursuing their long-continuing campaign of forcing flag of convenience vessels from the high seas.

The House of Lords, to whom this matter was eventually taken on appeal, were forced to consider the application of the facts to the Trade Union and Labour Relations Act 1974, as amended in 1976. Section 13 of the Act grants immunity to anybody for acts done 'in contemplation or furtherance of a trade dispute'. A trade dispute is defined in section 29(1) of the Act as being a dispute between employers and workers or between workers and workers connected with a stated list of defined situations, one of which is terms and conditions of employment. It was established as a fact that the crewmen on the *Nawala* were quite content with their terms and conditions of employment and it was entirely with the blessing of the Seaman's Union in Hong Kong that they had been originally engaged. Nevertheless, their Lordships considered that, applying the letter of the law strictly as they did, the ITF were entitled to immunity and that it was not their place to question the motives and possible underlying purposes of the ITF. Also, it was not their place to change the existing laws of the UK but merely to interpret and apply the law as it presently stands. Thus the owners of the *Nawala* lost their case. (*The Nawala* [1980] 1 Lloyd's Rep. 1, HL.) The effects of section 13 of the 1974 Act were, however, tempered by the coming into effect of the British Employment Act 1980 and particularly its section 17. The owners of the vessel *Hoegh Apapa* benefited from this in that they won (right up to and including the House of Lords: [1983] 2 Lloyd's Rep. 1) against the ITF when the latter had 'blacked' their vessel at Liverpool in July 1982. Her crew was Filipino and she was loading under time (and sub) charter. The blacking had the effect of interfering with the performance of the charterparty and thus was contrary to section 17 of the 1980 Act which withdrew from certain kinds of *secondary* action the wide-ranging immunity from actions in tort afforded under section 13 of the 1974 Act. The ITF *was* liable in tort.

Another case involving the ITF is as follows:

*The Uniform Star* [1985] 1 Lloyd's Rep. 173
The ITF claimed outstanding wages of the crew of the vessel *Uniform Star* on her arrival at Tilbury. Owners declined to pay and the ITF issued a writ against the owners. The owners applied for an injunction contending that the ITF might go beyond what they might lawfully do and would engage in or procure unlawful industrial action.

*Held*: In order to leave Tilbury the vessel would need the co-operation and assistance from tug crews, linesmen, pilots and lock-gate keepers. The threatened action by the ITF to induce or procure these people to break their contracts would afford the owners a cause of action at common law. The conduct threatened by the ITF was within section 13(1) of the Trades Union and Labour Relations Act 1974. The linesmen, tug-crews and lock-gate keepers had contracts of employment with employers who were not parties to the industrial dispute between the owners and the crew of the *Uniform Star*. It would be unlawful for the ITF to induce or procure linesmen, tug-crews and lock-gate keepers to refuse services to the *Uniform Star* in breach of their contracts of employment and the owners could rely on section 17 of the Employment Act 1980. The rules of the ITF prevented holding a ballot which complied with the Trades Union Act 1984. If the ITF could not and did not hold a ballot then the action was unlawful. If the owners gave a satisfactory bail bond in the Admiralty Court they should be entitled to an injunction.

## REGISTRATION

Perhaps the most attractive argument in support of the policy of registering ships is that it provides prima facie evidence of title to the vessel in disputes as to title. As registration of land has in the UK been the subject of legislation, so registration of ships which provides similar advantages is also subject to statutory control.

In addition to the evidence of rights of ownership or title (comparable to the advantages of the title deeds to property on land) registration brings other advantages, namely, rights in relation to mortgages and the right to fly a British flag and attendant benefits.

*Liverpool Borough Bank* v *Turner* (1860) 29 LJ Ch 827
The court emphasized two points relating to registration. First, it is in the interests of the nations of the world that it should be clearly known and recognized who shall be entitled to the privileges of a British ship, and, secondly, the object is to determine, as in the case of title to land, what should be proper evidence of title to maritime property.

Up until 1988, the legislation which has covered registration of British ships has been Part 1 of the Merchant Shipping Act 1894. Although the idea of compulsory registration has been in vogue in Britain since the mid-17th century, as from 1989 the idea of compulsory registration has been replaced by an entitlement to register dependent upon certain preconditions by way of qualification, mentioned earlier. The 1995 Act also states that registration is an entitlement.

The relevant Act governing the jurisdiction aspect of registration of British ships is the Supreme Court Act 1981 (particularly section 20(2)(b)), whereunder the right is vested in the Admiralty Court to hear and determine any questions or claims referring to 'possession or ownership of any share therein'.

A case whose facts illustrate well when the Admiralty Court thought it had jurisdiction to decide an issue is *The Bineta*.

*The Bineta* [1966] 2 Lloyd's Rep. 419
X, the registered owner of the motor yacht *Bineta* sold her to Y. Y was registered as owner but X remained in possession of the yacht due to Y defaulting in payments, thus exercising his unpaid seller's lien. Y subsequently failed to produce the money, so X, exercising his right under section 48 of the Sale of Goods Act 1893, sold the yacht to Z. Z then sought a declaration that he was entitled to be registered as owner in place of Y.

*Held:* That although X had ceased to be the registered owner he had passed a good title to Z who was entitled to be registered as owner in place of Y.

CHAPTER 2

# SHIP MORTGAGES

Briefly defined a mortgage could be said to be 'any charge by way of lien on any property for securing money or money's worth'. It is the creation of a charge or encumbrance in favour of the lender of money by the person wishing to borrow. Indeed, it is the essence of a mortgage that it is something more than a mere personal covenant.

Many shipowners in this, and indeed in any, day and age are undercapitalized and mortgages on their vessels are a recognized method of raising finance. The word 'mortgage', which is said to derive from the Latin *mortuum vadium* (a dead pledge), could be said to be a 'three-in-one' word since it covers the triple idea of the mortgage loan or transaction, the mortgage deed or document and the rights generally conferred by the document upon the lender of the money.

Thus a shipowner who wishes to obtain money may do so by borrowing money on the security of his ship, giving the person who is prepared to lend him the money an interest in the ship as security for the loan. The shipowner (the borrower) is known as the 'mortgagor' and the person lending the money is known as the 'mortgagee'. It is well to know at the outset that a *mortgagee* incurs *no* liabilities to third parties since the *mortgagor* remains the owner of the ship or the shares in it.

The mortgagor or owner is free to continue operating and trading the vessel as a profit-making possession provided that he does not act in such a way as to jeopardize or put at risk the ship as security for the mortgage loan and thus prejudice the mortgagee's position. The importance of the doctrine of the 'ship as security' is emphasized by the custom and practice of every mortgage containing a personal covenant by the mortgagor to repay the loan and the equally obvious fact that such a covenant might be of little practical value to the mortgagee. However, even as security a vessel is not, as we shall see, an ideal form of security, one reason being that certain privileged claims can rank against the vessel in priority before those of a mortgagee. A second reason is that, being a floating object, it will disappear from and escape out of the jurisdiction of the courts whose aid the mortgagee may be entitled to seek. A third reason for the precarious nature of a ship as security is its permanent exposure to partial damage or even total destruction through the perils of the seas. Lastly, it is also worth noting that if a *further* advance is given on the same security and a second independent mortgage has been effected *and* registered in the intervening period the latter may rank ahead of any *further* advance on the first mortgage.

A mortgage may be created to secure a current account and upon which a further extension of credit is given to the mortgagee *after* the intervening registration of an independent mortgage on the same security. Some argue that the further advance/extension of credit should rank even before the subsequently created but prior registered other mortgage. Even this, however, would appear to be caught by the 'notice' rule which is the whole essence of registration, and every mortgagee, whether he has actual notice or not, is deemed to have notice of a previously registered mortgage and, before extending credit even under the current account, would be prudent to examine the register closely.

## MORTGAGE OF SHIP AT COMMON LAW

In olden times, the mortgagor absolutely conveyed (i.e. transferred) the ship to the mortgagee under the terms of an agreement by operation of which if the mortgagor paid off the mortgage debt and interest in accordance with the agreement the mortgagee would reconvey the ship to the mortgagor there and then. This method was substituted in 1825 in the case of ships by a special form of mortgage introduced by statute.

## MODERN FORM OF STATUTORY MORTGAGE

Acts governing ship mortgages are the Merchant Shipping Act 1894 with minor amendments by the Merchant Shipping Act 1988. The relevant sections of the 1894 Act are sections 31 to 46 inclusive. Section 31 reads as follows:

> '31.—(1) A registered ship or a share therein may be made as a security for a loan or other valuable consideration, and the instrument creating the security (in this Act called a mortgage) shall be in the form marked B in the first part of the First Schedule to this Act, or as near thereto as circumstances permit, and on the production of such instrument the registrar of the ship's port registry shall record it in the register book.[1]
>
> (2) Mortgages shall be recorded by the registrar in the order in time in which they are produced to him for that purpose, and the registrar shall by memorandum under his hand notify on each mortgage that it has been recorded by him, stating the day and hour of that record.'

Subsection (1) above has been amended to read (see the 1988 Act, Schedule 1, paragraph 21):

> '(1) A registered ship, or a share in any such ship, may be made a security for the repayment of a loan or the discharge of any other obligation; and on production of the instrument creating such security (referred to in this Act as a mortgage) the Registrar of the ship's port of registry shall record it in the Register.'

Part 1 of Schedule 1, referred to in the original subsection (1894), has been repealed which means that the statutory forms of mortgage and transfer of mortgage in their crystallized form are a thing of the past. The forms are included in Part 2 of the Schedule and are to be henceforth 'on such forms as are to be prescribed by the Commissioners of Customs etc.'. These mortgage forms, like

1. The word 'book' in this context has been deleted from current statutory language on this subject.

the bill of sale form, will in future be subject to intermittent review and revision.

The inability of a mortgagee of a non-British ship thus to register his mortgage as a legal mortgage under the provisions of the 1894 Act should not, however, worry non-British shipping interests. The facilities of borrowing under a mortgage agreement are just as readily available and on similar customary terms but by pure technicality of law such mortgages are regarded by British law only as equitable in nature.

The Merchant Shipping Act 1894 thus provides that only registered ships (or shares in ships), can be subject to the statutory legal mortgages. Any other mortgage relating to ships or shares must take effect as a purely *equitable mortgage*. Simply put, an equitable mortgage is that which a mortgagee has if he has merely received an *equitable* interest. It could be described as a mortgage created otherwise than by deed. If an equitable mortgage is effected on a registered ship, or shares therein, the big disadvantage is that it cannot be taken into account when deciding the priorities in relation to other legal (and properly registered) mortgages of that same ship or share(s). Typical circumstances where equitable mortgages can and do exist are:

(1) on an unregistered British ship or a share in such;
(2) on foreign vessels; and
(3) on unfinished vessels. As unfinished vessels cannot be registered, so also no mortgage on them is capable of being registered.

It is perhaps in connexion with a partly constructed vessel that the equitable mortgage is most in demand. For example, the prospective buyer may have agreed to pay by instalments but needs to borrow money to do so and has nothing else to offer by way of security except the partly constructed ship. This the lender may be willing to accept as security. On the other hand, the shipbuilder may have signed a building contract under which the buyer is not required to pay any instalments before completion, so he, the builder, may seek a loan to finance himself whilst constructing the ship.

The Merchant Shipping (Registration etc) Act 1993 ('1993 Act') received the Royal Assent on 1 July 1993 and came into force on 21 March 1994 (SI 1993 No 3137). The Merchant Shipping (Registration of Ships) Regulations 1993 ('1993 Regulations') came into force on 21 March 1994. Section 6 and Schedule 1 of the 1993 Act as supplemented by the 1993 Regulations set out private law provisions for registered ships including provision as to the title to, and registration of mortgages over, such ships. These Regulations only apply to British ships registered under Part I of the 1993 Act and not to small ships, fishing vessels which opt for simple registration or bareboat chartered-in ships, or other ships excluded by regulations (s.3(4)(a)).

Now, under section 16 of the Merchant Shipping Act 1995 (the '1995' Act) Schedule 1 (which makes provision relating to the title to, and the registration of mortgages over, ships) shall have effect (as from 1 January 1996). Schedule 1 does not apply in relation to ships which are excluded from its application by registration regulations under section 10(4)(a). The 1995 Act is a consolidating Act. By virtue of the Interpretation Act 1978, s.17(2)(b) regulations made under the repealed legislation are continued in force unless otherwise stated.

Paragraph 7 of Schedule 1 of the 1995 Act states that 'A registered ship, or share in a registered ship, may be made a security for the repayment of a loan or the discharge of any other obligation'. The mortgage must be in a form approved by the Registrar at the General Registry of Shipping and Seamen. (See Chapter 1 for further details of the central registry.)

Mortgages are registered in the order in which they are produced to the Registrar for the purposes of registration.

## HOW MAY AN EQUITABLE MORTGAGE BE EFFECTED?

An equitable mortgage may be effected by a deposit of the legal deeds relative to a registered mortgage with another person in consideration of a loan. Alternatively, it may be made by an agreement to create a legal mortgage in consideration of a loan being made. Also, where an unfinished ship is concerned, it may be effected by the deposit of a builder's certificate relating to the vessel.

The effect of the equitable mortgage is to give the equitable mortgagee a preferential right over the thing charged (or mortgage). The fact that the 'thing' is movable makes no difference.

Supposing the builder/borrower is a limited company he may issue a debenture charging all the company's assets including the ship in his yard. A debenture is a voucher certifying that a sum of money is owing to the person designated in it. It could take the form of a bond issued by a corporation or company acknowledging that it is indebted to the holder in the sum of money specified.

## REGISTRATION OF STATUTORY MORTGAGES

There is no legal obligation to register a mortgage. However, to have proper legal effect registration is necessary. Any mortgagee who does *not* register his mortgage gains none of the benefits available under the Merchant Shipping Acts. For obvious reasons if a ship is unregistered there can be no registration of a mortgage on it. Mortgages on foreign ships cannot be registered in the United Kingdom. But it must be emphasized that failure to register a mortgage does not render the mortgage void.

Buyers of unregistered ships could have unregistered mortgages enforced against them, even though they did not know that a mortgage existed.

*The Shizelle* [1992] 2 Lloyd's Rep. 444

The vessel *Shizelle* was mortgaged to the plaintiffs and the vessel and mortgage were both unregistered. Subsequently the vessel was sold to the defendants 'free from any encumbrances'. The purchasers did not have any knowledge, actual or constructive, of the mortgage and were bona fide purchasers. The defendants registered their ownership of the vessel on the Small Ships Register maintained by the Secretary of State for Transport in accordance with the Merchant Shipping (Small Ships Register) Regulations 1983. That register did not provide for registration of mortgages or other security. The plaintiffs then advised the defendants of their undischarged mortgage and arrested the vessel.

The question raised was whether the bona fide purchasers for value of an unregistered vessel were liable to the mortgagees under an unregistered mortgage of the vessel where he has neither actual nor constructive notice of the mortgage at the time of the purchase of the vessel. The purchasers argued that the only legal mortgage of a ship was a registered mortgage and as the mortgage was unregistered it was equitable only and would not bind a bona fide purchaser for value. The High Court disagreed. The fact that the vessel was unregistered and therefore the mortgage was incapable of being registered did not prevent the mortgagees from acquiring a legal interest in the vessel. The purchasers would be bound by what was a legal mortgage and not an equitable mortgage.

### *Legal mortgage of a registered ship (or share)*

Since 1894 a legal mortgage must have been made and entered on the stated statutory form. Any attempt to use any other method could result in the registrar's refusal to register it. Where a registered ship or share is mortgaged but the mortgage is not registered, the mortgage will only take effect as an equitable mortgage.

Under a statutory mortgage, the actual ownership of the vessel does *not* pass to the mortgagee. However, the property in the ship or share does pass to and invest in the mortgagee and, in circumstances where it may be required to make the ship available as security for the debt, the mortgagee can be considered as owner of the ship (or share) to that extent.

The mortgage deed must be executed under seal in the presence of one or more witnesses, but there is no necessity for the deed to be stamped.

### *The vital significance of registration*

The most important advantage of registration is the obtaining of priority. The ranking of one mortgagee against another mortgagee is governed simply and solely by the date of registration of the mortgage.

Registration, which may be aptly described as 'notice to all the world', protects the mortgagee against all *later* secured creditors of the shipowner and against all *non*-registered mortgages. Failure to register does not invalidate the mortgage but it must give precedence to later *registered* encumbrances. One very good reason for the devising of the mortgage registry system was the common requirement of a vessel owner to seek *further* advances on the security of the *same* property.

In view of the existence of the registry system, persons intending to lend money to shipowners are best advised to search the register carefully.

Regulation 59 of the 1993 Regulations allows intending mortgagees of a registered ship or a share in a registered British ship to give notice of his interest which it is intended that he should have under the proposed mortgage to the Registrar. Once this priority notice has been given the Registrar records that interest on the register. Once notice of this intended mortgage is given and recorded on the register the mortgage will, if later executed and registered, take priority over another registered mortgage even if the other registered mortgage was fully registered in the first place. The priority notice lasts for 30 days although it can be renewed. Subject to priority notices, where two or more mortgages are registered in respect of the same ship or share, the priority of the mortgages between themselves is determined by the order in which the mortgages were registered (paragraph 8 of Schedule 1 to the 1995 Act).

### *Priorities*

Registration gives a mortgagee priority over: (a) earlier unregistered mortgages, whether or not he has knowledge of them; (b) later registered or unregistered mortgages; (c) unregistered debentures of earlier creation, even though he knew of them; and (d) additional advances subsequently made under a prior registered mortgage whereunder the agreement was that the mortgage should cover present *and* future advances by the mortgagee (this right does not arise under statute but at common law under such a mortgage the mortgagee obtained priority in respect of advances made under the mortgage deed only up to the time he had notice of a later mortgage; registration in this case is notice to the earlier mortgagee of the establishment of a later mortgage).

A mortgagee, even if the mortgage is registered, does not have priority over: (a) mortgages registered earlier; (b) any mortgages entered into under current certificates of mortgage where notice of the certificate of mortgage appeared on the register at the time when the mortgagee entered into his mortgage; (c) any claims in connection with which the vessel had already been arrested at the time when the mortgage was entered into; (d) any possessory lien of a ship repairer; and (e) maritime liens, whether earlier or later. As mentioned above, under the 1993 Regulations there is no provision for giving priority notices.

*The Ioannis Daskalelis* [1974] 1 Lloyd's Rep. 174, Supreme Court of Canada
On 20 December 1961 the vessel *Ioannis Daskalelis* was mortgaged to the defendants. In March 1963 the plaintiffs rendered necessary repairs to the vessel at New York, but the sum due to them was not paid. In June 1964 the vessel was sold, and the question arose whether the plaintiffs' claim in respect of the repairs had priority over the defendants' mortgage.

*Held*: that the plaintiffs' claim for necessary repairs gave rise to a maritime lien in the USA and in that country would have taken precedence over the mortgage, but in Canada a claim for necessary repairs did not entitle the claimant to such a maritime lien under the law in Canadian Admiralty Courts. The necessary repairs furnished by the plaintiffs in New York gave rise to a maritime lien enforceable against the defendants in Canada. The question whether the lien took precedence over the mortgage must be determined according to the law of Canada, i.e. the lex fori, and accordingly the lien did have priority.

The mortgagee may also have no priority over an unprivileged claim in circumstances such as in *The Pickaninny*, below.

*The Pickaninny* [1960] 1 Lloyd's Rep. 533
A 'necessaries' (see page 120) claimant may be preferred to a mortgagee if that mortgagee had stood by knowing that the shipowner was insolvent and that the claimant was carrying out work in supplying materials which were directly benefiting his interest.

An interesting insight into the difference between French and English law on this issue is given by the *Colorado*, below.

*The Colorado* (1923) 14 Ll.L.Rep. 251
Under French law, the mortgagee of a vessel, although not having the same right of

property as that given by the Merchant Shipping Act 1894, has the right to arrest the ship in the hands of a subsequent owner. The claim, however, is postponed to that of a necessaries man. Upon a motion it became necessary to determine priorities between *English* claimants in respect of necessary repairs done to a French ship and *French* claimants under a French mortgage.

*Held*: that as rights given under the French mortgage must be determined according to French law which gave wider rights than English law to a necessaries man who has merely the right to sue in rem, the claim of the necessaries man according to the lex fori, by which the question of priorities must be determined, was postponed to the claims of the mortgagees.

## WHAT IS A COLLATERAL DEED?

There may be several details which both parties to a mortgage wish to be included in the mortgage deed and such details are usually contained in a collateral deed. The basic statutory form should contain a reference to such collateral deed as containing further particulars (compare the 'rider' or addendum to the main charterparty document). The sort of matters which appear in a collateral deed are:

(a) the time for the repayment of the principal sums;
(b) the interest payable on the capital sum loaned;
(c) the method of payment of such sum;
(d) who is to be responsible for insuring the vessel;
(e) any restriction which the mortgage may place on the manner in which the ship is to be used; and
(f) such things as will be considered default by the mortgagor and allow the mortgagee to repossess and sell the mortgaged security.

## TRANSFER OF A REGISTERED MORTGAGE

Under the 1988 Act a registered mortgage of a ship may be transferred to any person, provided that the transfer is made out in the form prescribed in the Act or any form closely resembling it. The deed of transfer must be produced to the Registrar at the ship's port of registry (now the central register) so that he can note it in the register book. The Registrar must also endorse the instrument of transfer to the effect that he has recorded the transfer, entering the day and hour of the entry.

Where in the event of death, marriage or bankruptcy the interest of the mortgagee is transmitted to another person, that other person must declare the fact to the Registrar. The declaration must state how the transmission happened and must be supported by evidence. The Registrar must enter the name of the person benefiting under the transmission in the register book as the new mortgagee.

Paragraphs 11–12 of Schedule 1 of the 1995 Act and Regulations 60–61 of the 1993 Regulations deal with the transfer and transmission of registered mortgages, should the private law provisions apply. The transfer or transmission must be in a form approved by the Secretary of State and given to the Registrar

General of Shipping and Seamen. Evidence is needed as to the transmission of the registered mortgage by operation of law. Such evidence is the same as required on transmission of a registered ship. For example, if the transmission was consequent on death, a copy of the grant of representation must be produced to the Registrar. Once this information is produced then the Registrar must register the transferee or the name of the person to whom the registered mortgage is transmitted in the register as mortgagee of the ship or share in question. He must also endorse on the instrument the date and time when the entry is made.

### *What is transferred under the mortgage?*

Under the statutory form of mortgage the number of shares in the ship 'and in her boats, guns, ammunition, small arms and appurtenances' are mortgaged to the mortgagee as security in express terms. In this context the term 'appurtenances' covers all articles appropriated to the vessel and which are necessary for her navigation or for the performance of her voyages and which were present on the vessel at the time when the mortgage was entered into. It does *not* include cargo which is on board the ship at the time of the mortgage and which belongs to the mortgagor or to a third party.

The question of whether a vessel's bunker fuel should rightly be included in a mortagee's security was considered in:

*The Honshu Gloria* [1986] 2 Lloyd's Rep. 67
Clause 4 of the mortgage document meticulously set out the various items or appurtenances of the vessel which were to be transferred as security. The list did *not* include fuel. The mortgagee plaintiff (or bank) argued that Clause 1 of the same document, wherein a definition of the vessel was given, expressly mentioned fuel as part of the vessel's definition and as the vessel itself was transferred so also should those items which fell within the definition of the vessel.

*Held*: that Clause 4 would have had little significance if it was merely repeating 'parrot fashion' the items listed as per the definition. The fact that the list in Clause 4 did repeat some of the Clause 1 items but expressly excluded others, e.g. fuel, the word at issue here, underlined the fact that fuel *was* meant to be excluded in the context of this particular mortgage agreement.

### *Fishing nets on trawlers*

A mortgagee taking possession is entitled to the nets actually on board at the time of the mortgage but not to any nets acquired subsequent to the mortgage being entered into.

*The Humorous, The Mabel Vera* (1933) 45 Ll.L.Rep. 51
A claimed from B £2,706 advanced as mortgage on the steam drifters *Mabel Vera* and *Humorous* and their respective appurtenances. A also demanded interest and a declaration that all fishing gear was included in the mortgage.

*Held*: that the mortgages covered the ships and fishing gear (or the gear in substitution therefor) actually appropriated to the vessels at the time of the mortgages and that the evidence showed that the marking of the gear in store with a ship's number did not necessarily imply appropriation to that vessel.

## WHAT HAPPENS WHEN A MORTGAGE IS DISCHARGED?

Where a registered mortgage is discharged in the ordinary way by all the instalments due on a loan having been repaid, the mortgagor gives notice of this fact to the Registrar General of Shipping and Seamen. The Registrar, when he has received the mortgage deed duly signed and attested, and containing a receipt for the mortgage money, or evidence of the discharge, makes an entry in the register to the effect that the mortgage has been discharged in this matter and returns the full rights in the mortgaged property to the mortgagor. Failure to observe this procedure means that the Registrar has no authority to delete an entry relating to a mortgage simply because it has in fact been discharged.

The relevant provisions are paragraph 13 of Schedule 1 to the 1995 Act and Regulation 62 of the 1993 Regulations. Regulation 62 goes on to say 'if for good reason the registered mortgage cannot be produced to the Registrar, he may, on being satisfied that the mortgage has been properly discharged, record in the Register that the mortgage has been discharged.

## WHAT ARE THE RIGHTS OF THE MORTGAGOR?

Perhaps the most significant right of the mortgagor is that he remains the owner of the vessel. The only limitation of this is that it may be necessary to make the ship or share available as security for the mortgage debt (Merchant Shipping Act 1894, section 34). As Lord Mansfield said at the end of the 18th century: 'In general, till the mortgagee takes possession, the mortgagor is owner to all the world; he bears the expenses and he is to reap the profit.'

As he remains the owner, the mortgagor is able to enter into contracts for the use of the vessel and these contracts will be valid and can be enforced. The manner in which the ship is used must not, however, prejudice the mortgagee's security. If a mortgagee attempts to interfere with a charterparty entered into by the owner and which is advantageous, he may be restrained by injunction. The mortgagee who actively obstructs the performance of a beneficial charterparty may find himself liable in damages plus costs to the mortgagor.

*The Heather Bell* [1901] P 272, CA
Where a mortgagor in possession had entered into a beneficial charterparty, the mortgagee was restrained by injunction at the suit of the charterer from dealing with the security so as to interfere with the execution of the charterparty.

Section 34 of the 1894 Act was replaced by Schedule 1, paragraph 10 to the 1995 Act (if the private law provisions apply) which deals with protection of registered mortgagees. It provides that where a ship or share is subject to a registered mortgage then (a) except so far as may be necessary for making the ship or share available as security for the mortgage debt, the mortgagee shall not by reason of the mortgage be treated as owner of the ship or share; and (b) the mortgagor shall be treated as not having ceased to be owner of the ship or share. It is thought that this change in wording does not affect the position that the mortgagor is still treated as the owner of the ship.

## Ship mortgages

### *Insurance*

Insurance is usually taken out by the mortgagor who is declared to have an insurable interest in the full value of the property. A stipulation that the mortgagor will keep the vessel fully insured usually appears in the collateral deed. If it does not, it should be expressly stipulated in the mortgage deed. A breach of this duty may entitle the mortgagee to insure the ship and charge the costs on to the mortgage debt.

*The Basildon* [1967] 2 Lloyd's Rep. 134
In this case it was held that the right of the mortgagee to insure the vessel and add the cost of the insurance to the mortgage debt *must* be expressly stipulated for in either the mortgage deed or the collateral deed.

The Admiralty judge said that it was clear that a mortgagee who had entered into possession of a vessel had the right to insure it and charge the insurance against any freight he received, but no such implied right exists in favour of a mortgagee who has not thus taken possession.

*The Maira* [1985] 1 Lloyd's Rep. 300
In a dispute involving the vessel *Maira* the Court of Appeal in December 1984 reinstated an arbitrator's decision in favour of the ship's owners. To finance the building of the vessel the owners had to raise 70 per cent of the purchase money by securing the sum by two mortgages in Japanese currency. Both mortgages provided that the vessel was to be insured 'for the full insurable value of the vessel and in any event not less than 130 per cent of the amount of the mortgages'.

Her owners initially insured her for 10 million dollars which at the time was sufficient to cover the minimum requirements. But the following year, because of the appreciation of the yen against the dollar, an insurance for the same sum was insufficient to cover that minimum requirement. The second year's insurance was placed by a management company brought in under a tripartite agreement between the owners and the second mortgagee and the managers because of a default under the mortgage agreement under which the managers were under a duty to act in the best interests of the owners and the bank and to place all hull and machinery insurance in accordance with the respective insurance clauses of the mortgage in favour of the bank.

A little while later the vessel became a total loss. The Court of Appeal, in endorsing the arbitrator's decision for the owners, found that he had made no error of law in finding that the managers were duty bound to comply with *both* mortgages, treating them as having combined effect and not, as the managers had argued, merely bound to have regard to the second mortgage only. The error, said the appeal judges, was rather that of the High Court judge who had appeared to conclude that the renewal of the insurance policy for the same sum of 10 million dollars was sufficient compliance with the shipowners' obligations because it covered the outstanding liabilities of each mortgage severally even if not under the two mortgages combined. The arbitrator had therefore been correct in finding that the management company's duty was to insure the second year for 12 million dollars to cater for the appreciation of the yen against the dollar.

### *Power of a mortgagor to sell the ship*

The mortgagor may sell the vessel to another person even though the vessel is mortgaged, since he remains the legal owner. If the sale is to a *British* subject, the buyer takes with notice of the mortgage since it is registered and he would be unable to resist an action by the mortgagee to have the ship sold to recover the money due. In that event, the surplus of any proceeds from the sale would be held in trust for the new owner of the ship by the mortgagee after he had satisfied his own account.

Section 16(4) of the 1995 Act and Regulation 63 of the 1993 Regulations provide that where the registration of a ship terminates by virtue of any provisions of the Registration Regulations, the termination of that registration shall not affect any entry made in the register of any undischarged registered mortgage of that ship or any share. So if a ship is transferred to someone not qualified to be an owner of a British ship, the unsatisfied registered mortgage, may, if the ship comes within the jurisdiction of a court in the UK which has jurisdiction to enforce the mortgage, or would have had jurisdiction had the vessel not been sold, be enforced.

Where, however, a ship is sold by order of the court, the position of the mortgagee is different. He is barred from proceeding against the vessel under her new ownership to recover any outstanding balance due under the mortgage before the sale. The new owner, being an innocent purchaser for value, takes the ship free of all encumbrances. The mortagee's recourse is restricted to the proceeds of sale only.

*The Acrux* [1962] 1 Lloyds's Rep. 405
The vessel was sold by the Admiralty Marshal to satisfy an Admiralty Court judgment. Proceedings in rem were instituted by Italian mortgagees who applied for judgment against proceeds of sale. The proceeds of sale, however, were less than the sum claimed by the mortgagees. The court was advised that the buyer of the vessel was unable to secure permanent registration of the vessel in the country of his choice because he was unable to obtain a certificate of deletion from the Italian register.

*Held*: that the title to the vessel was given to the innocent purchaser and that if the sum representing the vessel was insufficient to satisfy all the claims, that was no fault of the court and the loss must fall on the creditors for advancing money against inadequate security; that the mortgagees, by claiming against fund, approbated the process of the court in effecting the sale. Hence it would be inequitable if the mortgagees were able to proceed against the ship under her new ownership. Accordingly an undertaking from mortgagees was required and, the undertaking having been given, judgment would be entered for the mortgagees.

In the course of the judgment it was said: 'It would be intolerable, inequitable and an affront to the court if any party who invoked the process of the court and received its aid, and, by implication, assented to the sale to an innocent purchaser should thereafter proceed or was able to proceed elsewhere against the ship under her new and innocent ownership. The court recognizes proper sales by competent Courts of Admiralty or Prize, abroad—it is a part of the comity of nations as well as a contribution to the general well-being of international maritime trade.'

*The Blitz* [1992] 2 Lloyd's Rep. 441
In 1989 the plaintiff lent £10,000 to the then owner of the vessel *Blitz* and the mortgage was entered on the register. In 1991, *Blitz* was arrested by the Thanet District Council for unpaid harbour dues and pursuant to their powers under section 44 of the Harbours, Docks and Piers Clauses Act 1847, the Council sold the vessel to the defendant for £4,000. The plaintiff claimed the monies due under the mortgage and the question for decision was whether the sale of the vessel pursuant to section 44 of the 1847 Act was a sale free from encumbrances.

*Held*: that if the Council had been required to find out whether the vessel was mortgaged and to advertise the sale subject to the mortgage the vessel would have been unsaleable; an owner of a ship could effectively deprive a harbour authority of its remedy under section 44 by mortgaging the vessel for her full value; the risk of non-payment should be borne by the person who voluntarily lent an unwisely large amount on the security of a ship rather than the harbour authority or an innocent purchaser without notice of the mortgage; a harbour authority could not be expected to clear any unsatisfied mortgage affecting a ship which they wished to sell pursuant to section 44 and a purchaser of that ship could not be expected to investigate the register which might be in some foreign land. The plaintiff's claim accordingly failed.

### *To what extent has the mortgagor the right to redeem?*

The mortgagor has the right to redeem the property from the mortgagee as soon as the time for redemption has elapsed. This is usually six months after the date of the mortgage. Payment of all the moneys outstanding under the mortgage must be made. The right still vests although the mortgagee may have taken possession of the security. However, the right cannot be exercised once the mortgagee has sold the vessel for the purpose of realizing his security. A mortgagee who wrongfully refuses to allow a mortgagor to redeem and proceeds to sell the property may be liable in damages to the mortgagor.

## WHAT ARE THE RIGHTS OF THE MORTGAGEE?

The mortgagee has the right to receive repayments of the principal sum together with interest, where applicable, at the time stipulated in the mortgage deed or the collateral deed as agreed. It is usually expressly stipulated in the deed that should the mortgagor fail to repay the sums at the agreed times the mortgagee is free to seize the security and sell it to realize the sum owing to him (see *Fletcher and Campbell* v *City Marine Finance* [1968] 2 Lloyd's Rep. 520).

Secondly, the mortgagee has the right to insure the security. Section 14(1) of the Marine Insurance Act 1906 provides that the mortgagee has an insurable interest in respect of any sum due or to become due under the mortgage. Section 14(2) gives a mortgagee the right to insure on behalf and for the benefit of other persons the interest in the security (viz. the mortgagor) as well as for his own benefit. The courts have, however, insisted that the right to insure and add the cost of the insurance to the mortgage debt *must* be expressly stipulated in either the mortgage deed or the collateral deed.

### *Default in mortgage repayments*

There is apparently an inherent right in the mortgagee to take possession if the mortgagor should default in making payment. It is, however, usual to stipulate for such in the mortgage deed.

### *Endangering the security*

If the mortgagor behaves in such a way as to endanger the security or place it in jeopardy the mortgagee has the right to intervene and take possession of the security (i.e. the vessel). This principle was clearly recognized by the courts as far back as the beginning of this century.

*The Manor* [1907] P 339, CA
If a mortgagor's activities with his vessel are of such a nature as to be inconsistent with the sufficiency of the security, the mortgagee may be free to take possession despite the absence of any actual default by the mortgagor under the agreement.

For example, if the mortgagor has failed to insure the vessel, despite having agreed to do so, the mortgagee may take steps to prevent her sailing until the mortgagor has insured her. Also, as already explained, where the mortgagor entered into a charterparty that is not at all beneficial the mortgagee may take possession of the security.

*Law Guarantee & Trust Society* v *Russian Bank for Foreign Trade* [1905] 1 KB 815, CA
If the mortgagor enters into a charterparty which is not beneficial the mortgagee may take possession of the security.

An exception to this is where the charterparty had already been fixed when the mortgage was entered into and the mortgagee was at the time aware of the fact.

The sailing of the vessel out of the jurisdiction is not *in itself* an act jeopardizing security.

Where the mortgagor allows the vessel unreasonably to become and remain encumbered by maritime liens, this will be regarded as a circumstance which puts the security in jeopardy, *but* the mere giving of a bottomry bond does not necessarily ipso facto allow the mortgagee to enter into possession on the grounds that his security is endangered.

What effects the letting out of a mortgaged vessel under a speculative charterparty have was examined in the *Myrto*, below.

*The Myrto* [1977] 2 Lloyd's Rep. 243
On 26 April 1974 a merchant bank agreed to advance US$1,650,000 to a company to facilitate its purchase of the *Myrto* which it intended to register in Liberia. On 6 May the vessel was duly purchased and registered. On 19 June the mortgage was executed by the company in favour of the merchant bank. In September 1974, by mutual agreement, the ship was transferred to the Greek registry and on 7 November a provisional certificate to that effect was issued by the Greek authorities. In December 1974 the merchant bank agreed to advance a further US$300,000 on the vessel to be secured by a second mortgage which was executed on 10 December in accordance with Liberian law. Not until 3 June 1976 was the certificate of permanent Greek registration issued. On 2 March 1976 both mortgages were registered in Greece. On 22 September the vessel's owners let the ship out to an organization known as NAMSA. The shipowner/mortgagor failed to pay sums due under the two mortgages and so the mortgagees arrested the ship and applied for an order for appraisement and sale of her on the ground that she was a wasting asset whilst under arrest and all parties should therefore be interested in her prompt sale. The mortgagor opposed the claim on the ground that the mortgages were void and the vessel's charterers applied to have the ship released from arrest on the ground that it constituted unlawful interference with their rights.

As to the application to release from arrest, the Admiralty Court decided that the mortgagees' security had been impaired by the mortgagor's handling of the vessel for several reasons. (1) The contract for her employment was speculative and improvident. (2) Her owners were impecunious. (3) The ship was already under arrest at the suit of a creditor in respect of a substantial debt (an unpaid bunkers bill). And lastly, (4) the owners had sundry other accrued debts and liabilities enforceable both in the UK and elsewhere. These included £20,000-worth of unpaid crew's wages carrying a maritime lien and thus taking precedence over the bank's mortgages.

For authority to dismiss the application for these combined reasons, the court only had to apply the ruling in *The Manor*. The application for release from arrest by the charterer was denied. There were other issues material to this decision which need not be specifically mentioned.

As to the order for the appraisement and sale of the ship, the principle by which the court was guided was that an order for appraisement and sale is, generally speaking, made where there is a default in appearance or defence. In the normal course of events, a defendant to an action in rem whose ship has been arrested and who intends to defend the action will obtain release from arrest by giving bail or furnishing some alternative security satisfactory to the plaintiff. The merchant bank's argument in the *Myrto* case was that the continuing costs of maintaining the ship under arrest would gradually erode and diminish the value of the ship as security and in any case in these particular circumstances the shipowner was not in a financial position to meet any of the running costs. The court felt committed to finding 'a good reason' within the meaning of the Rules of the Supreme Court but equally felt that that good reason was the very fact that the ship should not be kept under arrest at great expense for possibly up to $1\frac{1}{2}$ years pending litigation. If that was allowed to happen all interested parties would either directly or indirectly be adversely affected, including the third party charterer.

On appeal, the judges slightly modified the lower court's order in that they allowed the cargo-owners to take quick delivery of cargo against suitable guarantees for the payment of costs of so doing. The idea was to stop the unnecessary mounting-up of costs.

The rules of law which emerge from the decided cases (*De Mattos* v *Gibson* (1859) 4 De G & J 276; *Collins* v *Lamport* (1864) 11 LT 497; *The Innisfallen* (1866) LR 1 A & E 72; *Johnson* v *Royal Mail Steam Packet Co* (1867) LR 3 CP 38; *Keith* v *Burrows* (1877) 2 App Cas 636; *Cory Bros & Co* v *Stewart* (1886) 2 TLR 508, CA; *The Blanche* (1888) 58 LT 592; *The Fanchon* (1880) 5 PD 173; *The Celtic King* [1894] P 175; *The Heather Bell* [1901] P 272, CA; *Law Guarantee & Trust Society* v *Russian Bank for Foreign Trade* [1905] 1 KB 815, CA; *The Manor* [1907] P 339; *The Lord Strathcona* [1925] P 143) are that a shipowner is at liberty to deal with the ship in the same way as he would have done if the ship was not under mortgage. This would include employing her under contract to a third party such as a voyage charterer. The only exception to this general rule would be the obligation that a shipowner who is tied to a mortgage must not deal with his ship in such a way as to impair it as security. Further, where a shipowner contracts with a third party for the employment or use of his ship, the nature and circumstances being such as not to prejudice the mortgagee's interests and the shipowner is both able and willing to perform the contract, the mortgagee may not, in attempting to exercise his rights, take possession of or sell or arrest the ship by action in rem so as to cause interference with the contract under performance. Such action could only validly be taken by a mortgagee in disregard of such third-party contract if either the contract was of such a kind or made under such circumstances which endangered the mortgage security or if, whether or not this was so, the shipowner was either unwilling or unable to perform the contract. A mortgagee with no such reasonable excuse for interfering with the due performance of a contract may find himself to have committed a tort, in so doing, actionable at the suit of the aggrieved third party. The latter's remedies lie in either seeking an injunction to restrain the mortgagee from possessing and/or selling the ship, or where the interference takes the form of arrest under action in rem, in applying for an order to release the ship from arrest, or thirdly and by way of an alternative, to seek damages.

What does or does not impair the security is always a question of fact in each case; as also are the allied questions whether in any given circumstances a shipowner is impecunious or encumbered with liabilities, operating on credit only, etc. His inability or lack of desire as the case may be to perform a particular contract is also a question of fact which it is open to the court to find.

### *The mortgagee in possession*

#### Actual possession

Actual possession involves the mortgagee seizing the vessel through his representative who may actually go on board. In this event, the Master may be dismissed by the mortgagee or he may be retained on board and become the agent of the mortgagee.

#### Constructive possession

Constructive possession may take place when the vessel is not within the jurisdiction and it is thus impossible for the mortgagee to take actual possession. In this event, the mortgagee may take possession 'constructively' by giving notice of his intention to the mortgagors, charterers, underwriters and any other persons known to be interested in the vessel. Whatever happens, the mortgagee by his actions must clearly express his intention to take possession.

Once having entered into possession either actually or constructively the mortgagee becomes entitled: (a) to take over any freight which is in the process of being earned even though some of it will relate to services given prior to his taking possession; he will not be entitled to freight which has actually fallen due but is still unpaid at the time of his taking possession; and (b) to continue to work the vessel, but he must use the ship as a prudent man would; thus, if he continues to work the ship after taking possession and before sale, he will be responsible to the mortgagor for any damage which the security may suffer due to his (i.e. the mortgagee's) imprudent use of her.

### *The right of a mortgagee to foreclose on the mortgage*

A mortgagor has an equitable right to redeem the security by paying off what is owing even after default on his part and subsequent entry into possession by the mortgagee. So as to give the mortgagee the power to extinguish this right to redeem by the mortgagor, the common law allowed a mortgagee to bring an action for foreclosure. 'Foreclosure' means the action of foreclosing, that is to say proceeding to extinguish the right of redeeming the mortgaged property.

Thereunder, the mortgagee asks the court to make a foreclosure order nisi. This means that the court directs that the accounts between the parties be settled and that if the mortgagor fails to pay the sum due within a certain period (normally six months from the settling of the account) then the mortgage will be foreclosed. The mortgagor is thus effectively deprived of his equity of redemption; i.e. excluded from his entitlement to redeem. Once this date has been reached without the mortgagor settling the account, his right to redeem is lost forever and the mortgagee becomes the absolute owner of the property.

Although the Merchant Shipping Act 1894 makes no provision for the foreclosure action, there is in principle no reason why the mortgagee should not exercise his common law right, and such a course of action is not entirely unknown in respect of ships' mortgages.

*Tuck* v *The Viking Prince* [1974] AMC 921
In this case it was held, by the US District Court of New York, that, under the Federal Ship Mortgage Act, Title 46, U.S. Code, the parties may agree on a rate of interest. Therefore a mortgagor may not defend a foreclosure action on the ground that the stated 8 per cent interest rate was usurious and unconscionable because he was required to purchase allegedly worthless scows from the mortgagee-lender as part of the loan transaction.

### *Power of sale of a mortgagee*

Section 35 of the Merchant Shipping Act 1894 expressly gives the mortgagee a right of sale which is independent of any special provision in the mortgage deed. The wording of section 35 is:

> '35.—Every registered mortgagee shall have the power absolutely to dispose of the ship or share in respect of which he is registered, and to give effectual receipts for the purchase money; but where there are more persons than one registered as mortgagees of the same ship or share, a subsequent mortgagee shall not, except under the order of a court of competent jurisdiction, sell the ship or share, without the concurrence of every prior mortgagee'.

That these powers must, however, be exercised with care and discretion is illustrated by the *The Calm C*, below.

*The Calm C* [1975] 1 Lloyd's Rep. 188, British Columbia Court of Appeal
In June 1969 the mortgagees of a fishing vessel took possession for purposes of operating the vessel and subsequently selling it. The vessel was sold in October 1970 for $35,000. The mortgagors contended that they were entitled to offset this amount against losses occasioned by the mortgagees' failure to observe the expected standards of care and foresight due from a mortgagee in possession of the vessel.

*Held*: that there was evidence that the sale was imprudent but that the mortgagors *were* entitled to offset due to failure of the mortgagees to show reasonable care and precaution and due to their conduct being unreasonable, unfair and prejudical to the interests of the mortgagors.

Such power of sale is exercised with the aid of the Admiralty Court which gives authority to the Admiralty Marshal.

*The Halcyon the Great* [1975] 1 Lloyd's Rep. 518
The Admiralty Court made an order for valuation and sale of the ship and, resulting from

the mortgagee's application, the Admiralty Marshal was authorized to invite bids and sell the ship for a price in foreign currency as well as in sterling. Bids were invited and bids were made, all substantially below the appraised value. The Admiralty Marshal applied for leave to sell the ship. The application was approved by the court.

Subsequent to sale, the proceeds of sale should be dealt with by the mortgagee as follows: he should deduct:

(a) all moneys (principal sum and interest) still owing under the mortgage agreement;
(b) all expenses incurred in the course of taking possession;
(c) any *extra* expense to which he may have been put in taking possession, e.g. the paying of crew's wages or ship's Master's wages and disbursements; and
(d) costs of sale.

If anything is left, the mortgagee becomes a constructive trustee of the remaining balance either for subsequent mortgagees (if any) or for the mortgagor. The mortgagee as such may not make any charge on his own behalf for carrying out the sale of the ship.

Section 35 of the Merchant Shipping Act 1894, as has been mentioned, provides that second or subsequent mortgagees of a ship or share may not sell the ship or share without the agreement of every prior mortgagee, unless he has obtained an order of a court of competent jurisdiction. Where the second or subsequent mortgagee does obtain either the agreement of a prior mortgagee (or the prior mortgagees) or a court order, he will have to account to the prior mortgagees for the sum realized from the sale and their claims will be satisfied first from such proceeds of sale.

Financial institutions are becoming much more actively interested in the day-to-day management of vessels, enlarging their interest beyond the closely defined limits of simple mortgagees to a more active participating role in the management and operation of the ship (i.e. their security).

It is this increased interest which has fortunately greatly reduced the risk of mortgagees ultimately resorting to such drastic procedure as foreclosure and, although this chapter has described foreclosure and outlined its availability and scope, it should be emphasized that far more commonly every effort is made on both sides to find a more mutually beneficial solution short of foreclosure. For example, ship managers may be changed hopefully to advantage or the handling of claims may be taken over by and put under the control of the mortgagee. Perhaps even mortgagors' personal guarantees might be acceptable in certain cases.

An example of action by a mortgagee for the general benefit of all interested parties was:

*Hobbs Savill & Co* v *The Vasilia (Owners), Albaran Bay Corp* [1972] 1 Lloyd's Rep. 51
A motion was entered by the plaintiffs, who were mortgagees, in default of appearance by the defendant shipowner seeking leave to make payment through the Admiralty Marshal to the Greek Master and crew to enable them to be signed off and repatriated back to Greece. The crew had continued to live on board after their ship had been arrested at Fleetwood. A previous order had been made for her appraisement and sale but this had been directed to be held in abeyance until the crew had been repatriated. The ship had

been valued at about £41,000 and total claims by Master and crew were put at about £17,000. Tentative agreement had also been reached which would enable the crew to leave and the ship to be sold. It was accepted that in this sort of situation unless the ship is eventually sold nobody would recover anything and in the light of this it was clearly in the general interest that the mortgagees should put up the money.

UK shipowners can apply for moratoria on UK-built ships under certain circumstances. The moratorium scheme, originally a creation of statute in the UK, allows for an extended period during which defaulting mortgagors may attempt to remedy their default, thus creating a more amicable atmosphere in which mortgage disputes may be resolved without the unpleasant alternative of taking foreclosure action.

Section 35 of the 1894 Act has been reworded in Schedule 1, paragraph 9 of the 1995 Act. This provides:

'9(1) Subject to subparagraph (2) below, every registered mortgagee shall have power, if the mortgage money or any part of it is due, to sell the ship or share in respect of which he is registered, and to give effectual receipts for the purchase money.

(2) Where two or more mortgagees are registered in respect of the same ship or share, a subsequent mortgagee shall not, except under an order of a court of competent jurisdiction, sell the ship or share without the concurrence of every prior mortgagee.

The above new wording no longer gives the registered mortgagee power 'absolutely' to dispose of the ship or share. His power of sale is only exercisable 'if the mortgage money or any part of it is due' presumably once the legal date for redemption of the loan has passed. It would seem that the money is due once the date for redemption of the loan has passed.

### *The position of mortgagee when vessel removed from British registry*

If the ship is removed from the British registry, what is the mortgagee's position? Schedule 1, paragraph 12 of the 1980 Act provided that where any action is taken to remove a ship from the register under powers vested in the Secretary of State, the termination of its registry shall not affect any entry made on the register so far as relating to any undischarged registered mortgage or any existing certificate of mortgage of that ship or any share in it. It seems that the legislators intended positively to protect mortgagees' interests to an extent without feeling any need to notify them that their interests were being tampered with. Regulation 63 of the 1993 Regulations provides that where the registration of a ship terminates under these Regulations, that termination shall not affect any entry in the register of any undischarged registered mortgage of that ship or any share in it. (See also s.16(4) of the 1995 Act).

It should also be borne in mind that under the 1993 Regulations there is only a fixed five-year period of registration which is renewable. If there is no application to renew, the Registrar only has a duty to notify the mortgagees after registration has expired. On the other hand, the Registrar has to notify the owner of the ship three months before the expiry of the registration period and give him a renewal notice. The owner of the ship in applying for a renewal must provide to the Registrar a declaration of eligibility and a declaration that there have been no changes to any registered detail of the ship that have not been notified to the

Registrar (Reg. 42). If the mortgagee is concerned that registration is not renewed by the owner then he should ensure that he has the above documentation to support an application for renewal of registration.

### *Improper exercise of a mortgagee's powers*

If a mortgagee wrongfully exercises his powers he will be liable in damages to the mortgagor. Examples: (1) a mortgagee who wrongfully arrests a vessel on the grounds that his security had been placed in jeopardy when it has not been so placed. (2) A mortgagee who wrongfully prevents the mortgagor from exercising his power of redemption.

*Fletcher and Campbell* v *City Marine Finance* [1968] 2 Lloyd's Rep. 520
Mortgage repayments were duly paid until April 1967 when Fletcher defaulted. Fletcher was notified that the mortgagee was taking possession and that the vessel would only be released on payment of the outstanding balance. Campbell, acting as Fletcher's agent, tendered the balance. The mortgagee rejected the offer and sold the vessel. Fletcher sued the mortgagee on the grounds that it was an implied term of the mortgage that he would be permitted to pay off sums due in order to redeem.

*Held:* that the claim succeeded since the right to redeem was prevented by the wrongful act of the mortgagee. The court commented that it is usual to stipulate expressly in the mortgage deed that the mortgagee has the right to take possession where the mortgagor defaults on mortgage repayments.

A further example of a wrongful exercise of powers by a mortgagee might be: (3) a mortgagee who sells a ship whilst arbitrators were in the act of investigating the balance of accounts between the parties.

## WHAT IS A CERTIFICATE OF MORTGAGE?

A certificate of mortgage is designed to cover those circumstances where the owner of a vessel (or of shares in her ) desires to mortgage the vessel (or shares) *outside* the country in which the port of registry of the ship is located. The shipowner in this event is permitted to apply to the registrar at the port of registry to issue a certificate of mortgage.

### *Contents of certificate*

Since a certificate of mortgage is in the nature of a power of attorney it must contain:

(a) the name of the person(s)/attorney to exercise the power;
(b) the maximum amount of the charge to be created;
(c) the place where the power is intended to be exercised, if designated, or alternatively a reference to the effect that the power may be exercised in any place;
(d) a time limit to the exercise of the power; and
(e) details of any registered mortgages in existence at the time and any certificates of mortgage.

Further information on required details may be found in section 42 of the Merchant Shipping Act 1894.

Particulars as under heads (a), (b), (c) and (d) above must also be entered by the registrar in the book of registry. This is to allow anyone inspecting the registry in Great Britain to be aware immediately of the existence of such certificate and the powers granted under it.

Section 41 of the Merchant Shipping Act 1894 provides:

(1) That the certificate may not be granted so as to authorize a mortgage of the ship *within* the country of registry.
(2) That the certificate may not authorize the power of mortgage to be exercised by any person not named in the certificate.

A mortgagee under a mortgage created under the powers granted by a certificate of mortgage enjoys all the powers of a mortgagee where the mortgage has been created in the customary manner and the mortgage registered in the book of registry.

When such a mortgage is *discharged*, an endorsement to that effect is noted in the certificate by a registrar or British consular official, after suitable evidence of discharge has been produced. When the certificate is finally delivered to the registrar, he must enter in the book details of any unsatisfied mortgages entered into under the certificate. He then must cancel the certificate and note the fact in the book. The certificate then stands vacated.

An owner's power of revocation of powers exercisable by virtue of the certificate is set out in section 46 of the Merchant Shipping Act 1894.

Provision in the Merchant Shipping Act 1894 is also made in the event of loss, destruction or obliteration of the certificate (section 45). Evidence of such may be presented to the Commissioners of Customs and Excise who may in their discretion direct the registrar to issue a new certificate or insert appropriate replacement entries in the registry.

The forging or fraudulent alteration of a certificate of mortgage is a criminal offence. So, also, is a false declaration.

Jurisdiction in mortgage disputes was originally the exclusive province of the Courts of Chancery but the Admiralty Court eventually was granted jurisdiction and section 20(2)(c) of the Supreme Court Act 1981 provides that the Admiralty Court has the right to hear and determine any claims in respect of a mortgage or charge on a ship or any share therein (see page 117). Whether the mortgage is or is not registered is immaterial.

Disputes involving maritime mortgages seem very rarely to feature in the pages of *Lloyd's Law Reports*. One of these rare occasions was:

*The Yolanda Barbara* [1961] 2 Lloyd's Rep. 337

All 64 shares in a motor yacht were mortgaged on a statutory form in 1960 in consideration for a loan of £8,000. The mortgage was duly registered. In a collateral agreement the mortgagor also agreed to make the vessel available to the mortgagee for sales promotion purposes if the latter would waive the interest due in consideration. At all times the vessel was made available if required. Subsequently the mortgagor sought to redeem the mortgage by payment of an £8,000 cheque. The mortgagee nevertheless failed to deliver up, endorse or cancel the mortgage.

The mortgagor took his complaint to the Admiralty Court seeking, inter alia, an order that the mortgage be delivered up or cancelled as he wished to sell the yacht free of encumbrances. The order was granted.

Although the ship is basically the primary security, because of the very fickle nature of the security and the fact that values of vessels are subject to frequent and unpredictable market fluctuations, lenders of money, be they banks or other financial houses, frequently seek further additional and very likely more reliable security. One very obvious (and in practice, common) example being the existence of a long-term charter by way of time or demise, taken out with a charterer of known reliability; the mortgagee/lender's requirement would perhaps require an assignment of the charter hire for the whole or at the least a substantial part of that charter period. Such a charter is known colloquially by practitioners as a 'bankable charter'. Under such an arrangement the loan would become, it might be said, self-liquidating and the ship itself would become security to fall back on only in the event that the assignment agreement fell through. Security, in other words, hopefully never to be realized.

Litigation arising from such an arrangement came before the courts in March 1978 in the *Gator* case, below. The facts arose from the oil market collapse of 1976 and was yet another dispute arising from the massive financial difficulties in which the Maritime Fruit Carriers group found themselves.

*Gator Shipping Corp* v *Trans-Asiatic Oil Ltd SA and Occidental Shipping Establishment (The Odenfeld)* [1978] 2 Lloyd's Rep. 357
X, a subsidiary of the Maritime parent group, chartered their vessel to Y under a charterparty for a period of years stipulating hire at a fixed rate with a guaranteed minimum. Maritime's underlying purpose in negotiating this business through the medium of X was to furnish additional security for a loan they desperately needed from Z, a finance company, to which they intended to assign the charter hire as back-up security to the vessel itself. By 'side letter' arrangement between X and Y, and unbeknown to Z, the arrangement for hire payments were varied by Y only being required to pay market rates for the last three years of the charter period, this in turn being countersecured by funding arrangements also unknown and entirely undivulged to the lender, Z. The vessel's owner, X, was a 'one-ship' company and had no assets other than the mortgaged vessel. In consideration of a second mortgage on the vessel and an assignment of the charter hire to it, Z loaned in excess of $6,000,000. Sometime during the currency of the charter Y refused to continue to pay full hire and treated the charter as terminated. Thereafter Z declared the loan in default, called it in but received nothing. The ship was laid up, having no positive orders for employment.

The ensuing litigation in which Z was plaintiff and X and Y were defendants involved several issues not all of which were directly relevant to the loan default. One issue which was so relevant was the question whether the repudiation of the charterparty agreement, regardless of its rights or wrongs, prejudiced the position of the lender, Z, an innocent third party, bearing in mind that X had expressly covenanted to do all necessary to secure the performance of the charterparty to Y. To accept repudiation of the charterparty was a direct breach of such covenants. X was not free in his relationship with Y but was under obligations to Z, and furthermore Y was fully aware of this. X by his very conduct and attitude towards Z from the outset was estopped from denying that the charterparty alone was the entire content of the bargain between X and Y since both parties had knowingly concealed an independent side arrangement from the plaintiff, Z. As Lord Denning said in an earlier case 'where a man, by his words or conduct has led another to believe in a particular state of affairs, he will not be allowed to go back on it when it would be unjust or unequitable for him to do so'. The plaintiff's losses were the direct result of this deliberate concealing of material information—this misrepresentation—and there had been no break in the chain of causation as a result of the happening of the repudiation of the charterparty.

The court ordered that the plaintiff was free to enter judgement for $600,000 plus interest. The defendants seemingly lost the heart to appeal and were reported to have settled out of court in a sum which exceeded this figure.[2]

## CONVENTION

In May 1993 the International Convention on Maritime Liens and Mortgages was adopted. This will enter into force six months after 10 States have expressed their consent to be bound by it.

The 1993 Convention deals with the recognition and enforcement of mortgages, hypotheques and charges created in accordance with the laws of the state of registration. The ranking of registered mortgages, hypothèques or charges as between themselves and their effect with regard to third parties shall be determined by the law of the state of registration. All matters relating to the procedure of enforcement is regulated by the law of the state where enforcement takes place. With the exception of a forced sale a vessel cannot be deregistered unless all registered mortgages, hypothèques or charges are previously deleted or the written consent of all holders of such mortgages, hypothèques or charges is obtained. Where the deregistration of the vessel is obligatory in accordance with the law of a State party otherwise than as a result of a voluntary sale, the holders of registered mortgages, hypothèques or charges shall be notified of the pending deregistration in order to enable such holders to take appropriate action to protect their interests; less the consent, the deregistration shall not be implemented earlier than after a lapse of a reasonable period of time which shall be not less than three months after the relevant notification to such holders.

2. For further information on ship mortgages the reader is referred to *Ship and Aircraft Mortgages* by Nigel Meeson (Lloyd's of London Press, 1989).

CHAPTER 3

# SALE OF SHIP AND SHIPBUILDING CONTRACTS

## SALE OF SHIP

The Sale of Goods Act 1979 came into force on 1 January 1980 in the UK. This Act does not change the substantive law applicable to sale of goods. Rather it consolidates in a single statute the significant legislation specifically relating to sale or supply of goods which has emerged over the years and to which reference will be made, where relevant, throughout this chapter—namely the Sale of Goods Act 1893 and the Supply of Goods (Implied Terms) Act 1973. In addition to its consolidating role, the 1979 Act looks backward and forward. By 'looking backward' is meant that it covers all contracts of sale made at any time between 1 January 1894 and the present day. It should be understood that Schedule 1 to the Act does contain certain minor modifications which have to be taken into account and applied to the terms of any contract of sale of goods made between 1973 and 1978 (that is to say the years specifically covered by the effect of the Supply of Goods (Implied Terms) Act as a statute standing on its own before the introduction in February 1978 of the Unfair Contract Terms Act). These minor modifications will, as this chapter should reveal, have very little relevance to contracts for the sale of ships which are almost invariably contracts where both seller and buyer are acting in the course of business.

The reader is warned at the outset of this chapter that its scope is limited to agreements to buy and sell ships and that it is not intended to set out a comprehensive treatment of the law of contract generally. Only where strictly required to explain the contractual relationship between sellers and buyers of vessels is the law of contract put before the reader.

Ships are 'goods', a chattel within the meaning of section 61 of the Sale of Goods Act 1979. That this is so was confirmed in *Behnke* v *Bede Shipping Co* [1927] 1 KB 649 and, generally speaking, the sale of a vessel is subject to the terms of the Sale of Goods Act. Where, however, the sale concerns a ship which by law requires registration as a British ship the terms of the Act are not easy to apply in practice. The passing of property in the ship is effected by transfer of a normal bill of sale from seller to buyer. On this point section 24 of the Merchant Shipping Act 1894 is the ruling section.

Indeed it would not be too wide of the mark to define the procedure of selling ships as lying approximately between the procedure for the sale of goods and that for the sale and conveyance of real property. The sale of a ship is merely one way of effecting a change in its ownership.

## Sale of ship and shipbuilding contracts

### *What is a sale?*

By section 2 of the Sale of Goods Act 1979, a sale is defined as a contract whereby the seller transfers or agrees to transfer the property in the goods to the buyer for a money consideration. Distinguished from a sale is a mere agreement to sell; one of the basic differences being that a *sale* causes the property in the goods to be passed at the time when the contract is made, whereas an *agreement to sell* means that some contingency must take place or some condition be fulfilled or performed before a transfer of property can take place.

### *When is a binding agreement reached?*

One source of frequent contention between prospective sellers and buyers is the question of determining at what point a binding agreement has come into existence between them which is enforceable at law by either against the other.

*Lovegrove* v *Campbell* (1948) 82 Ll.L.Rep. 615
A dispute arose as to whether there had been a firm offer and acceptance so as to form the sound basis of a contract. A prospective buyer offered to buy a yacht. The owners replied that they were 'a little undecided' as to that offer but later accepted it. The buyer then repudiated the offer.

*Held*: that since there was no unequivocal revocation of the buyer's offer before it was accepted by the yacht's owners and they had accepted his offer within a reasonable time, a firm contract had been made between the parties and the buyer was liable in damages.

An interchange of correspondence or telex messages in itself may not amount to the reaching of that stage because the all-important 'consensus ad idem' or meeting of minds may not thereby have necessarily been achieved. However, if agreement between the parties has been reached on certain basic significant points, even though the entire transaction is subject to one condition being eventually fulfilled, the law will regard a binding contract as having been made and allow either of the parties to the agreement to obtain redress if the other is in breach of any of the stipulations. The following case well illustrates this.

*The Merak* [1976] 2 Lloyd's Rep. 250, CA
The joint owners of the vessel *Merak* decided to sell her and commenced negotiations for sale with a potential buyer, concluding the negotiations by telex and via brokers. An offer by the sellers was made quoting the price of US$210,000 and agreement on significant points was reached subject to inspection by the buyers at a port and date to be agreed. The Norwegian Saleform as revised in 1966 was to be used and London arbitration was agreed to in the event of a dispute arising. The conditions for inspection were not fulfilled and as the market for ships had risen the sellers contended that they were not bound to sell the ship to the buyers since no contract had been concluded.

*Held*: that a binding contract *had* been concluded and that the failure by the sellers to provide a reasonable opportunity for the buyers to inspect was a breach of a binding obligation. The dispute should go to arbitration.

Another more recently reported case also concerned the issue whether negotiations between the prospective buyer and seller conducted by means of exchange of telex messages had culminated in a binding contract enforceable by either party. It was:

*The Buena Trader* [1977] 2 Lloyd's Rep. 27
Negotiations took place in November 1971 for the sale of the *Buena Trader*. They were conducted by an exchange of telex messages and were based on the provisions of the Norwegian memorandum of agreement form. One significant term was that the ship was to be delivered with continuous machinery survey cycle[1] up to date at the time of delivery. Another significant provision was that the vessel should be delivered 'charter free, class maintained free of recommendations, free of average damages affecting class with all trading certificates clean and valid at the time of delivery'. Offers and counter-offers were made culminating in January 1972 in a message from the buyers to the sellers confirming purchase at $680,000 cash as per sellers' final offer but in view of the requirement of survey cycle being up to date at the time of delivery this would be anticipated to be 75 per cent or even more. The ship was tendered on 7 April 1972 but the buyers refused to accept delivery because, inter alia, the continuous survey cycle was not up to date as required by the terms of the agreement in that one-fifth of the machinery had not been examined each year as the system required. Another reason for rejection was that the sellers were alleged to be aware, prior to the delivery date, that the ship had suffered wear and tear affecting the maintaining of her class and were in breach of an implied obligation to notify their classification society of that fact. The dispute went to arbitration and the arbitrator found in favour of the seller but stated his award in the form of a special case on two points of law. (1) Was there a concluded contract for the sale of the ship? And (2), if so, whether on the established facts the buyers were liable in damages to the sellers by reason of their refusal to accept delivery.

*Held*: that the concluding wording of the buyers' telex of January was merely expressive of their expectations and had no binding contractual effect upon the sellers. The references in the agreement to the continuous machinery cycle were clear enough and on the facts the sellers had not complied with the provisions despite the fact that the extent to which they had fallen short of the requirements had not produced any serious machinery defects. Items affecting her class were not serious enough to go to the root of the contract. Thus there was a concluded contract. The buyers were not, however, liable to the sellers in damages.

Two things which this case spotlights particularly are, first, that the conduct of the parties towards the conclusion of the negotiations is of vital importance to resolve any existing doubt as to whether a contract has been concluded. The final telex of the buyers which was in fact sent after the deadline set by the sellers in the previous counter-offer constituted technically only another counter-offer; but the conduct of the parties generally overrode this technicality to make the buyers' final telex in effect the acceptance of the sellers' offer. Secondly, that the buyers in the course of their arguments were not saying that the failure to comply with the rules and regulations laid down for the facility of the continuous machinery survey cycle was not of itself a ground for treating the contract as at an end but that the sellers were not tendering their ship in the condition which it was agreed it should be in and that they had the opportunity to remedy that between the tendering date and the agreed subsequent cancelling date. The sellers, in other words, only had themselves to blame for not putting their ship into proper

1. This is a facility available to shipowners as a result of amendments to the Classification Society's rules in March 1966 which allowed owners to spread the cost of surveying machinery evenly rather than having to incur all the expense at one time at the end of every five years. In effect it means that the various items of machinery should be open for survey in rotation, so far as practicable, to ensure that the interval between consecutive examination of each item will not exceed five years. The rule specifically provides that approximately one-fifth should be examined each year.

condition before tendering her for delivery. It is on this basis, then, that the court seems to have found that the buyers were not liable to the sellers in damages. This theme will be developed further in the pages which follow.

The sellers appealed and the Court of Appeal allowed their appeal. It took the view that the requirement that one-fifth of the machinery be examined each year under the cycle system was not a contractual stipulation and that in the light of business practice it could not be said that the expression 'up-to-date' in the contract wording meant an even spread of examination of individual items of machinery over the five-year period. Furthermore, there was no call to imply a term construable against the sellers that they would notify Lloyd's of any 'wear and tear' items which might have an effect on the ship's class. Leave to appeal to the House of Lords was refused ([1978] 2 Lloyd's Rep. 325).

In sale and purchase transactions the expression 'subject details' is used for the same purpose as a conveyancer would say 'subject to contract'. This expression was considered in *The Nissos Samos* [1985] 1 Lloyd's Rep. 378 where Leggatt J said the expression was intended to allow a party to resile from a contract if, in good faith, either party was not satisfied with the details as discussed. Subsequently, in *The Junior K* [1988] 2 Lloyd's Rep. 583 which was a dispute regarding a charterparty where the negotiations were 'sub-details' and 'sub-details Gencon c/p', Steyn J held that the parties were not committed until negotiations had taken place about the details of the charterparty. Steyn J, giving the judgment in *The Junior K*, stated that the qualification made by Leggatt J in *The Nissos Samos* was obiter and that it was a statement of the broking view and not the strict legal position. Steyn J.'s judgment was approved by Potter J in *The CPC Gallia* [1994] 1 Lloyd's Rep. 68.

The question of whether a binding contract had been reached was also considered in *Ignazio Messina* v *Polskie Linie Oceaniczne* [1995] 2 Lloyd's Rep. 566. The plaintiffs, who were intended purchasers, alleged that the defendants had entered into binding ship sale contracts either on their own behalf or on behalf of principals. The defendants said that they were negotiating 'subject BOD approval' and on 'NSF' 87 subject to amendments to be mutually agreed, subject to further minor amendments'. The court held there was no contract. In obiter the judge also said he accepted a submission that using the expression 'subject to Norwegian saleform' (as to which, see below) prevented a binding contract coming into existence until the contract was signed. This is in line with a decision in *The Gladys* [1994] 2 Lloyd's Rep. 402 where the purchasers were negotiating subject to their standard terms and conditions 'to be mutually agreed'. The sellers had previously dealt on the buyer's standard terms and claimed there was a binding contract. The court held that both parties anticipated the final form of the contract was to be agreed and therefore there was no contract.

### *Representations*

In the negotiations leading up to any contract there are always *representations* made on each side. On the strength of these the terms of the contract are worked out and agreed, or as might be said, they are intended to *induce* the contract. Let us consider first the nature and effect of representations, or, as they are more commonly known, *'misrepresentations'*.

By definition misrepresentations are either *innocent* or *fraudulent*.

### *Innocent misrepresentations*

Where a statement is made negligently and is thus an innocent misrepresentation, the position is governed, depending upon the facts, circumstances and relationships of the parties, by either

(a) the Misrepresentation Act 1967, or
(b) the *Hedley Byrne* doctrine.

The former, self-evidently, contains statutory remedies, the latter is a rule of the common law formulated by the courts in *Hedley Byrne & Co Ltd* v *Heller & Partners* [1964] AC 465, HL.

## The rule in Hedley Byrne

This rule was fashioned on the basis that a special relationship may arise between persons (one might say a pre-contractual relationship); not only that type of relationship which exists professionally between a solicitor and his client, or a banker and his customer, but also between ordinary businessmen engaged in normal commercial transactions, such as the sale and purchase of ships. From that relationship, in turn, arises a duty of care in the making of statements during a pre-contractual negotiative situation. Thus, it is not difficult to contemplate a situation where there exists, side by side, both a contractual relationship and a relationship giving rise to a duty of care. Simply expressed, a relationship in tort creates a duty towards persons generally, whereas in contract duties are created towards particularly specified persons. There is no reason why these two relationships should not co-exist in the same factual situation.

The rule in *Hedley Byrne* v *Heller* embraces the idea that he who possesses special knowledge or skill and makes a representation to another on the strength of it with the object of inducing that other to enter into a contract with him is under a duty to use reasonable care to see that his representation is correct and that the advice, information or opinion given is reliable. If he negligently gives advice which is poor, information which is misleading or an opinion which is mistaken and as a direct result induces the other to contract with him, he will be liable in damages. This duty of care is quite independent of any possible future contractual relationship between the same parties. As Lord Denning said in *Candler* v *Crane, Christmas & Co* [1951] 2 KB 164, CA, 'a duty to use care in a statement does exist apart from a contract'. It could be said as a result of this trend in the law that, providing a special relationship is proved, a plaintiff who has entered into a contract relying on an innocent misrepresentation which can also be proved to have been negligent will be able to recover damages.

In the non-maritime case of *Esso Petroleum Co* v *Mardon* [1976] QB 801, CA, which concerned the taking of a tenancy of a petrol-filling station and centred around an alleged misrepresentation as to its estimated annual throughput, it was Lord Denning again who volunteered the suggestion that 'the duty to use reasonable care arises not only in contract but is also imposed by the law apart from contract and is therefore actionable in tort'. In 1974 the same judge said (*McInerny* v *Lloyds Bank* [1974] 1 Lloyd's Rep. 246, CA) 'since the *Hedley* rule in 1964 it seems that if one person by a negligent misstatement induces another to enter into a contract—with himself or with a third person—he may be liable in damages'.

## Economic loss under Hedley Byrne

Under the *Hedley Byrne* rule a person who has suffered economic loss by reason of having placed reliance upon a careless statement made by another under circumstances where he who made that statement could reasonably have foreseen that such reliance would be placed may establish a claim for economic loss. Thus *Hedley Byrne* may be regarded as the precedent for a statement of law that there is no general rule, nor probably in truth ever has been, that financial loss is irrecoverable in a negligence action. There are, however, according to judicial opinion other tests which properly should be applied in determing liability for the consequences of a careless statement: (a) the test of a special relationship of close proximity (see *Junior Books* [1983] 1 AC 520 HL), or (b) the test of directness of damages (*Spartan Steel* [1973] QB 27, CA), i.e. that an action for damages in respect of economical loss *only* should lie provided such was reasonably foreseeable *and* was a direct result of the failure in the duty of care contemplated by the *Hedley Byrne* doctrine. Where the liability may arise under contract or in a situation 'equivalent to a contract' it must be expected that an objective test will be applied when asking the question whether, in a particular case, responsibility should be held to have been assumed by the defendant to the plaintiff; see *Caparo Industries* v *Dickinson* [1990] 2 AC 605 at 637. In general the courts are now seeking to limit the classes of cases in which a claim for economic loss could be made. For example in *The Aliakmon* [1986] 1 Lloyd's Rep. 1 the House of Lords overruled *The Irene's Success* [1981] 2 Lloyd's Rep. 635 on the basis that, in order to make a claim for damage to property in tort, the plaintiff must have a proprietary interest in the damaged property at the time the claim arose.

Lord Denning, however, in *Spartan Steel* warned of the danger of a spread of claims for economic loss on the ground that whereas claims for physical damage or harm were, by their very nature, contained within reasonable limits by the law of nature itself, claims for economic loss could create ripples and ramifications over a potentially limitless area, generating thereby the lodging of often remote if not baseless claims.

This principle is independent of the Misrepresentation Act 1967 which deals only with misrepresentations made by a party to the contract. Thus where the Act only covers the relationship between the two contracting parties and a negligent misstatement made by one or other of them, the common law rule is extended to the 'triangular' situation where one party placing reliance on negligent advice given by another makes what turns out to be a disadvantageous contract with a third person.

## Misrepresentation Act 1967

Relief under section 2(1) of the 1967 Act is available if the following three conditions are satisfied: (a) the two parties concerned are parties to a contract. It is *not* necessary to establish that any special relationship exists between them; (b) the statement (or misstatement) must be one of fact; (c) the person who made the statement cannot show that he had reasonable cause to believe that it was sound.

The introduction of the Unfair Contract Terms Act 1977 caused a small alteration to the provisions of the Misrepresentation Act 1967. Section 8(1) of the 1977 Act provides for the substitution of the existing section 3 of the 1967 Act with the following revised wording:

> '8.—(1) In the Misrepresentation Act 1967, the following is substituted for section 3—
>
> 3. If a contract contains a term which would exclude or restrict—
>
>    (a) any liability to which a party to a contract may be subject by reason of any misrepresentation made by him before the contract was made; or
>
>    (b) any remedy available to another party to the contract by reason of such a misrepresentation,
>
> that term shall be of no effect except in so far as it satisfies the requirement of reasonableness as stated in section 10(1) of the Unfair Contract Terms Act 1977; and it is for those claiming that the term satisfies that requirement to show that it does.
>
> (2) The same section is substituted for section 3 of the Misrepresentation Act (Northern Ireland) 1967.'

Thus under the present law, terms which would tend to avoid liability for the results of misrepresentation will be subject to a test of reasonableness and, if they fail to pass the test, will be of no effect.

The rules relating to damages for negligent misrepresentation differ according to whether liability is in tort or under contract. Rescission is essentially discretionary, being an equitable remedy, and can be defeated, if claimed, by the contract being affirmed. Damages are, however, available under section 2(1) of the 1967 Act. The Court of Appeal in the *Esso Petroleum* case felt that the damages should be the same whether the action was based in tort or under contract and that whatever be the cause of action the damages recoverable by the aggrieved party in this type of predicament should be the losses he directly suffers through having been induced to enter into the contract. As the law develops, and this is true of contract and tort generally, the 'pigeon-hole' distinction between the two branches of the law is becoming less marked and the tendency is for the courts to allow concurrent allegations in tort and contract to be brought and dealt with on their merits in the same dispute. (See also the courts' changing attitude towards the treatment of sea passengers' death or injury claims in Chapter 12, *post*.)

The special feature of damages awarded in tort is the application of the 'foreseeability' test (for the measure of damages, see Chapter 9, *post*), i.e. the aggrieved party can recover damages or losses which were reasonably foreseeable by the wrongdoer. In contract, the principle is different; the damages recoverable are restricted, in the normal course, to what would reasonably be deemed to have been in the minds of the principal parties to the contract.

The Misrepresentation Act received one of its rare testings late in 1977.

*Howard Marine Dredging Co Ltd* v *Ogden & Sons (Excavations) Ltd* [1978] 1 Lloyd's Rep. 334, CA
Sewage contractors wanted to hire barges to dump unwanted earth out at sea. They negotiated for two barges recently acquired from German owners. As a result of preliminary inquiries the hirers were satisfied and entered into a charterparty hire agreement. The agreement contained, inter alia, a provision that the charterer/hirer's acceptance of the barges was to be conclusive evidence of the craft being fit for the intended purpose. After six months' use the hirers began to suspect that the carrying capacity of the barges was less than had been advised to them at the preliminary negotiation talks. The error was said to have arisen because the barge owners' representative did not have with him at the time the official documentation giving the correct payload but merely the Lloyd's Register figure on which he relied. At this juncture the hirers withheld hire payments. This was met by a withdrawal of the barges by their owners. The hirers promptly counterclaimed £600,000, alleging misrepresentation resulting in costly delay in carrying out their contract. The trial court found for the barge owners. The contractors appealed. The Court of Appeal by majority decision allowed the appeal. The Act, they said, was clearly worded. It did not require that negligence should be proved. Liability lay with the barge owners unless they could show that their representative had reasonable cause to believe that his statement in regard to the barges' carrying capacity was true. The court found that the barge owners had failed to show that their representative had reasonable ground to believe his statement was true at the time when it was made. Liability lay under the terms of the Misrepresentation Act 1967, and there was no need to look at any common law rules on misrepresentation in this case.

To summarize, the innocent party is entitled to recover damages provided that he can show that he has suffered loss as a direct result of the innocent misrepresentation. The only way the person making a careless statement can escape liability is to prove that he had reasonable grounds in believing and continuing to believe the truth of his statement. If the innocent party has not performed his part of the contract, he may refuse to do so; but if both parties have fully performed, the innocent party may apply to a court for rescission which may be granted *if reasonable*. It would probably not be considered reasonable if third parties have acquired interests or rights in the subject of the contract.

*Goldsmith* v *Roger* [1962] 2 Lloyd's Rep. 249, CA
The defendant offered to sell his fishing boat to the plaintiff for £400. The plaintiff said he had examined the boat and found certain defects. He therefore offered £100 which was accepted. This statement was not correct and on discovering that the plaintiff had not examined the boat at all, the defendant refused to perform the contract.

*Held*: that the defendant was entitled to treat the contract as rescinded because of the innocent misrepresentation by the buyer. The misrepresentation was considered to be innocent because the seller did not allege fraud.

It is interesting to speculate as to whether the court, in reaching its conclusions in this case, was foreseeing the introduction five years later of the Misrepresentation Act.

Where, however, the misrepresentations alleged were never of a kind which were intended to have any contractual basis then the position may be different.

*Dawson* v *Yeoward* [1961] 1 Lloyd's Rep. 431, CA
When selling a motor yacht, the seller informed the buyer that the vessel had been recently scraped and painted in dry dock, meaning and being understood to mean that nothing

abnormal was detected. The buyer was satisfied and the vessel was not inspected. Later there was discovered serious bottom damage.

*Held*: that the seller's statements were mere representations which were never taken to have any contractual basis, and that while they might have induced the contract they never formed part of its terms and that evidence did not establish a warranty.

Generally speaking, what constitutes a representation intended to form part of a contract depends on the circumstances of each case and the intentions of the parties. In *Harrison* v *Knowles & Foster* [1918] 1 KB 608, CA, a memorandum stating that two steamships had a joint deadweight capacity was not part of the contract and therefore the sellers were not liable when it was found that the statement was in error.

### *Fraudulent misrepresentations*

A statement made recklessly and careless of whether it is true or false may constitute a fraudulent misrepresentation. Similarly, a statement made knowing it to be untrue or without a reasonable belief in its truth. The remedy available to the innocent party in this circumstance is to claim damages or rescission of the contract or both. Rescission may not be granted if innocent third parties subsequently acquire an interest in the subject-matter.

*Mason* v *Wallasea Bay Yacht Station* (1939) 65 Ll.L.Rep. 204
A fraudulent misrepresentation made during negotiations for the purchase of a yacht by the plaintiff from the defendant under a hire purchase agreement. A promissory note was given to the finance company as collateral security. The plaintiff buyer claimed rescission of the agreement and also indemnity by the defendant seller in respect of any liability under the promissory note. The plaintiff had relied on a representation as to the seaworthy condition of the yacht. The yacht was found in fact to be completely unseaworthy.

*Held*: that a representation *was* made as to the seaworthiness of the yacht and on the strength of that representation a hire purchase agreement was entered into. The representation was false and recklessly made. The plaintiff was entitled to rescission *and* indemnity.

## BREACHES OF CONTRACT MAY BE CONDITIONS, WARRANTIES OR INTERMEDIATE TERMS

Terms and stipulations in a contract are treated as conditions, warranties or intermediate terms, and they may be either express or implied.

### *What is a condition?*

A 'condition' is a fundamental term of the contract, which if there is a failure in its observance, causes the contract itself to be substantially different to that which the parties originally intended.

A breach of a *condition* entitles the other party to refuse to perform (if he had not already performed) a contract, or to return the goods to the seller (if he has already performed). Damages may also be claimed. In cases of ship sales, the buyer is entitled to a reasonable time in which to examine the ship but once having examined her, if he retains the ship, he is deemed to have accepted her.

## Sale of ship and shipbuilding contracts

### *What is a warranty?*

A 'warranty' is a term not fundamental to the contract, but only *collateral* to it. The innocent party is entitled to damages only for a breach of warranty; there is no right to reject the ship.

Generally speaking, whether any particular term is a condition or a warranty depends on the intention, interpretation and construction of each individual contract.

The use of the actual words 'conditions' or 'warranty' in the agreement is *irrelevant* to determining the status of any particular stipulation in dispute. It is the intention of the parties which matters and the way in which the breach of the particular stipulation affects the whole purpose of the contract.

*Wills* v *Ambler* [1954] 1 Lloyd's Rep. 253
A four-berth motor boat had been sold. An innocent statement by the seller that the hull was sound was held to be a warranty; the buyer had entered into the contract in reliance on that statement and the hull was in fact rotten. He was awarded damages.

*Sullivan* v *Constable* (1932) 48 TLR 369
A yacht was the subject of sale and an assurance as to its seaworthiness was a condition but as the yacht had been accepted the assurance could only, under the circumstances, be treated as a warranty.

*Willis* v *Claxton* [1951] 1 Lloyd's Rep. 70
A speedboat was advertised as having had 'a complete overhaul' and was sold. A receipt for the purchase money stated that the engine had been 'reconditioned'.

*Held*: that the buyer was not entitled to damages for breach of warranty in respect of there having been no complete overhaul since the buyer's agent had been fully aware of that when negotiating the sale. But since the engine had not been reconditioned the buyer was entitled for breach of warranty ex post facto on the receipt.

This case should, however, be contrasted with *Ecay* v *Godfrey* (1946) 80 Ll.L.Rep. 286 where a similar statement amounted only to an innocent misrepresentation in the case of the sale of a motor cruiser, and the buyer's claim failed.

### *What is an intermediate term?*

This is a term of the contract for which the parties will expressly, or more usually impliedly, agree that the effect of non-performance will depend on the nature and consequences of the breach (*Bunge Corporation* v *Tradax Export SA* [1981] 2 Lloyd's Rep. 1 at 7).

### *Implied conditions and warranties*

Under the Sale of Goods Act 1979, and in so far as a ship is 'goods' within the meaning of the Act, certain conditions and warranties are implied if the contract contains no express provisions to the contrary. Section 12 (in relation to contracts made before 18 May 1973, see Schedule 1, paragraph 3), possibly the most significant section in the entire Act, stipulates that there is: (1) an implied condition on the part of the seller that in the case of a sale he has a right to sell the goods at the time when the property is to pass; (2) an implied warranty that the goods are free, and will remain free until the time when the property is to pass, from any charge or encumbrance not disclosed or known to the buyer before the contract is made; and (3) an implied warranty that the buyer will enjoy quiet possession of the goods except so far as it may be disturbed by the owner or other person entitled to the benefit of any charge or encumbrance so disclosed or known.

Different terms are applied to contracts of sale where the seller only disposes of a limited interest in the goods.

Mortgages and maritime liens are examples of the charge or encumbrance referred to in section 12 but the term does *not* include personal obligations, i.e. under a charterparty. *Kelman* v *Livanos* [1955] 1 Lloyd's Rep. 120 (see page 60, *post*) ruled that the use of the expression 'free from average' was intended to mean 'free from claims against her'.

Section 13(1) of the Sale of Goods Act 1979 covers the situation of a sale by description and provides for an implied condition that where the goods are sold by description they will correspond with that description.

By section 14(3) of the Sale of Goods Act 1979 (as to contracts made between 18 May 1973 and an appointed day, see Schedule 1, paragraph 5) there is an implied condition that a ship is reasonably fit for the purpose for which it is bought (e.g. sea-going) if the seller sells the ship in the course of his business and the buyer, expressly or by implication, makes known to him the particular purpose for which the ship is being bought. This condition is not implied, however, where it is shown that the buyer did not rely, or that it was unreasonable for him to rely, on the seller's skill or judgement. As such skill and judgement are not inherent in every shipowner, the seller must be a person whose business it is to supply ships for this legal rule to have effect. This leaves virtually only shipbuilders, as 'ship-dealers' as such rarely, if ever, exist.

Subsection (2) of section 14, which provides for goods to be of merchantable quality, rarely, if ever, applies to contracts of sale of ships.

Breach of an implied warranty of fitness for the purpose intended was found by the Supreme Court of Ontario in March 1977 when they considered a plea of caveat emptor (let the buyer beware) by the seller in answer to an allegation that the latter had committed a fundamental breach of contract or alternatively a breach of warranty in that the boat which was the subject of the sale was found, after having been used for a period by the buyer, to be blistered on the hull below the waterline. The sellers brought an action claiming the balance of the purchase price which by the terms of the sale contract was payable in instalments.

The Court of Appeal confirmed the trial court's decision which was that although the buyer had taken the opportunity of examining the boat at a boat show and had not noticed any defects in the exterior of the hull, nevertheless the plea of caveat emptor could not be applied to the facts since it could not be reasonably expected of the buyer that he should have retained a consulting chemist to analyse the hull. Nothing less than that would have revealed the defect which was eventually said to be a defect in the composition of the skin material which reacted adversely when in contact with the water. This was vital to the fitness of the craft and there had been a breach of the implied warranty as to the fitness of the boat for the purpose for which it was sold, thus entitling the buyer to damages which were assessed at $5,000, being the estimated cost of putting the boat in a fit condition (*Canadian Yacht Sales* v *MacDonald* [1977] 2 Lloyd's Rep. 298).

## Express conditions

One type of express condition is that which must be fulfilled before the agreement itself can ever become effective. For example, an agreement stated to be 'subject to contract' is not binding and either party can withdraw.

*Howard (John) & Co (Northern)* v *Knight (JP)* [1969] 1 Lloyd's Rep. 364
In the sale of a ship there was an alleged breach of contract. The buyer agreed to buy 'subject to satisfactory running trials' and the agreement generally was 'subject to contract'. A dispute arose as to whether a binding agreement had been reached.
*Held*: that the relevant correspondence between the two parties merely confirmed that what was said was subject to contract. The minds of the two respective parties were not ad idem. There was no binding agreement at law.

But the words in a contract for the sale of a ship 'subject to satisfactory survey' have been held to be of no legal significance and the matter is one of the proper interpretation of the word 'satisfactory' by the buyer.

*Astra Trust* v *Adams and Williams* [1969] 1 Lloyd's Rep. 81
The sale of a ship was 'subject to satisfactory survey'. A dispute arose as to whether a contract had been concluded and whether the dissatisfaction of the buyers entitled them to withdraw from the contract.
*Held*: that the word 'satisfactory' did not add to or detract from what would have been the meaning and effect in law in the absence of the word. The court said (obiter) that dissatisfaction must in any case be bona fide. Even if an objective test was applied, the plaintiffs were not unreasonable in taking the view that the survey report was not satisfactory. Judgment was given for the plaintiffs.

Where the expression 'if any material defect or defects shall have been found' appears, the word 'found' means 'found in fact', that is to say the test is objective and to be determined by arbitration and, if not so found to be material, there will be no right of rejection by the buyer. See *Docker* v *Hyams* [1969] 1 Lloyd's Rep. 487, CA.

Another expression commonly used is 'subject to satisfactory running trials'.

A clause stating that a vessel is to be delivered 'free from average' means 'free from claims against her'. It is not equivalent to the mere everyday expression 'free from damage'.

*Kelman* v *Livanos* [1955] 1 Lloyd's Rep. 120
A contract of sale of the steam trawler *Goodmar* was entered into in March 1953. The sale was on 'Priam terms' ('Priam terms' include provisions for an inspection of a vessel's bottom and underwater parts) which provided, inter alia, that the sellers should deliver the steamer to the buyers 'free from average and with clean swept holds and class maintained'. Other provisions included drydocking and drawing of the tail shaft and express agreement that if any bottom damage was found the purchasers could require it to be made good to the satisfaction of a Lloyd's Register surveyor (Clause 6 of the agreement). A Lloyd's classification certificate after special survey of the vessel in September 1949 referred to some bottom damage but said that it did not affect the maintenance of the class. A surveyor to Lloyd's Register made a further inspection in accordance with the sale agreement provisions and was still of the view that there was no deterioration and that the

ship was fit to maintain her classification. A dispute arose between buyer and seller as to the cost of repairs and an estimated sum was paid into a joint account pending a decision by arbitrators. The buyers argued that they were entitled to refuse to accept the ship until repairs were effected. They also contended that the sellers had broken their obligation to deliver the vessel 'free from average'. The arbitration was in favour of the sellers but a case was stated.

*Held*: that Clause 6 must be construed in the light of the entire range of clauses and as such there were two contingencies: (1) if the surveyor after inspection approved the condition of the underwater parts and found the ship to be generally seaworthy then she should be deemed ready for delivery; (2) if after underwater inspection he found parts damaged to the extent that the condition of the ship was inconsistent with seaworthiness then she should not be deemed ready for delivery until such time as the repairs were carried out to his satisfaction. It was also held that 'free from average' in this context meant free from claims against the ship and the sellers were not in breach of that provision.

In *The Alfred Trigon* [1981] 2 Lloyd's Rep. 333 the court defined the contractual provision 'free from average damage affecting class'. The word 'average' in that context must have some meaning attributed to it; otherwise its use is meaningless. It must restrict the word 'damage' so that 'damage' when qualified by the word 'average' should only be such damage as is occasioned by a peril insured against and not just *any* damage, e.g. general wear and tear or sheer old age.

As a follow up to *The Alfred Trigon* the sale of the vessel *Star of Kuwait* brought about judicial review of the phrase 'the vessel is to be delivered . . . free of recommendations and average damage or defects affecting class . . . '. The question for the court was—did the word 'average' govern the word 'defects' additionally or only the word 'damage'? The court admitted that the construction of sentences rested to a large extent on impressions gained from just looking at the phrase, particularly first impressions. In regard to this particular phrase the impression was that the word 'average' was intended to describe *only* the word 'damage'. For the word 'average' to be applied to the word 'defects' was practically unheard of and it would be unnatural for the phrase to be interpreted to mean that 'average' covered both words. The parties must have intended that so far as defects were concerned, the vessel was to be free from defects affecting class.
(*Lips Maritime Corporation* v *National Maritime Agencies Co (The Star of Kuwait)* [1986] 2 Lloyd's Rep. 641.)

In *The Great Marine (No. 2)* [1990] 2 Lloyd's Rep. 250 the court held that propeller damage was 'average damage' because the classification society would have imposed a recommendation relating to class if the damage had been reported to it.

### *Contract term implied by court to give 'business efficacy'*

In order to add substance to and give 'business efficacy' to a particular contract it may be necessary for a court to imply a term in the contract that both parties should reasonably be deemed to have intended even though it was not expressly included, as in *The Lady Tahilla*.

*The Lady Tahilla* [1967] 1 Lloyd's Rep. 591
The plaintiff sold his motor yacht to the defendant in April 1960 for £8,000. The defendant paid £5,000 and it was agreed that the balance should be met, at the

defendant's option, in one of three ways: (a) by allowing the plaintiff free use of the yacht for one month during each of the years 1962, 1963 and 1964, subject to the plaintiff giving the defendant three months' notice of the month in which he required the yacht; or (b) by paying the plaintiff £1,000 for any year in which the yacht was not available for use under method (a); or (c) by payment in cash if the vessel was disposed of by the defendant. In April 1960 the defendant secured the balance due from him by executing a mortgage in favour of the plaintiff. In 1966 the plaintiff sued. The defendant denied liability and contended that the yacht was made available for the plaintiff in 1962, 1963 and 1964, but the plaintiff had not given notice of the month he required her.

*Held*: that the plaintiff was entitled to the £5,000 plus interest. As a general proposition where X had an option to perform a contract in more than one way and the obligations of Y depended on which way X chose and could only effectively be performed by Y if he had notice beforehand, then X would be under an implied obligation to give Y proper notice. So on these facts in order to give business efficacy to the contract it was necessary to imply a term that the defendant would give the plaintiff reasonable prior notice whether or not he was choosing method (a) in respect of any of the three relevant years. No notice had been given, therefore the mortgage remained undischarged and the plaintiff was entitled to judgment.

### *The ability of a seller to exclude his liability*

The Sale of Goods Act 1893 as originally enacted contained provisions for certain conditions to be implied if not expressly stipulated to the contrary. If, however, such express clauses were not worded in clear language the burden of showing that liability had thereby been excluded was on the party seeking to rely on the particular stipulation. If there was ambiguity it was to be interpreted in favour of the other party. A seller could exempt himself from almost anything provided he used clear meaningful language. An extreme example of how a seller might 'get away' with selling a ship with perhaps quite serious faults is in an agreement to sell a ship 'as she lies' or 'as is, where is'. A purchaser under such an agreement has little, if any, protection. The vessel must conform with the seller's basic description of it.

*Shepherd* v *Kain* (1821) 5 B & Ald 240
A ship was sold as 'copper bottom' and 'teak built' and classed at Lloyd's. The terms of the contract also said the vessel was sold 'with all faults'.

*Held*: that such an exclusion clause did not go so far as to allow the seller to escape liability for the vessel not complying with the basic description under which it was sold.

This case is in sharp contrast, however, to *Taylor* v *Bullen*, below.

*Taylor* v *Bullen* (1850) 5 Ex 779
A ship was sold 'with all faults' and 'without any allowance for any defect or error whatever'. It was also stipulated that she was 'teak built and in A1 condition'. These two items of description proved to be untrue.

*Held*: that the seller had expressly excluded his liability and the buyer was without a remedy as fraud was not proved.

So, too, in certain circumstances a buyer should be able to rely on the seller's skill and judgement.

*Cammell-Laird & Co Ltd* v *Manganese Bronze & Brass Co Ltd* [1934] AC 402, HL
The sellers were in breach of the Sale of Goods Act 1893, section 14. The buyer was entitled to rely on the sellers' skill and judgement. This need only be *partial* reliance. The

facts were that the *thickness* of the propeller was left to the discretion of the sellers although plans and general dimensions were supplied by the buyer. But to answer the question of law raised in the special case justice required that the case should be remitted to the arbitrator for further findings of fact.

However, a seller's ability to 'contract out of' his implied obligations under sections 12, 13 and 14 of the Sale of Goods Act 1893 was radically affected by the Supply of Goods (Implied Terms) Act 1973. This Act significantly modified the 1893 Act. The 1973 Act concentrated mainly on consumer sales and international sales. It is not now possible for a seller to exclude expressly section 12 of the Sale of Goods Act 1979 (the one guaranteeing quiet possession, freedom from encumbrances, etc.). Nor is it possible now, in a *consumer* sale, to exclude sections 13 and 14. In a non-consumer sale a seller *may* rely on such an exclusion clause providing he can show that his enforcing of the clause is reasonable and fair under the circumstances. (See 1979 Act, Schedule 1, para. 11.)

### *What is a consumer sale?*

A 'consumer sale' is a sale of goods, not by auction or some similar competitive method, in the course of business when (a) the goods are of a type ordinarily bought for private use or consumption, and (b) are sold to someone who is not buying them in the course of business.

### *What is an international sale?*

Where the parties are habitually resident in different States, and the goods as a result of the sale contract must be carried from one State to another, and delivery is to be made in a State different to that in which the offer (or perhaps acceptance) was made.

*Rasbora Ltd* v *JCL Marine* [1977] 1 Lloyd's Rep. 645
By the terms of a contract the defendant boat builders agreed to build a power boat. The agreement was with A. A was not the buyer, who was not a UK resident. A clause in the contract stated: 'It is agreed that the company's liability for warranty of the craft is limited to the terms and conditions set out in the warranty certificate given to the purchaser on acceptance of the craft. Any implied condition or warranty is expressly excluded, and the company shall not be liable for any loss, damage, expense or injury howsoever arising, except as accepted under the terms and conditions of the warranty certificate.' The warranty certificate stated that the defendants would replace and/or repair any items which in their opinion were defective owing to faulty materials or workmanship, provided that the items were manufactured by or to the specification of the defendants. Several months after the date of the contract A went to the builders' yard, acceptance trials took place and he signed an acceptance certificate. Six days later the plaintiffs, a company incorporated in Jersey and wholly owned by A, communicated with the defendants who sent documentation necessary to give effect to the sale, including invoices showing the plaintiffs substituted for A as buyers. Two weeks later A and others boarded the boat and sailed to the Hamble River. On the following day the boat caught fire and became a total loss. The plaintiffs claimed damages alleging breach of the implied condition contained in section 14(2) of the Sale of Goods Act 1893, as amended by the Supply of Goods (Implied Terms) Act 1973, that the boat was of merchantable quality in that the fire was caused by defective electrical systems. The defendants relied on the contract clause.

*Held*: that the plaintiffs were proper parties to the contract of sale and the boat was not of merchantable quality. The exclusion clause was of no effect because the sale was a consumer sale and the implied condition of merchantable quality could not be excluded.

This case admirably illustrates how a boat can be the subject of a consumer sale in circumstances where the buyer does not hold himself out to be buying it in the course of business. The court also came to the conclusion that the sale was not an international sale of goods. That the eventual buyer turned out to be a Jersey-registered company did not of itself have the effect of transforming the sale into an international one. Had it been so definable the builders would have been entitled to rely on their exclusion clause since the Sale of Goods Act, as amended, allows the parties to a contract for the international sale of goods to negative or vary any right, duty or liability which would otherwise arise by implication of law under the relevant sections of the statute (see section 61 of the 1893 Act, as amended).[2]

The Unfair Contract Terms Act 1977 (amended in a minor way by the Sale of Goods Act 1979) further restricted the ability of parties to a contract to exclude or limit their liability by expressed contract terms. Part 1 of the Act applies to England, Wales and Northern Ireland, Part 2 to Scotland and Part 3 contains provisions which apply to the whole of the UK.

Many of the provisions of the Act concern consumer sales and thus are irrelevant to contracts to buy and sell ships where both parties could be said to be selling/buying in the course of business. The Act has not, to the best of the author's knowledge, been tested in the field of maritime claims generally or in particular in respect of a sale/purchase contract of a ship.

Liability arising from sale or supply of goods (and by definition at the beginning of this chapter it has been stated that ships are 'goods' within the meaning and intent of the Sale of Goods Act 1979) is dealt with under sections 5 and 6 specifically of the 1977 Act.

Section 5 which concentrates entirely on the 'consumer' type of sale is not here quoted in full; section 6, however, which follows up directly the earlier provisions of the 1973 Supply of Goods (Implied Terms) Act is given in full:

'6.—(1) Liability for breach of the obligations arising from—

(a) section 12 of the Sale of Goods Act 1979 (seller's implied undertakings as to title, etc.);

(b) section 8 of the Supply of Goods (Implied Terms) Act 1973 (the corresponding thing in relation to hire purchase)

cannot be excluded or restricted by reference to any contract term.

(2) As against a person dealing as consumer, liability for breach of the obligations arising from—

(a) sections 13, 14 or 15 of the 1979 Act (seller's implied undertakings as to conformity of goods with description or sample, or as to their quality of fitness for a particular purpose);

(b) sections 9, 10 or 11 of the 1973 Act (the corresponding things in relation to hire-purchase)

cannot be excluded or restricted by reference to any contract term.

2. This right in relation to the contract for the international sale of goods does, however, exist only in relation to contracts made between 1973 and 1978 since the relevant section in the 1973 Supply of Goods (Implied Terms) Act is not preserved in the 1979 Sale of Goods Act so as to apply to international sales made after 1978. See also the opening paragraph to this chapter.

(3) As against a person dealing otherwise than as consumer, the liability specified in subsection (2) above can be excluded or restricted by reference to a contract term, but only in so far as the term satisfies the requirement of reasonableness.

(4) The liabilities referred to in this section are not only the business liabilities defined by section 1(3), but include those arising under any contract of sale of goods or hire-purchase agreement.'

Section 7 of the Act specifically is confined to miscellaneous contracts which govern the transfer of ownership of goods but which are not regulated by the law of sale of goods or hire-purchase. It would therefore seem to be not directly relevant to sale or purchase of commercial vessels. In any event this section, in so far as non-consumer sales are concerned, merely reiterates the general tone of the Act generally that liability can be excluded or restricted by reference to an express term but only if that term is found to be reasonable under the circumstances.

It is worthy of note generally that the 1977 Act gives, in section 1, a clear explanation of the meaning of the word 'negligence' within the framework of the Act. The word includes (a) a breach of any obligation, expressed or implied from the terms of the contract, to take reasonable care or exercise reasonable skill in the performance of the contract; (b) a breach of any duty under the common law to take reasonable care or use reasonable skill; and (c) (though this can obviously have no relevance to sale and purchase contracts) a breach of the duty of care imposed by the Occupiers' Liability Act 1957 (see Chapter 12 on Passengers).

The 'reasonableness test' itself and how it should be applied is explained in section 11. Section 11(1) lays down that so far as Part I of the Act is concerned the term in question must be fair and reasonable having regard to the circumstances which were or ought reasonably to have been, known to or in the contemplation of the parties when the contract was made.

### *When does property pass?*

Sections 17 and 18 of the Sale of Goods Act 1979 provide the key to when property passes as per the following provisions:

'17.—(1) Where there is a contract for the sale of specific or ascertained goods the property in them is transferred to the buyer at such time as the parties to the contract intend it to be transferred.

(2) For the purpose of ascertaining the intention of the parties regard shall be had to the terms of the contract, the conduct of the parties, and the circumstances of the case.

18.—Unless a different intention appears, the following are rules for ascertaining the intention of the parties as to the time at which the property in the goods is to pass to the buyer.

Rule 1.—Where there is an unconditional contract for the sale of specific goods in a deliverable state the property in the goods passes to the buyer when the contract is made, and it is immaterial whether the time of payment or the time of delivery, or both, be postponed.

Rule 2.—Where there is a contract for the sale of specific goods and the seller is bound to do something to the goods for the purpose of putting them into a deliverable state, the property does not pass until such thing be done and the buyer has notice that it has been done.

Rule 3.—Where there is a contract for the sale of specific goods in a deliverable state but the seller is bound to weigh, measure, test, or do some other act or thing with reference to the goods for the purpose of ascertaining the price, the property does not pass until such act or thing be done, and the buyer has notice that it has been done.

Rule 4.—When goods are delivered to the buyer on approval or on sale or return or other similar terms the property in the goods passes to the buyer:

(a) When he signifies his approval or acceptance to the seller or does any other act adopting the transaction;

(b) If he does not signify his approval or acceptance to the seller but retains the goods without giving notice of rejection, then, if a time has been fixed for the return of the goods, on the expiration of that time, and, if no time has been fixed, on the expiration of a reasonable time.

Rule 5.—(1) Where there is a contract for the sale of unascertained or future goods by description, and goods of that description and in a deliverable state are unconditionally appropriated to the contract, either by the seller with the assent of the buyer or by the buyer with the assent of the seller, the property in the goods then passes to the buyer; and the assent may be express or implied, and may be given either before or after the appropriation is made.

(2) Where, in pursuance of the contract, the seller delivers the goods to the buyer or to a carrier or other bailee or custodier (whether named by the buyer or not) for the purpose of transmission to the buyer, and does not reserve the right of disposal, he is deemed to have unconditionally appropriated the goods to the contract.'

It is extremely important to determine the time of passing of the property as it may well play a significant role in deciding when the risk passed from seller to buyer.

The basic criterion is: when did the parties intend that the property should pass? This, in turn, can only reasonably be determined by examining the terms of the contract and studying the actions of the parties.

In *Pierce* v *Wood* (1934) 48 Ll.L.Rep. 26 the buyer required the seller to make certain alterations, but nevertheless used the boat before the alterations were completed. The court inferred that the parties had intended the property to pass immediately on completion of the contract. This is an exception to the general rule.

As can be seen above, rules for ascertaining the intentions of the parties are contained in section 18 of the Sale of Goods Act 1979.

*NV & 'Vredobert'* v *European Shipping Co Ltd* (1926) 25 Ll.L.Rep. 210, HL
The House of Lords, in considering an agreement to sell five secondhand vessels, decided that the words 'buy now' in the agreement did not have such a dominant meaning as to govern the whole of the document. The contract was nevertheless a 'contract to sell' and *not* a 'sale'. The agreement was a *present* agreement to 'buy now' but that was quite consistent with a *subsequent* passing of the property.

An equally insignificant view would likely be taken of expressions such as 'today sold' or 'today bought' in a customary form of sale agreement.

The use of the bill of sale in connection with ships' sales solves much doubt as it has been confirmed by the Merchant Shipping Act 1894, section 24, that property only passes when the bill of sale is executed and transferred and the 1988 Act in no way detracts from or alters this rule. This gives rise to the legal fiction that when a ship is sold to an 'unqualified' person, that is to say a person who is not qualified to own a British ship, it operates as an agreement to sell only since if it was a proper sale contract the ship, by British law, would be subject to forfeiture.

Section 71 of the Merchant Shipping Act 1894 operates to ensure that an attempt to sell a ship to an unqualified person (i.e. a foreigner) means that the latter's legal or beneficial interest is forfeited. In practice, section 71 could mean that a *sale* automatically operates only as an agreement to sell until the legal rule can be circumvented (see *The Naamlooze* case, above).

One important point is that the actual possession of the vessel is irrelevant where there is an unconditional contract of sale. The property prima facie passes at the time the contract is entered into and the retention of possession of the vessel by the seller does not affect this happening. The risk also prima facie passes; this means that in the event that the ship is damaged or destroyed the buyer must bear the loss (unless, of course, such damage or loss is caused through the seller's fault) (Sale of Goods Act 1979, s.20).

#### *What are the seller's duties?*

The seller must deliver the ship in accordance with the terms of the contract. The time of delivery may or may not be an essential part of the contract. Unless it is expressly stipulated it is highly unlikely to be regarded as of fundamental significance. There is nothing to prevent a buyer inserting a clause in the contract making the time of delivery an essential feature and allowing him the option to cancel the contract with immediate effect if delivery is not made by the stipulated date.

#### *What are the buyer's duties?*

The buyer must pay the purchase price. The time of payment, like that of delivery, is not, generally speaking, an essential factor unless expressly made so. The buyer must also accept delivery (Sale of Goods Act 1979, s.27). Section 28 provides that payment and delivery be concurrent unless otherwise stipulated.

#### *What are the seller's remedies?*

The Sale of Goods Act 1979 empowers an unpaid seller to exercise a *possessory* lien until payment by the buyer (s.41). In addition to this possessory lien, section 48 empowers an unpaid seller to resell the goods. Resale under these circumstances will bestow upon an innocent purchaser a good title as against the defaulting buyer. There can, however, be a technical drawback arising owing to the statutory use of bills of sale and the statutory requirements of registration, because the transfer and execution of a bill of sale to X will enable X to register and, if he wishes, immediately to resell to Y by executing a bill of sale in Y's favour despite having defaulted in payment to the original seller. Such a tricky situation could probably be sorted out under section 20(2)(a) of the Supreme Court Act 1981; see also *The Bineta* [1966] 2 Lloyd's Rep. 419.

An unpaid seller may bring an action to recover the price where the purchaser has acquired the property in the ship but refused or failed to pay the price. Possession is irrelevant.

If there is a day stipulated for payment of the price and that day is past, the seller may institute proceedings. It is irrelevant in this situation whether or not property has passed. Lastly, a seller can sue a buyer for damages if he refuses to accept the ship (see *The Buena Trader*, page 51, above). Special damages are assessed on the basis of a ship's market value where applicable and should cover whatever the seller's financial loss may be directly resulting from the buyer's breach of contract.

A recent case illustrating legal action by an unpaid seller under a memorandum of agreement and counteraction by a buyer restraining sale to an alternative buyer is the following:

*Neptune Navigation Corporation* v *Ishikawajima-Harima Heavy Industries Company Limited* [1987] 1 Lloyd's Rep. 24, CA
Under contract terms the purchase price of a ship was to be paid in four instalments, the largest (85 per cent) was the final. The first three were duly paid, but as the market value for the type of ship sharply dropped before the final instalment was due the buyers found difficulty in raising the necessary cash. The sellers refused to extend the time to pay and the option to register under the Swiss flag, which the buyers held under the sale agreement was proving difficult to exercise. Due to the buyers' failure to pay, the sellers gave notice that they considered the sale terminated and when the buyers protested they were merely told that the ship was being sold to an alternative buyer for eight and a half million dollars. The first buyer offered to buy it for the same, but subject to certain conditions. The sellers refused, so the buyers obtained ex parte an injunction restraining the sale of the ship which was effective for a period of 10 days.

On appeal by the sellers, the Court of Appeal *held*: that as by their conduct in attempting to get the ship at a lesser contract price they had demonstrated that they did not want the contract in its original terms specifically performed, but rather wished somehow to obtain judicial backing to get the contract into a condition where they could insist on receiving delivery of the vessel, paying only the lesser price, coupled with a guarantee that no further claims would be made against them, the circumstances were not those suitable for allowing the buyers to obtain such relief nor was this a proper case for the granting of an injunction. The injunction would therefore be discharged.

Furthermore, the seller may sue the buyer for any deposit he has agreed to pay but not advanced and forfeit a deposit which has been paid and sue for damages insofar as they exceed this deposit. But see *The Blankenstein* [1985] 1 Lloyd's Rep. 93 where the seller could not claim substantial damages as well as forfeiting the deposit when the loss did not exceed the amount of the deposit.

### *What are the buyer's remedies?*

A buyer may take action for non-delivery of the ship and claim damages. This is the exact reverse of the damages action by the seller against the buyer for non-acceptance (Sale of Goods Act 1979, s.51).

*The Ile Aux Moines* [1974] 2 Lloyd's Rep. 502
On 5 September 1972 the buyers bought the vessel *Ile Aux Moines* from the sellers for US$617,500. Delivery was to be made not later than 15 December 1972. The vessel was not delivered by that date, so on 16 February 1973 the buyers bought for $1,000,937 a sister ship named *Crystal Diamond* for delivery about 15 July 1973. The buyers claimed: (a) $260,000 in respect of the difference between the value of the vessel on 15 December 1972 and the contract price; (b) loss of profit from the use of the vessel at the daily rate

of $871 for 212 days from 15 December 1972; and (c) $771 as interest due on the deposit made by the buyers representing 10 per cent of the contract price. The sellers denied that the buyers could recover under both heads (a) and (b) and counter-claimed $12,000 in respect of wrongful arrest of the vessel by the buyers. In a final award the arbitrators, to whom the dispute had been referred, ordered that the sellers should pay the buyers $171,271 which represented: (1) the difference in the value of the vessel at 15 December 1972 and the contract price which they found to be $182,500; (2) interest of $771 on the deposit; and (3) a lump sum of $6,300 by way of interest. In a further award the arbitrators made an award in the form of a special case in favour of the buyers for $119,350 on the ground that the buyers were entitled to recover as damages for non-delivery both the difference between the contract price of the vessel and her market value at the date of the breach and damages in respect of loss of profits. The buyers applied for the award to be remitted as they now claimed $3,821,593 under the first head. The sellers contended that under the Sale of Goods Act 1893, section 51(3), the loss of profit was not recoverable, and sought to uphold an alternative award in their favour.

*Held*: that the buyer's first claim was for $260,000 in respect of the difference in value of the vessel of 15 December 1972 and the contract price and no claim for any higher figure could be allowed.

In *The Solholt* ([1981] 2 Lloyd's Rep. 574) a buyer had cancelled a contract because of late delivery occasioned by a seller having taken a calculated risk to squeeze every drop of profit from trading his ship before handing it over. The buyer sought full damages for non-fulfilment. But, conversely, the buyer had a duty to mitigate his losses. The court found that the damages amounted to half a million dollars, the difference between the contract and the market prices, but applied the test of 'had the buyer acted reasonably' and found he had not in that he failed to offer to buy the ship while it was still available for sale without prejudice to his right to claim damages. Thus he was not entitled to recover $500,000. Ironically the seller subsequently resold his ship for 5.8 million dollars; a capricious result, commented the presiding judge.

The buyer may also sue to recover the price if he has paid it but not received the ship. He may also seek specific performance. This remedy is usually granted by a court where damages would be insufficient, inappropriate, or unrealistic.

*Onassis and Calogeropoulos* v *Vergottis* [1968] 2 Lloyd's Rep. 403, HL

The first and second plaintiffs claimed for specific performance of an order for transfer of shares in a vessel alleging under an agreement between the parties for purchase of the vessel that the second plaintiff had paid £60,000 for 25 shares, or that £60,000 was to be treated as loaned with option to take up shares. The defendant denied that the money had been paid for the shares and argued it was loaned. Had the second plaintiff effectively exercised the option to take up shares?

The lower court found for the plaintiff. The defendant appealed. The Court of Appeal ordered a new trial. The House of Lords held that this was improper and allowed the plaintiff's plea not to retry the case.

The consequences flowing from a *sale* as opposed to an *agreement to sell* are: (a) the seller is divested of his legal right to the ship; (b) the rights of the seller under his insurance policies are terminated; (c) the prima facie risk of destruction of or damage to the vessel is transferred from the seller to the buyer; and (d) the rights of the seller's creditors to any benefit from the vessel in the event of the seller's subsequent bankruptcy are removed.

***What is the position when the ship is under charter at time of sale?***

Charterparties are essentially *personal* obligations and *not* the subject of rights in rem. The buyer of a ship which is under charter at the time of the sale is not bound to perform the charter. But where he knows that the ship is under charter (and that should normally be the case) he must not employ the ship in violation of the charterparty. If he attempts to do so, he can be restrained by the charterer applying to the court for an injunction (see *Lord Strathcona SS Co Ltd* v *Dominion Coal Co Ltd* [1926] AC 108, PC; *Greenhalgh* v *Mallard* [1943] 2 All ER 239; *Port Line* v *Ben Line Steamers* [1958] 1 Lloyd's Rep. 290).

In *Isaacs (M) & Sons* v *William McAllum & Co Ltd* [1921] 3 KB 377 the sale of a chartered ship to a foreign owner was held to be a breach of the charter by the owner who was liable to the charterer in damages.

## SALE AND PURCHASE PRACTICE

Some practical as well as legal comments would probably be of value, particularly to practitioners. In many ways it would be reasonable to compare the law applicable to the sale and purchase of ships with that applicable to the sale and purchase of real property and the sale and purchase shipbroker has certain things in common with an estate agent. Such a broker is or should be an expert in his field and is of valuable assistance to the prospective seller or purchaser, as the case may be. To the buyer, the ship's particulars are all-important. They can be obtained by a study of the Lloyd's Register or the equivalent registers of other Classification Societies (e.g. the American Bureau of Shipping, Germanischer Lloyd or the Bureau Veritas). Significant features are the draught and deadweight, the number and layout of the decks (e.g. whether the ship is an 'open' or 'closed' shelterdecker), the date when and the place where the ship was constructed, the number and positioning of the compartments for carrying cargo, details of the vessel's machinery, the speed, and the fuel consumption both at sea and in port. Buyers looking for ships purpose-built for special categories of goods (e.g. motor vehicles) will require information on the relevant carrying capacity. General cargo ships will have cubic capacities, grain ships grain capacities, and so on.

Another matter of vital interest to the potential buyer is the position concerning the survey requirements of the vessel according to the requirements of the relevant Classification Society for the maintenance of the ship in her class (see *The Buena Trader*, page 51, above).

For his protection the prudent buyer will request an inspection of the vessel, possibly before meaningful negotiations for purchase take place. He may either instruct one of his superintendents to carry out the inspection or engage a consultant surveyor.

Next, the price and delivery date. Eventually the buyers will make a firm offer stipulating delivery on a fixed date and place with the option in his favour to cancel in the event of failure to meet an agreed cancellation date which will be a reasonable time subsequent to the delivery date. This elasticity serves, among other things, to give the seller the opportunity to effect any repairs which might have been put off which are necessary for the maintenance of the ship in class.

The buyer may require the ship to be put into dry dock so as to have the chance to examine the underwater parts of the ship; many sale agreements contain a clause to that effect of which a typical wording is:

> 'The Sellers shall place the vessel in dry dock at port of delivery and if rudder propelled bottom or other underwater part or parts be found to be broken, damaged or defective so as to affect the vessel's clean certificate of class same shall be made good at the Seller's expense to Classification Society's satisfaction to retain vessel's class without qualification.
>
> While the vessel is in dry dock and if required by the Buyers the tail-end shaft shall be drawn and should same be condemned or found defective so as to affect the vessel's clean certificate of class it shall be renewed or made good at the Seller's expense to Classification Society's satisfaction to retain vessel's class without qualification. The cost of drawing and replacing tail-end shaft shall be borne by the Buyers unless Classification Society requires tail-end shaft to be renewed or made good.
>
> The expense of putting in and taking out of dry dock and the dry dock dues shall be paid by the Buyers unless rudder propeller bottom or other underwater part(s) or tail-end shaft be found broken, damaged or defective as aforesaid in which event the Sellers shall pay these expenses.
>
> Sellers shall pay all costs of transporting the vessel to the dry dock and from the dry dock to the place of delivery.'

It should be emphasized that it is the seller's responsibility under this clause to get the ship to the dry dock and to pay for the expense of so doing; but the expenses of actually entering the dock and leaving it are customarily for the prospective buyer's account. For the buyer's account also is the expense of the drawing of the tail-end shaft for inspection if so required by him (the tail-end shaft is the part of the ship which links the propeller with the main engine).

As soon as agreement is reached the seller's broker will draw up a memorandum of agreement containing clauses which will include the following:

1. A preamble giving the names of the buyers and the sellers, the name of the ship and a brief description of her.
2. Price and times for payment. Payment is normally made by a 10 per cent deposit on signing memorandum of agreement in joint names of buyers and sellers or their agents and the balance, together with the release of this deposit is paid on delivery, which is usually within three days after readiness for delivery.

In *The Selene G* ([1981] 2 Lloyd's Rep. 180) an interpretation was placed by the court on the nature of a 10 per cent deposit required expressly under MOA terms to be paid within 48 hours of signing the document. A separate clause required the purchase money to be paid 'on delivery of the vessel but no later than three days . . . after the vessel is ready for delivery'. Another separate clause gave the seller the right to cancel in the event of failure thus to pay. This carried with it forfeiture of the deposit.

The buyers failed to remit the *deposit* in due time. The sellers cancelled. The dispute went to arbitrators who decided for the sellers on the ground that the deposit had a 'dual character' which included being a prepayment of part of the purchase price thus triggering off the seller's right to cancel.

On appeal by the buyers the Commercial Court judge found a clear distinction between purchase money and deposit, the latter being dignified by a separate clause. The clause containing the right to cancel had reference to the paying of the purchase money (the whole balance) *not* to the deposit. To *this* extent the arbitrators' reasons were wrong.

*But,* this was a *non-returnable* deposit in the event of non-performance and thus payment of it within the due time stipulated went to the root of the sale agreement. The appeal was dismissed.

3. Conditions of sale, also time and place for delivery.
4. Drydocking clause.
5. Additional payments for bunkers and stores.
6. Exclusion of hired items such as wireless, radar, if not the ship's property, and particularly in passenger ships it is usual to exclude badged articles.
7. All plans and classification certificates to be handed to buyers.
8. Ship to be at seller's risk until time of delivery.
9. A caveat emptor clause, absolving sellers from all faults or deficiencies of any description after delivery, subject, of course, to the conditions of the contract being fulfilled.
10. Clauses dealing with default on either side. If the buyers default the sellers can cancel the contract, retain the deposit and obtain compensation for any further loss, all expenses, plus interest thereon. If the sellers should default buyers may cancel the contract and the deposit will be returned with interest. In addition sellers would be required to make due compensation for any loss caused to the buyers.
11. Automatic cancellation of the contract and return of the deposit to the buyer in the event of the loss of the ship before delivery.
12. An undertaking to change the ship's name and funnel marking before trading under new ownership.
13. Arbitration clause.
14. A clause providing for commission to be paid to the brokers concerned.

### *Norwegian Saleform 1993*

The form most commonly in use in the world is the Norwegian Saleform of which the most recent revision was in 1993. Its text may be found in Appendix 5. This revision to the Saleform has made some important changes to the previous 1987 amended form.

One of the most important amendments introduced by the NSF is the new provision in Clauses 3 and 5 that the vessel must be physically ready for delivery at the time that the sellers give the three days' notice of readiness required under the agreement. As a result the decision of the High Court in *The Aktion* [1987] 1 Lloyd's Rep. 283 where it was held that the ship need not be ready when notice is given does not apply to contracts under NSF 93.

Following *The Al Tawfiq* [1984] 1 Lloyd's Rep. 598 (a case on NSF 66) the NSF was amended in order to make it clear that Clause 14, which requires 'proven negligence' on the part of the sellers in order for the buyers to claim damages, overrides the provisions regarding delivery, now in Clause 5. Therefore, in relation to non-delivery and late delivery the buyers must show negligence on the part of the sellers in order to claim damages. Where non-delivery is prevented by events over which the sellers have no control, e.g. accidental damage to the vessel, the buyers will not succeed.

There are also important variations in the NSF 93 at Clause 11. There is no longer a requirement on the part of the sellers to advise the classification society of damage affecting class. This provision which appears in NSF 87 was in issue in *The Niobe* [1995] 1 Lloyd's Rep. 579. There was a dispute between buyers and sellers as to whether this duty arose at the time of the contract or at the time of the last special survey (a major inspection by the vessel's classification society). The House of Lords said it was the date of the special survey. It is interesting to note that judicial opinion was evenly divided on the point.

The NSF 93 provides at Clause 11 that the vessel is to be in class without any recommendations. That means, as far as the classification society is concerned, the vessel is in class. There may be items of damage of which class are unaware. However, buyers can rely on the words 'free of average damage affecting the vessel's class' which have been added to Clause 11 and which, following *The Alfred Trigon* [1981] 2 Lloyd's Rep. 333, mean damage affecting class occasioned by an insured peril. This excludes wear and tear. Clause 11 is not, apparently, overruled by Clause 14, and if that is correct there is no need for the buyers to prove negligence on the part of the sellers. Certainly it appears that after *The Al Tawfiq* there was no intention to make Clause 14 override Clause 11, but Clause 14 does also refer to sellers' failure 'to be ready to validly complete a legal transfer' which may be wide enough to cover any breach under the NSF. The point seems to be open to argument.

The NSF provides for vessels to be delivered free of encumbrances. Whilst it is a relatively easy matter for buyers to satisfy themselves as to what mortgages exist on the ship's register and to ensure that those are discharged simultaneously with payment of the purchase price there are, of course, a number of other liabilities attaching to the ship which may not be so apparent. Claims which confer maritime liens will follow the ship even if she has been transferred to new owners.

In common law jurisdictions, where a writ is issued before the transfer of title but not served until after delivery, the vessel is still liable in rem even though the claim made under the writ does not confer a maritime lien—*Monica S* [1967] 2 Lloyd's Rep. 113. In this way claims for, for example, chandlery which do not confer a lien under English law can affect a new owner if the writ was issued before the ship was sold. Buyers could, of course, search in the Admiralty Registry in London to see what writs have been issued and carry out similar searches in other registries conferring admiralty jurisdiction in England and abroad. This would be an expensive process to undertake and, given that writs can be renewed, it is difficult to assess how far back the search should be conducted. Buyers might also wish to satisfy themselves that major items of expenditure, e.g. repairs, insurance, classification fees, crew wages, bunkers and other suppliers are paid. One would doubt whether sellers would be prepared to produce this information or whether the buyer would be willing to undertake an extensive and expensive audit.

A persistent cause of difficulties during closing has been the price to be paid for bunkers and lubricating oils remaining on board. The NSF 93 now minimizes the scope for disputes by providing in Clause 7 that they are to be paid for at the buyers' net price excluding barging.

Other new provisions of note in NSF 93 are:

Definitions of, inter alia, 'Banking days' which appear in the preamble for the first time;
Clause 2 which provides that the deposit is to be released on joint written instructions of buyers and sellers;
Clause 4 which has an alternative provision for the sale on the basis that the buyer has inspected the classification records and that the sale is outright, i.e. not subject to further inspection;
Clause 5 where there is a provision for the parties to agree extensions where the sellers are unable to meet the delivery date;
Clause 6 which now defines the underwater parts to be inspected in drydock and makes a new provision for divers' inspection as an alternative to drydock;
Clause 8 where the list of documents which sellers are to provide has been expanded;
Clause 14 which now deals with the position where the vessel ceases to be ready between notice of readiness and the date of delivery;
Clause 15 which allows buyers to place representatives on board after the MOA is signed; and
Clause 16 which provides for alternative arbitration venues.

An interesting case and one involving the Norwegian Saleform is to be found in the pages of *Lloyd's Law Reports* for the year 1988 and the facts and court's findings were as follows:

*The Troll Park* [1988] 1 Lloyd's Rep. 55
The case hinged upon the interpretation put upon the words 'built—Jan 1971' which form part of an MOA on the Norwegian Saleform. Evidence shows that the ship was substantially built by the end of 1970, but during the month of January 1971 she had to have two auxiliary engines replaced and a third repaired. This was as a result of her undergoing sea trials. The sole arbitrator found there had been no misdescription. The buyers appealed on the grounds that the arbitrator had misdirected himself or alternatively had made a finding of fact which no arbitrator, if he had reasonably directed himself, would have made.

The Commercial Court judge ruled in favour of the arbitrator's findings basing his dismissal of the buyers' appeal on the following points:

(a) The words 'built' or 'building' are ordinary language without the need to read into them any special meaning. 'Built—January 1971' must mean built *in* January 1971, and that in turn must mean building *completed* in January 1971. Few, if any, ships could be built in the space of one month. The arbitrator had attempted two alternative constructions of the controversial words, the second of which had not involved a misdirection, i.e. that a ship which was not in a condition to put to sea in mid-January 1971, could not be said to be completed (building-wise) by 31 December 1970. The de minimis rule (i.e. that the law does not take account of trifles) was not relevant.

(b) A further point as to whether an extract from the British registry describing the ship as having been built in 1970 was surplantable by other evidence was decided in the affirmative, i.e. that the entry in the registry was only determinant if no other evidence outweighed it, and there was plenty on hand to show that the building was not completed (other than de minimis) until after the end of 1970.

### *Execution of bill of sale*

Although the agreement to sell does not require executing under seal, the transfer and execution of the bill of sale from seller to buyer must be so executed. Under English law seals are no longer required although they may still be used, see the Law of Property (Miscellaneous Provisions) Act 1989 for personal seals and section 36A of the Companies Act 1985 inserted pursuant to section 130 of the Companies Act 1989. As a matter of practice foreign registers usually prefer to see a seal on the bill of sale. Usually there is a 'closing' meeting attended by all parties at which transfer of the bill of sale, together with other documents (e.g. class certificates) and payment take place simultaneously. Payment is often confirmed by Bankers' Payment Letter authenticated with copies of the banks authorized signature books. This is because the physical transmission of funds can take some time, particularly as US dollars have to clear through New York. There are often concurrent meetings at the relevant registries where the ship is currently, and will be after the purchase, registered. Representatives are standing by to delete any mortgages and register new ones with immediate effect from the passing of title. Risk passes with the passing of the property, as cannot be too heavily emphasized, i.e. coincidentally with the delivery and transfer of the bill of sale. The law relating to registration is dealt with in Chapter 1, and suffice it to say here only that under British law where the buyer is a foreign national the bill of sale should be signed in the presence of a notary public and bear the stamp of the local consulate of the country of the buyer.

### *Examples of broker's involvement legally*

The broker's legal position in the course of negotiations can be of significance, particularly when, as is customary, a deposit on the purchase price is paid by the buyer to the seller and placed in some form of specially opened joint trust account. Should the contract of sale eventually be repudiated, ownership of the 10 per cent deposit may be contested. It may then become necessary to determine the actual role which the joint holders of the bank account were playing or were intended to play when they agreed to the use of their names as holders of the account. A case in point is *The Ranger*, below.

*The Ranger* [1970] 1 Lloyd's Rep. 32
A ship was sold by the plaintiffs to the first defendants under contract requiring first defendants to pay a deposit into the joint account of the plaintiffs' agents and first defendants. The vessel was subsequently sold by the first defendants to the second defendants. A deposit was paid into the joint account of the plaintiffs' agents and the second defendants. The second contract was cancelled because of late delivery of the ship. The first contract was wrongfully repudiated by the first defendants. A claim was lodged by plaintiffs for the release of the deposit. The question arose whether the second defendants were stake-holders of the deposit.

*Held*: that the second defendants had consented to their name being used as one of the two names in which the joint account was opened, the other name being that of the plaintiffs' agents. In ratifying the use of their name as one of the two joint account holders they were ratifying its use as that of agents for the first defendants. Since as between the plaintiffs and the first defendants the plaintiffs were entitled to the deposit, the second defendants had no claim to it as against the plaintiffs.

In the following year litigation arose out of a similar situation involving a motor fishing vessel, the *Ocean Queen*, below.

*Goodey and Southwold Trawlers Ltd* v *Garriock, Mason and Millgate* [1972] 2 Lloyd's Rep. 369

The three co-owners of a motor fishing vessel, the *Ocean Queen*, decided to sell her and one of them contacted a sale and purchase broker, giving him instructions to find a buyer. Subsequently, after seeing an advertisement circulated by the broker, a potential purchaser contacted them and by mutual arrangement the purchaser inspected the vessel. An agreement to buy her for £4,000 subject to survey was made. The purchaser told the broker of this arrangement and he asked for a £400 deposit. This was paid into the broker's account. The survey revealed that work needed performing on the vessel and the estimated cost was in the region of £400. Subsequently agreement was reached between the buyer and the sellers that this cost should be split 50/50 and that the ship would cost the buyer in effect £3,800. Later the buyer gave a further cheque to the broker in the sum of £3,400. (Southwold Trawlers was a company controlled by the purchaser which was formally joined as co-plaintiff with himself.) Next, the broker told the defendant vessel owners that he had received no money from the purchaser and had in fact sold the *Ocean Queen* to another buyer for £4,000. He asked the defendant owners to confirm this second sale, which was done.

In an action by the plaintiff first purchaser to recover his money the court found that there had been a contract concluded between the first purchaser and the owners of the *Ocean Queen* and that no property in the vessel had passed to the second purchaser by that time. It was, therefore, still open to the first purchaser to sue on his contract. The court found further that it was the custom of the trade that a deposit of the purchase price was given and held by the broker acting as the sellers' agent. Similarly, the balance of the money paid by the first purchaser was also held by the broker acting as the sellers' agent. Although, the court said, the first purchaser (the plaintiff) had no cause of action against the broker against whom he had already taken legal action and failed, this did not preclude him from maintaining a successful action against the ship's owners themselves who were in any event the *disclosed* principles of the broker.

In *Atlas Shipping Agency* v *Suisse Atlantique and others* [1995] 2 Lloyd's Rep. 188, the court was considering a broker's claim for commission. This is not usually referred to in the MOA (c.f. a charterparty where the commission is set out). The court affirmed the rule that the parties create a trust for the benefit of the broker and if the commission is unpaid, the broker can, effectively, sue for breach of that trust.

### *The use of 'Mareva' jurisdiction*

Aggrieved sellers, like any claimant, have access to *Mareva* jurisdiction. It has never been the purpose of this jurisdiction to interfere disproportionately with a defendant's routine and, it is presumed, innocent business activities. The *Mareva* could perhaps be described in 'lay' language merely as the plaintiff keeping a watchful eye on likely 'debt-dodgers', aiming to hamper or irritate and so bring pressure on such people hoping perhaps *that* way to obtain their security.

*The Niedersachsen* case [1983] 2 Lloyd's Rep. 600 was the subject of a sale agreement which included a term that the ship was 'free of average damage affecting class'. According to the ruling in *The Alfred Trigon* (see page 61, above), average damage affecting class means only that type of damage which is capable of insurance coverage (i.e. not fair wear and tear) and about which the ship's Classification Society's surveyor knew or should have known. The *Niedersachsen* had leaks in her boiler tubing and defects in her stern tube and tail-shaft. Just prior to paying the purchase price and taking delivery the buyers applied ex parte for an injunction to prevent the sellers from 'dissipating' the purchase money as soon as it was paid. The Commercial Court judge refused this request because there were as yet no assets within the jurisdiction on which to impose an injunction. Accordingly, on 3 March 1983 the buyers paid the purchase money and then reapplied for the injunction. This time it was granted but only on $787,000 of the total price paid of over $3½ million. The cause of action, a prerequisite of the granting of a *Mareva* injunction, was alleged breach of warranty in the sale contract because of the existence of defects of that kind before and at the time of delivery.

The sellers applied successfully to have the injunction lifted and the injunction was discharged. The buyers appealed. The Court of Appeal reviewed the many dicta derived from case law on *Mareva* jurisdiction and reaffirmed what they considered to be a correct consensus of views that the plaintiff applicant must have a good arguable case on his cause of action. Having established that, he had to show that there existed a real risk and not merely an illusory fear that the defendant would remove or dissipate his assets. On the first of these two points there is, obviously, a danger that the *Mareva* judge may *pre*-judge the claim (on the merits) itself. He could look at *The Alfred Trigon* decision as precedent. Goff J had said there that defects under this particular sale agreement warranty were only those which actually did affect or should, if known to a surveyor, have affected, class and which arose from a cause capable of being covered by insurance. The decision in *The Alfred Trigon* is, however, not the 'last word' on this point and arbitrators to whom any dispute on *The Niedersachsen* might be referred might be persuaded only with difficulty and in turn be successfully challenged on appeal. What, therefore, Mustill J had had to guide him realistically was not so much the likely interpretation of the warranty given by the sellers but the presentation of the facts regarding the defects (leaks) themselves. The evidence before him included known leaks, allegedly repaired—communications addressed by the buyers to Germanischer Lloyd expressing worry about the state of the boiler tubes—known differences of opinion on the tubes between a surveyor for Germanischer Lloyd and a surveyor for Det Norske Veritas (*another* Classification Society). The interest of *two* societies in itself raises possibilities of defects likely to be the subject of serious dispute. Lastly there seemed to be a conflict of evidence as to whether the defective boiler tubes were due to mere wear and tear or were caused by crew negligence. All in all, Mustill J had concluded that the buyers had a good arguable case and a strong chance of recovering from the sellers any losses they might suffer (e.g. repair costs and other consequential losses flowing from the alleged breach of MOA warranty). The appeal judges spent no time on that point. Instead they pondered on whether, if they lifted the injunction, the buyers would be exposed to being unable to get any judgment in their favour satisfied. The West German sellers had not shown any prior tendencies to dodge debts, were not a company difficult to locate, nor were likely to be. Mere reticence as to their financial affairs did not of itself imply that they had 'something to hide'.

The buyers had not made out a sufficient case that there was a real risk such as to justify the continuing of the *Mareva* injunction. The buyers' appeal thus failed and leave to appeal to the House of Lords was refused.

A practice began to develop in sale and purchase transactions where the seller was an offshore corporation of obtaining a *Mareva* injunction prior to the closing of the sale in relation to alleged breaches of the contract and serving it immediately after the payment had been effected. This allowed the buyer to secure himself, but, at the same time, obtain delivery having paid for the ship. It is clear that the buyer cannot obtain a *Mareva* where he does not have a cause of action—*Siskina* [1978] 1 Lloyd's Rep. 1. In the *Veracruz I* [1992] 1 Lloyd's Rep. 353 that principle was reaffirmed by the Court of Appeal where the injunction was allowed to stand in relation to a claim for late delivery where the buyers had a pre-existing cause of action but not for a claim for breach of condition which would only exist on delivery.

## SHIPBUILDING CONTRACTS

Shipbuilding contracts by definition concern the sale of *future* goods so the property obviously cannot pass at the time the contract is concluded. Therefore a ship*building* contract cannot in practice ever amount to more than an agreement to sell (Sale of Goods Act 1979, section 18, rule 5(1), is particularly relevant and the word 'unconditionally' of particular significance).

> '(1)—Where there is a contract for the sale of unascertained or future goods by description, and goods of that description and in a deliverable state are unconditionally appropriated to the contract, either by the seller with the assent of the buyer or by the buyer with the assent of the seller, the property in the goods then passes to the buyer; and the assent may be express or implied, and may be given either before or after the appropriation is made.'

It has been said that a contract for the complete construction of a ship or for supplying materials therefor is a non-maritime contract and *not* within the Admiralty jurisdiction. Contracts to construct entirely new ships are non-maritime because insufficiently related to any rights and duties pertaining to sea commerce and/or navigation. Such reasoning also applies to agreements made *after* the hull is in the water for the work and material necessary to consummate a partial construction and bring the vessel into a condition to function as intended.

*Laing & Sons Ltd* v *Barclay, Curle & Co Ltd* [1908] AC 35, PC
A contract was entered into to build two ships on the Clyde. It contained a provision for the purchase money to be paid by instalments at specified stages as construction work proceeded. Another clause stipulated that the ship should not be deemed as having been delivered to the buyers until construction was complete and they had performed successfully their pre-acceptance trials.

*Held*: that the property in the ships passed only when they were completed and not before official trials. The contract was for a complete ship.

When a ship is to be built, the property, generally speaking, passes to the buyer only when the ship has been completed. This can create difficulties, and to avoid them provision can be made for the property to pass in stages in the process of development and construction. It is usually coupled with a counter-obligation of the buyer to pay instalments on the price. This can be seen to be a different principle to most hire-purchase agreements where the seller retains property in the whole until the payment of the final instalment.

By section 18 of the Sale of Goods Act 1979, where there is a contract for sale of unascertained or future goods by description and goods of that description and in a deliverable state are unconditionally appropriated to the contract either by the seller with the assent of the buyer or by the buyer with the assent of the seller, the property in the goods then passes to the buyer.

*Re Blyth Shipbuilding & Dry Docks Co Ltd* (1926) 24 Ll.L.Rep. 139, CA
The Blyth Shipbuilding and Dry Docks Co agreed to build a ship for an Italian company. Clause 6 of the contract stated that 'from and after payment to the builders of the first instalment on account of the purchase price, that the vessel and all materials and things appropriated to her shall become the absolute property of the purchaser'. Construction continued until debenture-holders appointed a receiver. At that point the vessel had been partly constructed and two instalments of the purchase price had been paid. Certain material which was ready to be incorporated into the hull of the ship had been brought into the builder's yard. This material had been approved by the buyer's surveyor. There was also some unworked material in the yard which had not been approved. The question arose whether the worked and/or the unworked material was the property of the buyer.

*Held*: that the property in neither type of material had passed to the buyer for neither had become so inextricably part of the vessel as to be 'appropriated to her' within the wording of clause 6. Appropriation to the contract must be complete in the truest sense. Mere approval of material by a surveyor on behalf of the buyer may not be sufficient.

### *Formation of contract*

A shipbuilding contract may be written or oral. It differs from a simple contract for the sale of a ship under which property cannot pass without the transfer also of a bill of sale in statutory form. The parties are at liberty to agree the law by which they wish the contract to be governed. There are a number of standard form contracts. The most commonly used are the Association of West European Shipbuilders form of July 1972 (AWES), the Shipowners of Japan form of January 1977 (SAJ), the Maritime Subsidy Board of the US Department of Commerce (Marine Administration) form of 1980 (MARAD) and the Association of Norwegian Marine Yards and the Norwegian Shipowners' Association form of October 1981. Yards tend to use the form promulgated by their domestic trade Association.

A prospective buyer will endeavour to write a term into the contract that the materials brought into the shipyard for use in the construction of the ship shall become his property. This will serve as added protection for him in the event of any danger that the builder may become insolvent and thus unable to complete. But bare words in the written contract may not necessarily produce this desired effect. It may take a more objective test to determine from the facts or circumstances whether a particular contract is a mere agreement to sell a completed ship, or is a contract for the sale from time to time of a ship in stages of construction. The parties must be very clear and precise in their choice of words in this respect so that their real intentions may be properly interpreted. For example, the mere expression by words in the contract that the property in materials properly approved and intended to be used in the construction should pass at a given moment may not necessarily be taken at face value. The Sale of Goods Act 1979 has clear provisions about the requirement to 'appropriate' goods (e.g. materials) to the contract. Although there has always been a view held by some that a shipbuilding contract should be regarded as a contract for work and labour and sued upon as such the prevailing view is that the work and labour aspect is ancillary only and it is seldom, if ever, that any court regards the nature of a shipbuilding contract as being a contract for a whole range of materials to be assembled into a complete ship. Rather it is, in essence, an *eventual sale of a completed ship* or a sale from time to time of a ship in its stages of construction. It is traditionally and deeprootedly interrelated to the sale of a finished product. On this basis, something more than mere intention is necessary before property and materials can effectively pass. There must be a *definite* act which usually comprises the affixing of the materials to the ship itself of some specially detailed collateral agreement to the same effect.

*Seath & Co* v *Moore* (1886) 11 App Cas 350, HL
Shipbuilders had contracts with Campbell & Sons to supply them with engines, bodies and machinery. Campbell became bankrupt and the shipbuilders commenced an action for delivery of pieces of machinery in a more or less limited condition and materials obtained for such machinery but lying loose on the bankrupt contractor's premises.

*Held*: that it is in order for parties to agree for a valuable consideration that a specific article shall be sold and become the property of the purchaser as soon as it has reached a certain stage but it is a question of construction in each case at what stage the property shall pass and a question of fact whether that stage has been reached. However, materials provided by the builders, whether wholly or partly finished, cannot be regarded as appropriated to the contract and 'sold' unless they have been 'affixed' or in a reasonable sense made part of the 'res'.

*Reid* v *MacBeth and Gray* [1904] AC 223, HL
In a shipbuilding contract there was an agreement that during construction all materials earmarked for the vessel whether or not physically in the builder's yard should vest in the buyer as his property.

*Held*: that certain plates lying in a railway yard, although marked with the ship's number by instruction of the builder, were nevertheless the property of the builder's creditors, not the buyer's. Therefore creditors of the buyer could not attach these materials.

Certainly, mere agreement by the respective parties that the purchase price is to be paid by instalments will not suffice to imply beyond a doubt that the property in the various parts will pass stage by stage. Over the years, the courts have been reluctant to hold that the property in materials has passed to the buyer unless the expressed wording is very precise, clear and unambiguous. The alternative for the buyer to negotiate a refund guarantee or, if that is not available, a provision that the ship is security for the repayment of the instalment. Where appropriate this may require registration—see *The Annangel Glory* ([1988] 1 Lloyd's Rep. 45) where a lien on sub-freight due to an English charterer who was in liquidation was unenforceable for non-registration with the Registrar of Companies. This guarantee is an important provision as can be seen from *Gyllenhammar* v *Sour Brodogradevna Industrija* [1989] 2 Lloyd's Rep. 403. The contract provided for a performance guarantee on behalf of the builder, failing which the contract was void. The buyer had an option to have another vessel built on the same terms, but was unable to enforce the option because the builder could not obtain the guarantee.

That there *is* a construction element in the nature of contract is, however, illustrated in *The Atlantic Baron* [1979] 1 Lloyd's Rep. 89 where increases in the commercial credit opened by a builder in favour of a customer for repayment of any instalments paid in the event of default by the builder, resulting in eventual non-delivery of the finished product, were held to be consideration, as indeed was the original credit itself.

### *Duties of a builder*

No responsibility can rest upon a shipbuilder if he builds in accordance with the design and specification given to him by the buyer. He must, however, always warrant that the materials he uses are fit for the purpose required, and must carry out the work to the general standard of skill expected of a shipbuilder.

This principle should be contrasted sharply with the reverse idea that when the buyer asks a builder to 'build him a ship', he, the buyer, is entitled to rely on the builder's skill and judgement.

Ships nowadays are built subject to the safety requirements laid down in the more recent Merchant Shipping Acts; the relevant Acts being the Merchant Shipping Act 1974, the earlier Merchant Shipping (Safety Convention) Act 1949 and the Merchant Shipping Act 1964.

### *Doctrine of frustration*

The doctrine of frustration can apply to shipbuilding contracts as is well illustrated by the *Fisher Renwick* case, below, where supervening events rendered the contract commercially impossible of effective fulfilment.

*Fisher Renwick & Co* v *Tyne Iron Shipbuilding Co* (1920) 3 Ll.L.Rep. 201, 253
The issue in this dispute was whether the plaintiffs were entitled to recover damages from the defendants for failure to build a screw steamer, under a contract dated 8 February 1913, for delivery in January 1916. Default was made. The vessel was in fact not even commenced at the date she should have been delivered. The contract provided that in the event of any cause beyond the control of the builders the defendants should be allowed one day's extension of the contract period for each day's delay so caused. The defendants argued that by reason of government interference the contract became impossible of performance. They contended that the Admiralty had directed them to give preference to Admiralty rather than private work and that the war had depleted their staff, etc.

*Held*: that the circumstances had so drastically changed from the time when the contract was entered into that the doctrine of frustration applied. Whether there has been inordinate delay so as to frustrate the mutual intentions of the parties depends on the circumstances. In this case there clearly had been. The plaintiffs' continued insistence on the performance of the contract was unjustified and their claim failed.

Given the fact that shipbuilding contracts can extend over lengthy periods, delay, in order to be frustrating, would have to be similarly lengthy. The matter may also be covered in the contract. The AWES form provides for delay as a result of 'force majeure' in Article 6(c).

### Passing of risk

The general rule that risk passes at the same moment as the property could produce unfair results to a purchaser of a partially built ship. To obviate this it is customary for parties to agree expressly that the risk does not pass until delivery of the completed ship.

### Destruction of ship being built

When a ship in the course of construction is destroyed by reason neither of fault on the part of the builder/seller nor of the buyer, one cannot look to section 6 or section 7 of the Sale of Goods Act 1979 for an answer for they deal with situations involving the destruction of specific goods. The general rules of the law of contract determine who bears responsibility in the event of a partially constructed ship being destroyed through fault of neither party. In deciding whether a shipbuilding contract has thus been frustrated consideration will be given to the stage of completion reached and to the degree of urgency with which the buyer requires the completed vessel for some particular purpose of which the seller may be aware. The presence of wording in the agreement to the effect that property should pass in stages would be irrelevant to the determining of this issue which is the total destruction before risk has passed of the contemplated subject-matter of the agreement.

Delay as a result of 'force majeure' may be covered in the contract (see above). Alternatively the contract may provide for a loss of the vessel under construction. The SAJ form at Article 12, provides either for the outlay of the builders' insurance recovery on rebuilding or for the refund of the buyer's instalments.

### What are the builder's remedies?

If the buyer fails to pay, the builder may: (a) exercise his possessory lien; (b) resell as a result, exercising his lien; (c) exercise a common law right of stoppage in transit; and (d) sue for the price. These rights of the builder are, of course, the same as those of a seller generally.

In *Hyundai* v *Pournaras* [1978] 2 Lloyd's Rep. 502 the subject of the extent of a guarantor's liabilities was discussed.

The plaintiffs were shipbuilders who had entered into contracts of shipbuilding and sale with two buyers who were Liberian registered companies. Having little knowledge of the integrity or financial capabilities of the buyers, the plaintiffs' yard accepted guarantees from Piraeus-based guarantors as an inducement for them to conclude the contracts. There were four buildings the subject-matter of the contracts and, under the terms of the contracts, payment was to be in five instalments. The buyers in fact defaulted on the first instalment and failed totally to pay the second instalment. Exactly a year after the contracts were entered into, the plaintiff builders regarded the contracts as at an end and sought to recover under the guarantees.

The trial judge, (confirmed later by the Court of Appeal) found for the plaintiffs. The guarantees had to be construed upon commercial lines. The fact that the contracts were at an end did not free the buyers from their duty to pay what was already due and thus did not absolve the guarantors' several liabilities for the accrued but unpaid instalments. It was right to hold the guarantors to their guarantees and wrong that they should be granted any form of equitable relief from having to pay over huge sums, although ultimate performance of the contracts had failed.

On facts very similar to the above case, in *Hyundai* v *Papadopoulos* [1980] 2 Lloyd's Rep. 1, the House of Lords emphasized their full endorsement of the judicial reasoning given in the earlier *Hyundai* case. It would be difficult to believe that commercial men would have intended that the guarantor was to be released from his liability for payments already due and in default just because the plaintiff builder had made use of his contractual remedy to cancel the contract for the future. The buyer's default indeed had the effect of triggering the defendant guarantors' liability and made the letters of guarantee operative at that moment and not at some final day of account-reckoning in the distant future.

If the buyer fails to take delivery, the builder may sue for failure to accept. The builder also, of course, has the usual remedies available where the buyer has been in breach of a condition of warranty.

Refusal to take delivery was well illustrated in *The Diana Prosperity*, below, although it should be emphasized that in that case the contractual relationship was one of eventual owner and charterer in disagreement over a newly constructed vessel and not one between the builder of the vessel and its purchaser. The point illustrated, however, is relevant to either relationship.

*The Diana Prosperity* [1976] 2 Lloyd's Rep. 60, CA
In 1972 the third party defendant, Sanko, planned to build 50 tankers to be delivered from 1975. They raised money by granting time-charters. In August 1972 the first defendant chartered from Sanko a vessel to be built by Osaka Shipbuilding Co. The first defendant sub-chartered it in October 1973 to the plaintiff with delivery date 1 April 1976. The vessel was to be of 87,600 tons. However, Osaka Shipbuilding could not handle the building of ships over 45,000 tons, for which reason the ship was built at the Oshima Yard of which Osaka Shipbuilding owned 50 per cent of the shares. The ship *Diana Prosperity* was due to be delivered on 1 April 1976, but the plaintiff rejected the tender on the ground that the ship they had chartered had been built by a different company (Oshima) from that stated in the charterparty (Osaka). A summons was taken out to determine the issue.

*Held*: (in the lower court) that the plaintiff and the first defendant were not entitled to refuse to take delivery merely because the ship was built by a different shipyard to that stated in the charter. An appeal was lodged against the decision and the Court of Appeal decided that the stipulation to 'build in Osaka Yard' was not a strict condition precedent which had to be exactly fulfilled. The charterer and sub-charterer were getting in substance the vessel they bargained for and fit for the purpose for which they wanted it. The fact that it was not built in the stipulated yard was incidental and a 'mere misdescription of nomenclature'.

Another dispute which was very similar on the facts to *The Diana Prosperity* but yet which differed in certain respects was *Sanko Steamship Co Ltd* v *Kano Trading Ltd* [1978] 1 Lloyd's Rep. 156, CA. *The Diana Prosperity* rule was applied, but the actual wording of the agreement differed from that in the earlier case. In the later case charterers sought to escape from their contractual obligations because of the collapse of the tanker market due to the oil crisis of 1974. Perhaps this case as well as any other in the field of shipbuilding contracts illustrates how very close scrutiny must be made of the actual wording of the contract clauses, both individually and read as a whole, in order to determine the true intentions of each party to the agreement. Also emphasized is what might perhaps be described as the very individual nature of the agreement covering the very specialized needs and requirements of the purchaser/receiver of the completed vessel. The interest in the *Sanko* case was the particular and peculiar significance of the word 'at'.

*Sanko Steamship Co Ltd* v *Kano Trading Ltd* [1978] 1 Lloyd's Rep. 156, CA
The charterers, faced with possibly disastrous results on a falling market, sought to rescind the charter they had entered into on the ground that the vessel tendered did not correspond to the contractual description. The charter agreement contained, inter alia, two clauses: one in the preamble to the agreement stating that 'it is agreed between the owners of the Good Newbuilding tank vessel known as Osaka Shipbuilding Co Ltd hull no 352 until named . . . described as per clause 24 hereof [which provided for the description of the vessel on a special annexed form] and the charterers . . . '; and the other, much later on in the document, stating 'this charterparty is for a motor tank vessel to be built at Osaka Shipbuilding Co Ltd hull no 352, described as about 87,600 tons . . . summer deadweight . . . '. The vessel was in fact not built at Osaka but at a yard at Oshima, a half-subsidiary company of Osaka, about 30 miles away. The owners, Sanko, sought US$11,000,000 damages.

The Commercial Court of the Queen's Bench Division found for the owners and this was confirmed on appeal. The Court of Appeal said that the words in the preamble to the agreement were words of identification only and could not on any reasonable construction of the wording be said to impose a contractual obligation on the owners to provide a vessel actually constructed in the Osaka yard. One judge said that to rest the case on the discrepancy between the use of the word 'at' in a clause and the word 'as' in the preamble should not redound to the charterers' benefit. 'At' may have been an inappropriate word to use in the circumstances but it could not of itself put a different commercial construction on the agreement and the intentions of the parties therein expressed as to allow the charterers to treat the delivery of a ship built in another shipyard as a breach of the agreement. It was mere conjecture as to what would have been the commercial judgement of the charterers before they had entered into a bonding agreement if they had known that such a vessel would eventually be constructed in the Oshima yard.

*Dixon Kerly* v *Robinson* [1965] 2 Lloyd's Rep. 404
A new design of yacht was built by the plaintiff in the action. During the negotiations the builder/seller wrote to the buyers enclosing drawings and specifications of class. He wrote again later confirming that the vessel was built generally in accordance with marine specifications. The buyers argued that they were entitled to off-set damages for breach of express terms of the contract and implied terms that the vessel should be seaworthy and reasonably fit for sailing at sea and/or for cross-Channel trips.

*Held*: that the builder's obligations were to build generally according to the drawings. The defendant buyers had failed to establish any of the allegedly implied terms.

### *What are the buyer's remedies?*

If the builder fails to deliver, the buyer may either (a) seek specific performance, or (b) sue for non-delivery.

Where there may be an express term in the contract that property is to pass in whole or partly by stages to the buyer *before* delivery, this does not deprive the buyer of his right to reject the ship if it fails to meet up with the required standard.

*Admiralty Commissioners* v *Cox and King* (1927) 27 Ll.L.Rep. 223
The defendants contracted to build a motor boat for the Admiralty. The engine was to be supplied by the Admiralty but the speed was guaranteed by Cox and King. The engines

failed to attain the necessary brake horse power and consequently failed to reach the guaranteed speed. The Admiralty put in a claim for the return of the contract price. Their claim was allowed.

Their Lordships commented that the respective rights of the parties depend upon the true inference which is to be drawn from the correspondence which forms the basis of the contract between them.

The Sale of Goods Act 1979 allows an examination of the goods by the buyer before he is obliged to signify acceptance (section 34). Having accepted, however, the right of rejection is lost and the buyer's only redress if he discovers fault is by way of damages.

Delivery usually takes place at the place agreed for the acceptance trials. The builder must notify the buyer of the ship's readiness for trials. (Inasmuch as this specialized arrangement is covered by the Sale of Goods Act 1979, it is by section 29.) It is up to the buyer to arrange to take delivery in that place. The costs are for his account.

The time of delivery is usually stated and indeed usually constitutes a material or essential term of the contact. If it is not mentioned at all or if the delivery date, if mentioned, is not considered an essential term with the 'force' of a condition, then the builder must deliver within a reasonable time. What is 'reasonable' in any given circumstances is relative to those circumstances only. Every set of facts may be slightly different and must be construed on its own merits. (Again section 29 of the Sale of Goods Act 1979 is, if anything, the relevant section on this point.)

*Gabela* v *Vergottis* (1926) 26 Ll.L.Rep. 238
A contract was made on 23 June 1925, but subsequently the buyer refused to be bound by the contract and claimed back his deposit and damages.

*Held*: that the sellers were to blame because they had delayed for an unreasonable period of time in carrying out the terms of the contract and that the deposit should be returned.

It seems to be well established that when the delivery date is a term of the contract and not only has it passed but also a reasonable time thereafter has elapsed, the buyer is entitled to rescind the contract and recover the money he has paid.

*McDougall* v *Aeromarine of Emsworth* [1958] 2 Lloyd's Rep. 343
A contract for the construction of a racing motor yacht provided: (a) that best endeavours be made to complete construction by 1 May 1957, but no delivery date was guaranteed; (b) that the buyer was to be notified in writing that the yacht was ready for acceptance trials; (c) that the builder should be deemed to have contracted in accordance with specification requirements and the buyer's satisfaction was to be indicated in writing after the trial run; (d) the yacht was to become the absolute property of the buyer including all machinery, fittings and equipment earmarked for construction upon the first instalment of the purchase price being paid; and (e) any defective workmanship or defect in materials if discovered by the buyer within six months after the acceptance trials should either be made good by the builders or, alternatively, the builders should pay to the buyer a sum equal to reasonable costs of repair. Every warranty, condition or guarantee implied by statute or common law was expressly excluded from the contract.

The plaintiff buyer during construction decided to have the top-sides varnished and the defendant builder accordingly advised splining of the seams. The plaintiff agreed to meet the additional cost involved. The yacht's launching and acceptance trials were postponed until 3 June 1957. Subsequently, gaps were observed in the seams and the builder was requested to rectify them. The builder assured the buyer that the seams would close up naturally and on 5 June requested the buyer to accept. The buyer refused and the builder by way of compromise agreed to spline the seams without charge. Later still, further modifications were requested by the buyer and eventually on 17 July his surveyor discovered defects in the bolts and seams. Again the builder offered to rectify the defects provided that the buyer would accept the yacht thereafter. The buyer refused, demanding the return of his money and disclaiming the property in the yacht. Offers and counter-offers were rejected.

*Held*: that when the vessel was tendered for delivery on 3 June and 17 July she was neither seaworthy, nor of merchantable quality, nor fit for the use intended. The buyer was not unreasonable in refusing in July to be satisfied with the construction. No evidence was given that by November 1956 the construction of the vessel had started or that any equipment had been purchased by the builder for the construction. Thus, the buyer was not divested of his right to reject the vessel and disclaim any property in it. That even if the property had passed as the construction of the vessel proceeded and equipment was purchased the buyer was entitled to refuse to accept an incomplete vessel and, if he did so, any right of property in the incomplete vessel was revested in the builder. That the builder was under a duty to deliver within a reasonable time after 1 May 1957 and that it was a condition of the contract and not a mere warranty that the builder should deliver the vessel within that reasonable time. That the failure of the builder to tender the yacht for delivery in accordance with the contract by 5 September was a breach of condition and entitled the buyer to rescind the contract. That the meaning of the word 'performance' in the terms of the contract included the standard of workmanship and materials and the compliance of the yacht with the specifications. Judgment was given for the plaintiff buyer.

*Vosper Thornycroft Ltd* v *Ministry of Defence* [1976] 1 Lloyd's Rep. 58
The plaintiffs contracted to build a ship (HMS *Amazon*) the first of a new class of frigate, for the defendants for a price of just over £5,000,000. The contract provided, inter alia: 'Clause 66. Arbitration. Any dispute or difference between the parties . . . whether in regard to the carrying out of the work under the contract or as to the construction or meaning of the contract . . . shall be referred to the Controller of the Navy who may enter upon the reference . . . '. 'Price variation. Addition A. The price . . . tendered by the contractor and accepted by the Ministry of Defence for the construction of the vessel . . . shall be subject to the following proviso . . . '. 'Proviso 6. In the event of exceptional dislocation and delay arising during the construction of the vessel due to modifications . . . or any other cause beyond the contractor's control, the effect thereof shall be assessed by mutual agreement between the Ministry and the contractor, failing which the Ministry may pay for the vessel on an "actual cost" basis, subject to cost investigation by the Ministry, plus a fair and reasonable sum for profit'. The contract acceptance date of 20 April 1972 was delayed until 19 July 1974 due to a number of matters beyond the plaintiffs' control. The ship was delivered on 19 July 1974. The defendants paid the plaintiffs £2,000,000 extra in respect of the force majeure delays, but the plaintiffs claimed a further £4,000,000. The defendants contended that the plaintiffs' entitlement to payment was conditional on mutual agreement and if no mutual agreement was achieved, nothing could be due to the plaintiffs and, further, a failure to agree did not amount to a 'dispute' within the meaning of the arbitration clause.

*Held*: that the action succeeded. The arbitration clause was wide in that it referred not only to 'disputes' but also to 'differences'. It was essential for the business efficacy of proviso 6 to imply a term that, in default of agreement, the effect of the exceptional dislocation and delay be determined by arbitration pursuant to and under the arbitration clause. There was nothing in the context of the proviso or price variation condition 'A' in its totality which suggested that a restrictive interpretation should be placed upon the ordinary meaning of the word 'effect'. Since the plaintiffs had no right to claim compensation on the ground that the contract had been broken, in view of the fact that the cause of dislocation and delay did not amount to a breach, such a right had to be found in the provisions of the contract if it was to make commercial sense.

The judge in the *Vosper Thornycroft* case is quoted as having said: 'The fact that a particular construction leads to a very unreasonable result must be a relevant consideration. The more unreasonable the result, the more unlikely it is that the parties can have intended it, the more necessary it is that they shall make that intention abundantly clear'.

The buyer may have the benefit of an option to cancel written into the agreement and how such a situation is dealt with if it becomes a disputed issue is illustrated in the *Harland & Wolff* case, below.

*Harland & Wolff Ltd* v *Lakeport Navigation Co Panama SA* [1974] 1 Lloyd's Rep. 301
On 15 August 1969 the plaintiffs, shipbuilders, entered into a contract with the defendants to build a steam turbine tanker for them at the basic price of £9,070,000. Clause 4(1) of the contract was entitled 'delayed delivery' and stated, inter alia, that 'if the delay in delivery continues for a period of more than 150 days after the date of delivery set forth in this agreement, the buyer may at his option cancel the agreement by serving upon the builder written notice of cancellation. The buyer may serve such written notice by cable or telex . . . if the buyer has not served such notice . . . within . . . the . . . 150 days' period delay in writing . . . the builder and the buyer shall negotiate and agree within 30 days after such notice received by the buyer from the builder either to cancel or consent to delivery and accept the vessel at a future date under the conditions mutually agreed by the buyer and the builder in the course of negotiation'.

It was agreed that the plaintiffs should use due diligence to deliver the vessel by 28 February 1973. The vessel was not delivered by that date. Shortly before that date the parties agreed that the plaintiffs would deliver the vessel on completion, and that the matter would be referred to arbitration. On 29 July 1973 the plaintiffs, purporting to act under clause 4(1) of the agreement, made a written demand on the defendants to elect whether they would cancel the contract or would accept the vessel under conditions to be mutually agreed in the course of negotiations within the next 30 days, with a view to the defendants paying for the increased cost of the vessel's construction. On 7 September 1973, the vessel was tendered to the defendants, who accepted. The defendants had always made it clear that they were willing to take delivery at any time, and never purported to cancel the contract. The arbitrator to whom the matter was referred made an interim award in the form of a special case, the question for the decision of the court being whether the plaintiffs were entitled (1) to give notice under clause 4(1) demanding that the defendants should make an election, and (2) to require that negotiations should take place.

*Held*: that the answer to both questions was 'yes'. The defendants, by communicating their intention to the plaintiffs not to exercise the option to cancel, could not reprieve the plaintiffs of the right or discharge them from the obligation under clause 4(1) to make the demand. The plaintiffs in giving the notice were entitled to require that the negotiation should take place.

A collateral agreement commonly included in a shipbuilding order is contained in a promise, supported perhaps by a deposit of money to pay for extras in the way of equipment which may eventually be required by the purchaser.

*John Helmsing Schiffahrts GmbH & Co KG* v *Malta Drydock Corp* [1977] 2 Lloyd's Rep. 444
Some German shipowners ordered two small vessels from a Maltese shipyard. A 'plus-up' of 10 per cent on the agreed basic of each ship was also agreed to pay for any extras the buyers might want, such as radio equipment. The extra 10 per cent was returnable if not used by the buyers. The buyers eventually purchased what extras they required in Germany and requested the return of their 10 per cent extra deposit. The shipyard refused but later settled out of court. The other issue in the dispute was interest payable from delivery of the vessels to the time of repayment; more than four years. The shipyard argued that the money was not due to be repaid until four years after delivery in any case. The amount of interest was also in dispute. This centred round the arrangement for financing the vessels at the outset. The buyers could only contribute 40 per cent in cash towards the cost and the Investment Bank of Malta agreed to advance 50 per cent leaving a balance of 10 per cent. The shipyard accordingly had consented to leave the 10 per cent balance undrawn for four years receiving only 4 per cent interest, which arrangement they said should be applied by parallel agreement to the repayment under dispute.

*Held*: that the defendant shipyard's argument failed and repayment was due at or about the time of delivery; preferably a mean date between the delivery of the two respective ships. The amount of interest depended on the country and the currency in the context of which the interest was to be awarded. Under the principle enunciated in the *Miliangos* case interest is payable in the currency of account and the German shipowners' actual loss was that through the Maltese shipyard's failure to pay they had had to find the equivalent sum in Germany at the commercial borrowing rates prevailing. They were, therefore, entitled to interest payable in Maltese pounds but calculated in accordance with prevailing German borrowing rates.

It is customary for the parties to stipulate in the agreement which law and/or jurisdiction should control and govern any dispute which might arise out of the agreement but some agreements are drawn up without such express stipulation. In the absence of an express clause, the proper law is to be found by asking with what country has the transaction 'the closest and most real connection': per Lord Denning in *Sayers* v *International Drilling Co NV* [1971] 1 WLR 1176, CA.

In summary of the concluding section of this chapter, the features which set shipbuilding contracts apart from contracts of sale generally are these. The nature of the contract, being one for construction and ultimate sale, means that the performance of the agreement is likely to be spread over a considerable period of time and the risk of supervening events of a force majeure nature interfering significantly with the original commercial intentions of each party is that much the greater. This would seem to underline the need for shipbuilding agreements to be accurately 'tailored' with this in mind.

There are two specific risks, the risk of partial or total destruction of the subject matter of the contract and the risk of financial embarrassment of, or at worst bankruptcy of, either party at any stage during building. The latter risk, as we have seen, is partly catered for by the introduction of appropriate wording, sufficiently unambiguous, to represent the intentions of the parties that property may pass in stages during construction, reinforced by a counter-commitment that the price be paid by instalments. That this may be said to run roughshod through the basic rules contained in the Sale of Goods Act regarding the passing of property is neither here nor there because what surely *really* matters is the clear and accurate expression of intention of the parties.

As to the risk of partial or total destruction, it would be a very unwise shipbuilder who omitted to take out insurance cover on the ship he was constructing in accordance with the Institute Clauses for Builders' Risks. In this respect and as regards this particular risk it surely must be the builder/seller who is on risk until such time as the ship is a completed entity ready for delivery and fit for the purpose intended. That the intentions of the parties run counter to the general rules laid down in the Sale of Goods legislation emphasizes the more clearly the specialist nature of these agreements. The need to build to specifications, to conform to and observe the stipulations laid down either nationally or internationally, e.g., the Safety of Life at Sea Convention which now renders obligatory the carrying of up-to-date navigational equipment and the meeting of other requirements, further bears witness to this.

Shipbuilding contracts need very careful drafting of provisions in contemplation of the likely event of damage before delivery which may need remedying but would not perhaps be so drastic as to entitle the buyer to refuse to take delivery. Objections raised by technical experts, surveyors, officials of government are very foreseeable and a properly drafted agreement should bear such eventualities in mind. Extreme delay, through fault perhaps of neither party, could cause the need for an adjustment in the price from the originally agreed figure. A clause covering this likely happening should be a regular feature of the agreement.

Precise accurate drafting of stipulations is perhaps as vital in this type of contract as in any other because, rare though may be the disputes arising from them which find their way into the tribunals, the few which do are likely to concern sums in the millions rather than the thousands. There is a strong argument for putting shipbuilding contracts more forcefully than hitherto on the agendas of international discussions.

CHAPTER 4

# ADMIRALTY JURISDICTION, MARITIME CLAIMS, LIENS AND SOVEREIGN IMMUNITY

## ADMIRALTY JURISDICTION

Before 1852 in England at common law all actions were by way of proceedings in personam. Since then an action in rem has been available in certain circumstances in maritime disputes. Admiralty Court Acts in the 19th century (1840 and 1861) introduced into English law the statutory right to arrest, originally conferring it upon claimants in respect of necessary materials supplied or services such as towage rendered to foreign vessels. The in rem jurisdiction was expanded in 1873–75 by the Supreme Court of Judicature Acts and the right was next consolidated by the Supreme Court of Judicature (Consolidation) Act 1925. This last mentioned statute was replaced by the 1956 Administration of Justice Act, itself being replaced by the Supreme Court Act 1981.

To understand how Admiralty jurisdiction is exercised in England it must thus be borne in mind that Britain is a *common* law country and that *Admiralty* law has been superimposed over the years by various statutory enactments from time to time. The right to seize a vessel by legal process is therefore partly based on rights conferred by general maritime law and partly upon the right to take legal action of this nature granted by statute. The 1956 Act was the United Kingdom's attempt to give recognition to the International Convention on the Arrest of Sea-going Ships, 1952. Much of shipping law is based on international Convention and post-World War Two this Arrest Convention was a significant development. As this chapter will relate, however, the 1956 statute was a half-hearted attempt only to adopt the Convention and caused dilemmas and necessitated much subsequent judicial interpretation, which problems became resolved only after the elapse of some 30 years in 1982 by amending legislation contained in the 1981 Supreme Court Act. The essence of the in rem procedure is that the 'res' itself becomes, as one might say, the defendant, and ultimately the 'res' (i.e. the ship) may be arrested by legal process and sold by the court to meet the plaintiff's claim; always provided, of course, the validity of the claim is eventually proved to the satisfaction of the court. The full claim may not necessarily be satisfied because the proceeds from the sale may not be sufficient, and/or there may be other claimants with prior-ranking claims. The primary object, therefore, of the action in rem is to satisfy the claimant out of the 'res'. It should be understood that the vessel itself is not the only 'res' against which action may be taken. Under certain circumstances it may also be (a) the cargo, or (b) the freight, or even (c) the proceeds of sale.

The advantages of an action in rem over an action in personam (i.e. directly against the *person* allegedly at fault) is that the action in personam is dependent entirely upon the plaintiff X being able properly and effectively to serve a writ of summons on the defendant Y in connection with the legal complaint he has against Y. This is unlikely to cause problems when X and Y are both in the same jurisdiction, but may create difficulties when they are in different jurisdictions unless the defendant Y is domiciled in an EU or EFTA country. Ships, however, which are perhaps their owners' most valuable assets, sail between nations and move from jurisdiction to jurisdiction. Thus the maritime shipping industry contains within its sphere the concept of legal action being available to an injured party through the machinery of the Admiralty jurisdiction which allows, under certain clearly defined circumstances, the vessel to be 'sued in rem'.

The modern writ in rem has become a piece of legal machinery directed against the ship alleged to have been the instrument of wrongdoing in cases where it is sought to enforce a maritime or statutory lien or in a possessory action against the ship whose possession is claimed. A judgment in rem is a judgment good against 'all the world'.

This does not mean that the vessel itself is the wrongdoer but that it is the means by which the wrongdoer (its owner) has done wrong to some other party. It is also logically the means by which the wrongdoer is brought before the court as a defendant to what may thereafter turn into an action in personam. It has been said that the purpose behind the original granting of Admiralty jurisdiction was the protection and promotion of the shipping industry.

English legal theory has accepted that an action in rem is *procedural*, the purpose being to secure the defendant owner's personal appearance. Action in rem is distinguished from 'maritime attachment' which is directed against the *person*.

Some very pertinent comments were made by the court in *The Capricorn* (*Antares Shipping Corp* v *Delmar Shipping and Portland Shipping Co Inc* [1977] 1 Lloyd's Rep. 180), a case heard in the Supreme Court of Canada. The matter involved an action for possession of the vessel. Quoting a previous judgment (*The Atlantic Star* [1973] 2 Lloyd's Rep. 197, HL) it was said that: 'Ships are elusive. The power to arrest in any port and found thereon an action in rem is increasingly required with the custom of ships being owned singly and sailing under flags of convenience. A large tanker may by negligent navigation cause extensive damage to beaches or to other shipping: she will take very good care to keep out of the ports of the "convenient" forum. [It should be understood that the expression "forum non conveniens" is used to describe the position where the competent court of a State will not exercise its jurisdiction if it is a seriously inconvenient forum or place for the action to be tried *provided that* a more appropriate forum is available to the plaintiff in the action.] If the aggrieved party manages to arrest her elsewhere, it will be said forcibly that the defendant has no sort of connection with the forum except that she was arrested within its jurisdiction. That, however, will frequently be the only way to secure justice.'

'Forum shopping' is a phrase much used in everyday language in the maritime world and it is inextricably linked with the principles of the action in rem and the availability of maritime liens. The word 'forum' in the Latin meant 'market-place' where men met to discuss everything from politics to cattle. Every port is potentially a legal forum in Admiralty. The system, inconvenient though it may be to some, has overall lent itself to the preservation of justice.

For an action in rem to be entertained in the Admiralty Court, however, the writ must be served on the 'res' in England or be deemed to have been duly served on the defendant.

*The Soya Margareta* [1960] 1 Lloyd's Rep. 675
An Italian company chartered a Swedish vessel, the *Soya Lovisa*, for a voyage from Texas to Venice with a cargo of solvents. The charterparty contained a clause stipulating that the contract was to be governed by Swedish law. After the ship arrived in Venice, the charterer discovered that the cargo had become contaminated while on board ship. He therefore issued a writ in rem against the *Soya Margareta*, also belonging to the owner of the *Soya Lovisa*, claiming damages. The writ was served on the *Soya Margareta* in England.

*Held*: the court had jurisdiction.

Hence a writ which commences action in rem *cannot* be served outside the jurisdiction. This is not so with a writ in personam although, as mentioned above, effective service outside the jurisdiction may prove difficult, unless the defendant is based in any EU or EFTA country.

## SUPREME COURT ACT 1981

Admiralty jurisdiction is governed by the Supreme Court Act 1981, namely sections 20–24. This Act took effect as law on 1 January 1982 and replaces the Administration of Justice Act 1956 which was passed to ratify and comply with the international obligations accepted by States which were parties to the International Convention relating to the Arrest of Sea-going Ships in 1952. The purpose of that Convention was to provide uniform rules as to the right to arrest sea-going ships by judicial process to secure maritime claims against the shipowner. What types of claim or dispute (s. 20(1)) are in the power of the English Admiralty Court to hear and determine are set out and defined in a list which may be found in section 20(2) of the Supreme Court Act 1981. It is appropriate here to quote that subsection in full:

'20(2) The questions and claims referred to in subsection (1)(a) are—
(a) any claim to the possession or ownership of a ship or to the ownership of any share therein;'

The court's jurisdiction may be invoked in such cases by an action in personam or in rem. There is jurisdiction to hear an action for a declaration that the plaintiff is entitled to be registered as owner of a British ship (see *The Bineta* [1966] 2 Lloyd's Rep. 419). There is nothing whatsoever to prevent the Admiralty Court hearing a dispute between two foreigners as to who should have possession of a ship. The more recent case of the *Ocean Enterprise* [1997] 1 Lloyd's Rep. 449 concerned a complicated dispute over the ownership of the vessel *Ocean Enterprise*. The court made a declaration that Warrick Shipping was now and had at all times since 14 December 1994 remained the beneficial owner of the vessel and the entry in the British Register of ships would be rectified. The defendant Bradstoan was not and had never been the owner of the vessel. The court has discretion to allow the release on bail of a ship subject to arrest for a claim to possession. An example of this can be seen in the case of *The Gay Tucan* (see page 118).

> '(b) any question arising between the co-owners of a ship as to possession, employment or earnings of that ship;'

By reason of section 20(4) the court has power to settle any account outstanding and unsettled between the parties in relation to the ship and to order that the ship or any share thereof be sold and to make such other order as the court thinks fit.

> '(c) any claim in respect of a mortgage of or charge on a ship or any share therein;'

This paragraph covers all mortgages and charges, whether registered or not, and whether legal or equitable, including mortgages and charges created under foreign law (s.20(7)(c)).

In the case of the *Maule* [1997] 1 Lloyd's Rep. 419 the Privy Council had to decide whether the plaintiffs were entitled to arrest the vessel *Maule* pursuant to mortgage whereby the vessel was mortgaged as security for the performance of the defendants' obligations under the loan agreement. The loan was repayable by instalments over five years. The plaintiffs argued that they were entitled to arrest the vessel under an express power in the Deed of Covenant dated the same day as the mortgage. The defendants argued that they were not so entitled because there was no instalment outstanding under the loan agreement on the day the writ was issued. The plaintiffs' power to accelerate repayment of the loan was not exercised until the following day. The Privy Court allowed the appeal from the decision of the Court of Appeal of Hong Kong. It stated that in the case of ships' mortgages the rights and duties of the parties were overwhelmingly dominated by contract. There was nothing in sections 101 and 102 of the Law of Property Act 1925 (which were concerned with powers conferred on the mortgagee) which touched on or restricted express powers conferred on the mortgagee by the mortgage deed itself. It was accepted by the defendants that if the contract was clear enough an express power of sale might be exercised even though there was nothing due under the loan. There was nothing in the first part of clause 7 of the Deed of Covenant under which the mortgagee was entitled 'to put it to force and to exercise' the power of sale, which suggested that the exercise of the power was to be dependent on anything other than an event of default. There was no room for an implied requirement or condition. Money should first have become due under the loan agreement; nor could any such requirement be extracted from the words 'all the powers possessed by it as mortgagee'.

> '(d) any claim for damage received by a ship;'

This includes damage done by something other than a ship, such as a collision with a pier or buoy. There is no provision for proceedings in rem in respect of claims falling within this paragraph but in practice many claims will also fall within paragraph (e).

> '(e) any claim for damage done by a ship;'

What seems to have emerged through judicial interpretation is that these words are not intended to limit such instances to direct contact between two vessels, viz.

a collision (see *Currie* v *M'Knight* [1897] AC 97, HL). The phrase 'done by a ship' must not be taken too literally, nor out of its context. The ship may have been the offending instrument, but the act of mischief can only be that of those on board her, e.g. a negligent act of navigation. By applying this concept, it is not stretching the imagination too far to contemplate physical damage resulting from an act whereunder the ship was the immediate instrument but not in direct physical contact with the damaged property. For instance, a ship may negligently cause a wash by which some other ship or property on shore is damaged.

The following case is on this point although it came before the courts long before either the 1956 Act or the 1981 Act.

*The Minerva* (1933) 46 Ll.L.Rep. 212
This was an appeal by the Grain Elevating and Automatic Weighing Company of Liverpool against a decision by the Liverpool District Registrar setting aside a writ in rem issued by the company against the *Minerva* (Norwegian flag) in respect of damage to its elevator alleged to have been caused by the breaking of a ship's derrick at Birkenhead docks in January 1933. The shipowners argued that the ship at the time was not being navigated and for that reason there was no right to arrest. The 'res' was not a ship but a 'floating warehouse'.

*Held*: that the criterion was, was the damage done by the ship or a part of the ship? If so, the claim fell under the heading of the Admiralty jurisdiction which could be exercised by action in rem or in personam.

Also, Lord Diplock, in the case of the *Eschersheim* [1976] 2 Lloyd's Rep. 1, stated:

'The figurative phrase "damage done by a ship" is a term of art in maritime law. Its meaning is well settled by authority; see The *Vera Cruz* [1884] 9 PD 96; *Currie* v *Knight* [1897] AC 97. To fall within the phrase, not only must the damage be the direct result or natural consequence of something done by those engaged in the navigation of the ship, but the ship itself must be the actual instrument by which the damage was done. The commonest case is that of collision, which is specifically mentioned in the Convention; but physical contact between the ship and whatever object sustains the damage is not essential—a ship may negligently cause a wash by which some other vessel or some property on shore is damaged.'

More recently Mr Justice Clarke in the case of the *Rama* [1996] 2 Lloyd's Rep. 281 said (deferring to Lord Diplock's dictum):

'The crucial aspect of that passage is Lord Diplock's insistence upon the fact that not only must damage be the direct result of acts done by those engaged in the navigation of the ship, but the ship itself must be, as he put it, "the actual instrument by which the damage was done". On the facts of that case, the tug *Rotesand* cast off the *Erkowit*, which she had in tow, with the result that she was beached in an exposed position and subsequently sustained damage . . . . In my judgment, the cases show that to be "damage done by a ship" and thus to qualify as giving rise to maritime lien, three criteria must be satisfied: 1. The damage must be caused by something done by those engaged in the navigation or management of the ship in a physical sense; 2. The ship must be the actual or noxious instrument by which the damage is done; 3. The damage must be sustained by a person or property external to the ship. . . . In short, the physical navigation or management of the vessel must cause the alleged loss or damage and the vessel or part of her must be in a physical sense, as Lord Cairns and others have put it, the active cause, the noxious instrument or the instrument of mischief . . . In my judgment, as the cases to which I have referred show, it is not sufficient for the ship to have been used "in some way as a means of causing damage".'

The case of the *Rama* concerned a claim by charterers for damages on the grounds that the owners knew, when they entered into the charter and when they persuaded the charterers to advance funds for bunkers, agency expenses and replacement parts, that they were not in a financial position to complete the voyage. The charterers also claimed damages for conversion and breach of charter, in that the vessel failed to complete the contractual voyage and to deliver the cargo to its destination.

The charterers argued that their claims gave rise to a maritime lien over the vessel and that they had priority over the claims of the mortgagees. The vessel *Rama* was of the Cypriot Registry and, since Cypriot law applied the law of England as it was in 1960, the charterers argued that they had a maritime lien under the law of Cyprus and under the relevant conflict of law rules in Panama. The mortgagees had sought an order of sale of the vessel in the Maritime Court of Panama and the vessel had been sold by judicial sale. The mortgagees applied for a declaration from the English court that under English law the charterers did not have a privileged maritime lien over the vessel *Rama*.

The High Court decided they had jurisdiction to make an appropriate declaration and the determination of the contested issues between the parties were likely to be of assistance to the Panamanian court i.e. whether the charterers' claim gave rise to a maritime lien under English law. It decided that none of the losses suffered by the charterers was done or caused by the vessel *Rama* as a physical object. The vessel *Rama* was not the active cause of the damage or the noxious instrument or the instrument of mischief in a physical sense. The loss was not caused by the physical act of the whole or part of the ship nor was it done by those engaged in the navigation or management of the ship in a physical sense. Accordingly, the charterers' claim did not give rise to a maritime lien.

Normally there is a maritime lien for claims involving damage done by a ship, i.e. in a collision scenario. This is not necessarily so and an action in rem can still be brought and the ship arrested under section 20(2)(e). For instance, a maritime lien does not attach to a government ship, nor where the claim arises under the Nuclear Installations Act 1965 (amended by the 1969 Act) in connection with an occurrence relating to the carriage of nuclear matter in a ship.

The principle that the damage need not necessarily be caused by direct contact is now well recognised. The damage need not be physical damage. In the case of *The Dagmara and Ama Antxine* [1988] 1 Lloyd's Rep. 431 the plaintiffs brought a claim because their fishing vessel was forced to leave fishing grounds due to the alleged dangerous navigation of the defendants' vessel.

Subsection (2)(e)—damage done by a ship—also extends to claims in repect of a liability for oil pollution (see the Merchant Shipping Act 1995).

'(f) Any claim for loss of life or personal injury sustained in consequence of any defect in a ship or in her apparel or equipment, or in consequence of the wrongful act, neglect or default of—
  (i) the owners, charterers or persons in possession or control of a ship; or

(ii) the master or crew of a ship, or any other person for whose wrongful acts, neglects or defaults the owners, charterers, or persons in possession or control of a ship are responsible,

being an act, neglect or default in the navigation or management of a ship, in the loading, carriage or discharge of goods on, in or from the ship, or in the embarkation, carriage or disembarkation of persons on, in or from the ship;

(g) Any claim for loss of or damage to goods carried in a ship;'

The expression 'goods' includes baggage (see s.24(1)). However, 'baggage' only covers that baggage belonging to passengers or travellers and not the Master and crew's personal effects.

'(h) Any claim arising out of any agreement relating to the carriage of goods in a ship or to the use or hire of a ship;'

This paragraph covers claims whether in contract or in tort arising out of any agreement relating to the carriage of goods in a ship.

In *The Antonis P Lemos* [1985] 1 Lloyd's Rep. 283, HL the claim endorsed on the writ in rem was a single claim for damages based on alleged negligence of the defendant. The Admiralty Judge had set the writ aside on the grounds that the subject-matter of the writ was not a dispute arising from an agreement between the plaintiff and the defendant. The Court of Appeal, sitting to hear the plaintiff's subsequent appeal reversed the Admiralty Judge's ruling. Provided that the claim in question arose out of an agreement of the nature specified, it did not necessarily have to be an agreement between the plaintiff and the defendant. The House of Lords decided that the phrase 'arising out of' should be given the broader meaning of 'connected with' and not the narrow meaning of 'arising under'. There were no limiting words in the text of sub-paragraph (h) and the 1952 Convention itself never implied any such restrictive interpretation. The Court of Appeal were right in holding that if the claim arose out of an agreement of the relevant kind it did not matter if the agreement was not directly between the plaintiffs and defendants.

In *The Hamburg Star* [1994] 1 Lloyd's Rep. 399 it was decided that claims for indemnity and contribution under the Civil Liability (Contribution) Act 1978 were claims arising out of an agreement for the carriage of containers and their contents.

*The Eschersheim* [1976] 2 Lloyd's Rep. 1, HL
Two ships collided in the Bay of Biscay. A salvage tug, under the provisions of an agreement made with the owners of the *Erkovit*, took her in tow. The tug beached the ship on the north coast of Spain and, after fruitless attempts by the salvors to patch her up, she became a total loss together with her cargo. Various cross-claims resulted (for full details of which the full report of the case should be studied). An action in rem was instituted against a sister ship of the tug.

*Held*: (confirming the Court of Appeal's decision): that there were no grounds for giving a restricted meaning to the words 'agreement relating to the use or hire of a ship' or to the words 'damage done by a ship' in the Administration of Justice Act 1956. The High Court did have jurisdiction. The salvage agreement related to 'the use or hire of a ship', that ship being a tug. There was also a claim in rem for 'damage done by a ship', although the ship was only an instrument in taking the ship to the shore. Accordingly, the claims were within the terms of section 1 of the 1956 Act and the High Court has jurisdiction to determine them.

This paragraph covers, inter alia, claims for damages for breach of a charterparty, bill of lading contract or towage contract. It does not cover a claim by shipowners for hire under a container leasing agreement (*Gatoil International Inc* v *Arkwright-Boston* [1985] 1 All ER 129. A particular vessel has to be identified (see the case of the *Lloyd Pacifico* [1995] 1 Lloyd's Rep. 55).

> '(j) Any claim in the nature of salvage (including any claim arising by virtue of the application, by or under section 87 of the Civil Aviation Act 1982, of the law relating to salvage of aircraft and their apparel and cargo);'

Salvage gives rise to a maritime lien. Salvage is dealt with in Chapter 7, and reference should be made to s.20(6) of the Supreme Court Act 1981 and s.224 of the Merchant Shipping Act 1995. This section does not cover a claim by the owners of the property salved against salvors for negligence in the salvage operations but such a claim falls within section (h) (*The Eschersheim* [1976] 2 Lloyd's Rep. 1). Nor does it cover a claim by salvors against shipowners for failure to use their best endeavours to obtain security from cargo owners before cargo is released under the Lloyd's Open Form 1990 or 1995 as this is not a claim for salvage.

> '(k) Any claim in the nature of towage in respect of a ship or an aircraft;'

*The Leoborg* [1962] 2 Lloyd's Rep. 146.
The owners of the tug *Jelezee* claimed against the owners of the motor tanker, the *Leoborg* for towage services performed at the request of the *Leoborg* when the *Jelezee* escorted the *Leoborg* from outside the Hook of Holland to Schiedam. The *Leoborg* was sold by order of the court. The tug owner moved for payment out of the proceeds of sale in default of appearance.

*Held*: that there was Admiralty jurisdiction for any claim in the nature of towage in respect of a ship; that the escorting services in this case were in the nature of towage and that the tug owners were entitled to judgment for such services.

This case clarified what may have been in doubt previously, that escorting services, without making fast, were in the nature of towage and should be regarded as such.

Towage in relation to aircraft means towage when it is waterborne (see s.24(1)). Also, this section covers a claim for damages for breach of a contract of towage, or for negligence in performing the towage contract.

> '(l) Any claim in the nature of pilotage in respect of a ship or an aircraft;'

Pilotage in relation to aircraft means pilotage when the aircraft is waterborne (see s.24(1)).

> '(m) Any claim in respect of goods or materials supplied to a ship for her operation or maintenance;'

This may include claims for 'necessaries'. 'Necessaries' is a term found only in common law or old statutes. It is not found in the Supreme Court Act 1981. The word has been defined as covering payment by way of advances to enable necessaries to be purchased.

Examples of what could reasonably be described as 'necessaries' for the effective prosecution of a ship's voyage are:

(a) bunker fuel;

(b) crew's clothing;
(c) repairs; and
(d) expenses of destroying contaminating or rotting cargo.

A comprehensive test for deciding what comes within the term 'necessaries' is 'all that is fit and proper for the service in which the ship is engaged and that the owner, as a prudent man, would have ordered if he had been present.' Though an unpaid 'necessaries man' (a supplier of necessaries) does not enjoy the privilege of being a maritime lienor, the Master of a ship who has disbursed money for such purposes in time of necessity has a lien for his disbursements. This is yet another example of the role of a ship's Master from time to time as agent of necessity for his owner.

*The Fairport (No 5)* [1967] 2 Lloyd's Rep. 162
It was decided that advances made to enable necessaries to be purchased were 'necessaries' within subsection (m).

Judicial consideration was given to this particular sub-section in a case involving the ship *River Rima*.

*The River Rima* [1988] 2 Lloyd's Rep. 193
The owners of the *River Rima*, a vessel equipped to carry both containers and general dry cargo, were accustomed to lease containers from their owner. One of them, the plaintiff in the case, issued a writ in rem claiming damages for the conversion of certain containers leased to the Nigerian National Line and also for failing to maintain the containers in a good state of repair in breach of contractual obligation. The Court had to consider whether these claims were maintainable by action in rem and section 20(2)(m) was the relevant subsection of the Supreme Court Act 1981.

*Held*: by Sheen J: that the court did have in rem jurisdiction, that the containers were goods . . . supplied to a ship for her operation . . . He dismissed the application to set aside the writ.

The Court of Appeal allowed the defendants' appeal and on appeal to the House of Lords, their Lordships concluded that the contracts for the lease of the containers were made with the shipowner, but not with reference to a particular ship. It was an essential ingredient that sub-paragraph (m) should contemplate claims relating to necessaries supplied to a particular ship. This was the historical intent right back to the legislation of 1925 (Supreme Court of Judicature (Consolidation) Act 1925). The plaintiffs did not know what ship their containers would eventually be carried on. Therefore the required specific identity was lacking. Subsection 20(2)(m) was irrelevant. The appeal was dismissed.

'(n) Any claim in respect of the construction, repair or equipment of a ship or dock charges or dues;'

*The D'Vora* [1952] 2 Lloyd's Rep. 404
The plaintiff supplied fuel oil to a vessel at Haifa and issued a writ claiming the purchase price.

*Held*: that the court had no jurisdiction to enter into the action, the claim was not one in respect of the 'equipment' of the ship.

This case illustrates the interpretation of subparagraph (n) of the Supreme Court Act 1981, which gives the High Court jurisdiction to determine 'any claim in respect of the construction, repair, or equipment of a ship'. Equipment in this sense connotes something of a more permanent nature and not the supply of consumable stores such as fuel oil.

However, it has been decided that a classification society's claim for their charges in issuing a certificate fell within this section (*Stinne Peter* [1986] Folio 171, referred to in the Supreme Court Practice 1995, Volume 2, page 341).

> '(o) Any claim by a master or member of the crew of a ship for wages (including any sum allotted out of wages or adjudged by a superintendent to be due by way of wages);'

There is a maritime lien for wages earned on the ship. Wages include emoluments such as taxes, national insurance contributions, payable by the shipowners. A master's claim for wages ranks pari passu (equally) with seamen's claims for wages (*The Royal Wells* [1984] 2 Lloyd's Rep. 255). Severance pay does not give rise to a maritime lien (*The Tacoma City* [1991] 1 Lloyd's Rep. 330).

> '(p) Any claim by a master, shipper, charterer or agent in respect of disbursements made on account of a ship;'

There is a maritime lien for disbursements properly incurred by a master on account of the ship but shippers, charterers or agents do not have a similar lien. Agents' out of pocket disbursements are included in this paragraph as well as their fees, charges or commission which is illustrated by the case of the *Westport.*

*The Westport (No 3)* [1966] 1 Lloyd's Rep. 342
The ship's agent claimed against the owners of the proceeds of sale of the vessel in respect of disbursements. The ship had been sold following an order for appraisement and sale.

*Held*: that the claimant was entitled to include a reasonable figure for his services in his claim in respect of disbursements.

This paragraph does not include insurance premiums as it is not a disbursement made on account of the ship. It is not necessary for the physical operation of the ship but only required for the financial benefit or comfort of the shipowners (see *The Sea Friends* [1991] 2 Lloyd's Rep. 322).

*The Sea Friends* [1991] 2 Lloyd's Rep. 322.
A firm of Lloyd's brokers had incurred a liability to Lloyd's underwriters in respect of hull insurance on the vessel *Sea Friends* and claimed US$15,615 from owners. They issued a writ and applied to arrest the ship *Sea Friends* on its arrival at Garston.

*Held*: by the Court of Appeal: that section 20(2)(p) was not wide enough to cover this case and the vessel could not be arrested.

It had been thought that solicitors or barristers could bring an action in rem to recover their fees as they were an agent who performed a service specifically for the benefit of the ship. (Hong Kong case of *The Atlantic Trader* [1991] 2 Lloyd's Rep. 324). This is not now the case, in view of the Court of Appeal's comments in *The Sea Friends*. In the case of the *Lloyd Pacifico* [1995] 1 Lloyd's Rep. 54 it was decided that a claim did not relate to a particular ship and the court did not have jurisdiction under paragraph (p) and s.21(4).

> '(q) Any claim arising out of an act which is or is claimed to be a general average act;
> (r) Any claim arising out of bottomry;'

Bottomry bonds were given to lenders of money whereby the ship was pledged for the loan, the payment of which depended on the ship arriving safely. Bottomry is practically obsolete in modern times but nevertheless gives rise to a maritime lien.

> '(s) Any claim for the forfeiture or condemnation of a ship or of goods which are being or have been carried, or have been attempted to be carried, in a ship, or for the restoration of a ship or any such goods after seizure, or for droits of Admiralty;'

Sub-section 20(7) states that it matters not whether ships or aircraft are British or not or registered or not or where the place of residence or domicile of their owners may be. However, this paragraph applies only to aircraft referred to in sections 20(2)(j)(k)(l). Neither does it matter where the claim arises.

In addition, the Admiralty Court has jurisdiction by virtue of section 20(1)(b) and section 20(3) in relation to:

(a) any application to the High Court under the Merchant Shipping Act 1995;
(b) any action to enforce a claim for damage, loss of life or personal injury arising out of—
   (i) a collision between ships; or
   (ii) the carrying out of or omission to carry out a manoeuvre in the case of one or more of two or more ships; or
   (iii) non-compliance on the part of one or more of two or more ships with the collision regulations;
(c) any action by shipowners or other persons under the Merchant Shipping Act 1995 for the limitation of the amount of their liability in connection with a ship or other property.

By virtue of section 20(1)(c) the court has Admiralty jurisdiction which it had immediately before the commencement of the 1981 Act. It seems that this section may preserve jurisdiction over, inter alia, claims for what were known before 1 January 1982 as 'necessaries'.

Section 20(1)(d) states that Admiralty jurisdiction applies to 'any jurisdiction connected with ships or aircraft which is vested in the High Court apart from this section and is for the time being by rules of court made or coming into force after the commencement of this Act assigned to the Queen's Bench Division and directed by the rules to be exercised by the Admiralty Court'.

### *Supreme Court Act 1981, section 22*

The manner in which jurisdiction in personam is exercised in collision and allied cases is the subject of section 22 of the Supreme Court Act 1981. Limitation is placed on the powers of the High Court in England and Wales to deal with actions in personam. They are claims for damage or loss of life or personal injury after a collision between ships or arising from non-compliance of any ship, whether there is contact or not, with the collision regulations or arising from the carrying out or failure to carry out a manoeuvre by one or more of two or more ships.

The prerequisites required by section 22(2) to found jurisdiction in personam are:

(a) the defendant has his habitual residence or a place of business within England or Wales; or
(b) the cause of action arose within the inland waters of England and Wales; or
(c) an action arising out of the same incident or series of incidents is proceeding in the court or has been heard and determined in the court.

In *The World Harmony* [1965] 1 Lloyd's Rep. 244 the court decided that the relevant date for applying the provisions of head (c) above was the date of the issue of the writ. It is also clear from reported cases that if two actions are commenced in separate places on the same day neither is deemed to be before or after the other.

## EXERCISE OF JURISDICTION

The Admiralty jurisdiction may be exercised in personam or in rem. An action in personam is effectively no different from any other action in the Commercial Court or in the Queen's Bench Division. It is issued and served on the person/company liable for the claim provided the claim lies within the jurisdiction (mentioned above) of the Admiralty Court. If the person/company liable for the claim resides out of the jurisdiction there are certain Supreme Court Practice Rules (RSC Order 11) which govern the right to serve the writ out of the jurisdiction. An in personam and an in rem writ can be issued for the same claim but only one writ can be served. An in rem writ is against the res, i.e. the vessel, as opposed to a person/company. Both in rem and in personam actions are governed by RSC Order 75 and many of the Commercial Court Practice Rules apply.

### *Nature of action in rem*

An action in rem is separate from an action in personam. It has for many years been the view that the action in rem under English jurisdiction is entirely independent of an action in personam. It is not ancillary to it. The action is against the ship, or in appropriate circumstances other properties such as cargo, freight and not its owner. Judgment may eventually be given against the ship, the owner perhaps having never appeared to answer the writ. Although the owner's personal liability is, under English legal thinking, irrelevant, an action in rem can be concluded (though in practice seldom is) by judgment in rem which is 'good as against all the world'. An owner may take part in an action in rem if he considers it to be appropriate to defend his property, but it is essentially an action against his property (in rem), not against him.

### *Advantages of in rem action*

The question then arises as to why an in rem action enjoys such popularity amongst maritime claimants around the world. Because it is of immense convenience and can bring advantages which are lacking in an action in personam which may be difficult, if not impossible, to institute. Leave of the court is needed to serve a writ of summons outside the jurisdiction unless the defendant is domiciled in an EU or EFTA country. This may be difficult to obtain as one has to prove that the claim falls within Order 11 of the Rules of the Supreme Court and that there is a serious issue to be tried (see, e.g. *Seaconsar Far East Ltd* v *Bank Markazi Jomhouri Islami Iran* [1994] 1 Lloyd's Rep. 1, HL).

With regard to an action in rem, one only has to establish that the claim falls within the Admiralty jurisdiction and the ship is within the English jurisdiction. But to issue a writ in rem and to wait and (in your own time, subject to the validity of the writ) to 'pounce' on the 'res' when it comes within an issuing court's territorial jurisdiction is an excellent method of getting the owner of the 'res' within your grasp. It founds jurisdiction (subject to a shipowner being in certain circumstances entitled to obtain a stay of the proceedings) and opens the way to obtaining adequate security in lieu and any peace of mind of knowing that if you do, eventually, obtain a judgment against the owner of the 'res', you will, within and subject to the terms of the security, get ultimate satisfaction. Alternatively, if security is not provided the court may sell the 'res' in order to satisfy the judgment for the claim (subject to the question of priorities).

### *Procedure for an action in rem*

An Admiralty action in rem can be commenced for most claims falling within the Admiralty jurisdiction under the Supreme Court Act 1981. However, only actions in personam are available for any claim for damage received by a ship (s.20(2)(d)) as there is no property against which it can be brought. However, claims falling within this head of jurisdiction often fall within another head of jurisdiction in respect of which an action in rem can be brought, for example, a claim for damage done by a ship (s.20(2)(e)). Actions in personam can only be brought in respect of limitation actions and applications under the Merchant Shipping Act.

An action in rem of the Admiralty Court of the Queen's Bench Division of the High Court of Justice must be commenced by a writ in the prescribed form and is issued by the Admiralty and Commercial Registry. If it is desired to commence proceedings both in rem and in personam, separate writs must be issued. Various writs in rem against different ships may be issued in respect of the same claim or one writ naming more than one ship can be issued. However, only one ship can be served with a writ in rem or arrested in respect of a claim which falls within paragraphs (e)–(r) of section 20(2) of the 1981 Act (see s. 21(8)). This follows the case of *The Berny.*

*The Berny* [1977] 2 Lloyd's Rep. 533
The claimants were owners of a cargo of bagged sugar carried from Duluth to Dares-Salaam in the Finnish ship *Berny.* She had no less than 18 sister ships. Supporting their claim for shortage, the cargo-owners brought an action in rem against the *Berny* and an

action in personam against her owners, but prior to that had also instituted an action in rem against a large number of her sister ships. The writ in personam had not been served, nor had leave been sought to serve it out of the jurisdiction. Since neither the *Berny* nor any of her sister ships had visited a port within the jurisdiction, the plaintiff cargo-owners applied to renew the writs in rem within the year. The writ against the *Berny* was eventually served on the ship and her owners moved to have the action stayed or dismissed on the grounds that the plaintiffs had already previously invoked the court's jurisdiction by issuing writs against her sister ships. They also argued that the renewal of the *Berny* writ was improper under the circumstances.

*Held*: that there was nothing to prevent the claimants instituting proceedings in rem against more than one of the shipowner's ships provided that they went on to serve a writ on and/or arrest only one. The rule in *The Banco* (see below) was applied. It would be wrong to force the claimant to continue an action against one of the sister ships rather than against the actual offending ship merely on the ground that the 'sister ship writ' was issued prior in time. In the course of his judgment, Brandon J referred to the rule of practice in regard to renewal of writs within the Admiralty registry that where the registrar is satisfied on the affidavit evidence that one or more of the ships proceeded against has not visited and indeed will not visit a port within the jurisdiction during the currency of the writ he will renew the writ. Of course, if a ship has called or may call at a place within the jurisdiction (bearing in mind that there is a subtle difference between 'place' and 'port') there must be a reasonable time and opportunity available to the plaintiff to serve the writ. Thirdly, the ship available to be served must, naturally, be of sufficient value to provide adequate security for the claims. In *The Banco* [1970] 2 Lloyd's Rep. 230 far more drastic action, relatively speaking, had been taken. The offending ship and all of six sister ships were actually arrested. The court set aside the service of the writ on the six sister ships allowing only the ship featuring in the cause of action to be proceeded against. This decision was confirmed by the Court of Appeal ([1971] 1 Lloyd's Rep. 49).

Where the writ has been issued naming more than one ship, immediately after service the writ must be amended by striking out the name of all ships save for the one served. (See *The Freccia del Nord* [1989] 1 Lloyd's Rep. 388). However, if a ship is mistakenly served with a writ in rem and arrested in the belief that it was a ship against which an action can be brought, this does not bar a subsequent action against and arrest of a ship against which an action can be properly brought. The previous mistake, and reasons for it, must be mentioned in the affidavit in support of the second arrest (*The Stephan J* [1985] 2 Lloyd's Rep. 344).

The parties need not be named on the writ provided that they are adequately described. For instance, the plaintiffs may be described as the 'owners of the ship A' or the 'owners of cargo lately laden on board the ship A'. The defendants are often described as 'the owners or demise charterers of the ship B'. If full particulars of the claim are not endorsed on the writ (normally by a statement of claim) then there must be a concise statement of the nature of the claim made. In the case of *The Tuyuti* [1984] 2 Lloyd's Rep. 51 Sheen J, the then Admiralty Judge, criticized a vague statement as to a cargo claim.

A writ in rem is valid for 12 months but can be renewed for a further period of time if the writ cannot be served on the ship in the meantime (see below), whereas a writ in personam is only valid for four months if the defendants are based in the UK or an EFTA or EU country, otherwise six months.

The writ is served upon the ship or other property against which the claim is brought. Alternatively, the defendant can acknowledge the issue or service of the writ or the defendant's solicitor can endorse on a writ his acceptance of service on behalf of the defendant. This must be done within 14 days after service of the writ by filling in the acknowledgment of service which is attached to the writ and returning it to the Court office from whence the writ was issued (the High Court of Justice in London or a District Registry). The defendant should state his intention either to contest or not to contest the proceedings.

A writ in rem may not be served out of the jurisdiction, nor may an order for substituted service of the writ in rem be made. If the ship is to be arrested, the writ in rem is normally served by the Admiralty Marshall who normally requests the assistance of the Customs at the port at which the ship is. If the defendant does not acknowledge service of the in rem writ within 14 days or does not later submit a defence to the plaintiff's claim, the plaintiff cannot enter judgment against the defendant in default of acknowledgment of service or defence. However, this is possible in an in personam action or in other proceedings such as commercial actions. Instead, the plaintiff must apply by motion for judgment in default and the plaintiff must prove to the court that his claim is well founded and he is entitled to judgment. The plaintiff submits an affidavit supporting his motion for judgment in default. It is not possible to make an application for summary judgment in an Admiralty action in rem.

### *Renewal of validity of writ in rem*

There is nothing to prevent a plaintiff applying to extend time in which to serve a writ, but it should be remembered that an extension is not granted as a matter of course, even if it is applied for during the currency of the writ. Usually it is only granted if an affidavit is filed stating that the ship has not been within the jurisdiction. It is incumbent upon a plaintiff who issues a writ to serve it promptly. It must be remembered that a long delay in the service of the writ can seriously prejudice the defendant's chances of successfully defending himself against the claim concerned. The following cases illustrate the court's views towards an extension of the writ.

*The Johnny Two* [1992] 2 Lloyd's Rep. 257.
On 17 May 1990 the plaintiffs issued a writ in rem in respect of an alleged cargo claim against the vessel *Johnny Two*. The writ was valid for service for a period of one year and during the currency of the writ *Johnny Two* visited Felixstowe on five occasions. The writ was not served at any time. On the last day of the validity of the writ the plaintiffs applied for its renewal. That application was supported by an affidavit which contained no information about the steps taken to effect service of the writ. Nevertheless, the writ was renewed and the *Johnny Two* was arrested on 30 July 1991. The owners applied for an order that the order extending the validity of the writ be discharged and that the service of the writ on *Johnny Two* be set aside on the grounds that (1) there was no good or sufficient reason for the validity of the writ to be renewed; (2) the plaintiffs had had reasonable opportunity for effecting service of the writ on the vessel during the currency of the writ; and (3) on the application for extension of the validity of the writ there was no proper disclosure, in particular it was not disclosed that the vessel was engaged on a regular and widely-advertised liner service with periodic calls at Felixstowe.

*Held:* that, on the facts and the evidence, it was impossible for the court to say that reasonable diligence was exercised during the period for which the writ was valid for service: There were no 'time constraints' which made it impossible to arrest the vessel on each of her previous five visits to Felixstowe and it was not impossible to obtain information as to the entry of the vessel into an English port before she departed. If this evidence had been seen by the Admiralty Registrar in considering the application to renew the writ, he would have declined to renew it. Therefore, the order extending the validity of the writ was discharged and the service of the writ set aside.

The then Admiralty Judge, Sheen J, also set out in this case a note on current procedures for the arrest of a ship (see below at page 117).

It should also be borne in mind that a writ must be issued, as opposed to served, within certain time limits, such as one year if a cargo claim is governed by the Hague or Hague/Visby Rules. Various claims, such as collision and salvage, must be commenced within two years under the Merchant Shipping Act 1995. In very limited circumstances, the court may extend the time in which a writ may be served beyond the two years prescribed.

### *Arrest of a ship*

On any occasion where there is a maritime lien or other charge on the ship, then an action in rem may be brought in the Admiralty Court and that ship arrested (see s.21(3) of the Supreme Court Act 1981). It does not matter if the ownership of the ship has changed between the time when the maritime lien attached to the ship and the time when the ship was arrested. In the case of any claim falling within section 20(2)(a), (c) or (s), or any question mentioned in section 20(2)(b), an action in rem may be brought against the ship or property in connexion with which the claim or question arises and the ship or property can be arrested (s.21(2) of the Supreme Court Act 1981). However, in the case of claims falling within section 20(2)(e) to (r) it is necessary to show an in personam link between the ship or property against which the in rem action and the arrest is brought.

Section 21(4) of the Supreme Court Act 1981 provides:

'In the case of any such claim as is mentioned in section 20(2)(e) to (r), where—
- (a) the claim arises in connection with a ship; and
- (b) the person who would be liable on the claim in an action in personam ("the relevant person") was, when the cause of action arose, the owner or charterer of, or in possession or in control of, the ship

an action in rem may (whether or not the claim gives rise to maritime lien on that ship) be brought in the High Court against—
- (i) that ship, if at the time when the action is brought the relevant person is either the beneficial owner of that ship as respects all the shares in it or the charterer of it under a charter by demise;

  or
- (ii) any other ship of which, at the time when the action is brought, the relevant person is the beneficial owner as respect all the shares in it.'

The word 'charterer' in section 21(4) is not restricted to demise charterers but includes a time charterer. The time when the action is brought means when the writ is issued (*The Carmania II* [1963] 2 Lloyd's Rep. 152). If the vessel is sold after the claim arises but before the writ is issued the ship cannot be arrested because the relevant person is no longer the beneficial owner of that ship.

### *'Alternative ship arrest'*

Britain's enactment of the Arrest Convention, introduced statutorily the idea that the right to arrest an alternative vessel, as opposed to the offending or involved vessel, rested on the determination as to whether that ship selected as alternative was owned as respects all its shares by the person who would be liable on the claim. The actual wording of the provision (known as the 'sister ship' provision in the statute) may be found in section 21(4) of the Supreme Court Act 1981. Prior to the bringing into effect of the 1981 Act, English courts had placed a restrictive interpretation on the right to seek out and arrest an alternative vessel, so restrictive that the provision allowing for such alternative arrest in the 1956 statute (section 3(4)) was known as the sister ship provision. This was because the courts had required there to be a *common ownership link* between the offending or involved vessel and the alternative ship selected for arrest (see: dicta in *The Eschersheim* [1976] 2 Lloyd's Rep. 1, HL). The two vessels had to be under the *same beneficial ownership* as respects all their shares.

This restrictive interpretation placed a bar on arrest procedure in the following hypothetical but in reality very likely situation. Shipowner A time-charters his ship X to B. B commits a breach of charter. A wishes to arrest ship Y wholly beneficially owned by B. He cannot, under the judicial interpretation of the 1956 Act (section 3(4)) because there is no common property ownership between ship X and ship Y.

Just prior to the bringing into effect of the Supreme Court Act 1981 a significant lawsuit received a hearing in the English Admiralty Court subsequently being taken to appeal—*The Span Terza* ([1982] 1 Lloyd's Rep. 225). The dispute almost pre-empted the about-to-be-introduced statute. The facts (very similar to the hypothetical example given earlier) were:

> The plaintiffs owned ship X which they had time-chartered to the defendants. The defendants owned ship Y (the *Span Terza*). They were allegedly liable for unpaid hire and damages to the plaintiffs in respect of ship X charter. The plaintiffs sought, pursuant to in rem rights under the 1956 Act, to arrest ship Y (the *Span Terza*) under the 'sister ship' provision (section 3(4)). What was the real issue to be determined was whether section 3(4) could be successfully used to arrest a vessel under the ownership (beneficial) of someone *not* the beneficial owner of the offending, or more correctly on these facts, the involved vessel.

The case had the unique experience of being 'rushed' from the court of first instance to the Court of Appeal on the same day because of the urgency, so far as the plaintiff arrestor was concerned, of the need to know. The Court of Appeal, by a majority only, decided that there did not have to be an ownership link between the involved ship and that selected alternatively for arrest. Strangely enough, one of the very few precedents which the appeal judges had to go on and which conformed with their eventual decision was a decision of the *Singapore* Court of Appeal (*The Permina 108* [1978] 1 Lloyd's Rep. 311) where on similar facts the court had concluded that there was no reason why the offending and alternative ships should be under common ownership for the arrest action to succeed.

So at last after 30 years of restrictive interpretation of the section 3(4) statutory provision, the courts adopted the liberal interpretation. But as at 1 January 1982 the new statute took effect and seems to have 'liberalized' the procedure statutorily anyway.

Perhaps it is the word 'charterer' and the meaning of it as used in the statute that has caused much of the conflict in judicial views. The 1952 Arrest Convention quite clearly in its Article 3, para 4, allows the arrest of a ship *owned* by a demise charterer who is potentially liable on the claim. English statute law, developed as a result of the 1952 Convention, failed to draw such a clearcut distinction between a charterer by demise and any other variety of charterer and as a result the restrictive interpretation became the vogue and the requirement of common ownership between the offending and the alternative 'arrestable' ship also became the vogue to the extent that the expression 'sister ship' arrest became common talk, misleading though that expression now is in the 1980s as a result of the introduction of the 1981 statute. None of this judicial conflict would have arisen if England's legislation drafters had, in designing the 1956 statute, included in their draft Article 3(4) of the Convention reading as follows:

'When in the case of a charter by demise of a ship the charterer and not the registered owner is liable in respect of a maritime claim relating to that ship, the claimant may arrest such ship or any other ship in the ownership of the charterer by demise, subject to the provisions of this Convention, but no other ship in the ownership of the registered owner shall be liable to arrest in respect of such maritime claims.'

The following words also appear at the conclusion of the above paragraph:

'The provisions of this paragraph shall apply to any case in which a person other than the registered owner of a ship is liable in respect of a maritime claim relating to that ship.'

These concluding words quite clearly and categorically indicate that there need not be an ownership link between the involved ship and the alternative ship. The English statute, however, either deliberately or inadvertently, did not implement that particular paragraph of the Convention and thus English law 'went off at a tangent' and was diverted easily into the restrictive judicial interpretation as to what alternative ship could be arrested.

Let us now look at the equivalent provision in the 1981 statute. Section 21(4) reads:

'In the case of any such claim as is mentioned in section 20(2)(e) to (r), where—
- (a) the claim arises in connection with a ship; and
- (b) the person who would be liable on the claim in an in personam ("the relevant person") was, when the cause of action arose, the owner or charterer of, or in possession or in control of, the ship

an action in rem may (whether or not the claim gives rise to a maritime lien on that ship) be brought in the High Court against—
- (i) that ship, if at the time when the action is brought the relevant person is either the beneficial owner of that ship as respects all its shares or the charterer of it under a charter by demise; or
- (ii) any other ship of which, at the time when the action is brought, the relevant person is the beneficial owner as respects all the shares in it.'

The main difference between arresting the offending ship and the alternative ship is that the relevant person when the action is brought (writ issued) must be the beneficial owner of the ship being arrested. It is not sufficient that he is the demise charterer.

The 'key' person whose identity is vital to the determination of whether an alternative ship has been *correctly* selected or not is the 'relevant' person, i.e. the person who would be (potentially) liable.

A case law illustration is:

An application was made to the Admiralty Court by the owners of the vessel *Mara* which was the new name of that same vessel as previously owned by a different company. Under her old name and previous ownership action in rem had been taken against her and she had been arrested in pursuit of a claim by the owners of a cargo which had been lost on the carrying vessel *Stanley Bay*, herself a total loss. The *Mawan* (subsequently renamed *Mara*) was one of seven ships named in the writ in rem and was the one finally selected for arrest. The vessel was released in exchange for security. The application was to set aside the writ and warrant and to release the security given on the ground that the plaintiff arrestor had failed to show that at the time the action was brought 'the relevant person' as defined in section 21(4) of the Supreme Court Act 1981 was the beneficial owner of the *Mara*.

On that particular issue (there was another) the court concluded that the claim arose in connection with the *Stanley Bay*. The person who would be *personally* liable to the plaintiff was the registered owner and he did not, at the time when the action was brought, nor indeed had he in the past, owned any shares in the ship *Mawan* against which in rem action was brought. The writ/warrant will therefore be satisfied and the security released.

*Mawan* (*now named Mara*) [1988] 2 Lloyd's Rep. 459.

The question of corporate veil was also considered in the case of the *Evpo Agnic* [1988] 2 Lloyd's Rep. 411. Here a cargo claim arose against the ship *Skipper I*. An action in rem was taken against the ship *Evpo Agnic*. Company 'A' was the registered owner of *Skipper I*, the shareholders being Mr X and Mr Y and the president and vice-president Mr P and Mr Q. Evidence was brought by the plaintiffs that these four indiviudals bore the same relationship to the corporate ownership of the *Evpo Agnic* or in other words the two separate companies owning the two ships were a sham and were designed to conceal assets. The court decided that there was no evidence of a sham and that the one-ship company had only been created for good financial reasons. The 'relevant person' (for the purposes of the Admiralty Jurisdiction) was the registered owner of the *Skipper I*, i.e. company 'A' which was not the beneficial owner of *Evpo Agnic*, and accordingly there was no right to arrest her (being only a ship owned by a sister company of the owners of the offending ship).

An alternative ship cannot be arrested for any claim falling within section 20(2)(a), (b), (c) and (s).

Although the section as it is literally worded still leaves a slight possibility that the court *could* apply the 'restrictive' interpretation, it would be a very narrow-minded judge of a conservative frame of mind who dared to do so now that demise charterers are categorized in their own right and that the word 'charterer' itself is thus the more naturally open to being defined as any type of charterer. It should not be thought that the words in brackets ' . . . whether or not the claim gives rise to a maritime lien on that ship . . . ' changes the character of a maritime lien at all. They do not. All these words mean is that a plaintiff who happens to have a lien against a particular ship *may*, if *that* vessel is unavailable, take in rem action against an alternative ship, provided that he complys with s.21(4).

### *Meaning of 'beneficially owning'*

What is meant by 'beneficially owned as respect all shares therein' in section 21(4) of the Supreme Court Act 1981? One judge's view was that it meant more than legal or equitable ownership and embraced into its meaning 'beneficially owned by a person who, whether he was the legal or equitable owner or not, lawfully had full possession and control of her, and, by virtue of such possession and control, had all the benefit and use of her which a legal or equitable owner would ordinarily have'. Whether the words 'as respects all the shares therein' suffice to exclude a demise charterer being such a person was considered in *The Andrea Ursula*, below.

*The Andrea Ursula* [1971] 1 Lloyd's Rep. 145
The plaintiff ship repairers who had repaired the *Andrea Ursula* at the request of the demise charterers and who claimed the cost of the repairs under section 1(1)(n) of the 1956 Act were held to be entitled to proceed by an action in rem against the ship on the basis that at the time when the action was brought the demise charterers were beneficial owners as respects all the shares therein.

This view was not, however, fully shared in *The I Congreso del Partido* [1977] 1 Lloyd's Rep. 536 where the court felt that the meaning which should naturally be given to the expression is that of ownership such as is vested in a person who, whether or not he is the legal owner of the vessel, is in any case the equitable owner. This would exclude a demise charterer or any other person who has merely possession or control, however full or complete that possession might be. A demise charterer has within limits defined by the contract the beneficial use of a vessel but does not have the beneficial ownership as respects all the shares in the ship. Thus there is strong ground for arguing that section 3(4) of the Act is concerned with title to the vessel and the use of the word 'beneficial' is resorted to by analogy with the English law concept of trust. Robert Goff J said in *The I Congreso del Partido* 'the intention of Parliament in adding the word "beneficially" before the word "owned" . . . was simply to take account of the institution of the trust, thus ensuring that if the ship were operating under the cloak of a trust, those interested in the ship should not thereby be able to avoid the arrest of the ship.' Following this same argument, it must be accepted that the use of the words 'owner . . . or any share therein' in the Merchant Shipping Act 1894, section 502, 503 (see further Chapter 9), must be different and a wider construction placed on them since it has long since been established they could include the demise charterer of a vessel.

Thus the State enterprise which may have had the possession and control of the *I Congreso del Partido* was not the party which was the beneficial owner in respect of all the shares therein, which was the Republic of Cuba, and therefore the plaintiffs in the action were not entitled to invoke the Admiralty jurisdiction of the High Court by an action in rem against the vessel in which Mambisa (the State enterprise referred to) are identified as the defendants.

A case of judicial value, though prior to the coming into effect of the 1981 Act, is *The Father Thames* [1979] 2 Lloyd's Rep. 364. The *Father Thames* was demised by her owners, who were London-based and owned all 64 shares, to Bandeck for two years. The rights and liabilities were subsequently assigned to Pindergate Ltd. During the charter period she collided with the *Office* (another vessel) and was promptly arrested. This posed a question for the court—can you proceed in rem against a vessel after a collision when the Master and crew were employees of the *charterer*, bearing in mind that maritime collisions, if fault there is at all, are approximately caused by negligence of Master or crew, i.e. human fallibility?

Admiralty Judge Sheen J, although acknowledging that there was a conflict in case law decisions about whether a demise charterer came within the definition of 'beneficially owning all the shares in' which forms part of the text of section 3(4) of the Administration of Justice Act 1956, said that *that* section dealt with the right to arrest sister ships and what was at issue in this case was the right to enforce the maritime lien by arresting the *offending* ship to which the 'leech-like' lien stuck, i.e. section 3(3) of the same Act. His answer was yes. The maritime lien although founded admittedly on the notion of owners' (presumably personal) vicarious liability could and should have that notion 'stretched' to include a demise charterer's liability since he at the time of the collision was to be regarded as the 'temporary' owner or owner 'pro hac vice'. The owners of the *Father Thames* should not suffer anyway, said Sheen J, because of a fully comprehensive indemnity clause in their favour given by charterers in the charterparty document.

*The Father Thames* ruling is, however, only of relevance when it is the *offending* ship which is arrested and only when it is a maritime lien which is being enforced.

Further discussion on the meaning of beneficial ownership was held in the Admiralty Court in August 1977 in the case of *The Aventicum*, below.

*The Aventicum* [1978] 1 Lloyd's Rep. 184
The matter involved a motion by the shipowners, inter alia, that a writ in rem and subsequent arrest proceedings taken under section 3(4) of the Administration of Justice Act 1956 should be set aside. The cause of action arose from alleged wet damage to newsprint carried as cargo in the vessel which at the time of carriage was called the *Ivory Neptune*. The plaintiffs, who were consignees of the cargo, maintained that although the vessel in the intervening time had apparently been through various processes of change in registered ownership, this had not truly brought about a change in the beneficial ownership. The Admiralty judge in the face of strong opposing arguments ruled that the court had the power to look beyond the registered ownership to the real or beneficial ownership, to see who really reaped the profits from the ship's trading, who had the right as true shareholders to the dividends. In *The Aventicum* matter, the vessel and its owning company had been through various processes of change of registered ownership which might not necessarily, so the plaintiffs argued, have involved a real change of beneficial ownership for true and valuable consideration. Mere changing from one flag of convenience to another was certainly not a change of ownership within the sense contemplated by the Act. Pertinent words from the judgment were—'Section 3(4) of the Act intends that the court shall not be limited to a consideration of who is the registered owner or who is the person having legal ownership of the shares in the ship. The directions are to look at the beneficial ownership. In a case where there is a suggestion of a trusteeship or a nominee holding there is no doubt that the court can investigate it.' The court found to its satisfaction that the persons who beneficially owned the shares in the *Aventicum* were not the persons who were the owners at the time the cause of action arose and the defendants' application was granted, the writ and all subsequent proceedings being set aside and the vessel released from arrest.

The Supreme Court Act 1981 draws a clear distinction between 'demise charterer' and 'beneficial owner'. Therefore it is clear that 'beneficial owner' cannot encompass 'demise charterer' which is in line with the earlier decision of *The Father Thames*.

The need to determine beneficial ownership to satisfy the requirements of English law (as opposed to international Convention) and that there has been no improper or wrongful arrest causes problems in English jurisdiction which do not arise in jurisdictions of those countries which have no concept of trust ownership. It is here, basically, that English law has always been 'out of step with' international trends. The 1952 Arrest Convention refers throughout to 'owning', 'ownership', 'owned by'—a simpler concept than the more complex English notion, avoiding the need in some cases to 'pierce' the 'corporate veil' of corporate ownership (as English judges have described it) to determine true, real, underlying or beneficial ownership. Because of the requirement of English statutory (Admiralty) law to determine *beneficial* ownership, the courts have reserved for themselves the discretionary power to investigate beneficial ownership, to 'pierce the corporate veil' or 'front' registered ownership and look behind in rare cases. In *The Maritime Trader* [1981] 2 Lloyd's Rep. 153 the Admiralty judge stated his view that a court should only use that power if there was a genuine likelihood that the owning company (legally registered as such) was formed merely as a device to hide the ship away from being used as security or sold to satisfy a judgment. *But*, can the necessary evidence be adduced other than through the process of court-ordered discovery? And how or where can such an order be secured at the early stage before the writ in rem has been issued?

The facts were that the disponent owners of the vessel *Antaios* had chartered her to MTO. MTO breached the charter, giving disponent owners a potential claim pursuant to which they issued a writ in rem against the *Maritime Trader* of which, they alleged, MTO was beneficial owner. The registered owner of the *Maritime Trader* was MTS, a wholly owned subsidiary of MTO. The court had to decide whether MTO was beneficial owner. Ostensibly, no. It is a principle of English company law that a shareholder in a company (e.g. MTO in MTS) has no property rights in the assets (*Maritime Trader*) of that company. The only way around this would be to 'pierce the corporate veil'. The court reiterated the views of earlier courts that they had the power to do this but that it should only be exercised in the event of a genuine likelihood that the registered owning company is a 'sham' to conceal true ownership, e.g. a company specially formed to own a ship with the aim of shielding it from the chances of being seized as security. It should be emphasised that in both the above cases there was an allegation that there was a change in beneficial ownership.

The meaning of 'beneficially owned as respect all shares therein' contained in section 21(4) of the Supreme Court Act 1981 is of topical interest bearing in mind the dissolution of the Soviet Union and the transfer of former Soviet property to independent republics.

In the case of the *Nazym Khikmet* [1996] 2 Lloyd's Rep. 362 the *Nazym Khikmet* carried a cargo of tobacco from India to Ukraine. The cargo owners brought a claim against the contractual carriers Blasco, a Ukraine company, and arrested another vessel operated by Blasco, the *Zorinsk* in Newport, Gwent. Blasco and the State of Ukraine contended that the vessel *Zorinsk* on the day the writ was issued was not beneficially owned by Blasco. They applied for the proceedings to be set aside and the vessel released from arrest. Expert evidence was produced by various Ukraine lawyers. The Admiralty judge decided that the *Zorinsk* had not, as at the date of issue of the writ, been beneficially owned by Blasco, and an appeal was made to the Court of Appeal.

The defendants relied on written evidence of two Blasco officials to the effect that the *Zorinsk* was the property of the Republic of Ukraine and that vessels were allocated to Blasco as operating managers. They also relied on evidence of two legal experts who said the vessel *Zorinsk* was owned by the state. The Court of Appeal decided that the evidence clearly showed that Blasco was at no time what English law would recognize as the legal owner of the *Zorinsk*. Legal ownership was a matter of title, and title to the vessel at all times belonged to the State. It was also clear that the State did not own the vessel as legal owner for the benefit of Blasco. It was more apt to regard Blasco as exploiting the vessel for the ultimate benefit of the public.

The evidence made it plain that the process of liberalization which took place in the Ukraine once it became independent had led to a loosening of the bonds of State control, but not to a severance of them. The State retained its ownership of the income-earning assets of enterprises such as Blasco, and had retained the right and power of ultimate decision over the use and exploitation of those assets. Even if in practice Blasco enjoyed a wide measure of commercial discretion, it did not enjoy what English law would recognize as the rights of an equitable owner. Therefore the Court of Appeal decided that the plaintiffs were not entitled to arrest the *Zorinsk*.

For the purposes of these proceedings, the Court of Appeal concluded that the court must give subsection (4)(ii) the meaning which Mr Justice Robert Goff gave in the case of the *I Congreso Del Partido* [1977] 1 Lloyd's Rep. 536. Therefore it was necessary to enquire whether, when action was brought, Blasco was, under the law to which it was subject, what English law would regard as the beneficial owner as respects all the shares in the *Zorinsk*. The Court of Appeal accepted that section 21(4)(ii) was enacted in order to implement the judgment of Mr Justice Robert Goff in the *I Congreso Del Partido* case on the effect of section 3(4) of the Administration of Justice Act 1956. Mr Justice Robert Goff at page 563 stated ' . . . as I read section 3(4), the intention of Parliament in adding the word "beneficially" before the word "owned" in section 3(4) was simply to take account of the institution of the trust, thus ensuring that, if a ship was to be operated under the cloak of a trust, those interested in the ship would not thereby be able to avoid the arrest of the ship'.

There have been two other recent cases concerning 'beneficial ownership'. In the case of the *Kommunar* [436 LMLN] the plaintiffs entered into an agreement with the Leningrad Fishing Industry Production Association (Lenrybprom) whereby the plaintiffs agreed to discharge expenses incurred by Lenrybprom's vessels operating in Latin America. The plaintiffs arrested the vessel *Kommunar*. Lenrybprom made an application to set aside the arrest of their vessel *Kommunar*. They said that at the time the relevant goods and services were supplied to the vessels Lenrybprom was an unincorporated association (referred to as POL) whereas by the time the cause of action arose it had become incorporated and was now a separate legal entity (referred to as AOL). In 1993, POL had been privatized under Russian legislation which involved its being converted into a public joint stock company and renamed AOL. The question of whether AOL was the same legal entity as POL for the purposes of section 21(4) of the 1981 Act had to be made by reference to Russian law.

The High Court decided that the effect of the Russian legislation appeared to treat the joint stock company as a totally different entity to the state enterprise. Whilst AOL was certainly expressly designated as the successor of POL in relation to such assets and liabilities as had not been stripped out by the privatization plan, its position as assignee or transferee under the law of its incorporation did not necessarily mean that it was the same legal entity. There was a fundamental difference between the two entities. Although there could be no doubt that there was legal succession of AOL to POL's assets and liabilities, there was nothing inconsistent between that and the discontinuity of legal personality. The arrest of *Kommunar* was set aside.

The New Zealand courts have also been concerned with a similar point in relation to the Novorossiysk fishing fleet in the case of the *Efim Gorbenko*. P.O. Novorossiskirybprom (PON) had been privatized and A.O. Novorossiskiryb-prom (AON) had emerged. The vessel proceeded against was owned by AON when the action was brought but by PON when the cause of action arose. Section 5(2) of the New Zealand Admiralty Act 1973 was similar to section 21(4) of the Supreme Court Act 1981. The argument that AON was not the same legal entity as PON was rejected.

The court decided that they were satisfied by the evidence, on affidavit, of the plaintiffs' experts that what occurred was not a substantive change of legal entity but a transformation of a state owned enterprise into a privately owned joint stock company in accordance with a government decree. That change did not bring about any real change in the nature of the owner of the vessel. The change was more consistent with a change of name or a form of legal succession where the same substantive legal entity existed but it was given a new form to recognize a new reality because of the changes in government and legal organization in a Russian State. The shipowners' application for the arrest to be set aside alternatively for a stay of the proceedings was dismissed.

By way of comment, beneficial ownership is a concept peculiar to common law countries such as England wherein ownership can exist under the 'cloak' of a trust, thus disguising the beneficiary from easy recognition.

## PROCEDURAL ASPECTS OF ARREST OF A SHIP

In the early days, an aggrieved person could arrest a shipowner or his ship or the goods on his ship: the former being an action 'in personam', the two latter being actions 'in rem'. The effect of either would be to force the offender into furnishing bail as security pending any judgment which might be given in favour of the complainant. Arrest of a person in these circumstances eventually became obsolete and was not permitted under the common law. Only the ship itself could be the subject of an arrest. As we have seen, the circumstances wherein arrest of a vessel may be permitted are presented in statutory provisions in the Supreme Court Act 1981.

It should be emphasized that, normally, arrest itself is not necessary to found jurisdiction. It is sufficient to institute in rem action only which, in practical language, means the issuing and serving on the named property of a writ in rem. The arrest process, as distinct from mere in rem proceedings, gives the added advantage to the arrestor/claimant of obtaining from the owner of the arrested property adequate alternative pre-judgment security. However, if the owner of the ship is domiciled in an EU country which has ratified the 1968 Brussels Convention (or a country which has ratified the Lugano Convention) then it will be necessary for the plaintiff to arrest the ship unless English jurisdiction has been agreed or unless the writ is acknowledged and the owners put up a bail bond. The effect of these Conventions is discussed below. In strict legal procedure, and since 1883, a writ in rem and a warrant of arrest are two separate documents but in practice, in the vast majority of cases, they are served at the same time on the res.

A person, or corporate person, contemplating making an arrest will, assuming he has a valid claim and that claim entitles him to proceed in rem, be required to prove on oath that he is so entitled. It is not necessary to prove the validity of the claim. It is only necessary to state on affidavit the nature of the claim and the circumstances giving rise to the claim.

Under the Rules of the Supreme Court (RSC) Order 75, rule 5, the affidavit must state the nature of the claim or counterclaim and that it has not been satisfied. It should also state, if the claim arises in connection with a ship, her name and port of registry. Alternatively, it must specify the nature of the property to be arrested, including the name and port of registry, if a ship. If a claim gives rise to a writ in rem and is brought under section 21(4) of the Supreme Court Act 1981, giving rise to a statutory right of action in rem, then the affidavit must also specify the name of the person who would be liable in an action in personam, that this person was, when the cause of action arose, the owner or charterer of, or in possession or control of, the ship in connection with which the claim arose, and that, when the writ was issued, the relevant person was either the beneficial owner of all the shares in the ship to be arrested or, if the offending ship is to be arrested, then the relevant person was the demise charterer of the ship.

There is a duty of full and frank disclosure in relation to the facts stated in the affidavit. However, the duty of full and frank disclosure only applies to the facts required to be stated under the Rules of the Supreme Court Act (RSC Order 75) (see *The Varna* [1993] 2 Lloyd's Rep. 253). If it transpires that there has not been full and frank disclosure then the arrest can be set aside and the security relinquished. In the case of *The Johnny Two* [1992] 2 Lloyd's Rep. 257, at page 117 above), Sheen J underlined the necessity for full and frank disclosure. If the plaintiff complies with the statutory procedural requirements he is entitled to issue the warrant of arrest. The issue of a warrant of arrest is not a discretionary remedy. Also in the case of the *Lloyd Pacifico* [1995] 1 Lloyd's Rep. 54, the Admiralty Court stated that it was important that parties should recognize that they ought not to seek to arrest a vessel unless they complied properly with the provisions of Order 75, rule 5(4) and (9): the affidavit had to state clearly whether the claim was put on a sister ship basis or not. The defendants or prospective defendants or other persons interested in the ship to be arrested were entitled to know the basis on which the property was arrested.

The procedure is that, subsequent to the issue of a writ in rem, a warrant for arrest of the property is issued on the request of the plaintiff and is executed by the Admiralty Marshal. Before a warrant of arrest is issued, the plaintiff must search the caveat book to see if there is a caveat in force against arrest. A caveat against arrest is issued by a party who does not want the ship to be arrested. If a limitation fund has been constituted in accordance with Article 11 of the Convention on Limitation of Liability for Maritime Claims 1976, then a caveat can be entered by the person (owner) relying on the limitation fund (RSC Order 75, rule 6(1A)). This rule came into force after the *Bowbelle* disaster. The caveat does not prevent the plaintiff arresting the ship but, if he does not have good and sufficient reasons for arresting them, upon the application of the caveator the court will order the ship to be released and may order the plaintiff to pay damages for any loss suffered as a result of the arrest (RSC Order 75, rule 7).

A person who wishes to prevent the arrest of property and undertakes to enter an appearance in any action which may be instituted against the property will, after the commencement of action, be required to give bail or some form of security. A bail bond can be provided to the court, though this is not so commonly done as it used to be. Under a bail bond the court is empowered to 'call it in' whereas other types of security are given personally to the claimant who would eventually be obliged to bring an action to enforce a guarantee if the guarantor subsequently displayed reluctance to honour it in accordance with its terms. Whatever the nature of security being sought, the arresting party must be reasonable in his demands.

Similarly, a third person may wish to prevent the release from arrest of any property detained in an action in rem, or alternatively, to forestall the paying out of any money held by the court as a result of the proceeds of sale. Such party may apply by motion for a caveat against release. Such procedure is a delaying tactic available to parties with complaints against property already under arrest. Any person taking such action should, however, ensure that he has good and sufficient reason for so doing: otherwise he may find himself liable for costs and damages.

A warrant of arrest will not be executed unless a written undertaking is lodged with the court to pay on demand the fees of the Admiralty Marshal and all expenses incurred by him in respect of the arrest and subsequent care of the property whilst under arrest. If security is provided, there is usually an agreement as to who (plaintiff or defendant) pays the expenses of the Admiralty Marshal. If the shipowner does not put up security promptly or at all, the ship may be under arrest for quite some time and considerable expenses may be incurred, i.e. in moving the ship to a lay-berth. These will be for the account of the arresting party, although they will be paid first out of the proceeds of sale if the ship is sold by the court. Also, the arresting party should consider insuring the ship against port risks for the amount of their claim and the inclusion in any policy of a 'held covered' clause, in case the ship moves or is moved outside the area covered by the usual port risks policy. The Admiralty Solicitors Group in London have negotiated an open cover through the London market covering arrest, salvor's lien, collision lien and general average disbursements.

If service of a warrant of arrest is to be effected it is performed by the Admiralty Marshal in London or by a Deputy, who will be a Regional Customs Officer, in other ports within the jurisdiction (i.e. an English or Welsh port). The High Court, situated in London, has 'branches' all over the jurisdiction. There are, thus, District Registries throughout the country capable of performing the duties undertaken by the London Admiralty Registry. These District Registries are empowered to issue arrest warrants but, once issued, all arrests are procedurally channelled through the Admiralty Marshal in London and a warrant can only be served through his good offices. The warrant must be served on the property itself which involves, in the arrest of the ship, the warrant being affixed for a brief period to a mast or to any other suitable part of the vessel's superstructure and, after that, a copy of the warrant is left on board. If the property concerned is cargo already discharged ashore, the warrant is placed on the cargo. To arrest freight, the warrant may be served on the cargo in respect of which the freight is payable or on the vessel on which the relevant cargo is carried. Freight cannot be arrested separately. As a result of such service, the Admiralty Marshal has custody, though not possession, of the arrested property (see *The Arantzazu Mendi* [1939] AC 256, HL; *The Queen of the South* [1968] 1 Lloyd's Rep. 182). Any person interfering with this right of custody is exposed to a charge of contempt of court and is liable to prosecution.

*The Jarvis Brake* [1976] 2 Lloyd's Rep. 320
Pursuant to an order of sale made in the Admiralty Court, a commission of appraisement and sale was issued to the Admiralty Marshal in respect of a ship lying in the defendant's yard. Thereafter the defendant tried to sell the vessel himself and also temporarily removed the arrest documents from the ship in order to copy them. The Marshal applied to commit the defendant for contempt.

*Held*: that the defendant had undoubtedly acted in contempt of court but that since it appeared that he had acted out of ignorance rather than for any sinister motive, it was not reasonable to punish him other than to order that he pay the costs of the committal application.

*The Synova* [1976] 1 Lloyd's Rep. 40
The Master of a vessel owed £625 for equipment. On 16 May 1975, an officer acting for the Admiralty Marshal went on board the ship and fixed documents of arrest to her superstructure. The Master removed them and, on 19 May and 21 May, the documents were again fixed and again removed. In the meanwhile, the Master had repaid the debt but the question of costs was still outstanding. On a motion by the Admiralty Marshal for a penalty to be imposed for contempt of court:

*Held*: that any violation in the process of arrest should be punished. This, however, was not a serious case and there appeared to have been no attempt to defeat the ends of justice. The court imposed a fine of £100 and ordered the Master to pay the costs of the Admiralty Marshal.

In the case of *The Cerro Colorado* [1993] 1 Lloyd's Rep. 58 the court decided that any conduct which impedes or is likely to impede the ability of the Admiralty Marshal to achieve a fair market value upon the sale of the vessel (including but not limited to published statements that the vessel will, after sale, by the Admiralty Marshal, remain encumbered with existing claims) is an interference with the administration of justice. Such conduct may expose anyone responsible to proceedings for contempt of court.

Sheen J, in the case of *The Johnny Two* [1992] 2 Lloyd's Rep. 257 outlined the current procedure for the arrest of a ship as follows:

'Upon issue of the warrant the Admiralty Marshal telephones the relevant officer of HM Customs and Excise and instructs him to arrest the ship. He tells the Customs Officers his requirements for ensuring the security of the arrest. That is followed up by sending a "Note of Action" by fax confirming his instructions to arrest the ship and giving the folio number of the action, the name of the plaintiff and the name of the plaintiff's solicitors. An officer of HM Customs then arrests the ship by attaching the Note of Action to the ship. He then carries out the Marshal's instructions for keeping the ship safely under arrest. This can be carried out within a very short space of time.

The warrant of arrest and the writ are then sent by post to HM Customs for execution and service respectively. But frequently, of course, security will have been provided and service of the writ accepted by solicitors so that the ship will have been released before these documents are received by HM Customs.

If a ship is expected to arrive at a known port a warrant of arrest should be issued. A "Note of Action" instructing a Customs Officer to "Arrest on arrival" will then be sent to the relevant Customs Office. The ship will then be arrested on arrival by the "Note of Action" or the execution of the warrant if it has arrived at the Customs Office. In this way a ship may be arrested on a day when the Court Offices are closed.

Arrests in London are effected by the personal attendance of the Marshal's Officer who executes the warrant.

If a caveat against arrest is entered after a warrant is issued but before the arrest is effected, the plaintiff's solicitors will be informed. They will be asked if they still wish to arrest.

If a warrant of arrest is issued in respect of a ship when the port of arrival is not known, the warrant can be left with the Marshal with instructions, endorsed on the undertaking to pay his expenses, to arrest "at a port to be advised during normal working hours".

These procedures enable solicitors to arrest a ship at very short notice, particularly when they have taken the precaution of issuing a warrant in advance.'

The arrest of a vessel may cause hardship or inconvenience to innocent third parties and in *The Mardina Merchant* [1974] 2 Lloyd's Rep. 424 it was declared that it should be inherent in the jurisdiction of an Admiralty Court to allow a third party to intervene if the effect of an arrest was to cause that party serious hardship or difficulty, viz. the position of an arrested ship in a berth causing inconvenience in the running of the port.

It should also be borne in mind that a warrant of arrest may not be issued as of right in the case of property whose beneficial ownership has, since the issue of the writ, changed. If the ship is arrested then the 'new' owner should intervene in the action. In fact, any person who has an interest in the property or proceeds of sale, such as mortgagees and charterers, can apply to court by affidavit to intervene in the action to protect his interest. If the court grants leave to intervene, the intervener becomes a party to the action.

It may be prejudicial to the owner of a vessel that his ship remains under arrest in that the vessel, as property, is likely to deteriorate, thus endangering the interests of both arrestor and the defendant. That bail giving the security can be just as valuable to the arresting party as the vessel itself, as illustrated by *The Gay Tucan*, below.

*The Gay Tucan* [1968] 2 Lloyd's Rep. 245

A pleasure craft was arrested by the plaintiff who claimed that the vessel was held by the defendant on trust for the plaintiff. The plaintiff claimed possession of the vessel and an order for transfer of title. The plaintiff argued that the vessel had been grounded while in the possession of the defendant and might be grounded again and suffer damage. The defendant counter-argued that the vessel was liable to be damaged while under arrest and that unauthorized persons had been on board.

*Held*: that the authorities did not establish any clear basis on which the court's discretion should be exercised. Although the vessel was a pleasure craft, it should be taken into account that the defendant would be deprived of the use of the vessel and that the risk of deterioration was no greater if the vessel was released than if she remained under arrest. If the plaintiff received bail at the amount representing the present value of the vessel he would be in as good a position as if his security consisted of the vessel itself. The defendant's motion should be allowed.

This case also underlines the principle that arrest confers custodial rights but possessory rights can, and often should, if the circumstances dictate, remain with the defendant. Arrest is a prerequisite to the application to the court for an order to sell a ship.

Bail is rarely put up in order to secure release of a ship from arrest, or in order to avoid the threat of arrest. However, EU defendants may have difficulty in disputing jurisdiction of the English court in view of the recent cases of *The Prinsengracht* and *Anna H* (at pages 135 and 137) on the grounds that the defendants have submitted to the jurisdiction of the English courts by putting up bail without protest. What is far more common is the furnishing of security on behalf of the defendant owner of the ship in the form of a letter of undertaking by his 'Protection & Indemnity' (P & I) Club or a bank guarantee. The wording of the letter of undertaking often differs but one example might read as follows.

'In consideration of the owners of and other persons interested in the cargo referred to above (hereinafter referred to as the "cargo owners") consenting to the release from arrest and/or refraining from taking action resulting in the arrest of the above-named ship or any other ship in the same ownership, associated ownership or management, or possession or control . . . We hereby undertake to pay to you on demand such sums as may be adjudged by the English High Court of Justice or as may be agreed to be recoverable from the owners of the above-named ship in respect of the said claim, interest and costs of the cargo owners provided that the total of our liability shall not exceed the sum of . . . '

Such letter of undertaking invariably states a 'sum not exceeding £X' as opposed to an indefinite amount. It may also state the domicile of the defendant owners of the ship or may provide an agreement for jurisdiction both in respect of the claims covered by the letter of undertaking and any proceedings brought in order to enforce the letter of undertaking. Demands for security can be excessive in relation to the realistic value of the claim concerned and, particularly in cases where there may exist an undisputed right to limit liability, an application to reduce the amount of security sought may be made and the court can determine the appropriate amount of security. Security cannot exceed the value of the res.

Release from arrest can only be obtained by way of an instrument of release, that is to say unless the property has already been sold by court order. The obtaining of a release will normally be a simple formality provided that the bail, or alternatively security given, is considered sufficiently satisfactory. To release a ship from arrest a release must be filed in the Registry and the Admiralty Marshal's fees and expenses paid or an undertaking lodged. It is also necessary to obtain the agreement of the plaintiff and all caveators. The Marshal then instructs the release of the vessel.

If no security is provided by the owner of the ship (or his P & I Club), the Admiralty Marshal can sell the ship, usually by private treaty after appraisement. The proceeds of sale are distributed to the claimants in accordance with the priority of their claims. The purchaser of the ship obtains clear title free of all liens and other charges or encumbrances (*The Acrux* [1962] 1 Lloyd's Rep. 405). All existing claims are transferred to the proceeds of sale. In the recent case of *The Blitz* [1992] 2 Lloyd's Rep. 441 it was decided that a sale of the vessel *Blitz* by a local authority pursuant to its powers under section 44 of the Harbours Docks and Piers Clauses Act 1847 is a sale free from mortgages (and encumbrances).

### *Wrongful arrest*

A cause of action for wrongful arrest does potentially lie within English law, though it is very rarely pursued. Gross negligence or malice must be proved to establish wrongful arrest. Excessive demands for security will not be tolerated and an owner will be eager to obtain the release of his ship from arrest in any event. The affidavit which must support an application for an arrest warrant should also effectively help to nullify the likelihood that the wrong ship will have been selected for arrest.

### *What is a maritime lien?*

There are two alternative definitions of a maritime lien: (1) a right to a part of the property in the res; and (2) a privileged claim upon a ship, aircraft or other maritime property in respect of services rendered to, or injury caused by, that property.

A maritime lien attaches to the property at the moment when the cause of action arises and remains attached (rather like a leech to human skin), travelling with it through changes of ownership. It is, however, inchoate or of little 'positive' value unless and until enforced by action in rem. It is *not* dependent upon possession nor is it defeated or extinguished because the res may happen to be transferred to new ownership for value and without notice.

It is a right which springs from general maritime law and is based on the concept that the ship (personified) has *itself* caused harm, loss or damage to others or to their property and must *itself* make good that loss. The ship is, in other words, the wrongdoer, not its owners. This may make very little sense to the practical mind. How can a ship do wrong? It *is*, however, the instrumentality by which its owners or their legal servants do wrong. The most obvious and chronologically first original example of the arising of such a lien was the collision at sea—physical impact ship to ship or ship to fixed property. At the moment of impact and the causing thus consequentially of harm to others or to their property a maritime lien arises in favour of all those thus suffering, attaching to the ship. It is in this practical aspect of enforcement where the general maritime law, which incorporates this right of lien, assumes a similarity to the *statutory* right to arrest.

A maritime lien is a *proprietary* interest in the 'res'; it detracts from the absolute title of the 'res' owner. There has been a division of judicial opinion as to whether it is a right *in* the property (a jus in re) or a right *against* the property (a jus in rem) only. It is submitted that the lien is *both*, a right in the property perfected by action (in rem) against it.

## Maritime liens and the conflict of laws

Should maritime liens, recognized as a created right inherent in the claim by a *foreign* system of law, be recognized *at the time of enforcement* by an English court bringing it into effect against the object of the lien—the vessel? Furthermore, where there is a need to determine priorities amongst lien-holders whose liens attach to the proceeds of that same vessel sold to satisfy them, should the order of priorities be determined according to the law of the country where the lien was created (lex loci) or the law of the country exercising jurisdiction (lex fori)?

The problem attracted the attention of the Privy Council in *The Halcyon Isle* [1980] 3 All ER 197. It was considering an appeal to it from a Singapore court. It decided that the consensus of English case law authority concluded that liens are enforceable in actions in rem in English courts where *and only where* the events on which the claim is founded would have given rise to a maritime lien in English law if those events had occurred within the territorial jurisdiction of the English court. This was a majority decision (3–2). The majority acknowledged that a maritime lien followed the property through changes of ownership and was enforceable against an innocent purchaser, but nevertheless refused to define the lien as more than remedial and procedural. The question of priorities *was* purely jurisdictional and should be a matter for determination exclusively by the lex fori. The minority refused to accept this view, maintaining that a maritime lien is a right of property and that that was the original concept of a lien of this sort and was in keeping with the principles of the law of the sea. This latter view, it is submitted, is correct. Certain claims carry a lien, the lien travels with the ship and it would be a denial of this simple principle to say that the recognition and priority bestowed upon it were exclusively for the determination of the eventual lex fori. With *priorities* the procedural theory is *admittedly* logical and with the creation or nature of the lien the jurisdictional theory is logical as a prevailing determinator *if* there are several liens from various countries attaching to the same vessel. But what seems utterly irreconcilable is the premise that a right in the nature of a proprietary interest is nevertheless only a procedural or remedial right. *The Halcyon Isle* case does nothing to resolve or even clarify the question of how a conflict of laws should treat liens. The answer is that both views, majority and minority, have their flaws. For an English court to refuse to recognize foreign legal thinking on the nature and creation of a lien is to deny the reasonably smooth 'dovetailing' process of the conflict of laws, but on the other hand a forum should not be obliged to recognize a foreign right if it is against its established principles to do so.

*The Ioannis Daskalelis* [1974] 1 Lloyd's Rep. 174, Supreme Court of Canada

The question for decision in this case was as to whether or not a ship repairer's claim for necessary repairs gave rise to a maritime lien, thus having precedence over the subsequent mortgage of the vessel.

*Held*: that Canadian law did not recognize the existence of a maritime lien in these circumstances but that the law of the United States (where the repairs were effected) did. By its very nature, this lien follows the vessel wherever it may proceed and through any changes of ownership which the vessel may undergo.

This case illustrates very well how a certain type of claim may carry a maritime lien under the laws of one country but under the laws of another country the same type of claim may not carry a lien but merely a possible right in rem.

The essence of a maritime lien was expressed concisely by the court in *The Bold Buccleugh* (1852) 7 Moo PC 267 to be that it is a right which 'travels' with the ship into whosesoever possession it may subsequently go. The judge in that case might by way of explanation have added 'and *where*soever it and that subsequent possession may be'. Because it, the ship, is to 'pay for the wrong it has done' it must be compelled to do so by Admiralty process, by forced sale thus making the proceeds of sale available to satisfy the existing lien holders; if the proceeds are limited then each privileged creditor will receive satisfaction in a court-determined order of priorities until the available proceeds are exhausted. The buyer of the vessel in an *Admiralty* sale acquires a *clean*, unencumbered title.

*The Bold Buccleugh* (1852) 7 Moo PC 267
The facts of this case are not of significance but this was one of the early leading cases which decided that a maritime lien does not require possession. It can be defined to mean a claim or privilege upon a thing (res) to be carried into effect by legal process. It is the foundation for a proceeding in rem, the legal machinery to perfect a right born at the moment the lien attaches. It can, however, be defeated if the res is either (a) sold by order of a court, or (b) transferred to a foreign government who can plead sovereign immunity, or (c) the holder of the lien has been neglectful of his interest and thus deemed to have waived or forfeited his rights.

It is of the utmost importance to distinguish the maritime lien from the *possessory* lien which latter may be defined as: 'A right in one man to retain that which is in his possession belonging to another until certain demands of him, the person in possession, are satisfied.'

Since every proceeding in rem is in essence a proceeding against the owner of the ship, a proper maritime lien must have its root in the shipowner's personal liability, though some say that at least one exception to this principle is damage after a collision. The following is a quotation from the judgment in *The Parlement Belge* (1880) 5 PD 197:

'In a claim made in respect of a collision the property is not treated as the delinquent "per se". Although the ship has been in collision and has caused injury by reason of negligence or want of skill of those in charge of her, yet she cannot be made the means of compensation if those in charge of her were not the servants of her then owners, as if she was in charge of a compulsory pilot. That is conclusive to show that the liability to compensate must be fixed not merely on the property, but also on the owner through the property.

Thus, a claimant who holds a maritime lien may bring an action in rem against the ship under section 21(3), even though the ownership of the 'res' may have changed since the cause of action arose. The plaintiff has an unqualified right to take proceedings in rem against the ship, irrespective of ownership. But where no maritime lien has arisen in favour of the claimant his position is different if the vessel changes ownership. Judicial interpretation of the statutory authority (see *The Monica S* below) has confirmed that the right does not pre-exist the taking of the action and that until action is taken, e.g. by the issuing of a writ naming the 'res', the right does not come into being. This is a fundamental difference between the right in rem as granted by *statute* and the general maritime law lien.

Generally speaking, the holder of a maritime lien has a higher priority than other creditors in the event that the ship is sold with the intention that the assets should be distributed to satisfy the creditors.

Where the statute gives an unsecured creditor an action against the ship and does not clearly prescribe that his claim overrides that of a mortgagee, such creditor in *no* case obtains the ship as a security *until* he institutes suit in court. His right, in that case, is subject to any registered mortgage, and he must arrest the ship and thereby acquire the ship as security.

The arrest of the vessel under statutory right is only one of several possible alternative proceedings. No right in the ship or against the ship is created at any time before the arrest which does not relate back to any earlier period. But an arrest of ship in enforcement of a *maritime lien* gives effect to the pre-existing lien.

*The Monica S* [1967] 2 Lloyd's Rep. 113
This case raised the question of whether a cargo damage claimant, who has issued a writ in rem against the carrying ship at a time when she was still owned by the carrier but has not yet served the writ or arrested the ship, has a right to proceed with the action despite a subsequent transfer of the ownership of the ship to a third party.

*Held*: that the preponderance of authority tends to show that the defendant's contention that under pre-1956 law a change of ownership after the issue of a writ but before service or arrest defeated a statutory right in rem was *wrong*. There was no reason why, once a plaintiff had properly invoked jurisdiction under the 1956 Act by bringing an action in rem, he should not, despite a subsequent change of ownership of res, be able to prosecute it through all its stages up to judgment against the res and payment out of the proceeds. That this may be hard on the innocent buyer would only be countered by the argument of caveat emptor. It is up to him to obtain appropriate guarantees from the seller and/or to search the Admiralty registry well before he agrees to buy. He would be faced with substantial problems if the seller subsequently became bankrupt or otherwise could not be legally pursued.

Indeed, it has been said, a purchaser (of a ship) always has to reckon with the possibility of maritime liens or other charges and under many foreign laws all or most of the claims which in England only give a right of action in rem give rise to liens (Sheen J in the *The Helene Roth* [1980] 2 Lloyd's Rep. 477). The lien is a secret right, not capable of being registered (though there has long since been a powerful lobby for this to be remedied), and whose existence cannot be determined by a mere glance at the ship's registry.

More issues on changes of ownership and the effect of arrest were discussed in *The Alletta*, below.

*The Alletta* [1974] 1 Lloyd's Rep. 40
The *Alletta* had been in collision in December 1963 in the River Thames with the motor vessel *England*. The owners of the *England* obtained judgment in October 1965 in their claim for damages against the *Alletta's* owners. Later, the *Alletta's* owners sought to limit

their liability but were unable to do so because the collision had not occurred without their actual fault or privity. In June 1973 the *Alletta* was sold, the buyers knowing nothing of any actual or potential claim against the previous owners. The ship was re-named and the sale contract included a covenant by the seller to the buyer to give indemnity in respect of any claims incurred prior to the time of delivery. In July the *England's* owners applied successfully for a warrant to arrest the *Alletta* (now renamed) to enforce the still unsatisfied judgment on the now increased value. The new owners of the *Alletta* sought to set aside the order for arrest arguing that the plaintiffs' (the owners of the *England*) right to arrest their ship either under a maritime lien arising on the collision had been lost by laches, for the vessel had visited British ports several times between 1963 and 1973 and many opportunities to arrest her had not been taken. They also contended that the right to arrest had been lost by the fact that the plaintiffs had obtained judgment against the original owners of the *Alletta*.

*Held*: that the defence of laches failed owing to the indemnity provisions in the contract of sale, but that the plaintiffs' right to arrest the ship was nevertheless lost since it had become 'merged in the judgment'. It was commented that it is always wise for a purchaser of a vessel, who always may be in danger of inheriting maritime liens attaching to the ship he buys, to procure for himself indemnity from the seller against any claims which might have accrued before the date of the sale, thus fully protecting his position. On the subject of re-arrest to enforce the judgment or to secure an increased sum (which was the reason in this case) earlier case law conflicts on the validity or otherwise of such action. Reference is made to the case of *The Point Breeze*.

*The Point Breeze* (1928) 30 Ll.L.Rep. 229
A collision took place in 1927 and on 6 December the plaintiffs issued a writ in rem and security was given in the sum of £3,500. The blame was assessed entirely against the *Point Breeze* and the matter referred out for assessment of damages. Towards the end of December, it was decided the security was insufficient to cover the damages and a warrant for arrest was issued.

*Held*: that a warrant for arrest of a vessel could not be properly served *after* liability had been determined by the court.

One thought which emerges from both *The Point Breeze* case and *The Alletta* case is that if a ship may be arrested *after* judgment on liability has been obtained against her and is by the date of the arrest the property of a third party who had bought her without knowledge of the maritime lien, grave injustice may be done.

It is important to realize that whether or not a particular cause of action confers upon the claimant a maritime lien is determined by reference to the *common* maritime law. Nowhere will this question be answered in the wording of any statute, either the Administration of Justice Act 1956 or any previous statute. In English law it is customary to regard the following causes of action as conferring a maritime lien: (1) damage resulting from a collision; (2) bottomry (and respondentia) (it is interesting to note that the Admiralty Court has not heard a case concerning bottomry for many years and the Admiralty jurisdiction in this type of claim might be regarded as obsolete); (3) salvage (see *The Tequila*, below, which, although not a decision of an English court, illustrates this point); (4) wages of seamen (see *The Halcyon Skies*, below); (5) ship's Master's wages and disbursements (this is a product of statute rather than the common law; whether the Admiralty court would willingly entertain a claim for wages brought by the Master or crew of a non-British ship would, in olden time, have been contingent upon the consent of the parties, or at least someone representing their native country (these days an English court would require to know that notice to the relevant consul had been given before it would agree to issue an arrest warrant)); and (6) fees and expenses incurred by a receiver of wreck.

*The Tequila* [1974] AMC 860
A salvor claimed a maritime lien in respect of a salvage operation in attempting to free from a strand in Honduras the motor ship *Tequila*. The claim was opposed by the holder of a foreign preferred mortgage which had been obtained four months after the alleged salvage.

*Held*: that where the salvage was hired at a daily rate under a contract which did not contain a 'no cure—no pay' provision, the owner of the salvage vessel was entitled to a maritime lien for salvage. Other issues decided by the court though not specifically on the issue of lien were that where two salvors were involved, the initial salvor has the burden of proving that his efforts contributed to the second salvor's ultimate success in freeing the vessel (on the facts of this case the first salvor failed to discharge this burden) and that the salvor's failure to remove the vessel from the strand was not excused either by adverse weather or by the alleged ineptitude of the stranded vessel's Master, but, although the salvor's efforts to free the stranded vessel were unsuccessful, he would be allowed an award for bringing food and supplies to the crew who might otherwise have abandoned ship. $5,000 was awarded.

*The Halcyon Skies* [1976] 1 Lloyd's Rep. 461
X was employed under a special contract, not being an ordinary mariner's contract, as a deck officer and crew member of the tanker *Halcyon Skies*. Y, his employer, failed to pay agreed contributions to the pension fund, and subsequently went into liquidation.

*Held*: that his claim was a claim by a crew member for wages within the meaning of the Administration of Justice Act 1956, for he had a good claim in debt for those wages, so that the damages recoverable were protected by a maritime lien despite the fact that the employment was under a special contract.

In determining how different claims which carry maritime liens should rank in priority against each other, they are divided into two distinct categories: contractual liens and damage liens.

In the absence of any specific priority rating (salvage liens, for example), it is logical that damage lien holders should be given higher priority then holders of contractual liens for a very good reason. A contractual lien holder, being a claimant who has a cause of action in his favour arising from breach of contract by the other party, is a person who originally entered (presumably) quite voluntarily into the contract and with his eyes open and thus is deemed to have been aware at the time, as any reasonable person should be, that there were risks involved and inherent in entering any agreement. Thus, in a sense, he had some forewarning of the possibilities of suffering loss, harm or damage.

The damage lien holder, on the other hand, being a person who has suffered loss or damage by reason not of a broken contract but as a result of another's wrongful or tortious act has not, by the very nature of the incident, this benefit of such forewarning or foreknowledge of the likelihood of such loss or damage; the innocent, injured passenger after a collision at sea is an obvious example. That damage lien holders should rank for priority, generally speaking, before the holders of contractual liens is not only logical but also is the basic rule.

In relation to the ranking of claims it is interesting to note that salvage has priority over (a) earlier salvage, (b) earlier damage, (c) earlier wages, (d) earlier claims to forfeiture by the Crown, (e) subsequent possessory liens, (f) necessaries, and (g) mortgages. A *salvor's* lien ranks first (and in reverse order of time if there is more than one salvor—i.e. later before earlier) simply because without the emergency services he renders there would be no funds preserved out of which anybody could be satisfied.

Excellently illustrative of the relative priorities of wage claimants and salvors against the proceeds of sale of a vessel is the case of *The Lyrma*. Both classes of claimants were holders of maritime liens.

*The Lyrma* [1978] 2 Lloyd's Rep. 27
Whilst on a cargo-carrying voyage from Antwerp to the Republic of Ireland the *Lyrma* developed steering trouble. Her cargo shifted and she took on a list. Her Master sent distress signals. A tug came to her aid off the south-west coast of England in atrocious weather conditions and towed the ship, already abandoned by her crew, to safety. The vessel was subsequently arrested to secure the tug-owner's claim for salvage and, in default of an appearance by her owners, was ordered to be sold. She fetched £32,000. This was thought to be considerably less than her salved value after her ordeal which was put at £55,000. The court viewed the tug-owner's claim for salvage in a most favourable light. It had been a difficult operation, involving much skill and the ship and her cargo had undoubtedly been saved from almost certain total loss. A salvage reward was assessed at £22,000.

The next problem was that out of the proceeds of sale, there were other claimants seeking satisfaction—the ship's Master and crew, for their unpaid wages, and the Master additionally, for disbursements. Wages claimed were earned before and after the salvage operation and the crew also sought to recover repatriation expenses. The wages claimants' aggregate claim was for £17,000. Thus £17,000 and £22,000 were sought from the net proceeds of sale which worked out at just under £25,000. The court was therefore asked to determine priorities. Obviously the delay in sale meant that the ship lying idle deteriorated and thus fetched far less than it should have done. The award of salvage, as it happened, itself almost swallowed up the net proceeds of sale leaving practically nothing for the wage claimants. Even this seeming injustice did not influence the court to depart from the established principle that a salvor's lien took precedence over a wage claimant's lien regardless of whether those wages were earned before or after the salvage service.

*The Tacoma City* [1991] 1 Lloyd's Rep. 330
The extent of the crew wages maritime lien was considered by the Court of Appeal. In 1985 the world shipping group, Reardon Smith Line, became insolvent and ceased trading. The *Tacoma City* was owned by a subsidiary company and mortgaged to a London bank. The vessel was arrested and the bank was required by court order to pay the crew all the sums due to them under their contracts of employment except those which in the opinion of the bank did not qualify as wages. The vessel was sold by the court subsequently and the Master and officers claimed severance pay against the sale proceeds. The officers had been employed under a contract which incorporated the National Maritime Board Agreement. These contracts provided that an officer with 'a minimum of two completed years of company service' would qualify for severance pay in the event of his becoming 'surplus to requirements'.

The Court of Appeal decided that the officers had no contractual entitlement to severance pay. If severance pay had been due, would this have qualified as a maritime lien? The officers contended that severance pay accrued due as a result of service aboard a ship and was therefore within the definition of 'wages'. The Court of Appeal disagreed. When a maritime employment contract includes an entitlement to pension payments upon retirement the sums due as a pension could not possibly be regarded as 'wages'. Modern contracts of employment provided for such matters as bonuses, sick pay and notice of termination of employment, all of which represented the value of the current service on the ship by the seafarer. Severance pay, on the other hand, was a payment in respect of earlier service aboard the ship or different ship. Severance pay was compensation for the termination of employment and not wages.

In the earlier case of *The Halcyon Skies* it was decided that the wages lien extends beyond bare wages to include other matters such as sick pay, leave pay and the employers' contribution to pension funds. However in view of *The Tacoma City* case it seems that it is necessary to examine precisely how each entitlement under the contract of employment arises. A maritime lien will not exist for severance pay, or a medical severance pay or pensions as opposed to agreed pension contributions.

At one time it was thought that seamen's wages had priority to Master's wages. This is not now the case in view of *The Royal Wells* [1984] 2 Lloyd's Rep. 255. It was decided that by the then section 1 of the Merchant Shipping Act 1970 the Master, crew and officers were all employees of the shipowners. As the Master was no longer liable by law to pay the seamen their wages, the seamen's claim against the vessel for wages was no longer to be preferred to his wages or disbursements. The seamen's and Master's wages should rank pari passu, i.e. equally.

But, as already explained, there are causes of action *additional* to this which confer rights in rem, and under the Supreme Court Act 1981, the right to arrest. Damage to cargo and towage are examples of these causes of action.

If a ship is sold the first things paid out are the Admiralty Marshal's charges and the plaintiff's costs of arrest.

In May 1993 the International Convention on Maritime Liens and Mortgages ('1993 Convention') was adopted. This will enter into force six months after 10 states have expressed their consent to be bound by it. This replaces the Liens and Mortgages Conventions of 1967 and 1926 which were never brought into force in English law. It remains to be seen whether the 1993 Convention will ever be brought into force. The 1993 Convention does not define maritime liens but only lists them under Article 4 (Convention liens), namely:

(a) Master and crew wages including costs of repatriation and social insurance contributions;
(b) claims for loss of life or personal injury in direct connection with the operation of the vessel;
(c) salvage;
(d) claims for port, canal and other waterway dues and pilotage dues;
(e) claims based on tort arising out of physical loss or damage caused by the operation of the vessel other than loss of or damage to cargo, containers and passengers' effects carried on the vessel.

Oil pollution claims falling within other Conventions and claims based on radioactive materials are excluded. There is no Convention lien for wreck removal or General Average contribution. Convention liens recognised under Article 4 'follow the vessel' and (apart from entitlement to compensation under an insurance contract) the claim. These liens are extinguished after a period of one year unless, prior to the expiry of this period, the vessel has been arrested or seized and such arrest has led to a forced sale.

Article 6 provides that a Convention state may grant other maritime liens on a vessel to secure claims in addition to those referred to in Article 4 subject to various provisos which rank in priority after the Convention maritime liens and registered mortgages hypothèques or charges (complying with Article 1).

Article 7 provides that a Convention state may grant under its law a right of retention in respect of a vessel in the possession of either (a) a shipbuilder to secure claims for the building of the vessel and (b) a ship repairer to secure claims for repairs effected during such possession. Such right of retention is extinguished when the vessel ceases to be in the possession of the shipbuilder or ship repairer, otherwise than in consequence of an arrest or seizure.

The 1993 Convention sets out the various priorities between Convention maritime liens (under Article 4), other maritime liens (under Article 6), mortgages and rights of retention. The order of priority is Convention maritime liens, rights of retention in favour of ship repairers or shipbuilders, registered mortgages, hypothèques and charges and other maritime liens. With regard to maritime liens, salvage has priority over all other maritime liens which have attached to the vessel prior to the time when the operations giving rise to the said liens were performed. Salvage liens rank in inverse order of the time when the claims secured thereby accrued. The other liens rank in the order listed above but as between themselves rank pari passu. Other maritime liens under Article 6 rank after the maritime liens set out in Article 4 and also after registered mortgages, hypothèques or charges which comply with the provisions of Article 1. These liens are extinguished after a period of six months from the time when the claims secured by them arose or at the end of a period of 60 days following a sale to a bona fide purchaser of a vessel.

## 'Other charge'

What the words 'other charge' in section 21(3) of the Supreme Court Act 1981 are intended to cover is not clearly defined by the Act. Certainly not a charge by way of mortgage, as this is specifically catered for by subsection (2) of section 21. They could refer to types of charges mentioned in other statutes, e.g. the Merchant Shipping Act 1894, section 513(2).

What they do *not* include is a possessory lien for repairs available, for example, to an unpaid shipbuilder or repairer.

## 'Ship repairer's lien'

The special status of a ship repairer is worth comment. He has two rights: (a) a possessory lien which is a product of the common law and (b) a right to proceed in rem against the ship.

His possessory lien, if he exercises it, is subordinate to any maritime liens which may have accrued against the ship earlier, e.g. Master's or crew's wages overdue at the time the possessory lien is exercised. If he forgoes his possessory lien by losing physical possession of the ship and leaves himself merely his right to proceed in rem against the ship he may find himself worse off in the order of priorities.

*The Narada*, below, provides an interesting illustration of the efficacy of a *ship repairer's lien* and of what facts and circumstances must exist to constitute its effectiveness.

*The Narada* [1977] 1 Lloyd's Rep. 256
This was a claim by ship repairers for a declaration that they had a possessory lien in respect of repair costs. The question for the court was as to whether there had been a sufficient hand-over of possession by the owners to the repairers to enable them to assert a possessory lien where the Master and crew remained on board. The judge said that it was a question of fact and degree and the merits of each case. It should depend on the extent and character of the repairs which are done and on whether the repairs are of such a kind as to necessitate the repairers being in overall or effective possession of the ship despite the presence of the Master and crew on board. The repairers' declaration was granted.

## The Civil Jurisdiction and Judgments Act 1982 (The Brussels Convention)

What follows includes the analysis of the difficulties of reconciling the provisions of the Brussels Convention and the 1952 Arrest Convention, with examples of recent and relevant case law.

The Brussels Convention on Jurisdiction and the Enforcement of Judgments in Civil and Commercial Matters 1968 has been ratified by various Member States of the European Union over the course of several years. This Convention has been enacted in the UK by virtue of the Civil Jurisdiction and Judgments Act 1982. The Lugano Convention on Jurisdiction and the Enforcement of Judgment in Civil and Commercial Matters 1988 is now in force between various member states of the European Union and various Member States of the European Free Trade Association. This has been enacted in the UK due to an amendment in 1991 (the Civil Jurisdiction and Judgments Act 1991 which came into force on 1 May 1992). It is not necessary to consider both Conventions separately as they are encompassed by the same Act. Both are referred to as the Brussels Convention. The contracting States to the Brussels Convention include Belgium, Denmark, France, the Federal Republic of Germany, the Hellenic Republic, the Republic of Ireland, Italy, Luxembourg, The Netherlands, Portugal, Spain and the UK. The Contracting States of the Lugano Convention include Austria, Belgium, Denmark, Finland, France, the Federal Republic of Germany, the Hellenic Republic, Iceland, the Republic of Ireland, Italy, Luxembourg, The Netherlands, Norway, Portugal, Spain, Sweden, Switzerland and the UK. Arbitration is excluded from the effect of the Brussels Convention.

The impact of the Brussels Convention has been consideration in relation to admiralty actions in rem, particularly in relation to whether an action in rem can be commenced and, if so, whether the action can be stayed. It is important to ascertain whether the defendant is domiciled in a Contracting State and, if so, then one has to consider whether the Brussels Convention has any impact.

In the case of the *Anna H* [1995] 1 Lloyd's Rep. 11, Hobhouse LJ said at page 16:

'The primary purpose of this Convention is to give effect to Article 220 of the Treaty of Rome and to secure the simplification of formalities governing the reciprocal recognition and enforcement of judgments within the European Community. To this end, it was necessary to provide a scheme for determining which courts were to have jurisdiction over what matters and to avoid conflicting decisions of the courts of different countries. The scope and basic principle of the Convention are laid down in Articles 1–3, in each case with exceptions which are not material for present purposes.

1. This Convention shall apply in civil and commercial matters whatever the nature of the court or tribunal . . .
2. Subject to the provisions of this Convention, persons domiciled in a Contracting State shall, whatever their nationality, be sued in the courts of the State . . .
3. Persons domiciled in a Contracting State may be sued in the courts of another Contracting State only by virtue of the rules set out in Sections 2–6 of the title.'

The main rule regarding the appropriate forum in which to commence proceedings is that a defendant should be sued in the Contracting State of his domicile. Proceedings commenced in breach of this rule may be stayed or dismissed. However, there are other rules which give a court jurisdiction, such as the place of performance of a contract or where the harmful event occurred in relation to a tort claim (Articles 5(1) and (3)). The relevant sections regarding domicile are as follows:

Article 2

'Subject to the provisions of this Convention, persons domiciled in a Contracting State shall, whatever their nationality, be sued in the courts of that State.'

Article 20

'Where a defendant domiciled in one Contracting State is sued in a court of another Contracting State and does not enter an appearance, the court shall declare of its own motion that it has no jurisdiction unless its jurisdiction is derived from the provisions of this Convention.

The court shall stay the proceedings so long as it is shown that the defendant has been able to receive the document instituting the proceedings or an equivalent document in sufficient time to enable him to arrange for his defence, or that all necessary steps have been taken to this end.

The provisions of the foregoing paragraph shall be replaced by those of Article 15 of the Hague Convention of 15 November 1965 on the Service Abroad of Judicial and Extra-judicial Documents in Civil and Commercial matters, if the document instituting the proceedings or notice thereof had to be transmitted abroad in accordance with that Convention.'

Further provisions relating to domicile are a follows:

Article 52

'In order to determine whether a party is domiciled in the Contracting State whose courts are seised of the matter, the court shall apply its internal law.

If a party is not domiciled in the State whose courts are seised of the matter, then, in order to determine whether the party is domiciled in another Contracting State, the court shall apply the law of the State.'

The domicile of a corporation can be the state in which it is incorporated and has its registered office or official address, alternatively the state where its central management and control is exercised.

Article 53 of the Brussels Convention provides:

'For the purposes of this Convention, the seat of a company or other legal person or association of natural or legal persons shall be treated as its domicile. However, in order to determine that seat, the court shall apply its rules of private international law . . . '

Section 42 of the 1982 Act (as amended) provides:

'(1) For the purposes of this Act the seat of a corporation or association (as determined by this section) shall be treated as its domicile.

(2) The following provisions of this section determine where a corporation or association has its seat—

(a) For the purpose of Article 53 (which for the purposes of the 1968 Convention or, as the case may be, the Lugano Convention, equates the domicile of such a body with its seat); and

(b) For the purposes of this Act other than the provisions mentioned in Section 43(1)(b) and (c).

(3) A corporation or association has its seat in the United Kingdom if and only if—

(a) it was incorporated or formed under the law of a part of the United Kingdom and has its registered office or some other official address in the United Kingdom; or

(b) its central management and control is exercised in the United Kingdom.

. . .

(6) Subject to subsection (7), a corporation or association has its seat in a state other than the United Kingdom if and only if—

(a) it was incorporated or formed under the law of that state and has its registered office or some other official address there; or

(b) its central management and control is exercised in that state.

(7) A corporation or association shall not be regarded as having its seat in a Contracting State other than the United Kingdom if it is shown that the courts of that state would not regard it as having its seat there.

(8) In this section—

. . .

"official address", in relation to a corporation or association, means an address which it is required by law to register, notify or maintain for the purpose of receiving notices or other communications.'

Therefore, it is apparent that under Article 2 of the Brussels Convention the main forum in which to commence proceedings is that of the Contracting State where the defendant has his domicile. For instance, if a cargo claim is being brought against a shipowner based in Germany and there is no exclusive jurisdiction clause which stipulates another forum the claim should be brought in the German courts. The rules in the Brussels Convention do not apply to arbitration i.e. if there is a clause in the bill of lading or charterparty contract which provides for disputes to be determined in arbitration, then the claim should be brought in arbitration. There are other rules in the Brussels Convention which confer jurisdiction to a particular court such as the place of performance of the contract (see Article 5). (See for instance the cases of *Union Transport* v *Conti Lines* [1992] 1 Lloyd's Rep. 229 and *Atlas Shipping* v *Suisse Atlantique* [1995] 2 Lloyd's Rep. 188.)

However, Article 2 is 'subject to the provisions of this Convention'. The Convention contains a number of exceptions including Article 57 of the Brussels Convention (added to by the Accession Conventions of 1978 and 1989).

Article 57 provides that:

(1) This Convention shall not affect any conventions to which the Contracting States are or will be parties and which, in relation to particular matters, govern jurisdiction or the recognition or enforcement of judgments.
(2) With a view to its uniform interpretation, paragraph 1 shall be applied in the following manner: (a) This Convention shall not prevent a court of a Contracting State which is a party to a convention on a particular matter from assuming jurisdiction in accordance with that convention, even where the defendant is domiciled in a Contracting State which is not a party to that convention . . . .

The International Convention relating to the arrest of seagoing ships signed at Brussels on 10 May 1952 (Arrest Convention) is a Convention referred to in Article 57. The primary purpose of the Arrest Convention was to agree on the circumstances in which a ship flying the flag of one Contracting State could be arrested in the jurisdiction of a Contracting State. The right of arrest exists in respect of maritime claims and extends to sister ships. Article 1(2) defines arrest as: 'Arrest means the detention of a ship by judicial process to secure a maritime claim, but does not include the seizure of a ship in execution or satisfaction of a judgment'. Article 7 also deals with the jurisdiction of the country of arrest to determine the merits of the claim. Article 7 provides:

'(1) The Courts of the country in which the arrest was made shall have jurisdiction to determine the case upon its merits if the domestic law of the country in which the arrest was made gives jurisdiction to such courts, or in any of the following cases, namely: (a) if the claimant has its habitual residence or principal place of business in the country in which the arrest was made; (b) if the claim arose in the country in which the arrest was made.'

In the case of the *Anna H* it was said at page 23: 'So Article 57 and the Arrest Convention preserve the jurisdiction of England as "the country in which the arrest was made" when, among other cases, it has jurisdiction under its domestic law'. It was also said that the Brussels and Arrest Conventions have to be read together.

The Arrest Convention, however, only applies to *in rem* actions and not to *in personam* actions. Before the Brussels Convention came into force in the UK, jurisdiction could be founded for a claim if a writ was served on a vessel. The vessel need not be arrested. It was quite common for Owners' P & I Clubs to put up security for a claim when an arrest was threatened and then to undertake to accept service of the writ through solicitors.

If the owners are now based in the European Union, then the claimants must actually arrest the vessel as opposed to serving a writ in rem on the vessel in order to bring themselves within Article 57 and the Arrest Convention, being an exception to the rule in Article 2 of the Brussels Convention that a claim should be brought in the court of the defendant owners' domicile. Alternatively, if the claimants want to establish English jurisdiction they should insist upon the Owners' P & I Club undertaking to give security and not merely undertaking to accept service of the in rem writ but agreeing to submit claims to the jurisdiction of the English court which complies with Article 17 or 18 of the Brussels Convention. This was established in the case of the *Deichland* [1989] 2 Lloyd's Rep. 113.

The facts were that Verwaltungs GmbH & Company KG let their vessel

*Deichland* in May 1995 on demise charter for a period of two years to Deich Navigation S.A. Deich were incorporated in Panama but its central management and control were exercised in Germany. In February 1986, the plaintiffs' cargo of steel coils being carried on the vessel was allegedly damaged. In January 1987, the plaintiffs issued a writ in rem against the vessel *Deichland* and the writ was served on the vessel in November 1987 but the vessel was not arrested as the defendants' P & I Club had provided the plaintiffs with security by a letter of guarantee. The demise charterers only acknowledged service of the writ for the purpose of contesting the jurisdiction of the Admiralty Court. The demise charterers applied to the court for an order that the court decline jurisdiction or declare that they had no jurisdiction by reason of the fact that they (Deich) were domiciled in the Federal Republic of Germany and accordingly the claim should be brought there in accordance with Article 2 of the Brussels Convention.

The issues which had to be decided by the Court of Appeal were as follows:

1. Whether the 1968 Convention had any application at all to an Admiralty action in rem while it remained solely in rem.
2. If the 1968 Convention applied to the action, whether, for the purposes of Article 2 of the 1968 Convention, Deich were domiciled in Germany (as they contended) or in Panama (as the plaintiffs contended).
3. If the 1968 Convention applied to the action and Deich were domiciled in Germany for the purpose of Article 2, whether nevertheless the High Court had jurisdiction by reason of the combined effect of Article 57 of the 1968 Brussels Convention, section 9 of the 1982 Act and the provisions of the 1952 Arrest Convention.

With regard to issue 1, the Court of Appeal decided that the Brussels Convention was intended, inter alia, to regulate the circumstances in which a person domiciled in one Contracting State might be brought before the courts of another Contracting State in civil and commercial matters. All forms of proceedings in civil and commercial matters were intended to be covered except insofar as some special provisions such as Article 57 might otherwise prescribe. It covers proceedings which are solely in rem. Deich were being sued in these proceedings even though the proceedings were solely in rem.

Lord Justice Neill said at page 119:

> 'It is true that in the present case the vessel is no longer chartered to Deich and that the jurisdiction to entertain the action in rem is based upon the provisions of section 21 of the Act of 1981. But looking at the reality of the matter it is Deich who is interested in contesting liability and against whom the plaintiffs would wish to proceed in personam if an appearance is entered . . . . I find it impossible to conclude that on the proper construction of Articles 2 and 3 of the (Brussels) 1968 Convention Deich are not being "sued" in these proceedings even though at this stage the proceedings are solely in rem. Deich are liable to be adversely affected by the result of the proceedings and wish to contest the merits of the plaintiffs' claim.'

With regard to issue 2, it was clear from section 42(3) to (6) that for the purposes of the 1982 Act a corporation may have its seat in relation to more than one state. Deich were domiciled in Germany because the seat of the company was there as this was where central management and control were exercised (see section 42(6)(b)).

With regard to issue 3, the Court of Appeal decided that the 1982 Act and the 1968 Brussels Convention provided a comprehensive code. If a defendant was domiciled in a Contracting State, he must be sued in the State unless the case fell within the exceptions contained in sections 2–6 of the 1968 Convention or under Article 57 which, for the purposes of this case, meant the 1952 Arrest Convention. However, as the vessel had not been arrested, Article 57 did not prevent the Brussels Convention from applying. Therefore, the English courts did not have jurisdiction over Deich.

In the course of argument, emphasis was placed on the common practice whereby ships are not actually arrested but some security or undertaking is furnished to prevent an arrest. Whilst Neill LJ saw the force of the argument that the jurisdiction given by Article 7 of the 1952 Arrest Convention should not be confined to cases where an arrest has actually been effected, he rejected this argument. He had in mind that the word 'arrest' in Article 7 of the Arrest Convention did not include a process which falls short of an actual arrest. He also had in mind that the word 'arrest' is defined in Article 2 as meaning the 'detention of a ship by judicial process to secure a maritime claim, but does not include the seizure of a ship in execution or satisfaction of a judgment'.

He also had in mind that under Articles 3 and 6 reference is made to 'bail or other security' given 'to avoid a threatened arrest' or to 'prevent the arrest'. He also thought Professor Schlosser's comments on Article 5 in the report on the Accession Convention was consistent with the view that Article 7 did not confer jurisdiction where bail or other security was given to avoid arrest. Whilst it was common ground that, had it not been for the Brussels Convention, the High Court would have jurisdiction to try the action under sections 20–21 of the Supreme Court Act 1981, the Court of Appeal decided that the jurisdiction governed by Article 7 of the 1952 Convention is governed by the word 'arrest'. The Court of Appeal were all of the view that there would have been a different result if the vessel had been arrested because the claimants could then have relied upon the Arrest Convention and Article 57 of the Brussels Convention. The matter was succinctly expressed by Stuart-Smith LJ at page 126 as follows.

> 'The practical consequences of allowing this appeal do not seem to me to be as far reaching as Mr. Aikens (for the plaintiffs) suggested. If a plaintiff for some reason is determined to litigate in the English Admiralty Court he can easily secure this; either he arrests the ship, or he secures express agreement by the defendant owner or demise charterer to submit to the jurisdiction of the English court to avoid arrest, no doubt at the same time obtaining security. In the present case, the plaintiff did neither of these things'

The case of the *Bergen* [1997] 1 Lloyd's Rep. 380 involved a claim by cargo owners and the bill of lading provided for disputes to be referred to Germany. The vessel was arrested and proceedings brought in England. The High Court decided that Article 7 of the Arrest Convention was preserved by Article 57 of the Brussels Convention. A court, where a vessel has been arrested, could determine the merits in accordance with their domestic law. The English court had jurisdiction under English domestic law, the vessel having been properly served and arrested in England. The position under English domestic law was that the court retained jurisdiction to determine the plaintiffs' claim on the merits, even in a case where there was an exclusive jurisdiction clause which provided for the determination of the dispute in a foreign court, but the court had a discretion to stay the action which it would exercise unless strong cause why it should not do so was shown, in the light of the *El Amria* case. There was a conflict between Article 17 of the Brussels Convention and Article 7 of the Arrest Convention and that by reason of Article 57 of the Brussels Convention, Article 7 had to prevail. The English court had jurisdiction over the cargo owners' claim under the Arrest Convention. The effect of the shipowner's argument was that the court was being asked to refuse to assume jurisdiction because of Article 17. If it were to do so, the Brussels Convention would, by Article 17, be preventing the English court from assuming jurisdiction in accordance with the Arrest Convention, which was the very thing which was expressly prohibited by paragraph 2(a) of Article 57 of the Brussels Convention. The court's conclusion was supported by the reasoning of the Court of Appeal in *Continental Bank* v *Aeakos SA* and the *Anna H* and was not inconsistent with the reasoning of the European court in the *Maciej Rataj*. The English court had jurisdiction by reason of Article 7 of the Arrest Convention.[1]

The Court of Appeal in the *Deichland* case recognized that jurisdiction can be established by arresting the ship or by agreement. If a ship is not arrested but security is provided in lieu of arrest then such security should stipulate English jurisdiction, should this be required, to determine the claim. Sometimes a bail bond is provided instead of security. In these circumstances the defendants cannot avoid English jurisdiction under the Convention. When a bail bond is lodged the defendants have to acknowledge the writ by which they voluntarily submit to the English jurisdiction.

In the case of the *Prinsengracht* [1993] 1 Lloyd's Rep. 41 the shipowners unsuccessfully sought to avoid English jurisdiction by providing a bail bond to the court as opposed to the more usual provision of a P & I Club letter of undertaking. When a bail bond is lodged with the court the defendant shipowners have to acknowledge the writ by which they voluntarily submit to the English jurisdiction. The plaintiffs claimed damages against the defendant Dutch shipowners in respect of a cargo shipped on board the vessel. A writ in rem was issued by the plaintiffs but not served initially. The plaintiffs asked for security from the shipowners but, instead of providing security, a bail bond was issued in the High Court by which the defendants' P & I Club agreed to submit to the jurisdiction of the court and consented that if the defendants did not pay what might be adjudged against them, execution might be issued against them. The defendants' solicitors acknowledged issue of the writ in rem prior to service.

Then the plaintiffs' solicitors arrested the vessel despite the fact that a bail bond had been lodged in the High Court. The vessel was released from arrest shortly thereafter. The defendants contended that, as they had voluntarily given bail as security, the plaintiffs had no right to arrest the *Prinsengracht* and, accordingly, the arrest was invalid and should be set aside. They also argued that the English courts did not have jurisdiction to determine the claim which should have been brought in the courts of the Netherlands (albeit time-barred) where the shipowners were domiciled under the Brussels Convention.

1. See also page 166.

The Admiralty judge at the time, Mr Justice Sheen, said at page 42:

'This motion raises a question of great importance to Admiralty practitioners. The question of course is this: if shipowners who are domiciled in one of the Contracting States of the European Economic Community voluntarily give bail for the purpose of avoiding the inconvenience of the arrest of one of their ships, is the consequence of putting up bail that this court is deprived of jurisdiction to hear and determine the plaintiffs' claim? As bail is a solemn undertaking to satisfy a judgment of this court, there would be more than an element of absurdity in the rules and practice of this court if the answer to that question is "yes".'

The Admiralty Court decided that the defendants took the voluntary step of acknowledging the issue of the writ. They thereby became a party to the action which from that moment became in personam as well as in rem. By acknowledging the issue of the writ, the defendants voluntarily submitted to the jurisdiction of the court because they desired to take part in the proceedings. The Admiralty judge had in mind the statement of Lord Justice Stuart-Smith in the *Deichland* where, in reference to the shipowner, he said 'If he acknowledged service, he submits to the jurisdiction'. The voluntary act of the defendant in acknowledging the issue of the writ at a time when no action by them was called for, because the writ had not been served, was the clearest submission to the jurisdiction.

At the time the writ was acknowledged, the plaintiffs had not invoked the jurisdiction of the court, because the writ had not been served. The defendants' solicitors could only acknowledge the issue of the writ if they desired to take part in the proceedings. At the time the defendants' solicitors acknowledged issue of the writ, there were no grounds upon which the defendant could dispute the jurisdiction of the court because there was no irregularity in the writ and the claim endorsed on the writ was within the Admiralty jurisdiction, which could be invoked by a writ in rem. At the time of acknowledgment of service no attempt had been made to arrest the vessel.

The Admiralty judge went on to say that contractual security may be given without submitting or agreeing to submit to the jurisdiction of the Admiralty Court as in the case of the *Deichland* but bail cannot be given without submitting to the jurisdiction. Under the current procedure, a person who desires to prevent the arrest of his property must acknowledge the issue or service of the writ as the defendants had done. There were no grounds for suggesting that there is any irregularity in the writ. Its issue had been voluntarily acknowledged. Before the arrest, the defendants had submitted to the jurisdiction. He went on to say at page 46:

'It would be absurd, and it would bring the law into disrepute, if a defendant could procure a bail bond in which there is a solemn undertaking to satisfy a judgment of the court and then say to the plaintiff "Of course, you cannot obtain a judgment against me, because you cannot arrest my ship and I have not submitted to the jurisdiction of the court". Fortunately that is not the effect of the decision in the *Deichland*. The defendants have, by acknowledging the issue of the writ, shown their desire to take part in the proceedings. They are free to do so.'

With regard to the caveat against arrest, the Admiralty judge decided that a person who enters a caveat against arrest undertakes to acknowledge service and submit to the jurisdiction. The defendant had submitted to the jurisdiction. The defendants also argued that upon the provision of bail the ship is released from the action and cannot thereafter be arrested. The arrest in the present case lasted less than a day and the Admiralty judge decided that the arrest was not vexatious or oppressive. The Admiralty judge went on to say:

'Indeed, the ship was arrested solely because the defendants declined to agree expressly to submit to the jurisdiction of this court and because it was thought that the decision in the *Deichland* might have made it necessary to arrest the ship, even though bail had been given. In looking after the interests of the plaintiffs, it was natural for Mr Evers to make quite sure that he did everything which was necessary. In arresting *Prinsengracht* he was doing just that and no more. If the arrest of the ship is necessary to preserve the jurisdiction of this court, it cannot be wrongful to arrest the ship. Put in another way, if the case on which the defendants rely does show that in order to found jurisdiction in this court a plaintiff must arrest a ship and cannot achieve that result by accepting bail, that would show that bail is not the equivalent of the ship except in money terms. Bail can only be the equivalent of a ship if it provides equivalent security without adverse effect upon the plaintiff. If, contrary to the views I have expressed, bail can be given without submitting to the jurisdiction, it remains necessary for the plaintiff to arrest the ship that arrest cannot be unlawful.'

The defendant shipowners' application was dismissed.

In the case of the *Anna H* [1995] 1 Lloyd's Rep. 11, the plaintiffs' solicitors followed the advice in the *Deichland* and arrested the vessel. The plaintiffs' claim arose from a shipment of steel coils on the vessel *Anna H* in December 1990. On 17 September 1991 their solicitors gave notice of the claim to the solicitors representing the owners' P & I Club and invited them to give security and submit to the jurisdiction of the English courts. The owners offered security for the judgment of a competent court but refused to submit to the English jurisdiction. Instead 'they tried to navigate between the Scylla of arrest and the Charybdis of submission by resorting to the antique ceremony of entering a caveat against arrest under RSC Order 75, Rule 6'. They issued a præcipe containing an undertaking on behalf of the owners to acknowledge issue or service of the writ and to give bail. A caveat was entered on 19 September 1991.

On 17 November 1991 the plaintiffs' solicitor learned that the vessel was due to arrive in the UK but, as he had not been given any undertaking to submit to the jurisdiction, he decided to arrest the ship. He discovered the caveat but still arrested the ship. Then presumably satisfied with the undertaking in the præcipe to give bail, he released the ship after an hour without obtaining further security. The owners duly gave bail and acknowledged service of the writ. The owners then issued a summons under RSC Order 12, Rule 8 to set aside service of the writ on the ground that the owners were domiciled in Germany and therefore under Article 2 of the Convention they could only be sued in Germany. The plaintiffs relied upon Article 57 and the Arrest Convention. The plaintiffs further submitted that the defendants had submitted to the jurisdiction of the court when they filed the præcipe for the caveat or when they put up bail or when they acknowledged service of the writ.

The Admiralty Court dismissed the owner's application because the arrest was 'the detention of a ship by judicial process to secure a maritime claim' within Article 2 of the Arrest Convention even if it could be shown that the motive of the plaintiff in arresting the vessel was to found jurisdiction and not to obtain security. Article 57 of the Brussels Convention saved Article 7 of the Arrest Convention and these excluded the exclusive jurisdiction of Germany under Article 2. The claim fell within Article 7(1)(b)—the damage occurred as a result of events in England and Wales where the arrest took place. The Admiralty judge went on to say that the filing of the præcipe could not itself amount to a submission to the jurisdiction of the court. However, the putting up of bail amounted to a submission to the jurisdiction of the Admiralty Court.

An appeal was made to the Court of Appeal. The question was—does the Arrest Convention require only that the legal consequence of judicial detention of the ship should be that it becomes security for a maritime claim or does it require that the plaintiff's commercial motive must be to obtain security? The Court of Appeal decided that the Arrest Convention required only that the legal consequences of judicial detention of a ship should be that it became security for a maritime claim. The first meaning was therefore correct.

The definition of arrest in the Arrest Convention is concerned with the character of the legal process, not with the motivation of the party that initiates the process. It was beside the point that the plaintiffs in the present action may have been primarily motivated by the need to satisfy the requirements of founding an action in rem within the jurisdiction of the Admiralty Court. Likewise, it was irrelevant that the plaintiffs shortly afterwards chose to release the vessel. The purpose of the Arrest Convention was to harmonize the laws of the Contracting States as to the type of claims which could form the basis for an arrest and the words 'to secure a maritime claim' were part of the scheme to prevent the use of arrest for securing other kinds of claim. The Arrest Convention prevailed over the Brussels Convention.

Another question was whether Article 7 requires the court to have jurisdiction under its domestic laws. The plaintiffs argued that Article 2 of the Brussels Convention is also part of domestic law and restricts the court's jurisdiction conferred by the Supreme Court Act 1981. The Court of Appeal decided that 'domestic law' in the Arrest Convention must be contrasted with treaty law i.e. the Brussels Convention. The shipowner's application was dismissed.

It was not necessary for the Court of Appeal to decide the other question raised by the plaintiffs that the defendants had submitted to the jurisdiction of the Admiralty Court. However, Hobhouse LJ commented that there were problems about treating a mere acknowledgment of service or an undertaking to acknowledge issue or service as being a waiver of the right to challenge the jurisdiction of the court. Also, since it is accepted that it is possible to put up bail conditionally, reserving the right to challenge the jurisdiction of the court, there are problems about treating the provision of bail, without more, as precluding the shipowner from thereafter exercising his right to challenge the jurisdiction of the court.

Although the general rule is that persons domiciled in a Contracting State of the Brussels Convention should be sued in the court of their domicile, there are various exceptions to this rule. For instance, under Article 17 of the Brussels Convention, if the parties have agreed that the Court of a Contracting State is to have jurisdiction to settle disputes then that Court shall have exclusive jurisdiction. A clause in a charterparty or bill of lading agreeing English jurisdiction may fall under Article 17 (see also page 165).

In a collision action, however, arrest is not necessary to found jurisdiction. If security is provided in lieu of arrest although the ship was in the English jurisdiction and could have been arrested this is sufficient. (See Article 1(b) of the 1952 Collision Convention).

*The Po* [1991] 2 Lloyd's Rep. 206
The vessels *Bowditch* and *Po* collided in the harbour of Rio de Janiero in 1987. In 1988 the owners of the *Bowditch* served a writ in rem on the *Po* in Southampton but she was not arrested because of the letter of undertaking given by the P & I Club. The Italian owners of the *Po* applied for a stay of the English proceedings under Article 2 of the Brussels Convention.

*Held* (CA): the English court had jurisdiction under the 1952 Collision Convention. Article 1(b) provides that one of the courts which has jurisdiction to decide a collision action is a court of a place where the defendant's ship has been arrested 'or where arrest could have been effected and bail or other security has been furnished.' The *Po* could have been arrested in Southampton and security had been furnished. Article 57 of the Brussels Convention applied and that Convention did not deprive the English courts of jurisdiction.

## Stay or dismissal of proceedings

Although the plaintiffs may have commenced proceedings in England, they may still find that jurisdiction is declined or their proceedings stayed or dismissed in favour of another Contracting State by reason of Articles 21 or 22 of the Brussels Convention.

Article 21 of the Brussels Convention provides:

'Where proceedings involving the same cause of action and between the same parties are brought in the courts of different Contracting States, any court other than the court first seised shall of its own motion stay its proceedings until such time as the jurisdiction of the court first seised is established.

Where the jurisdiction of the court first seised is established, any court other than the court first seised shall decline jurisdiction in favour of that court.'

Under Article 21, it is necessary to establish that there are proceedings in different Contracting States which involve the same cause of action and are between the same parties, in which case the court not first seised (the second court) must decline jurisdiction. A court is first seised when the writ in rem is served (as opposed to issued) or the vessel is arrested, whichever is the earlier (see the case of the *Freccia del Nord* [1989] 1 Lloyd's Rep. 388). Also in the case of the *Sargasso* [1993] 1 Lloyd's Rep. 424 it was decided that a court was not seised of proceedings until a writ was served whether or not the defendant was within or outside of the jurisdiction. As the Rotterdam court was first seised the English proceedings were stayed under Article 21.

Article 22 of the Convention provides:

'Where related actions are brought in the courts of different Contracting States, any court other than the court first seised may, while the actions are pending at first instance, stay its proceedings.

A court other than the court first seised may also, on the application of one of the parties, decline jurisdiction if the law of that court permits the consolidation of related actions and the court first seised has jurisdiction over both actions. For the purposes of this Article actions are deemed to be related where they are so closely connected that it is expedient to hear and determine them together to avoid the risk of irreconcilable judgments resulting from separate proceedings.'

Under Article 22, the court has a discretion to stay proceedings. In *Overseas Union Insurance* v *New Hampshire* (European Court of Justice) [1992] 1 Lloyd's Rep. 204 it was stated that the aim of Articles 21 and 22 was to prevent parallel proceedings before courts of different Contracting States and to avoid conflict between decisions which might so result. The circumstances in which in rem proceedings in England can be stayed in favour of other Convention countries has been the subject of considerable debate. There has relatively recently been a very important decision of the European court in the case of the *Maciej Rataj* (see below). However, it is useful to consider some of the earlier cases.

In the *Nordglimt* [1987] 2 Lloyd's Rep. 470, Hobhouse J decided that an English Admiralty action in rem and proceedings in personam in Belgium did not fall within Article 21 because the proceedings were not between the same parties i.e. when the action was originally commenced. It would only become an action between the same parties when and if a shipowner liable in personam chose to appear in and defend the action.

In the *Sylt* [1991] 1 Lloyd's Rep. 240, an action was commenced in the Admiralty Court by cargo owners to obtain security. The vessel was arrested and released from arrest after a bail bond was given by the shipowners as security. The cargo owners applied for an order pursuant to section 26 of the Civil Jurisdiction and Judgments Act 1982 (dealt with in more detail below) that the bail bond should stand as security for the satisfaction of any judgment given by the Sierra Leone court which was seised of the dispute between the plaintiffs and defendants, provided the judgment was enforceable in England and Wales. They also applied for an order pursuant to the inherent jurisdiction of the Admiralty Court that the action be stayed. The High Court decided that the court's power to grant an application for a stay under section 26 was on the ground that the dispute should be submitted to the determination of a court of an overseas country. The English court had not been asked to stay the action in favour of the courts of Sierra Leone and, if that application had been made, it would have failed. The owners of the *Sylt* were domiciled in Germany and should have been sued there under Article 2 of the Brussels Convention. Article 17 gave the German court exclusive jurisdiction by reason of clause 3 of the bill of lading and the English court had no jurisdiction to stay the action in favour of the courts of Sierra Leone.

The court then gave further reasons as to why the plaintiffs' sought order could not be granted. The reality of the matter was that the action had been brought to obtain satisfaction of a judgment in personam given in Sierra Leone. The claim endorsed on the writ was a claim for damages in respect of the loss or damage to cargo which fell within the Admiralty jurisdiction. But that claim had already been the subject of litigation in personam. The question then arose as to whether an action in rem is an action between the same parties as an action in personam. An action in rem cannot be brought against a ship for the purpose of enforcing a judgment in a personal action.

The plaintiffs argued that the cause of action was the same as the cause of action in respect of which the court of Sierra Leone had given judgment and that the plaintiffs were the same in both actions and that they could not now bring proceedings against the same parties. The court was referred to the case of the *Nordglimt*—that an action in rem and an action in personam is not an action between the same parties on its inception. However, a different view was taken by the Court of Appeal in the *Deichland*, namely that the action in rem was against the owners of the ship and not merely against the ship even before those owners submit to the jurisdiction.

The Admiralty Court in the *Sylt* followed the decision of the *Deichland* and said that it was clear that the action in the Admiralty Court was between the same parties as the parties to the action in Sierra Leone. Since judgment had been given in Sierra Leone, the action in the English Admiralty Court ought not have been brought.

However, in the *Al Tawwab* [1991] 1 Lloyd's Rep. 201, Lord Justice Lloyd said: 'The whole point of the action in rem is that it is an action against the ship itself or the cargo, as the case may be, and not a personal action against the owners'. This conflicts with the views expressed by the Court of Appeal in the *Deichland*. In the latter case, Lord Justice Stuart-Smith said at page 126 ([1989] 1 Lloyd's Rep.):

> 'Notwithstanding that the action is begun as an action in rem, a defendant can contest the court's jurisdiction on Convention grounds and is not to be taken to have submitted to the merits jurisdiction of the English court, and he is not obliged so to submit or see the action against the ship go by default . . . If a defendant is domiciled in a Contracting State he must be sued in that state.'

Sir Denys Buckley said at page 128:

> 'In reality, distinguished from formal aspects, the instant action is, in my judgment, as much a suit against (Deich) as would be an action in personam against them found on the same complaint.'

In the *Kherson* [1992] 2 Lloyd's Rep. 261, the cargo owners commenced proceedings against the owners/operators of the vessel *Kerch*—the Georgian shipping company. There was a treaty between the USSR and the Netherlands which prohibited the owners of cargo from arresting the ship if the owners of the ship chose domicile in the Netherlands. The defendants elected domicile in the Netherlands and the plaintiffs refrained from arresting the vessel *Kerch* when she was in Rotterdam.

Subsequently the plaintiffs arrested a sister ship of the vessel *Kerch*, the *Kherson*, in England and the owners, P & I Club provided security. The defendants applied for an order that the Admiralty Court decline jurisdiction on the basis that the Netherlands was to have exclusive jurisdiction under Article 17 of the Brussels Convention. This was declined.

Alternatively, the defendants contended that the court of the Netherlands was already seised of proceedings involving the same cause of action and between the same parties and the court must decline jurisdiction in favour of the court of the Netherlands in accordance with Article 21 of the Brussels Convention. The plaintiffs submitted that Article 21 did not apply to an action in rem: that an action in rem was not of the same character as a cause of action in personam, and that the action was not between the same parties, in that the action began as an action in rem but after the owners acknowledged service of the writ it continued as an action in rem as well as in personam.

The Admiralty Court decided that there can be no doubt that this action (in England) was founded upon and involved the same cause of action as the proceedings in Rotterdam. At the time of the hearing, the action was proceeding in rem and in personam because the vessel was still under arrest. There are differences in character between an action in rem and an action in personam but there were no differences between the essential elements of the cause of action in the two types of proceedings.

The next question was whether the two sets of proceedings were between the same parties. The Admiralty Court decided that the only differences between an action which is based in personam and in rem (because the ship remains under arrest) and an action which is solely in personam lie in the remedies available to a successful plaintiff and the procedure which must be followed to obtain these remedies. The action in Rotterdam and the English action involved the same cause of action, even though the plaintiffs have two different remedies available to them. The two actions were between the same parties and the English court declined to exercise its jurisdiction in favour of the District Court of Rotterdam under Article 21.

In the case of the *Havhelt* [1993] 1 Lloyd's Rep. 523, the vessel was arrested in relation to an alleged cargo claim arising under bills of lading which stated that disputes were to be decided in Norway and Norwegian law was to apply. The defendant shipowners argued that the proceedings in England had been brought in breach of the jurisdiction clause, and applied to set aside or stay the writ and for an order that the vessel be released. The plaintiffs argued that they would be prejudiced by having to sue in Norway because they would be deprived of security for their claim. Under section 26 of the Brussels Convention implemented by the Civil Jurisdiction and Judgments Act 1982, the court has power to order that security obtained in England should be retained as security for the foreign court (see below). The issue for decision was whether the action should be stayed and whether the arrest should be continued.

The Admiralty Court decided that the English proceedings should be stayed as the parties had expressly agreed that disputes should be determined in Norway under Norwegian law. It was suggested in argument that it might be relevant that the proceedings with which the court was concerned are in rem proceedings (in England) whereas any proceedings in Norway would be or would be likely to be in personam proceedings. However, the Admiralty Court said that in the present context it seems that no material distinction can be drawn between the two types of proceedings and he adopted the approach of the courts in the case of the *Sylt*, the *Deichland* and the *Kherson*.

In the *Maciej Rataj* [1992] 2 Lloyd's Rep. 552, the Polish shipowners of the vessel *Tatry* commenced proceedings in the Netherlands (the place of discharge) seeking a declaration that they were not liable for cargo claims and also sought to limit liability. The cargo claimants commenced in rem proceedings in England claiming damages and arrested a sister ship *Maciej Rataj*. The shipowners applied for an order that jurisdiction be declined or stayed in favour of the Rotterdam court, relying on Articles 21 and 22 of the Convention. The Court of Appeal decided that the two proceedings involved the same cause of action, i.e. the same contractual relationship and the same subject matter—whether the cargo was contaminated. If the English proceedings were to be regarded solely in personam, Article 21 would apply. However, it was decided that, even after the shipowners had acknowledged service of the writ in England, the nature of the action there was hybrid and, although in personam did not, even after the release of the 'res', lose its previous character of being an action in rem. The Court of Appeal did not decide whether the proceedings in England and in the Netherlands concerned the same cause of action or involved the same parties. The European court then considered the various questions raised by the Court of Appeal [1995] 1 Lloyd's Rep. 302.

One question raised was whether, if a vessel is arrested by cargo owners in a Contracting State (in this case England) can such state retain jurisdiction despite the fact that proceedings have previously been brought by the shipowners in another Contracting State (Rotterdam) under Article 57 of the Brussels Convention. Or, in other words, can England retain jurisdiction despite Articles 21 and 22 of the Brussels Convention? The European Court decided that Article 57 means that 'where a Contracting State is also a contracting party to another Convention on a specific matter containing rules on jurisdiction' that specialized Convention precludes the application of the provisions of the Brussels Convention only in cases governed by the specialized Convention and not in those in which it does not apply.

Another question was whether Article 21 applies in the case of two sets of proceedings brought in different Contracting States involving the same cause of action and some but not all of the parties are the same. This question arose because the shipowners in 1988 brought proceedings in the Rotterdam court against various cargo interests (groups 1 and 3) with the exception of Phibro, seeking a declaration that they were not liable for the alleged contamination of the cargo. On 15 September 1989 cargo interests (group 3) started an action in England and arrested a sister ship *Maciej Rataj* and security was provided (folio 2006). The cargo interests (group 3)—Phibro—also arrested the *Maciej Rataj* (folio 2007). Only subsequently did the shipowners bring proceedings in the Rotterdam court against group 2. The shipowners also commenced limitation proceedings.

The European Court of Justice decided that the second court seised (i.e. England) is only obliged to decline jurisdiction under Article 21 when the parties to the two sets of proceedings are identical. Where some of the parties are the same as the parties to an action which has already been started, Article 21 requires the second court seised to decline jurisdiction only to the extent to which the parties to the proceedings pending before it are also parties to the action previously started before the court of another Contracting State (i.e. the Netherlands). It does not prevent the proceedings from continuing between the other parties.

Another question was whether, under Article 21, the action brought by cargo interests for alleged damage had the same cause of action and the same object as the earlier proceedings brought by the shipowners in the Rotterdam court seeking a declaration that they are not liable for the alleged claim. The European Court of Justice decided that the shipowners' action for a declaration of non-liability and another action, such as that brought subsequently by the cargo interests in England on the basis of shipping contracts which are separate but in identical terms, concerning the same cargo transported in bulk and damaged in the same circumstances were the same cause of action. The action in England had the same object as the shipowners' action in the *Netherlands*, since the issue of liability was central to both actions. The fact that one action was couched in negative terms and the other in positive terms was irrelevant.

Another question was whether, for the purposes of Article 21, the same cause of action was involved where the first action in the Netherlands is in personam and the second action in England is either an in rem and in personam action or solely in personam. The European Court of Justice decided that the distinction drawn by the law of a Contracting State between an action in personam and an action in rem was not material for the interpretation of Article 21. The subsequent action in England did not cease to have the same cause of action and same object and to be between the same parties as the earlier in personam proceedings brought by the shipowners in the Netherlands seeking a non-liability declaration. This is consistent with the earlier High Court decisions of the *Havhelt, Sylt, Deichland* and the *Kherson*.

Finally, the question was whether Article 22 could apply if an action is brought by one group of cargo owners against a shipowner in one Contracting State and another action brought in another Contracting State against the same shipowners by another group of cargo owners, such cargo being shipped under the same conditions and under contracts which are separate from but identical to those between the first group and the shipowners. Group 1 of the cargo owners did not bring any action before the English court. Instead, on 29 September 1989, they brought an action for damages in the Rotterdam courts against the shipowners. At about this time, groups 2 and 3 (with the exception of Phibro) brought actions in the Rotterdam court as a precautionary measure, should the English courts decide to decline jurisdiction.

The European Court of Justice decided that under Article 22 the court has a discretion to stay proceedings. This question as to staying proceedings under Article 22 only arose if Article 21 did not apply. The European Court of Justice decided that 'related actions' must be broadly interpreted and should cover all cases where there is a risk of conflicting decisions even if the judgments can be separately enforced and their legal consequences are not mutually exclusive. The objective of Article 22 was to avoid conflicting and contradictory decisions by different courts even where the separate enforcement of each decision was not precluded. Article 22 would apply if the actions brought by the cargo owners in different Contracting States against the same shipowner related to cargo shipped under contracts which are separate from but in identical terms.

The effect of the European Court of Justice's decision appears to be that the English courts should decline jurisdiction under Article 21 in relation to folio 2006, the same cause of action being involved and the same parties being involved (the shipowners and group 3 of the cargo owners). Article 21 could not apply to folio 2007 because the shipowners had not commenced an action against group 2 prior to the arrest of the *Maciej Rataj*.

A more recent case is as follows: In the case of the *Lake Avery* [1997] 1 Lloyd's Rep. 540, the salvors had a good arguable case that the Master agreed to salvage in the River Scheldt on the terms of the LOF 1995. The salvors had obtained the appointment of an arbitrator in London and wished their claim for salvage remuneration to be assessed under the LOF. The owners submitted that the English court should decline to exercise jurisdiction under Article 21 or 22 of the Brussels Convention, as proceedings had been brought by them against the salvors in the Dutch court. The High Court decided that the salvors had a good arguable case that the Master agreed LOF 95 and that the parties agreed to a contract which was governed by English law and subject to English arbitration and that England was at least a, if not the, natural forum for the determination of this dispute.

The issue was whether or not there was an effective agreement to arbitrate; if so, there was no issue as to the validity of the appointment of the arbitrator, and the proceedings were ancillary to arbitration proceedings. The relief sought was ancillary to or an integral part of the arbitration process, and Article 1.4 of the Convention applied so that the case was outside the Convention, relying on the case of the *Atlantic Emperor*. The Convention did not apply to these proceedings, and the owners were not entitled to a stay under either Article 21 or Article 22 nor would it be appropriate for the court to decline jurisdiction under Article 21. If the matter proceeded in Holland, the salvors would or potentially would be deprived of a legitimate juridical advantage, namely the right to have their claim arbitrated if LOF 95 was agreed. In all the circumstances and having regard in particular to the fact that, if LOF 95 was agreed, the court in Holland might not enforce the arbitration clause; viewed objectively, England was clearly the more appropriate forum for the determination of the issue as to whether or not LOF 95 was agreed both for the interests of the parties and for the ends of justice. The action was stayed on the grounds of lis alibi pendens or forum conveniens.

## Position where there is a pre-existing arbitration clause

Many charterparties and bills of lading provide that disputes are to be determined by arbitration. It is 'private' litigation (as opposed to litigation in the public sector provided by the courts). The authority of the arbitrators and the jurisdiction within which they carry out their task spring solely from the contractual arrangement between the parties. The arbitrators have no power to arrest a ship. So what is the judicial position when a ship is arrested in the High Court by a writ in rem for the twin purpose of founding jurisdiction and obtaining security when there is an arbitration agreement which pre-exists the arrest?

On the face of it, there is a clash of concepts in that an in rem action, which is a creature of statutory powers and pursued on the basis of court jurisdiction, should not, by definition, be used pursuant to a matter which the parties themselves have already agreed to take before a private tribunal. Article 26 of the Brussels Convention (see below) now provides that if a ship is arrested and these proceedings are stayed in favour of arbitration or in favour of another Contracting State to the Brussels Convention then the property arrested can stand as security or alternative security can be granted. Section 26 of the Brussels Convention came into force in late 1984 due to the Civil Jurisdiction and Judgment Act 1982.

## Article 26 of the Brussels Convention

Prior to the implementation of section 26 of the Brussels Convention, a vessel could be arrested and security sought in aid of other proceedings, not pending in the English High Court, for instance London arbitration proceedings. The fact that security was being sought for a claim in arbitration had to be considered by the court in exercising its discretion whether or not to arrest the vessel. Once the vessel was arrested, there was uncertainty as to whether any security obtained should be released or whether the security should be retained or whether any alternative security should be ordered in its place. In the case of the *Cap Bon* [1967] 1 Lloyd's Rep. 543, the court decided that security obtained as a result of proceedings in rem against a vessel could not be used to satisfy an arbitration award. However, one school of thought was that if English proceedings were stayed in favour of arbitration, the English court had power to order that sufficient security be provided to cover the eventual arbitration award.

In the case of a domestic arbitration agreement, the court has a discretion to stay English court proceedings, whereas in the case of a non-domestic arbitration agreement a stay is mandatory under the Arbitration Acts 1950 and 1975. It should be borne in mind that the Arbitration Act 1996 came into force on 31 January 1997 but the same principles will apply. In due course, the relevant sections of the 1996 Act could be repealed as being discriminatory under the Treaty of Rome as between UK and EU nationals.

In the case of the *Rena K* [1978] 1 Lloyd's Rep. 545, a vessel was arrested and security given in relation to an alleged cargo claim arising under a bill of lading which incorporated an arbitration clause of the charterparty. The English court stayed the proceedings and decided that it could not impose terms such as security being retained as a pre-condition for the stay. However, the court was not obliged to release the vessel from arrest or release the security already given to secure its release. The judge qualified this by saying that there should be an unconditional release of the security if the distinct probability was that the stay of proceedings in favour of arbitration would be final.

The Admiralty Court's view that security should only be retained for an English court judgment as opposed to an arbitration award or other proceedings started to erode in 1984 in the case of the *Vasso* [1984] 1 Lloyd's Rep. 235. In that case, it was decided that the English Admiralty Court had jurisdiction to arrest or maintain an arrest of a vessel when the purpose of the arrest was simply to obtain security for an award in arbitration proceedings. The motive for arresting was, however, relevant when deciding whether or not the English court would exercise its discretion to arrest. Nevertheless, in the affidavit leading up to the arrest, the arbitration agreement had not been cited and the security provided following the arrest was discharged due to the non-disclosure.

In the case of *Tuyuti* [1984] 2 Lloyd's Rep. 51, the High Court decided that the English proceedings must be stayed if they contravened the arbitration agreement but the warrant of arrest was not set aide.

Article 26 of the Brussels Convention has been implemented into English law by section 26 of the Civil Jurisdiction and Judgment Act 1982 (as amended). It provides:

'26(1) Where in England and Wales or Northern Ireland a court stays or dismisses

Admiralty proceedings on the ground that the dispute in question should be submitted to arbitration or to the determination of the courts of another part of the United Kingdom or of an overseas country, the court may if in those proceedings property has been arrested or bail or other security has been given to prevent or obtain release from arrest—

(a) order that the property arrested be retained as security for the satisfaction of any award or judgment which—

  (i) is given in respect of the dispute in the arbitration or legal proceedings in favour of which those proceedings are stayed or dismissed; and

  (ii) is enforceable in England and Wales or, as the case may be, in Northern Ireland; or

(b) order that the stay or dismissal of those proceedings be conditional on the provision of equivalent security for the satisfaction of any such award or judgment.

(2) Where a court makes an order under subsection (1), it may attach such conditions to the order as it thinks fit, in particular conditions with respect to the institution or prosecution of the relevant arbitration or legal proceedings.'

When the ship is still under arrest section 26(1)(a) applies, whereas where security has been given to prevent the arrest of the ship or to obtain its release, section 26(1)(b) applies. This section provides that where Admiralty proceedings are stayed (or dismissed) in favour, not only of arbitration but of an overseas forum, the court may order that any security furnished may be retained or that alternative security must be provided to secure an eventual arbitration award. An example of security being ordered for an overseas forum is the case of *The Emre II* (at page 152). The purpose of section 26 is to ensure that the plaintiff is secured against all eventualities. If the arbitral process 'collapses' or is somehow incapable of performance, the plaintiff can use the security by going back to the Admiralty Court to complete his Admiralty action since the action was only stayed, not dismissed. If the arbitral process succeeds, the security obtained can be used legally to enforce that award.

Section 26, however, is a procedural mechanism and does not state expressly that it sanctions arrest of a vessel solely for the purpose of obtaining security for an arbitration award. However, in the case of *The World Star* [1986] 2 Lloyd's Rep. 274 the vessel was arrested by charterers solely to obtain security for arbitration proceedings. The defendant shipowners applied for a stay and for an order that the vessel be released from arrest. Sheen J decided that since the case procedurally fell within Section 26 the court could order the retention of the vessel as security for the satisfaction of the arbitration award under paragraph (a) of section 26(1). As the arbitration was not a domestic arbitration the court was required to make an order staying the proceedings by section 1 of the Arbitration Act 1975. However, it should be borne in mind that there is a new Arbitration Act 1996 which came into force on 31 January 1997. In these circumstances it was not open to the court to impose conditions and to order alternative security under paragraph (b).

*The Jalamatsya* [1987] 2 Lloyd's Rep. 164
Arbitration of a charterparty dispute was well under way when the plaintiff realised that he had no security for any award which might be made in his favour. He therefore sought to arrest a ship also owned by the defendant. Being a claim within the Admiralty jurisdiction of the UK's High Court, the arrest was allowed and took place. No application to stay the action was made, but one to set aside the action was made on the ground that the arrest

was an abuse of court process. The defendant argued that section 26 did not alter the previous case law on this subject in that it provided a procedural remedy in cases where an application for a stay was made. If no application for a stay was made then section 26 could not apply. The defendant also argued that section 26 could not apply because the arbitration had already been commenced.

Sheen J dismissed both these arguments and decided that the vessel could be detained under arrest 'until security is given'. It was quite irrelevant in determining the interpretation and application of section 26 to particular circumstances or to distinguish between circumstances where an arbitration has not been commenced and those where it has. The purpose was to allow plaintiffs, if they proceeded by way of arbitration rather than by way of court action, to obtain security by way of an in rem procedure. The court's process had not been abused. Section 26 was enacted to enable plaintiffs to obtain security if they proceeded by way of arbitration rather than by action, whether or not arbitration has been commenced. If an arbitration had been commenced and if the plaintiffs in the arbitration had not obtained security for any possible award they could quite properly issue a writ in rem if they knew that a ship belonging to the defendants in the arbitration was coming within the jurisdiction and they might arrest that ship in order to obtain security.

The effect of section 26 of the 1982 Act was considered more recently in the following cases.

*The Bazias 3 and The Bazias 4* [1993] 1 Lloyd's Rep. 101.
A dispute under two bareboat charters of vessels employed on a cross-channel ferry service were referred to arbitration. The vessels were arrested as security for the arbitration claims and taken into the custody of the Admiralty Marshal. The defendant shipowners applied for a stay under section 1 of the Arbitration Act 1975. Initially the vessels remained under arrest but were allowed to return to their employment on the cross-channel service. The defendants argued that the pre-existing practice was preserved by section 26 so that, when a claim was subject to an arbitration clause, the court had a discretion to release the vessel without requiring equivalent security depending on whether the defendants were likely to be able to meet an arbitration award in the plaintiffs' favour. The defendants contended that the effect of section 26 was to assimilate claims in arbitration with in rem proceedings in the Admiralty Court so that the discretion was the same in both classes of case.

The Court of Appeal decided that there was no longer a wider discretion in relation to arbitration cases. On an application for the release of a vessel from arrest the usual practice had always been that the vessel would only be released on the provision of sufficient security to cover the amount of the claim plus costs on the basis of the plaintiff's reasonably arguable best case. None of the matters relied on by the defendants, and in particular their ability to meet any award that might be made against them, took this out of the usual run of cases or justified anything other than the usual order. The defendants' submission that it was impossible to find liquid resources in time to enable them to put up security would be rejected. There were no grounds for departing from the usual order. Therefore, the vessels were to remain under arrest until further order of the Admiralty Court and the action was stayed pursuant to section 1 of the 1975 Arbitration Act. A vessel could not remain in the custody of the Admiralty Marshal and be allowed to trade outside the jurisdiction.

In the case of *The Havhelt* [1993] 1 Lloyd's Rep. 523 the vessel was arrested in relation to an alleged cargo claim arising under bills of lading which stated that disputes were to be decided in Norway and Norwegian law was to apply. The defendant shipowners argued that the proceedings in England had been brought in breach of the jurisdiction clause and applied to set aside or stay the writ and for an order that the vessel be released. The plaintiff cargo interests argued that they would be prejudiced by having to sue in Norway because they would be deprived of security for their claim. The issues for decision were whether the action should be stayed and whether the arrest should be continued.

*Held* (Admiralty Court): that the English proceedings should be stayed as the parties had expressly agreed that disputes should be determined in Norway under Norwegian law. The submission by the defendants that any proceedings brought in Norway would be time-barred in that the one-year limitation under the Hague Rules had expired and the security should be released was rejected as the question of Norwegian law had not yet been proved. The plaintiffs argued (based on the case of *The El Amria* at page 173) that a court should take into account the plaintiffs being prejudiced by having to sue in a foreign court, without being able to obtain security, when deciding whether or not to give effect to a jurisdiction clause. The Admiralty Court decided that 'it seems to me that that particular factor has somewhat been overtaken by section 26'. Pending this question being determined, the court ordered that the vessel should remain under arrest under section 26 as security for the satisfaction of any award or judgment which might be obtained in Norway. However, as a condition of continuing the arrest, the plaintiffs were required to provide security for the defendants' losses in the sum of £30,000.

## What is the appropriate forum?

The English High Court can stay or strike out an action or other proceedings in England on the basis that England is an inappropriate forum (forum non conveniens). There must be another forum to whose jurisdiction the defendant is amenable, which is clearly or distinctly more appropriate than the English forum, i.e. is a forum in which the case may be tried more suitably for the interests of all the parties and the ends of justice.

If the Brussels Convention applies then there are specific rules for determining the appropriate jurisdiction, which is dealt with above. In the leading case on forum non conveniens of *Spiliada Maritime Corporation* v *Cansulex Limited* [1987] 1 Lloyd's Rep. 1 the House of Lords said that:

> 'The basic principle is that a stay will only be granted on the ground of forum non conveniens where the court is satisfied that there is some other available forum, having competent jurisdiction, which is the appropriate forum for the trial of the action, i.e. in which the case may be tried more suitably for the interests of all the parties and the ends of justice.'

The considerations which are taken into contemplation by courts when they are deciding whether or not to exercise jurisdiction in any given situation are (1) whether access to sources of proof is relatively easy; (2) the availability and/or costs of obtaining willing, and unwilling, witnesses; (3) the question of whether, if judgment is eventually obtained, it could, in practice, be enforced; and (4) any other incidental practical matters which would effect the speed of holding a trial and have an influence on the expenses. Such factors are not exhaustive and the facts of each particular case must be considered in detail.

A well known case in the Admiralty Court on the forum non conveniens issue is *The Abidin Daver* [1984] 2 WLR 196. This arose out of a collision between a Turkish ship and a Cuban ship in Turkish territorial waters (the Bosphorus). The Turks arrested the Cuban ship in Turkey, thus commencing an action in the jurisdiction where the accident occurred. Subsequently, the Cubans arrested a sister ship of the Turks in a UK port, thus commencing a second action in England. The English Admiralty Judge stayed the English proceedings.

On appeal, the Court of Appeal reversed that and let the English action continue. On final appeal, the House of Lords restored the trial judge's decision to grant a stay in favour of the existing Turkish action. The Lords, using to help them the so-called 'MacShannon formula' (from the *MacShannon* v. *Rockware Glass Limited* case [1978] AC 795) framed two basic prerequisites for the granting of a stay in a tort action—(a) that there should be an alternative forum which was either the natural one with which there was a substantial connection on the facts or where there would be considerably less inconvenience and expense than in the one from which a stay was being sought. The burden of proving this was on the defendant seeking the stay; and (b) that there must be neither a personal nor juridical advantage accruing to the plaintiff in the action which he stood to lose if the stay was granted. The burden of proving this was, naturally, with the plaintiff.

As to how much, if at all, the defendant would be disadvantaged by a stay not being granted cannot be excluded as a factor going to influence the judge's eventual decision. In *The Abidin Daver* case, the 'lis alibi pendens' (the Turkish action) could be regarded in this light but it is difficult to think readily of another specific disadvantage which a defendant might suffer.

Having established that there is (a) a natural alternative forum and (b) no relevant legitimate advantage to the plaintiff, then a stay should be granted. But, it is not quite that simple. There should, hinted Their Lordships, be a balancing of interests of the plaintiff and defendant respectively (what Lord Wilberforce in *The Atlantic Star* [1973] 2 Lloyd's Rep. 197, HL called a 'critical equation'), that the court, in the exercise of its discretion, should involve itself in a balancing up of those factors which support on either side the case for and against the stay. One surely noticeable factor in *The Abidin Daver* is that to allow the English action to proceed would have meant the continuation of two independent proceedings in two independent jurisdictions arising from one collision incident—surely an unwarranted and unjustified extravaganza of costs overall. Thus the lis alibi pendens factor (the prior-commenced Turkish proceedings), which indeed was, perhaps, the one influencing factor in the original Admiralty Judge's mind must be an important factor weighing in the scales.

In *The Forum Craftsman* [1984] 2 Lloyd's Rep. 102 the decision of the Admiralty Judge to refuse to stay proceedings brought in rem in England by a plaintiff cargo owner of Angolan nationality was upheld by the Court of Appeal which dismissed the subsequent appeal of the Panamanian shipowner to have the matter referred to the Tokyo District Court. The vessel was Greek flagged and Piraeus managed. It was strenuously argued by the shipowner that Japan was the natural forum because the ship loaded there and it was cargo damage after loading but before sailing which was the subject matter of the dispute. The plaintiff was suing in tort not in contract, bills of lading not having been issued at the time the damage to cargo was inflicted. Whilst accepting the principle that the place where the tort was committed was, generally speaking, the natural forum, the appeal judges found on these facts that the assumption was displaced by the fact that the loading had been completed and that the accident happened in the hold of the ship which was of Greek nationality. Whilst, therefore, Japan might be a natural forum it was not the natural forum.

In *The Sidi Bishr* [1987] 1 Lloyd's Rep. 42 an action in rem in London's Admiralty Court arose out of a collision in Alexandria harbour. One ship was Moroccan, the other Egyptian. It was the Moroccan which took action in rem and also took out a warrant of arrest against a ship under common ownership with the Egyptian ship. The Egyptians applied for a stay of proceedings in England in favour of Alexandria on the ground that it was not only competent but also natural and appropriate.

The court held that although there was no doubt that Alexandria was the more natural forum, the scene of collision being the harbour there, one ship being Egyptian and Arabic being the crew's native language and that of the court, these considerations were overridden by the behaviour of the defendant Egyptian who, if he had seriously wanted the matter tried in Egypt, would not have gone to the lengths of instructing English solicitors to file a preliminary act in the collision claim. Furthermore, costs had already been incurred which would be wasted if the matter were to be re-enacted over again from 'square one' in an Egyptian forum. The application for a stay was refused.

As mentioned above the leading case on the question of forum non conveniens, although this was not heard in the Admiralty Court, was *The Spiliada* [1987] 1 Lloyd's Rep. 1. The decision and facts were:

The shipowners commenced legal action against the shippers of a cargo of sulphur as a result of damage done by the sulphur's corrosive qualities to the holds and tanktops. The claim bore much similarity to *The Cambridgeshire* action pending in England where the circumstances were essentially the same. The voyage was from British Colombia, the sulphur was of Canadian origin. The crucial question was—was Canada or England the more appropriate forum? The trial judge gave great weight to what he called the '*Cambridgeshire* factor' whereunder much expertise, particularly legal, was centred in England and was available for use if required in *The Spiliada* dispute. Balanced against this, the *Cambridgeshire* was British-owned whereas the *Spiliada* was Greek/Liberian owned with the only English connection being that the vessel was partly managed by a British company. Far more witnesses would have to be transported to Canada if the forum was determined to be Canada than would have to be transported in the opposite direction if the more appropriate forum was found to be England.

In the Court of Appeal, the judges emphasized that the test should not be one of mere practical convenience, but rather one of suitability or appropriateness, i.e. is there some other forum which is competent and above all appropriate? They cited the '*Cambridgeshire* factor' as a consideration, but not decisive. The House of Lords, overturning the Court of Appeal's decision, concluded that the High Court judge (who had actually presided over *The Cambridgeshire* case) was well placed to weigh the importance of the '*Cambridgeshire* factor' and rightly regarded it as paramount and one able to tip the balance of appropriateness. They said that the legal burden of proof rested on the defendant to persuade the court to exercize its discretion to grant a stay, although the evidential burden will rest on the party who seeks to establish the existence of matters which will assist him in persuading the court to exercize its discretion in his favour. If the court is satisfied that another available forum is prima facie the appropriate forum then the burden shifts to the plaintiff to show that there are special circumstances by reason of which justice requires that the trial should nevertheless take place in England. Also, the burden on the defendant is not just to show that England is not the natural or appropriate forum but to establish that there is another forum which is clearly or distinctly more appropriate than the English forum. The court will look at factors which point towards another forum being the natural forum, i.e. that with which the action has the most real and substantial connexion. These include convenience or expense (such as availability of witnesses) and such other factors and the law governing the transaction and the places where the parties reside or carry on business. If the court decides that there is no other available forum which is clearly more appropriate then the court will ordinarily refuse a stay. If the court decides that there is some other available forum which prima facie is clearly more appropriate it will ordinarily grant a stay unless there are circumstances by reason of which justice requires that a stay should not be granted. A stay will not be refused simply because the plaintiff would therefore be deprived if 'a legitimate personal or juridical advantage' provided that the court is satisfied that substantial justice will be done in the available appropriate forum.

*The Coral Isis* [1986] 1 Lloyd's Rep. 413 involved a collision between two ships—the *Celtic Sky* and the *Coral Isis*. The collision occurred in international waters. A month after the collision the owners of the *Coral Isis* arrested the *Celtic Sky* off Flushing commencing action in Dutch jurisdiction. A month later the reverse happened in English jurisdiction, the owners of the arrested *Coral Isis* tried to get the English proceedings stayed because of the prior-instituted Dutch proceedings, because it would be less expensive there and because justice could perfectly well be achieved. Using *The Abidin Daver* as a role model, Sheen J said that whereas Turkey had been a natural appropriate forum in that case, the same could not be said of the dispute when there was no natural forum. The Dutch forum was no worse or better than an English forum. Just to show that a balance of convenience favoured The Netherlands was not good enough. The defendant in the second (English) proceedings had to satisfy the court that there was another forum where justice could be gained at significantly less cost and inconvenience. That could not be shown here.

In the case of *The Emre II* [1989] 2 Lloyd's Rep. 182 the mortgagees issued a writ in rem against the vessel *Emre II* claiming a sum from owners of the vessel which was secured by a mortgage. They applied for an order that the vessel be appraised and sold by the Admiralty Marshal. The defendant owners applied for an order staying the action on the grounds that the parties had agreed Turkish jurisdiction. Sheen J decided that there was no agreement in the mortgage to refer disputes to Turkey. He then had to consider whether the action should be stayed on the grounds that Turkey was a more appropriate forum in which justice could be done between the parties at substantially less inconvenience and expense. In exercising his discretion whether or not to grant a stay, Sheen J applied the following principles.

(1) A mere balance of convenience is not a sufficient ground for depriving a plaintiff of the advantages of prosecuting his action in an English court if it is otherwise properly brought.
(2) In order to justify the stay, the defendant must satisfy the court that there is another forum, to whose jurisdiction he is amenable, in which justice can be done between the parties at substantially less inconvenience or expense.
(3) The stay must not deprive the plaintiff of a legitimate personal or juridical advantage which would be available to him in this court.
(4) In considering inconvenience the court must have regard to every aspect of the litigation. In particular the court should have in mind (a) the convenience of the parties themselves, (b) the convenience of the witnesses, (c) the disruption caused to others by the absence of the witnesses from their normal place of work, (d) the costs involved in litigation in London as compared with litigation in the other forum.

In the present case both parties were Turkish, the issues are likely to raise questions of Turkish law. Save for the fact that security had been provided by the arrest of the ship, all the other factors pointed to a trial in Instanbul as being the more convenient and cheapest forum. Documents will be in Turkish; questions of Turkish law can be decided in their natural forum; and a trial in Istanbul will be far more convenient for the witnesses. However, in view of section 26 of the 1982 Act it was decided that the court would not stay an action against a ship which had been mortgaged as security for a loan unless the defendant provides equally good security in 'the other forum'. The juridical advantage which the plaintiff had by retaining the vessel under arrest would be preserved by ordering that the vessel remained under arrest until the proceedings in Turkey had reached finality.

In the case of *The Vishva Ajay* [1989] 2 Lloyd's Rep. 558 a collision occurred between the plaintiffs' and defendants' vessels at a port in India. The plaintiffs founded jurisdiction in England by arresting a sister ship of the defendants. The defendants applied for an order that the action be stayed on the grounds of forum non conveniens. Sheen J decided that the court in India was the natural forum for the action in the sense of being that with which the action had the most real and substantial connection. Since India was clearly more appropriate, the High Court would grant a stay unless there were circumstances by reason of which justice required that a stay should nevertheless not be granted, relying on the *Spiliada* case.

It appeared that a successful litigant in India would not be awarded costs upon a realistic basis and would have to bear a substantial portion of the litigation costs himself: if this was so, then there was for both parties an advantage in litigating in England; the plaintiffs should not be deprived of part of the sum awarded by paying a large sum in costs and the defendants should not be under pressure to settle the action for fear of paying a large sum in costs even if he had been successful; there was also a substantial body of evidence that, if this case was to proceed in the High Court of Bombay, the trial would be delayed for many years. It was in the interests of justice that actions should come to trial at a time when witnesses could reasonably be expected to have some recollection of the events in question. In these circumstances a stay of the English action would not be granted.

In the case of *The Vishva Abha* [1990] 2 Lloyd's Rep. 312 the question as to whether an Admiralty action should be stayed arose out of a collision in the Red Sea. There was litigation in a number of jurisdictions including South Africa and England. The cargo interests issued proceedings in England and served a writ on the sister ship of the *Vishva Abha*. The defendants contended that the English court was not the appropriate forum for the hearing of the action and applied for a stay on the ground that they had already commenced proceedings in South Africa and had arrested the other collided vessel, *Dias*, there. If the defendants were to invoke limitation in South Africa there was evidence that the limitation fund would be much lower in South Africa than in England.

*Held*: that it was relevant that the litigation in England was not between the same parties as the litigation currently being pursued in South Africa and that the plaintiffs should not be prima facie deprived of litigating in the forum of their choice merely because others had chosen to litigate in South Africa. The defendants were Indian shipowners with ships that came to England regularly and they would not be put to any more inconvenience or expense by having their witnesses attend the English courts than they would in attending a court in South Africa. The court was not convinced that South Africa was the more appropriate forum and that the interests of justice did not demand that the plaintiffs' action be heard in South Africa merely because of the chance that the defendants, who had an interest in pursuing the vessel *Dias* were only able to bring an action against her in South Africa. Therefore the application for a stay of the English proceedings was dismissed.

In the case of *The Lakhta* [1992] 2 Lloyd's Rep. 269 there was a dispute as to the ownership of the vessel *Lakhta* between Latvian plaintiffs and Russian defendants. A Russian arbitration award decided that the vessel was owned by the defendants although the plaintiffs were not a party to this arbitration and complained against the award.

Subsequently, the plaintiffs arrested the vessel *Lakhta* in England claiming a declaration that they were the sole owners of the vessel. The defendants applied for an order staying the action on the grounds of forum non conveniens.

*Held*: that a stay would only be granted if the court was satisfied that there was some other available forum which was the appropriate forum, and if so, then it was for the plaintiffs to show that there were special reasons why justice required that the trial should nevertheless take place in England. The case was in every respect connected with Russia and the Baltic States and it had no connection with England; the plaintiffs were Latvian and the defendants were Russian and the language of the documents was Russian; all the witnesses would have to come from Russia thereby greatly adding to the expense and causing them personally great inconvenience. All these factors indicated that a Russian forum would be clearly and distinctly more appropriate than an English court. The plaintiffs' submission that the case would not be heard on its merits in Russia was rejected. Accordingly, the Admiralty Court declined to exercise its jurisdiction to resolve a dispute which could be resolved at far less expense and with far greater convenience to those involved in the appropriate court in Russia. The English action was stayed.

In the case of *The Falstria* [1988] 1 Lloyd's Rep. 495 the vessel *Falstria* collided with the quay and gantry crane in Felixstowe in August 1986. At the time the *Falstria* was owned by a Danish company and on demise charter to the plaintiff charterers. The dock company of Felixstowe commenced proceedings in Denmark against both the owners and the charterers. On 4 February 1987 the charterers issued a writ claiming, as demise charterers, to have their liability limited pursuant to the provisions of the Merchant Shipping Acts 1894 to 1984 (i.e. the Merchant Shipping Act 1979 only came into force subsequently on 1 December 1986). In Denmark the higher limit of liability agreed in the Convention on Limitation of Liability for Maritime Claims 1976 was in force at the time of the occurrence. The dock company applied to stay the limitation proceedings.

*Held*: (Sheen J) that, if this limitation action was instituted because several claims were apprehended in respect of the liability of the charterers, the court did not have an inherent jurisdiction to stay the action upon the application of only one of those claimants; if the charterers were entitled to a decree limiting their liability there was no basis upon which the charterers could be deprived of that right by an order that the action be stayed on the application of the dock company. If the only question was whether the owners or the charterers could show that the damage occurred without their actual fault or privity, the submission that the most appropriate court for the trial of that issue would be a court in the country in which the owners or charterers were domiciled would be understandable. However, the relief claimed by the charterers did not relate to Denmark and could not be obtained in a Danish court. The relief claimed by the charterers was a decree that in respect of all claims brought in this country there was a limit to the liability of the charterers and that decree could only be granted by the English court. The dock company's application for a stay of the limitation proceedings was dismissed.

*Varna No. 2* [1994] 2 Lloyd's Rep. 41
A dispute arose under a charterparty as a result of which proceedings were brought in Bulgaria and England. The owners applied to stay the English action on the grounds: (1) that some or all of the issues which were the subject matter of the English action had been finally determined by a competent court in Varna; (2) that there was a lis alibi pendens, i.e. an action proceeding in Varna; and (3) that in any event the court in Varna was the more appropriate forum for the trial of the action.

*Held*: The plaintiffs' submission that their action was properly and validly brought by action in rem and they were entitled to prosecute it unless the owners showed that there was another available forum which was the appropriate forum in the sense of being clearly or distinctly more appropriate for the interests of the parties and the ends of justice would be accepted. The principles laid down in *The Spiliada* applied to a case where there was a lis alibi pendens. There was no basis for saying that the plaintiffs would not receive justice in Bulgaria.

The District Court of Varna had been scrupulous throughout the interlocutory stages to ensure that the plaintiffs were afforded every opportunity of putting their case and adducing evidence. The owners had already indicated that they intended to rely on the decision of the Bulgarian court as giving rise to an issue estoppel. This question would be avoided if the claim was litigated in Bulgaria. The existing Bulgarian proceedings pointed in favour of Bulgaria as the natural and appropriate forum for the trial of this action. The owners had established not only that the English court was not the natural or appropriate forum but that the District Court of Varna was clearly the more appropriate forum for the trial of this action. There were no circumstances which would make it unjust to grant a stay of the action.

The significance of limitation proceedings being brought in another country in relation to an action to stay English proceedings arose in the following cases. In the case of *The Hamburg Star* [1994] 1 Lloyd's Rep. 399:

Various containers were lost whilst the vessel *Hamburg Star* was proceeding between Rotterdam and Hamburg. Some of the goods were shipped in Felixstowe and some of them were destined for Cyprus. The vessel was arrested in Cyprus and security obtained. The Owners issued proceedings in Cyprus claiming a declaration that they were not liable and in the alternative a declaration that they were entitled to limit their liability. Various claims were brought by cargo interests in England and Owners applied for a stay on the ground that Cyprus was a more appropriate forum. Cyprus had not ratified the 1976 Convention and accordingly any limitation fund established there would be lower than a fund established in England. Cargo interests argued that if the English action were stayed in favour of Cyprus they may be deprived of a legitimate juridical advantage by being deprived of the benefit of the limitation fund in England.

The High Court decided that the existence of a limitation action in Cyprus was no ground for a conclusion that Cyprus was clearly the more appropriate forum than England. There was little relevant evidence in Cyprus as to the state of the vessel or the condition of most of the cargo although there may be evidence as to the value of the goods. The damaged containers were discharged at Hamburg and repairs were done there. Any evidence available at Hamburg or Antwerp (where some of the goods were shipped and where the Court surveyor carried out a survey) could as readily, if not more readily, be made available in London as in Nicosia. There was little connection with Cyprus and it would be more appropriate for the cargo claims to be tried in England. The stay application was refused.

However, in the case of *Caltex* v *BP* [1996] 1 Lloyd's Rep. 286 a collision took place in Singapore waters. BP admitted liability for the collision in limitation proceedings which had been commenced in Singapore. The Singaporean plaintiffs brought proceedings in England. The limit of liability in Singapore was likely to be less than that in England, and the plaintiffs, inter alia, resisted the defendants' application for a stay of the English proceedings as they would be deprived of a substantial legitimate juridical advantage, with which the court agreed. The plaintiffs had established that to be deprived of the larger limit of liability was a relevant special circumstance as a result of which justice potentially required that the action be allowed to proceed in England. The action was stayed temporarily in order to enable the issues of quantum to be determined in Singapore.

The statement made by Mr Justice Clarke in *Caltex* v *B.P. Limited* that the Singapore right to limit was not substantive but procedural was agreed with by Mr Justice Longmore in the case of the *Happy Fellow* [1997] 1 Lloyd's Rep. 130. Mr Justice Longmore said:

'A shipowner's right to limit (at any rate in a multiparty case) does not attach to or qualify the substantive right of the claimant but, rather, limits the extent to which that right can be enforced against a particular fund. I also agree that the position under the 1976 Convention (with which I am here concerned) is no different from that under earlier legislation such as the 1894 Act.'

This case involved a collision near the mouth of the Seine between the vessels *Darfur* and *Happy Fellow*. On 28 November 1995, *Darfur* was arrested at Le Havre by the *Happy Fellow* interests and, on 22 December, a writ was issued in the Commercial Court of Le Havre on behalf of seven French claimants including the owners and three members of the Unigas Pool who were the operators of the vessel. Damages were claimed against the owners of *Darfur*. Then in March 1996 the time charterers of *Darfur* issued a writ against the owners of *Darfur*, and a few days later the owners of *Darfur* instituted a limitation action namely as the defendants the owners of *Happy Fellow*, the bareboat charterers of *Happy Fellow*, time charterers of *Darfur* and all other persons claiming or being entitled to claim damages by reason of the collision. In April 1996 the plaintiffs purported to constitute a limitation fund in England. *Darfur* was still under arrest at Le Havre but was released on 2 May 1996 after security had been given. Then one member of the Unigas Pool which operated the vessel *Happy Fellow* applied by summons for a stay of further proceedings in the English limitation action. This member, Slomand Neptun, contended that the English proceedings involved the same cause of action as the French proceedings and that, since the French court was the court first seised, the English proceedings should be set aside or stayed pursuant to Article 21, alternatively the proceedings were related and should be set aside or stayed pursuant to Article 22 of the Brussels Convention.

In considering whether the same cause of action arose, the court considered that a limitation action was a special proceeding to which all potential claimants were made party and includes a power to stay proceedings to enforce any judgment which may have been obtained in other proceedings. In a multiparty situation, a shipowner's right to limit is not an incident or attribute of a claimant's claim but an altogether different right to have all claims scaled down to their proportionate share of a limited fund.

In the case of the *Happy Fellow* [1997] 1 Lloyd's Rep. 130, Longmore J said at page 133:

'. . . It is necessary to say what an English limitation action is. It needs first to be said that the limitation action is unnecessary and, thus, undesirable if only one claim is made on a shipowner and no other claims are expected. In such a case, the shipowner's right to limit can (and usually should) be dealt with in proceedings to which those two persons are parties. This is not this case. In the present case, the owners of *Darfur* are faced with claims in France from *Happy Fellow* interests, claims from owners of cargo on board *Darfur* (which had not yet become pending in any particular jurisdiction) and claims from the time charterers, Baco-Liner (which are currently pending in England). In circumstances such as these, the question of a right to limit cannot be determined between the shipowner and only one of the claimants and, as a matter of English law, a limitation action becomes necessary. The nature of such an action was explained in the *Penelope II* [1980] 2 Lloyd's Rep. 17 by Lord Justice Brandon whose judgment in this respect, despite being a dissenting judgment with regard to the precise order made by the Court of Appeal in that case and despite being given in relation to earlier legislation than the current (1995) Merchant Shipping Act was in no way inconsistent with the judgments of the other members of the court and reflects the current law . . . A limitation action is thus a special proceeding to which all potential claimants are made parties and includes a power to stay proceedings to enforce any judgment which may have been obtained in other proceedings. That power can now be used to enforce Article 13 of the 1976 Limitation Convention, which is entitled "Bar to other actions". It seems to me, therefore, that, in what I may call a multi-party situation, a shipowner's right to limit is not an accident or attribute of a claimant's claim but an altogether different right to have all claims scaled down to their proportionate share of a limited fund.'

The High Court went on to say that a shipowner's right to limit did not qualify or attach to the substantive right of the claimant but operated to limit the extent to which an unqualified right could be enforced against the limitation fund: the right to limit was procedural and did not affect the substantive rights of the French claimant; the English proceedings purported to invoke a right which was good against all possible claimants while the French proceedings sought only to invoke rights between the parties to those proceedings. The French and English proceedings did not involve the same cause of action and Article 21 of the Convention did not apply. If they had involved the same cause of action, the French court was the court first seised. The English action and the French action did seem to be related, in that no admission of liability had been made by the owners of *Darfur* and it was likely that the French court would take the view that it was first seised of limitation issues. The actions were so closely connected that it was expedient to hear and determine them together to avoid the risk of irreconcilable judgments from separate proceedings and the actions were related. The cause of the failure of the steering gear on board *Darfur* would be a primary fact in both jurisdictions and there would be an inevitable risk of irreconcilable judgments if both actions proceeded. The French and English proceedings were related proceedings, and, pursuant to Article 22, the English proceedings should be stayed insofar as they affected Sloman Neptun.

The Court of Appeal decided ([1998] 2 Lloyd's Rep. 13) that Longmore J had been justifiably satisfied that the French court would conclude that it could and should deal with limitation. From that it inevitably followed that there was a risk of irreconcilable judgments and thus that the actions were related. The appeal was dismissed.

In the case of *The Owners of the Herceg Novi* v *The Owners of the Ming Galaxy* [1998] 1 Lloyd's Rep. 167 involving consideration of whether English proceedings in rem should be stayed on the ground of forum non conveniens following a collision in the Straits of Singapore in 1996, the defendants had begun an action in rem in Singapore which applied to the 1957 Limitation Convention, and the limitation fund of the *Ming Galaxy* was half that in Singapore compared with that under the 1976 London Convention which applied in London. The High Court decided to temporarily stay the English proceedings pending the determination of issues of responsibility and quantum. The case of the *M.C. Pearl* [1997] 1 Lloyd's Rep. 566 involved cargo owners disputing salvage and the bill of lading providing for disputes to be determined in South Korea. There was a strong cause for concentrating all claims arising out of a single casualty (here there were 62 bills of lading) in a single jurisdiction, which in the circumstances could only be England. The failure to commence proceedings in time in South Korea was either a deliberate, but reasonable, decision to concentrate on England, or it was the result of overlooking the jurisdiction clause followed by failing to realize that the relevant time limit was one year or it was the result of first overlooking the clause followed by a deliberate decision to leave the action in England. A stay would not be enforced purely on the grounds of the existence of the time bar in South Korea. A plaintiff's failure to preserve a time limit in the contractual forum could not assist them to find jurisdiction in England where he did not have a strong case for it separately from the time bar point; and, even where he did have a strong case of jurisdiction in England apart from the time bar, the fact that he had allowed the time bar to go by default in the contractual jurisdiction always required some consideration or explanation. If there had not been a strong cause for refusing a stay, the existence of a limitation defence in South Korea would not have saved the action or caused it to be stayed on terms that the South Korean limitation defence be waived, but the plaintiffs had shown strong cause why the jurisdiction clause should not be enforced and all the relevant parties' disputes should be concentrated in a single jurisdiction. The application to enforce the exclusive jurisdiction clause was dismissed.

The case of *Ultisol* v *Bouygues* [1996] 2 Lloyd's Rep. 140 concerned a dispute under a towage contract, and the competing jurisdictions were England and South Africa. Ultisol argued, inter alia, that, if the merits of the dispute were determined in South Africa, there was a serious risk that a different and less favourable regime of limitation would be applicable since South Africa applied the 1957 Convention whereas England applied the 1976 Convention.

The High Court decided that the Ultisol's right to seek to limit its liability in accordance with the law of the chosen forum and thus under the 1976 Convention was a potentially very valuable right and was a right of which Ultisol should not lightly be deprived. An injunction was granted restraining Bouygues from continuing proceedings in South Africa in relation to claims under the towage contract provided that Ultisol gave a satisfactory undertaking with regard to security which Bouygues had obtained by attaching bunkers in South Africa.

However, if the defendant is a member of the EU to which the Brussels Convention applies it seems that the English court has no discretion to stay English proceedings in favour of the courts of other Contracting States to the Brussels Convention except in accordance with Articles 21 to 23. The question as to whether the English courts still had a discretion despite the clear provisions of the Brussels Convention was referred to the European Court in the case of *Re Harrods (Buenos Aires) Limited* [1991] 4 All ER 334. However, this reference lapsed because the actions were settled. Also in the case of the *Nile Rhapsody* [1994] 1 Lloyd's Rep. 383 the Court of Appeal declined to refer to the European Court the question whether an English court still retained the power to stay proceedings in a case whether there was an exclusive jurisdiction clause or on forum conveniens grounds, the plaintiffs having argued that the Brussels Convention prevented this.

Furthermore, another case in point is—

*The Xin Yang and An Kang Jiang* [1996] 2 Lloyd's Rep. 217
A collision occurred at Vlaardingen in Holland on 20 November 1995. *Xin Yang* was arrested in Rotterdam for security. On 22 November, the vessel *An Kang Jiang* was arrested in England and on 24 November the defendants submitted a petition to the district court in Rotterdam to limit their liability for the collision. The defendants applied for a stay of the English action on the ground of forum non conveniens. They contended that the action could be tried more suitably for the interest of all the parties and the ends of justice in Rotterdam. The plaintiffs argued that the court had no jurisdiction to stay the action because it was the court first seised within Article 21 of the Brussels Convention. The defendants argued that the English court retained its discretion to stay an action on the ground of forum non conveniens where the defendant was not domiciled in a Contracting State. Here, the defendant Chinese owners were not domiciled within a Contracting State.

It was decided that the English court had jurisdiction under the Supreme Court Act 1981 which was preserved by Article 4 of the Brussels Convention and nothing in the Convention restricted the right or duty of the English court to decline to exercise that jurisdiction on the ground of forum non conveniens. However, there was no room for the exercise of a discretion to decline jurisdiction on the ground of forum non conveniens where a defendant was domiciled within a Contracting State. Holland was more appropriate, particularly in relation to the determination of issues of quantum, proceedings having been commenced there and the defendant had not shown that England was more appropriate. There were no special circumstances which required that the trial should take place in England; there was another available forum having competent jurisdiction which was the appropriate forum for trial of this action—i.e. where the case might be tried more suitably for the interests of all parties and the ends of justice and that forum was Holland.

The principles relevant to the exercise of the Court's discretion to stay an action are derived principally from the *Spiliada*, which was summarized by the High Court in the above case as follows:

1. The court will only grant a stay where it is satisfied that there is some other available forum having competent jurisdiction which is the appropriate forum for the trial of the action. That is where the case may be tried more suitably for the interests of all the parties and the Inns of Justice.
2. The problem should be approached in two stages. At stage one the burden is on the defendant to show both that England is not the natural or appropriate forum for the trial of the action and that there is another forum which is clearly or distinctly more appropriate than England.
3. If the defendant discharges that burden, it is necessary to move to stage two. It is then for the plaintiff to persuade the court that there is some special circumstance which requires that the trial should take place in England.

In the case of *Sarrio SA* v *Kuwait Investment Authority* [1997] 1 Lloyd's Rep. 113, the plaintiff appealed the High Court decision staying English proceedings in the action brought by the plaintiffs for damages in tort for negligent misstatement. The Court of Appeal decided that Articles 21 and 22 of the Brussels Convention did not apply, as the English and Spanish proceedings did not involve the same cause of action nor were they related actions. The plaintiff also contended that the court could not order a stay on the *Spiliada* principles where proceedings are pending in a foreign state which is a party to the Brussels Convention (Convention country) and where the English writ has been served on the defendant 'as of right' within the English court, as opposed to service outside the jurisdiction under the provisions of RSC Order 11. The defendant, the Kuwait Investment Authority, was domiciled in Kuwait, being a non-Convention country, although they had been served with a writ in England through the Kuwait Investment Office.

The Court of Appeal had in mind the case of *Re Harrods (Buenos Aires) Limited* involving an alternative forum which was not a non-Convention country. In these circumstances it was not inconsistent with the letter or spirit of the Convention for the English court to stay proceedings on the grounds of the alternative forum, if more appropriate, in accordance with the *Spiliada* principles. Section 49 of the Civil Jurisdiction and Judgments Act 1982 preserves the powers of the court to order a stay of the English proceedings in these circumstances. However, in the present case the plaintiffs submitted that the alternative forum is another Convention country, Spain, and the plaintiffs argued that the discretion of the court to stay proceedings on the ground of forum non conveniens was excluded by the Brussels Convention.

However, the Court of Appeal stated that even if Article 21 would require the Spanish court to decline jurisdiction in any future proceedings by the plaintiff against the defendant in respect of the same cause of action then the correct analysis is not that the *Spiliada* principles are excluded but that, in the application of those principles, the Spanish courts could not be regarded as an alternative forum which was 'available' for hearing the dispute between the parties. The Court of Appeal agreed with the view expressed in Dicey and Morris that forum non conveniens of the national law are not excluded by the Convention when the defendant is not domiciled in a Convention country. In exercising the court's discretion whether to stay the proceedings in the light of the *Spiliada* principles, the Court of Appeal decided that the defendants could not say that they are placed at any substantial disadvantage by having to defend the proceedings in London rather than in Spain and a stay was not ordered. The appeal was allowed.

## Jurisdiction clauses

If a contract provides that all disputes between the parties are to be referred to the jurisdiction of the English courts then an action arising under this contract will be determined in England. However, it is quite common for a contract to provide that all disputes are to be referred to the jurisdiction of a foreign court or arbitration tribunal. In these circumstances the English court will stay proceedings brought in England in breach of such agreement unless the plaintiff establishes that it is just and proper to allow them to continue. It is also necessary to consider whether the Convention applies and, in particular, whether the jurisdiction agreement is an exclusive jurisdiction agreement within Article 17 of the Convention.

First, dealing with non-Convention cases, there have been various applications to the High Court by shipowner defendants to stay proceedings instituted by cargo interests in favour of the forum selected by agreement by the parties to the bill of lading contract. One of these is *The Eleftheria* [1969] 1 Lloyd's Rep. 237.

The vessel had carried goods from Galatz (Romania) to Hull (UK). She was Piraeus registered and owned jointly by three Greek nationals. The relevant bills of lading provided for disputes to be decided in the country in which the carrier had its principal place of business and also stipulated that the law of the same country should be applied (a combined law and jurisdiction clause). The cargo was off-loaded at Rotterdam and the bill of lading holders sought to recover from the carrier the costs of on-forwarding to Hull. The ship was served with a warrant of arrest and her owners applied to stay the proceedings which were commenced in London, pleading the validity of the jurisdiction clause in the bill of lading contract.

*Held*: that the plaintiff's arguments were not compelling enough to justify the court in exercising a discretion to refuse to stay proceedings. A stay was granted subject to satisfactory arrangements regarding security.

The court summarized the individual factors which should be taken into account by a court when exercising its discretion to grant a stay or otherwise. These are:

(a) in what country the evidence is more readily available, and the effect of that on the relative convenience and expense of trial as between the English or foreign court;
(b) whether the law of the foreign court applies and, if so, whether it differs essentially from English law;
(c) with what country either party is connected and how closely.
(d) whether the defendants generally wish a trial in a foreign country or are only seeking procedural advantages;
(e) whether the plaintiffs would be prejudiced by having to sue in the foreign court because they might either be deprived of security for their claim or be unable to enforce any judgment they might obtain or be faced with a time bar not applicable in England.

*The Eleftheria* case was one of those considered when the Admiralty Court sat to hear an application by the owners of the vessel *El Amria* for a stay of proceedings brought by cargo interests in the case of *Aratra Potato Company Limited and Morello International Limited* v *Owners of the El Amria* [1980] 1 Lloyd's Rep. 390. The facts are:

Goods were discharged damaged in Liverpool, surveyed by a British surveyor reporting in the English language. The bills of lading were also in English and the receivers of the goods were British. The relevant bills of lading contained a clause stipulating that any dispute arising should be referred to the courts of Alexandria—i.e. the carrier's place of business. The owners of the vessel applied for a stay of proceedings which had been brought by cargo interests in London on the ground that there was an exclusive jurisdiction clause in the contract of carriage stipulating for Egyptian jurisdiction.

*Held*: that the court, in refusing to grant a stay, found favour in the argument that the substantial connexion of the whole matter was to England and that it was material that much of the evidence if forced into Arabic translation for the benefit of an Egyptian court would lose its significance.

What emerges from these cases and others preceding these is that the underlying factor is the principle that he who voluntarily agrees to a jurisdiction clause should be bound by it, unless there are strong reasons why he should not be so. It is a feature of English legal theory that the jurisdiction conferred on an Admiralty Court to issue writs in rem or warrants of arrest exists independently of any jurisdiction established by contractual agreement between the parties to a contract or, alternatively, to there existing a more proper convenient 'forum' elsewhere in the world, taking account of the facts and circumstances surrounding the incident which gave rise to the claim. Thus, the arresting court in practical terms may be neither of these things. Nevertheless there is no pre-existing requirement of the jurisdiction to arrest that the arresting court should be properly the court contractually picked to examine the merits or the 'right place' to consider a claim in tort. Once jurisdiction has been founded by proceedings in rem it is in the judge's discretion to decide whether he and his court should go on to examine the merits or to stay and/or transfer the proceedings to another foreign forum or, perhaps, to another type of forum (e.g. arbitration in the same jurisdiction).

Lord Denning in *The Fehmarn* [1957] 2 Lloyd's Rep. 551 said, 'I do not regard the choice of law in the contract as decisive; I prefer to look to see with what country the dispute is most closely concerned'. Very compelling arguments would have to be put before the court if a successful attempt was made to retain jurisdiction in the face of an exclusive jurisdiction clause (i.e. one agreeing to the use of some foreign forum) in e.g. a contract of carriage contained in a bill of lading. In the *El Amria* [1980] 1 Lloyd's Rep. 390 it was said that the parties cannot oust the jurisdiction of the (arresting) court by agreement. A plaintiff must show strong reason why the court should not give effect to an existing agreement to refer to a foreign jurisdiction.

If an English court whose aid has been invoked or more correctly taking into account the language of the Supreme Court Act 1981 before whom an action in rem has been brought is informed that the plaintiff (arrestor) and the defendant (whose property has been served with the writ and who has probably given security in lieu) had voluntarily agreed with each other in e.g. their contract of carriage, that any disputes arising would be referred to a selected foreign forum, the matter is at the English judge's discretion as to whether he grants the defendant's application to stay proceedings in favour of that foreign court or whether he considers that the interests of achieving a just solution for both parties would be better served by retaining jurisdiction in defiance of the contractual arrangement. A summary of the way the courts think on this point is found in Brandon J's decision in *The El Amria* [1980] 1 Lloyd's Rep. 391:

> 'Where plaintiffs sue in England in breach of an agreement to refer disputes to a foreign court, and the defendant applies for a stay, the English court, assuming the court to be otherwise within its jurisdiction, is not bound to grant a stay but has a discretion whether to do so or not. The discretion should be exercised by granting a stay unless strong cause for not doing so is shown.'

This was supported by (to take a random example) Sheen J in *The Atlantic Song* [1983] 2 Lloyd's Rep. 394. Lord Denning, whilst Master of the Rolls (senior judge in the Court of Appeal) let it be known that he preferred to look at the facts, circumstances and evidence thereon put before him and to see with which jurisdiction the issue(s) is/are most *closely connected.* Clearly, such factors as the location and availability of witnesses and/or documentary evidence, the overall estimate of costs expected if the case was transferred to that contractually selected forum as compared with those if it was retained, and—a very important factor—the question of whether, if it was transferred, the plaintiff's interests would be seriously and unfairly prejudiced, e.g. because he might find himself time-barred and left wholly without a remedy, will be relevant in this regard.

The party (plaintiff) opposing the application to stay must, therefore, show 'good cause' (words being used in their legal sense) why the proceedings should not be stayed if he is to defeat the natural inclination of an English judge to respect and uphold the foreign jurisdiction clause which, after all, contains the original voluntary mutual wishes of the disputants.

One of the cardinal rules of Admiralty jurisprudence is that mere balance of convenience is not a sufficient ground for depriving a plaintiff of the advantages of an action properly brought in the arresting court. In this respect English judges still draw inspiration from the case of *MacShannon* v *Rockware Glass Ltd* [1978] AC 795. In the vast majority of occasions there is no natural forum resulting from the consensus of facts and circumstances surrounding the incident. In *The Traugutt* [1985] 1 Lloyd's Rep. 76 the bill of lading law was Belgian if cargo was shipped from a Belgian port, otherwise it was to be Polish law. The ship was Polish, her officers were Polish, the owners' principal place of business was in Poland. An action in rem had been brought in England against a sister ship in respect of alleged loss/damage to cargo shipped from Antwerp to Bombay. The defendant shipowners sought to stay the English action on the grounds that England was not a convenient forum, that in any event a dispute to be resolved in accordance with Belgian law should appropriately be brought before a Belgian court. There was admittedly, so the court was told, a difference between Belgian and English legal attitudes towards the question of a corporate shipowner's personal fault depriving him of his limitation rights but that fell short of saying that justice could substantially be done at less inconvenience and expense than in England. English was the language of the contractual documents, England was the place of residence of relevant 'expert witnesses'. The 'balance of convenience' favoured England.

Another more recent example is the following case of *The Al Battani* [1993] 2 Lloyd's Rep. 219.

The plaintiff alleged that the owners were in breach of an oral agreement that the vessel would proceed direct to Hamburg, as a result of which their cargo had deteriorated. The defendant owner denied that there was any oral agreement and argued that the cargo was carried under the terms of the bills of lading which stipulated that any dispute shall be decided in the carrier's principal place of business, namely Egypt. The plaintiffs served a writ on the vessel *Al Battani* in the English jurisdiction. The defendant owners then applied to stay the action on the grounds that the parties had agreed that disputes should be decided in a court in Egypt. They further contended that, whatever the terms of the contract, this was case in which not only was England not the natural or appropriate forum for the trial, but that an Egyptian court was clearly and distinctly more appropriate for the trial of their action and the court should grant a stay.

It was held, inter alia, that the plaintiff had founded jurisdiction in the English courts as of right and that it was for the defendants to show that England was not the natural or appropriate forum and to establish that Egypt was more appropriate (relying on *The Spiliada*). Egypt was a more appropriate forum. However, on the facts, the financial burden of litigating in Egypt was so heavy that justice required that a stay should not be granted. If the contract of carriage was contained in the bill of lading the Egyptian court under Article 245 of their law would regard the jurisdiction clause as null and void and there was no reason why, as a matter of comity, the English court should enforce that contractual clause. The court's discretion should be exercised by granting a stay unless strong cause for not doing so was shown and that the burden of proof was on the plaintiffs. Although the natural forum for the trial was Egypt, justice required that a stay should not be granted. There was strong cause for not granting a stay and the application by the defendant owners was dismissed. The case of *The El Amria* was applied.

In the case of the *Rothnie* [1996] 2 Lloyd's Rep. 206 it was decided that the legal burden of proof rested on a defendant to persuade the court to exercise its discretion to grant a stay and the defendant must establish that there was another forum which was distinctly or clearly more appropriate than the English forum. The fact that the parties had agreed to the agreement being governed by and construed in accordance with the laws of Gibraltar and had agreed to submit to the non-exclusive jurisdiction of the courts of Gibraltar created a strong prima facie case that the forum was an appropriate one. It was for the plaintiffs to show that there were special circumstances by reason of which justice required that the trial take place in England.

The action had the most real and substantial connection with Gibraltar; the repairs were done in Gibraltar and it would be highly disruptive to the workings of a shipyard in Gibraltar to have to bring a number of key personnel to give evidence in England. There were no circumstances by reason of which justice required that a stay should not be granted.

Also in the case of the *Nile Rhapsody* [1994] 1 Lloyd's Rep. 383 the Court of Appeal agreed with the High Court that there was an agreement for Egyptian law and jurisdiction and the English action was stayed. Furthermore, Egypt was the natural forum for a trial. The High Court decided that, although in respect of costs and to a small extent in respect of delay and interest the plaintiffs would suffer juridical disadvantage if the actions were stayed in England this fell far short of establishing that the plaintiffs would be deprived of substantial justice if the actions were stayed.

The Court of Appeal said that even if it was legitimate to take procedural disadvantages into account in a situation here, the parties had chosen the forum. The disadvantages relied on by defendants were wholly insufficient and the judge's decision that Egypt was the appropriate forum would be upheld.

In the case of *Citi-March Limited* v *Neptune Orient Lines Limited* [1997] 1 Lloyd's Rep. 72, bills of lading contained an exclusive jurisdiction clause in favour of Singapore. The cargo interests brought a claim for loss of goods delivered in Felixstowe in the English court whereas the claim was already contractually time barred in Singapore. The High Court decided that, in an exclusive jurisdiction clause case where a plaintiff had failed to issue protective proceedings in the contractual forum, a stay would be ordered or service set aside unless strong cause was shown as to why English jurisdiction should be maintained. Consideration of those factors (other than the time bar defence) material to the question of whether England, as distinct from the contractual forum, was the place where, in the interests of justice and of all the parties, the disputes ought to be tried, led to the view that strong cause was shown for a trial in England. If, in the circumstances existing prior to the effluxion of time in Singapore, strong cause could be shown in favour of maintaining the proceedings in England, a plaintiff was entitled to take the view that it was unnecessary for him to take steps to preserve time in contractual forum. Mr Justice Coleman said at page 75:

'In international commercial litigation, where in the interests of all the parties and the aims of justice between the parties it is substantially more appropriate that the issues between the parties should be determined in the English courts than in the contractual forum, a stay will not be ordered merely to protect the defendants' rights to the contractual forum. Accordingly, if a plaintiff utilises the English courts, and in so doing, ignores the contractual forum and permits the claim to become time barred there, it is open to the English court, when asked to stay the proceedings, to look at the plaintiffs' conduct in permitting the time bar to arise in order to ascertain whether such conduct was justifiable.'

As mentioned above, the main rule in the Brussels Convention is Article 2 which provides that the defendant should be sued in his country of domicile. However, under Article 17 the English court has no jurisdiction to determine a dispute if one or more of the parties is domiciled in a Contracting State and the parties have agreed in accordance with Article 17 that the courts of a Contracting State other than England are to have jurisdiction to settle such dispute, in which case such foreign court is to have exclusive jurisdiction, that is unless the defendant submits to the English jurisdiction. Alternatively, the English court has no jurisdiction if none of the parties is domiciled in a Contracting State and the parties have agreed in accordance with Article 17 that the courts of a Contracting State other than the UK are to have jurisdiction to settle any such dispute and the courts chosen have not declined jurisdiction. If there is an exclusive jurisdiction agreement under Article 17, the question of a stay under Articles 21 and 22 of the Brussels Convention does not arise, nor does the court have an inherent power to stay proceedings (see the case of *Continental Bank* v *Aeakos Company Naviera SA* [1994] 1 Lloyd's Rep. 505).

In the case of the *Sylt* [1991] 1 Lloyd's Rep. 240, a bill of lading provided 'any dispute arising under this bill of lading shall be decided in the country where the carrier has his principal place of business'. The shipowners had their principal place of business in Germany and were domiciled there for the purposes of the 1968 Convention. The High Court decided that Article 17 gave the German courts exclusive jurisdiction by reason of the bill of lading in relation to alleged cargo claims against the shipowners.

Cases in which an Article 17 argument succeeded include: *Mark Edmund Denby* v *The Hellenic Mediterranean Lines Co Ltd* [1994] 1 Lloyd's Rep. 320; *Continental Bank* v *Aeakos Compania Naviera SA* [1994] 1 Lloyd's Rep. 505. Cases in which an Article 17 argument did not succeed include the *Rewia* [1991] 2 Lloyd's Rep. 325; *New Hampshire* v *Strabag Bau AG* [1992] 1 Lloyd's Rep. 361.

In *Toepfer* v *Molino Boschi* [1996] 1 Lloyd's Rep. 510, it was decided that where there was an exclusive jurisdiction clause, Article 17 applied and had precedence over Articles 21 and 22. In *Lexmar Corporation* v *Nordisk Skibsrederforening* [1997] 1 Lloyd's Rep. 289, the High Court decided that there was a blanket exclusion of the application of Articles 21 and 22 when Article 17 of the Brussels

Convention applied, having been referred to the case of *Continental Bank NA* v *Aeakos Compania Naviera SA*.

The case of the *Bergen* [1997] 1 Lloyd's Rep. 380 was concerned with Article 17 of the Brussels Convention and Article 7 of the Arrest Convention. This involved a claim brought for damage to cargo and the bill of lading provided that disputes should be brought in the country where the carrier has his principal place of business, namely Germany. The vessel was arrested by the plaintiff cargo owners and proceedings were brought in England. The shipowners argued that the proceedings should be set aside for want of jurisdiction under Article 17 of the Brussels Convention. The plaintiffs argued that where Article 17 applied its effect was to deprive the English court of jurisdiction in accordance with its domestic law and, if Article 17 was allowed to have this effect, they would be deprived of their right to have their claim determined on the merits under Article 7 of the Arrest Convention in accordance with English domestic law whereas that right was expressly preserved by Article 57 of the Brussels Convention.

The High Court decided that Article 7 of the Arrest Convention was preserved by Article 57 of the Brussels Convention. It confers jurisdiction upon the courts of the state in which the arrest is made to determine a case upon its merits in accordance with the domestic law of that State. As the vessel was properly served and arrested in England the English court had jurisdiction to determine the plaintiffs' claims on the merits in accordance with English domestic law. The court retains jurisdiction to determine the plaintiffs' claim on the merits even in a case where there is an exclusive jurisdiction clause which provides for the determination of the dispute in a foreign court, but the court has a discretion to stay the action, which it will exercise unless strong cause why it should not do so is shown in the light of the decision of the *El Amria* [1981]. The plaintiffs were right in their submission that there was a conflict between Article 17 of the Brussels Convention and Article 7 of the Arrest Convention but, by reason of Article 57 of the Brussels Convention, Article 7 must prevail. Where Article 17 applied, the jurisdiction agreement deprived the courts of other Contracting States of jurisdiction; it would therefore deprive this court of discretion under Article 7 of the Arrest Convention and would fall foul of Article 57 (2) of the Brussels Convention.

The effect of Article 17 where it applied was to deprive the court of original jurisdiction; accordingly its effect was not that another court must decline to exercise jurisdiction which it would otherwise have, but that it must decline jurisdiction on the ground that it never had it. Article 17 did not apply to the facts of the case, and the court had retained jurisdiction by reason of Article 7 of the Arrest Convention. Whilst the court reached this decision in principle, the court mentioned that the decision was unlikely to have farreaching consequences because the practical result of applying Article 17 on the one hand and the principles of English domestic law on the other is likely to be the same. The questions as to whether the plaintiffs were able to show strong cause why the action should not be stayed in the light of the *El Amria* case was adjourned.[2]

2. The later application is at [1997] 2 Lloyd's Rep. 710. The plaintiffs had not shown that they had acted reasonably in failing to protect the time limit in Germany and the action was stayed.

## IMMUNITY OF STATE-OWNED VESSELS

The UK has not ratified the Brussels Convention of 1926 relating to the arrest of State-owned ships. Foreign State-owned vessels used in commerce, however, are not immune from arrest. Ships owned by the British government and used for government purposes may not be arrested, but proceedings may be brought against the Crown to recover damages in respect of wrongful acts committed by Crown servants in the operation of such ships.

## SOVEREIGN IMMUNITY

The granting or otherwise of sovereign immunity to a foreign government which finds itself named as a defendant in a commercial or Admiralty Court has been regulated as much by practical reasons as by legal principles. It has been the custom for the courts of the UK not generally speaking to 'handle' a claim against a foreign sovereign, sovereign State or government, unless such a defendant voluntarily agrees to submit to the jurisdiction. The practical reason for this is that there is very little point in hearing a dispute and pronouncing judgment in the dispute unless there is a very real likelihood of that judgment being enforced and when the defendant against whom that judgment may be given is a foreign sovereign, the chances of enforcement are far from great. Enforcing it by execution against the government's property in the country where judgment was given could lead to embarrassing diplomatic difficulties unjustified under the circumstances and perhaps escalating to international repercussions beyond the confines of the two countries directly concerned.

### *Historical development*

The doctrine of absolute immunity, as this is sometimes described, was established more than a century ago in the English legal system.

Perhaps the first shipping case of significance on the issue of sovereign immunity was *The Parlement Belge* (1880) 5 PD 197. In that case a Belgian mail packet steamer belonging to the Belgian king was in collision with a British vessel in the harbour at Dover. The Court of Appeal found that the Belgian vessel, although not exclusively used in public service, could not be sued in the courts of the UK. Forty years later a similar dispute came before the courts and was destined to be another leading case on the subject:

*The Porto Alexandre* (1919) 1 Ll.L.Rep. 191
A Portuguese government vessel used exclusively for trading purposes was held also to be immune from process of the courts of the UK.

Four years later the courts considered:

*Compania Mercantil Argentina* v *United States Shipping Board* (1924) 18 Ll.L.Rep. 369, CA
A ship owned by the defendants was chartered by the plaintiffs and the charterparty contained an arbitration clause. As the result of a dispute arising, the two parties appointed arbitrators but later the defendants withdrew theirs. The plaintiffs pursued legal action.

*Held*: that the defendant company were US government representatives and in such capacity were immune from legal process in the courts of England.

The next case on sovereign immunity of great significance came in 1938.

*The Cristina* [1938] AC 485, HL
The facts were that the ship, of Spanish nationality registered in a Spanish port (Bilbao), was, at the height of the Spanish Civil War in accordance with a decree requiring the requisitioning of all vessels registered at that particular port, requisitioned whilst lying in the port of Cardiff in Wales. ('Requisition' is a term used to describe the compulsory taking by a government, generally for public purposes of the user, of the direction and control of the ship with or without possession.) The Spanish consul boarded her and replaced the serving Master with a man of governmental choice. This gave the Spanish government de facto possession and rendered somewhat irrelevant at that time the validity or otherwise of the consul's action in a foreign country. The ship's commercial owners promptly issued a writ in rem to claim possession. The dispute finally reached the House of Lords who set aside the writ appearing to be still in those days influenced by the fact that the principles of international law still embraced the seemingly sacrosanct concept that publicly owned vessels should enjoy immunity despite the employment to which they were put. The days of heavily increased participation by governments and government departments were still in the future at that stage. The *Cristina* had been requisitioned by a government for governmental purposes and beyond that the courts should not and need not look. It is not a valid counter-argument that requisitioning involves an interest very much less than ownership and may not necessarily involve a proprietary or even possessory interest at all.

It may be noted here that in 1926 an International Convention for the Unification of Certain Rules concerning the immunity of State-owned ships was drawn up. Its objects were to provide that ships owned or operated by States were to be subjected to the same rules of liability as privately owned vessels, ships of war, State-owned yachts and various other vessels owned or operated by a State; government and non-commercial service to be excepted. Although Great Britain signed the Convention she has never ratified it or adopted its provisions into her legal system by statutory enactment.

There are, of course, certain time-honoured and recognized exceptions where a court will unhesitatingly implead a foreign sovereign, obvious ones being where he has taken an interest in land or property in a different country and incurs debts or other legal responsibilities. Similarly, if a foreign sovereign incurs debts in respect of services rendered to his property within the jurisdiction of a different independent State, whether the property be land-based or maritime—he must expect his ship perhaps to be arrested under the circumstances.

However, what has been most relevant to the vast majority of situations is the question of whether or not immunity should be granted when a foreign sovereign enters voluntarily into a commercial deal with a merchant or trading company in another State and a dispute arises as a result. This becomes crucial where a commercial fleet may be owned by a department of the government—viz. Ghana, Kuwait, India. Ships are chartered in a world shipping market such as the London Baltic Exchange. It is perhaps stating the obvious that those who enter into the commercial sphere and have the advantages arising therefrom should also abide by the rules and codes of the commercial world in respect of any obligations they may thereby inherit, and foreign sovereigns and governments should *basically* not be excepted from that principle.

*Petrol Shipping Corporation* v *The Kingdom of Greece, Ministry of Commerce, Purchase Directorate* [1966] 2 Lloyd's Rep. 431, US Court of Appeal
The motor vessel *Atlantic* was chartered by the defendants from her owners, who were a United States company. A dispute subsequently arose and the shipowners appointed their own arbitrator in accordance with the provisions of the arbitration clause in the charterparty which stipulated New York arbitration. The charterers claimed sovereign immunity.

*Held*: that the charterers' claim was denied on the basis that the Purchase Directorate of the Greek Ministry was at the material time engaged in commercial dealings.

Lord Denning in a 1958 judgment (*Rahimtoola* v *Nizam of Hyderabad* [1958] AC 379, HL) summarized concisely and admirably this idea. He said

'sovereign immunity should not depend on whether a foreign government is impleaded, directly or indirectly, but rather on the nature of the dispute. Is it properly cognizable by our courts or not? If the dispute brings into question, for instance, the legislative or international transaction of a foreign government, or the policy of its executive, the court should grant immunity if asked to do so; but if the dispute concerns, for instance, the commercial transaction of a foreign government (whether carried out by its own department or agencies or by setting up separate legal entities) and it arises properly within the territorial jurisdiction of our courts, there is no ground for granting immunity.'

These words, which would seem to be a fully comprehensive test for any set of circumstances where sovereign immunity might be pleaded, also imply that one would have an eye also to the substantive laws of the country which is asked to exercise jurisdiction and not so much to its procedural laws or rules of procedure.

A legal point which must inevitably be considered is whether the two parties to the dispute had, when they entered into the original contractual relationship, mutually agreed that a particular State's law should apply to the dispute or the jurisdiction of any particular State should rule.

*The Dunelmia* [1969] 2 Lloyd's Rep. 476, CA
It was held in this case that the existence of an arbitration clause in the contract implied a voluntary submission to the jurisdiction of the arbitrators and to the supervision of them by the courts.

*The Evje* [1974] 2 Lloyd's Rep. 57, HL
An undertaking was given by the Indian High Commissioner in London.

London arbitration might have been stipulated in a charterparty, but the circumstances out of which the dispute arose may have absolutely no connexion whatsoever with Britain either geographically or as a place of residence of any persons or corporations involved as third parties in the affair. This is particularly so when the legal proceedings are in personam and there is no 'res' within the jurisdiction. What has been clearly established over the years in English courts is that the mere act of a foreign government/sovereign entering into a commercial relationship with a trader resident in a different country, even if voluntary submission to arbitration is incorporated in the agreement, has not in *itself* necessarily deprived that foreign sovereign of its right to immunity from process in that different country's courts.

Where proceedings are in rem and where the 'res' is or comes within the jurisdiction of the court and the dispute arises from a contract or commercial transaction entered into voluntarily by a foreign sovereign government then the atmosphere has been far more conducive to the court's feeling justified in not granting sovereign immunity even if the cause or causes of action arise from situations occurring entirely outside the territorial jurisdiction of the court concerned.

*The Philippine Admiral* [1974] 2 Lloyd's Rep. 568
In 1956 a treaty was concluded between the Philippines and Japan whereby Japan agreed to make available US$5,000,000 by way of war damage reparation. As part of this, Japan agreed to build a ship subsequently named the *Philippine Admiral* for the Philippine Reparation Commission. The commission entered into a contract to sell the vessel to X & Co. Under the terms of this contract it was expressly stipulated that the commission was to retain ownership of her until the full price had been paid, but remained the registered owner. X & Co operated her in the course of their business until some time in 1972. In December 1972, Y & Co chartered her. At that time she was undergoing repairs in a dockyard in Hong Kong. Y & Co sued in rem for damages for breach of contract. Z & Co sued in rem in respect of necessary disbursements made during the ship's stay in Hong Kong. X & Co entered an appearance. Later, the Philippine Reparation Commission, also a defendant in the action, applied for both writs to be set aside on the grounds that they were the owners of the ship and were entitled to sovereign immunity. Part of the purchase price was still owed to them.

*Held:* that the writ should be set aside. There were no firm rules concerning sovereign immunity, but it was clear that to support a claim for immunity there must be such an interest that the claimant could fairly claim also the exercise of dominion over the ship. On these facts, the commission's right to possession was realistic and not merely illusory. Certainly, immunity should not be granted where a vessel was not destined for public use, and there was no evidence to support such a conclusion.

The Judicial Committee of the Privy Council, before whom this matter was finally brought on appeal, ruled that the doctrine of restricted immunity did apply to actions in rem (viz. the arrest of a ship); see [1976] 1 Lloyd's Rep. 234.

One case to receive the attention of the Court of Appeal in England was *Trendtex Trading Corp* v *Central Bank of Nigeria*, below, which was one of the numerous pieces of litigation which arose out of the massive congestion which existed in 1975 outside the ports of Lagos and Apapa in Nigeria owing to large numbers of cement-carrying vessels waiting for a discharging berth. At the time it was popularly known as 'the cement queue'.

*Trendtex Trading Corp* v *Central Bank of Nigeria* [1977] 1 Lloyd's Rep. 581, CA
The facts were that the Nigerian Ministry of Defence had, in April 1975, agreed to buy 240,000 tons of cement from an export/import company in London and instructed their bankers to open a letter of credit in the seller's favour in an amount of US $14,400,000. The letter of credit, which was arranged through the Nigerian bank's London correspondents who were under no personal liability, was irrevocable. The London firm entered into a contract with the plaintiff company (Swiss) to supply thetttcement, agreeing at the same time to transfer the letter of credit. Six of the consignments comprising the total contracted quantity were shipped though not actually delivered. Four of these only were paid for by the London correspondent bank. The remaining two, together with demurrage

payments due, were not paid for in accordance with instructions received from the Nigerian bank.

The plaintiffs, Trendtex, issued a writ under which they claimed the price of the last two cement consignments and demurrage sums due generally on all six vessels. Other sundry additional losses were also claimed. Trendtex based their claim on the contract contained in the letter of credit itself independently from the contract of sale. This procedure was of itself allowable under the terms of the Uniform Customs Rules issued by the International Chamber of Commerce. The bank applied to have the writ set aside and their application was granted by the court of first instance. Trendtex appealed and argued that the defendant corporation was fundamentally in character a bank and because it happened to handle the financial affairs of the Nigerian government this did not change its character in any way. The bank argued that it was merely the servant of the federal government of Nigeria and in these particular circumstances was no more than the instrument by which the government acted. The issuing of the letter of credit, in other words, was a mere act of government.

*Held:* that the bank was not entitled to enjoy the immunity which it sought. The letter of credit arrangements was a separate independent transaction within the court's jurisdiction and as this was the basis of the plaintiff's claim, sovereign immunity was not available to the defendant bank.

This case gave the opportunity to the court to review the question of sovereign immunity generally. It has been widely thought that international legal rules are incorporated into English law so long as they do not come into conflict with English statute law. In favouring this theory, the court said that as the rationale of sovereign immunity had gradually changed over the years with governments and government departments becoming more and more engaged in commercial activities, so it was necessary for the English courts to adapt themselves to this changing concept. What should be considered in these modern times is not so much a doctine of absolute immunity but rather one of 'restrictive' immunity. This would be more in keeping with the purely commercial activities of governments and would enable courts to restrict their recognition of immunity to acts purely of a governmental nature.

There was only one serious obstacle in the way of the free application of the 'restrictive' immunity doctrine and that was the rule established and confirmed in *The Philippine Admiral* that the 'absolute' immunity rule should apply to all actions in personam. 'Restrictive' immunity could only be applied in connexion with actions in rem. However, if the theory of international law being smoothly and easily adopted into English law was followed, even this obstacle should be overcome and evaporate generally.

It is interesting to note that one of the judges in the Court of Appeal in the *Trendtex* case did not find it necessary to base his decision on, or indeed go deeply into, the question of absolute or restrictive immunity, because as he pointed out the evidence showed that the bank was never intended to be an 'emanation, arm, alter ego or even department of the government'. Indeed, its very name had an exclusively commercial 'ring' to it. Its affiliation to the government itself was restricted, if at all, solely to its role as banker and/or financial adviser.

The law was more fully clarified and confirmed when certain motions were brought by the Republic of Cuba to set aside writs and subsequent proceedings in three actions in rem brought against the vessel *I Congreso del Partido* [1981] 2 Lloyd's Rep. 367, HL, by the owners of cargo loaded on board two other vessels, both chartered by the Cuban State enterprise. The claims were for non-delivery and the circumstances arose during the period of the Chilean change of government in 1973, the buyers being Chilean. The full facts are, for the purpose of these comments, not material but the question of ownership and the nature of the acts of the Republic of Cuba which brought about the failure of the carrying vessels to deliver their sugar cargo to the rightful bill of lading holders are of great significance.

At the time of the hearing of the motions (*The I Congreso* was arrested in Sunderland, England) the law on sovereign immunity rested on *The Philippine Admiral* doctrine and the very much more recent *Trendtex* decision. *The Philippine Admiral* case established that in an action in rem against an ordinary trading vessel the rules of international law gave effect to the doctrine of restricted immunity, putting into 'the waste paper basket' the old ideas of *The Parlement Belge* and *The Porto Alexandre*, i.e. that no matter how the ship was employed, sovereign immunity was available. *The Philippine Admiral* decision 'split' the law into two seemingly irreconcilable propositions: (1) that in actions in personam a foreign sovereign is absolutely entitled to invoke sovereign immunity, and (2) that in actions in rem against an ordinary trading ship, a foreign sovereign who can be shown to own the ship may, by execution on his property, be effectively held liable in a claim in personam. It was *The Trendtex* v *Central Bank of Nigeria* case which concluded that the doctrine of restricted immunity applies to all cases whether in rem or in personam. It is now openly argued that once a sovereign descends from his throne and enters the marketplace he voluntarily divests himself of his sovereign status and is therefore no longer immune to the domestic jurisdiction of the other country's law courts.

In *The I Congreso* dispute the House of Lords had to consider whether the Republic of Cuba could rely on sovereign immunity. The act of the Republic of Cuba in withdrawing the vessel *Playa Larga* and denying the cargo to the purchasers was not an act done jure imperii (a sovereign or public act). This should be compared with an act jure gestionis (a private act). Everything done by the Republic of Cuba in relation to *Playa Larga* could have been done, and, so far as evidence goes, was done, as owners of the ship: it had not exercised, and had no need to exercise, sovereign powers. It acted, as any owner of the ship would act, through Mambisa, the managing operator. It invoked no governmental authority. If immunity were to be granted the moment that any decision taken by the trading state was shown to be not commercially, but politically, inspired, the 'restrictive theory' would almost cease to have any content and trading relations as to state-owned ships would become impossible. It is precisely to protect private traders against politically inspired breaches, or wrongs, that the restrictive theory allowed states to be brought before a municipal court. The House of Lords accepted the decision of *The Philippine Admiral* in that as regards state-owned trading vessels, actions, whether commenced in rem, are to be decided according to the 'restrictive' theory (albeit too restrictive). The existence of a governmental purpose or motive will not convert what would otherwise be an act jure gestionis, or an act of private law, into one done jure imperii.

In considering under the restrictive theory whether state immunity should be granted or not the court had to consider the whole context in which the claim against the state is made with a view to deciding whether the relevant act(s) upon which the claim is based should, in that context, be considered as fairly within an area of activity, trading or commercial, or otherwise of a private law character in which the state has chosen to engage, or whether the relevant act(s) should be considered as having been done outside that area, and within the sphere of governmental or sovereign activity.

As regards the vessel *Marble Island* which was not allowed to enter the port of Valparaiso, the House of Lords decided that the actions of the Master in connexion with the discharge and sale of the cargo in Vietnam, carried out on the instructions of the Cuban government and under the supervision of its representatives, were properly to be regarded as having been done under private law and not as an exercise of sovereign powers.

These events gave rise to a further dispute between the sellers and buyers of the cargo in *The Playa Larga* [1983] 2 Lloyd's Rep. 171. The Court of Appeal rejected the defence of act of state. The decisions implemented by Cubazucar, a state-trading enterprise in Cuba, were jointly made with the Cuban government. This activity was a trading rather than a governmental activity. What the Cuban government did was to induce breaches of contract by Cubazucar and it was the nature of the act that mattered not the motive behind it.

The gradual development and shaping of the rules of sovereign immunity in respect of ships by process of court interpretation of actions in rem and in personam over the years has now been interrupted and presumably crystallized by statute in the UK by the passing of the State Immunity Act 1978. This Act is intended, amongst other things, to set out provisions in the UK with regard to legal proceedings whether it be by or against other sovereign states. It is further intended to give recognition to judgments given against the UK in the court of sovereign States who are party to the European Convention on State Immunity, described briefly in the statute's text as the Brussels Convention. In this respect, the statute is another inevitable development arising from the entry of the UK into the European Union and its becoming a full member thereof.

Section 10 of the Act is devoted to ships used for commercial purposes. The full text of this section is as follows:

10(1) This section applies to—
(a) Admiralty proceedings; and
(b) Proceedings in any claim which could be made the subject of Admiralty proceedings.

(2) A State is not immune as respects—
(a) an action in rem against a ship belonging to that State; or
(b) an action in personam for enforcing a claim in connection with such a ship, if, at the time when the cause of action arose, the ship was in use or intended for use for commercial purposes.

(3) Where an action in rem is brought against a ship belonging to a State for enforcing a claim in connection with another ship belonging to that State, sub-section (2)(a) above does not apply as respects the first-mentioned ship unless, at the time when the cause of action relating to the other ship arose, both ships were in use or intended for use for commercial purposes.

(4) A State is not immune as respects—
(a) an action in rem against a ship belonging to that State if both the cargo and the ship carrying it were, at the time when the cause of action arose, in use or intended for use for commercial purposes; or

(b) an action in personam for enforcing a claim in connection with such a cargo if the ship carrying it was then in use or intended for use as aforesaid.

(5) In the foregoing provisions references to a ship or cargo belonging to a State include references to a ship or cargo in its possession or control or in which it claims an interest; and, subject to sub-section (4) above, sub-section (2) above applies to property other than a ship as it applies to a ship.

(6) Sections 3 to 5 above do not apply to proceedings of the kind described in sub-section (1) above if the State in question is a party to the Brussels Convention and the claim relates to the operation of a ship owned or operated by that State, the carriage of cargo or passengers on any such ship or the carriage of cargo owned by that State on any other ship.

In *The Philippine Admiral* litigation there was a clear-cut difference in treatment between an action in rem and an action in personam. The House of Lords in *The I Congreso* stated:

'I would unhesitantly affirm as part of English law the advance made by *The Philippine Admiral* with the reservation that the decision was perhaps unnecessarily restrictive in, apparently, confirming the departure of made to actions in rem. In truth an action in rem as regards a ship, if it proceeds beyond the initial stages, is itself in addition an action in personam— . . . It should be borne in mind that no distinction between actions in rem and actions in personam is generally recognized elsewhere so that it would in any event be desirable to liberate English law from an anomaly if that existed. In fact there is no anomaly and no distinction. The effect of *The Philippine Admiral* if accepted, as I would accept it, is that as regards state-owned trading vessels, actions, whether commenced in rem or not, are to be decided according to the "restrictive" theory.'

Subsection (2) of section 10 of the 1978 Act makes no such distinction between actions in rem and actions in personam. The criterion is not the type of legal action commenced but the simple question as to whether or not, at the time when the cause of action arose, the ship was either being used or intended to be used for commercial purposes. Slight protection is given to sovereign States by subsection (3) whereunder a State may still receive immunity from legal process against a sister ship unless that sister ship is also being used commercially or intended to be so used. Subsection (5) clarifies any doubt which may still exist about the expression 'belonging to' which is designed to include the possession or control of a vessel or the existence of an interest in it.

In the case of *Alcom* v *Republic of Columbia* [1984] 1 Lloyd's Rep. 368 (albeit not an Admiralty case) the Court of Appeal decided that one had to regard the transactions under scrutiny rather than to the reasons why the transactions were undertaken for the purposes of the State Immunity Act 1978. This point was taken in *The I Congreso* in which the House of Lords gave an example of a commercial trading or private law transaction as the ordering of uniforms for the maintenance of the army, the latter being a sovereign function. It is the nature of the act and not its purpose that is decisive. In *The I Congreso* case, Lord Wilberforce quoted with approval the following passage in the German case of the claim against the Empire of Iran:

'As a means for determining the distinction between acts jure imperii and jure gestionis one should rather refer to the nature of the State transaction or the resulting legal relationships, and not to the motive or purpose of the State activity. It thus depends upon whether the foreign State has acted in exercise of its sovereign authority, that is in public law, or like a private person, that is in private law.'[3]

*Kuwait Airways Corporation v Iraqi Airways Company and Republic of Iraq* [1995] 2 Lloyd's Rep. 317

During the Iraqi invasion of Kuwait, the Iraqi Airways Company (IAC), a corporation owned and controlled by the Republic of Iraq, at the direction of the Iraqi Minister of Transport and Communications arranged for IAC personnel to fly 10 civilian aircraft owned by Kuwait Airways Corporation from Kuwait Airport to Iraq. Six of the aircraft were flown to Iran where they were interned. The House of Lords decided that the taking of the aircraft and their removal from Kuwait Airport to Iraq constituted an exercise of governmental power by the State of Iraq: the participation by IAC in supplying engineers and pilots who performed the mundane tasks of preparing the aircraft for flying and then flying them from Kuwait to Iraq was not a job of work but was so closely involved with the state of Iraq in the last stage of the enterprise which entailed both the seizure of the aircraft and their removal to Iraq to be used for such purposes as the government of Iraq should direct. IAC in so acting was acting in the exercise of sovereign authority. The possession and control of the aircraft were unlawfully transferred to IAC. The House of Lords decided that it could not be said that IAC's retention and use of the aircraft as its own constituted acts done in the exercise of sovereign authority; they were acts done by it in consequence of the vesting or purported vesting of the aircraft in it by legislative degree. The fact that Resolution 369 was itself a governmental act by the State of Iraq could not of itself render IAC's consequent retention and use of the aircraft a governmental act; the characterization as an act juri imperii of the earlier involvement by the entity in the act of seizure could not on the facts be determinative of the characterization of the subsequent retention and use of the property by the state entity following the formal vesting of the property in the entity by a legislative act of the State. IAC in treating the aircraft as its own was doing so pursuant to the Iraqi legislation which vested the aircraft in IAC and by so doing it could not be said to have acted in the exercise of sovereign immunity. Default judgment was granted against IAC and the action remitted to the Commercial Court so that it could proceed against IAC in relation to those claims of the plaintiffs in respect of which IAC could not rely on state immunity.

3. See now the State Immunity (Merchant Shipping) Order 1997, which came into force on 1 November 1997.

CHAPTER 5

# CHARTERPARTIES

A charterparty is *the* contract, a private contract between two principal parties. It is this one basic fact that distinguishes a voyage charterparty from what is too loosely described as a bill of lading contract. A bill of lading is *never the* contract. It is, when first issued, the best available evidence of the contract of carriage between carrier and shipper (almost certainly the only written evidence) and at best only eventually is said to *contain* the contract when it reaches the hands, properly and unconditionally, of an 'innocent' third party for value.

Thus a charterparty is a private agreement between two parties, individual or corporate. Like any other contract only those who entered into it can sue or be sued upon it. Charterparties fall basically into three categories—demise (or to use an American expression, bareboat), time and voyage.

## DEMISE CHARTERPARTIES

It is not intended to comment in depth on this type of charter but merely to describe its distinctive features briefly. Demise charterparties (or 'bareboat' —being an expression coined by American oil companies) are agreements whereunder the charterer literally 'takes over' the ship and has possession of it together with the right of management and control. One of the main features of such a charterparty is that the charterer has the right to engage and pay the Master and crew so that they are his, the charterers, employees for the period of the charter. The charterer will also be responsible for victualling and supplying the ship. Thus, the shipowner fades into the background, as it were, and merely collects his hire payments for the period of the charter. It is for these reasons that a demise or bareboat charterer is virtually on a par with the owner of a ship in regard to the scope and range of his exposure to liabilities and thus a demise charterer would more advantageously obtain his liability or P & I insurance in a shipowner's P & I Association despite the fact that he is only a charterer and not the actual owner. By reason of the fact that the charterer is the engager and employer of the Master and crew, the demise charterer is the principal party to the contract of carriage contained in bills of lading covering cargo carried on the chartered ship. In practical terms a demise charter is used as a method of financing the acquisition of newly constructed ships. The party providing the finance whether it be a bank or financial institution takes on the role of shipowner (in name only) and the charterer by demise operates the vessel and trades it for his own account in the normal way. It would be fair to say that the nature of a demise or bareboat charterparty is a lease of the ship, similar to a hire purchase arrangement, rather than a simple agreement for the hire or use of the ship.

## TRIP CHARTERS

Charterparty contracts which go under this heading are a 'hybrid'. Being on a time form and remuneration being by way of a daily rate of hire, they logically fall within the broader genus of time charterparties. However, they have features which give them the flavour of a voyage charter, not the least of which is that the geographical route, together with named ports, is included in the charterparty wording. Thus the voyage which the charterer intends that the ship is to perform is delineated together with the charterer's estimate of how long that performance is likely to last. Very frequently after that stated number of days, two extra words are inserted e.g. 'about 50/60 days *without guarantee*'.

The logical effect of these two extra words has been the subject of discussion in legal circles for a long time but, strangely, judicial pronouncements have been rare. Since the previous edition, however, London's commercial court has dealt with the point in the *Lendoudis Evangelos 2* ([1997] 1 Lloyd's Rep. 404). The wording in that case was 'about 70/80 days without guarantee'. The trip in fact lasted 103 days and the shipowner claimed for wrongful detention for the excess. The case was put before an arbitrator in the first instance. The shipowner argued that the estimate of duration should be given both in good faith and upon reasonable grounds. The arbitrator said that the displaying of good faith was the only requirement of the charterer. He went on to say that the test of good faith was whether or not the statement was made reasonably at the time of making the trip charter fixture. The arbitrator awarded damages against the charterer on the basis that there had been no reasonable grounds for that estimate, i.e. the charterer had failed the good faith test. In the subsequent court case the court held that it was solely required of the charterer that he made his estimate in good faith, that the test of good faith was *not* whether it had been made on reasonable grounds, but merely that the charterer should have 'genuinely believed' at the time of fixing that the trip contemplated would last (on those facts) between 70 and 80 days. The owner's claim failed. This decision, in the author's view, leaves loose ends. What, for example, constitutes genuine belief? How much 'checking up' on previous experience should a charterer be expected to do before his estimate becomes indisputably the product of genuine belief? Whereas the test of good faith has been defined, the test of genuine belief remains not so. The *Lendoudis* case follows the decision in another (unreported) in 1988 when the court said that the words in question should be classed merely in the category of representation which in turn required only the exercise of good faith in its making.

One frequently encountered dispute emerging from the use of trip charters is the question of determining the correct measure of damages flowing from a repudiation by the charterer because of e.g. an inability by the charterer to supply the intended cargo (this may be because a sub-charterer has defaulted in that regard). Trip charters do not ordinarily specify the *amount* of cargo to be carried. They will, of course, specify the type of cargo, e.g. fertilizer. Thus in assessing the damages flowing from a repudiation of a trip charter, regard should be had not to the notional loading of a full and complete cargo and the subsequent length of a notional voyage to carry and discharge and the daily hire payment over that estimated period, but rather to what are the minimum obligations which the defaulting charterer should be content to discharge. This legal principle was put forward in the *World Navigator* ([1982] 2 Lloyd's Rep. 23). In other words, it is wrong to have in contemplation the voyage (with cargo) which might have been performed and use that as a yardstick for calculating a measure of damages. Rather the question should be asked—what was the least unfavourable method (to the charterer) of performing what was his original contractual obligation, however reasonable or unreasonable that might appear to be?

## SLOT CHARTERPARTIES

This has reference to the carriage of containers, or to use current jargon, TEUs (20-foot equivalent units). The shipowner or operator 'rents out' or hires a 'piece' of space (a percentage of the total space available on the vessel) for carrying TEUs in return for which he receives hire calculated in accordance with the number of slots (accommodation for each TEU) payable whether or not those slots or spaces are actually used.

## TIME CHARTERPARTIES

As the word implies they are agreements to hire a vessel for a period of time. Under the provisions of the time charterparty the shipowner agrees that the ship named in the document, including her Master and crew, shall be placed at the disposal of the charterer for his use and employment over a defined period of time. His use of the ship may be subject to certain restrictions, e.g. he may only employ the ship in lawful trades, only within defined trading limits and he may also be limited as to the types of cargoes he will be permitted to carry during the charter period. The owner remains responsible for insurances on his ship. The remuneration for the use of the ship in this manner is customarily paid on the basis of an agreed daily hire rate payable monthly or semi-monthly in advance. A fundamental feature of a time charter is that the charterer has no possession or control of the vessel. The Master and crew remain in the employment of the shipowner and at all times are his servants in law. It is this very feature that sets apart from a simple time charter (or period charter as it is sometimes called) the demise (or to use an American oil company coined word 'bareboat') charter under which form it is a fundamental term that the charterer may engage, employ and pay the Master and crew. It is this fact together with the legal principle that a Master (the legal meaning of the word) is accountable in law for the consequences of the act, neglects and defaults of his servants which puts the range of liabilities which a demise (or bareboat) charterer is exposed roughly on a par with a head owner's range of liabilities. It is for this reason that a demise charterer seeking liability insurance by way of Club (as opposed to market) is recommended to approach for membership/cover a shipowner's Club rather than obtain charterers' liability insurance whether by way of market cover or a mutual.

To draw an analogy from the use of land property, actual ownership of a ship could be said to be akin to freehold ownership, a demise charterer roughly akin to a leasehold owner of unfurnished property with an option to purchase and a time charterer tenant renting furnished property.

## SUBJECT DETAILS (CHARTERPARTIES GENERALLY)

A vexed question has been to what extent is a charterparty agreement binding when the parties, as a result of recapitulating exchanges are 'ad idem' on significant/major terms but have stipulated 'subject details'. The answer (see *The Junior K* [1988] 2 Lloyd's Rep. 583) is that it is not. The intention of the parties derived from the use of the qualifying expression 'subject details' is that they do not regard themselves as legally bound until *all* details are agreed. Certainly the printed Gencon form contains options which need clarifying and also in its fully concluded form usually contains many insertions, riders and amendments. Where, however, in a voyage charterparty the two parties during the course of negotiations failed to make use of the phrase 'subject to details' although they appreciate the significance of it, and nothing of importance has in fact been left unagreed, the assumption would be that a binding contract has been concluded (*Granit SA* v. *Benship* [1994] 1 Lloyd's Rep. 526).

## OBLIGATIONS OF SEAWORTHINESS (TIME OR VOYAGE CHARTERPARTIES)

Ensuring that his vessel is seaworthy is one of the most fundamental obligations of an owner (or of a disponent owner if the vessel is sub-chartered). The duty may be an absolute one (it is under the common law of England) or it may be tempered by the need only to exercise due diligence to make the ship seaworthy (e.g. the minimum inescapable standard required) when the Hague (or Hague Visby) Rules are voluntarily incorporated in the charterparty by a clause paramount. Seaworthiness is a subject so vast that only a cursory mention can be included in this text. A broad definition might be a fitness of the ship to withstand the expected hazards of the contemplated voyage laden with cargo. Thus the various aspects of seaworthiness would include the 'unofficial' concept of 'cargo worthiness' which reflects the fitness of the vessel in those parts which have direct reference to, and direct contact with, cargo, e.g. the holds being clean and generally fit to receive the chartered cargo (*The Good Friend* [1984] 2 Lloyd's Rep. 586).

Generally speaking under a voyage charter (in the absence of a clause paramount, i.e. a clause incorporating the Hague Rules) the owner's duty is to furnish a seaworthy ship when it is presented for loading. Under a time charter (again in the absence of any governing Hague or Visby Rules) the ship is to be delivered to the charterer in a seaworthy condition. This, however, is not a continuing warranty but there is normally in any time charterparty a separate and independent obligation placed upon the owner, namely to maintain the ship in a thoroughly efficient state throughout the currency of the charterparty. Thus the exact wording in the NYPE charterparty reflecting this duty is ' . . . maintain her class and keep the vessel in a thoroughly efficient state in hull, machinery and equipment for and during the service'.

A frequently used test to determine whether or not an unseaworthy condition exists is 'would the owners had they known of the particular defect, have sent the ship to sea without first remedying it?' Aspects of unseaworthiness range over a wide area and can be as serious as extensive cracks in the shell plating or as seemingly minor as a third engineer who is uncertificated.

Whereas generally under the voyage charterparty terms the owner gives an absolute undertaking that his ship is seaworthy when presented for loading and indeed such has been symbolically and traditionally expressed in the charterparty itself by words descriptive of the ship such as the 'good ship' or an expression such as 'tight, staunch and true', the commonly used Gencon form contains in its printed Clause 2 a significant variation from this, very much more in the shipowner's favour. It provides that in respect of loss or damage to or delay in delivery of goods (cargo) the shipowner shall only be exposed to liability if such loss or damage or delay results from his *personal* want of due diligence or that of his manager in making the ship seaworthy. If the want of due diligence to which the loss/damage is causally linked is that of the Master, crew or an agent, then the owner shall not be liable. The Gencon, like any other charterparty, is not mandatorily subject to a regime of rights and liabilities such as the Hague or Hague Visby Rules but if such was voluntarily incorporated it would have the effect of widening the owners' liability for unseaworthiness from the very narrow position to the minimum requirement under the international regimes that the carrier shall ' . . . use due diligence to make the ship seaworthy . . . '. This would include the diligence (or lack of it) of the carriers' servants or agents.

## TIME CHARTERS

Being aware of the limited space in this book which is earmarked for the subject of charterparties, I intend to analyse and comment upon selected important provisions of the time charterparty, taking as role model the NYPE form although occasional references to other forms of time charterparties may be made.

### *Performance—speed and consumption*

The preamble to a time charterparty contains words which describe the capabilities of the vessel, e.g. that she is 'capable of steaming fully laden throughout the period of the charterparty under good weather conditions about 14.5 knots on a consumption of about 14 tonnes IFO etc.'.

The word 'about' is not merely casual wording, it has a significance which the English Courts have habitually interpreted as a tolerance of half a knot on the speed and five per cent on the daily rate of consumption of bunkers. Arbitrators in London also tend to apply the same interpretation. It is, however, not an exact definition and the tolerance may be varied in accordance with the type and size of the vessel. The effect of *deleting* the word 'about' from the printed wording would seem to have the effect of making the warranty more precise. The 'spin-off' from this would be that arbitrators would tend to disregard a 'de minimis' defence by owners of a formulated under-performance claim by the charterers which was in a very modest amount only.

The charterparty warranted speed and consumption rates are to be taken to relate to good weather conditions, i.e. free of the beneficial or adverse effects of current, wind and waves.

In *The Gas Enterprise* [1993] 2 Lloyd's Rep. 352 the time charterer drew up speed calculations on the basis that if the vessel has under performed in periods of good weather, she must have under performed in bad weather as well to the extent that the under performance was not entirely due to the bad weather. Conversely, the owners' calculations were based on the charterparty containing an undertaking as to the performance on each sea passage, but confined to periods of weather up to and including Beaufort force four of wind and wave. The Court of Appeal confirmed the lower court's finding for charterers. If this owner intended to warrant a ship's performance only in good weather conditions, he should have so stated in clearly express language. Unless he does so there is no reason to confine the vessel capacity to perform to periods when the weather was force four or less. The warranty should apply in this case to all voyages whether cargo-laden or in ballast. In order to determine properly whether there has been truly a breach of either speed or consumption warranty, reference must be made to the vessel's deck log books for the voyage in question supplemented by weather data supplied by a reputable weather routing organisation such as Ocean Routes.

Originally there was doubt as to whether the warranted speed stated in the charterparty referred to (a) the time when the charterparty was concluded or (b) the time when the ship was delivered into the hands of the charterer at the commencement of the charter period or (c) was a continuing warranty. Case law dealt with this point as follows:

*Lorentzen* v *White* (1943) 74 Ll.L.Rep. 161
The speed warranted in the charterparty was the speed which this vessel was capable of performing at the time the charterparty was concluded (i.e. the date of the charter).

But in *The Apollonius* [1978] 1 Lloyd's Rep. 53 the court held that the speed described (or warranted) in the charterparty applied at the date of *delivery* under the charter. The facts in this case were that a vessel's bottom had become fouled and seriously affected the ship's performance. The fouling occurred between the concluding of the relevant charterparty and the taking of delivery by the charter.

The idea that the warranty continues throughout the charter period has ceased to find favour (see *The Al Bida* [1987] 1 Lloyd's Rep. 124.

Thus case law witnesses to speed and consumption warranties not continuing throughout the period of the charter, but applying only initially. It is accepted, however, that an additional cause of action could lie, additional that is to a breach of warranty, on the basis of a breach of obligation (in standard time charterparties) to maintain the ship in an efficient and fit state (which can be said to include the maintenance of the warranted speed under the stated fair conditions).

### *How should speed and consumption claims be calculated?*

There are two alternative methods used by arbitrators in London and the author does not intend to comment upon which is the more widely used or the more favoured. Neither does he propose to venture an opinion upon which is the better method. He merely describes below each of the alternative methods of calculation (with hypothetical illustrations) and leaves the readers to decide for themselves. The basic data on each side can be derived from the ship's logbook on the one hand and the data furnished by an independent weather bureau on the other. In an ideal world, the data from these two sources should match, but in practice that is rarely the case. Once an under-performance in good conditions has been established a loss can be proved for *all* conditions (*The Didymi* [1987] 2 Lloyd's Rep. 166 and [1988] 2 Lloyd's Rep. 108).

## Method (a)

Assuming that the charterparty warranties relate to fair weather conditions in calm water (i.e. not taking into account any adverse, or even favourable, effects of current) the following process should be followed:

(1) Ascertain the vessel's performance in calm water in good weather conditions (as defined by the charterparty terms, e.g. very commonly winds not exceeding Beaufort force 4).
To achieve this (a) calculate the vessel's day's run for each day of the voyage in question (evidence provided by the ship's logbooks) (b) narrow this down to the day's run in *calm* water by removing the effect of any current.

(2) Next, calculate the total distance steamed through the water (free of the effect of current).

(3) Subtract from the figure achieved in (2) above the distance steamed on any days on which winds in excess of force-4 were recorded (this may be none too simple in that the log books may not record similar figures to the weather bureau on wind speed). Also to be subtracted at this stage should be the distance steamed during any periods of deliberately reduced speed at the charterer's orders.

(4) The figure reached in (3) above will provide the 'good weather distance'.

(5) Next, the 'good weather *speed*' should be calculated. This is done by dividing the good weather distance by the good weather steaming time. The good weather steaming time is the time obtained by subtracting the *bad* weather day's steaming time from the total voyage time. Prior to the above subtractions, there should be subtracted from the good weather steaming time, any time steamed at reduced speed on the charterer's orders.

(6) At this point it will be now possible to calculate an under performance claim—i.e. where the time which the vessel would have taken at her good weather speed exceeds the time she would have taken at her warranted speed (adjusted by the allowance representing the word 'about'—customarily, though not universally, taken as half a knot). The value of the claim is obtained by multiplying the time lost by the charterparty daily (or pro rata) rate of hire.

Re bunker consumption, the procedure for determining whether or not a performance claim lies will be to take the vessel's daily rate of consumption in good weather, calculated by recording her consumption on those days when the wind speed was force-4 or less, then calculate, by using that rate, how much bunkers would have been used up had the whole voyage been performed in good weather conditions at the good weather speed. Then work out the maximum consumption (allowing a margin, e.g. 0.5 per cent) representing the word 'about' in the charterparty terms with the vessel steaming at the *warranted* speed. When the good weather consumption exceeds the warranted consumption a claim for over consumption could be presented.

It is arguable, conversely, that when the ship's consumption for the voyage under scrutiny is less than the minimum allowed under the charterparty, the shipowners could claim for 'under' consumption.

*Illustration*

| | | | |
|---|---|---|---|
| Total Distance: | 3594 | Steaming Time: | 302 |
| Slow steaming | -425 | | -38.5 |
| | 3169 | | 263.5 |
| Good Weather Distance | 2597 | | |
| Good Weather Steaming Time | 213.5 | | |
| Good Weather Speed: | 12.16 | | |

| | | |
|---|---|---|
| Time For Voyage at Good Weather Speed: | 3169/12.16 | = 260.608 |
| Max. Time Allowed at C/P Speed: | 3169/14 | = 226.360 |
| Actual Time Lost: | | = 34.248 |

Performance Speed Claim: 34.248hrs. @ $6225/day = US$ 8883.075

Bunker Consumption

Good Weather Consumption per day: 119.3/213.5×24 = 13.43 tons

Total consumption if good weather had prevailed: $\frac{3169 \times 13.43}{12.16 \times 24}$ = 145.832 tons

Max. Allowed Consumption per C/P: $\frac{3169 \times 14.7}{14.5 \times 24}$ = 133.863 tons

Excess Consumption: = 11.969 tons

Bunker Claim: 11.969×$75 = US$ 897.675

TOTAL CLAIM: US$ 9780.75

**Method (b)**

(1) Take charterparty warranted speed.
(2) If word 'about' qualifies the figure, subtract half knot.
(3) Subtract something from the figure in (2) above to represent 'weather and current factor'.

(4) Resultant figure is required average speed.
(5) Take the voyage distance (in nautical miles).
(6) Take the time actually taken to perform that distance.
(7) If the time actually taken is longer than the time which should have been taken at the required average speed, the difference represents the time lost and this forms the speed claim.

An illustration of a speed and consumption claim using this method is given below:

| | | |
|---|---|---|
| C/P Speed Knots | : | 12.0 knots |
| 'About' factor | : | –0.5 knots |
| Weather – – : : – – | : | –0.7 knots |
| Current – – : : – – | : | –0.1 knots |
| Required av. speed | : | 10.7 knots |
| Distance | : | 2474.0 nautical miles |
| Time en route | : | 270.8 hours |
| Voyage should have taken | : | 2474.0/10.7 = 231.2 hrs |
| Time lost | = | 270.8 – 231.2 = 39.6 hrs |
| Speed claim | = | 39.6 hrs = 1.65 days |
| Warranted consumption | : | 19 LT = 19.3 mt IFO per day |
| Calculated cons | = | 231.2/24×19.3 = 185.9 mt IFO |
| As reported | = | 192.4 mt IFO |
| Over consumption | = | 192.4 – 185.9 = 6.5 mt IFO |
| Warranted consumption | : | 2.0 mt Do per day |
| Calculated cons | = | 231.2/24×2.0 = 19.3 mt MDO |
| As reported | = | 23.0 mt MDO |
| Over consumption | = | 23.0 – 19.3 = 3.7 mt MDO |

### *Charterparty bunkering disputes*

Under the terms of a time charterparty the charterer is obliged to provide and pay for bunker fuel (the term 'bunkers' derived from the old days when vessels were driven by coal). Clause 2 of the NYPE charterparty includes the words 'the charterer shall provide and pay for all fuel except as otherwise agreed . . . ' That the charterers are supplying and paying for the bunkers for the duration of the charter period (appropriate financial adjustments are made for bunkers on board at delivery and conversely ROB at re-delivery) means that the law regards the time charterer as owner of the bunkers with all the disadvantages that that implies, e.g. the risk of an arrest of bunkers to secure some claim against that charterer possibly wholly unconnected with the ship upon which the bunkers are or with the owner of that same ship.

These comments shall be restricted to two points of legal concern.

(1) To what extent is a time charterer legally liable for supplying fuel to a vessel which is of sub-standard quality and (2) what legal action can a shipowner take if he thinks his ship's engines have been damaged by poor quality fuel?

Regarding (1), is the charterer under an absolute duty to supply quality fuel or is he merely obliged to use due diligence? There is a lack of reported case law on this point which hampers the making of a clear-cut answer. However, London arbitrators have been known to favour the alternative of absolute duty/strict liability. Leave to appeal was recently granted from an award favouring an absolute duty which indicates that the due diligence theory was at least arguable, but the award was not after all disturbed.

Casual observers might say that an absolute duty is too much of an imposition to put on a charterer particularly as he may not have been given any clue as to what degree of quality was acceptable. The trend, however, throughout the 1980s and into the 1990s has been towards one of absolute duty to provide fit bunkers with no sign of a contrary view in the courts.

Regarding (2), the shipowner wishing to claim damages for physical damage to his ship's engines may sue either the charterer who has supplied the bunkers, his cause of action being breach of charter, or the bunker supplier, but in the latter event his cause of action would be in tort because he, the owner, has no contract with the supplier. If he elects to sue the charterer he might find the first hurdle easy to clear, i.e. to persuade the arbitrators that the charterer had an absolute duty to provide fit bunkers but would likely find it difficult to discharge the burden of proof (which would be his as claimant) that there was a link in the chain of causation between the sub-standard fuel supplied and the damage caused to the engines, e.g. (a) was the damage to, e.g. piston rings excessive or merely the result of fair wear and tear and (b) was it solely caused by impurities in the fuel or could it perhaps have been inadequate or faulty lubricating, e.g. negligence of the ship's own engineering staff. The burden of proof on this issue is heavy and the shipowner would need persuasive evidence from reputable technical experts to assist him towards possible success.

### *Safe ports*

In a time charterparty there is usually in the printed terms a warranty given by the charterer that he will only trade the vessel between good and safe ports. The word 'good' is in the context archaic and can be dismissed from this commentary as of no modern day significance. A *safe* port is defined in the classic case of *The Eastern City* [1958] 2 Lloyd's Rep. 127, 131 in this quotation from the judgment of Sellers J.

'A port will not be safe unless, in the relevant period of time, the particular ship can reach it, use it and return from it without, in the absence of some abnormal occurrence, being exposed to danger which cannot be avoided by good navigation or seamanship.'

A port can be considered unsafe for two broad general reasons:

(1) a physical feature (e.g. an underwater obstruction to navigation);
(2) a political happening (e.g. a riot causing the throwing of bombs).

Additionally, if the *system* of the port itself, as contrasted to the individual negligent acts or omissions of individuals within the port administration, is defective, the port will be held to be unsafe (see *The Khian Sea* [1977] 2 Lloyd's Rep. 439.

The question as to whether a port is safe or unsafe is one of fact. The question as to whether there has been a breach of warranty is one of law. The safety or otherwise of a particular port must be related to the particular ship which is used and which is the subject of the charterparty which contains the safe port warranty under scrutiny, e.g. if a ship is physically too big to manoeuvre reasonably within the confines of the harbour waters of a relatively small port, it is hardly likely to be the characteristics of the port or its administration which is deficient.

As per *The Eastern City* definition, if the sole and only cause of the damage which has resulted from what is alleged to have been a breach of the safe port warranty is a failure of the Master and crew to exhibit the standard of navigation and seamanship expected of them, then there has been no breach of warranty.

Extensive discussion of the safe port warranty in time charterparties took place in the House of Lords on the final appeal of *The Evia (No 2)* [1982] 2 Lloyd's Rep. 307 which became (and has remained) the classic case law on this legal issue. The root of the dispute which the court deeply analysed was at what point of time, if at all, has the safe port warranty been breached or conversely at the time when the charterers order the ship to proceed to port X should port X be *prospectively* safe? Their Lordships said yes to that question, meaning that the charterer is making a forecast promise that when the ship reaches the nominated port, that port will be safe. The second obligation imposed upon the charterer is that if the nominated port becomes unsafe after the nomination has been made but before the ship reaches it, the charterer must make a fresh nomination of an alternative (safe) port and redirect the ship to it. If the ship has already reached the originally designated port and it then becomes unsafe, the charterer has a residual obligation to order it out if there still remains an opportunity to do so.

Safety of a port, because of the political angle, is heavily interrelated to the existence of war risk-type situations. *The Evia* case itself was born out of the sudden eruption of the Iran/Iraq war in 1980, destined as it was to last for 10 years, rendering 'overnight' the port of Basra unsafe.

In *The Product Star (No 2)* the charterparty contained a clause which excluded ports which the owners in their own discretion believed to be dangerous. The Commercial Court ruled that an expression of that belief must be made honestly and reasonably on the facts available. The word 'dangerous' was to be construed by reference to the circumstances existing at the date of the time charter and to the time charterparty terms as a whole. This included knowledge that certain ports (within a war zone) were permitted and the charterers had funded a part of the owner's war risk insurance premium.

In an appeal hearing in 1993, the judges commented that the exercise by the owners or their Master of a contractual discretion to decline to proceed to a port perceived by them to be unsafe must be done honestly and bona fide and having regard to the other provisions of the contract which gave them the discretion initially. Discretion must not be used arbitrarily, capriciously or unreasonably.

In reference to the extent of the risk likely to be encountered, the Court of Appeal in *The Saga Cob* [1992] 2 Lloyd's Rep. 545 ruled that a port will not be considered to be prospectively unsafe because of guerrilla attack unless the political risk is sufficiently serious to cause a reasonable shipowner or Master to decline to send his ship there. In ruling thus they reversed the lower court's decision that the determination as to whether a guerrilla attack was a characteristic of the port was made on the basis of whether at the date the vessel was ordered there was a foreseeable risk of guerrilla attack. A risk a little more than negligible was sufficient to put charterers in breach.

### *Off-hire*

The right of a charterer to put a ship 'off-hire' is an express contractual right and is contained in specific charterparty wording. In the NYPE form the printed off-hire clause is Clause 15. It reads as follows:

> 'That in the event of the loss of time from deficiency of men or stores, fire, breakdown or damages to hull machinery or equipment, grounding, detention by average accidents to ship or cargo, dry-docking for the purpose of preventing the full working of the vessel, the payment of hire shall cease for the time thereby lost; and if upon the voyage the speed be reduced by defect in or breakdown of any part of her hull, machinery or equipment, the time so lost, and thereof, and all extra expenses shall be deducted from the hire'.

## Net loss of time

It is known by those who are required to interpret it (e.g. lawyers, defence club claims men) as a 'net loss of time' clause. This means that only the actual (net) loss of time is taken into account when calculating the period over which it is intended to place the ship off-hire. The principle of net loss of time can produce the anomaly that a ship can be wholly or partially disabled but still the charterer may not have suffered a loss of time in actual fact.

In the *Ira* [1995] 1 Lloyd's Rep. 103 there was an agreement between the parties that after discharge of cargo at Ravenna the vessel would be dry-docked (at Piraeus). Dry-docking was completed on 24 January 1992 and the owners offered the ship back to charterers on dropping off of pilot off Piraeus at noon the next day. The charterers argued that the time actually lost to them was from dropping off of pilot off Ravenna. Owners said the voyage Ravenna/Piraeus was not time lost to the charterers because her next engagement was loading in the Black Sea and a deviation to Piraeus after leaving Ravenna was only a slight geographical deviation off that route. The arbitrator favoured the owners' argument. On appeal by the charterers, the court upheld the arbitrator and said that the burden is upon the charterer to prove the off-hire event and its causative effect, and to prove that thereby he had actually lost time (not merely a paper loss). It was not simply a matter of showing an off-hire event and its duration and complaining that the time was automatically lost therefrom.

The right to off-hire is only available when one of a specific expressed list of incidents has occurred which causes the ship to be in less than full working order in turn depriving the charterer of the use of the vessel (for which he is paying valuable hire money) for the purposes for which he is immediately requiring it. Basic illustrations of immediate requirements are that an engine breakdown when the ship is in port working cargo does not prejudice the charterer's continued use of the ship. Conversely, the fact that a winch is out of action whilst the vessel is at sea does not affect the charterer's uninterrupted use of the vessel at that time.

## Events preventing the full working of the vessel

It is well established case law that the incident which gives rise to the forming of an intention in the charterer's mind to off-hire the ship is one which, if the charterer's action is to succeed, must prevent the full working of the vessel. As in the interpretation of any clause which is the basis for any dispute, there are 'grey' areas, probably the most commonly met being when there are difficulties with the cargo on board resulting in delay to the ship. *The Aquacharm* [1980] 2 Lloyd's Rep. 237 is a case in point. The vessel was performing a time charter trip on the NYPE form. The Master was under instructions to load to maximum draft contemplating passage to the Panama Canal, but omitted to allow for the transiting of a fresh-water lake being part of the canal system. He was denied entry and forced to discharge some cargo to adjust his draft for canal transit. The charterers contended that the lack of a correct draft caused the ship to be unfit for performing the service immediately required. The court decided that the ship in 'itself' was fit to perform and therefore was not off-hire.

From the facts it can be seen that although time was lost to the charterer the full working of the vessel was not hindered. At all times the ship was capable of performing the service which the charterer was entitled to expect from it.

Similarly, where cargo is damaged and discharge takes longer than it would have done had the cargo been sound, this cannot be causally related to any full or partial disability in the ship itself affecting its full working potential.

Another illustration of the operation of the NYPE off-hire clause is *The Marika M* [1981] 2 Lloyd's Rep. 622 where the vessel had grounded at Bahrain on 17 July whilst proceeding to her allocated berth. She remained aground until refloated on the 27th and thereafter had to wait for a berth until 6 August. The court decided that although she was rightly off-hire during the period she was grounded, upon being refloated she became fully efficient again and although the extra time waiting for an alternative berth was due to the delay caused by the grounding it was not a proper 'off-hire' period and she was back on hire upon refloating. The charterers might, of course, have had a right to claim back by way of damages the hire they had been obliged to pay during the waiting period if they could prove that the grounding was caused by the shipowner's fault or breach, unless the charterparty incorporated the Hague (or Visby) Rules which contains an exception to liability for neglect or default of the Master in the navigation or management of the ship.

The cause of the accident giving rise to the alleged off-hire pleaded by the charterer must be fortuitous and not one that could be said to originate from the natural use which the charterer makes of the ship. Illustrative of this is *The Rijn* [1981] 2 Lloyd's Rep. 267, the facts of which were that the ship's bottom became fouled by barnacles/growth during a prolonged waiting period before loading cargo at a Red Sea port. The charterparty off-hire clause included the words 'any other cause preventing the full working of the vessel'. The charterers alleged a reduction of speed because of this fouling which had caused a sluggish performance. This they claimed came within the definition of 'defect in hull'. There is nothing fortuitous about the accumulating and clinging of marine growth to a ship's hull during her service under a charterer. That, unless it is an extraordinary example of fouling (which this was not), is a natural consequence of a ship's trading operations. Whereas it might be described as a defect *on* hull, it is certainly incorrect to call it a defect *in* hull.

### Deficiency of men

This phrase means what it says—a numerical insufficiency of officers and crew, i.e. short of the correct establishment for that ship. It does not mean 'inefficiency' of the men nor their inadequacy as individual members of the crew.

### Detention by average acts

Accidents to ship or cargo. For this cause to be realized as a true ground for placing the ship off-hire there must be more than merely delay to the ship; there must be some physical or geographical restriction on the vessel's movements disabling her from performing as a fit ship. Thus merely an extra long discharge period due to cargo having been wetted because of leaking hatch covers would not be sufficient to off-hire. An average accident to cargo is not *of itself* sufficient cause (*The Mareva AS* [1977] 1 Lloyd's Rep. 368).

### What is meant by the words 'any other cause preventing the full working of the vessel'?

Does the eiusdem generis rule apply? i.e. are any other causes to be limited to only those of the same genus or species as those specifically described earlier in the clause. Certainly other causes to which that phrase might be contemplating would be likely restricted to causes *internal* to the ship and not external (e.g. the cause which failed to place *The Aquacharm* off-hire). In order to make even *external* causes the subject of off-hire the addition of the word 'whatsoever' after the word 'cause' would have to be made, though it is doubtful that even that comprehensive wording would embrace all other causes whether external or not.

In *The Berge Sund* [1992] 1 Lloyd's Rep. 460 the arbitrator and, on appeal, the High Court adjudged the vessel to be off-hire by reason of 'any other cause preventing efficient working of the vessel', the cause on the facts being cleaning between cargoes being accidentally required and involving the fault of neither owner nor charterer. However, this was overturned on appeal ([1993] 2 Lloyd's Rep. 453) on the basis that the *cleaning itself* was part of the service given by the owner to the charterer.

The court in the *Laconian Confidence* (*Andre and Cie SA.* v *Orient Shipping* [1997] 1 Lloyd's Rep.139) strictly scrutinized an unusual set of facts. The vessel had suffered 18 days' delay because Bangladesh port authorities had refused it permission to sail due to the presence on board of 15.75 tonnes of sweepings of bagged rice. The NYPE form contained the customary clause 15 and the words 'any other clause' were not extended by the additional word 'whatsoever'. The arbitrators found the ship *not* to be off hire despite the charterers' 'two-pronged' approach that it should be, either under the words 'detention by average accidents to cargo' or 'by any other cause'. They found that the true cause of the delay was the 'remarkable' (unreasonable under the circumstances) conduct of the port authority, i.e. a cause unconnected directly with the cargo and not one which was eiusdem generis with the string of causes specifically enumerated in clause 15.

The charterers' subsequent appeal failed on two points, but succeeded on one. The success was that the phrase 'preventing the full working of the vessel' which qualified the causes enumerated in the clause could be activated not only by physical means but by legal means also. But the charterers failed to show that the interference by the port authority which was the relevant cause in this case was either an average accident or any other cause of a like and similar nature to the specifically enumerated list. The court hinted that had the word 'whatsoever' been inserted after the words 'any other cause' the decision might well have been different.

#### *A right to make deductions from hire*

These rights, which are either expressed or equitable, which latter expression means that the courts have discretion over the right to deduct from hire if certain pre-conditions (explained below) are met, one of which being that the deduction in question would have been exercised in good faith.

### Express deductions

As the expression itself implies, clear and unambiguous wording must exist in the charterparty providing the charterer with a contractual right to deduct in respect of certain costs/expenses, a common example of which is owners' disbursements (money advanced by charterers in a foreign port for goods or services to enable the ship to prosecute its voyage(s)).

### Equitable deductions

These have been the subject of controversy for years whilst the courts were 'fishing' for a basis upon which to found the granting of a right to deduct. Eventually the case of *The Nanfri* [1978] 2 Lloyd's Rep. 132 gave them a basis when in Lord Denning's words, 'a charterer should in fairness be able to recoup himself by making a deduction from the next month's hire so as to compensate him for the loss of use for those days equivalent to the loss of hire for those days'. He intended those words to refer to circumstances which *might* fall outside the specific list of incidents in the off-hire clause.

In *The Leon* [1985] 2 Lloyd's Rep. 470 the judge elaborated on this view by saying that equitable set-off should be allowed where the charterer had been denied the use of the ship in circumstances which did not in fact fall within the off-hire clause.

The following recent case further defines the extent of the right of a charterer to make deductions from hire by way of equitable set-off.

The *Aditya Vaibhav* [1993] 1 Lloyd's Rep. 63 where the Shelltime 3 form was used. The charterer had deducted a sum representing his loss resulting from a delay of 14 days due to the owners having failed to clean the holds properly. The owners did not contest the charterer's right to deduct but did complain that the deduction exceeded the amount of hire payable for those 14 days. The charterers argued that all losses/expenses (including wasted time) flowing from the owner's failure/breach could be deducted.

The court held that the charterers could only deduct an amount equivalent to the hire which would have been earned during the period of deprivation of use of the ship and *not* other consequential losses.

### *Delivery of cargo without production of original bills of lading*

It is not in the scope of this book to go deeply into the nature and function of the bill of lading other than briefly to repeat what textbooks have been saying 'since time began', that it has a three-fold purpose:

(1) it is a document of title with negotiable characteristics;
(2) it is a receipt for goods shipped on board a named carrying vessel;
(3) it is the best available evidence of the terms and conditions of the contract of carriage of goods as between shipper and carrier.

A bill of lading has the effect of creating a contractual relationship as between shipper (of cargo) and carrier, the inevitable question arising being who is the carrier when a ship is under time charter. Whereas most aspects of shipping law are founded upon international Convention, the answer to the above posed question varies from jurisdiction to jurisdiction. Suffice it to say briefly this (because this section is devoted to a commentary on charterparties not bills of lading) English law takes heed of the following in answering the questions:

(1) Is the bill signed by or for the Master?
(2) Which courts have jurisdiction (as agreed by the principal parties in the bill of lading jurisdiction clause)?
(3) Does the bill itself expressly identify the carrier by way of an 'identity of carrier' clause on the reverse side?

Bearing in mind the document of title role of the bill of lading, physical possession of at least one of the original set of bills of lading must be obtained by any party who seeks to take delivery of the cargo described and enumerated in that bill from the Master or his authorized agent. Thus a negotiable bill of lading is used rather in the same manner as a cloakroom ticket when an overcoat is left in the care of an attendant at the theatre. The owner of the coat is given a ticket, sees the show, returns to the cloakroom, offers his ticket without necessarily saying anything nor needing to identify himself and is handed back his coat. In the same manner, presentation of the bill, not identification of the consignee by other means, is what is required to obtain delivery. So sacrosanct did this requirement become and proportionately so grave became the risk of delivery to the wrong party when a bill of lading could not be timely produced by the party purporting to be the rightful receiver, that the P & I Clubs expressly excluded recovery from Club funds for claims resulting from the adverse consequences of delivering cargo without production of an original bill of lading. All Club managers were prepared to do to assist their members in what was a commercial predicament (because they were facing a calculated commercial risk, not a marine risk) was to recommend acceptance of a suitably worded letter of indemnity, endorsed by a first class bank.

Recently has come a court ruling which threatened initially to distrust that deep-rooted thinking.

*The Houda* [1993] 1 Lloyd's Rep. 333

The circumstances arose out of Iraqi invasion of Kuwait in August 1990. The owner of a chartered ship refused to deliver cargo in default of presentation of the original bill of lading because he had doubts about the legality of the order given by the charterer (the Kuwait Petroleum Company—effectively the Kuwait Government—to give the order to deliver without production of the bill. The owners maintained their refusal for 36 hours, which period was thus wasted hire time from the charterers' point of view. They sought to off-hire the vessel for that wasted period. The shipowner argued that he was entitled to a reasonable time to consider his position. The charterparty form was Shelltime 4 which contained a special provision as follows:

Clause 13

> '. . . The master . . . shall be under the orders and direction of charterers as regards employment of the vessel . . .
> charterers hereby indemnify owners against all consequences or liabilities that may arise from . . . ( . . . delivery of cargo without presentation of bills of lading . . . ) . . . Letter of Indemnity to Owners' P & I Club wording to be incorporated in this Charterparty.'

The presiding judge confirmed the long-held view that: (a) the Master can only be obliged to deliver cargo against actual production of a bill of lading (see also *The Sormovskiy* 3068 [1994] CLC 433); and (b) that a time charterer cannot lawfully order a Master or shipowner to deliver cargo to a receiver who is not entitled to possession of the cargo, but emphasised that there was a 'loophole' in those established rules which is that there is no authority to say that a time charterer may not lawfully order delivery of cargo without presentation of the relevant bill of lading in circumstances where the charterer is *himself* entitled to possession or gives the order with the authority of any third party who is entitled to possession. However, the judge granted a declaration that the vessel was off-hire for a substantial part of the period between arrival on the 8 August 1990 and the commencement of discharge on 27 September 1990. The shipowner appealed and in July 1994 the appeal judges had to consider three issues:

(1) Must an owner comply with time charterer's order immediately or does he have a reasonable time to consider what compliance might involve if he has doubts about the origins or lawfulness of the order?
(2) If no time to consider is permitted, what are the consequences of failing to comply immediately?

(3) (The basic root point). Can a time charterer lawfully demand that an owner deliver cargo without production of an original bill of lading?

The charterer submitted that only in exceptional circumstances could failure to comply immediately be excused, e.g. (a) when to comply immediately might endanger either vessel, crew or cargo; (b) when delay was necessitated by a need to clarify an ambiguous order; (c) where the owner had some knowledge which the charterer did not, which might affect the latter's orders and so confirmation was required.

The court concluded that the right (or duty) to pause and reflect could not be confined to a limited category of situations. A broad comprehensive view should be taken based on the hypothetical question—'how would a reasonably prudent man have acted under these particular circumstances?' The case was remitted to the lower court for determination as to how much of delay was reasonable, using these guidelines. The court accepted the owner's argument that only a bill of lading holder (and no-one else) may demand delivery of the cargo. There was no reason to depart from this principle.

But the sacrosanctity of this rule has on occasions been shaken by court rulings in other countries. One that received a measure of publicity was the decision of the *Guang Zhou* Maritime Court in 1994. The carrying vessel was the *Kota Maju*. The contract for sale of Sudan crude cotton had been concluded under which an irrevocable documentary letter of credit had been issued. On arrival of the vessel the cotton was stored in a port warehouse. After declarations to customs, the buyer took delivery (without production of the bill of lading) against a guarantee supplied by a third party. The buyer, whilst this was going on, was refusing to pay the value of the cargo and discussions were entered upon with the seller to fix a compromise price based upon the quality of the cotton as delivered. There resulted an agreement to make a down payment of US$600,000 with the balance to be 'paid shortly'. The balance was never paid, so the sellers sued the guarantor and the discharge port agent for their lost balance either in kind (cotton) or in money.

What probably distinguishes this case from the traditional view of sacrosanctity is that there was, in addition to the carrier/shipper legal relationship of which the bill of lading was an integral part, i.e. the Master delivers only against that document or otherwise at his peril, an international contract of sale. Although international shipping practice has been violated by the delivery of cargo without production of the original bill of lading (still in the possession of the seller), nevertheless the seller and buyer were negotiating with each other on the matter of the true price for the quality of the cotton which had been delivered into the buyer's possession. The seller was seemingly happy to do this rather than sue the carrier or his guarantor. Not only had he altered the letter of credit to a T/T payment, his actions were indicative of his intentions to continue performing the sale contract. The bill of lading had virtually lost its status as a document of title. Under circumstances such as these, the carrier, or his agent or guarantor, although still being at fault, should not be considered so at fault that he should be saddled with liability for the failure of the sale contract. The carrier should not, in short, be liable for the seller's loss of cargo value.

### *Deck cargo*

The deck is generally speaking not the proper space for carrying cargo for the obvious reason that it exposes cargo to the extra risks of being damaged by heavy weather on voyage, not to mention the risk of being lost overboard. There are exceptions to this general rule, e.g. where containers have been carried on deck of a purpose-built container ship it has been held that they are carried there lawfully and without there being a breach of the contract of carriage (or as is more commonly known a 'deviation' from the contract of carriage). In regard to the responsibility for negligent stowage under a time charter as between the shipowner and the time charterer, the case of *The Fantasy* [1991] 2 Lloyd's Rep. 391 has recently produced an interesting decision. In that case there were at least three clauses in the NYPE charterparty which were relevant to the responsibility for stowing cargo on the ship generally including a printed Clause 8 which placed responsibility for the consequences of negligent stowage upon the charterers. Apart from this there were two typewritten rider clauses which shifted responsibility for stowage back on to the shipowner and even a third typewritten rider clause which specially provided for the crew during the voyage to attend to the deck cargo and to check from time to time on the lashings. That same clause also specifically provided for the cargo to be carried 'at charterers risk'. The charterparty did not incorporate and was therefore not subject to the Hague Rules. The Commercial Court held that in regard to the cargo actually placed on deck, the shipowner had not (despite the existence of the other clauses in regard to responsibility for stowage) assumed responsibility for negligent stowage of the deck cargo before the voyage began, but that the shipowner was liable (under the third additional clause quoted above) for negligence of the crew in checking and attending to the deck cargo during the voyage. This decision was affirmed by the Court of Appeal ([1992] 1 Lloyd's Rep. 235) and seems to point to the fact that cargo stowed on deck should be subject to clear-cut provisions about responsibility for stowage and lashing and that it should not be automatically assumed (by the charterer) that because there are other clauses referring to stowage of cargo generally which seem to place responsibility on the owners that those same clauses should necessarily also have reference to cargo stowed on deck.

*Darya Tara* [1997] 1 Lloyd's Rep. 42
This case minutely examined the extent to which charterers should be held responsible for the consequences of deck cargo shifting in heavy weather when the charterparty (on an NYPE form) contained the following clauses: Line 25—charterers to have the option to load a full deck cargo . . . at their own risk and expense. Clause 8 (the unamended printed wording). Clause 57 charterers' option deck cargo O.K. . . . but vessel had no lashing materials on board and cargo to be loaded always at charterers' risk and expense. Steel beams were loaded under and on deck at UK ports for Hong Kong discharge. The vessel met heavy weather off Ushant and the deck cargo shifted. After vain attempts to remedy at sea, the vessel put into Brixham to restow. Very briefly, resulting from this incident there was damage to cargo, damage to ship, a deviation involving loss of time, expenses of restowing and relashing, the cost of surveys at Brixham and Hong Kong and finally disbursements at Brixham. How should these various items of loss/damage be allocated as between disponent owner and sub-charterer. Initially the sole arbitrator allowed a recovery by disponent owners of the hire lost due to the deviation to Brixham and the survey fees and disbursements. Thus the owners obtained indemnity for expenses which were not directly referable to the cargo or to the loading and stowing of it.

Charterers appealed on the ground that the combination of the deck cargo clauses in the charterparty had the effect of restricting the charterers' responsibility to those risks and expenses flowing directly from the loading, stowing (and carriage) process.

This interpretation would exclude the expenses at the intermediate port of refuge. They distinguished, in short, between losses/damage directly referable to deck cargo and arising from the exercise by the charterer of the option to use the space for cargo. The clauses should not be considered a basis for the owners to claim full indemnity for whatever are their own losses.

The court rejected the right of virtually full indemnity found by the arbitrator and accepted the restrictive interpretation argued by the charterers. The right of *full* indemnity in circumstances such as these needs clauses composed of much clearer language, unambiguously declaring that such are the parties' intentions.

### *Liens*

Earlier in this book we have examined the nature, purpose and effect of the maritime lien. Now we should look at another type of lien—the possessory lien. A brief definition of this type of lien would be 'a right which a person has to retain possession of goods which do not belong to him until such time as certain outstanding charges which are due to him have been satisfied'.

What needs emphasis is that the possessory-type lien to be found in time charterparties is entirely contractual in nature. It creates a right only as between the two parties which are principals to the charterparty contract. In contrast, a maritime lien is a creation of the Admiralty or general maritime law or even statute.

On the face of it and based on the premise that a charterparty lien creates a right to be exercised only between the two contracting parties, no lien could be exercised on cargo which was not owned by the offending time charterer. But case law has shown that the right of lien is not interpreted in quite such a minimal way. The problem lies in reconciling (a) the protection of the shipowner's interests by the exercise of the charterparty lien on cargo in support of his demand for unpaid overdue charterhire and (b) protection also of the rights of what may be 'innocent' third-party holders of bills of lading who might consider that they have an unfettered right to immediate delivery of their cargoes on presentation of a properly endorsed original bill of lading. No conflict between these two seemingly opposed interests occurs, of course, if the bill of lading incorporates the charterparty lien clause because the lien is expressly granted as against the time charterer and exercisable on cargoes actually owned by him but also as against all third-party bill of lading holders independently through the contractual relationship between shipowner/carrier and shipper/receiver. Such bill of lading holders would be deemed to have had prior notice of the existence of a right of lien against their cargo and thus be aware of the possibility when they purchased the bill for value.

The problem does, however, persist when bills of lading do not contain lien clauses and the so-called innocent holder has no prior notice. Case law varies on this point. In *The Agios Giorgis* [1976] 2 Lloyd's Rep. 192 the court said that a lien for unpaid charterhire was not exercisable on cargo not owned by the time charterer. But a year later in *The Aegnoussiotis* [1977] 1 Lloyd's Rep. 268 the court took a different view, saying that as the charterers have granted the shipowner a contractual right of lien on *all* cargoes (customary wording) then a lien can be exercised on any cargo irrespective of independent ownership. Third parties (innocent) may indeed have a cause of action for interrupted delivery. But nevertheless the charterers cannot, ran the courts thinking, benefit from their own breach of contract in granting the shipowner a lien 'with one hand' and preventing him from exercising it 'with the other'. An aggrieved 'innocent' cargo-owner, said this court, should have a right of indemnity from the shipowner from being wrongfully deprived of his ability to lay hands on his cargo when he sought delivery. If the bill of lading makes no reference to a charterparty lien and is endorsed 'freight prepaid' the owner must deliver the cargo without further payment from the bill of lading holder (*The Alev* [1989] 1 Lloyd's Rep. 138).

### Where and when should a possessory lien on cargo be exercised?

Another conflict in obligations, rights and duties arises as a result of a possible 'clash' between a shipowner/carrier's common law and contractual duty to proceed with a reasonable despatch to the contractual destination (and there to deliver the cargo) and the shipowner's right to withhold delivery of cargo by exercise of a valid possessory lien. The simplest example of when and where *not* to lien cargo is during the course of a loaded voyage. Carrying ships have 'stopped' for two or three days, e.g. south of the Suez Canal on a carrying voyage so as to pressurize a charterer into paying overdue hire. This is quite wrong and should never be supported by an English court or London arbitration tribunal (*The Mihalios Xilas* [1978] 2 Lloyd's Rep. 397 and [1979] 2 Lloyd's Rep. 303).

The only possible similar circumstances which might constitute an exception to this would be when a Master anchors off the named destination port and refuses to proceed to a discharging berth knowing that if he does so he, and so his owners, would inevitably lose possession or effective control of the cargo intended to be liened. This possibility received the court's blessing in *The Chrysovalandou Dyo* [1981] 1 Lloyd's Rep. 159.

### Lien on sub-freights

In addition to cargoes as a subject (or object) of lien, the charterparty may confer the right to lien sub-freights, i.e. either (a) freight due to a time charterer under bills of lading or (b) freight due to a time charterer under the terms of a sub-charter. Because of the very nature of the subject-matter the exercise of this lien is not effected by retaining possession but rather by timely interception of the targeted monies before they have been paid over to the time charterer. See *The Lancaster* [1980] 2 Lloyd's Rep. 497 where the High Court judge drew a clear distinction between a lien on cargo which is a possessory lien and a lien on sub-freights, which is not. Interception is customarily effected by sending an appropriately worded notice to the party who is due to pay the freight, so that it reaches him *before* he has paid over the money to the charterer or to anyone authorized to receive the money on the charterers' behalf. A suitable form of wording for such a notice, which would normally be drafted and sent by the owners' solicitors, would be as follows:

> We are instructed on behalf of the owners of the above mentioned vessel, ....................(name of owners). The vessel was chartered by our clients to....................under the terms of an (name of charterparty form) dated.................. .

Hire is outstanding under the terms of the said charterparty in the amount of................ . In breach of the terms of the said charterparty, the charterers (name of charterer) have failed to pay such sum.

By clause...................of the said charterparty, the charterers granted to the owners a lien over 'all sub freights for any amount due' under the terms of the charterparty.

Accordingly, pursuant to clause...................of the charterparty the owners hereby give notice to you to pay direct to them, without deduction, any sum or sums due to be paid by you to (name of charterers) until further notice.

Where a ship is under time charter but the bills of lading issued pursuant to the authority in the charterparty are deemed to be 'owner's' bills (that is those whose printed terms and conditions are evidence of or are eventually contained in the contract of carriage of goods between the shipper) (or the eventual rightful holders of the bill) and the shipowner as the other principal party, the ability of the shipowner to intercept sub-freights as security for unpaid charterhire is founded upon rights contained in the bill of lading itself and is not dependent upon the existence of a charterparty clause conferring such a right. Only if the sub-freights are rightly due to the (head) charterer would the shipowner have to rely on the charterparty to exercise his right of interception. In any event, the shipowner is bound to account to the charterer for any excess balance after he has secured the full amount of overdue charterhire he was seeking. The role of the agent who may be collecting freight will have to be carefully understood, since he may have been appointed by the charterers but in circumstances we are now discussing, he will have to be instructed specially to receive the freight on the *owners'* behalf. The vessel's agent must be well aware on whose behalf he is acting when he performs any task in the course of his agency duties.

In *The Attika Hope* [1988] 1 Lloyd's Rep. 439 the issue was whether a third-party assignee by the time charterer of sub-freights did or did not have priority in regard to receipt of that freight as against the notice constituting the exercise of their lien given by the owners to the sub-charterers. It was a fact that the notice of assignment had been given before the notice of an exercise of lien. The court held that the third-party assignee *had* priority and thus the sub-charterer, having already paid the freight to the owners direct, had to pay it again to the assignee.

## Right to lien sub-sub-freights

The beneficial effects of a fully comprehensive lien clause can be enjoyed by the head owner still further down the charterparty chain provided that co-extensive clauses are present in the sub-charterparty. This principle was firmly established in *The Cebu* [1983] 1 Lloyd's Rep. 302, where there was a charterparty chain all on the NYPE form. Sub-freights were judicially construed as including sub-sub-time charterhire as well as sub-charter hire.

The principle of extending these lien benefits right down the 'chain' was founded upon the idea that the 'owner's' lien took the form of an equitable assignment in respect not only of the hire due to the head-charterers, but also the hire due to the sub-time charterers. The head-charterer, by operation of the equivalent lien clause in the sub-time charterparty, was deemed to have assigned the right 'up the chain' to the head-owner. Where the charterers are incorporated in England or Wales or have a place of business there, the lien must be registered at Companies House or it will be void against a liquidator—*The Annangel Glory* [1988] 1 Lloyd's Rep. 45.

### *Authority to sign bills of lading*

One of the most vexed questions in shipping law and one to which there has never been an adequately formulated uniform and standard reply reached under international Convention (the basis, it is generally acknowledged, for shipping/Admiralty/maritime law of the vast majority of the world's sovereign nations) is who is the carrier under the terms and conditions of the bill of lading where the ship is under time charter.

English law has for years been clear about the answer. England is a 'common law' country with rules of law and judicial thinking basically different from many of the other fellow members of the European Union whose territories form the land mass of mainland Europe and whose judicial systems were founded upon the 'thoughts of Napoleon'. A basic premise of the common law provides that a ship's Master has general authority to sign bills of lading on behalf of his owners. Thus, the Master's personal signature on the bill of lading will bind the owners providing the Master is signing within the scope of his general authority. (This he was not in the old case of *Grant* v *Norway* (1851), which sparked off the introduction of the Bills of Lading Act 1855 which itself through sheer lapse of over much time, has been replaced by the Carriage of Goods by Sea Act 1992 which has modernized the legal rules regarding the passing of title to goods whilst afloat; *Grant* v *Norway* has thus been consigned to 'museum' status.)

Case law supporting this view is too numerous to list here. *The Berkshire* [1974] 1 Lloyd's Rep. 185 is a representative case as well as being one which established the validity under English law of the demise or 'identity of carrier' clause which is very widely, if not almost universally, to be found in standard printed forms of bills of lading. A customary wording of this clause is as follows:

> The contract evidenced hereby is between the merchant (the shipper) and the owner or demise charterer of the vessel designated to carry the goods. No other person or legal entity shall be liable under this contract and the protection of Article 4 bis of the Hague Visby rules and any other statutory exemption from or limitation of liability shall inure also to the benefit of stevedores and other servants or agents of the carrier. For the purpose of this clause all such persons and legal entities are deemed to be parties to this contract made on their behalf by the carrier.

This particular wording has two purposes, one is to ensure that the contract of carriage evidenced by or contained in the bill of lading is one between the shipper and the shipowner (or demise charterer as the case may be) and not with the time charterer who will be considered to be merely an agent and under no personal liability whatsoever. At a casual reading, this clause appears to have a bold rather presumptuous flavour about it, since it appears that the Carrier A is virtually saying to the shipper merchant B—'although you have entered into a contract of carriage of the enumerated goods with me, the charterer of the named ship, you have not really contracted with me but with the owner (or charterer by demise) of the ship on whose behalf I am merely acting as agent'. However, the fact that

English courts endorse its validity coupled with the common law notion that the Master is, under a time charterparty (*not* on demise terms) the employee and/or agent of his owners and that the bill of lading is almost always signed by either him or on his behalf, means almost equally invariably that the bill of lading is considered under English law to be an 'owner's' bill.

Bills issued at the bidding of a time-chartered (or disponent) owner are regarded differently in many of the Western European Continental countries where the charterer is more commonly held to be the carrier, particularly so if the charterer's 'logo' appears on the face of the bill in bold lettering.

## What are the duties of a Master re signing bills?

The general principle is simply that the ship's Master should sign bills of lading as and when presented to him for signature. However, he could, by signing without question or protest be 'letting his owners in' for liabilities greater, possibly significantly greater, than the owner might be exposed to under the terms and conditions of the time charterparty itself. Thus the owners need protection and this is usually 'built in' to the charterparty by a standard clause known as: the Employment and Indemnity clause. This clause is to be found expressed in the Baltime form. In the NYPE form, however, an indemnity provided by the charterer to the owner in consideration of the Master signing bills of lading as presented is only implied (see *The Caroline P* [1984] 2 Lloyd's Rep. 466).

It has been held that a Master may refuse to sign bills which are *manifestly* inconsistent with the charterparty terms by reason of extraordinary terms and conditions contained in them. What is manifestly inconsistent would probably mean terms which went against the whole tenor of the background charterparty. In *The Vikfrost* [1980] 1 Lloyd's Rep. 560 it was held that a difference between the charterparty jurisdiction (Oslo arbitration) and the bill of lading jurisdiction (English court) was not to be construed as 'manifestly inconsistent'.

It is well established in English law that a Master has general implied authority to sign bills of lading on his owners' behalf. His signature personally will bind his owners, creating a contractual relationship between those owners and the then holder of the bill or any who subsequently, through lawful transfer, become rightful holders of the bill. An exception to this rule would be if the vessel at the material time was under demise charter since a charterer on such terms has not only the right to employ the ship but also takes over possession and control. The Master there is effectively the charterer's servant and/or agent (*The Venezuela* [1980] 1 Lloyd's Rep. 393).

So strong is the rule that a Master's signature on a bill of lading where the ship is under time charter *not* demise binds his owners that for his signature to bind the time charterer, there would have to be a clear expression of intent that in signing he was signing on behalf of the charterer and as his agent.

The question of whether a shipowner owes an implied contractual duty to a charterer to exercise reasonable care when signing bills of lading or mates' receipts, was reviewed in the *Arctic Trader* [1996] 2 Lloyd's Rep. 449. The charterer in question was a time charterer and the ship had been sub- and sub-sub-chartered. The entire chain of charterers were parties to the litigation. The cargo was salt and because it was found by the port authority in the country of discharge (Nigeria) to be contaminated, the ship was impounded for four months. Evidence was available that the salt was contaminated at the time of loading (in Alexandria). The charterers took legal action on the basis that the Master had breached an implied term by failing to clause the mates' receipts when it should have been obvious to him that the salt was in a less than good order and that was directly causative of the four months' delay and the consequent disruption to the charterer's business programme. The arbitrator found that the Master had been 'wrongly persuaded' to regard the cargo as in an acceptable condition. He found for the charterers. On appeal by the owners, the court reasoned, inter alia, that on these facts so far from owing a duty to the charterer to sign mates' receipts which accurately reflected the true condition of the cargo at the time of loading, the charterer should have been deemed to have known of the condition of the cargo and indeed, conversely, it was the charterer who prevailed upon the Master to omit a reference to the contamination when he signed the mates' receipt. A charterer cannot be seen to object to a Master's conduct if and when he fails to describe the condition of the cargo accurately when he, the charterer, knew or should have been aware of the condition anyway.

The *Arctic Trader* should be viewed together with, but distinguished from, the *Nogar Marin* [1988] 1 Lloyd's Rep. 410 and the *Almak* [1985] 1 Lloyd's Rep. 559. In the *Nogar Marin*, the Master carelessly signed mates' receipts clean when the cargo was physically not. When the ship was subsequently arrested at the suit of holders of *clean* bills of lading, signed (against mates' receipts) by the owners' agents, the owners claimed an indemnity from the charterers. On final appeal, the appeal judges held the Master's carelessness broke the chain of causation between the charterers' breach (in presenting bills of lading for signature) and the owners losses. In the *Almak*, the Master had similarly been careless in signing a bill of lading containing a wrong date. The arbitrators initially allowed the charterers' claim based upon the owners' breach of an implied duty of care. On appeal the High Court decided there was no such duty, the reasoning being, inter alia, that if the wrongly dated bill had been signed by the Master and issued by the owners at the request of an independent shipper, the owners were entitled to be indemnified by the charterer and this would cause the charterers' claim to fail for circuity. What appears to emerge from these cases is that although there may well exist an implied duty to take care re signing bills of lading and/or mates' receipts towards the owners or towards innocent third parties, no such duty exists vis-à-vis the charterer or person presenting such bills of lading.

## To what extent may the Master delegate his authority to sign?

He may expressly delegate his authority or it may be implied from the wording of the charterparty. In the NYPE form such implication may be derived from the words:

'.......................................*Captain to sign Bills of Lading as presented*......................................' (lines 78, 79) combined with: '.......................................*Captain to be under the orders and direction of the charterers as regards employment and agency*.......................................' (line 77).

The latter set of words gives the charterers liberty to sign themselves on the Master's (and thus his owners) behalf. It is this additional liberty which makes it the more vital that the owners protect themselves by way of an express or reliably implied indemnity against the consequences of a bill of lading signature exposing them to liabilities more onerous than they would be exposed to under the charterparty itself.

## How far down a charterparty 'chain' may this authority extend?

This depends on what is expressed in the head charterparty or what can be implied from its provisions. *The Vikfrost* gives guidance on this point. In that case the head owner A had chartered to the (head) charterer B who had sub-let to (sub) charterer C. These agents were expressly authorized to sign bills of lading on the Master's behalf and to include a demise clause and B had express liberty to sub-let. However, the head charter was silent on the question of C or B's agent signing bills or including a demise clause. C's sub-agent *did* sign bills which *did* include a demise clause. The Court of Appeal ruled that C's agent had implied authority and that should have been in the reasonable contemplation of A when he gave dispensation to sub-let.

In this modern highly pressurized trading atmosphere where chartering is an attractive idea (as opposed to owning), particularly chartering on a time basis, and it has become the norm for charterers, or more likely their agents to sign on the Master's behalf and with the Master's implied authority, a shipowner can find himself bound to a contract he did not personally enter into in the first place. The following case illustrates this:

*The Nea Tyhi* [1982] 1 Lloyd's Rep. 606
The vessel was chartered on a NYPE form. A rider clause provided owners with an express indemnity against the consequences of charterers' agent (or even the Master) signing Bills. Wood loaded on deck (covered by 'under-deck' bills) was water-damaged. Faced with a claim from cargo receivers the owners tried to argue that the charterers' agents had no authority to issue 'under-deck' bills for cargo shipped on deck and thus had no liability.

*Held*: that there was no *actual* authority but there was 'ostensible' authority and the owners were liable. One can presume that the word 'ostensible' in this context must mean that degree of authority which a third party would be excused for assuming that a person had conferred upon him.

### *Shipowner's implied right of indemnity*

*The Island Archon* [1994] 2 Lloyd's Rep. 227
This case is an excellent illustration of the courts' current attitude towards the existence or otherwise of an implied right of indemnity arising in favour of an owner who has obeyed the lawful orders of a time charterer in regard to loading of cargoes and sending his ship to destinations designated by the charterer. The case involved a voyage to Iraq with cargoes destined for its ports. Prior even to arrival, let alone discharge, the Iraqis demanded security from the shipowner in the form of anticipatory guarantees in case cargo was found eventually to be lost or damaged (which as it happened it was eventually found not to be). On the ground it seemed that when a charterer, despite the fact that he has in no way breached the charterparty, has options which he is fully entitled to exercise(i.e. types of cargo, range of ports to direct the ship to) and he chooses options

with which the shipowner is bound to comply which option lets the owner in for an expense or causes him to suffer a loss which he will not otherwise have suffered, he, the owner, may rightfully claim to be indemnified. Only if there has occurred (through some fault or failing of the owner) in the meantime a break in the chain linking the charterer's order with the eventual loss, can the owner's claim be defeated. In an earlier case —*Athanasia Comninos* [1990] 1 Lloyd's Rep. 277 the courts had already given thought to an implied indemnity when the charterparty was silent on any express indemnity. There had been an unexplained explosion of a coal cargo. In answer to the question 'why was there an explosion?', the court decided that a perfectly reasonable and logical answer was 'because the time charterer called upon the vessel to load coal'. This, it said, was sufficient to found an indemnity, irrespective of who, if anybody, may have been at fault or of the properties, usual or otherwise, of coal.

### *To what extent can the question of identity of the carrier be resolved when the vessel is under time charter?*

Only by applying guidelines to the facts.

Thus:

(1) If the bill of lading is signed by the Master personally or it is signed on his behalf by the charterer or his agent, then the contract of carriage evidenced by (or eventually contained in) the bill of lading would be likely considered one with the registered shipowner. Or (if the ship happens to be under *demise* charter) with the demise charterer.
(2) In those rare circumstances where the time charterer has signed the bill in his own name and where the intention appears to have been that he was signing on his own behalf with no indication that he was signing for the Master or as agent for the owner, then he, the charterer will be considered the carrier.
(3) A clue as to the carrier's identity may be found in the charterparty itself by way of some provision pointing to the true and intended identity *provided that* such a provision is incorporated into the bill of lading itself, thus giving the shipper and/or third-party holder of the bill constructive notice of that information.

### *The Inter-Club agreement*

Commentary on the 1984 version has been retained so that comparisons with the 1996 version may be made (see page 207).

## General description

This was an agreement drawn up by the P & I Clubs which formed what was then known as the 'London' Group and subsequently was widened and re-named the 'International' Group. The main purpose of the agreement was to provide a 'mechanical' formula for dividing responsibility as between owner and charterer for cargo claims brought by third parties. This in turn was considered to be necessary because of the lack of clarity in the printed form of the NYPE charterparty as to responsibility for cargo claims. The cargo responsibility clause in the NYPE form is Clause 8 of which line 78 reads:

... and charterers are to load, stow and trim the cargo at their expense under the supervision of the Captain'.

This wording gave rise to practical doubts as to where ultimate responsibility actually should be when the charterers were under obligation to load/stow (and discharge) and yet the Master (the *owner's* agent) was under a duty to supervise, e.g. was this to be active or 'passive' supervision? Could he be *positively* at fault or only negatively? If he *actively* intervened in the stowage was his active intervention the sole and only cause of the damage to the cargo? Such issues used to give rise to disputes and the need to hire lawyers. Thus the Inter-Club agreement was introduced to eliminate disputes of this sort or at least to keep them to a minimum. No contract or agreement in writing has ever been made so perfect that it has *completely* eliminated all disputes, nor is it ever likely to be. In retrospect, it largely achieved this aim, but not entirely, as will be seen. The agreement contained two alternative formulae, the respective texts of each of which may be found in Appendix 7.

The basic formula (that positioned in Clause (2) of the agreement) is to apply where the cargo responsibility clauses (which are 8 and 26) have *not* been 'materially' amended. A 'material' amendment is said to be one which makes responsibility for cargo claims clear as between the parties where before it was uncertain. There are two examples of this commonly used in practice:

(1) the addition of the extra words 'and responsibility' inserted between the word 'supervision' and the words 'of the Captain' in line 78 (clause 8);
(2) the insertion of the words 'cargo claims' in Clause 26.

Example (1) is far more common than example (2).

The 'basic' formula then sets out a logical apportionment, simply attributing claims arising from unseaworthiness 100 per cent to owners and claims arising from faults or failings in the overall cargo handling process 100 per cent to charterers. Shortage, short delivery and over-carriage are to be divided on a 50/50 basis.

The insertion of a material amendment (e.g. as described, the addition of the words 'and responsibility' in Clause 8)—or, it is emphasized, similarly effective wording introduced as a rider clause—triggers off the application of the alternative formula (that positioned in Clause 1(c)), the significant difference between the two being that the basic one attributes bad stowage and handling claims 100 per cent to charterers whereas the alternative formula divides responsibility for this type of claim 50/50.

In the printed wording of Clause 8, the word 'discharge' does not feature. But frequently, if not universally, it is inserted so as to complete the overall cargo handling process. The addition of this word does *not* rank as a 'material amendment'.

On the other hand the addition of the words 'cargo claims' into printed Clause 26 thus causing it to read: ' . . . the owners to remain responsible for the navigation of the vessel, insurance, crew, cargo claims and all other matters same as when trading for their own account' causes the agreement to be generally inapplicable as will be obvious from the amended clause itself.

### Is the Inter-Club agreement legally binding?

As the signatories to the agreement are all Clubs, the only binding feature is that the Clubs bind themselves as between each other to recommend to their members on each separate occasion that they accept the terms of the agreement. What, however, is becoming increasingly common is for the terms of the ICA to be incorporated into the NYPE charterparty as a rider clause. This then, like any other contractual provision, is binding upon the parties themselves. If such express incorporation takes place, the agreement can be subject to judicial or arbitral interpretation in the context of the charterparty as a whole. Such occurred in *The Strathnewton* [1983] 1 Lloyd's Rep. 219 where the Court of Appeal pronounced upon a situation where the charterparty contained the Hague Rules expressly incorporated (which includes a one-year time limit for bringing suit in cargo claims) and the Inter-Club agreement limit of two years for notifying claims. In view of the traditional 'overriding' nature of the paramount clause, one party argued that the one year prevailed over the two-year (agreement) period. The court did not accept this argument and ruled that the Inter-Club agreement was a mechanical division of responsibility for cargo claims which 'cut across' the Hague Rules and was to be regarded as wholly independent from them. Other cases followed *The Strathnewton* which dealt with other aspects of the inter-relation between the agreement and the remainder of the charterparty.

*The Benlawers* [1989] 2 Lloyd's Rep. 51 in which the facts showed a conflict between the provisions of the agreement and the charterparty terms generally where a cargo of onions had deteriorated due to a defective ventilation system. Clause 48 obliged the charterer to indemnify the owner for cargo claims in consideration of including a demise clause in the covering bill of lading. Clause 47 incorporated the Inter-Club agreement. Applying very much the thinking in *The Strathnewton* that however comprehensive and clear-cut appear the indemnity provisions in the charterparty, the mechanical apportionment provided the boundaries for the limiting of the charterers' responsibility to indemnify. It was held that failure of a ship's ventilation system was an aspect of unseaworthiness and therefore 100 per cent owners' liability.

In *The Holstencruiser* [1992] 2 Lloyd's Rep. 378 the court was asked to determine how and to what extent the agreement could be adopted to cover apportionment of cargo claims arising from container carriage and particularly multi-modal journeys. Answer: only applicable to cargo claims which arose under bills of lading issued by charterers pursuant to rights granted to them by the charterparty itself. To show this the charterers would have to demonstrate through production of Mates' receipts that the cargo had been handed over to the Master/owners' care and custody. In the absence of Mates' receipt because of modern transport custom, the charterers would need to discharge this burden of proof by some other means. The agreement, in short, should be co-extensive in scope with the period of carriage responsibility which the named owner had under the charter.

Regarding damage caused by condensation, the court in *The Holstencruiser* ruled that where there is doubt as to the true cause of damage (e.g. as to whether there has been condensation or fresh-water damage by rain) but nevertheless the claim is compromised with the third-party claimant, this does not absolve the charterer (when he seeks recovery under the Inter-Club agreement) from the burden of proving that his claim under the ICA was one for *condensation* damage. Once settled with the prior approval of the owner, subsequent proof that it could have been successfully rejected does not of itself invalidate the charterer's claim.

### What is meant by a 'properly settled' claim?

It is provided in the agreement that a condition precedent for one or other party claiming an indemnity from the other is that the claim shall have been 'properly settled' (i.e. with the third-party claimant). In the absence of a formal judgment on liability, this will, in most cases, be an amicable, probably compromised, settlement. This invites the thought: (a) has the defendant merely acknowledged the claimant's theory of liability or has he compromised on his own version and, if so, who is correct?; (b) has a best terms settlement been achieved or could the quantum have been reduced further with a little more effort?

In the author's opinion the Inter-Club agreement has little hope of continuing to act as an effective eliminator, or at least minimizer, of disputes unless each party (or more relevantly each Club concerned) places trust in the manner in which the party actually handles the third-party claim with the primary claimant. Clubs were the original signatories to the agreement (i.e. those 'Group' Clubs in existence at the time of its coming into force and subsequently formed independent Clubs in principle adhere to the agreement) and those same Clubs should acknowledge the capabilities of the managements of other Clubs to handle claims with skill and attention and achieve best possible settlements not only on their own Club's behalf but also on behalf of any other Club involved under the ICA. It is, of course, open to possibility that two opposing Clubs may argue about the nature or type of damage which is the subject of claim. The nature of the damage is the criterion upon which apportionment of responsibility under one or other formula is made.

### What happens about recoverability of legal costs under the agreement?

One answer to this lies in the judgment of Hobhouse J in *The Holstencruiser*. On page 388 of his judgment he says that Clause 1(i) of the agreement contains the words ' . . . the cargo claim, including any legal costs incurred thereon . . . '. Although this phrase could be interpreted in two ways (i.e. (1) the third-party claimant's costs or (2) the charterer's costs against the owner—or (vice versa), C: common sense dictates that it must mean the primary claimant's costs since the very underlying aim of the agreement is to minimize, if not entirely eliminate, the incurring of costs by charterer against owner (or vice versa). The agreement makes no reference to costs as between owner/charterer or charterer/owner. Costs must refer only to those costs which the third-party claimant has occurred in pursuing his claim and which he would be entitled to 'tack on' to the cargo claim itself.

### *Inter-Club Agreement—1996 Version*

Because of the uncertainties created by the 1984 version and which were left to be judicially resolved, a restructure of the wording was made and is now in use: the 1996 Agreement. Such hitherto unresolved points as:

(a) an accurate definition of legal costs;
(b) to what carriage documents should the agreement apply; and
(c) what does 'cargo claims' include,

have been addressed and clarified in this latest version.

Item (b) above has been clearly resolved. The *Holstencruiser* case decided that for the 1984 Agreement to apply, the cargo document must be a bill of lading issued by a charterer strictly in accordance with charterparty terms. Through transport or combined transport documents fell outside its scope. In clause 4 (a) of 1996 the Agreement applies to any contract of carriage *whatever its form*. Thus, way-bills, voyage charters, traditional bills, or through transport documents, are all documents to which the agreement can apply if cargo claims arise. Such claims must, of course, be in reference to loss/damage arising between the commencement of loading and the completion of discharge. Re item (c), clause 3 of 1996 clearly defines cargo claims. Customs' fines or dues are *in*cluded. The *Holstencruiser* had *ex*cluded them from the scope of the previous version. Item (a)—legal expenses. The 1996 version endorses the decision in *Holstencruiser* by defining legal expenses as those incurred in defence of or settlement of the third party (primary) cargo claim (including Club correspondents' and experts' costs) and *not* legal costs incurred in the secondary claim as between owner and charterer in attempting to resolve doubts about correct apportionment.

Another doubt now resolved under the 1996 version is 'what must the party seeking apportionment actually prove to justify its claim under the Agreement'. In other words, what constitutes a 'properly settled' (with the third party claimant) claim, so as to make it 'packaged' and ready for apportionment in accordance with the formula provided in the Agreement, e.g. the shipowner might have made a compromise settlement on the primary claim on the same basis as the claim was presented to him—unseaworthiness, but in subsequently trying to obtain indemnity from the charterer, he might try to override that theory of liability by arguing bad stowage in turn being the cause of the unseaworthy condition. Such moves have been forestalled by the 1996 version in that claims under the Agreement must be based on the 'actuality of the facts' and not simply on how they were pleaded by the cargo interests.

The time bar question is addressed in the 1996 version, primarily so that the extended influence of the Hamburg Rules can be duly catered for. The Hamburg Rules themselves have a two-year time limitation period for cargo claims (twice as long as the Hague or the Hague/Visby Rules) and in recognition of this the Agreement extends the period for the notifying in writing of indemnity claims under the Agreement to 36 months where, and only where, the Hamburg Rules are *compulsorily* applicable to the primary claim by operation of law. Thus there is a two-tier limitation period for indemnity claims—two years where the Hague or Hague/Visby Rules apply to the primary claim and three years where the Hamburg Rules are compulsorily applicable.

One other concession to the increased use of the Hamburg Rules in potential cargo loss/damage disputes can be seen in that section of the 1996 version which is subheaded 'The Apportionment' (section 8). In subsection (a) claims arising out of unseaworthiness *and/or error in fault in navigation or management* are apportioned 100 per cent to owners. The words emphasized feature a cause which under the Hague or Visby Rules provided a firm defence to a carrier's liability but which under the Hamburg Rules do not.

The wording of the apportionment section generally has been tightened up and instead of two separate apportionments (as in the 1984 version) it is merged into one but contains a proviso that the inclusion of the words 'and responsibility' in clause 8 of the NYPE vary the apportionment of bad stowage and handling claims to 50/50 instead of 100 per cent upon charterers. This raises an interesting question as to how the words 'and responsibility' can be introduced into the equivalent of clause 8 in the 1993 NYPE without coming into direct conflict with the words 'at their (charterers') risk'. Presumably the latter three words would have to be deleted in order to allow the words 'and responsibility' to have their intended significance.

There is, in the 1996 version of the Agreement, an anomalous contradiction which fortunately has merely academic but no practical significance. In the apportionment section itself (at section 8(b)) it is provided as to how the mechanical apportionment is varied according to whether or not the words 'and responsibility' are inserted and used, and yet under section 4(b)(i) the insertion of those two words is described as *not* a material amendment, prompting the silent question—if it is not a material amendment (and it *was* considered to be so under the 1984 version) why does it have the effect of altering the mechanical apportionment? Having observed this point, it can be dismissed as of no practical importance.

The 1996 apportionment includes a final subsection which provides that all *other* cargo claims whatsoever, including claims for delay to cargo, are to be divided 50/50 between charterers and owners unless there is clear and irrefutable evidence that the claim arose out of the act or neglect of one or the other (including their servants or subcontractors) in which case that particular party shall then bear 100 per cent of the claim.

### *Obligation to pay hire and the right of withdrawal of vessel for non-payment*

It is customary for the payment of hire to be made in advance. Line 58 of the NYPE form provides for this and requires it to be made semi-monthly (in advance). Hire is the consideration given by the charterer to the shipowner for the use and employment of the ship and the services of its Master and crew and as such it is of prime importance for the shipowner that he receives payment regularly and punctually and in full.

## Payment to be made in cash

A further charterparty stipulation is that hire instalments are to be paid in cash and this has been interpreted to mean unconditionally, i.e. without any strings attached, meaning that the owner has immediate control of the full cash value of the instalment without having to wait for any final stage of the bank transfer process (see *The Chikuma* [1981] 1 Lloyd's Rep. 371).

As to the point of time beyond which the payment of an instalment is legally overdue, it was held in *The Afovos* [1983] 1 Lloyd's Rep. 335 that the words 'on or before the (specified) date' is to be interpreted to mean the entire (specified) day, i.e. the charterer has until midnight to effect payment. The incidence of a weekend and/or banking holiday places the onus on the charterer to properly effect payment not later than the immediately preceding bank working day (see *The Laconia* [1977] 1 Lloyd's Rep. 315).

## Withdrawal must be permanent, not temporary

The standard remedy available to a shipowner in the event of failure to pay hire regularly and punctually (the customary wording used) is to exercise his express right (granted in the charterparty itself) to withdraw the vessel from the charterer's service. It should be realized that this right to withdraw is granted *expressly* by the charterparty itself. Under the English common law no such remedy is available to a shipowner. Such withdrawal, if exercised, must be permanent and not merely temporary. One example of a *temporary* withdrawal would be an instruction by the owners to their Master to stop loading or discharging until further notice. This is often done as a pressurizing tactic to induce the charterer to pay up an outstanding and overdue balance of hire. Temporary withdrawal is wrongful and constitutes a breach of charter giving the charterers a claim in damages for whatever losses they could prove they had suffered as a direct result of the breach. But in the newly designed version of the NYPE-NYPE '93—the wording of Clause 11 has been enlarged in scope (see particularly line 154) to include the right of the shipowner to be entitled not only to withdraw his ship but to 'withhold the performance of any and all of his obligations hereunder . . . '. Presumably that would include a right to refuse to discharge cargo or to interrupt cargo as a lawful counter-action to the charterer for failing to pay hire instalments as they fell due. (The further comments upon the '93 version of the NYPE charter are found on page 215.)

Because of the harsh consequences that a charterer might suffer as a result of a permanent withdrawal in mid-period, especially if he had sub-let the ship under a liberty to do so and/or had entered into carriage contracts for cargoes on planned voyages for the immediate future, the English courts were asked to look into the question of how to alleviate the harshness of the consequences of a summary withdrawal, particularly when the failure to pay punctually and regularly may have been due not so much to the charterer's failure, but to the failure of his bankers promptly to implement payment instructions given to him.

A shipowner may be deemed to have waived his right of withdrawal in certain circumstances, e.g. if he has accepted previous late payment of hire instalments and thus by his conduct led the charterer to believe that he is content with late tenders of hire instalments.

The consequences of a failure by the charterers to pay instalments of hire punctually and regularly were closely examined by English courts (up to and including the House of Lords in *The Laconia* [1977] 1 Lloyd's Rep. 315). In that case, a charterer was due to pay a hire instalment by 3pm on a certain Sunday afternoon (a non-banking day). In effect this meant payment by close of banking hours on the preceding Friday if the contracted commitment was to be fulfilled. By late afternoon on the following Monday (a banking day) the owner's bank still had not received the remittance. Despite a late tender by the charterer, the House of Lords defined the law as being that once the default had accrued, i.e. the payment was unpaid and the material deadline for payment passed, the default cannot be erased by late offer of payment by the charterers (even an offer of the full amount). As a balance, however, their Lordships stipulated that the owner, in giving notice of his intention to with-draw, must give reasonably prompt notice. What is reasonable in these circumstances would have to take into account inter alia where each party is based in relation to each other.

## Anti-technicality clauses

As a result of the strict, if not totally harsh, interpretation by the courts, a clause known as 'an anti-technicality' clause has been devised and is now very commonly used so as to temper the strictness and give charterers a 48-hour 'breathing space' to pay up without being penalized for not doing so. (This clause in the NYPE '93 is entitled 'grace period' and is Clause 11(G).)

Although a ship may have been withdrawn for non-payment of hire under the provisions described above, the owner cannot just 'walk away' from any current responsibilities he may have towards innocent third parties under bills of lading as yet unaccomplished. A voyage, uncompleted at the time of withdrawal, must be completed and the contract of carriage contained in bills of lading issued for that voyage must be fully performed. (See *The Alev* [1989] 1 Lloyd's Rep. 138.)

In the *Pamela* [1995] 2 Lloyd's Rep. 249 the technicalities of the anti-technicality clause were examined. The High Court was asked to review a decision by London arbitrators who had been asked to say whether or not a telex sent by an owner's broker to the charterer's office and received on the telex machine at 19 minutes before midnight on a Friday when the office was closed for the weekend and the machine consequently unmanned, constituted effective 48 hours' notice as required by the charterparty's anti-technicality clause. The arbitrators said no and that notice was only effective as from the time of opening of the charterers business on the next working day. The court endorsed that view and said that common business sense decreed that it could not be expected of a charterer that he gave attention to a telex message received so clearly outside customary business hours.

The court also remarked that a message sent pursuant to an anti-technicality clause must be couched in clear unambiguous terms and constitute an unmistakable ultimatum that default must be remedied within 48 hours or withdrawal will take place.

### *Redelivery*

This generally presents more problems than delivery. The longer the charter period, obviously the trickier it will be for the charterer to plan voyages and cargoes for the vessel which will dovetail in nicely with the contractual redelivery date. Furthermore, from a commercial viewpoint a charterer is obviously going to squeeze as much employment out of the ship as he possibly can. In recognition of this, the parties themselves have been accustomed to fixing between them a marginal or 'grace' period, delivery within which would not be considered a breach. Thus phrases such as 'about 6 months', '6 months 10 days or less', 'minimum 8 months, maximum 10 months' are commonly found. Even if the charterparty contains no such tolerance, it is rare, if ever, that an English court would hold a charterer to the exact contractual date.

## What is meant by the 'illegitimate last voyage'?

A *legitimate* last voyage is one which at the time it is commenced the charterer could reasonably expect that redelivery could be made within the charter period, marginal tolerance, if existing, included. Under this scenario the owner was bound to follow the charterer's direction, perform the voyage and hire would be payable at the charterparty rate right up to redelivery even if that eventually fell beyond the original charter period.

Conversely, a last voyage is classified as *ill*egitimate if at the time of its commencement it could not reasonably have been expected that the ship could be redelivered within the charter period (including marginal allowance, if relevant). The Master/his owners could refuse to perform the voyage and ask for alternative orders. If, despite the 'illegitimacy' the Master performed that voyage, the remuneration for the period between the latest contractual date for redelivery and the time/date of actual redelivery is to be calculated at the *market rate*.

The following cases are relevant on this point: *The Dione* [1975] 1 Lloyd's Rep. 115; *The Democritos* [1976] 2 Lloyd's Rep. 149; *The Matija Gubec* [1983] 1 Lloyd's Rep. 24; *The Black Falcon* [1991] 1 Lloyd's Rep. 77.

In *The Peonia* [1991] 1 Lloyd's Rep. 100 the Court of Appeal confirmed that when the parties do not expressly agree a margin, such margin will be implied if there is otherwise merely a rigid fixed redelivery date. The court construed the words 'further option to complete last voyage' as being confined to an *illegitimate* last voyage. It does not mean that an illegitimate voyage can or should be legitimized.

There is nothing to prevent the parties agreeing to include what some call a 'completion of last voyage clause' which applies whether the last voyage is legitimate *or* illegitimate. Such a clause may be found in the Shell Time 3 form (Clause 18). In *The World Symphony* [1991] 2 Lloyd's Rep. 251 it was held that the 'round voyage' alluded to in Clause 18 was, on the facts before the court, a combination of a cargo-laden and a ballasted voyage. Thus such a combined voyage, even if it could not reasonably be finally completed by the contractual redelivery date, was legitimate, made so by the express liberty in Clause 18. The owners' appeal against this decision was dismissed by the Court of Appeal [1992] 2 Lloyd's Rep. 115.

In *The Gregos* [1992] 2 Lloyd's Rep. 40 the Court of Appeal emphasized that the charterer has two separate obligations:

(1) To give a lawful order before the commencement of the last voyage. The shipowner may then accept the order and, if he does so, then cannot

later refuse to perform. He can, however, oblige the charterer to give revised instructions of what was originally a legitimate order but has become illegitimate before the time for commencing performance is actually reached.

(2) To redeliver at the conclusion of the agreed charter period, subject only to his right to redeliver later than the contractual date provided that it was a legitimate last voyage and the extended period was not due to his own fault.

The matter was appealed by the shipowner and the House of Lords rendered its judgment just prior to this edition going to press. Their Lordships decided the following:

(1) If, when the order to form a 'last' voyage is given, it is plain that the outcome will cause redelivery *after* the agreed expiry date of the charterparty (i.e. the order is categorized as illegitimate) the shipowner is at liberty to refuse to comply with it.

(2) If, however, the order is legitimate when given, then the shipowner may not refuse to comply with it *at that time*. But if by the time the performance (of that 'last' voyage) falls due it appears that the order, if carried out, will result in redelivery after the expiry date (i.e. the voyage categorized legitimate has become illegitimate) the shipowner is entitled to refuse to comply.
Their Lordships' decision seems to have been reached (a) on operational grounds that the balance of convenience is weighted more in support of the shipowner's arguments than the charterer's and (b) as most time charterparties are constructed, the risk of delay is *primarily* upon the charterer with contractual restraints being generally placed upon the charterer not only on time, but on geography, trading areas and permitted cargoes.

(3) If the charterer insists on compliance with an order which had started off by being legitimate but which had become illegitimate by the time performance of the voyage fell due, the shipowner could treat that as an anticipatory breach of charter and regard the charterparty contract as at an end.

Shipowners and charterers can now regard the following as generally being the current rule so far as they have to date been formulated by English case law taking into account particularly the House of Lords' decision as described above in *The Gregos* [1995] 1 Lloyd's Rep. 1.

(1) A precise redelivery date can be tempered by an expressly agreed margin of tolerance. If the parties have not expressly agreed such a margin, the courts will apply one, the amount varying according to the amount of the charter period.

(2) The charterer, assuming there were no specific provisions on the point, must give a legitimate order (legitimate at the time it was made) for the last voyage.

(3) He must redeliver within the charter period, tolerance included (either express or implied).

(4) An owner can refuse to perform an illegitimate last voyage. Alternatively he can opt to perform it, reserving his rights to claim damages for breach of charter by reason of late redelivery. Alternatively again, he can seek from the charterer a substitute order for a *legitimate* voyage (assuming this is still possible), failure to give which will entitle the shipowner to regard the charter as ended.

(5) If after giving what, at the time of giving it, was a legitimate order, the practical situation changes before the voyage is commenced and it becomes apparent that the intended last voyage could not be completed within the charter period, the shipowner is *at that time* entitled to refuse to comply with it.

(6) The measure of damages for late redelivery is:
   (a) regardless of any liability for damages for breach of charterparty, the charterer must pay hire at the contractual rate up to actual redelivery,
   (b) if the voyage runs beyond the redelivery date, (latest permitted by margin) and the market rate is currently higher, then the owner is entitled to additional damages being the difference between the contractual and the market rate for the extra days the charterer has in fact used the vessel. No loss will, of course, have been suffered if the market rate has dropped below the charterparty rate.

### *NYPE '93*

A newly introduced version of this NYPE form has recently been made available to the shipping community. The general impression gained from studying its provisions is that it is slanted more in favour of the owner than is the currently in-use form.

The following is a commentary upon its significant features:

8. Performance of Voyages

'(a) The Master shall perform the voyages with due despatch, and shall render all customary assistance with the Vessel's crew. The Master shall be conversant with the English language and (although appointed by the Owners) shall be under the orders and directions of the Charterers as regards employment and agency; and the Charterers shall perform all cargo handling, including but not limited to loading, stowing, trimming, lashing, securing, dunnaging, unlashing, discharging, and tallying, at their risk and expense, under the supervision of the Master.

(b) If the Charterers shall have reasonable cause to be dissatisfied with the conduct of the Master or officers, the Owners shall, on receiving particulars of the complaint, investigate the same, and, if necessary, make a change in the appointments.'

The alteration to the wording of Clause 8 (which clause is now in title 'performance of voyages'). Traditionally Clause 8 is the key clause to determine the responsibility for cargo claims as between owner and charterer. Under the old form it has been seen (see page 208) that apportionment of responsibility was not clear-cut but that the application of one or other formula contained in the Inter-Club agreement provided a 'painless' method of apportionment. Clause 8(a) in the '93 provision has the last three lines reading:

'. . . and the charterer shall perform all cargo handling, including but not limited to loading, stowing, trimming, lashing, securing, dunnaging, unlashing, discharging and tallying at their *risk* and expense under the supervision of the Master.'

There are two points to note in these words, one is that the whole cargo handling process in all its consecutive phrases is *expressly* mentioned (which it was not in the old printed version) and the word 'risk' is added in. Putting the entire cargo handling process at the charterer's risk would seem on the face of it to rule out any additional benefit gained by the charterer by the adding in of the words 'and responsibility' after the word 'supervision'. Indeed to add in those words into the revised wording would create a direct clash or conflict. So how would the Inter-Club agreement be used in connexion with the new revision? Pending the testing of this question, the author ventures to think that only that formula which is used in connection with the original *un*amended Clause 8 could still be logically used. To use the other formula effectively, would mean inserting 'and responsibility' appropriately and to do that effectively there would be a need to delete the word 'risk' from the printed wording.

9(b) The Charterers shall supply bunkers of a quality suitable for burning in the Vessel's engines and auxiliaries and which conform to the specification(s) as set out in Appendix A.
The Owners reserve their right to make a claim against the Charterers for any damage to the main engines or the auxiliaries caused by the use of unsuitable fuels or fuels not complying with the agreed specification(s). Additionally, if bunker fuels supplied do not conform with the mutually agreed specification(s) or otherwise prove unsuitable for burning in the Vessel's engines or auxiliaries, the Owners shall not be held responsible for any reduction in the Vessel's speed performance and/or increased bunker consumption, nor for any time lost and any other consequences.'

This is the first time in the history of the NYPE form that a positive attempt has been made to spell out the legal position when there is a question that the vessel's engines may have been damaged by poor quality bunker fuel. In modern times shipowners frequently complain that substandard bunkers are the proximate cause of damage to the main engines or auxiliaries and this newly drafted printed clause seems to reflect the frequency of that occurrence. Although the clause does reflect what in fact is happening already, it does beg the question as to whose is the burden of proof.

11. Hire Payment
(a) *Payment*
'Payment of Hire shall be made so as to be received by the Owners or their designated payee in ..... ..... ..... .... ..... ..... ..... ....., viz .....
..........................................................................................................................
..........................................................................................................................
..........................................................................................................................
in ............................................... currency, or in United States Currency, in funds available to the Owners on the due date, 15 days in advance, and for the last month or part of same the approximate amount of hire, and should same not cover the actual time, hire shall be paid for the balance day by day as it becomes due, if so required by the Owners. Failing the punctual and regular payment of the hire, or on any fundamental breach whatsoever of this Charter Party, the Owners shall be at liberty to withdraw the Vessel

from the service of the Charterers without prejudice to any claims they (the Owners) may otherwise have on the Charterers.
At any time after the expiry of the grace period provided in Sub-clause 11(b) hereunder and while the hire is outstanding, the Owners shall, without prejudice to the liberty to withdraw, be entitled to withhold the performance of any and all of their obligations hereunder and shall have no responsibility whatsoever for any consequences thereof, in respect of which the Charterers hereby indemnify the Owners, and hire shall continue to accrue and any extra expenses resulting from such withholding shall be for the Charterers' account.'

Clause 11(a) allows the shipowner to withhold performance (of the charter-party), e.g. the Master may legitimately refuse to discharge in circumstances where there has been non-payment of hire. Under the previous version of the NYPE form the owner has a right to withdraw the vessel permanently (thus terminating the charter) but has no right to withdraw the ship in any temporary manner in default of full payment of hire. To do so under the previous form would have constituted a breach of charter. Under the new version of the NYPE a temporary withdrawal of services is presumably allowed because it would come within the definition of 'withholding performance' as per the first line of the new Clause 11(a).

(c) *Last Hire Payment*
'Should the Vessel be on her voyage towards port of redelivery at the time the last and/or the penultimate payment of hire is/are due, said payment(s) is/are to be made for such length of time as the Owners and the Charterers may agree upon as being the estimated time necessary to complete the voyage, and taking into account bunkers actually on board, to be taken over by the Owners and estimated disbursements for the Owners' account before redelivery. Should same not cover the actual time, hire is to be paid for the balance, day by day, as it becomes due. When the Vessel has been redelivered, any difference is to be refunded by the Owners or paid by the Charterers, as the case may be.'

Clause 11(c) of the new form imposes an additional burden on the charterer in that whereas in the previous form he could make his own assessment (provided it was reasonable) of the likely time remaining for redelivery and calculate his final hire payment accordingly, the new form (by this clause) requires *agreement* on this period. This may introduce difficulties and the new clause does not make it clear what is to be done in the absence of any such agreement.

16. Delivery/Cancelling
If required by the Charterers, time shall not commence before ..... and should the Vessel not be ready for delivery on or before ...... but not later than .. hours, the Charterers shall have the option of cancelling this Charter Party.

*Extension of Cancelling*
If the Owners warrant that, despite the exercise of due diligence by them, the Vessel will not be ready for delivery by the cancelling date, and provided the Owners are able to state with reasonable certainty the date on which the Vessel will be ready, they may, at the earliest seven days before the Vessel is expected to sail for the port or place of delivery, require the Charterers to declare whether or not they will cancel the Charter Party. Should the Charterers elect not to cancel, or should they fail to reply within two days or by the cancelling date, whichever shall first occur, then the seventh day after the expected date of readiness for delivery as notified by the Owners shall replace the original cancelling date. Should the Vessel be further delayed, the Owners shall be entitled to require further declarations of the Charterers in accordance with this Clause.

Under the previous form the charterer may not cancel prior to the cancelling date having been reached nor, on the other hand, was he obliged to declare his intentions to the shipowner prior to presentation of the vessel. Clause 16 of the new version (entitled 'Extension of Cancelling') permits the shipowner to force the charterer to make an election under certain circumstances.

30(c) 'Bills of lading covering deck cargo shall be claused: "Shipped on deck at Charterers', Shippers' and Receivers' risk, expense and responsibility, without liability on the part of the Vessel, or her Owners for any loss, damage, expense or delay howsoever caused." '

Clause 30(c) provides that bills of lading issued for cargo placed on deck should be claused 'shipped on deck at charterers, shippers and receivers risk . . .'. The addition of *charterers* as well as shippers and receivers in this particular phrase is an innovation generally speaking but, as the subject of deck cargo is dealt with in a different part of this chapter (see page 201) no further comment will be made at this point.

31(d) U.S. TRADE—DRUG CLAUSE
'In pursuance of the provisions of the U.S. Anti Drug Abuse Act 1986 or any re-enactment thereof, the Charterers warrant to exercise the highest degree of care and diligence in preventing unmanifested narcotic drugs and marijuana to be loaded or concealed on board the Vessel.
Non-compliance with the provisions of this clause shall amount to breach of warranty for consequences of which the Charterers shall be liable and shall hold the Owners, the Master and the crew of the Vessel harmless and shall keep them indemnified against all claims whatsoever which may arise and be made against them individually or jointly. Furthermore, all time lost and all expenses incurred, including fines, as a result of the Charterers' breach of the provisions of this clause shall be for the Charterer's account and the Vessel shall remain on hire.
Should the Vessel be arrested as a result of the Charterers' non-compliance with the provisions of this clause, the Charterers shall at their expense take all reasonable steps to secure that within a reasonable time the Vessel is released and at their expense put up the bails to secure release of the Vessel.
The Owners shall remain responsible for all time lost and all expenses incurred, including fines, in the event that unmanifested narcotic drugs and marijuana are found in the possession or effects of the Vessel's personnel.'

In view of the considerable tightening up being made by the US Government through the medium of the US Coast Guard in regard to the smuggling of drugs into the United States of America the new form contains Clause 31(d) which provides for the proper placing of liability as between shipowner and charterer in the event that drugs are discovered on board and as a consequence fines are imposed upon the vessel. It should be noted that fines is one of the many risks covered by the shipowners' mutuals under their ordinary P & I cover.

35. *Stevedore Damage*
'Notwithstanding anything contained herein to the contrary, the Charterers shall pay for any and all damage to the Vessel caused by stevedores provided the Master has notified the Charterers and/or their agents in writing as soon as practical but not later than 48 hours after any damage is discovered. Such notice to specify the damage in detail and to invite Charterers to appoint a surveyor to assess the extent of such damage.

(a) In case of any and all damage(s) affecting the Vessel's seaworthiness and/or the safety

of the crew and/or affecting the trading capabilities of the Vessel, the Charterers shall immediately arrange for repairs of such damage(s) at their expense and the Vessel is to remain on hire until such repairs are completed and if required passed by the Vessel's classification society.
(b) Any and all damage(s) not described under point (a) above shall be repaired at the Charterers' option, before or after redelivery concurrently with the Owners' work. In such case no hire and/or expenses will be paid to the Owners except and insofar as the time and/or the expenses required for the repairs for which the Charterers are responsible, exceed the time and/or expenses necessary to carry out the Owners' work.'

Stevedore damage clauses have up to now normally been found as rider or additional clauses with specially designed wording but the new NYPE version has 'promoted' this type of clause to appear in the *printed* version and is Clause 35. Under this clause the charterer is made strictly liable for the damage caused to the vessel by stevedores. Charterers have traditionally tried to restrict their liability for this type of damage only to be in circumstances arising from the *negligence* of stevedores but if they are to continue to reap such a benefit when they charter ships on a time basis, then they will have to negotiate that additional advantage by introducing an amendment to Clause 35 to which the shipowner will have to be persuaded to agree.

41. *Stowaways*
(a) (i) The Charterers warrant to exercise due care and diligence in preventing stowaways in gaining access to the Vessel by means of secreting away in the goods and/or containers shipped by the Charterers.
(ii) If, despite the exercise of due care and diligence by the Charterers, stowaways have gained access to the Vessel by means of secreting away in the goods and/or containers shipped by the Charterers, this shall amount to breach of charter for the consequences of which the Charterers shall be liable and shall hold the Owners harmless and shall keep them indemnified against all claims whatsoever which may arise and be made against them. Furthermore, all time lost and all expenses whatsoever and howsoever incurred, including fines, shall be for the Charterers' account and the Vessel shall remain on hire.
(iii) Should the Vessel be arrested as a result of the Charterers' breach of charter according to sub-clause (a)(ii) above, the Charterers shall take all reasonable steps to secure that, within a reasonable time, the Vessel is released and at their expense put up bail to secure release of the Vessel.
(b) (i) If, despite the exercise of due care and diligence by the Owners, stowaways have gained access to the Vessel by means other than secreting away in the goods and/or containers shipped by the Charterers, all time lost and all expenses whatsoever and howsoever incurred, including fines, shall be for the Owners' account and the Vessel shall be off hire.
(ii) Should the Vessel be arrested as a result of stowaways having gained access to the Vessel by means other than secreting away in the goods and/or containers shipped by the Charterers, the Owners shall take all reasonable steps to secure that, within a reasonable time, the Vessel is released and at their expense put up bail to secure release of the Vessel.

Clause 41 is a fresh introduction to the NYPE charter and is concerned with liability for the costs/expenses incurred in dealing with stowaways located anywhere on the vessel. The presence of stowaways on board ships is becoming an increasing problem and it is in this risk also that the P & I Clubs are directly concerned. Normally when a stowaway is found on board, the responsibility for keeping him on board and affording him reasonable treatment and conditions until he can be disposed of is upon the shipowner. However, Clause 41 in the new NYPE version purports to involve the charterers in liability for stowaway expenses in circumstances where stowaways are discovered *inside containers.* It is perhaps hard on charterers that they should be held responsible merely because stowaways are found inside containers, particularly when they have had no chance to check upon the possibility of stowaways concealing themselves inside containers, but on the basis of the principle of freedom of contract if the shipowner can bring in charterers by way of the charterparty contract with some partial form of responsibility then he is free to do so. Charterers' liability to indemnify is based upon a want of due diligence to prevent the hiding away of stowaways in goods or containers. In the same way as the expenses resulting from the maintenance and disposal of stowaways can be recovered by shipowners from their P & I Club, so any time charterer under the new NYPE version would be well advised to seek similar cover from his Club and/or insurers on liability.

The above remarks are not an exhaustive examination of the new form, which space does not permit, but some significant points have been selected for commentary.

Since the publication of the 4th edition of this book there has been little sign of owners or charterers (or their respective brokers) making use of the 1993 version of NYPE. This is probably good news for charterers but certainly it testifies to the enduring popularity on both sides of the contractual fence of the traditional version.

## VOYAGE CHARTERPARTIES

These are contracts under which a vessel is to load at one or more named ports (or identified berth within a port) a particular specified cargo to be carried to a named discharging port or ports. The shipowner's remuneration for performing his obligations under the charterparty is known as freight. Methods of calculation of freight will be described later on.

It is convenient to think of the overall performance of obligations under a voyage charter as being divided into four stages:

(1) the approach voyage;
(2) the loading process;
(3) the carrying voyage;
(4) the discharge process.

The commentary which follows will therefore be divided into these four sections. First the approach voyage. A significant piece of information given by the shipowner up front in the charterparty is a statement that the named vessel is 'now at . . . ' and 'expected ready to load . . . '. If, at the time of the making of the statement the vessel is not where it is claimed to be, the owner is in breach fundamental enough to entitle the charterer to repudiate. A prediction of expected readiness is, of course, not a promise or guarantee, but must, at the time of the prediction, be made on the basis of a genuine belief. If proved not to be so, the charterer may treat it as a fundamental breach justifying repudiation.

In addition, the owner has an obligation to prosecute the approach voyage with 'all convenient speed' and this will almost certainly be expressly stated in the charterparty. Such an obligation is absolute in nature, meaning that if the approach voyage is held up due to an intermediate engagement, whether or not the owner is at fault, the charterer may rescind the contract and claim whatever damages he can prove as flowing direct from the ship's failure to present timely. As to what damages might be recoverable for late arrival at the loading port, or even for delay on the cargo carrying voyage resulting in late arrival at the loading port or even for delay on the cargo carrying voyage resulting in late arrival at the discharge port, the legal test under English law is, as has been for many years, such losses as would or should reasonably have been in the contemplation of the parties at the time when they concluded the contract (*Hadley* v *Baxendale* (1854) 9 Ex. 341). There has been a tendency in recent times for owners of tankers or gas carriers to be considered to have sufficiently 'inside' knowledge of the oil (or gas) industry to bring losses likely to be suffered by charterer for late arrival within the 'contemplation' envisaged by that test. In one case the Court of Appeal upheld an arbitration award (which had been reversed by the High Court) by saying that an experienced operator of gas tankers must be deemed to have known that the market in this commodity was very sensitive and would be affected by a sea transit delay and that the charterers were likely to have re-sold the cargo at a fixed price (*The Baleares* [1990] 2 Lloyd's Rep. 130, Commercial Court; [1991] 1 Lloyd's Rep. 349 and [1993] 1 Lloyd's Rep. 215, CA).

It will be less likely, however, that when general cargoes are being carried, an owner or operator of a general ship would be expected to possess intricate knowledge of a 'whole host' of commodity markets.

Anyone analysing the fine borderline between recoverability and remoteness of damages would have to distinguish clearly between how much general knowledge about a particular market an owner should have or be expected to have and whether or not he had or should have had knowledge of the particular transaction (i.e. contract of sale) relative to the cargo actually being carried.

### *The charterer's right to cancel*

In a voyage charterparty a clause universally found is a cancelling clause. If the ship fails to make the stated cancelling date, the charterer may cancel. This right of cancellation is not at all connected with any fault or breach which the owner may or may not have committed causing his ship's late arrival. The charterer may not exercise the option to cancel until the stated cancelling date is reached. There is, that means, no right to cancel in anticipation. Indeed, if he does so, he will, without justification, himself have repudiated the contract. If in the circumstances he could show that it would have been an impossibility for the vessel to have reached by the cancelling date, damages awarded against him for his repudiatory breach would be nominal (*The Mihalis Angelos* [1971] 1 Q.B. 164).

Conversely, if the shipowner could show that, despite what the charterer thought, the ship could have reached by the cancelling date, he can claim damages, provided that he mitigates his losses by re-employing his ship to best advantage or he can order his ship to maintain course and speed to the loading port and so compel the charterer to load and thus 'wipe out' his anticipatory breach (if he makes the cancelling date) or to cancel (if he arrives after the specified date).

### *Arrival at loading port*

**Where must a vessel have reached before it can be said to have arrived in the legal sense?**

Under a *port* charterparty, that is a charterparty whose provisions require the vessel to proceed to a named port or ports, case law has established that in order to be so arrived and to be in a position for the Master to be entitled to tender his notice of readiness, the ship must have satisfied a two-part test:

(1) she must have reached and be lying in a customary waiting area *within* the port;
(2) she must be at the immediate and effective disposal of the charterer.

This test was laid down by the House of Lords in *The Johanna Oldendorff* [1974] AC 479. In the author's opinion, the only defect in this test, which has stood now for 20 years is the word 'within'. There are many waiting areas which lie outside even the outer limits of a port, e.g. the Hook of Holland for Rotterdam, and thus the wording of the test might have been widened in scope to say 'whether within or without the port' but it was not.

If the charterparty provides that the ship shall proceed into a named or identified berth in a port, then the ship must be at or in that berth before she can be said to have 'arrived' and be in a position to present its NOR.

## Notice of readiness

At common law a written notice of readiness is only required to be given at the ship's arrival at the first port of loading. This is obviously to inform the charterer and so give him a chance to have the cargo ready for loading. At subsequent loading ports and at ports of discharge there is no common law requirement to tender a notice of readiness, though in practice almost all voyage charterparties, if not all, expressly require the Master to tender NOR at every port, both loading and discharge. The Master may not tender NOR until his ship has *legally* arrived as described above. An anticipatory notice, even though he may be confident of the accuracy of his imminent arrival time, is not permitted.

A Master may tender his notice of readiness if the only thing which obstructs his readiness to load or to proceed to a loading berth is a routine formality of which the most obvious example is free pratique.

In *The Linardos* [1994] 1 Lloyd's Rep. 28 discussion was had on the question of the 'black and white effect' (to use the presiding judge's own words) of the general principle that a valid notice of readiness cannot be given unless and until the vessel is in truth ready to load. The relevant charterparty contained, in addition to the usual stipulations for presenting a notice of readiness, a provision that any time subsequently lost through requirements for load readiness being unfulfilled, including a marine surveyor's certificate, should not count . . . . It also contained a separate clause incorporating load port (Richards Bay) regulations providing, amongst other things, that a notice of readiness would only be accepted after the receipt of certificate by an independent marine surveyor certifying that the holds were clean and dry. It also required that a Master's certificate that the holds had been washed and dried prior to tendering notice of readiness should be presented. Three-and-a-half days after tendering the notice of readiness the vessel berthed but the surveyor appointed locally failed her on load readiness because of water and rust in the hatches. It was a further 20 hours before the hatches were declared clean. The owners argued that the NOR was validly tendered when it was, the charterers conversely argued that the NOR only became effective when the hatches were declared clean. On appeal by the charterers from an arbitration award in favour of owners, the Commercial Court held that:

(1) The 'black and white' effect of the basic principle could be varied by express provisions in the charterparty.
(2) In giving the NOR the Master had to be acting in good faith. The charterparty wording providing as it did for presentation of NOR whether in berth or not (i.e. contemplating a possible port congestion on arrival) also provided very sensibly for the possibility that the holds might need a final cleaning prior to the mandatory passing as fit by an independent local surveyor. The vessel on the other hand might have had to wait weeks for a berth due to the congestion whereas the hold cleaning might have occupied only a few hours, as indeed it did. It would be commercially unreasonable to force an owner to lose all the benefits of wasted waiting time for the sake of merely a few hours hold cleaning. Thus the court held that it is possible to contract out of the 'black and white' effect of the general principle upon which the tendering of a notice of readiness is founded.

## Can an invalid NOR become validated when a ship does become ultimately in all respects ready?

*The Mexico I* [1990] 1 Lloyd's Rep. 507 dispelled any doubt. The facts were that the ship carried two part-cargoes for discharge at Luanda. Cargo A overstowed cargo B. In all other respects, i.e. other than the immediate inaccessibility of cargo B, the ship was ready to discharge. Thus an NOR for cargo B was invalid when tendered. The court said that (1) the NOR was invalid and (2) it could not automatically become valid when cargo B became accessible. The Master must *then* re-tender his NOR.

However, that there can be error in generalizing was demonstrated by the *Petr Schmidt* case (*Galaxy Energy International Limited* v *Novorossiysk Shipping Company* [1997] 1 Lloyd's Rep. 284) where on the facts and under an Asbatankvoy form the NOR was tendered outside the stipulated hours but nevertheless was a reflection of the truth that the vessel was in all respects ready. The charterer argued the *Mexico 1* ruling and said that as the NOR was ineffective, it had to be tendered afresh. The court, distinguished between a NOR which was 'ineffective' because it purported to offer a ready ship when it was not ready and a NOR which was ineffective solely because it was given outside stipulated hours. In the latter event, no fresh NOR need be given and the originally tendered NOR could become effective at the commencement of the stipulated range of hours which in this case was 06.00.

### *Laytime*

#### When does laytime commence?

Laytime, which is the time available to the charterer to load (or discharge) the chartered cargo free of any charge upon the charterer over and above the freight for the carriage of the cargo, cannot commence to run until three conditions have been satisfied:

(1) that the vessel has arrived (legally);
(2) that NOR has been tendered (it does not need to have been accepted);
(3) the vessel is *in all respects* ready to load (or discharge).

In *The Virginia M* [1989] 1 Lloyd's Rep. 603 readiness was held to mean readiness in the fullest commercial and business sense. Mere technical readiness (i.e. merely complying with formalities) is not sufficient. The facts in the case were that the vessel arrived with insufficient supply of fresh water to feed her boilers and run her auxiliaries.

Regarding (3) above, if a vessel was required to load at two load ports a valid NOR could be given even if the tanks required for loading at the *second* load port contained slops.

The fact that condition (2) has been satisfied does not *necessarily* mean that condition (3) is itself a true and actual fact. The Master may genuinely believe that the ship is completely ready, but he may be mistaken. This gives rise to a further query, below.

#### Does laytime commence immediately all three of these conditions are met?

This depends on the express wording of the charterparty. The Gencon printed form provides that if NOR is tendered before noon, laytime will commence at 13.00 hours. If given *after* noon within office hours, laytime will commence at 06.00 on the next working day. A commonly used tanker voyage form—Asbatankvoy—allows a six-hour period to elapse, (often called 'notice' time) between tender of NOR and commencement of the laytime 'clock'.

#### Who pays for waiting time?

So many ports are congested with charterers being unable to provide the ship with a berth on arrival that it is common for a ship to be kept waiting at anchorage. This is time wasted and time is money. In a *berth* charterparty an owner may protect himself and advance the commencement of laytime by inserting the expression 'Wibon' (whether in berth or not) to give him the right to tender NOR on arrival rather than have to wait until in berth. Similar expressions could alternatively be used e.g.:

Wipon (whether in port or not);
Wifpon (whether in free pratique or not);
Wiccon (whether in customs clearance or not).

Wibon was tested as to its effect in *The Kyzikos* [1989] 1 Lloyd's Rep. 1 which climbed the appeal ladder right to the House of Lords. The charterer eventually won due to the final decision being that where a berth was available on arrival but the named ship could not reach it by reason of fog (i.e. not because of congestion) the Master could not rely on Wibon to tender his notice in advance of berthing. It did not affect delay due to navigational difficulties.

Another expression frequently relied on by an owner to protect himself against time wasted in waiting is 'time lost in waiting for a berth to count as loading/discharging time (or sometimes "laytime")'. When the word 'laytime' is used there was for a long time doubt as to whether this could mean that laytime exceptions would apply to waiting time only if those same exceptions would have applied if the ship had been berthed and actually working cargo. The doubt was clarified in *The Darrah* [1977] AC 157, i.e. laytime exceptions *should* apply to the waiting period. Thus periods of rain (if they would have interrupted cargo work and if weather working days were the basis of laytime) were excepted and also Sundays or holidays. Such a ruling had a measure of morality also since if it had not been so the shipowner would have been financially 'better off' waiting than berthed.

Some tanker voyage charterparties, e.g. the Asbatankvoy and the Exxonvoy, provide that the charterer is to procure a berth 'reachable on arrival'. This places an absolute obligation on the charterer to obtain the berth as soon as the ship has concluded its approach or carrying voyage. Thus it is irrelevant whether or not the ship has become 'arrived' in the legal sense. Compensation will be payable for all time spent waiting and will be computed as damages for detention which will be calculated on the basis of the daily running costs of that ship. The word 'reachable' has been given a wider meaning than the word 'available' which, as we have seen in *The Kyzikos*, is restricted to the idea of the berth being vacant and thus available for use at the time of the ship's arrival. The word 'reachable', however, includes the additional notion that the ship can gain access to the available berth and/or has the ability or otherwise to proceed into that nominated berth. Both Exxonvoy and Asbatankvoy include a printed clause (Clause 9) which obliges the charterer to designate and procure a (safe) berth . . . reachable on arrival. It also contains a separate (also printed) Clause (6) which allows the interrupting of the running of laytime when the ship is kept waiting (to berth) in circumstances where the delay is beyond the charterer's control. However, the benefit of this latter clause is only available to the charterer if he has already designated and procured a vessel reachable on arrival. The logic of this is that the charterer should not gain benefit out of his failure to fulfil his primary basic duty of procuring a berth. These issues were analysed and were the subject of a House of Lords' decision in *The Laura Prima* [1982] 1 Lloyd's Rep. 1.

'Reachable on arrival' is probably therefore about the most effective way of a shipowner ensuring that if his ship has to wait on arrival the onus of waiting for a berth is passed over to a charterer. The culmination of clauses described above also placed the burden on the charterer of proving that the circumstances which caused the delay are beyond his control.

## How is laytime calculated?

The two most common methods are: (1) a fixed number of days or hours—which is usually clear and needs no interpretation, e.g. tanker voyage charters usually provide for 72 hours; (2) a calculation based on a rate of loading or discharging, e.g. wording such as 'cargo to be loaded (or discharged) at the average rate of x thousand tonnes on basis of six available working hatches pro rata, per weather working day of 24 consecutive hours . . . '.

Such forms of wording tend to 'lower the morale' of those who have to deal with ensuing disputes because of the need to 'translate' this calculation into a period of time so that all concerned know where they stand. Complexities of such wording were examined by the House of Lords in *The General Capinpin* [1991] 1 Lloyd's Rep. 1. In that case the charterer contended that the rate of discharge should lessen as the holds emptied of cargo and that thus the laytime allowed should be governed by and calculated according to the quantity of cargo in the 'heaviest' hold divided by 200 tonnes (i.e. 1,000) being the average rate for the ship divided by five being the number of available working hatches. Thus the hold into which the greatest quantity of cargo is stowed becomes the yard-stick for measuring the laytime period. A hatch with no cargo in was not an 'available' or 'working' hatch.

The wording in (2) above invites analysis of the words 'day', 'working' and 'weather'.

A 'working day' is one on which work at the port in question is customarily performed, e.g. not Sunday (or Friday if a Muslim country).

A 'weather working day' is a working day on which the weather conditions are such that work on cargo (i.e. that particular cargo) is able to be carried out, e.g. light rain might not prevent the discharge of general cargo in wooden boxes but it certainly would prevent the discharge of bagged cement. This expression should also be contrasted with a similar laytime phrase 'working day, weather permitting'. Originally it was thought that there were two distinctly different effects resulting from these two respective expressions:

(a) Weather working day—'weather' being the first word, the mind is concentrated upon that word rather than the word 'working'. The word 'weather' describes the type of day—it is characteristic of it. It is not relevant as to whether bad weather actually interrupted work nor even whether work was planned on the day in question, e.g. the ship could be waiting for a berth at anchorage and if waiting time is to be counted (as it frequently is) as laytime, then a day on which the weather substantially prevents cargo work (whether or not work was actually being carried out or being planned to be carried out was irrelevant) was not computed as and included in laytime (see *The Darrah* [1977] AC 157).

Thus the phrase was descriptive of the type of day (*Reardon Smith Line* v *Ministry of Agriculture and Fisheries* [1963] AC 691).

(b) Contrasting with this (as originally thought) waiting day, weather permitting concentrates the mind on whether work was being done or scheduled to be done. Thus an interruption by weather had the effect of suspending laytime. This expression was causative because the incidence of weather was said to have an effect on cargo operations.

However, *The Vorras* [1983] 1 Lloyd's Rep. 579 put an end to these two contrasting views and held that both phrases are contributors to the basic computation of laytime. They were therefore both descriptive expressions because both phrases have the same descriptive effect, according to current judicial thinking. What is the criterion now is that the test is 'did the weather conditions permit the loading (or discharging) of vessels of the same general type as the involved vessel?', i.e. the involved vessel need not necessarily be in its allotted berth, it could be waiting for a berth which is presently occupied.

Sometimes the expression 'running day' is found. This means consecutive calendar days *including* holidays and/or days when work is not normally done.

Another method of reckoning laytime is on terms known as COP/CQD (custom of port/customary quick despatch). The obvious disadvantage of this method from an owner's point of view is the absence of clarity and precision in calculation. There has been post Second World War very little, if any, case law on disputes arising under these terms and the only reported references are comparatively old, e.g. *Postlewaite* v *Freeland* (1880) 5 App Cas 559, where the terms were 'all despatch according to the custom of the port'. The court in those now far-off days took the view that the cargo must be discharged within a reasonable time under the circumstances. That means basically that the charterers on the one hand must use reasonable diligence and the shipowner (or disponent owner in the case of a sub-charter) must accept those obstacles to quick despatch which may manifest themselves by custom or practice in that port on that occasion and in the particular circumstances surrounding the voyage in question, i.e. *actual* circumstances and not merely hypothetical (see also *Hulthen* v *Stewart & Co* [1903] AC 389).

On the above case law and the dicta of the Law Lords in those early days it would seem that when CQD/COP terms are governing, the risk of delay due to port congestion is on the owner, unlike the situations where laytime is pre-calculable and defined.

The complete lack of modern day case law on this particular issue must presumably mean that disputes have been rare in post-war times and that the old Victorian decisions have not thus been challenged. With the emergence of China as a fast growing economic power with the Chinese Government in its various forms voyage chartering ships in ever increasing numbers and with the seeming insistence of the Chinese to take ships on COP/CQD terms, the immediate years to come may see some legal developments (either confirmation or variation) on this issue.

As it stands now, the shipowner may be left with little else to base a claim on than that the charterer had misrepresented the estimated discharge (or loading) period *prior* to fixing the vessel and that he had relied upon that misrepresentation when agreeing to COP/CQD terms.

### Excepted periods from laytime

Laytime does not run continuously, ticking away against the charterer, until loading or discharge is completed. Certain periods are 'excepted' from laytime and cause the 'laytime clock' to stop whilst those excepted periods last.

Examples of commonly excepted periods are:

(a) bad weather (as we have seen when studying the expression *weather* working days);
(b) strikes;
(c) time spent shifting from one loading berth to another. The ship is under navigation and thus time spent in that way should not and does not count against the charterer.

Much will depend upon the custom of the port concerned, e.g. although Sunday (in Christian areas) is universally a non-working day, there is doubt about Saturday or as to whether Saturday is only a half working day. Sometimes how Saturday is to be treated will be the subject of special wording or even a separate rider clause.

One interesting, if one-off, dispute which recently went to London arbitration merits mention at this point. It was a dispute as to whether a voyage charterer was entitled to except from laytime a period lost due to stevedores refusing to work in face of bees swarming. The charterer relied on a force majeure type of clause in the charterparty (a sugar charterparty form) reading as follows 'strikes or lock-outs of men, or any accident or stoppages on railway and/or canal, and/or river by ice or frost, or any other force majeure causes including government interferences, occurring beyond the control of the shippers, or consignees, which may prevent or delay the loading and discharging of the vessel, always excepted'. The charterer failed on that clause because 'other force majeure causes' were necessarily restricted under the eiusdem generis rule whereby general wording following specifically listed causes had to be of a like nature to the preceding causes. The charterer failed also in two alternative arguments, one being an attempt to invoke a clause purporting to make stevedores the owners' servants and freeing the charterer from responsibility for negligence, default or error or judgement of the stevedores. This failed because the arbitrators found that the stevedores' refusal to work was quite reasonable in face of the swarm of bees. The charterer's third approach was to say that as bees only swarmed in humid, sticky weather this in itself could be described as a 'weather condition' entitling him to rely on the (bad) weather exception. The arbitrators dismissed this argument also since there was not a sufficiently strong continuous link between hot sticky weather and bees swarming, i.e. bees did not inevitably swarm in such weather conditions.

Clear and precise wording for laytime exception is strongly encouraged. In *The Lefthero* [1992] 2 Lloyd's Rep. 109 the vessel was chartered for a voyage to Bandar Khomeini with a cargo of steel products and the charterparty contained clauses providing that, whether in berth or not, time was to account from arrival pilot station Bandar Abbas excluding actual steaming time to and from Bandar Khomeini and more importantly a clause providing that neither the vessel, nor the owners, nor the charterers/shippers/receivers shall be responsible for any loss or damage or delay or failure in performing hereunder, arising or resulting from . . . *restraint of princes* (author's emphasis) . . . At the time this voyage actually took place the Iran/Iraq war was well under way and there were dangers involved in sailing in the upper part of the Arabian Gulf. A convoy system was in operation when vessels arrived at Bandar Abbas and the vessel joined a convoy to proceed to Bushire where the next available convoy for Bandar Khomeini was to be assembled. However, the pilot refused to proceed further north. Without going into further detail on the facts, the issue in this case was regarding a claim by the charterers for damages due to shipowner's failure to deliver the cargo at Bandar Khomeini which was the contractual destination, as against the actual place of discharge which was Bushire. Claims and counterclaims arose from the failure to discharge at the contractual destination and also the additional period of delay caused by discharging at Bushire rather than Bandar Khomeini. The London arbitrators to whom this dispute was referred held that as the charterers' claim for damages could not succeed because of the restraint of princes clause, the owners' claim for accrued demurrage could not likewise succeed due to the same exceptions clause. The exception of restraint of princes protected the charterers from the consequences of the vessel not being permitted to proceed beyond Bandar Abbas.

Owners and charterers appealed against the arbitrator's decision and the High Court held, inter alia, that the restraint of princes clause was intended to operate in conjunction with the laytime demurrage provisions with the result that the charterers were not responsible in demurrage for the additional delay.

On this particular issue, again an appeal was taken by the shipowner and the Court of Appeal found that on the face of it the words of the restraint of princes clause were wide enough to cover delay by the charterers in discharging the vessel where the delay arose or resulted from restraint of princes. However, in order to protect the charterers against liability for demurrage, the language of the exception clause must be clearly worded to that effect. The decision reaffirmed the already established judicial view that a general exceptions clause will not normally be construed as applying to provisions for laytime and demurrage unless the language is very precise and clear. This in effect echoes the firmly established principle of 'once on demurrage always on demurrage' (unless there are absolutely clear contractual provisions to the contrary) and has it applying even though the vessel is not yet on demurrage.

### Used laytime

In *The Stainless Emperor* [1994] 1 Lloyd's Rep. 298 the issue was whether delay caused by the charterers in producing the complete cargo on arrival (as specially required under the charterparty) counted as used laytime in the face of another charterparty provision allowing Fridays and holidays as periods excepted from the running of laytime and where there was an overlap of holiday and the delay due to unavailability of cargo. The High Court judge confirmed the arbitrators' award stating that if the charterparty stipulated that delay due to non-availability of cargo was to be counted as used laytime, then the excepted period permitted under the charterparty terms should *not* be applied to that delay. Used laytime in this sense, the court commented, is intended to mean periods of time which are to be treated as if they had been used for loading and discharging. Thus Friday (or Sunday in Christian countries) and holiday periods are only to be excluded if they have not been used. Force must be given to the word 'used'.

### *What is demurrage?*

Demurrage is *liquidated* damages. The rate of demurrage is fixed, agreed between owner and charterer at the time of the concluding of the charterparty and the rate is stated in the charterparty. On the basis that it is fixed and unalterable the author prefers to think of demurrage as a penalty imposed upon the charterer for exceeding the laytime period and delaying the ship beyond the agreed laytime in order to complete loading or discharging. The rate of demurrage is linked in with the rate of freight so that the shipowner satisfies himself as far as he can that overall by the time the voyage is fully completed he will have balanced his books and made a reasonable profit.

Demurrage should be contrasted with *damages for detention* the latter being unliquidated, assessable damages payable by a charterer for detaining the ship for whatever reason (there may be reasons other than exceeding laytime—e.g. repairs necessitated after the causing of damage to the ship by charterers' stevedores for whose negligence the charterers are vicariously liable).

Due to the 'penalty' nature of demurrage, it runs continuously from the point when laytime expires. Laytime exceptions do *not* interrupt the running of demurrage. This is typified by the oft-used expression 'once on demurrage, always on demurrage'.

If demurrage itself, as opposed to laytime, is to be interrupted by any excepted period, such an exception must be expressly provided for in the charterparty. This was made clear in *The Dias* [1978] 1 Lloyd's Rep. 325. It cannot be assumed that laytime exceptions apply equally to demurrage as they do to laytime. They do not unless expressly stated as applying also to demurrage.

### *Despatch money*

This is in a sense the opposite to demurrage. It is reward money paid to a charterer for completing loading/discharging earlier than the expiry of laytime. The rate for despatch money is by custom one-half the agreed demurrage rate and this may or may not be specially provided for in the charterparty.

### *'Full and complete' cargo*

Many disputes arise out of the alleged failure of the charterer to load a 'full and complete' cargo. It is basic charterparty law that a voyage charterer's absolute duty is to furnish the 'intended' cargo to be ready and available on arrival of the vessel. But how is the expression 'full and complete' to be defined and how is the charterer to show that he has complied with this duty? He has to have occupied the entire capacity of cargo spaces on the ship either by way of space occupied or by making use of the ship's full dead-weight capacity available for cargo, bearing in mind that there are other items to be necessarily carried which weigh a vessel down, e.g. bunkers or water. The stowing of cargo is a skilled process and one which should be carried out with care and bearing in mind the nature of the cargo, its ratio weight/measurement, the custom of the port of loading and the charterparty terms. A failure to stow properly may result in that same party, whether owner or charterer, being at fault for a failure to load a 'full and complete' cargo.

On many occasions a min/max option is expressed. If an option of this nature is written into the charterparty together with the obligation to load a full and complete cargo, the latter duty prevails over the exercise of any option within the min/max range, the option merely precluding the shipowner from demanding more than the maximum and placing upon him the onus of having warranted that his vessel was capable of carrying the specified minimum.

The option, if clearly expressed, should define who is to exercise the option, either owners, with the Master physically exercising it on their behalf, or the charterer. If it is owner's option, this must be exercised within whatever time is stipulated (or a reasonable time if none is stated). Once exercised the option becomes a contract to load the selected amount.

#### *Freight*

This is money payable by the charterer in consideration of and as remuneration for carrying the cargo on the named ship. Under the common law freight is payable concurrently with delivery of the cargo at the port of destination or, as the traditional expression goes, on 'right and true delivery'. This does not mean in perfect condition but in accordance with the contractual terms re time and place. In early times, before crews' welfare and condition became protected by statute, the crew took a risk that if freight was not eventually paid they would not receive their wages. In modern times, of course, crews' employment contracts ensure there is no link between their entitlement to wages and the shipowner's receipt of freight. The common law time for payment of freight is, however, almost always varied by express contractual provision in the charterparty. There may be provision for a portion of freight to be paid (e.g. 90 per cent) on signing/issuing of bills of lading and the balance (10 per cent) on delivery of the cargo.

This places some risk on the owners because if between the issue of bills and the delivery at destination the ship sinks, the shipowner has got his 90 per cent but has no right to claim the 10 per cent balance.

There is no right to receive pro rata freight. Thus freight is not payable on a day-to-day basis as the voyage progresses.

### How is freight calculated?

Either:

(a) as a lump sum, i.e. a fixed figure regardless of the quantity of cargo actually loaded. The whole sum is thus payable in full even if the contracted quantity of cargo is not delivered in full; or

(b) on a per tonne of cargo basis—this could mean either on *intaken* quantity, i.e. at the time of loading, or *delivered* quantity, i.e. at the termination of the voyage.

## Can deduction be made from freight by way of equitable set off?

Case law has affirmed the principle that freight is 'sacrosanct' and that setting off counterclaims arising under the same charterparty against it is outlawed.

Case law in support of this well established rule of law is—*The Brede* [1973] 2 Lloyd's Rep. 333 and *The Aries* [1977] 1 Lloyd's Rep. 334.

In these two cases the owners of cargo had tried to set-off against what they owed in freight that which they calculated was their valid claim for short delivery of cargo. The respective courts ruled against this. The claim for freight was altogether separate from and could not be inter-related with by way of set off a counterclaim for loss of or damage to cargo. One very practical reason why it would be dangerous for a charterer to use his counterclaim for loss/damage to cargo as a defence or set-off against a claim for freight or balance of freight would be that different time bars may well apply to each of the claims (e.g. one year to the cargo loss/damage claim, six years (the general statute of limitations) to the claim for freight). The charterer might well find himself time barred in his counterclaim if he left it until the owner claimed for his freight.

An attempt to topple this principle of sacrosanctity was made more recently in *The Dominique* [1989] 1 Lloyd's Rep. 431. The shipowner had assigned freight and all other earnings to a bank and whilst on a cargo-laden voyage the ship was arrested. Her owners made no move to get the arrest lifted prompting the charterer to regard the charter as terminated and to seek other means of carrying the stranded cargo to its destination. The assignee bank demanded freight which the charterers refused to pay claiming an ability to set-off and arguing that their losses were a result of the owner's breach in failing to complete the cargo voyage and prematurely and wrongfully terminating the charterparty. The House of Lords, on final appeal, rejected the charterer's arguments, ruling that payment of freight was sacrosanct against all counterclaims resulting from owners' breaches, however serious.

## Deadfreight

This is damages payable by a charterer to a shipowner for failure to load a quantity short of the amount he is contracted to load under the charterparty terms. The computation of deadfreight is made up of the missing freight which would have been earned had the full cargo been loaded less the cost of earning that amount, i.e. the expense of loading and discharging that quantity which expense was saved for the benefit of the owner because the cargo was not loaded.

To justify his claim for deadfreight, however, an owner must, as in any claim of whatever nature, take reasonable steps to mitigate his loss and in respect of a claim for deadfreight, he must be seen to have taken any reasonable opportunity to load an alternative 'fill-up' cargo if a suitable one offers.

In a voyage charterparty a lien for deadfreight is usually expressly granted alongside a lien for freight and demurrage. The lien is possessory and is used in the manner described on page 197.

### *Clause 2 of the Gencon charterparty*

This clause, as even a cursory reading will reveal, is heavily weighted in the owner's favour. For claims in respect of cargo loss or damage, or even delay, the owners contractually exclude their liability except in the minimal of circumstances, these being only two:

(a) if and when the owners (not the charterers (as per Clause 5(a)) have improperly stowed the cargo; or
(b) when the loss/damage is caused by an unseaworthy condition of the vessel and this in turn is due to the personal lack of due diligence by the owner or his manager. If it is the employee/agents (including Master) lack of due diligence then the charterer is responsible and thus legally liable.

This printed clause may, however, be qualified or even wholly superseded by a rider typed clause (which generally have precedence where there is a conflict of wording over printed clauses). A clause paramount, incorporating the Hague (or Visby) Rules would thus have the effect of moderating the extreme 'owner-bias' of the bare unamended wording of printed Clause 2.

## What is meant by the word 'personal' in the context of clause 2?

Clause 2 on face value appears to 'drive a coach and horses' through the provisions of the Hague Rules, not that there is any relevance in that as the Hague Rules were never intended to govern the terms and conditions of charterparties unless the parties mutually intended so, in which case they would voluntarily incorporate them by clause paramount. The conflict then would be that the carrier of goods (i.e. under a Gencon either the owner or possibly the disponent owner) would have under the Hague Rules a non-delegable duty (see *The Riverstone Meat Company Pty* v *Lancashire Shipping Company Limited The Muncaster Castle* [1961] AC 807) *to exercise due diligence to make the ship seaworthy before and at the beginning of the voyage* . . . Because it is non-delegable (i.e. the work is delegable, e.g. to a shipyard, but the responsibility for possible adverse consequences is not) it matters not who performs the work physically, whether agent, employee or even independent contractor, the responsibility that the work is carried out with due diligence remains with the carrier personally.

Clause 2 cuts across this '*Muncaster Castle*' doctrine saying that owners are responsible for their own personal want but not for the want of those that they delegate to carry out the work, whether agent, Master, crew or independent contractor.

### *What is meant by repudiation?*

A contract (in the context of this chapter—a charterparty) may be terminated because of the conduct of one of the principal parties to it. The conduct must be of a sufficiently serious nature to entitle the other (innocent) party to treat the contract as terminated. It will be stating the obvious to say that breaches of contract occur in all shades and degrees of seriousness. Lawyers have divided breaches into two categories known as (a) warranties and (b) conditions. Warranties are those terms which are not essential to the fulfilling of the purpose of the contract. A breach of such a term will only entitle the innocent party to damages for whatever loss flows from the breach. Conditions are more serious. They are terms which go to the root of the contract and are fundamental to it. A classic example is the 'expected ready to load' provision to be found in voyage charterparties. Whether a particular term is a condition or a warranty is not necessarily advertised as such in the charterparty itself; (it would be helpful if it was), and mostly the intention of the parties has to be examined in order to make the correct classification. However, a breach of a condition (which in practice takes the form of an undertaking by one party to perform or a guarantee that something will happen as promised) should give rise to a right in the innocent party to terminate. It is thus a repudiatory breach.

The over-rigidity of two distinct classes in charterparty terms has caused difficulty in placing every breach into one or other of the two existing categories. A breach of the seaworthiness obligation is probably the best example of the difficulty faced in attempting correct classification because unseaworthiness covers a whole range of major or minor conditions of the vessel, some of which would be central to the purpose of the contract, others of which would be collateral only. In *Hong Kong Fir Shipping Limited* v *KKK Limited* [1961] 2 Lloyd's Rep. 493 Diplock LJ favoured the idea of examining the effect of a particular breach to determine whether it did go to the root of the contract and thus substantially disrupted the intentions of the parties, thus entitling the innocent party to terminate or whether it was minor, not adversely affecting the benefits potentially to be derived from the contract and thus causing the contract to continue intact, but entitling the injured party to seek damages for the breach. Contract terms which were not serious enough to be classed conditions when breached or minor enough to be classed warranties should be classed 'innominate' and dealt with according to the effect which the breach had upon the aggrieved party.

*Lack of clarity in charterparty text itself*

In determining what term of a contract, when breached, is or should be classed as a condition and not a warranty, most charterparties are lacking in an express categorization. It has in the past been largely left to the courts to make the determination. This failure of charterparty text to supply the answers 'up-front' leaves the innocent party under a repudiatory breach scenario (particularly where the breach is anticipatory) in an unpleasantly uncertain frame of mind as to how each should react to the other party's conduct.

## How is a repudiatory breach to be analysed?

It may either be (a) actual or (b) anticipatory. Simply defined, anticipatory breach is when one party has evinced a clear intention not to be bound by the charterparty terms and thus not to perform the contract according to its provisions. Conversely, an actual repudiatory breach would be an explicit act or statement about which there can be no doubt. Thus the anticipatory breach is implicit in the conduct of the party accused of the breach which suggests that he may have no intention of continuing with his performance of the contract.

A recent and suitably illustrative case is the *Santa Clara* (*Vitol SA* v *Norelf Limited* [1995] 2 Lloyd's Rep. 128. The facts were Norelf sold to Vitol propane cif North West Europe. The propane was to be loaded in the *Santa Clara* at an agreed freight rate within 1 and 7 March 1991. On 8 March Vitol despatched a message stating that they must reject the cargo and repudiate the contract on the ground that loading would not be finished until 9 March. This statement (with the reason supporting it) was held to be a repudiatory breach because the contract was held to be one for loading that cargo on that named vessel and not one for shipment within those stated dates. Placing reliance on Vitol's message, Norelf did not provide Vitol with bills of lading and sold the propane to alternative purchasers. Vitol made no message in reply accepting repudiation and stating their intention to terminate the contract. The matter just 'ground to a halt'. Some time later they put in a claim for US$ 1 million. In arbitration the claim succeeded but the manner in which the *Santa Clara* dispute subsequently 'seesawed' up the appeal ladder, up to the House of Lords, illustrates how finely balanced are the arbitral and judicial views as to how and in what manner an innocent party should react to an anticipatory repudiation if he does not want to be deprived of his full quiver of rights. Vitol was the repudiating party, Norelf the innocent party. On the facts as given, the decisions made at the various stages of appeal were as follows:

(1) arbitration for Norelf;
(2) High Court—for Norelf;
(3) Court of Appeal for Vitol;
(4) House of Lords—for Norelf.

The arbitrator originally found that Norelf had displayed conduct sufficient to indicate to Vitol acceptance of repudiation, even though such acceptance was not contained in a specific personal message to them. The High Court (of first instance) agreed. Acts could convey acceptance in some situations as well as specific words. The Court of Appeal disagreed in that the innocent party had a choice to exercise, either to accept repudiation or to affirm the contract as continuing. The choice *must* be exercised clearly and unequivocally. A mere failure to perform contractual obligations is always equivocal and can never, in law, constitute acceptance of an anticipatory repudiation by the other (innocent) party.

So on final appeal by Vitol, the correct answer was given to the question 'can an aggrieved party ever be said to have accepted a repudiation of a contract merely by a failure to perform'? Their Lordships endorsed the judicial view that acceptance of an anticipatory breach does not have to be couched in specific language of acceptance. It is sufficient that the communication or conduct clearly and unequivocally conveys to the repudiating party that the aggrieved party is treating the contract as at an end. In other words, he has made his election to terminate in a manner which should leave no doubt in the repudiating party's mind.

One of the most common voyage charterparty scenarios is the one involving a ship presenting itself at the loading port and the charterer failing to perform what is his absolute obligation—to provide a cargo. In the normal course the owner has a remedy built into the charterparty by way of demurrage or damages for detention which will cushion him to some extent against the frustration of having to wait for the cargo to materialize. But the uncertainty may still remain that the cargo may *never* materialize, and promises by a charterer that 'don't worry the cargo will be here tomorrow', may prove empty. When should he decide to call it a day and take his ship away to seek alternative, more reliable employment elsewhere? The dilemma from the owners' view point is that the charterer's failure to load may not be a repudiatory breach, because the cargo *may* eventually materialize and if the owner nevertheless loses patience and removes his ship (despite the charterparty allowing him compensatory damages for the delay) he, the owner, may face an accusation of wrongful termination so that at the end of the day it is not the charterer but the owner who may be held in repudiatory breach. The dilemma is illustrated in *Alfred Toepfer International* v *Itex Italgrani Export* [1993] 1 Lloyd's Rep. 360. This was a seller/buyer dispute. A sub-buyer had contracted to load 6,100 tonnes of maize on the same vessel as the head buyer, under contract with the seller, had fixed to load a full cargo of 22,000 tonnes up river, completing at Buenos Aries. The sub-buyer's parcel was to be loaded up river. The issue was as to whether the head buyer was in repudiatory breach vis-à-vis the seller by being either unable or unwilling to load the full cargo up river. The arbitrators decided there was a breach serious enough to go to the root of the contract, but nevertheless did not constitute a clear repudiation. The High Court, on appeal, supported this award on the ground, inter alia, because the sub-buyer had contracted to load other goods on the vessel this did not per se establish that the buyer could not perform; at most, merely that they *might* not perform. The judge said:

> 'what must be established (apart from the other requirements of repudiation) is that on the balance of probabilities the party in question cannot perform his obligations. The fact that that party has entered into inconsistent obligations does not in itself necessarily establish such inability, unless those obligations are of such a nature or have such an effect that it can truly be said that the party in question has put it out of his power to perform his obligations'.

One practical remedy would be for an owner to write into his charterparty a deadline provision beyond which date if the charterer still had given no positive indication of the appearance of any cargo, the owner could withdraw from the commitment.

*The innocent party may choose to affirm*

He may do so either by:

(a) expressly affirming that the contract should continue or
(b) by taking some kind of action which is unequivocal and clearly evinces

his intention to carry on with the performance of the contract despite the happening of the other party's repudiatory breach.

Merely to remain silent and inactive will not pass a clear message to the other party and will not be sufficient to effectively affirm continuance of the contract. What is in no doubt is that once the innocent party has made up his mind whether to terminate or to affirm, and so has conveyed his intentions in whatever clear manner he chooses (and he must do so within a reasonable time), he cannot change his mind and so his decision.

### *Maritime Arbitration (Commentary on significant aspects of London's arbitration service)*

To condense this vast subject into the limited space appropriate in this book would be an impossible task. Thus, selecting a few 'highlights' is all that is possible.

## General comments

*Private sector litigation*

Arbitration could be said to be litigation in the 'private sector'. The arbitral process, certainly for commercial or maritime claims was intended to be a commercial service provided by commercial men for commercial disputants who were unable to resolve their disputes amicably.

Arbitrators' powers and authority to act as arbitrators springs from contract, i.e. from the agreement to refer disputes to arbitration which is to be found enshrined in a particular clause in the contract (for maritime disputes usually the charterparty).

Arbitrators are judges appointed not by the State, but by the parties themselves. The law (originally the Arbitration Act 1950) required only a single arbitrator but traditionally and in deference to the freedom allowed to contracting parties arbitration agreements have called for each party to appoint his own arbitrator and in the event of disagreement for an umpire to act as final arbiter. Since the Arbitration Act 1979, the idea of a tribunal of arbitrators consisting of the two party-appointed arbitrators who then themselves select a third has become a more acceptable arrangement. The award will be that of the majority. Indeed this was given statutory blessing by section 6(2) of the 1979 Act.

*Commercial service*

Whereas in the 'old days' arbitrators were very much *commercial* men, preferably doing the same kind of work as is the subject-matter of the dispute to which they are being referred, in recent years there has been what many consider to be an unwelcome trend towards an increased involvement of the legal profession. Many maritime arbitrators in these present times are professional lawyers, although it has to be said that the challenging of an arbitrator's competence to act is a rare event. This may, however, be partly due to the requirement that arbitrators should be *commercial* men being less and less observed in arbitration agreements on potential maritime disputes. Generally speaking, unless a particular category of persons is stipulated in the arbitration agreement, e.g. 'arbitrators to be persons engaged in the shipping or grain trade' or 'to be members of the Baltic Exchange' or 'members of the LMAA (London Maritime Arbitrators Association)', the only qualifications are that they be not children nor of unsound mind. It goes without saying that in carrying out their work they must act impartially.

In *Pan Atlantic Group Inc.* v *Hassneh Insurance Company of Israel* [1992] 2 Lloyd's Rep. 120 the Court of Appeal dismissed the notion that an arbitrator who had been appointed pursuant to a clause requiring arbitrators to be 'disinterested executive officials of insurance or reinsurance companies . . .' should cease to be qualified to act or capable of acting in the reference when he retired from his employment in this capacity. The purpose of the clause was to ensure that the right sort of persons sat as arbitrators rather than that they remained in their jobs.

It was originally provided in section 7 of the 1950 Arbitration Act that where the arbitration agreement requires that each disputing party appoints his own arbitrator and one (presumably the respondent) despite being challenged to do so, fails to do so, the other (presumably the claimant) may after the lapse of seven clear days declare his own to be sole arbitrator.

It was in an attempt to address the still numerous shortcomings of the combined effectiveness of the 1950, 1975 and 1979 Arbitration Acts that the 1996 Act has been introduced.[1] It is effective as from 31 January 1997 and applies to any arbitration proceedings commenced (*not* arbitration agreements made) on or after that date. Many of the provisions contained in the new Act which are intended to improve and raise standards of the arbitration services provided in the United Kingdom (London being, of course, the maritime centre) are commented upon in these pages, but the author has retained pages from the previous edition which gave an overview of arbitration pre-1996. It is left to the reader to interrelate the pre-1996 to the post-1996 data.

### *Pre-1996 Right of appeal*

Arbitrators are primarily finders of fact and indeed it is implied by the provisions of the Arbitration Act 1979 that they are final arbiters of fact. Unless their decision is palpably wrong, their findings of *fact* cannot be challenged. As to their ability to apply the law, it is recognized and generally speaking (though there are, as said above, an increasing number of exceptions to this) they are not practising lawyers and therefore do not necessarily possess an intimate knowledge of the relevant law, and thus there is by statute a right of appeal from an arbitration award but only in respect of an error of law. The law also required that they furnish reasons for their award if requested to do so and more often than not the parties themselves would request a 'reasoned' award.

1. For Commentary see page 239.

The right of appeal was couched in the wording of section 1 of the 1979 Act and was available where in the opinion of the judge, to whom leave to appeal was being addressed, the alleged error of law is one the determination of which could 'substantially' affect the rights of one or more of the parties. The bare statutory wording left judges, saddled with the task, a considerable discretion and thus in *The Nema* [1981] 2 Lloyd's Rep. 239 guidelines were laid down as follows:

(1) If a disputed clause was at issue and it was a 'one-off' clause—no leave should be granted, unless in the judge's opinion the arbitrators were 'obviously wrong'. But if the arbitrators could have been right, then as they were the parties' own choice they should 'lie on the bed they had made'.
(2) Where the clause at issue is a standard clause and one in common use, the test should be less strictly applied.

Leave to appeal from the High Court to the Court of Appeal would only be granted where there was sufficient doubt about the correctness of the decision of the High Court judge and whether, if the Court of Appeal did agree to review the question of law, its decision would make a significant contribution towards making English commercial law clearer and more certain (*The Baleares* [1991] 1 Lloyd's Rep. 349, CA).

Depending upon the complexity of the issues in a dispute and upon the need to call 'live' witnesses, arbitration proceedings are conducted either by way of an oral hearing or on documents alone. Oral hearings in modern times in London have tended to take on the appearance of court rooms in that with the increasing complexity of issues and the ever heightening of the value of disputes, the parties are the more inclined to have stronger legal representation and with the English judicial 'gladiatorial' approach to the conducting of the hearing, i.e. examination and cross-examination of witnesses by professional advocates, the presence of professional lawyers (both solicitor and barrister) in an arbitration room is common place which brings with it increased and increasing costs and lengthening delays. The days when arbitration was a simple, quick and cheap method of resolving commercial disputes are long gone. It is anybody's guess whether the courts (public sector litigation) or arbitration (private sector) is the quicker or cheaper in present times.

Arbitration is still theoretically private and by the same token awards are confidential to the two involved parties, though many question whether this confidentiality is beneficial to the shipping community. (In New York arbitration awards are collated and published.)

Obviously if judicial review is made of an arbitration award, the confidentiality is to that extent lost as the matter may find its way eventually into the law reports. Parties may opt out of judicial review (this is allowed by the Arbitration Act 1979), but in respect of Admiralty (Maritime), commodity or insurance contracts *only* if the agreement to mutually exclude judicial review is made *after* a dispute has arisen and arbitration proceedings started.

Arbitrators have powers to award interest, grant security for costs and apportion costs. Costs generally speaking 'follow the event', i.e. the loser pays his and also the winner's costs, subject to taxation.

*Arbitrators' powers including power to dismiss cases for want of prosecution*

Up to 1 January 1992, arbitrators had no power themselves to dismiss for want of prosecution. Judicial thinking was that there was a mutual obligation on the parties to 'keep the ball rolling' (*Bremer Vulkan* [1981] 1 Lloyd's Rep. 253). The High Court could step in and declare the proceedings at an end in cases of extreme delay, only, however, as case law painfully fashioned, in very limited circumstances, this in effect being only if there were clear indications that one or other party had abandoned the arbitration agreement itself (*The Hannah Blumenthal* [1983] 1 Lloyd's Rep. 103).

Effective from 1 January 1992, power was granted to arbitrators by section 13A of the 1950 Arbitration Act which came into force on that day. The wording of section 13A is as follows:

13A.—(1) Unless a contrary intention is expressed in the arbitration agreement, the arbitrator or umpire shall have power to make an award dismissing any claim in a dispute referred to him if it appears to him that the conditions mentioned in subsection (2) are satisfied.

(2) The conditions are—(a) that there has been inordinate and inexcusable delay on the part of the claimant in pursuing the claim; and (b) that the delay—(i) will give rise to a substantial risk that it is not possible to have a fair resolution of the issues in that claim; or (ii) has caused, or is likely to cause or to have caused, serious prejudice to the respondent.

(3) For the purpose of keeping the provision made by this section and the corresponding provision which applies in relation to proceedings in the High Court in step, the Secretary of State may by order made by statutory instrument amend subsection (2) above.

(4) Before making any such order the Secretary of State shall consult the Lord Chancellor and such other persons as he considers appropriate.

(5) No such order shall be made unless a draft of the order has been laid before, and approved by resolution of, each House of Parliament.

In *The Boucraa* [1993] 2 Lloyd's Rep. 149 the Court of Appeal ruled that the power is not retrospective, meaning that the period of delay which the arbitrators may take into account in exercising their power of dismissal is only that occurring after 1 January 1992. This is not, however, to say that the statutory section is not applicable to arbitrations entered into before 1 January 1992. It is. However, on appeal to the House of Lords, Their Lordships ruled that the power to dismiss a claim for delay granted to arbitrators by section 13A of the Arbitration Act 1950 *is* partially retrospective. This means that, in deciding whether to exercise their new power, arbitrators may take into account delay by the claimant in pursuing his claim before the date on which the new Statutory power came into force (i.e. 1 January 1992), [1994] 1 Lloyd's Rep. 251). The result of this final appeal has been criticized as 'surprising' as it tends to offend against the general legal principles of retrospectivity, i.e. that it is on the face of it a rule of construction of the common law that a statute should not be interpreted retrospectively if thereby it would adversely affect an existing right or obligation unless that result is unavoidable on the language used.

## Time limits

Often a charterparty arbitration clause makes no mention of a fixed period of time within which a claimant must appoint an arbitrator. In that event the general statute of limitations applies providing for a six-year period of running from the date of the cause of action. If the claim has reference to cargo loss or damage and the charterparty is governed by the Hague or Visby Rules, then the one-year time period applies. A recent (1994) arbitration has provided a fresh view that claims which are *not* cargo claims are not subject to the Hague Rules time bar even if the time charterparty has the rules incorporated.

## Extension of time

Section 27 of the 1950 Arbitration Act allows the High Court to extend time beyond the fixed period provided in an arbitration agreement but it is up to the party applying for such an extension to satisfy the court that 'undue hardship' will result if an extension is not granted. Evidence of the applicant's own fault will not necessarily prevent the granting of an extension, provided the fault is not serious and the opposing party does not complain of prejudice thereby (*The Baiona* [1991] 2 Lloyd's Rep. 121).

### *The Arbitration Act 1996*

The Arbitration Act 1996 was given effect on 31 January 1997 and has the twofold purpose of consolidating the arbitration legislation that has preceded it (particularly the 1950 and 1979 Acts) and of introducing some new and innovative provisions, some of the more significant of which will be mentioned below.

It must be admitted that on paper it does a sound job of (a) consolidation and (b) fresh ideas, but whether those that are responsible for the providing, controlling and assisting in London's maritime arbitration service will have the courage and strength of mind to seize the new opportunities which the Statute offers, time alone will tell.

The author proposes here merely to list and briefly comment upon some new innovative ideas contained in the Act. One of its general principles is admitted to be (section 1 (a)) 'to obtain the fair resolution of disputes by an impartial tribunal without unnecessary delay or expense'. This is bold comment and hits back directly at two of the main criticisms that up to now have been levelled at London's maritime arbitration service—unreasonable delays (including delay in issuing the award after closing of submissions or conclusion of a hearing) and continually rising costs. It is unlikely that either of those two criticisms can be effectively addressed by the Statute alone. Arbitrators, lawyers and parties themselves will have to work together to achieve these things, making use whenever possible of the increased or widened powers granted by the Statute.

Section 5 provides that for the Act to apply arbitration agreements must be made *in writing*, and that the words or expression 'agreement', 'agree' and 'agreed' must be construed accordingly. This requirement applies not only to the arbitration agreement itself, but to any other agreement relative to any matter falling within the scope of the Act.

Section 7 recognizes the severability of the arbitration agreement from the main contract of which it forms a part. Thus if the main contract becomes invalid or ceases to exist, the arbitration agreement nevertheless has a life of its own which may continue. This section would seem to give statutory effect to the ruling of the Court of Appeal in *Harbour Assurance Ltd* v *Kansa General International Insurance Co Ltd* [1993] 1 Lloyd's Rep. 455 in which the dispute revolved around the question of whether the arbitration agreement was comprehensive enough to deal with the alleged illegality of a reinsurance contract. The Appeal Court ruled that the arbitration agreement was severable and that thus the arbitrator was capable to deal with the issue of illegality.

Section 12 recapitulates the court's powers to extend time upon application by a claimant who has missed the fixed time-bar stated in the arbitration agreement. The court will extend time only if it would be just to do so or if the conduct of one party makes it unjust to hold the other party to the strict terms of the relevant provision. This is a variation to the 'undue hardship' test introduced by the 1950 act (section 27).

Section 16(4): either party can call upon the other to appoint his arbitrator and the party so called upon has 14 days to make his appointment. If he fails to meet the deadline, the other party may give a *further* seven clear days' notice that he is treating his own arbitrator as sole arbitrator (section 17(1)). This has the effect of lengthening the overall time it may take to constitute a tribunal if one party is unco-operative.

Section 16(5) provides that where the intention is to form a tribunal of three arbitrators and both parties have duly appointed theirs, but they in turn fail to appoint a third (who should act as the tribunal's chairman) then either party may apply to the court to appoint a chairman (this procedure is provided for in section 18).

Section 20 consolidates the new popular structure of the tribunal consisting of three arbitrators, the third of which acts as chairman, which means that the third (chairman) arbitrator has a clear role that if the two party-appointed arbitrators fail to agree, he can be the determining voice. The three-man panel by now seems to have almost totally eclipsed the old idea of two arbitrators and an umpire, certainly in maritime disputes.

Section 29: an arbitrator is given immunity. That is to say he cannot be held liable for the consequences of anything done (or not done) in the discharge of his duties, provided that he shall not have acted in bad faith. This should increase an arbitrator's confidence in himself and thus add to the quality of deliberations and the ultimate award.

Section 30: arbitration panels may rule upon their own jurisdiction, e.g.

(a) the validity of the arbitration agreement,
(b) whether the tribunal is properly constituted,

(c) whether the matters in dispute have been correctly submitted under the Arbitration Agreement.

Sections 33–41: in this range of sections the conduct of the proceedings is dealt with. They considerably widen the powers exercisable by arbitrators, but (in section 33) they are bound to act 'fairly and impartially as between the parties' giving each one a reasonable opportunity of putting his case and dealing with that of his opponent.

Section 34(1): details the scope and extent of the panel's powers to take control of the arbitration proceedings. It is reproduced below in full because, in the author's opinion, it could be the section which more than any other provides the basis for a practical improvement in London's service. The section is prefaced (subsection (1)) by 'It shall be for the tribunal to decide all procedural and evidential matters, subject to the right of the parties to agree any matter'. Then in subsection (2) it lists the procedural and evidential matters which are contemplated:

(a) when and where any part of the proceedings is to be held;
(b) the language or languages to be used in the proceedings and whether translations of any relevant documents are to be supplied;
(c) whether any and if so what form of written statements of claim and defence are to be used, when these should be supplied and the extent to which such statements can be later amended;
(d) whether any and if so which documents or classes of documents should be disclosed between and produced by the parties and at which stage;
(e) whether any and if so what questions should be put to and answered by the respective parties and when and in what form this should be done;
(f) whether to apply strict rules of evidence (or any other rules) as to the admissibility, relevance or weight of any material (oral, written or other) sought to be tendered on any matters of fact or opinion and the time, manner and form in which such material should be exchanged and presented;
(g) whether and to what extent the tribunal should itself take the initiative on the facts and law, and
(h) whether and to what extent there should be oral or written evidence or submissions.

It can be seen that this section gives wider powers than ever to arbitrators to direct, control and handle the proceedings in a manner designed to provide a fair resolution at reasonable expense and avoid unnecessary delays.

Section 37 empowers arbitrators to appoint experts of whatever persuasion who will be entitled to attend the proceedings unless the parties expressly object. The parties shall be free to comment upon the advice, information or views given by such experts. The costs of these experts shall be part of the total cost of the arbitration. This is a novel idea and time will tell whether or not it proves beneficial.

Section 41(1) gives consolidating statutory confirmation to section 13A of the 1950 Arbitration Act which came into force on 1 January 1992 by virtue of the Courts and Legal Services Act 1990. Arbitrators are empowered to dismiss a claim if and when there has been inordinate and inexcusable delay by the claimant in presenting his claim. The nature of the delay must be such as to (a) give rise or be likely to give rise to a substantial risk that it is not possible to have a fair resolution of the issues in that claim, or (b) have caused or be likely to cause serious prejudice to the respondent.

Section 46(1)(a), (b) provides a fresh and healthily commercial innovation. In previous Arbitration Acts it is required of arbitrators that they come to their decision on the basis of and within the framework of the law of the contract (i.e. English law in the case of London arbitration—subsection (a)). However, the 1996 Act, under subsection (b) of section 46 allows that arbitrators may reach their decision in accordance with such other considerations as are agreed by them (the parties) or determined by the tribunal. What this must be intended to mean is that if justice is truly to be served in the determining of the dispute and strict adherence to the letter of the law fails to produce such just results, commercial considerations may be taken as a basis for determination, thus overshadowing the law. This, in the author's view, is one of the most enlightened innovations of the entire Statute, and emphasizes the fast being forgotten basic principle that arbitration is basically a commercial service and *not* a legal service.

The implication of this section and other sections dealing with procedures and control of proceedings is that the arbitrators are now freer than ever before to adopt an inquisitorial approach, to question witnesses themselves, and to take a more 'hands on' role, rather than to feel bound to play a more negative role relying solely upon the adversarial (examination and cross-examination) procedure which has been so much the accepted mode of proceedings in previous years.

## The award

Under section 52, the award must now be *reasoned* unless both parties have agreed to dispense with reasons. This is a slight amendment to the pre-1996 stipulation that the parties were obliged to *ask* for a reasoned award. Arbitrators who fail to produce reasons may be challenged (through the court) on the basis of 'serious irregularity'.

## Right of appeal

An appeal on a point of law remains unchanged (section 69), but, an agreement *not* to have a reasoned award excludes the right to appeal. The application for leave must be made within 28 days of the date of the award. By section 69(3) for leave to be granted, the court should be satisfied that the determination of the question will substantially affect the rights of one or more of the parties and that the question is one that the tribunal was originally asked to determine. This point gives statutory effect to the guidelines enshrined in the '*Nema*' case. Unless the point was raised before the arbitrators no application for leave to appeal may be made.

On appeal the court has certain options:

(1) it may confirm the award;
(2) it may vary the award;
(3) it may set aside the award, either wholly or partially;
(4) it may remit the award back to the arbitrators either in its entirety or relevant sections of it, for them to reconsider in the light of the court's decision.

**Can parties exclude judicial review**

Yes, provided they do so in writing, and in the case of a non-domestic (e.g. international charterparty) agreement, this may be done at any time. What, however, seems to be the more practical way for the parties to exclude the right of appeal is to agree between themselves not to have a reasoned award. If the tribunal produces reasons contrary to the parties' wishes (and one wonders why it should) similarly no appeal may be taken.

**Costs**

The way that the new statute deals with the manner in which costs should be allocated is contained in sections 59–65 inclusive. A summary of the rules is as follows:

(a) the parties may agree that one or other of them should pay all or part of the costs provided that they make such an agreement *after* the dispute has arisen (section 60);
(b) subject to (a) above, the tribunal may make an award allocating costs as between the parties (section 61(1));
(c) costs should follow the event as a general principle unless the parties otherwise agree. Under this subsection the arbitrators have discretion to vary any allocation of costs as they see fit and as may be appropriate to the circumstances of a particular case (section 62(2)). This is a restatement of what has been the custom and practice of arbitrators previously;
(d) where costs are made subject to an agreement between the parties, the costs shall be deemed to be *recoverable* unless otherwise expressly stated;
(e) the parties are free to agree what costs are recoverable (section 63(1)). But in the absence of any such agreement, the tribunal has power to determine what costs are recoverable in whatever manner it thinks fit (section 63(2) & (3));
(f) if they omit to do so, the parties may invoke the aid of the court (section 63(4)).

**What is meant by a 'sealed offer'?**

If one party, after commencement of arbitration proceedings and before the arbitrators have proceeded to their award, wishes to make an offer of settlement, he may conceal the amount of the offer from the arbitrators by placing it in a sealed envelope addressed to them. The effect of this is that if the amount of the award (principal plus interest) is found to be less than the offer, all costs incurred after the date of the offer will be for the account of the offeree and the arbitrators shall so award. Thus an arbitrator should have in mind only whether the claimant has achieved more in respect of principal and interest by forging ahead with the arbitration proceedings than by accepting the offer (*The Maria* [1992] 2 Lloyd's Rep. 167).

## Doctrine of precedent does not apply

The doctrine of precedent which applies to judicial decisions and under which the rulings of lower courts are bound by earlier rulings of the higher courts, does not apply to arbitrations. This is a matter also of common sense because of the confidential nature of arbitration proceedings. Arbitrators are not *technically* aware of previous arbitration awards, nor of the reason upon which they were based, although in practical terms information does circulate through newsletters and articles, though permission to do so should properly be obtained from the parties to the dispute which gave rise to the award. Though not bound to follow previous awards on similar subject-matters, arbitrators must reach their award within the framework of the law which governs their jurisdiction to act. What law that will be is normally expressed within the text of the agreement to arbitrate (e.g. the arbitration clause in the charterparty), viz. English law to apply if no choice of law is expressly made, then it is to be assumed that the law of the country of the venue for arbitration is to rule, e.g. if arbitration is to be in London, then English law is assumed to apply.

CHAPTER 6

# COLLISIONS

No matter how sophisticated navigational aids and safety devices become, no matter how automated, computerized and mathematically planned become the voyages of vessels (of whatever size and species), the element of human fallibility will always exist and will remain the prime cause of collisions in navigable waters. Rules of the road at sea have been laid down by statute in England since the middle of the 19th century (the first Act of significance was passed in 1846) and have been modified regularly as shipping has grown and developed through the years. Discussion of the latest rules so far as relates to the steering and sailing regulations and requirements for lights and shapes features later in this chapter (see page 253 *et seq, post*). There is an infinite variety of circumstances in which two or more ships can come into contact with one another causing anything from superficial scraping to total loss. The weather obviously plays a significant part in creating conditions of good, bad or restricted visibility as does also the incidence of night-time or daylight. Narrow or congested waterways create a greater likelihood of collision than open stretches (the English Channel and the Straits of Malacca are two notorious areas) but ultimately the seamanship, foresight and intelligent appraisal of others' moves by the ship's Master or watch officer on duty at the material time are always the prerequisites of safety at sea. An inescapable feature of collision disputes is that they are mainly involved with facts and findings of fact and the intricacies of navigation and skilled (or unskilled) seamanship. The navigator or merchant mariner may for this reason be more interested than the maritime lawyer but this does not mean to say that there is not plenty of law to apply, as the succeeding pages will show.

How often do we hear of the expression in everyday maritime conversation 'the vessel caused the damage'? This 'humanizing' or 'personifying' of the 'thing' (the 'res') is misleading, and partly springs from the Admiralty concept of attaching or arresting by legal process the ship itself as being the recognized method in Admiralty procedure whereby a claimant can secure his claim and establish jurisdiction over the offending shipowner (see further Chapter 4, page 91). The cause of action which arises as a result of a collision is based on negligence and this inherently includes a personal element. Such negligence is based on the failure of skill and care which should ordinarily be expected of a competent seaman and also a reasonable and prudent one.

Furthermore, the liability of the owner of a ship for damage caused to another as the result of a collision does not spring per se from the fact of his ownership but from the fact that those navigating the vessel at the time of the collision were his employees and that he was reaping the benefits of that employment. It should be remembered in this connection that the owner of a ship is not always the employer of the Master and crew (e.g. a ship under demise charter, where the Master and crew are engaged, employed and paid by the charterer). This point is of particular importance since a further prerequisite of vicarious liability is that the negligent act of which the sufferer complains must be an act within the scope of employment. Wilful or malicious acts of a ship's Master or crew resulting in collision are rare these days but would not in the normal course render the employer liable, as being wholly outside the concept of negligence and vicarious liability.

The burden of proof of negligence is on the party seeking to assert it, i.e. the plaintiff (*SS Heranger (Owners)* v *SS Diamond (Owners)* [1939] AC 94, HL. The rule applies in the common law and in Admiralty alike). He must also show that he has suffered loss or damage as a result of the negligence. Unless he can establish such a prima facie case beyond reasonable doubt he cannot hope to succeed. At that point, generally speaking, the burden of proof shifts to the defendant shipowner to show that his negligence (or that of his employees) neither caused nor in any way contributed to the loss or damage. The plaintiff may find it difficult to establish negligence to the satisfaction of a court, but often the facts speak for themselves (i.e. the well-known doctrine of res ipsa loquitur, first established perhaps in *Scott* v *London Dock Co* (1863) 3 H & C 596, where a barrel fell from the upper storey of a warehouse and injured a passer-by) and the burden of proof shifts without the need for the plaintiff to assert positive allegations. One test applied is that the circumstances should allow of a 'reasonable explanation which is at least as consistent with the absence of negligence as with negligence' (see *The Wakaw and The Woolviston* [1952] 2 Lloyd's Rep. 272).

## LOSS OR DAMAGE CAUSED WITHOUT ACTUAL CONTACT

Although the very word 'collision' (from the Latin) implies contact and/or impact between vessels (NB, it need not necessarily be between their respective hulls; contact with an anchor chain or with the fishing net of a trawler has been held to be contact within the meaning of the expression) a vessel may cause damage by its negligence to another vessel without actual contact. For example, a ship by proceeding at excessive speed can cause another ship to sink (see *The Royal Eagle* (1950) 84 Ll.L.Rep. 543; *The Royal Sovereign* (1950) 84 Ll.L.Rep. 549) or to suffer chafing damage against a wharf simply by the swell or wash she creates. About a hundred years ago a ship found it necessary to run itself aground to avoid colliding with another lying negligently unlit in a navigable waterway. She had an actionable claim for damages (see *The Industrie* (1871) LR 3 A & E 303).

An example of an attempt by one ship to impose liability on another for damage done to it through negligent navigation without there having been direct contact was *The Shell Spirit 2*, below.

*The Shell Spirit* 2 [1962] 2 Lloyd's Rep. 252
The owners of the Greek vessel *Patrai* accused the tanker *Shell Spirit 2* of being responsible for their vessel colliding with some moored barges by reason of her negligent navigation.

The matter involved the use of sound signals. The *Patrai's* owners, however, failed to prove their allegations.

See also *The Centurity* [1963] 1 Lloyd's Rep. 99 where the *Centurity* was accused of responsibility for the grounding of the vessel the *Pakefield* because of negligent navigation. The Admiralty Court cleared the *Centurity* of blame. Another example is the case of *The Eglantine, Credo and Inez.*

*The Eglantine, Credo and Inez* [1990] 2 Lloyd's Rep. 390
There was a collision between the vessel *Eglantine* and the vessel *Credo* in dense fog in the Dover Straits. The *Eglantine* had been proceeding into the Dover Straits at a speed of about 13 knots on a course of 020°. About half an hour before the collision the *Credo* was about 2.5 miles astern proceeding into the Dover Straits on a course of 039° at a speed of at least 16 knots. The vessels were then on a diverging course. They then became aware of the vessel *Inez* which was proceeding in breach of Rule 10 of the International Regulations for Preventing Collision at Sea 1972, in a south-westerly direction, down the lane of the traffic separation scheme reserved for ships proceeding in a north-westerly direction. At first it appeared that the *Inez* would pass down the starboard side of the *Eglantine* but in due course she was seen to alter her course to starboard. The Master of the *Eglantine* thought that the ship ahead was then on a collision course with his own. Accordingly he made a bold alteration of course to starboard and later when he thought he was safely clear of the *Inez* he started to bring his ship back to port. Before an appreciable alteration in the heading had been made, *Eglantine* collided with the port side of the *Credo.* After the first contact the vessels separated momentarily and then the port quarter of the *Credo* struck the starboard side of the *Eglantine.*

The question was the appropriate liability for the damages caused by the collision. The Court of Appeal decided that both the *Eglantine* and *Credo* were in part to blame for their excessive speed in dense fog. However, the vessel *Inez* was in the wrong lane, in breach of the Collision Regulations, and caused the *Eglantine* to make, albeit later than she should have done, a proper turn to starboard. Therefore the vessel *Inez* was 75 per cent to blame for the collision and the *Eglantine* and *Credo* were each 12.5 per cent to blame. The action of the *Inez* was likened to a motorist proceeding south on the north-bound carriageway of the M1. The comments of Lord Pearce in the case of *The Miraflores* [1967] 1 Lloyd's Rep. 191 are illustrative.

> 'It is axiomatic that a person who embarks on a deliberate act of negligence should, in general, bear a greater degree of fault than one who fails to cope adequately with the resulting crisis which is thus thrust upon him. This generality is subject, of course, to the particular facts. And it may be that the initial act was so slight or easily avoidable and the subsequent failure to take avoiding action so gross that the blame for the accident falls more largely or even (if the interval and opportunity for avoidance are sufficiently great) wholly upon the person who failed to avoid the consequences of another's negligence. Between the extremes in which a man is either wholly excused for a foolish act done in the agony of the moment as the result of another's negligence or is wholly to blame because he had plenty of opportunity to avoid it, lies a wide area where his proportion of fault in failing to react properly to a crisis thrust upon him by another must be assessed as a question of degree. But the driver who deliberately goes round a corner on the wrong side, should, as a rule, find himself more harshly judged than the negligent driver who fails to react promptly enough to the unexpected problem thereby created. For all humans can refrain from deliberately breaking the well-known safety rules: but, 'tis not in mortals not to command the perfect reaction to a crisis: and many fall short at times of that degree which reasonable care demands'.

Somewhat unusual circumstances involving damage to a vessel without any contact arose in the case of the *Carnival* [1994] 2 Lloyd's Rep. 14 (CA). Shortly after the vessel *Danilovgrad* was alongside the Setramar berth, north of the port of Ravenna but before she was securely moored, another vessel, *Carnival*, proceeded along the canal assisted by two tugs. When the *Carnival* passed the *Danilovgrad*, her headway caused movement of the water and the vessel *Danilovgrad* surged and came into contact with the edge of the quay. The shell plating of the vessel *Danilovgrad* pressed against a fender and the edge of the end plate pierced the vessel's shell plating. Water flowed into the Hold No. 7, damaging the vessel's cargo. The owners of *Danilovgrad* claimed damages from the owners of *Carnival* on the ground that the latter vessel was negligently navigated and caused damage. They also claimed against the voyage charterers of the vessel *Danilovgrad* on the basis that they had ordered the vessel to an unsafe berth. The defendants, inter alia, contended that the pilot of *Danilovgrad* had authorized the vessel *Carnival* to pass her and that the owners of *Danilovgrad* were also guilty of negligence which contributed to the causes of the damage, in that they advised by VHF that *Carnival* might proceed when it was not safe to do so and in failing to have sufficient moorings tensioned when *Carnival* passed and failing to have lines from the port side forward.

The Court of Appeal decided that the *Carnival* was negligent in passing *Danilovgrad* before the latter was securely moored and all lines were out and made fast. It found that the pilot did not pass on a message on VHF that the vessel *Danilovgrad* was alongside the berth with some lines ashore and did not give his consent. However, they found that the berth was also unsafe by reason of the design of the fender. The Court of Appeal agreed with the High Court's decision that the conduct of the owners of the *Carnival* was substantially more blameworthy than that of the voyage charterers of *Danilovgrad*. It was unlikely that the *Danilovgrad* would have suffered such damage if the *Carnival* had not passed too early. It was just and equitable that the owners of *Carnival* should recover from the voyage charterers of *Danilovgrad* one-third of the total damages paid to the owners of the *Danilovgrad*. The defendants' argument that the damage was too remote was rejected. The Court of Appeal decided that the true test was whether it was foreseeable that, as a result of negligence on the part of *Carnival* (if proved), *Danilovgrad* would suffer damage to her hull and it was unnecessary to pinpoint foreseeability by reference to the actual damage suffered.

There may even be a situation where there is doubt initially as to whether there has been direct contact between two vessels. In the winter of 1971, a tanker veered off course and struck a passenger ferry terminal in Newcastle alongside which a Customs launch was moored. As a result of the tremendous impact, which caused serious damage to the terminal, the launch capsized and sank. First reports were not sufficiently clear to determine whether or not the ship had made direct contact with the launch. Subsequent investigations revealed that there had been no direct contact.

Negligence charged in collision cases may, however, not necessarily be negligence in navigation. It could be negligence in the management of the ship. Failure adequately to care for equipment, a breakdown of steering gear due to neglect or carelessness or the parting of a mooring rope for the same reasons could amount to actionable fault (see *The Merchant Prince* [1892] P 179). Any successful defence to such an allegation would likely be that the defect was latent, i.e. not to have been discoverable even by the exercise of due diligence, or that the vessel had been sent to sea in as efficient and safe a condition as the exercise of reasonable care could ensure.

## THE 'AGONY OF THE MOMENT' DEFENCE

An argument which, however, has always tended to form the basis of a good defence to a charge of negligence or contributory negligence is the plea that the act alleged to be negligent was committed solely in the 'agony of the moment'. Proof of this can override the general obligation to exercise due care and skill which is expected of a seaman when he finds himself confronted by a dangerous situation. For the 'agony of the moment' defence to succeed, it must be shown that the Master had no time to think of imminent danger, no time to form a deliberate and properly calculated alternative form of action to avoid the critical situation with which he was suddenly confronted. Thus, it could be said that although the act committed in such an 'agony of the moment' was the proximate cause it was not a 'probable' cause attaching blame with it.

*The Bywell Castle* (1879) 4 PD 219, CA
The *Bywell Castle* was navigating down the River Thames at night and the *Princess Alice* was proceeding up the river. When very close to each other, the *Princess Alice* suddenly and negligently hard-a-ported her wheel. The *Bywell Castle* equally hastily, but wrongly, put her wheel hard-a-starboard and struck the *Princess Alice* on her starboard bow. The latter sank with the loss of 500 lives.

*Held*: that no blame attached to the *Bywell Castle*. Her Master's action was entirely excusable despite its being wrong action.

Another 'agony of the moment' case, *The Homer* [1973] 1 Lloyd's Rep. 501, CA, provides an example. A ship was found not to be at fault when she relied on VHF messages from another ship with which she was later in collision. A more recent example is *The Regina D.*

*The Regina D* [1992] 1 Lloyd's Rep. 543
On 1 December 1987 a collision took place between the plaintiffs' vessel, *Iran Nabuvat*, and the defendants' vessel, *Regina D*, in the River Scheldt in dense fog. Each ship was being navigated by a licensed River Scheldt pilot. There was no doubt that at the moment of collision and while covering the preceding mile, *Regina D* was on her correct side of the channel. It was also clear that *Iran Nabuvat* crossed onto the wrong side of the mid-channel about one minute before the collision and came into collision on the green side of mid-channel. The plaintiffs conceded that *Iran Nabuvat* was proceeding at an excessive speed. The issues for decision were whether *Regina D* was also at fault and how blame for the collision should be apportioned.

*Held*: (Court of Appeal): that there was no ground upon which the findings of the Admiralty Judge that the pilot of *Regina D* was not negligent could be disturbed. His decision that *Iran Nabuvat* was wholly responsible for the collision was correct. The pilot of *Regina D* had no warning in time to take the kind of crisis action which would necessarily involve damage to his own ship and which would not be taken by any prudent navigator until absolutely essential. There was no evidence of any unwholly unjustifiable decision taken by the pilot of *Regina D.*

## TYPICAL COLLISION SITUATIONS

A common reason for a collision at sea is failure to maintain a proper look-out.

*The Sabine* [1974] 1 Lloyd's Rep. 465
The vessel, *Ore Prince*, went aground in the River Schelde on her way to Antwerp. The *Sabine* had been obliged to anchor about six cables distance up river from the *Ore Prince* due to the failure of her steering gear. Late in the evening just after high water when it was dark but the visibility was clear and while the *Ore Prince* was being assisted by 13 tugs to refloat, the *Sabine* was also being assisted by tugs (six in number) to turn in the river with a view to proceeding upstream and into Antwerp port. The attention of those on each vessel was so concentrated on their own respective problems that each failed to observe what was happening so far as the other ship was concerned. The *Ore Prince* omitted to notice the *Sabine* swinging round until after she (the *Ore Prince*) had been refloated and was making headway up the river. At that point of time the *Sabine*, herself around 650 feet in length, was lying across the river which had a width there of around 900 feet only. Instead of holding back until the *Sabine* had fully swung round, the *Ore Prince*, with her attendant tugs, tried to edge through the limited space between the *Sabine's* stern and the river's edge. She failed, and the two ships collided. The *Sabine* could have checked her swing until the *Ore Prince* had passed but, incredibly, seemed to have been entirely oblivious of the movements and proximity of the *Ore Prince* and her 13 tugs.

*Held*: that both vessels were equally to blame, the proximate cause of the collision on both sides being failure to maintain a proper look-out.

*The Sea Star* [1976] 2 Lloyd's Rep. 477, CA
In December 1972 the *Sea Star* fully loaded with crude oil collided with the *Herta Barbosa* in ballast in the Gulf of Oman. Visibility was good. Both vessels' radar was in use. The *Sea Star* caught fire and was destroyed. Eleven of her crew were killed. Claims on either side amounted in total to £10,000,000.

*Held*: that the *Sea Star* had made an inexplicable alteration of course to starboard turning a safe situation into one of acute danger. She was therefore seriously to blame. It was to be inferred that this improper manoeuvre was the result of defective look-out. The fact that she did not sound a signal before altering course was *not* causative. The *Herta Barbosa*, however, contributed to the collision by reason of the second officer's failure to stay at his post in the crucial minutes before the collision. This resulted in the vessel not properly reacting to the position of danger created by the *Sea Star*. The *Sea Star* was 75 per cent to blame and the *Herta Barbosa* 25 per cent to blame.

Another factor liable to cause a collision is a failure to slacken speed in dangerous situations. Also, the actual knowledge and information possessed by the ship's Master, or rather the lack of it, particularly when navigating in areas unfamiliar to him, can be directly instrumental as a contributing cause. This might, in turn, reflect the shipowner's failure to provide his vessels with up-to-date current charts and notices to mariners relevant to those areas through which the ship was bound to pass in the course of its contemplated voyages.

*The Troll River* [1974] 2 Lloyd's Rep. 181
In 1969 the fairway leading to Nagoya harbour was extended to seaward for about a mile, with its new extremity marked by a buoy. This new fairway was shown on the new edition of the Admiralty Chart 2960 of April 1970. It was found that the plaintiffs' vessel, the *Shariff*, had been using the 1967 edition of the chart of Nagoya harbour which did not show the 1969 extension of the fairway. When the *Shariff* approached Nagoya harbour channel her Master had seen the outward-bound *Troll River* pass the buoys marking what

on his chart was the end of the channel; he naturally, but mistakenly, thought that the *Troll River* would soon turn to seaward. She did not turn, but continued on towards the end of the fairway and collided at speed with the *Shariff* which was proceeding to enter across the fairway.

*Held*: that the *Shariff* was solely to blame for the collision. Her Master had been misled as to the extent of the fairway by using an out-of-date chart.

The situation after a collision can be analysed in one of three ways. It might have arisen: (a) from the sole fault of one ship (see *The Boleslaw Chrobry*, below); (b) from the fault of both ships; or (c) it might have been an inevitable accident (see *The Merchant Prince*, below, and *James River Transport Inc* v *Nasenbulk* below).

*The Boleslaw Chrobry* [1974] 2 Lloyd's Rep. 308
On the evening of 28 November 1970 the motor vessel *Melide* was on a voyage from Lisbon harbour to Hampton Roads and was proceeding down the River Tagus in Lisbon harbour towards the sea. The motor vessel *Boleslaw Chrobry*, assisted by a tug, shifted from a jetty at the lower end of the Gara Maritima quay of Alcantara on the north side and was turning in the river in order to go to an anchorage on the south side. The weather was overcast with intermittent rain showers. A collision occurred between the two vessels at 18.43 hours, the stern of the *Boleslaw Chrobry* coming into contact with the starboard side of the *Melide* a little forward of midships. The angle of blow was between 90 deg and 80 deg leading forward on the *Melide*. Serious damage was sustained by both vessels.

*Held*: that the *Boleslaw Chrobry* was not at fault in failing to see the *Melide* when she herself left the jetty for she had left when the *Melide* was about $1\frac{1}{2}$ miles away, and visibility was reduced by rain, and there were a number of other vessels anchored in the vicinity of the *Melide* after she herself had embarked on the turning manoeuvre, for it was her duty to keep a good look-out for any vessel going down or coming up the river. The *Melide* was not at fault in altering course to port for it was not unreasonable to expect that the *Boleslaw Chrobry* would be aware of the *Melide's* approach early enough to avoid collision by her action alone and the *Melide* had reduced her speed which gave the *Boleslaw Chrobry* more time to act; nor had she altered course to starboard at an improper time. Accordingly, the *Boleslaw Chrobry* was solely to blame for the collision.

In *The Merchant Prince*, below, the defence of inevitable accident was not made out.

*The Merchant Prince* [1892] P 179, CA
In weather conditions which were by no means unusual and in clear daylight a vessel under way collided with a ship at anchor. Under the Admiralty Court thinking of those days, the onus lay with the moving ship to rebut the charge of negligent navigation. This meant showing that the accident was inevitable. In this case the moving ship's steering wheel had jammed and this caused the collision. The Court of Appeal reversed the decision on the ground that the probable cause of the jamming was that the chain connecting the steering-gear with the rudder had been allowed to get too loose, causing kinks in the links. The shipowner therefore had failed to show that the accident was inevitable and judgment was entered against him.

See further *The Norwalk Victory* (1949) 82 Ll.L.Rep. 539 where the breaking of steering-gear was held not to be an inevitable accident because of failure to look at the rudder indicator.

*James River Transport Inc v Nasenbulk* [1974] AMC 575
During a 56-knot typhoon in Sasebo, Japan, two ships lying at anchor in anchorage positions designated by the harbour authority collided after dragging their anchors.

*Held*: that neither ship was at fault, and each should bear its own damages.

Liability is based on fault but not all instances of negligence amount to such a degree of fault as to impose legal liability. Tests for determining fault can vary. Where there are recognized navigation rules in existence, whether they be local or international, the disobeying of such rules by a vessel will throw the obligation on the ship to excuse herself for such disobedience, but on the other hand the mere disobeying of a rule may not necessarily be the direct causative factor which caused the collision.

*The Estrella* [1977] 1 Lloyd's Rep. 525
The Cypriot vessel *Setubal* collided with the Finnish vessel *Estrella* off Cape St Vincent in April 1972. The *Setubal* was in breach of the recommendations as to the traffic separation zone, but the court found that this breach (although it was admitted had that ship proceeded correctly in the correct traffic lane the collision would not have occurred) was not causative of the eventual collision. There were no other ships about and both vessels were able to observe each other while still several miles distant. The only requirement for avoiding the collision was that each should comply with the crossing rules. Faults that were causative and constituted blameworthiness were, on the *Estrella's* part (as the 'give-way' vessel),[1] that when she did alter to starboard she should have made a larger and more rapid alteration. Nearer the moment of collision she committed a second fault by failing to put her engines full astern. The *Setubal's* culpability lay in her failure, as the 'stand-on'[1] ship in a crossing situation, to keep her course and later in altering her course to port in the face of the *Estrella's* showing of her red light more or less ahead.

Traffic separation schemes have become a feature of maritime traffic and routeing generally and their primary purpose is to lessen the chances of collision risks arising in areas where heavy concentrations of traffic proceeding in opposite directions are expected. Basically, a scheme involves separating ships proceeding in one direction from those proceeding in the opposite direction. Far greater risks, of course, exist in conditions of poor visibility, viz. fog, but even in clear weather the presence of several ships concentrated in one area will inevitably render navigation more difficult than when two vessels only are involved. But, of itself, violation of a traffic separation scheme by one or other of the vessels does not necessarily create liability because it may not be a fault causative of the collision. *The Estrella* case was an example of an area where a separation scheme was in force but at the material time the two ships involved in the collision were the only ships in the area and could clearly see each other even from a distance. *The Genimar*, below, shows that the existence of a separation scheme in a given area is not necessarily the governing criterion for determining causative fault.

*The Genimar* [1977] 2 Lloyd's Rep. 17
The Liberian flag *Genimar* collided with the Greek ship *Larry L* in the Dover Straits in the dark early morning hours of 1 October 1972. The *Genimar*, the very much smaller of the two ships, subsequently sank and, with her caro, was totally lost. Compliance with the Dover Straits Separation Scheme is not, so far as foreign ships are concerned, compulsory but failure to comply with the scheme could amount to a lapse of good seamanship which could amount, in turn, to negligent navigation. However, the scheme is not intended to, and does not, override the Collision Regulations. Evidence showed that at the time of the collision the *Larry L* was navigating in accordance with the scheme, the *Genimar* in

1. For an explanation of expressions 'give-way' and 'stand-on' vessels, see page 267.

contravention of it. As far as the Collision Regulations were concerned, there was a crossing situation involving risk of collision, the *Larry L* being 'give-way' vessel and the *Genimar* being 'stand-on' vessel. Neither ship complied with its respective obligations under the Crossing Rules.

After consultation with the Elder Brethren, the Admiralty judge found that the *Genimar* was guilty of falling below the standard of seamanship expected of her in that she did not act in accordance with the recommended scheme; but the fact that this initial fault might have prompted the Master of the *Larry L* to take improper action which he might not otherwise have taken did not necessarily make it causative. The fact that the visibility at the time allowed both vessels to be aware of each other at a considerable distance, both visually and by radar, also added favour to the argument of non-causativeness of this particular fault. However, in the final analysis the judge felt unable to regard it as entirely non-causative. It did partly contribute to the cause of the collision but only in a very small degree.

It also came out in evidence in *The Genimar* case that there was a third vessel which was navigating in the same area and whose presence was alleged to have had an influence on the alterations of course taken by one of the ships. This is one point on which the factual situation presented by *The Estrella* case differs from the situation in *The Genimar* case.

## INTERNATIONAL REGULATIONS FOR THE PREVENTION OF COLLISIONS AT SEA

Disputes heard in court and decided under the earlier 1960 Collision Regulations though illustrative of situations, are not valid or legally definitive of the 1972 revised Collision Regulations and this should be borne in mind when reading these pages.

The regulations were finally adopted and recommended for international use as far back as 1972 as a result of a determination by what was in those days the Inter-Governmental Maritime Consultative Organization (now IMO) that the then existing regulations (the 1960 Regulations) needed revising and updating to take into account the technical advances made in recent years, particularly in speed and draught of vessels and the increased use of specialist craft such as hovercraft, hydrofoils, etc.

Under international law any sovereign nation which is a party to an international Convention is bound to incorporate its terms into its own legal system. This does not occur automatically. The UK Parliament, so as to make the regulations have the binding force of law in the UK, originally adopted them in the Collision Regulations and Distress Signals Order 1977 (SI 1977 No 982). From then on the regulations applied to British ships 'on the high seas and all waters connected therewith navigable by sea-going vessels'. A vessel whilst within the territorial jurisdiction of any other sovereign State would, so far as the application of the regulations is concerned, be subject to any local law relevant to them. Conversely, all foreign ships whilst within UK jurisdiction would be required to observe the regulations incorporated into the Order.

In 1983 the 1977 Order was revoked when the Merchant Shipping (Distress Signals and Prevention of Collisions) Regulations 1983 was introduced. They were made effective as from 1 June 1983 by SI 1983 No 708. The object of the

1983 Regulations is to give effect to the amendments to the 1972 Collision Regulations which are contained in Resolution A464 (X11) of IMO. In 1989 the Merchant Shipping (Distress Signals and Prevention of Collisions) Regulations 1989 came into force by SI 1989 No 1798. These were slightly amended in 1991, implementing IMO Resolution A678(16) (Merchant Shipping (Distress Signals and Prevention of Collisions) (Amendment) Regulations, SI 1991 No. 638). These apply to UK vessels (wherever they may be) and any other vessels in UK waters are required to comply with the international regulations as so amended. The Secretary of State has extended these regulations to various relevant countries, such as Guernsey, and the Falkland Islands. The current collision regulations applicable in the United Kingdom and to United Kingdom ships elsewhere are the Merchant Shipping (Distress Signals and Prevention of Collisions) Regulations 1996 (SI 1996/75). These regulations revoked and replaced the Merchant Shipping (Distress Signals and Prevention of Collisions) Regulations 1991 (SI 1989/1798) as amended by SI 1991/638 as well as the 1983 and 1989 Regulations and related instruments. Regulation 2 of the 1996 Regulations applies, inter alia, to vessels—(a) United Kingdom ships wherever they may be, and other ships while within the United Kingdom or the territorial waters thereof.

Section 4 provides (1) that subject to paragraph (2) below (i.e. exemptions under Rule 38), vessels to which these Regulations apply shall comply with the provisions of Rules 1 to 36 of, and Annexes I to III to, the International Regulations. The signals of distress which are to be used are those in Annex IV. The International Regulations for Preventing Collisions at Sea are set out in the Merchant Shipping Notice No 1642 which incorporates changes to Rule 26 and Annexes I, II and IV adopted in November 1993 by the International Maritime Organisation (Resolution A736(18)).

Any breach of the Collision Regulations is of paramount importance in determining blame for a collision. It should also be borne in mind that where any of the collision regulations is contravened, the owner of the vessel, the Master and any person for the time being responsible for the conduct of the vessel are each guilty of an offence. A person so charged with any offence has a defence if he proves that he took all reasonable precautions to avoid committing the offence. Nevertheless, an offence under the 1989 Regulations is in addition to other offences, such as manslaughter, and failure to secure that the ship is operated in a safe manner.

It should be borne in mind that under section 85 of the Merchant Shipping Act 1995 the Secretary of State may by regulations (referred to as 'safety regulations') make such provision as he considers appropriate for all or any of the following purposes—

(a) for securing the safety of United Kingdom ships and persons on them, and for protecting the health of persons on United Kingdom ships;
(b) for giving effect to any provisions of an international agreement ratified by the United Kingdom so far as the agreement relates to the safety of other ships or persons on them or to the protection of health of persons on other ships;

(c) for securing the safety of other ships and persons on them while they are within United Kingdom national waters;

and the power conferred by paragraph (b) to make provision for giving effect to an agreement includes power to provide for the provision to come into force although the agreement has not yet come into force.

Section 85(3) provides, inter alia, Regulations in pursuance of subsection (1)(a) or (b) above may make provision with respect to any of the following matters, and Regulations in pursuance of subsection (1)(c) above may make provision with respect to any of the following matters so far as relates to safety, that is to say—

(k) the steps to be taken to prevent any collision involving a ship and in consequence of any collision involving a ship;

To give a detailed commentary on the entire current regulations would be quite beyond the limited confines of this work and it is intended, therefore, to confine comment to Parts B and C only (the rules for steering and sailing and the requirements for lights and shapes). The full text with commentary may be found in Sturt's *Collision Regulations* published by Lloyd's of London Press.

Section I of Part B contains Rule 5 (a new rule). It is designed to tighten up and properly to define the duties and responsibilities of a ship to maintain a look-out. The previous requirement in the 1960 Regulations (not to 'neglect to keep a proper look-out') is enlarged to the obligation to use *sight* and *hearing* and 'all available means appropriate in the prevailing circumstances and conditions so as to make a full appraisel of the situation and of the risk of collision.' These words are intended to be all-embracing in scope and to replace the more cumbersome idea of listing possible alternative methods of maintaining look-out.

*The Maritime Harmony* [1982] 2 Lloyd's Rep. 400

The 1978 the *Maritime Harmony* outbound from Antwerp collided with the *Anna Bibolini* inbound into Antwerp in the River Scheldt. Visibility was reduced due to fog. The Collision Regulations of 1972 were applicable but as they were intended not to interfere with any local rules for navigable inland waterways connected with the high seas the Belgian regulations for the Lower Scheldt was also applicable.

*Held*: (Sheen J) that the *Maritime Harmony* was found to be on her correct side and the *Anna Bibolini* had crossed into wrong water and remained so until the collision. However, the *Maritime Harmony*, although she had two radar sets both working, was maintaining no efficient radar watch. Any speed over five knots was excessive under the circumstances. She was in fact proceeding at $8\frac{1}{2}$ knots at the material time. The *Anna Bibolini's* radar watch was also found wanting and evidence showed that she was not being kept under control either by her own steam or by tugs. The predominance of fault lay with the *Anna Bibolini*—75 per cent—25 per cent only with the *Maritime Harmony.*

*The General VII* [1990] 2 Lloyd's Rep. 1

A collision occurred between the vessel *Rora Head* and motor tug *General VII* in the River Thames in 1985. The duties of ships navigating there were prescribed in the Port of London River Byelaws 1978 which incorporated the International Collision Regulations, Rule 5 being relevant. One minute before the collision *General VII* was on the starboard bow of the *Rora Head.* The white stern light of *General VII* would have been visible to those on the bridge of *Rora Head* and if that light had been observed and carefully watched it would have become apparent that its bearing was closing. The stern light of *General VII* was visible to, and should have been observed by, *Rora Head* at least two minutes before the collision. Likewise, the masthead lights and green side light for *Rora Head* should have been seen by *General VII* throughout the same period. The stern and starboard bow of *Rora Head* struck the portside of *General VII* about 19 foot from her stern with such force as to cause *General VII* to roll over to starboard and capsize with loss of life. It was apparent from the fact that *Rora Head* had been navigating near the centre of the fairway and came into collision on the edge of the fairway that the course steered when rounding Tilbury Ness must have been to starboard of the line of the fairway. *General VII* was proceeding upriver outside the fairway and close to the jetties which she passed.

*Held*: *General VII* was at fault for being on or near the fairway on a course which would take her into the fairway in view of Rule 9. *General VII* was also at fault for failing to keep a good lookout; her skipper ought to have looked all round, and particularly over his port quarter, to make quite certain that no ship was proceeding upriver along the fairway before he reached a position close to the outer edge of the fairway; it was his duty to keep well clear of the fairway. Neither the pilot nor the Master of *Rora Head* appreciated that *General VII* was converging on the starboard bow until half a minute before the collision; this was due to a deplorably deficient lookout. If the stern light of *General VII* had been observed even as late as one minute before the collision, the speed of *Rora Head* could have been and should have been reduced and the collision would have been avoided.

The overriding cause of the collision was the failure on the part of both ships to maintain a proper lookout in accordance with Rule 5. *General VII* was also at fault for approaching the fairway in a manner which obstructed *Rora Head*. It was the navigation of *General VII* which created the situation of difficulty and for which she must bear the greater proportion of blame. *General VII* was 60 per cent to blame and *Rora Head* was 40 per cent to blame for this collision.

*The Devotion and Golden Polydinamos* [1993] 2 Lloyd's Rep. 464
A collision occurred between the vessels *Devotion* and *Golden Polydinamos* at the northern entrance to the Panama Canal in 1989. *Devotion* was southbound and *Golden Polydinamos* was northbound. The navigation of both vessels was governed by the Collision Regulations subject to the provisions of the Panama Canal Regulations and the Marine Directive No 1–89. The effect of Marine Directive 1–89 as it applies to the vessels was that priority would normally be granted for *Devotion* to pass though the breakwaters first in order to avoid delay at Gatun Locks.

*Held*: on the facts and the evidence the angle of blow was probably about 30° or less. *Golden Polydinamos* was proceeding at about 2 to 2.5 knots at the moment of collision and the speed of *Devotion* was probably about 4.5 to 5 Knots. The collision occurred either in mid-channel or slightly to the west of mid-channel. The principal cause of the collision was the failure of *Devotion* to keep a proper lookout as a result of which she failed to observe that she had altered her heading to port until the Master thought it was too late to do anything about it; such alteration was probably caused by some inadvertence on the part of the helmsman which was not noticed and checked by the Master. *Devotion* was not keeping a proper lookout and as a result she did not see *Golden Polydinamos* until a considerable period after she should have; the alteration to port occurred at a time when the Master had time to correct it without running any risk of collision with any other vessel. The Master could and should have done so by putting the rudder to starboard and by putting his engines ahead in order to ensure that his vessel did not enter the channel. The principal cause of the collision was a breach by *Devotion* of Article 111.8 of the Panama Canal Regulations by reason of a failure to keep a proper lookout and properly to appreciate what was happening.

*Golden Polydinamos* was partly to blame because she failed to take immediate steps to alter to starboard in order to regain her starboard side of the channel when the green light opened and the red light shut out. It was insufficient merely to contact *Devotion* by VHF; she should have taken urgent action to take off her way and she should have put her engines astern significantly before she did; if she had taken off her way earlier it was probable that the collision would have been avoided. *Devotion* was very much more to blame than *Golden Polydinamos* both in terms of causative potency and in terms of blameworthiness. *Devotion* was three times as much to blame as *Golden Polydinamos* and liability would be apportioned 75/25 in favour of *Golden Polydinamos.*

The Court of Appeal held ([1995] 1 Lloyd's Rep. 589) that the learned judge was right in his conclusion that *Golden Polydinamos* was approximately in the centre of, or just to the west of, the centre line of the channel when she turned on to 000 deg. The evidence of the Master of *Golden Polydinamos*, that it was because he saw the lights of *Devotion* indicating that she was on a course that was likely to go across his bows that he made the first VHF call, was wholly consistent with the independent evidence of the pilot of another vessel. The judge was entirely justified in his conclusion that, before the VHF call, *Devotion* was already on a course between 10 and 20 deg. to port of the reciprocal of the course steered by *Golden Polydinamos*; and since *Golden Polydinamos* was on a course of 000 deg. at that time, *Devotion* must then have been on a course of between 170 and 160 deg. The plaintiffs' appeal as to what caused *Devotion* to turn to port before the collision, was dismissed. As to apportionment of blame, since, save in one respect, which was immaterial, the learned judge's findings of fact were accepted and endorsed, and, since no error of law was made, the High Court judge's decision on apportionment of blame was not disturbed (namely 75/25 in favour of *Golden Polydinamos*).

Another addition to Section I of Part B is Rule 6, which introduces the idea of *safe* speed (instead of moderate speed in the 1960 Regulations) and obliges such a speed to be maintained at all times and in all types of good or poor visibility. The idea of safe speed presumably is that the speed is adaptable to the circumstances prevailing and is not a generally controlled speed regardless of surrounding circumstances. As an added help to Masters in complying with the rule certain factors are specifically listed in paragraph (a) and must be taken into account by all vessels; additional factors are listed in paragraph (b) for vessels using radar. A failure to keep a good look-out, as well as being a breach of the Collision Regulations, may mean that the Master in certain circumstances is liable for an offence under section 58 of the Merchant Shipping Act 1995 (see also the 1996 Regulations).

If a vessel is proceeding at an unsafe speed this could mean that the vessel is unable to control herself, which is illustrated by the case of the *San Nicolas* and *Fraternity L* below.

*The San Nicolas and Fraternity L* [1994] 2 Lloyd's Rep. 582
On 12 July 1991 the plaintiffs' vessel, *San Nicolas,* came into collision with the defendants' vessel, *Fraternity L* at about 18.8 km in the access channel to the port of Buenos Aires. The main issue between the parties was where in the channel the collision occurred and why the heading of *Fraternity L* altered to port from 283.5 deg. gyro at 1.75 or 1.8 minutes before the collision to 258 deg. at the time of the collision.

*Held:* the *San Nicolas* was just to starboard of mid-channel. The *Fraternity L* overshot the bend of the channel at 22.2 km with the result that she was well to the north of mid-channel and it was for that reason that she came back to port. She then altered a little to starboard with the result that her heading was 280 and then 283.5 deg., which had nothing to do with the position of *San Nicolas.* It was caused by the necessity for *Fraternity L* to correct her course from a course to port of an up-channel heading which had in turn been caused by a correction as a result of overshooting the bend in the channel. Until about 2.5 minutes before the collision or less, nothing *Fraternity L* did was caused by the way in which *San Nicolas* was being navigated. Again, the heading of 283.5 deg. of *Fraternity L* on the edge of the channel had nothing to do with *San Nicolas*. The collision was caused entirely by the negligence of those on board *Fraternity L*, in that she negligently failed to correct her alteration to port in time and she allowed herself to approach too close to the bank at an excessive speed, as a result of which she failed to correct her course in time, altered her heading to port as a result of interaction with the bank and she was unable to correct her heading by starboard helm. *Fraternity L* was proceeding at an unsafe speed and it was that speed which caused her to be unable to control herself. The sole cause of the collision was the alteration of heading to port by *Fraternity L* and the collision occurred on the southern edge of the channel after *San Nicolas* had taken emergency helm and engine action. *Fraternity L* alone was to blame for the collision.

*The Roseline* [1981] 2 Lloyd's Rep. 410
In May 1978 the *Roseline* collided with the *Eleni V* six miles off the coast of Norfolk (England). The *Eleni V* was split in two and spilled much of her cargo of oil into the sea. Fog was thick at the time. Both ships carried radar in working order. Each ship knew of the other's presence at a distance of six miles. Three minutes before impact the *Eleni V* turned to port.

*Held* (Sheen J): that both ships were at fault in not proceeding at safe speeds under the circumstances. The *Eleni V's* turn to port was inexcusable and changed a dangerous 'passing' situation into a '*dramatically*' dangerous crossing situation. This meant that the substantial fault was with the *Eleni V* (60 per cent). *Roseline's* failure to react, however, was causative in part (40 per cent), particularly as it seems she was not making proper use of her radar at that crucial moment.

See also the *Coral I* (see page 278, *post.*)

*The E. R. Wallonia* [1987] 2 Lloyd's Rep. 485
A collision occurred between this vessel and the *Nedlloyd Seine* in the South China Sea on 23 October 1980. It was just before sunrise and shortly prior to the collision the weather had been good and with it the visibility. However, there was suddenly a rain downpour of tropical intensity causing a rapid reduction in visibility. Under the crossing rule in the Collision Regulations the *Nedlloyd Seine* was the give-way ship. Evidence revealed that her speed was in excess of what should have been under the circumstances a safe speed. In fact she maintained 18 knots right up to the impact. The *E. R. Wallonia* was proceeding at 14 knots, which speed was not reduced, even after sighting the *Nedlloyd Seine*. A last minute hard-a-porting of her wheel by the *E. R. Wallonia* failed to avert impact. Both vessels conceded that they were at fault by exceeding what should have been a safe speed and by not keeping a proper look-out, but each ship tried to get the other to take the preponderance of blame.

The Admiralty Judge held inter alia that when considering the fault of excess of speed it was relevant to take into consideration the excess over that speed which was regarded as being safe for that particular ship. Both ships were guilty of committing faults of navigation independently of each other. The *Nedlloyd Seine* was slightly more at fault for excessive speed and she also failed to take the correct action because she failed to keep an effective lookout. As to the *E. R. Wallonia*, when visibility was reduced there should have been a qualified officer, a helmsman and a look-out on the bridge, none of whom were there and on top of that the Master remained in his cabin. This in itself was a dereliction of duty and the apprentice who was on the bridge was not a qualified watch-keeper. The vessel should have reduced speed, and the helmsman should have taken the wheel.

The Admiralty Judge found the *E. R. Wallonia* 40 per cent to blame for the collision, the balance of blame being upon the other ship.

Rule 7 is largely new and lays emphasis on the importance of determining the 'risk of collision'. Every vessel shall use all available means appropriate to the prevailing circumstances and conditions to determine if a risk of collision exists. If there is any doubt such risk shall be deemed to exist. Again the importance of using radar and radar-plotting is underlined (see paragraph (b)). The danger of making assumptions on scanty information particularly scanty radar information is stressed by paragraph (c).

In the *Mancunium/Deepdale 2* [1987] 2 Lloyd's Rep. 627 the scene of the collision was the South-Eastern channel in the River Mersey. The *Mancunium* was a hopper laden with sludge and was out-bound. The *Deepdale* was in-bound with a cargo of tallow. Both ships were in waters covered by the International Regulations for Preventing Collisions at Sea 1972 (the version prior to the 1983 version). The stem of the *Mancunium* collided with the port side of the *Deepdale* about one-third of the way along her length.

The Admiralty Judge found that the *Mancunium* was substantially to blame because of the failure of those responsible for her navigation to hold her in control in a flood tide. The skill required to do so was within their competence and they had failed to exercise it. The *Mancunium* had created a risk of collision by the unreasonable actions of those in charge of her. The *Deepdale*, however, was initially an innocent party. She was maintaining her course at a reasonable speed on the correct side of the channel, but when she saw a risk of collision she put her engines hard astern which rather than reduce the risk of collision in fact increased it. Her fault was, however, less of a contributory factor than the *Mancunium* so that blame was apportioned two-thirds to the *Mancunium* and one-third to the *Deepdale*.

In *The Gannet* [1967] 1 Lloyd's Rep. 97, Karminski J, after having consulted the Elder Brethren (see page 290, *post*) on questions of navigation and seamanship, declared himself satisfied that plotting radar was the safest method of observing the bearing of an approaching vessel. It is an extra additional eye by way of security when watching by natural means may be only partly effective.

Paragraph (d) of Rule 7 states that in determining if risk of collision exists, the following considerations shall be among those taken into account:

(i) such risk shall be deemed to exist if the compass bearing of an approaching vessel does not appreciably change;
(ii) such risk may sometimes exist even when an appreciable bearing change is evident, particularly when approaching a very large vessel or a tow or when approaching a vessel at close range.

Rule 8, providing for action to avoid collisions, has been strengthened by the substitution of the word 'shall' in place of 'should' in describing the obligation to take positive action (paragraph (a)). Any action taken to avoid collision shall, if the circumstances of the case admit be positive, made in ample time and with due regard to the observance of good seamanship. Alterations of course or speed shall be large enough to be apparent to the other vessels observing visually or by radar. A succession of small alterations of course and/or speed should be avoided (paragraph (b)). Before action is taken two things should be borne in mind: the avoiding of a close-quarters situation (paragraph (c)), and the eventual passing at a safe distance (paragraph (d)). Checks should be made in the course of taking action to ensure that this is achieved, until it is in fact achieved. Paragraph (e) (which applies in all visibilities) requires a ship to slacken her speed or take all way off by stopping or reversing her means of propulsion where necessary not only to avoid a collision but also to allow more time to assess the situation.

In *The Sanshin Victory* [1980] 2 Lloyd's Rep. 359 both the vessels which collided were proceeding at unsafe speeds in restricted visibility, allowing a close-quarters situation to develop.

Rule 9 is concerned with navigating in narrow channels or defined limits. Paragraph (a) provides that a vessel proceeding along the course of a narrow channel or fairway shall keep as near to the outer limit of the channel or fairway which lies on her starboard side as is safe and practicable. Here it is relevant to quote *The Koningin Juliana*, and some more recent cases.

*The Koningin Juliana* [1974] 2 Lloyd's Rep. 353, CA; [1975] 2 Lloyd's Rep. 111, HL
A collision occurred in Harwich harbour between the plaintiff's vessel, the *Thuroklint* and the *Koningin Juliana*, owned by the defendants. The outward bound *Koningin Juliana's* usual down-channel course was obstructed by the inward-bound *Thuroklint*. The pilot of the *Koningin Juliana*, believing that the *Thuroklint* was not moving, steadied on a course with the *Thuroklint*, showing her red sidelights and masthead lights slightly open, fine on the *Koningin Juliana's* starboard bow. He thus created a 'crossing situation' and tried to cross ahead of the *Thuroklint*. He failed and the ships collided. The *Thuroklint* prior to the collision had navigated outside and to port of a dredged channel which is contained within the whole navigable channel. The question arose whether the *Thuroklint* was in her correct water? This depended on the meaning of 'mid-channel'—the dividing line to starboard of which the vessels had to keep. Did it mean the centre line of the whole navigable channel or of the dredged channel?

The trial court found that rule 25(a) (now rule 9(a)) did not solely apply to ships within the dredged channel. The 'narrow channel' meant the whole width of the navigable water. This was confirmed by the Court of Appeal. The nautical assessors (technical advisers) in both courts agreed that in Harwich harbour the line to starboard of which each vessel shall keep is the centre of the dredged channel. The trial court below found four faults in the *Thuroklint* and three faults in the *Koningin Juliana*. The three faults of the *Koningin Juliana* formed a single composite fault. There was clearly substantial blame on the part of the *Thuroklint* and liability was apportioned as to two-thirds to the *Thuroklint* and as to one-third to the *Koningin Juliana*.

The consolidating of three faults into one was criticized in the Court of Appeal, as was also the trial judge's mathematical apportionment of liability, since under the Maritime Conventions Act 1911 liability is proportional to the degrees of fault not to the number of faults on each side. (The Admiralty Court, it is said, 'rejects the lore of nicely calculated less or more'.) They could find no clear preponderance of blame on either side. Applying section 1(1) of the Maritime Conventions Act 1911, two judges re-apportioned the blame equally between the two ships and one preferred to keep the one-third/two-thirds apportionment considering the *Thuroklint's* breach to be the overriding consideration both as regards culpability and causation. Because of this disagreement leave was granted to appeal to the House of Lords. On the appeal by the owners of the *Koningin Juliana*:

*Held*: on the issues involved, that this case was one where an appellate court should not disturb the apportionment of the trial judge. It had not been shown that the trial judge had failed to give proper weight to the elements forming the composite fault of the *Koningin Juliana*. The House of Lords allowed the appeal.

*The Toluca* [1984] 1 Lloyd's Rep. 131
In April 1974 a collision occurred in the dredged channel of the river up which ships gain access to Bangkok. The involved vessels were the *Visahakit 1* inbound and the *Toluca* outbound. Visibility was excellent. There were no local rules as to navigation of the channel and thus compliance with the international rules (those applicable at the material time would have been the 1960 version) was required. The relevant rule for narrow channel navigation required 'every power driven vessel . . . where safe and practicable to

keep to that side of the fairway or mid-channel which lies on the starboard side of such vessel'. The collision occurred at a bend in the channel and at the moment of impact the angle between the centre lines of the two vessels was 38 degrees leading aft on *Visahakit 1*. The *Toluca* had difficulty in negotiating the bend, being three feet longer than the maximum ship length normally permitted in Bangkok. It was alleged that being unable to turn to starboard she continued on her course and thus cut across the channel. The *Toluca* contended that the *Visahakit 1* was proceeding in the wrong water and in endeavouring to regain the correct side cut across ahead of the *Toluca*.

*Held* (Sheen J): on the balance of probabilities the *Toluca* was solely to blame. The *Visahakit 1* did appear to be on her correct side of the channel and any alteration of course by the *Visahakit 1* was 'last minute' and an 'agony of the moment' decision. Causative negligence was solely that of the *Toluca* in not appropriately reducing her speed at the bend and in not taking care to keep to her side of the channel. The fact that she was an unusually large vessel gave the *Toluca* no right of priority over the much smaller (and local) *Visahakit 1*.

The decision was later affirmed by the Court of Appeal.

*The Nordic Ferry* [1991] 2 Lloyd's Rep. 591
A collision occurred between the plaintiffs' vessel *San Salvador* and the defendants' vessel *Nordic Ferry* in 1987 in an area over which Harwich Harbour Board had jurisdiction. The main issues for decision by the Admiralty Court were the geographical position of the collision, the speed of the vessels during the last three minutes before the collision and the degree of fault of each vessel, if any to the collision.

*Held*: on the evidence *San Salvador* was proceeding at approximately $6\frac{1}{2}$ knots through the water while the speed of *Nordic Ferry* at the moment of collision must have been not less than 10 knots and probably rather more. The position of collision was about one cable from the Fort Buoy in the dredged channel on the eastern side of mid-channel which was the correct side for *Nordic Ferry* and the wrong side for *San Salvador*. *Nordic Ferry* was not keeping as near to the outer limit of the channel as was safe and practicable as required by Rule 9 of the Collision Regulations. Whilst *San Salvador* was not being navigated at a safe speed in the prevailing weather conditions, a further and more serious fault was not keeping to her own side of the channel. This was the primary cause of the collision and the fault could not be excused and the pilot should have taken every available step to avoid getting into his wrong water. The navigation by the Master of *Nordic Ferry* indicated that he was not keeping a careful watch on the radar and did not appreciate as he should have done the imminent danger of the collision; one minute before the collision *San Salvador* was about 12° from the starboard of *Nordic Ferry* and only $2\frac{1}{2}$ cables of water separated the vessel. The Master of *Nordic Ferry* could not have appreciated properly that very dangerous situation because it was then that he further increased the speed and even later when he altered course to 015°. The Master's failure to keep a careful watch on the situation was another serious fault. Although the *Nordic Ferry* was guilty of a further fault in not sounding a prolonged blast in accordance with Rule 35 of the Collision Regulations this was not a fault which contributed to the cause of the collision. The liability to make good the damage caused by the collision had to be in proportion to the degree in which each vessel was at fault. This was a case in which although *San Salvador* created the difficulty, having regard to *Nordic Ferry's* share in responsibility for the damage both vessels were equally to blame for the collision.

*The Faethon* [1987] 1 Lloyd's Rep. 538
A collision arose between the vessel *Miaoulis* and *Faethon* in 1983 close to the entrance to the port of Piraeus. Ships entering or leaving the port had to comply with the Piraeus port regulations and the international Collision Regulations, Rule 9 being relevant.

*Held*: the collision was caused by faults in the navigation of both vessels. Both vessels were at fault for their failure to keep as near to the outer limit of the fairway which lay on their respective starboard sides as was safe and practicable in accordance with Rule 9. The fault of *Miaoulis* in crossing to the north of the axis (centre of the fairway) was the first fault in the navigation of either vessel but she did not create a situation of difficulty. There was plenty of room for her to regain her correct side of the axis and for the vessels to pass port to port. *Miaoulis* sounded a correct whistle signal to indicate that she was altering her course to starboard. Even if that signal was not heard on *Faethon* her manoeuvre would have been apparent if they had been keeping a proper lookout. The main cause of the collision was the very serious fault of *Faethon* in altering her course to port. That action was taken precipitately and it was purely wrong being in breach of Article 3(2) of the Piraeus Port Regulations and Rule 9 of the Collision Regulations. It limited the amount of water available for any incoming ship and it made a collision with *Miaoulis* virtually inevitable. The *Faethon* was 75 per cent to blame and the *Miaoulis* was 25 per cent to blame.

Rule 10 is based on developments in very recent years. Traffic separation schemes (even under the auspices of IMO) were originally merely recommended, but not compulsory. Rule 10 makes that transition, provided that they are adopted by IMO and implemented in English law.[2] Perhaps these ideas are closely akin to the special set of rules laid down for motor traffic using motorways, four- or six-lane highways with sophisticated controlled exits and entrances from and to the main traffic highway flow, etc. The points to be stressed particularly are:

(1) the need to proceed in the appropriate traffic lane in the general direction of traffic flow for that lane;
(2) the need to keep clear of the actual separation line or zone as far as practicable;
(3) to avoid crossing traffic lanes, as far as practicable but if it is necessary to cross a lane it should be done on a heading as nearly as practicable at right angles to the traffic flow; and
(4) as far as is practicably possible, ships should avoid actually anchoring within a traffic separation scheme (compare the obligation not to stop on a motorway except at designated points).

*The Nordic Clansman* [1984] 1 Lloyds's Rep. 31
The vessel, of British registry, used the southerly lane entering the Arabian Gulf through the Straits of Hormuz instead of the northerly lane for inbound traffic as required by the Traffic Separation Zone for that area. Her Master was charged with contravention of section 419(2) of the Merchant Shipping Act 1894 *and* with breaching rule 10(d) of the international regulations in that he had wilfully used the wrong traffic lane to approach the nearby Gray Mackenzie buoy which he considered meant that he need not regard his vessel as 'through traffic'. The Justices to whom the complaint was referred dismissed the charge against him but the prosecutor pursued the matter before the Queen's Bench Divisional Court, which held:

'Wilful default' under the Merchant Shipping Act had two ingredients by way of definition: (a) the act or omission which constituted a breach of regulation must have been deliberate, or (b) that he, the Master, was careless of whether an infringement of the Collision Regulations would result from his deliberate actions. His 'honest belief' that his

2. The traffic schemes referred to are those now listed in Notice to Mariners No 17. The rule applies to traffic separation schemes adopted by IMO and does not relieve any vessel of its obligation under any other rule.

ship was not 'through traffic' in that situation did not make his act innocent as opposed to wilful. The Justices had been wrong to absolve him. The hearing should be continued against him.

*The Century Dawn* v *Asian Energy* [1996] 1 Lloyd's Rep. 125
In 1988, the vessels *Century Dawn* and *Asian Energy* collided off Singapore. The collision occurred within a traffic separation scheme as defined by Rule 10 of the Collision Regulations. *Asian Energy* was navigated from east to west and should therefore have kept in the westbound lane of the traffic separation scheme. *Century Dawn* was navigating from her anchorage in order to proceed from west to east and she should have crossed the westbound lane as nearly as practical at right angles to the general direction of traffic flow in that lane before altering course to port, in order to proceed along the eastbound lane. The Admiralty judge held ([1994] 1 Lloyd's Rep. 138) that the collision occurred in the eastbound lane. *Century Dawn* was at fault in failing to keep a good lookout and in failing to appreciate the presence of *Asian Energy* until a very late stage: *Century Dawn* was also at fault in crossing the westbound lane on a course of 110 deg. The obligation in Rule 10(c) applied to vessels crossing any traffic lane, whether the purpose of crossing it was to cross the next lane or to join it; there was no reason why *Century Dawn* could not have crossed at right angles and *Century Dawn* was at fault, not for crossing the westbound lane at all but for doing so at significantly less than a right angle. *Asian Energy* was at fault in failing to observe the echo of *Century Dawn* at the latest when she was about to enter into the westbound lane: *Asian Energy* was in breach of Rule 10; the alteration of course was causative of the collision because it had the effect that the two vessels would pass very close to each other and it was not sufficient to say that if *Century Dawn* had been keeping a good lookout she would have seen what was happening. The action of both vessels was causative of the collision; it was the duty of *Asian Energy* to take early and substantial action to keep out of the way of *Century Dawn* under Rules 15 and 16; she failed to do so and took no steps until she saw her red light at about 8 cables: the collision would have been avoided if the wheel had been put and kept hard to starboard without the necessity of putting the engines full astern; both vessels were to blame for the collision. The root cause of all the faults of both sides was very poor lookout; if either had been keeping a proper lookout, she would have seen what the other was doing in ample time in order to avoid the collision: thereafter, when the two vessels did become aware of each other, *Asian Energy* made a decision which was radically wrong and which had an important causative effect on the collision and damage; she failed to take and maintain urgent starboard helm action but delayed and then went hard to port; as a result, instead of turning away from *Century Dawn* and avoiding the collision, she in effect turned towards her: *Asian Energy* was more to blame for the collision than *Century Dawn* and the apportionment was that *Asian Energy* was 60 per cent to blame and *Century Dawn* 40 per cent to blame.

The Court of Appeal decided ([1996] 1 Lloyd's Rep. 125) that it would not be just to criticize *Century Dawn* for failing to see *Asian Energy* at any position prior to her point of entry to the westbound lane. Rule 15 of the Collision Regulations applied irrespective of the fault of the other vessel and *Century Dawn* was therefore entitled to the status of a stand-on vessel notwithstanding her own fault. The failures by the vessels to keep a proper lookout were equally lamentable and their subsequent efforts to cover up by false entries on their charts equally blameworthy. *Asian Energy*, having (albeit inadvertently) crossed the separation zone and entered the wrong lane, thus herself creating a position of danger for a vessel proceeding down the eastbound lane in the correct direction, it was impossible to accept that this fault did not significantly contribute to the accident. The moment of sighting was two and a half minutes or so prior to the accident, during which the Master of *Asian Energy* had time first to set the helm hard to starboard and then change his mind and set it hard to port; this was not properly categorized as an agony of the moment case and such a change of course infringed Rule 15. The turn to port rendered the collision inevitable, the maintenance of the starboard helm would probably have avoided a collision, albeit narrowly, and the Admiralty judge's apportionment of blame for the collision would be upheld.

This Rule 10 covering traffic separation schemes has been amended in view of IMO Resolution A626(15) and A678(16) and A736(18). The IMO defines a traffic separation scheme as a routeing measure aimed at the separation of opposing streams of traffic by appropriate means and by the establishment of traffic lanes. Traffic separation schemes are listed in Notice to Mariners No 17. The Department of Transport has also issued an 'M' Notice regarding observance of traffic separation schemes. Also the Merchant Shipping (Distress Signals and Prevention of Collisions) Regulations 1996, reg 6(1) provides: Where any of these Regulations is contravened, the owner of the vessel, the Master and any person for the time being responsible for the conduct of the vessel shall each be guilty of an offence, punishable on conviction on indictment by imprisonment for a term not exceeding two years and a fine, or on summary conviction: (a) in the case of any infringement of Rule 10(b)(i) (duty to proceed with traffic flow in lanes of separation schemes) of the International Regulations (being an offence corresponding to an offence under section 419(2) of the Merchant Shipping Act 1894) by a fine not exceeding £50,000; and (b) in any other case by a fine not exceeding the statutory maximum.

In paragraph (d)(i) of the Collision Regulations it says that a vessel shall not use an inshore traffic zone when she can safely use the appropriate traffic lane within the adjacent traffic separation scheme, although vessels of less than 20 metres in length, sailing vessels and vessels engaged in fishing may use the inshore traffic zone. Prior to SI 1991 No 638 which implemented IMO Resolution 678 a somewhat ambiguous rule existed that inshore traffic zones 'should not normally be used by through traffic.' The exception to (d)(i) is that a vessel may use an inshore traffic zone when en route to or from a port, offshore installation or structure, pilot station or any other place situated within the inshore traffic zone, or to avoid immediate danger. New paragraphs (k) and (l) were added by the 1983 Regulations. Paragraph (k) provides that a vessel restricted in her ability to manoeuvre when engaged in an operation for the maintenance of safety of navigation in a traffic separation scheme is exempted from complying with this rule to the extent necessary to carry out the operation. Paragraph (l) provides that a vessel restricted in her ability to manoeuvre when engaged in an operation for the laying, servicing or picking up of a submarine cable, within a traffic separation scheme, is exempted from complying with this rule to the extent necessary to carry out the operation.

Section II of the Collision Regulations provides specific rules applicable to ships in sight of one another. (Rule 12 deals specifically with sailing vessels.) Rules 13 (overtaking), 14 (head-on situations) and 15 (crossing situations) cover the three situations likely to result in a collision.

It is for the facts themselves to determine which is the relevant situation in each given set of circumstances but, for the purposes of applying the collision prevention rules, one situation cannot change and become another by subsequent manoeuvres of either vessel. This idea is embodied in the maxim 'once an overtaking vessel, always an overtaking vessel'. Thus it was in the *Nowy Sacz/*

*Olympian* collision that the judge rejected the argument of the owners of the *Nowy Sacz* that it was an overtaking situation and should be treated as such. From the outset, he said, it was a crossing situation and remained such and it was in such a crossing situation that the risk of collision arose justifying the application of the Collision Regulations. The Court of Appeal took a different view. (See pages 270–271.) See *The Nowy Sacz* [1976] 2 Lloyd's Rep. 682.

Rule 13 confirms the old idea that the overtaking vessel shall keep out of the way of the overtaken one (paragraph (a)). Paragraph (b) retains the old test of deciding when ship A is overtaking ship B, i.e. when approaching from a direction 'more than 22.5 degrees abaft her beam'. Paragraph (c) provides that when a vessel is in any doubt as to whether she is overtaking another, she shall assume that this is the case and act accordingly. Paragraph (d) provides that any subsequent alteration of the bearing between the two vessels shall not make the overtaking vessel a crossing vessel or relieve her of the duty of keeping clear of the overtaken vessel until she is finally past and clear. This rule applies to ships in sight of one another.

*The Iran Torab* [1988] 2 Lloyd's Rep. 38
A collision occurred between the vessels *Tan* and *Iran Torab* in the Khor Musa Bar Channel whilst proceeding in convoy due to the Gulf War in 1984. The *Iran Torab* took steps to overtake ships in the line on their starboard side but a collision occurred with the vessel *Tan*.

*Held*: When the *Iran Torab* commenced to pass *Tan* she did so at a safe passing distance of about half a cable. As soon as the overtaking manoeuvre commenced there was a close quarters situation in which it was the duty of *Iran Torab* to keep out of the way of *Tan*. The Master of the *Iran Torab* should have appreciated that the vessels were much closer than he thought and should have altered his course to starboard. The main cause of the collision was that the *Iran Torab* failed to keep out of the way of *Tan* and this was because *Iran Torab* steered a converging course and failed to keep a lookout by watching a ship which was being passed very close on her port side. If a continuous and effective lookout could not be maintained the Master of the *Iran Torab* ought not to have set a course to port of an up-channel course until he was safely past and clear. The vessel *Tan*, being the overtaken ship, should have altered course sufficiently early to avoid the possibility of being drawn towards *Iran Torab* and the collision was caused partly by the fault of *Tan*. The Master of the *Iran Torab* took a decision to overtake *Tan* and his manoeuvres had to be judged on the basis that they were highly blameworthy and potently causative of the collision. The Master of the *Tan* failed to react correctly to the dangerous situation thrust upon her in that no effective lookout had been maintained. The *Iran Torab* was 80 per cent to blame and the *Tan* was 20 per cent to blame.

Rule 14 deals with the 'head-on' situation (when two ships in sight of one another are meeting on reciprocal or nearly reciprocal courses so as to involve risk of collision) as before, i.e. each ship to alter course to starboard thus to pass on each other's port side. Paragraph (c) is intended to avoid any possible conflict in manoeuvre by the respective vessels by providing that if there is any doubt as to whether a 'head-on' situation exists each ship shall assume that it does and act accordingly.

*The Argo Hope/The Bebington* [1982] 2 Lloyd's Rep. 559
A collision occurred in the Manchester Ship Canal, the port bow of the *Bebington* striking the port bow of the *Argo Hope* at roughly a 30-degree angle. It was dark but the weather was fine and visibility good. There were local by-laws for navigating the Canal including

a maximum permitted speed, but the rules for ships approaching each other from opposite directions were essentially the same as the international rules (i.e. rule 14).

*Held*: (Admiralty Judge) that the *Argo Hope* caused the collision by altering to port but the *Bebington's* failure to judge correctly the speed and approach course of the *Argo Hope* and her failure to allow the *Argo Hope* as much room as possible by keeping well over to her starboard side contributed to the eventual impact. The *Argo Hope* bore the substantial blame (85 per cent) by wrongly altering to port and the *Bebington* 15 per cent by not accordingly navigating with sufficient caution as expressly required by the Canal by-law.

Rule 15 relates to a crossing situation (i.e. two ships approaching each other from different angles so as to involve risk of collision) and again, the original rule applies: the one having the other on its starboard side to keep out of the way and, when applicable, to avoid crossing ahead of the other. This rule applies to ships in sight of one another.

*The Toni* [1974] 1 Lloyd's Rep. 489, CA

The Master of the *Toni*, on watch on the bridge, saw the white masthead lights of the *Cardo*, 13 miles off on his starboard bow. After this initial sighting, the Master of the *Toni* seemed to take no interest in her, until some 28 minutes later when his attention was called to her by the seaman look-out on the bridge with him. The Master of the *Toni* then saw that the *Cardo* was 'about 35 degrees to 40 degrees on his starboard bow and about half-a-mile away and heading straight for the *Toni*'. If the Master of the *Toni* had carefully watched the approach of *Cardo* he would have observed her red sidelight and, it is hoped, would have realized that it was his duty to keep out of the way of the *Cardo*. In a written statement, the Master of *Toni* said that from the aspect of *Cardo's* masthead lights and his later sighting of her green sidelight, he inferred that the two ships would pass clear starboard to starboard. He therefore kept his course, attempting to cross ahead of the *Cardo*, contrary to the Collision Regulations. The *Cardo*, being the 'stand-on" ship was bound by the Collision Regulations to keep her course and speed. Unfortunately the officer-of-the-watch on the *Cardo*, after sighting *Toni*, thought that the two ships would pass each other port to port. Thus he had altered course successively to starboard even though able to see the green sidelight to *Toni* on his port bow.

The trial court found that the officer-of-the-watch of *Cardo* seemed not to understand what a crossing situation under the Collision Regulations was or what ships in such a situation were supposed to do under the regulations. The Court of Appeal confirmed the lower court's conclusion that the faults on either side were equally blameworthy and equally causative and that the blame should be divided equally. There was no error of fact or of law.

Rules 16 and 17 lay down the respective obligations of the vessel which is required to keep out of the way (the 'give-way' vessel) and the other one (the 'stand-on' vessel) when they are in sight of one another. The former's requirements are emphasized by the wording of Rule 16 to read 'shall take early and substantial action to keep well clear, as far as possible'.

In *The Estrella* [1977] 1 Lloyd's Rep. 525, the two ships were in a crossing situation and the Admiralty Court decided that the primary blame lay with the *Setubal* being the 'stand-on' ship in failing to keep her course and instead making successive slight alterations to port when the two ships were still a considerable distance apart. The fault of the *Estrella*, which had less of the blame attributed to her, lay in her failure to take more positive action as the 'give-way' ship in ample time. This case illustrates the significance of the requirement of Rule 16 to take 'early and substantial action to keep well clear'.

*The Angelic Spirit* and *Y Mariner* [1994] 2 Lloyd's Rep. 595
In the evening of 10 August 1991, the vessel *Angelic Spirit* and the vessel *Y Mariner* came into collision off the west coast of California. The vessels' courses were initially crossing at an angle of about 16 deg. The collision occurred between the starboard bow of *Y Mariner* and the port side of *Angelic Spirit* in way of No 6 hold at an angle of about 40 deg. leading forward on *Angelic Spirit*.

*Held*: the evidence of *Y Mariner* was that there was an alteration of course to port because of a tug and tow. It was more probable than not that *Y Mariner* altered course to 300 deg. when *Angelic Spirit* was some miles distant and that she put her wheel hard to port shortly before the collision. The vessels were crossing so as to involve risk of collision when they came into sight of one another on courses of 307 deg. and 143 deg. within the meaning of Rule 15 of the Collision Regulations. It was the duty of *Y Mariner* to keep out of the way of *Angelic Spirit* and, if the circumstances of the case admitted to avoid crossing ahead of her. *Y Mariner* should have made a large alteration of course to starboard (or even to port) in order to keep well clear of the other vessel, and there was plenty of sea room in which to do so. Thereafter, the vessels continued to cross so as to involve risk of collision and it remained the duty of *Y Mariner* to keep out of the way of *Angelic Spirit* under Rule 15 and moreover to take early and substantial action to keep well clear, in accordance with Rule 16; she failed to take any such action until shortly before the collision, when she went hard to port; that failure was a significant cause of the collision and was the result of a failure to keep a proper lookout.

*Angelic Spirit* was also partly to blame for the collision, in that she altered 20 deg. to starboard when the vessels were about two miles apart; it was her duty to keep her course and speed in accordance with Rule 17(a)(i) of the Collision Regulations, and she was at fault for failing to take proper action and for lacking sufficient action instead. Both vessels should have sounded signals as required by Rule 34(d) of the Collision Regulations but such failure was not causative of the collision. Both vessels were to blame for the collision. *Y Mariner* was the giveway ship but failed to take early and substantial action to keep clear of *Angelic Spirit*; instead, she made a small alteration in course to port which was difficult to detect and thereafter failed to take bold action to keep out of the way of *Angelic Spirit*; finally, she failed to put her engines full astern at the last and she should bear the greater share of the blame.

*Angelic Spirit* was also partly to blame, in that she failed to keep a proper lookout and did not judge the situation correctly; when a stand-on ship took action as permitted by Rule 17(a)(ii) it had to be bold action which did not make matters worse; the action taken by *Angelic Spirit* was insignificant action which did not improve matters and she failed to put her engines full astern at the last. The failure to take engine action at the last was of comparatively little significance when compared with the fault which brought about a close quarter situation. *Y Mariner* was found to be 70 per cent to blame and *Angelic Spirit* was 30 per cent to blame for the collision.

Rule 17, paragraph (a) is divided into two subparagraphs. Subparagraph (i) requires the stand-on vessel to maintain her course and speed. Subparagraph (ii) fills what was originally a gap in the 1960 Regulations in that where previously, in a developing critical situation the 'stand-on' vessel might have been unable to gauge the alertness, speed of judgment and capability of manoeuvering of the vessel obliged to give way, she might have maintained course and speed until such time as it might be too late and the situation had become one of inescapable danger. The current wording allows for the 'stand-on' ship to take avoiding action by executing a manoeuvre herself as soon as it becomes clear the 'give-way' vessel is not taking action appropriate to the circumstances in accordance with the rules. Paragraph (b) provides that where the stand-on vessel finds herself so close that a collision cannot be avoided by the action of the give-away vessel alone, she shall take such action as will best aid to avoid collision. Paragraph (c) provides that a 'stand-on' vessel taking action under paragraph (a)(ii) (above) shall not in the normal course alter course to port for a vessel on her port side for reasons which will be obvious. Paragraph (d) merely reminds the 'give-way' vessel to execute independent manoeuvres, she is not relieved of her primary obligations laid down in Rule 16 i.e. to keep out of the way. Unless this was specifically clarified, a 'give-way' vessel might be tempted to maintain course and speed hoping that the 'stand-on' vessel would take remedial action under paragraph (a)(ii) (above), thus in effect reversing the roles of each vessel.

*The Savina* [1975] 2 Lloyd's Rep. 141, CA
In a crossing situation in Ras Tanura roadstead the *Savina* was the 'give-way' vessel and the *Forest Hill* was required to keep her course and speed. At the time of the collision the *Forest Hill* was doing about eight knots through the water and *Savina* about two knots. The question was whether *Forest Hill* was at fault in altering her speed or whether the *Savina* should have stopped engines.

*Held*: (1) that the findings of fact of the trial judge would be accepted, which were (a) that approximately eight minutes before the collision (c minus 8) the *Forest Hill* steadied on a course of 350 degrees (true bearing) and that from that moment there was a crossing situation to which the Collision Regulations applied; (b) that by c–8 when *Forest Hill* was steadied on her course and *Savina* on 80 degrees (T) the ships were crossing so as to involve a risk of collision; (2) that the trial judge was wrong in law (a) in holding that the bad look-out on the *Savina* and the failure to stop her engines could be regarded as a single fault instead of separate faults; (b) in holding that *Forest Hill* was not on a course, and the crossing rules did not apply, until she was steadied on a course of 350 degrees (T); (c) in failing to hold that *Savina's* failure to take action to avoid contact with the *Forest Hill* was the most blameworthy and causative fault committed on either ship; (3) accordingly, that *Savina* was the first of the two vessels on which the negligence of those aboard constituted a dangerous situation and as such was the more to blame of the two: blame to be apportioned as to 60 per cent against the *Savina* and 40 per cent against the *Forest Hill*.

As the judge in *The Savina* case said:

'For the duties under the crossing rules to apply so as to impose on a vessel the duty to give way both vessels must be keeping a steady course involving risk of collision and the 'give-way' vessel should be able to ascertain that the vessel is on such a course. Before that moment each vessel owes the other a general duty of careful navigation with good look-out on a basis of mutuality.'

Other examples involving breaches of Rule 17 are as follows:

*The Lok Vivek and Common Venture* [1995] 2 Lloyd's Rep. 230
A collision occurred on 19 May 1988 between the vessels *Lok Vivek* and *Common Venture* in the Gulf of Thailand. It was dark but the weather was fine and visibility good. The speeds of the two vessels at collision were about 13 knots. Both vessels were on full ahead until very shortly before the collision. *Lok Vivek* did not reduce speed at all, and *Common Venture* put her engines to Stop shortly before the collision. The stem and port bow of *Common Venture* struck the port side of *Lok Vivek* with numbers 4 and 5 holds at an angle of about 17 deg., leading aft on *Lok Vivek*. The crucial issue between the parties was whether this was a crossing case to which Rule 15 applied or a head-on case to which Rule

14 of the International Regulations for Preventing Collisions at Sea, 1972, as amended, applied.

*Held*: *Lok Vivek* was steering 345 deg. by gyro until she went hard to starboard. On the assumption that *Common Venture* was on a course of 157 deg. until the collision or very shortly before the collision when the wheel was put hard to starboard, or on the assumption that she was on a course of 157 deg. followed by a course of 152 deg. from the time when the vessels were about four miles apart until collision or very shortly before the collision, the vessels were crossing so as to involve risk of collision within the meaning of Rule 15 of the Regulations. *Common Venture* was the giveway ship under Rule 15 and it was her duty to keep out of the way of *Lok Vivek*. Under Rule 16 it was the duty of *Common Venture* to take early and substantial action to keep well clear, and she ought to have altered course boldly to starboard at an early stage and was seriously to blame for not doing so; she was also at fault for failing to redeem her earlier failure by failing to alter course to starboard; moreover, she failed to put her wheel to starboard until too late and failed to put her engines full astern when the ships were only about a mile apart as she should have done. *Common Venture* was very substantially to blame for the collision. *Lok Vivek* was the stand-on vessel under the Regulations and it was her duty to keep her course and speed under Rule 17(a)(i). *Lok Vivek* went hard to starboard when the vessels were less than a mile apart and, as a matter of good seamanship in the light of Rule 17(a)(ii) a bold alteration of course to starboard ought to have been made. Finally, the engines should have been put full astern and the wheel hard to starboard when the vessels were about a mile apart, whereas the only action the Master of the *Lok Vivek* took was to put the wheel hard to starboard. In failing to take that action, *Lok Vivek* was in breach of Rule 17(b). The *Common Venture* had to bear by far the greater share of the blame for failing to keep out of the way of *Lok Vivek* and for failing to take any proper steps until the last. However, the *Lok Vivek* had to bear some share of the blame for failing to make a bold alteration of course to starboard and for failing to put her engines full astern. *Common Venture* was 75 per cent to blame and *Lok Vivek* was 25 per cent to blame for the collision.

*The Koscierzyna and Hanjin Singapore* [1996] 2 Lloyd's Rep. 124
In 1991, a collision occurred in the Bay of Biscay between the plaintiffs' vessel, *Koscierzyna* and the defendants' vessel, *Hanjin Singapore*. The former was being overtaken by the latter. The weather at the time of the collision was fine and clear with visibility of at least four miles. The stem of the overtaking vessel struck the aft transom of the overtaken vessel on the starboard side of the central line and caused very considerable damage to the overtaken vessel for which her owners claimed. The High Court held that the overtaking vessel was wholly to blame for the collision and it was accepted that she failed to observe the overtaken vessel at any time before the collision. The defendants appealed and argued that in all the circumstances the overtaken vessel should have taken avoiding action before Rule 17(b) of the Regulations took effect, at a time when avoiding action by the overtaken vessel was feasible without significant risk of collision. The defendants argued that the overtaken vessel should have taken helm action to avoid the collision and that the learned judge had been wrong in failing to so find.

*Held*: (Court of Appeal) that, although Rule 17(a)(ii) was expressed in permissive terms, situations might arise in which the requirements of good seamanship required a vessel being overtaken to take avoiding action before the stage at which Rule 17(b) applied. The overtaken vessel was at fault in failing to alter course by 20–30 deg., preferably to port, when (about a mile away) the overtaking vessel failed to alter course despite sound and light signals, and, if such alteration was not made then, the overtaken vessel was at fault in failing to make the alteration at any time before the overtaking vessel was less than three-four cables distant. The fault of the overtaken vessel was relatively minor; on any showing, the great bulk of the blame lay with the overtaking vessel and, to some extent, any percentage must be arbitrary. Fifteen per cent of the responsibility for the collision would be apportioned to the overtaken vessel and, to that extent, the appeal would be allowed.

One factor to consider in determining whether the crossing rule applies is whether or not the one ship was pursuing a clearly defined course which would 'strike confusion' into the mind of the Master of the other vessel. An example of a vessel not pursuing a clearly defined course would be when it was manoeuvering to drop or pick up a pilot, perhaps altering its head and proceeding slow ahead or with engines just stopped.

*The Sestrière* [1976] 1 Lloyd's Rep. 125
A collision occurred in the River Plate. Both vessels had pilots on board and were manoeuvering to drop the pilots. The *Alonso* turned to a northerly heading and stopped her engines. The *Sestrière* was still approaching the pontoon and the *Alonso* saw the possibility of a collision. The *Alonso* then put her engines full ahead and went hard-a-starboard. Both ships sounded blasts but neither heard the other. At the moment of collision the *Sestrière* was making one to two knots, the *Alonso* three to four knots. The *Alonso's* owners alleged that the *Sestrière* was solely to blame, in that she did not keep a proper look-out, failed to keep out of the way of the *Alonso* which was on her starboard side and failed to comply with the Collision Regulations (Rules 19, 23, 27 and 29). The owners of the *Sestrière* defended and counter-claimed that the *Alonso* was to blame in improperly going full ahead and hard-a-starboard instead of either stopping her engines or going full astern.

*Held*: that for the crossing rules to apply the 'stand-by' ship should be on a clearly defined course apparent to the other ship. The *Alonso* was not, in that she was free to adjust her heading to suit the operation of dropping the pilot. Nevertheless, in accordance with Rule 29, it was the duty of the *Sestrière*, being the ship which arrived later at the 'dropping' area, to take timely action to keep clear. Both vessels were guilty of unseamanlike action and of faults which contributed to the collision. Blame was divided equally.

The greatest dilemma for the Masters of two respective vessels and subsequently for any court seized of the matter, is whether the situation is one of overtaking or of crossing. As a result of the Admiralty Court's treatment of the *Nowy Sacz/Olympian* collisions and the *Auriga/Manuel Campos* collision (below) two principles emerged: (a) 'Once an overtaking ship, always an overtaking ship'. An overtaking situation cannot be converted into a crossing situation (NB: this is quite clearly the intent of Rule 13(d)); (b) No overtaking situation arises and thus no overtaking rules apply unless there is a risk of collision. A similar principle applies to the crossing rules to come into operation.

*The Nowy Sacz* [1976] 2 Lloyd's Rep. 682
A collision occurred just south of Cape St Vincent between the *Nowy Sacz* and the *Olympian*. It was a clear night with good visibility and both vessels were proceeding northwards on roughly parallel courses. By 03.30 hours the second officer of the *Nowy Sacz* could see the red light of the *Olympian* in addition to her masthead light. At this point in time the bearing of the *Olympian* had ceased to be more than two points abaft the beam of the other vessel. Similarly the green light and masthead light of the *Nowy Sacz* was visible to the second officer of the *Olympian*. By 03.30, the relative positions of the two ships indicated a collision risk. At this juncture the *Nowy Sacz* appeared to be closing on a crossing course from port to starboard. Warning blasts were sounded by both vessels and action taken to reduce speed and stop. However, the collision ultimately occurred at 03.57 hours. Two opposing arguments were presented. On the one hand, the owners of the

*Olympian* argued that it was a crossing situation under which it was the responsibility of the *Nowy Sacz* to keep out of their ship's way. The *Nowy Sacz's* owners argued conversely that it was an overtaking situation whereunder the *Olympian's* duty was to keep clear of their ship which was the one being overtaken.

*Held*: that the situation was one of crossing not of overtaking. The court based its decision on the evidence before it that before 03.00 hours a risk of collision had not arisen. In thus deciding that it was a crossing situation at the time when the risk of collision was apparent, the court found that it was the duty of the *Nowy Sacz* to keep clear of the *Olympian* and the *Olympian's* responsibility to maintain her course and speed. The *Nowy Sacz* was under an additional duty to take clearly positive action in the form of slackening speed, stopping or even reversing as the situation might require.

Another case and equally illustrative of this point is *The Auriga*.

*The Auriga* [1977] 1 Lloyd's Rep. 384
The owners of the Spanish Vessel the *Manuel Campos* claimed damages from the owners of the Italian *Auriga* after a collision in January 1973 off the west coast of Spain. The dispute centred around whether it was an 'overtaking' or a 'crossing' situation, the Spaniards arguing that the overtaking rules applied, the Italians that the crossing rules applied. The collision was after dark and the weather was fine and visibility good. Both ships were proceeding in a generally southerly direction, but for some 10 to 15 minutes before impact their courses were converging at an angle of 24 degrees, which involved a risk of collision if those courses were maintained. The *Manuel Campos's* owners argued that since the *Auriga* was originally bearing more than two points abaft the beam of the *Manuel Campos* and was proceeding faster than her she was an overtaking vessel and that the principle 'once an overtaking vessel, always an overtaking vessel' applied, putting the onus on her to keep out of the way with the corresponding duty on the *Manual Campos* (the overtaken vessel) to maintain her course and speed.

Subsequent alterations of course did not and should not cause an overtaking relationship to be converted into a crossing relationship. The *Auriga's* owners argued that the crossing rules were in any event only applicable *after* a risk of collision had come into existence and that such a risk on these facts had only arisen when the *Auriga* altered course from 212 degrees to 181 degrees, by which time the *Auriga* was bearing less than two points abaft the beam of the *Manuel Campos*. At that point the two vessels were crossing so as to involve a risk of collision and at that point it was the duty of the *Manuel Campos* to keep out of the way of the *Auriga* and the *Auriga's* duty to maintain her course and speed.

The Admiralty Court came to the conclusion that there never was an overtaking situation within the meaning and intention of the Collision Regulations. The distance between the two vessels was too great during the initial period when the *Auriga* was bearing more than two points abaft the beam of the *Manuel Campos*. It was in fact entirely the fault of the *Auriga* that a crossing situation involving a risk of collision came into being when she altered course about c minus 13 or c minus 14. Having once created that situation, however, both ships were guilty of causative faults. Both ships' look-outs were seriously defective. The *Manuel Campos* was at fault as the 'give-way' ship in a crossing situation in failing to keep out of the way of the *Auriga*. The *Auriga* was at fault additionally in improperly resuming her course and as 'stand-on' ship in failing to take sufficient avoiding action in sufficient time. The interesting point about apportionment of blame was that although the substantial blame *after* the crossing situation had arisen was found to lie with the *Manuel Campos*, the *Auriga* being entirely responsible for creating the crossing situation involving risk of collision in the first place was overall the more substantially to blame of the two. Apportionment was thus fixed at 60 per cent to the *Auriga* and 40 per cent to the *Manuel Campos*.

The *Nowy Sacz/Olympian* case was taken to appeal where the judges ruled that the words 'coming up with another vessel' in the overtaking rule (Rule 13(b) in the 1972 Regulations, but Rule 24(b) in the 1960 Regulations), could involve a time before there was any risk of collision. As the prevention of collision regulations in general were intended not only to avoid collision but also to avoid the risk of collision, the overtaking rule could properly come into effect and apply at that early stage. The appeal judges reversed the trial court's findings that the *Nowy Sacz* should have kept clear of the *Olympian* and held that the *Olympian* should have kept clear of the *Nowy Sacz*. Thus it would seem that the courts regard overtaking situations and the application of the overtaking rule as arising even before the risk of collision.

Rule 18 combines into one rule the responsibilities of various types of vessels to keep clear of each other. Under it, a power-driven vessel underway shall, unless Rules 9, 10 and 13 require otherwise, keep out of the way of:

(1) a vessel not under command;
(2) a vessel restricted in her ability to manoeuvre;
(3) a vessel engaged in fishing;
(4) a sailing vessel.

In Section III, Rule 19 deals with requirements of ships in conditions of restricted visibility. Paragraph (a) of Rule 19 defines the area of applicability: not in sight of one another when navigating in or near an area of restricted visibility. Paragraph (b) re-emphasizes Rule 6, (to proceed at a safe speed) thought to be of such vital importance in all degrees of visibility that it needs specifically re-emphasizing in situations of restricted visibility. See *The Sanshin Victory* (page 260) and *The Roseline* (page 258). The final sentence is quite new. It requires power-driven ships to have their engines ready for *immediate* manoeuvre. More recent examples are the cases of *The Da Ye*, *Maloja II*, *Tenes*, *Pulkovo*, *State of Himachal Pradesh* and *Skyron*.

*The Da Ye* [1993] 1 Lloyd's Rep. 30
A collision occurred between the vessels *Professor Vladimir Popov (Popov)* and *Da Ye* in the approaches to Port Said in 1987. The visibility was variable. At about three minutes before the collision, *Da Ye* altered course for starboard. *Da Ye* did not advertise her turn by sounding one short blast as was her duty. *Da Ye* struck the starboard side of *Popov* at an angle of 54° leading forward. The bulbous bow of *Da Ye* penetrated *Popov* below the water-line causing great damage.

*Held*: *Da Ye* was not keeping an efficient radar lookout; the greatly excessive speed and the deplorable failure to keep a proper radar lookout were two separate faults in that even if a good radar lookout had been kept her speed was unsafe and the failure to keep a lookout led to another serious fault. *Popov* was not maintaining a proper radar lookout: if a proper lookout had been kept it would have been seen that although a close-quarters situation was developing, the vessels would have passed each other starboard to starboard and no engine action was then necessary. At six minutes prior to the collision (C–6) *Popov* was almost directly ahead of *Da Ye* and either crossing on the *Da Ye's* starboard bow or would have done if *Da Ye* had not altered course a few degrees to starboard.

The same situation which existed at C–6 was transformed into a very serious situation by the unexplained turn to starboard by *Da Ye*. It was that alteration of course which created the risk of collision and was a very serious fault which seemed to have been the result of a bad lookout. Although *Popov* was not maintaining a proper lookout during the last ten minutes before collision, no complaint could be made about her navigation before C–3; the situation was safe and a collision would not have occurred if *Da Ye* had not altered course to starboard: there was no need for *Popov* to reduce speed before C–3; *Popov* ought to have been sounding signals of one prolonged blast at intervals of not more than two minutes but it was not contended that this was causative of the collision.

The faults in the navigation of *Da Ye* were undoubtedly the dominant causes of the collision; she was proceeding at 14 knots through an anchorage area in poor visibility when a safe speed would have been six knots: one of the results of that speed was that it led to a hasty and wrong decision to alter course to starboard; that decision was hasty because no proper lookout was being maintained and *Da Ye* was at fault for turning to starboard thereby creating a dangerous crossing situation: no ship was entitled in face of another ship seen to be approaching to turn on to a crossing course so as to force that other ship to keep out of the way. The fault in the navigation of *Popov* was not reacting correctly to the emergency thrust on her. The *Da Ye* was 80 per cent to blame and *Popov* was 20 per cent to blame for the collision.

*The Maloja II* [1993] 1 Lloyd's Rep. 48
A collision occurred between the vessels *John M* and *Maloja II* off the coast of Newfoundland in conditions of reduced visibility in 1988.

*Held*; on the totality of the evidence, on the balance of probabilities, the vessels came into sight of each other at a distance of six or seven cables and then *John M* turned hard to starboard and very shortly thereafter *Maloja II* turned hard to port. The collision was caused by faults in the navigation of both vessels and accordingly the liability to make good the damage had to be divided in proportion to the degree in which each ship was in fault. Where both vessels had been guilty of several faults in navigation it was wrong to apportion blame in proportion to the number of faults committed by each vessel and the court had to consider the blameworthiness and causative potency of the various wrongful acts and omissions and then make a comparative appreciation of the degree in which the faults of the respective vessels contributed to the damage.

*Maloja II* made the first attempt to avoid the close-quarters situation but the action she took was not in accordance with the Collision Regulations; that alteration of course was made at a distance of nine miles so that there was plenty of time for *John M* to assess the situation; no action was taken by *John M* until the vessels were six miles apart and the action taken by *John M* was insufficient. If after the two alterations of course a careful radar lookout had been maintained on both vessels, they both would have realised by the time the range had closed to four or three miles that a dangerous situation was building up. It was then the duty of both the vessels to make bold alterations to starboard and their failure to take this action was the most blameworthy fault in the navigation of each vessel. This fault was also the direct and immediate cause of the very close-quarters situation which led to the collision and in both vessels this fault was self-induced. Having failed to take that action both vessels continued to approach each other at a combined speed of 28 knots whereas both vessels should have reduced speed. The result of these faults in both these vessels was that they reached a situation in which measures were taken in panic. Neither vessel could contend that these basic faults were the result of being put in a position of difficulty created by the other vessel. Accordingly it was decided that both vessels were equally at fault. The Admiralty Judge stated that the structure of the Collision Regulations is designed to ensure that whenever possible, ships will not reach a close-quarters situation in which there is a risk of collision and in which decisions have to be taken without time for proper thought.

*Held*: (Court of Appeal) [1994] 1 Lloyd's Rep. 374, the action taken by *Maloja II* of altering course to port at a distance of about nine miles was wrong and such fault was serious but such fault would only have added a small percentage to her share of the blame. The Admiralty Court's decision was affirmed.

*The Tenes* [1989] 2 Lloyd's Rep. 367
The vessel *Tenes* was proceeding on a course of 261° at a speed of 15 knots. Her engines were stopped shortly before the collision. As the *Darion* sank as a result of the collision there was no evidence as to her course before action was taken in relation to the approach of the *Tenes.* Having regarded the voyage he was engaged on it was clear that her course must have been opposite to that of the *Tenes* or within a few degrees. Her speed was not less than 10 knots. A collision occurred between the stem and bulbous bow of the *Tenes* and the port side of the *Darion* and the *Darion* sank. Both vessels failed to comply with Rules 8(b) and 19(b) of the Collision Regulations.

*Held*: The master of the *Darion* gave unclear and unseamanlike instructions to avoid a close quarters situation to the mate, who was the only man on the bridge of the *Darion* which was on automatic steering in dense fog. The mate made two small alterations to starboard, but did not appreciate that by doing so he was putting the *Darion* on a crossing course and that because *Tenes* was proceeding at a higher speed than *Darion, Tenes* would, if each vessel maintained its course, cross ahead of *Darion. Tenes* should not have been proceeding at more than 10 knots with her engines ready for immedate manoeuvre and *Darion* should not have been proceeding at more than eight knots. Neither vessel was proceeding at the safe speed as was required by Rule 19(b) of the Collision Regulations. The real mischief which created the close-quarters situation was the fact that the *Darion* made two small alterations of course to starboard which would not have been readily apparent to *Tenes.* It was a breach of Rule 8(b) by *Darion* which created the very close quarters situation and a ship which created the difficulties inherent in such a situation should in general bear the greater proportion of the blame. The *Darion* was 60 per cent to blame and *Tenes*, 40 per cent.

*The State of Himachal Pradesh* [1987] 2 Lloyd's Rep. 97
In 1975 a collision occurred between the plaintiffs' vessel, *Capulonix*, and the defendants' vessel, *State of Himachal Pradesh*, (*Pradesh*) off the port of Bombay in the hours of darkness.

*Held* (Court of Appeal): although it had not been found possible to prepare a plot which established beyond doubt precisely how the vessels moved into collision, the final plot produced by the plaintiffs was consistent with, and reinforced the Admiralty Judge's finding that, at five minutes before the collision the vessels were green to green and in a position of safety. The ships were navigating in the approaches to a port; *Pradesh*, to the knowledge of *Capulonix*, was engaged in dropping her pilot, and *Capulonix* had the constraints of her draught, a fact of which *Pradesh* was aware. As soon as *Capulonix* showed her green light to *Pradesh* there was no risk of collision unless *Pradesh* made a prolonged and substantial alteration of course to starboard; it was a question of fact whether it was right to say that the ships had crossed; by the time *Pradesh* came to resume her voyage increasing speed and altering course for the Bombay Floating Light, the crossing rules had ceased to apply.

No useful purpose would have been achieved by the *Capulonix* going full astern when the *Pradesh* turned to starboard and her red light was visible; a collision was inevitable; on the other hand, to go full ahead and hard-a-port might have reduced the angle of collision and the resultant damage. As that manoeuvre could not possibly avoid a collision, the Master of *Capulonix* was not negligent for seeking as he thought to minimize the effects of the impending collision. The fact that the damage sustained might have been different was not a matter which was relevant in the circumstances in determining the question of whether the Master of *Capulonix* was negligent. Accordingly, the *State of Himachal Pradesh* was wholly to blame for the collision, the *Capulonix* being not at fault in any way.

*The Pulkovo and Oden* [1989] 1 Lloyd's Rep. 280
A collision occurred between the vessels *Pulkovo* and *Oden* on 10 March 1986 in the Baltic Sea in restricted visibility.

*Held*: the International Regulations for Preventing Collisions at Sea were designed to prevent the risk of collision by prescribing navigation which would avoid a close quarters situation. It was when a close quarters situation could not be avoided that a vessel was required to reduce her speed to the minimum at which she could be kept on her course or if necessary take all her headway off. The collision was caused by the negligent navigation of both vessels. The *Pulkovo* was at fault in proceeding at an excessive speed in conditions of restricted visibility contrary to Rules 6 and 19(b). She did not take action to avoid a close quarters situation as required by Rule 8. When action was taken, it was the wrong action in two respects, namely that it was a succession of small alterations of course contrary to Rule 8(b) and it consisted of altering course to port contrary to Rule 19(d)(i). The radar observation was inadequate in that the substantial alteration of course made by the *Oden* a few minutes before the collision was not observed. If it had been observed the *Pulkovo* would probably not have altered course to 10° to port between two and three minutes before the collision.

The *Oden* was at fault in failing to maintain a proper look-out by radar, in breach of Rule 5, and in breach of Rule 7(b) which requires long-made scanning to be carried out. The greater the distance at which an approaching ship is detected, the greater is the chance of making a proper appreciation of the situation and of avoiding a close quarters situation. She also proceeded at an excessive speed in conditions of restricted visibility contrary to Rules 6 and 19(b). Furthermore, she made assumptions as to the course and the speed of the *Pulkovo* on the basis of scanty radar information contrary to Rule 7(c). It was impossible to draw any distinction between the very serious breaches of the Regulations of which each vessel was guilty and liability was apportioned equally.

*The Skyron* [1994] 2 Lloyd's Rep. 254
In 1987 a collision occurred between the vessel *Skyron* and the vessel *Hel* in the North Sea in restricted visibility. At no time was either vessel able properly to see both mastheads of the other vessel. Although the vessels, until the last, were not in sight of one another their navigation was governed by Rule 19 of the Collision Regulations. The question for decision was how blame for the collision should be apportioned.

*Held*: At the material time the *Skyron* was proceeding at about 12.5 knots through the water and the *Hel* was proceeding at about 16 knots. Neither vessel made any significant reduction in speed. Neither vessel was sounding whistle signals for fog as she should have done but this failure was not causative of the collision. Both vessels were guilty of appalling lookout and proceeding too fast. *Hel* could only justify a faster speed than *Skyron* if she took positive early action to reduce her speed when necessary, which she did not. *Hel* was apparently concentrating on the vessels on her starboard bow whereas she should have appreciated that she would soon be crossing the north-eastbound route and that there were likely to be large deep-drafted vessels closing on her port bow; neither vessel reduced her speed before the collision and they were thus both seriously at fault so far as speed was concerned. Both vessels failed to take positive early helm action to avoid a close quarter situation as they should have done; *Skyron* failed to alter course as she should have done; *Hel* not only failed to alter course as she should have done but made a number of small alterations of course which caused the vessels to approach each other on collision courses. Although the situation was never safe and both vessels should have been proceeding more slowly and taken action when they were 4.5 to 5 miles apart, *Hel* made a number of alterations of course which had the net effect of putting the vessels on collision course; but for that action there would have been no collision. A fair apportionment was that *Skyron* was 40 per cent and *Hel* 60 per cent at fault for the collision.

Paragraph (d) of Rule 19 requires vessels detecting by radar alone to take avoiding action in ample time if a close-quarters situation is developing or there is a collision risk, such action being mandatory whereas under the 1960

Regulations it was merely permissable if thought necessary. When such action consists of an alteration of course, so far as possible, the following shall be avoided: (1) an alteration of course to port for a vessel forward of the beam, other than for a vessel being overtaken; and (2) an alteration of course towards a vessel abeam or abaft of the beam. Paragraph (e) also provides more positive guidance than the equivalent provision in the 1960 Regulations. It gives more scope for the efficient use of radar and requires a ship which has detected forward of her beam another vessel potentially indicating a close-quarter situation to reduce speed to a minimum consistent with keeping on course, unless there is absolutely no risk of collision. If this is insufficient she must take off all her way and in any event navigate with extreme caution until the danger of collision is over.

*The Ercole* [1977] 1 Lloyd's Rep. 516
The Greek ship *George S Embiricos* collided with the Italian ship *Ercole* in the South China Sea in October 1970. Initially, they approached each other on nearly opposite courses but as a result of the *Ercole's* altering to the starboard and the *Embiricos* to port, the stem of the *Ercole* struck the starboard after side of the other ship. Both ships were substantially damaged. Both vessels were using radar as visibility was restricted.

The court, sitting with two Elder Brethren of Trinity House as assessors, decided that the changes in bearing of each ship were very slow and should have warned the navigating officer of both vessels that a close-quarters situation was developing. Had both ships kept their original course and speeds they would have passed on parallel courses starboard to starboard. On the evidence the court found that the *Embiricos* was at fault in two respects, firstly defective appreciation of the situation on radar and, secondly, for not reducing speed when the visibility worsened. The *Ercole* was at fault in four ways: defective use of the radar, failing to stop her engines and navigate with caution when she lost the other vessel's echo, thirdly for altering course 10 degrees at an improper time and fourthly going hard to starboard at the last moment instead of going hard-astern. The serious element in the fault of both ships lay in allowing themselves to come into a close-quarters situation at high speed in conditions of restricted visibility.

Some further examples in recent years of failures which can amount to fault-producing liability including failure to sound appropriate signals when manoeuvering or in conditions of bad visibility or navigation on the wrong side of a channel are set out below.

*The Aldebaran/The Esso Brussels* [1972] 1 Lloyd's Rep. 286; [1973] 2 Lloyd's Rep. 73 CA
Both ships were fully loaded and both were engaged in moving in discharging berths in the canal dock system in Antwerp. Shortly before the collision the weather had been fine with good visibility but then dense fog developed. The *Aldebaran* on her way through the canal via Lille Bridge anchored when she encountered fog. The *Esso Brussels* following some 20 minutes later and somewhat faster reduced speed when she met fog and whilst coming to anchor she struck the *Aldebaran*. Subsequently, both Masters said they had their radar switched on but felt that it was not safe to rely on the readings in the prevailing circumstances. The risk of false echoes was considerable.

*Held*: that no fault lay in not using radar in the circumstances. The *Aldebaran* was not lying at a dangerous angle. The *Esso Brussels* was acting under the misguided assumption that the *Aldebaran* had already passed through the bridge and that consequently she (the *Esso Brussels*) had plenty of room in which to anchor. The *Aldebaran* should have sounded a blast as a warning which would have allowed the *Esso Brussels* to know the situation and to take action accordingly. The *Esso Brussels* was at fault for failing to appreciate that the *Aldebaran* might have anchored *before* reaching the bridge and in failing to take off way and anchor more quickly and earlier. The *Aldebaran* was at fault for not sounding attention signals. The *Esso Brussels* was 75 per cent to blame, the *Aldebaran* 25 per cent to blame. On appeal the *Esso Brussels* was found solely to blame.

*The Martin Fierro* [1975] 2 Lloyd's Rep. 130, CA
On 26 May 1970 the vessel *Joaquin Ponte Naya* was proceeding up the River Parana in Argentina. The *Martin Fierro* was coming down river. At approximately 19.10 hours the ships were 1,400 metres apart. The *Joaquin Ponte Naya's* wheel was put hard to starboard and it was about this time that the *Martin Fierro* first saw the green and red light of the *Joaquin Ponte Naya*. Shortly afterwards, on losing sight of the light, those aboard *Martin Fierro* went hard to port and sounded two short blasts. About half a minute later when *Martin Fierro* saw the starboard light of *Joaquin Ponte Naya* close and the port light re-open she went hard to starboard, sounding one short blast. Thereafter a collision occurred between the stem and port bow of the *Martin Fierro* and the port side of *Joaquin Ponte Naya*, at an angle of 35 degrees.

*Held*: (affirming the decision of the lower court) that (1) the *Joaquin Ponte Naya* was at fault in navigating the wrong side of the channel in breach of local regulations and the Collision Regulations, in failing to sound one short blast when altering course to starboard, but it was not wrong for her to turn to starboard to regain her proper side of the channel; (2) the *Martin Fierro* was at fault in not reducing speed as the situation became more dangerous and putting her wheel to port without sufficient knowledge of the other vessel's intention; (3) also, that the *Joaquin Ponte Naya* was additionally at fault (a) in deviating to port and (b) in going hard to starboard when she did; and that *Martin Fierro* was additionally at fault in failing to alter course to starboard before *Joaquin Ponte Naya* opened her green light, but the most serious fault was the initial bad navigation by the *Joaquin Ponte Naya*; (4) blame should be apportioned 85 per cent to the *Joaquin Ponte Naya* and 15 per cent to *Martin Fierro*. The appeal and cross-appeal were dismissed.

Failure to evaluate logically the movements of the other ship can constitute a fault and is a factor which becomes the more significant the narrower or more constricted the area of water in which the two ships are proceeding, manoeuvering or anchored at the material time.

### *Exhibiting of lights and shapes*

The majority of changes brought about by the introduction of the 1972 Collision Regulations are centred in Part B and few alterations of any significance are to be found in the other parts. However, a few comments on Part C of the regulations may be of value; that is the part dealing with lights and shapes. It is not intended to deal with Part D which deals with sound and light signals. It is indeed in Part C that the 1983 and 1989 (as amended) Regulations introduced some changes. The present regulations are the Merchant Shipping (Distress Signals and Prevention of Collisions) Regulations 1996.

The opening rule in Part C (Rule 20) describes the application of this part. It applies in *all* weather conditions. No light may be exhibited which could be mistaken for the lights specifically mentioned in the rules. The period of applicability is sunset to sunrise except that, in restricted visibility conditions, the same lights should be used between sunrise and sunset (and also in all other circumstances when it is deemed to be necessary). Presumably the customary tests of 'reasonableness' would apply.

In *The Coral I* [1982] 1 Lloyd's Rep. 441 the *Coral I* was at fault for not exhibiting anchor lights in Suez Bay waiting area and the *Neil Armstrong* was also at fault for not keeping a proper look-out and proceeding at excessive speed (breaches of Rules 5 and 6).

*The Ouro Fino* [1988] 2 Lloyd's Rep. 325
The *Rimac* collided with a dumb barge in care of the tug *Ouro Fino* moored port side of the barge. The barge was loaded with units of platform piling. The *Rimac* was proceeding down river out of Antwerp and was in the charge of two pilots, one specially to take her through the Weilingen Channel. The barge lay between two buoys marking the north side of the channel. It was exhibiting a stern light only which was not visible to a ship approaching from an easterly direction. The questions for the Admiralty Court to answer were (1) was the barge anchored in an improper position? (2) was the failure of the barge to exhibit anchor lights causative of the collision? (3) was there any negligence on the part of those in charge of the barge? (4) whether those on board the *Rimac* failed to keep a proper look-out? (5) was *Rimac* proceeding at an unsafe speed? (6) were those in charge of *Rimac* guilty of any other faults of navigation?

*Held* (in the Admiralty Court): that (1) the barge *was* anchored improperly and particular care should have been taken to advertise her presence to passing ships by, e.g. exhibiting anchor lights; (2) the tug should have kept a proper look out; (3) the *Rimac* was guilty of navigation faults, specifically a failure to maintain a proper look out and setting a course too close to a vessel on her starboard bow (the latter failure flowed from the former failure); (4) the barge (and tug) created the dangerous situation and therefore should bear the greater portion of blame (60 per cent) but the *Rimac* was also at fault which contributed and she must bear 40 per cent of the blame.

The barge-owners appealed seeking that the *Rimac* should be found solely to blame or alternatively that the blame percentage should be reversed. Held by the Court of Appeal: for 40 years the law had been settled that the question of causation was settled by simply asking—whose act caused the damage? Answer here, both parties committed acts which contributed to the collision. Secondly unless the apportionment of the lower court was plainly wrong, it should not be interfered with. To say that the only negligence of the tug was not to light the barge adequately was wrong. The fault lay also in anchoring in the fairway.

Rule 21 contains the definition of each type of light. Each one is specified as to colour, position and arc of visibility in the six sections of Rule 21. It should be noted that the current rules delineate the required area of visibility in terms of degrees rather than the points of the compass.

The placing of the sternlight is not quite so hard-and-fast a requirement as under the 1960 Regulations. Some vessels (viz. tugs, supply vessels) may have difficulty in placing the light absolutely at the stern so that the words 'as nearly as practicable at the stern' have been introduced into the positioning requirements.

The range of visibility is dealt with in Rule 22, where the change from feet to metres to describe the length of vessels is another feature of the new regulations. A new subparagraph (d) was originally introduced by the 1983 Regulations requiring inconspicuous partly submerged vessels or objects being towed to display a white all-round light visible at a minimum range of three miles. Rule 23 deals with the lights which must be exhibited by power-driven vessels underway.

Rule 24 covers the requirements for pushing or towing and the 1972

Regulations as amended enlarged and tightened up the equivalent 1960 rule. Introduced in paragraph (b) of Rule 24 is a reference to the 'composite unit' formed by a pushing vessel being rigidly connected to the vessel which it is pushing. The lighting requirements for such a 'unit' are the same as those required of any power-driven vessel. Paragraph (c) introduces the procedure for vessels towing alongside as well as pushing ahead (except in the case of a composite unit) and requires the displaying of two masthead lights forward in a vertical line (instead of the one light required for an ordinary power-driven vessel underway; see Rule 23 (a)(i)).

Paragraph (f) of Rule 24 requires vessels being towed alongside or pushed *in a group* to be lighted as one vessel.

The 1983 amendments write in a new subparagraph (g) relating to inconspicuous, partly submerged vessels or objects, or combination of such vessels or objects being towed, requiring them to exhibit:

(a) if less than 25 metres in breadth, one all-round white light at or near the forward end and one at or near the after end except that dracones need not exhibit a light at or near the forward end;
(b) if 25 or more metres in breadth, two additional all-round white lights at or near the extremities of its breadth;
(c) if more than 100 metres in length, additional all-round white lights between the lights prescribed in the previous subparagraphs so that the distance between the lights shall not exceed 100 metres;
(d) a diamond shape at or near the aftermost extremity of the last vessel or object being towed and if the length of the tow exceeds 200 metres an additional diamond shape where it can best be seen and located as far forward as practicable.

In a fresh subparagraph (i) recognition is given to the fact that vessels not normally engaged in towing operations sometimes find themselves towing or otherwise assisting another vessel in distress. They are relieved of the obligation of displaying the prescribed lights but *are* required to take all possible measures to indicate the nature of the relationship between the towing vessel and the vessel being towed, in particular by illuminating the towline.

Rules 25 and 26 lay down requirements respectively for sailing vessels, vessels under oars and fishing vessels.

Rule 27 requires special lights and shapes to be exhibited by ships not under command or restricted in their ability to manoeuvre. Included in the rule is a special reference to a towing operation where the towing vessel may be unable to deviate from her course, a form of restriction of manoeuvre. Vessels engaged in mineclearance operations are exempted from the light-exhibiting requirements of vessels restricted in their ability to manoeuvre as prescribed in this rule. The special requirements for vessels engaged in mineclearance are provided by a special subparagraph (f). With the advent and increased use of the hovercraft it is now accepted that 'vessel' includes non-displacement craft (see Part A, Rule 3(a)). The meaning of the words 'not under command' is given extended significance by the inclusion of the qualifying words 'through some exceptional circumstances is unable to manoeuvre as required by these rules and is therefore unable to keep out of the way of another vessel' (see Part A, Rule 3(f)). Dredgers, for example, engaged in underwater operations and restricted in their ability to manoeuvre are given special mention in paragraph (d) of Rule 27.

Subparagraph (g) of Rule 27 exempts vessels of less than 12 metres in length, except those engaged in diving operations, from exhibiting lights and shapes prescribed in this rule.

Rule 28 permits a vessel constrained by her draught to exhibit a special additional identification signal. The rule ties in with Rule 3(h) of Part A.

An alternative test for establishing negligence, in the absence of laid-down navigation rules, might be what a prudent navigator would have done under similar circumstances. The reasonable man, or, as English law has described him, the 'man on the Clapham omnibus' is the mythical being who sets the standards for determining negligence shown by any human being to his neighbour and if he falls below that standard of care which is expected of him and which he owes to his neighbour, the law may find him guilty of negligence and so responsible for loss or damage to persons or their property resulting directly from that negligent act.

There is perhaps no area of the 'world' of loss or damage to others' property generally where the 'human fault or failing' element plays a greater part or must inevitably bear a larger share of responsibility than in collisions between ships at sea.

What must be one of the most significant comments ever made by an Admiralty Court judge was made in 1967 by Cairns J in *The Fogo* [1967] 2 Lloyd's Rep. 208. He said:

> 'automatic steering is a most valuable invention if properly used. It can lead to disaster when it is left to look after itself while vigilance is relaxed. It is on men that safety at sea depends and they cannot make a greater mistake than to suppose that machines can do all their work for them.'

No matter how clear, detailed and comprehensive the regulations for preventing collisions may be, human fallibility and weaknesses are factors which may regrettably override even them. One inevitable contributing factor which has been noted and commented on in the course of sifting of evidence after a collision, particularly where there is a 'close-quarters' situation, is the diversity of languages, a misunderstanding that can so easily arise between the Masters or watch officers of two ships on a possible collision course because their native languages are different.

Furthermore, under section 92 of the Merchant Shipping Act 1995 a Master of a United Kingdom ship or a Master of a foreign ship in United Kingdom waters has a duty, in every case of collision between two ships, if and so far as he can do so without danger to his own ship, crew and passengers (if any)—

(a) to render to the other ship, its Master, crew and passengers (if any) such assistance as may be practicable, and may be necessary to save them from any danger caused by the collision and to stay by the other ship until he has ascertained that it has no need of further assistance; and
(b) to give to the Master of the other ship the name of his own ship and also the names of the ports from which it comes and to which it is bound. If the Master is in breach of his duty then there is no presumption that the collision was caused by the Master's wrongful act, neglect or default.

If the Master without reasonable excuse fails to comply with his duty, he commits an offence. Under section 93 the Master has a duty to assist ships etc in distress.

## CAUSATIVE POTENCY

There must be proved negligence causing or at least contributing to the collision. The judge's role these days in determining the apportionment of blame is to examine the evidence with a view: (a) to evaluating culpability; and (b) to deducing its 'causative potency'.

*The Statue of Liberty* [1971] 2 Lloyd's Rep. 277, HL
In the summer of 1965 the motor vessel *Andulo* collided with the tanker *Statue of Liberty* in good visibility at night off Cape St Vincent. It was argued on the *Andulo*'s behalf that the masthead and green lights of the other ship were sighted bearing 20 degrees on the port bow between five and six miles away. Five minutes later the bearing narrowed to 10 degrees. At about seven cables' length distant and when the other vessel's green light was just starboard of the foremast, the *Andulo* altered course for Casablanca. The *Statue of Liberty* altered to starboard, whereupon *Andulo* altered to port and then hard-a-port resulting in the collision.

The *Statue of Liberty*'s argument was that she first sighted *Andulo* on her starboard bow on a 20-degree bearing, observing her red and masthead lights. When distant about three miles she altered to starboard to bring *Andulo* on her port bow. About three-quarters of a mile distant her bearing broadened on the port bow but suddenly the green light opened up and the red disappeared causing *Statue of Liberty* necessarily to put her course suddenly to starboard. It was because *Andulo* thereafter swung further to port that the collision occurred.

*Held* (on an appeal by the *Andulo*'s owners and a cross-appeal by the *Statue of Liberty*'s owners): that fault lay with *Andulo* in failing to take more accurate observations earlier but that such fault had no 'causative potency' and should not be taken into the reckoning when assessing blame overall. Her causative fault did, however, lie in her unjustified assumption that *Statue of Liberty* would be making no further change in her course. The substantial causative fault was attributable to the *Statue of Liberty* for failing to give way earlier. Their Lordships upheld the percentage apportionment of fault which had been fixed by the Court of Appeal at 85 per cent on *Statue of Liberty* and 15 per cent on *Andulo*.

The accurate pinpointing of blame in a specific percentage becomes the more crucial to determine fairly and equitably the greater the aggregate total of claim value. One distinction which must frequently be drawn is between a fault occasioned by a positive fault of commission and a fault of omission. An example of the former is an intentional breach of a Collision Regulation and of the latter a defective look-out. Neither is necessarily more blameworthy than the other.

## THE 'LAST OPPORTUNITY' RULE

The word 'contributing' has itself many decades in the past created problems for jurists trying to reconcile the case law and common law which has been built up over the years and which applied to situations where more than one party has been, as we say, 'contributorily' negligent in the given situation. As early as 1842 a case established that where one party had created a negligent situation which was fixed and stabilized and another party had later also been negligent and as a result of the latter's negligence loss or damage had been caused, then provided that the latter person had the opportunity to avoid the loss or damage being caused, he (i.e. the latter party) was solely to blame.

*Davies v Mann* (1842) 10 M & W 546
The owner of a donkey, which had been negligently left hobbled and unguarded on a highway, sued the defendant, by the negligence of whose servant in driving along the highway at too rapid a speed the donkey was run over and injured.

*Held:* that the donkey-owner could recover, his negligence notwithstanding.

The suggestion was that in the case of collision between ships, negligence, such as that of the defendant in *Davies* v *Mann*, would render the shipowner liable, although no collision would have occurred if the other vessel had been navigated or managed with ordinary care.

This rule of law became so deep-seated in English law that lawyers in disputes concerning collisions at sea used it as a defensive argument in similar situations. However, the courts gradually came to the view that a fairer rule to apply to the collisions of ships at sea should be not who had the last opportunity of avoiding the mischief but whose act caused the wrong. It was not, however, until the period between the two world wars that the courts finally felt confident of circumventing the 'last opportunity' rule by applying two simple rules for colliding ships.

First, if the negligence of both parties to the litigation continues right up to the moment of collision each party is to blame for the collision which is the result of the continued negligence of both. Secondly, if the negligent act of one party is such as to cause the other party to make a negligent mistake that he would not have otherwise made, then both are to blame (*Admiralty* v *The Camroux* [1958] 1 Lloyd's Rep. 378).

In a speech when giving judgment in the *Admiralty Commissioners* v *SS Volute* [1922] 1 AC 129, Viscount Birkenhead summarized the position as clearly and concisely as could be expected by saying that in that particular case 'there seems to me to be no clear dividing line between the operation of one act of negligence and the other. Both were in operation at the same time and both seem to me to have contributed to the accident.' It is very easy to differentiate between the 'stabilized factor' set of circumstances as clearly illustrated by the fettered donkey in *Davies* v *Mann* and the contemporaneous continuing dual acts of negligence of two moving vessels up to the point of impact.

*The Eurymedon*, below, is probably one of the best illustrative cases this century to show how two 'pieces' of vessel negligence resulting in collision between those same vessels, even though they could be separately identified as independent acts of negligence, should be regarded as inter-related acts jointly contributing to the resulting collision, and that unless the one party has actually observed and is or should have been fully and clearly aware of the earlier act of negligence of the other and has ample opportunity to avoid it, the *Davies* v *Mann* principle of last opportunity creating sole fault should not be applied.

*The Eurymedon* [1938] P 41, CA
The vessel *Corstar* was anchored in the River Thames in a position of danger at night, properly lit but nevertheless forming an obstruction. The *Eurymedon*, proceeding up river, struck her. The court found both ships negligent. The negligence of the *Corstar*, though to some extent in a fixed situation, was inextricably bound up with the subsequent negligence of *Eurymedon* in failing to identify the lights and to take consequent action to avoid the danger. Both vessels had contributed to the resulting accident and their negligence was too inter-related to separate and free the one from blame altogether.

*The Boy Andrew* v *St Rognvald (owners)* (1947) 80 Ll.L.Rep. 559, HL
Two ships were sailing on parallel courses in daylight in a defined channel. The larger of the two started to overtake the smaller and had almost drawn level at a distance of only about 100 feet between them when the vessel being overtaken suddenly swerved hard to starboard and despite a movement hard to starboard and a simultaneous effort to stop by the other ship the two vessels collided, causing the sinking of the smaller, the *Boy Andrew*. The fluid state of the law in those days was reflected in the various appeals against the findings. The court of first instance (in Scotland) found the *Boy Andrew* two-thirds to blame and the *St Rognvald* one-third to blame. The appellate court absolved *St Rognvald* altogether but the House of Lords reinstated the original apportionment of blame. The facts of this case were easily distinguished from the hobbled and helpless donkey in *Davies* v *Mann*, a stabilized situation. This was a continually moving unified act of joint negligence continuing right up to the moment of collision.

The courts tend to be reluctant to condemn a shipowner or those charged with responsibility in a shipowning company as having acted unreasonably if, when faced with a crucial decision after a casualty at sea involving danger to life and property, they choose the path of caution rather than risk the path of the gambler.

It is fault causing or contributing to the *collision* which is material. Fault causing or contributing to the *resulting loss* only was not counted although it did count towards the dividing of damages under the Admiralty rule of equally divided damages (see page 296, *post*); see *The Margaret* (1881) 6 PD 76, CA, where the only fault of a schooner at anchor was that the anchor was improperly suspended in such a position as to hole and sink the barge which collided with it. The basis of the rule of equally divided damages is that a ship's negligence may contribute to the loss or damage which is the actual cause of action, though not contributing to the collision itself.

It should be noted also that in circumstances where damage is caused to one vessel by, for example, grounding subsequent to a collision and the grounding damage was caused partly by the collision and partly through a subsequent intervening fault on the part of the grounded vessel herself, then liability for the grounding can be sub-apportioned in the same percentage ratio as the collision blame bears to the subsequent intervening fault (see *The Calliope* [1970] 1 Lloyd's Rep. 84).

As Lord Pearce said in *The Miraflores* and *The Abadesa* [1967] 1 Lloyd's Rep. 191, HL, it is axiomatic that a person who embarks on a deliberate act of negligence should, in general, bear a greater degree of fault than one who fails to cope adequately with the resulting crisis which is thrust upon him. Between the extremes in which a man is either wholly excused for a foolish act done in the agony of the moment as the result of another's negligence or is wholly to blame because he had plenty of opportunity to avoid it, lies a wide area where his proportion of fault in failing to react properly to a crisis thrust upon him by another must be assessed as a question of degree.

## PRESUMPTION OF FAULT

Inevitably in the past there has tended to arise a presumption against a moving vessel if the other vessel involved is moored or anchored. To counteract such a presumption the owner of the moving vessel would probably have had to bring conclusive evidence of one or more of the following lapses on the part of the stationary vessel: (a) that the anchored ship was improperly positioned, (b) that the anchored ship was unlit or improperly lit at night; (c) that the anchored vessel had failed to maintain a watch where the circumstances required it; or (d) that the anchored ship had failed to take adequate steps to avoid the collision.

Presumption of fault also used to arise when a ship's Master had breached any one of the Collision Regulations. That such infringement per se should establish prima facie fault in law could lead to injustice and this injustice was remedied by section 4(1) of the Maritime Conventions Act 1911, which abolished the statutory presumption of fault by repealing subsection (4) of section 419 of the Merchant Shipping Act 1894, which had provided that a ship was deemed in fault in a case of collision where any of the Collision Regulations had been infringed by that ship.

## THE 1910 COLLISION CONVENTION AND THE MARITIME CONVENTIONS ACT 1911

Apportionment of blame arising from collisions was the subject of a Convention held at Brussels in 1910. In the document drafted and signed by the attending delegates in 1910 the following words appeared:

'Damages caused whether to vessels or to their cargoes or to effects or other property of the crew, passengers, etc. are borne by the vessels in fault in said proportion without solidarity as regards third persons.'

Many European countries ratified the 1910 Convention, the United Kingdom in the very next year, 1911, by passing the Maritime Conventions Act. Section 1 of that Act contained the following words:

'If, having regard to all the circumstances of the case, it is not possible to establish different degrees of fault, the liability shall be apportioned equally.'

What section 1 has been said to mean truly is that the court *must* apportion liability in proportion to the degree in which each vessel was at fault, unless it is impossible to do so (*The Anneliese* [1970] 1 Lloyd's Rep. 355).

*The Peter Benoit* (1915) 85 LJ 12, HL

A collision occurred between two ships off the mouth of the River Tees. The trial court found that both ships were at fault and apportioned the blame at one-fifth and four-fifths respectively. On appeal, however, the Court of Appeal considered that the evidence was not clear enough to determine blame so accurately, and apportioned the blame equally between the two vessels. The principle on which this decision was based was that the conclusion that it is possible to establish different degrees of fault must be a conclusion proved by evidence, judicially arrived at and sufficiently made out.

In *The Linde* [1969] 2 Lloyd's Rep. 556, in the Admiralty Court, blame was apportioned equally in a situation where, although each vessel was guilty of three serious faults, there was, looking at the case as a whole, no clear preponderance of blame.

The expression 'clear preponderance of blame' derives from language used by the court in *The Peter Benoit.*

However section 1 of the Maritime Conventions Act 1911 has been repealed and replaced by section 187 of the Merchant Shipping Act 1995 as follows—

187 (1) Where, by the fault of two or more ships, damage or loss is caused to one or more of those ships, to their cargoes or freight, or to any property on board, the liability to make good the damage or loss shall be in proportion to the degree in which each ship was in fault.

(2) If, in any such case, having regard to all the circumstances, it is not possible to establish different degrees of fault, the liability shall be apportioned equally.

(3) This section applies to persons other than the owners of a ship who are responsible for the fault of the ships, as well as the owners of a ship and where, by virtue of any charter or demise, or for any other reason, the owners are not responsible for the navigation and management of the ship, this section applies to the charterers or other persons for the time being so responsible instead of the owners.

(4) Nothing in this section shall operate so as to render any ship liable for any loss or damage to which the fault of the ship has not contributed.

The USA did not ratify the 1910 Convention and thus their law has diverged from European laws since 1910. The Americans continued to total up the damages in the case of mutual fault and divide them equally against each offending vessel until a US Supreme Court ruling (see page 299) began to break down this rigid theory. Equal division of damages was the English court's policy prior to the legislation of 1911 and now the legislation of 1995.

As section 187 of the Merchant Shipping Act 1995 only has relevance to the establishment of the degrees of blame of the vessels respectively and actually at fault, by the same token it does not restrict the right of any innocent vessel to sue either of two negligent vessels jointly or severally for its entire loss. No liability, of course, attaches to any ship whose fault has in no way contributed to the loss. 'Freight' for the purposes of the 1995 Act includes passage money and hire money. 'Damages' includes salvage or other expenses directly resulting from the collision. Section 187 is concerned with property damage and/or loss and has no application to personal injury or loss of life. These matters are dealt with under section 188 of the 1995 Act. Each claimant under this head is able to sue either of the two vessels at fault for his full losses. Conversely, the defendant to the action is free to use any defences available to him in addition to his right to limit. Section 189 extends to the defendant shipowner whose fault is only partial but who has had to pay out damages for loss of life or personal injury in excess of his proportion of fault the facility to claim contribution from the other vessels whose faults contributed to the damage/loss. A condition precedent to the exercising of this right is that the other ships concerned should have been liable directly to the innocent claimant in the first instance. The following case came before the courts at a time when section 3 of the 1911 Act was still the law pertaining to its subject matter.

*The Giacinto Motta* [1977] 2 Lloyd's Rep. 221
In 1967 the *World Mermaid* and the *Giacinto Motta* collided on the high seas due to negligent navigation resulting in the loss of the *Giacinto Motta* and her cargo and damage to the *World Mermaid.* Proceedings were commenced in the United States and in England, the former instituted by cargo-owners whose claim was eventually paid in full by the non-carrier (*World Mermaid*), the latter by the respective shipowners in a collision action counter-claiming against each other. It was agreed that both ships should be considered equally to blame. One of the questions in dispute in the English litigation was whether and, if so, how much the damages paid by the *World Mermaid*'s owners in respect of the cargo loss were recoverable from the carrying vessel's owners.

It was clear that by suing in the USA cargo-owners successfully recovered 100 per cent from the partly-to-blame non-carrier, whereas had they sued in the UK they would have recovered 50 per cent only. The rationale of the difference between US and UK law on this point is that, following a collision between two blameworthy vessels, the cargo is considered in the USA as an innocent party with the right to sue either guilty vessel on a 'joint and several basis' for full damages (although the carrier would have the benefit of the defence of negligent navigation). In the UK, however, the cargo is identified with the fault of the carrying ship and it can only recover from the non-carrier an amount of fault. Thus, in this case, the question to be decided was whether the cargo claim paid by the *World Mermaid*'s owners was loss or damage to them within the meaning of section 1 of the Maritime Conventions Act 1911, for which *Giacinto Motta*'s owners would be liable under that same section unless protected by proviso (c), which reserves the right to use whatever defences to exclude or limit liability may be available to the defendant vessel.

The judge rather interestingly based his answer to the problem on the 'foreseeability' test. Could it be said reasonably that the *Giacinto Motta*'s owners should reasonably have foreseen that cargo-owners would have sued in the USA (rather than in the UK or some other country with similar rules) so as to recover their full loss rather than merely half? If so, then the *World Mermaid*'s claim against *Giacinto Motta* could validly include the cargo claim as being damage or loss to them resulting from the collision for which *Giacinto Motta* was 50 per cent liable. Having decided this, however, he went on to say that the owners of *Giacinto Motta* were protected by proviso (c) in that they should have the benefit of any defences available whether they were to be used against a primary claimant or a secondary claimant, such as the partly-to-blame other vessel in the collision action. The other question of law in the case concerned the *World Mermaid*'s limitation fund which is not directly relevant to the subject presently under discussion.

## LOSS OF LIFE/PERSONAL INJURY CLAIMS

The position of the personal injury/loss of life claimant differs from the claimant in respect of property damage where their respective claims arise as a result of a collision between two (or more) vessels. Where death has resulted, the cause of action for wrongful death will, if British jurisdiction is contemplated, be framed within the provisions of the Fatal Accidents Act 1976.

*The Esso Malaysia* [1974] 2 Lloyd's Rep. 143
As a result of a collision on the high seas between a Latvian trawler and a Panamanian tanker 24 crew members of the trawler were killed. On behalf of the deceased crew action was taken in rem against a sister ship based on the Fatal Accidents Acts 1846–1959. It was agreed that the collision and resulting deaths were directly caused by the negligent act of

the tanker which was found to be 85 per cent to blame. The trawler was only 15 per cent to blame. The question for the court was whether the Acts (now the Fatal Accidents Act 1976) applied to the claim.

*Held:* that on their true construction they did. Whether death or merely injury had resulted, a claimant was at liberty to pursue his claim against either of the two offending vessels (or any of them if there were more than two) for full damages or, as the relevant legal expression would have it, he might sue 'jointly or severally'. Having once recovered full damages or a suitably negotiated compromise from the one party at fault, however, any concurrent action he might be taking against the other, or others, would be discontinued. The unsuccessful defendant then had a right to seek a contribution by way of indemnity from the other vessel(s) at fault, but only if the other vessel(s) would have been directly liable to the original claimant in the first place.

Section 187 of the Merchant Shipping Act 1995 has no application to this type of claim. The provisions described in the preceding paragraph are contained in sections 188 and 189. Besides these, section 188 also reserves to the defendant to the action any right he may have to limit his liability and/or any other defence which might be available to him.

## CONTRIBUTION BETWEEN JOINT TORTFEASORS

Under the old common law rules, before legislation began effectively to alter the maritime position just before the First World War, there was no right of contribution between parties who were together guilty of having contributed to a wrong resulting in loss or damage to an innocent third party. The innocent plaintiff having sued successfully an only-partly-at-fault defendant could not then proceed against one or more other guilty parties. The Maritime Conventions Act 1911, and now the Merchant Shipping Act 1995, radically changed the common law so far as the relationship between two or more vessels at fault in causing loss or damage are concerned. And so the Admiralty rules of law diverged from the common law rules. The common law itself, so far as non-Admiralty matters were concerned, did not undergo radical change on this particular point until 1935 when the Law Reform (Married Women and Tortfeasors) Act was passed which controlled and governed legal proceedings against, and any subsequent legal claims seeking contribution between, individual parties who had contributed to the wrong causing the loss or damage, viz. joint tortfeasors. The matter of contribution between joint tortfeasors in non-maritime cases is now governed by the Civil Liability (Contribution) Act 1978.

### *The Law Reform (Contributory Negligence) Act 1945*

The common law of the land originally took the view that there was only one cause of loss, not more, either the negligence of the plaintiff or of the defendant and that if there was found to be fault on both sides then the resulting losses lay where they fell, however small the degree of fault of the one party may have been and however much this tended towards an unjust result. This situation, though not applying in Admiralty when the effects of both parties at fault were to create an equal division of loss, continued through until 1945 when the Law Reform (Contributory Negligence) Act was enacted and applied to situations arising after

15 June 1945. Section 1 of that Act is as follows but it should be remembered that it does not apply to circumstances which fall within the scope of section 187 of the Merchant Shipping Act 1995.

'1.—(1) Where any person suffers damage as the result partly of his own fault and partly of the fault of any other person or persons, a claim in respect of that damage shall not be defeated by reason of the fault of the person suffering the damage, but the damages recoverable in respect thereof shall be reduced to such extent as the court thinks just and equitable having regard to the claimant's share in the responsibility for the damage:

Provided that–

(a) this subsection shall not operate to defeat any defence arising under a contract;

(b) where any contract or enactment providing for the limitation of liability is applicable to the claim, the amount of damages recoverable by the claimant by virtue of this subsection shall not exceed the maximum limit so applicable.

(2) Where damages are recoverable by any person by virtue of the foregoing subsection subject to such reduction as is therein mentioned, the court shall find and record the total damages which would have been recoverable if the claimant had not been at fault.

(3) Section six of the Law Reform (Married Women and Tortfeasors) Act, 1935 (which relates to proceedings against, and contribution between joint and several tortfeasors), shall apply in any case where two or more persons are liable or would, if they had all been sued, be liable by virtue of subsection (1) of this section in respect of the damage suffered by any person.

(4) [subsection (4) has been repealed].

(5) Where, in any case to which subsection (1) of this section applies, one of the persons at fault avoids liability to any other such person or his personal representative by pleading the Limitation Act, 1939, or any other enactment limiting the time within which proceedings may be taken, he shall not be entitled to recover any damages or contributions from that other person or representative by virtue of the said subsection.

(6) Where any case to which subsection (1) of this section applies is tried with a jury, the jury shall determine the total damages which would have been recoverable if the claimant had not been at fault and the extent to which those damages are to be reduced.'

The common law rule (*not* the Admiralty law as applied in the Admiralty Court) was that a party who had suffered loss or damage could not recover damages if his loss was caused entirely or partly by his own negligence. This rule is replaced by the 1945 Act which said in effect that no person was barred from claiming damages merely because he was partly to blame himself. This Act would not, however, be required to operate in favour of a claimant who already had the benefit of the Admiralty rule of divided damages and the jurisdiction of the Admiralty Court.

As the law now stands it would seem that there is no longer any divergence or difference between the Admiralty rules and those of the common law as to the rights and liabilities of parties where contributory negligence is involved.

## MULTIPLE COLLISION SITUATIONS

A common occurrence is the multiple collision situation, or a slight variation of this whereunder a third vessel might be forced through the negligence of two other vessels in collision to take evasive action which, combined possibly with additional negligence on her part, results in damage or loss to herself either by, for example, going aground or by coming into contact with property belonging to yet another party such as a harbour wall or a pier or wharf. Such a situation is contemplated by section 187 of the Merchant Shipping Act 1995 at page 288 above, which repealed section 1 of the Maritime Conventions Act 1911, which expressly allows for the apportionment of fault where loss or damage is caused to one or more vessels as a result of the fault of two or more vessels.

*The Oldekerk* [1974] 1 Lloyd's Rep. 95
A multiple collision took place in the Nieuwe Maas area of Rotterdam in October 1969. The ships involved were the Belgian vessel *Anvers*, the Dutch vessel *Oldekerk* and the South American vessel *Perija*, all motor vessels. All three ships had pilots on board. The *Anvers* was moving up river on the south side, the *Perija* was going down river on the north side and the *Oldekerk*, without her own motive power, was being towed by a tug from a southside berth to a northside berth further downstream. Her intention to leave the berth was communicated via shore radar transmitter to the other two ships. She indicated that she was leaving the berth and would be proceeding to port. Accordingly, *Anvers* proceeded at half speed altering slightly to port. Next, the tow ropes parted and *Oldekerk* went across the river at some speed. The *Anvers* hit her and then both *Oldekerk* and *Anvers* collided with *Perija*. The owners of *Oldekerk* admitted liability but sought and obtained a decree to limit their liability to £200,000 on the basis that the accident had occurred without their actual fault or privity. This made it relevant for the owners of the *Perija* to try to establish the partial fault of the *Anvers* which they attempted to do by alleging that the *Anvers* had failed to stop her engines when it was clear the *Oldekerk* was not holding back but coming out into the river, had failed to keep to her own side of the river, had failed to put her engines 'full astern' early enough and finally had failed to let drop her anchors.

*Held*: that *Anvers* was not negligent in not stopping her engines, for her pilot could not be expected to have foreseen that she was incapable of carrying out the manoeuvre which she had given notice that she intended to carry out. Neither was she in breach of local regulations or of the 1960 Collision Regulations which would require her to keep to the starboard side of the channel when it was safe and practicable to do so. The *Oldekerk's* announced intention to come out into the open river made it unsafe and impracticable to keep her on her otherwise safe course and by going to port a little it became unsafe to remain on the south side at all. The *Anvers* could not have put her engines astern any earlier since the time between the tow ropes breaking and the first collision was about $1\frac{1}{4}$ minutes only. Lastly there was no negligence in failing to let go her anchors because the orders to do so were drowned by the noise of *Oldekerk's* own anchors being let go. Sole blame for the collisions rested with *Oldekerk*.

The danger when applying section 187 of the 1995 Act is to look upon two of the vessels, especially when they are in collision initially resulting in another or possibly more than one other being subsequently damaged or being caused to suffer loss, as being one 'unit' rather than as two separate and distinct vessels.

The essence of section 187 is that, however many be the vessels at fault, their individual faults, however continuing and apparently inter-related, should be treated and assessed separately. The 'unit approach' has been condemned as being out of keeping with the spirit and letter of section 1 of the Maritime Conventions Act 1911, (now section 187 of the Merchant Shipping Act 1995).

*The Miraflores/The Abadesa* [1967] 1 Lloyd's Rep. 191, HL
The vessel *George Livanos* went aground as a result of taking evasive action when the ships *Miraflores* and *Abadesa* collided in the River Scheldt. The *Miraflores* and the *George Livanos* were inbound to Antwerp. A small coaster sheered violently to starboard when caught in

a cross-current. The *Miraflores* accordingly reduced speed and *George Livanos* following astern closed to about half-a-mile of her. Eventually the cross-current adversely affected *Miraflores* and in the ensuing difficulty of manoeuvre the stern of *Abadesa* struck the starboard side of *Miraflores*. Oil escaped and caught fire. In manoeuvering to turn down river *George Livanos* grounded, requiring 10 tugs to refloat her.

In consolidated actions, *George Livanos* claimed against *Miraflores* and *Abadesa*; the *Miraflores* claimed against the *Abadesa*; and *Abadesa* counterclaimed against *Miraflores*. In applying section 1 of the Maritime Conventions Act 1911, the trial court found *George Livanos* 50 per cent to blame, and that she could recover the remaining 50 per cent from the other two offending vessels as to two-thirds (*Abadesa*) and one-third (*Miraflores*) proportions respectively.

The Court of Appeal varied the apportionment on the ground that the trial judge had erred in treating *Miraflores* and the *Abadesa* as 'one unit'. Apportionment was fixed as *Abadesa*—45 per cent; *Miraflores*—30 per cent; and *George Livanos*—25 per cent.

On appeal by the *Miraflores*, the House of Lords apportioned blame for the grounding of the *George Livanos* as *Abadesa*—two-fifths; the *Miraflores*—one-fifth; and the *George Livanos*—two fifths. Doubt was expressed whether there had in fact been a significant error of apportionment in the trial court.

True apportionment can never be made unless both 'blameworthiness' and 'causative potency' are given equal consideration in the investigation. The 'unit approach' to the problem of apportionment would be more logical if the Law Reform (Contributory Negligence) Act 1945 applied to this particular type of situation. But it does not. In fact, section 1 of that Act expressly excludes section 1 of the Maritime Conventions Act 1911 (now section 187 of the 1995 Act). The purpose of the 1945 Act was to permit a plaintiff, although being negligent himself to some degree, to recover damages, albeit reduced to whatever extent a court might consider fair and reasonable in the light of his having been to some extent 'contributorily negligent'.

The advantage of the provisions of the 1995 Act is that in practice the whole assessment of both fault and damages can take place at one time and early on as between the plaintiff and the defendants, however many of the latter there may be.

## ELDER BRETHREN AND NAUTICAL ASSESSORS

A judge in the Admiralty Court has Elder Brethren to advise him on technical points of relative speeds, proposed alterations of course, etc.

Nautical Assessors act as advisers to the Court of Appeal in Admiralty matters, as distinct from the Elder Brethren who advise the Admiralty Court. The Court of Appeal is not bound to accept the advice of the assessors. It is merely free to consult them. Nautical Assessors occupy much the same position as do skilled witnesses with one significant difference, namely that they are not brought forward by one side or the other. They also may not necessarily have heard the whole of the evidence or have had the advantage of having heard it, or any of it, given orally.

Wilmer LJ in the course of his judgment in *The Fina Canada* [1962] 2 Lloyd's Rep. 445, CA, said:

'We are just as free to consult our assessors as the judge was to consult the Elder Brethren.

We are not bound to accept their advice any more than we or the learned judge would be bound to accept the advice tendered by the Elder Brethren. If there is a divergence of view between the assessors advising this court and the Elder Brethren who advised the Admiralty Court, those advising us are not to be regarded as speaking with any greater authority because they happen to be advising the court of Appeal. This, I understand, is what is meant by the phrase that there is no appeal from assessors to assessors. If there is such a divergence of view, the position is that this court must make up its own mind as to which advice ought to be accepted.'

The role of the Elder Brethren was concisely defined by the Court of Appeal in *The Fritz Thyssen* [1967] 2 Lloyd's Rep. 199, CA. It was said there:

'. . . the Elder Brethren are in a unique position to advise the judge in the Admiralty Court in the light of their experience; indeed, it is for this very purpose that they are summoned to assist the judge at the trial of an Admiralty suit. Their advice is, of course, in no sense conclusive; it becomes in effect part of the evidence in the case which has to be weighed in conjunction with all the other evidence. It always remains for the judge himself to decide whether he accepts the advice that is tendered to him.'

*The Antares II and Victory* [1996] 2 Lloyd's Rep. 482
There were disputes as to the admissibility of expert evidence, where the court was assisted by nautical assessors as to the place of collision in the river Great Ouse in the Lynn Cut, the angle of collision and the navigation of the vessel.

*Held*: that the collision occurred just up channel of Buoy 17 and well to the west side of the channel. Although there was a rule that, when the court was assisted by nautical assessors, then expert evidence on matters of navigation and seamanship might not be adduced, this rule was not absolute. The parties were allowed to admit the evidence of their experts although the order for directions were only intended to allow the parties to produce a speed and angle of blow report. Danger in the present case was created by the *Victory* proceeding down channel at speed without the pilot being able to ascertain properly and accurately her heading and course made good or her position relative to mid-channel. A reliable bearing of *Antares II* was never taken, which led to a total misapprehension on the pilot's part as to the position in the channel of *Antares II* which he assumed was on her wrong side when in fact she was on her correct side. The quality of her lookout was also criticized. Given the narrowness of the channel, a safe passing was best ensured by both vessels proceeding at slow speed and passing clear port to port. *Victory*, although she slowed down, continued on in about mid-channel without clarifying the situation, there was total misapprehension of the situation as to the heading and position of *Antares II* and under that misapprehension course was altered to port, in itself a wholly incorrect and dangerous manoeuvre. In terms of the collision regulations, *Victory* was in breach of Rules 5, 6, 7 and 8. *Antares II* was at fault primarily in failing in good time to comply with Rule 9(b) in failing to move right over on her starboard side of the channel and to proceed slowly and with utmost caution until danger of collision was over and the two ships passed safely port to port. The alteration of course of *Victory* to port must have come as a complete surprise but *Antares II* ought to have been further over to starboard. The failure of the vessels to use VHF radio was not a fault on the facts of this case where both vessels were in sight of each other in a narrow channel and no such communication was necessary. If a good lookout had been kept and each vessel had kept to its starboard side, all they had to do was comply with the Collision Regulations to ensure a safe passing and safety was assured. Both vessels were at fault. The faults of *Victory* were far greater than those of *Antares II*. *Victory* was 75 per cent to blame for the collision and *Antares II* 25 per cent. The plaintiffs, owners of the *Antares II*, were awarded the costs of their action.

## LIMITATION PERIOD

Section 8 of the Maritime Conventions Act 1911 provided that legal proceedings in a collision suit should be commenced within two years from the cause of action. The court has discretion to extend the period in circumstances which justify it. This is unlikely to be done if the delay has occurred solely through the claimant's own lack of knowledge of his legal rights.

The English High Court has been asked to consider whether to extend time on various occasions. A couple of relatively recent decisions which illustrate the court's thinking are set out below:

*The Anna L* [1994] 2 Lloyd's Rep. 379
Following a collision, a writ was issued claiming damages for the damage suffered by the vessel *Anna L* but named as the plaintiff the managers instead of the owners. The writ was served in Monaco on the defendants' managers. The defendants applied to the court to set aside the action. They argued, inter alia, that there was no cause of action after the two-year time limit had expired under the Maritime Conventions Act 1911. The plaintiffs applied, inter alia, for an extension of time.

The High Court stated that the intention of the plaintiffs' solicitors was to issue a writ in the name of the registered owners of the *Anna L* and it should have been clear to the defendants that the writ had been issued in the name of the wrong plaintiffs. It was necessary to show 'a good reason' for extending time under section 8 of the 1911 Act. The defendants' argument that if time had been allowed to expire because the plaintiffs' solicitor has made a mistake, that can never constitute good reason for granting an extension of time was rejected. Section 35 of the Limitation Act 1980, in effect, permits the extension of procedural time limits imposed by the Act where an action has been commenced in time, but is rendered defective by reason of a misnomer which should not have deceived the defendants. Such a situation can constitute a special reason for extending time under section 8 of the 1911 Act. Nor should the fact that the misnomer is attributable to fault on the part of the plaintiffs' lawyers automatically preclude the granting of an extension. The history of the delay was lamentable but it had occasioned no prejudice to the defendants. Justice did not demand that the owners of *Anna L* should be precluded from prosecuting their claim. The present action was struck out but Navigator Maritime Inc. (the true owners of *Anna L*) were granted a sufficient extension of time under section 8 of the 1911 Act to enable them to commence a fresh action in their own name.

*The Alter Tabith and Alan Fushi* [1995] 2 Lloyd's Rep. 336
Following a collision, negotiations took place between the respective P & I Clubs of the vessels, and time extensions were granted, but the plaintiffs' P & I Club case handler made a mistake in noting down the time limit. The plaintiffs applied for an extension of time of the limitation period provided by section 8 of the Maritime Conventions Act 1911. The Court of Appeal held that the court had to consider first whether good reason for an extension had been demonstrated by the plaintiff which was essentially a question of fact. Only if the plaintiffs succeeded in establishing good reason did the court proceed to exercise its discretion, taking into account the balance of hardship, as to whether such extension should be granted. Mere carelessness had never been a good reason for an extension, and a valid explanation for the failure to issue a protective writ was imperative. The failure to issue the writ was entirely due to the plaintiffs' P & I Club case handler's own mistake and this was no good reason for an extension of time.

However, section 8 of the Maritime Conventions Act 1911 has now been repealed. The present position is contained in section 190 of the Merchant Shipping Act 1995.

## BRIEF SUMMARY OF LEGAL PROCEDURE IN PURSUIT OF A COLLISION CLAIM

A brief résumé of the chronological order of procedure in taking Admiralty action after a collision is: (a) each claimant party will issue a writ so that 'time' is preserved; (b) each party will seek security for his claim from the other as early as possible; (c) if the security put up is satisfactory in each case, service of the respective writs will likely be accepted on each respective party's behalf by solicitors instructed to do so. Failure to put up adequate security will expose that party to having the writ served on his vessel resulting in arrest; (d) thereafter the action will begin to take shape similar to any other action in the High Court; (e) first, however, in collision actions, after entering appropriate appearances, a preliminary act must be filed by each party, with the Admiralty Registry. This sets out significant details of, for example, the weather conditions at the time, the place where the collision occurred, or the course which the vessel was following. The object is to obtain some measure of certainty since the preliminary act once registered cannot be amended without extreme difficulty and each party is prevented from changing any details, having perhaps seen eventually in the other party's pleadings evidence which could be more favourable to his own case; (f) next will come statements of claim, defence and counterclaim; and (g) next, discovery, including agreement about perhaps calling a handwriting expert if, for example, there is any question of discrepancy in a log book entry.

## 'TUG AND TOW' SITUATIONS

Let us now look at how the law deals with a situation where one vessel is under the tow of a tug when a collision with another vessel occurs. Here we see a slight divergence from the rule of vicarious liability, the liability springing from the employer/employee relationship based on the equitable principle that when A employs B and reaps the profits derived from his work he should conversely be responsible for the loss or damage to others caused by his act, defaults or neglect. Although the tug-owning company is an independent legal entity whose actions and policies are carried out independently of the shipowner who engages the services of its tug and crew for value, the tendency is for the towing and towed vessel to be considered as one unit which, in its joint character, may come into negligent contact with a third ship.

It has long been a legal maxim that 'the tug is the servant of the tow'. This principle is heavily emphasized and confirmed by the wording of the customary form of towage contract which purports absolutely to allow to the tug-owner complete indemnity from the tow-owner for any loss or damage he might cause to a third person's property whilst in the course of performing his duties under the towage contract, resulting from his negligence or that of his employees. Whilst such towage contracts are regarded by UK law with favour, US law takes a less favourable view, seeing them as being contrary to public policy.

The Admiralty law of the UK, in treating tow and tug as one vessel, regards the control and responsibility for the operation as resting with the tow although the motive power is provided by the tug. In addition to the expressed terms which appear in the towage contract, there are implied terms, these being that the tug shall implicitly obey the orders of the vessel in tow and that the tug shall exercise reasonable care, skill and diligence. There is, additionally, an implied warranty that the tug is seaworthy. The exact extent of this warranty has not been fully clarified by the courts, i.e. whether it is absolute or only implies a duty to make the tug as fit for service as care and skill can reasonably do. It is the responsibility of the tow to control the movements of the tug, to direct her course and maintain a proper look-out.

There are circumstances, however, where the owners of the tow are not liable to third parties; and it has become the courts' policy to base their decisions on this point on the facts of the individual case and not on some presumption of law that, regardless of where in fact responsibility lay, the tow-owner was to be considered as liable to innocent third parties. An example would be where a wrongful act of a tug is performed so suddenly as to prevent the tow from controlling its movements. No liability falls on the tow-owner.

The concept of the tow in the ordinary course having control over the tug and being responsible for damage to others' property caused by the tug was confirmed by *The Niobe* dispute, below.

*The Niobe* (1888) 13 PD 55

The tug *Flying Serpent* was towing the vessel *Niobe* under towage contract terms. Both tug and tow collided with the ship *Valletta*. The *Niobe* was keeping a poor look-out. Had she observed *Valletta*, the collision would not have occurred. The *Niobe's* owners denied liability for the negligence of *Flying Serpent* on the grounds that they were not their servants but independent contractors.

*Held*: that the *Niobe* was responsible for the *Flying Serpent's* negligence on the basis that in law the tow had control over the tug. *But*, as emphasized above, the courts have since given themselves much more latitude to look at the facts to determine where responsibility really lies.

Where the collision is with a third innocent ship, the various situations can be briefly stated as follows: (a) If the collision is with the tug and the fault lies with the tug alone, the tug is liable. (b) If the collision is with the tow and the fault lies solely with the tow, the tow alone is liable. (c) If the tow collides with a third ship and partial blame was attributable to the tug/tow unit and partial blame to the third ship, the court need not feel itself obliged to apportion blame as between tug and tow. Tug and tow are jointly and severally liable to make good the third ship's damage/loss (as having jointly committed a tort) in respect of that portion equivalent to their degree of fault, and conversely the third ship is liable to make good tug and tow's damage/loss which they have respectively sustained in the same ratio as the third ship's degree of fault.

The Maritime Conventions Act 1911, now replaced by the Merchant Shipping Act 1995, made no provision for apportioning fault as between tug and tow for this same reason, i.e. that both vessels are jointly and severally liable. Nevertheless, it has been known for a court to apportion out fault between all three vessels, especially when the tug is one of the colliding vessels and where the respective faults can be easily separated and effectively distinguished. It is probable that an English court would also have the power to apportion fault under the Civil Liability (Contribution) Act 1978, but such a procedure would likely be unnecessary in favour of the tug due to the protection provided by the terms and conditions of the towage contract, and unable to be applied in favour of the tow for the same reasons.

A case in the Canadian court involving a collision with tugs and tow and another vessel and the question of limitation of liability is *The Rhone and Peter A.B. Widener.*

*The Rhone and Peter A.B. Widener* [1993] 1 Lloyd's Rep. 600.
A dumb barge, *Peter A.B. Widener* (*Widener*), was being towed by four tugs. Due to a navigational error by the Master on board the lead tug *Ohio* relating to the speed at which the flotilla was travelling, *Widener* collided with a moored ship, *Rhone* in 1980. The tug *Ohio* and another tug, *South Carolina*, were owned by Great Lakes Towing Company. One question was the appropriate limitation of liability under section 647(2) of the Canada Shipping Act.

*Held* (Canada Supreme Court): All the vessels within a flotilla belonging to an impugned shipowner need not be taken into account in determining the effect of that shipowner's liability. The intent of section 647(2) was to limit liability for navigational errors according only to the tonnage of those vessels causing the alleged damage. Apart from the vessel responsible for the overall navigation of a flotilla, only those vessels of the same shipowner which physically caused or contributed to the resulting damage formed a unit for which liability was limited. Only *Ohio* and *Widener* were found to have been negligent for the collision and the *South Carolina* was absolved from fault. Liability should only be limited to the tonnage of *Ohio.* As the Master of the *Ohio* was not the directing mind and will of Great Lakes, there was no actual fault or privity of Great Lakes and they were entitled to limit their liability.

## THE DIVIDED DAMAGES RULE

The operation of the traditional Admiralty rule on divided damages was summarized concisely in various ways in early times, for example: where both vessels are in fault, the sums representing the damage sustained by each must be added together and the aggregate divided between the two. This is in effect deducting the lesser from the greater and dividing the remainder. If one in fault has sustained no injury, it is liable for half the damages sustained by the other, though that other was also in fault. Or, according to the general maritime law in cases of collision occurring by the fault of both parties, the entire damage to both ships is added together and the total equally divided between them, and thereupon arises the liability of one party to pay to the other such sum as is necessary to equalize the burden.

### *Division of loss*

The following are three hypothetical examples of the division of loss where both vessels are to blame and the 1995 Act currently applies, and neither vessel limits her liability.

## (1) Collision involving damage to ship only

Ships *X* and *Y* collide and both are to blame, X $\frac{2}{3}$rds and Y $\frac{1}{3}$rd

| | |
|---|---|
| Ship *X* | |
| Cost of repairs | £9,800 |
| Detention due to repairs | £2,200 |
| Ship *Y* | |
| Cost of repairs | £15,000 |
| Detention due to repairs | £3,000 |
| Aggregate damage/loss | £30,000 |
| *X* is liable to *Y* for $\frac{2}{3}$rds of *Y*'s damage/losses, viz. | |
| $\frac{2}{3}$rds of cost of repairs | £10,000 |
| $\frac{2}{3}$rds of detention | £2,000 |
| | £12,000 |
| *Y* is liable to *X* for $\frac{1}{3}$rd of *X*'s damage/losses, viz. | |
| $\frac{1}{3}$rd of cost of repairs | £3,200 |
| $\frac{1}{3}$rd of detention | £800 |
| | £4,000 |
| Owner of ship *X* owes owner of ship *Y* | £8,000 |
| Owner of *X* is obliged to pay: | |
| His own losses | £12,000 |
| Balance due to owner of *Y* | £8,000 |
| | £20,000 |
| Owner of *Y* is obliged to pay: | |
| His own losses | £18,000 |
| (But he has credit for balance recovered from *X*) | £8,000 |
| | £10,000 |

## (2) Collision involving ship and cargo damage only

Ships *P* and *Q* collide and both are to blame, *P*$\frac{3}{4}$ths and *Q*$\frac{1}{4}$th

| | |
|---|---|
| Ship *P*'s losses | |
| Cost of repairs | £6,000 |
| Detention due to repairs | £2,000 |
| Cargo damage on ship *P* | £2,000 |
| Ship *Q*'s losses | |
| Cost of repairs | £12,000 |

| | |
|---|---|
| Detention due to repairs | £4,000 |
| Cargo damage on ship *Q* | £4,000 |
| Both ships' aggregate damages/losses | £30,000 |
| *P* is liable for $\frac{3}{4}$ths of *Q*'s losses, viz. | |
| $\frac{3}{4}$ths of cost of repairs | £9,000 |
| $\frac{3}{4}$ths of detention | £3,000 |
| *Q* is liable for $\frac{1}{4}$th of *P*'s losses, viz. | |
| $\frac{1}{4}$th of cost of repairs | £1,500 |
| $\frac{1}{4}$th of detention | £500 |
| Therefore, owner of ship *P* owes owner of ship *Q* | £10,000 |
| Owner of *P* pays $\frac{3}{4}$ths of claim of cargo-owner on board *Q*, viz | £3,000 |
| Owner of *Q* pays $\frac{1}{4}$th of claim of cargo-owner on board *P*, viz | £500 |
| In toto, owner of ship *P* is obliged to pay: | |
| His own losses | £8,000 |
| Balance due to owner of *Q* | £10,000 |
| His proportion of claim of cargo-owner on board *Q* | £3,000 |
| In toto, owner of ship *Q* is obliged to pay: | |
| His own losses | £16,000 |
| (But has credit for balance recovered from *P*) | £10,000 |
| His proportion of claim of cargo-owner on board *P* | £500 |
| Cargo-owner on board ship *P* pays: | |
| His own loss (unrecoverable from owner of carrying ship *P* because of bill of lading exceptions protecting carrier) | £2,000 |
| *But* he recovers from ship *Q* | £500 |
| Cargo-owner on board ship *Q* pays: | |
| His own losses (unrecoverable from carrier as above) | £4,000 |
| *But* he recovers from ship *P* | £3,000 |

### (3) Collision involving ship and cargo damage and loss of life and personal injury to crew

Ships *J* and *K* collide and both are to blame, *J* $\frac{3}{5}$ths and *K* $\frac{2}{5}$ths

| | |
|---|---|
| Ship *J*'s damages/losses | |
| Cost of repairs, etc. | £5,000 |
| Detention due to repairs | £1,000 |
| Cargo damage on ship *J* | £1,000 |
| | £7,000 |
| Ship *K*'s damages/losses | |
| Cost of repairs, etc. | £11,000 |
| Detention due to repairs | £4,000 |
| Loss of life/personal injury of crew | £3,000 |
| | £18,000 |

| | |
|---|---|
| *J* is liable for $\frac{3}{5}$ths of *K*'s losses, viz. | |
| $\frac{3}{5}$ths of cost of repairs | £6,600 |
| $\frac{3}{5}$ths of detention | £2,400 |
| | £9,000 |
| *K* is liable for $\frac{2}{5}$ths of *J*'s losses, viz. | |
| $\frac{2}{5}$ths of cost of repairs | £2,000 |
| $\frac{2}{5}$ths of detention | £400 |
| | £2,400 |
| Therefore, owner of *J* owes owner of *K* | £6,600 |
| Owner of *J* pays $\frac{3}{5}$ths of loss of life/personal injury claims of crew on board *K*, i.e. | £1,800 |
| Owner of *K* pays $\frac{2}{5}$ths of claim of cargo-owner on board *J*, i.e. | £400 |
| *and* balance of claim for loss of life/personal injury of crew on board *K* (because there is no defence to liability) | £1,200 |
| Owner of ship *J* is obliged to pay: | |
| His own losses | £6,000 |
| Balance due to owner of ship *K* | £6,600 |
| Proportion of loss of life/personal injury claims of crew of *K* | £1,800 |
| Owner of ship *K* is obliged to pay: | |
| His own losses | £15,000 |
| *but* has credit for balance recovered from owner of ship *J* | £6,600 |
| His proportion of loss of life/personal injury claims of crew of *K* | £1,200 |
| His proportion of claim of cargo-owner on board *J* | £400 |
| Cargo-owner on board ship *J* pays: | |
| His own losses | £1,000 |
| *but* has credit for amount recovered from ship *K* | £400 |

(N.B: the remainder is irrecoverable from the carrying shipowner because of exceptions to liability under the terms of the contract of carriage evidenced by the bill of lading. As to the limit of liability by the one party eventually liable to pay under the single liability theory, see page 392.)

### *Differences of United States law*

Another point about the divided damages rule in the United States is that it has been long established that it applies not only in cases of collision between two ships but also in cases of a vessel grounding because of mutual contributing faults of the vessel itself and another party who may not be a vessel-owner.

In 1975, however, the United States Supreme Court replaced this 120-year-old Admiralty rule of equally divided damages (established in the 19th century with *The Schooner 'Catherine'* v *Dickinson* decision in 1854, 58 US (17 How) 170) with a rule which decrees liability for damage to be allocated among the parties proportionately to the comparative degree of their fault, and only to be apportioned equally either when the parties are equally at fault or when it is impossible fairly and reasonably to measure the degree of fault. The dispute which caused this change in the law was the *United States, Petitioner* v *Reliable Transfer Co Inc* [1975] 2 Lloyd's Rep. 286. In the course of giving its opinion, the US Supreme Court in answering the argument that the creation of a new rule for damages in maritime collision cases was a matter for Congress and not for the courts, stated that the judiciary had taken the lead in formulating flexible and fair remedies in maritime law and that the Congress had left largely to the courts the responsibility for fashioning such rules. The Supreme Court described the old rule as archaic, unfair and inequitable. For example, it meant that when one ship's fault in causing a collision was relatively slight and her damage was small and when the second ship was grossly at fault and suffered extensive damage, the first ship must still make a substantial payment to the second. This hardly commends itself to a sense of justice. Also, the long-held theory that the equally divided damages rule encouraged out-of-court settlements is neither persuasive nor logical.

As a result of the *Reliable Transfer* decision the way has been opened up for US law to come fully into line with the legal thinking in the other leading traditional maritime countries who have long since allowed for the proper apportioning of fault between colliding ships with damages being divided in a similar proportion.

This radical change in their law does not, however, mean that the traditional 'both to blame' collision clause will become obsolete. It may indeed paradoxically become the more significant in that it could be the very instrument by which the US legal rules on the issue could be brought fully on all fours with those of other countries. Whereas the clause is at present invalid in the eyes of the US courts as being contrary to public policy, it could now come into favour and be recognized as valid for this very reason. By the combination of a 'new-look' reinstated 'both to blame' collision clause and the new divided damages rule, US maritime law could implement the rules which have been in vogue since 1911 in Britain and the other countries which ratified the Collision Convention of 1910 in regard to the cargo interests' right of recovery after a collision as being proportionate only.

## MEASURE OF DAMAGES AFTER COLLISION

Generally speaking, it is incumbent upon the negligent party to put the injured party in the same position as he was before the collision, so far as this is possible in terms of money. Any loss or damage flowing naturally and directly from the negligent act or neglect causing the collision can be validly included as an item of damages. However, the injured party must not be placed in a better position than he was and so, if his ship is totally lost as a result of the collision, he cannot expect so much money by way of compensation as would enable him to buy a new ship. Rather, the correct measure of damages in this 'total loss' situation would be the market value of the ship at the time of the casualty. This may, however, be difficult to assess and the other basis for calculation of a fair measure of damages would be the value of that ship to its owner as a 'going concern'. The latter is in many ways a more logical and equitable measure of compensation in that it may not have been remotely in the mind of the 'innocent' owner to sell his vessel in the open market at the time when the ship was negligently damaged so as to become a total loss. She may have been engaged in a healthy and profitable long-term charter at the time. On the other hand, in attempting to arrive as such a value, it could be 'over-assessing' merely to add current and prospective freight or hire earnings to the market value of the ship. Such a method of assessment could amount to a duplication of damages unjustly in favour of the innocent owner. A case regarding the question of damages is *The Argonaftis*.

*The Argonaftis* [1989] 2 Lloyd's Rep. 487
The vessel *Ifrikia* was laid up in Grand Harbour, Valletta at a cost exceeding US$30,000 per month. The plaintiff owners entered into negotiations with many potential clients in the hope that employment could be found for her but those negotiations were unfruitful. If a contract had been obtained the financial rewards would have been very substantial. While she was lying at her moorings, the defendants' vessel *Argonaftis* collided with her causing damage. The plaintiffs obtained judgment on liability and the issue before the court was the amount of damages which the plaintiffs were entitled to recover from the defendants. The Admiralty Register reached the conclusion that the market value on the day of the collision of the *Ifrikia* was US$900,000. After the collision the vessel was sold for scrap for US$700,000 and the damage done by *Argonaftis* by the collision reduced her value by US$200,000, which the plaintiffs were entitled to recover. The plaintiffs appealed to the Admiralty Court.

*Held*: on the evidence the approach of the Admiralty Registrar as to the value of the vessel at the time of the collision was correct. There was some prospect then that employment would be found for the vessel and if the plaintiffs had thought otherwise they would not have expended over US$30,000 each month to keep and maintain the vessel; they would have sold her for scrap immediately and the market value of the vessel at the date of the collision was US$900,000. In deciding what sum of money the plaintiffs were entitled to recover, the main principle to be applied was that the plaintiffs were entitled to receive as damages such a sum of money as would place them in as good a position as they would have been in if the collision had not occurred.

Repairs were not carried out to the vessel after the collision because the plaintiffs decided to wait until contracts had been obtained for the charter of the vessel when the repairs and the pre-planned alterations could be executed more economically. Several months after the collision the Harbour Authorities advised the plaintiffs to find an alternative berth for the vessel. However the cost of removing the vessel to some other berth would have been high and the plaintiffs disposed of the vessel for scrap. These events would have happened whether or not the vessel had been damaged by the collision. After the collision the plaintiffs had a vessel which they sold for scrap for US$700,000. They should be compensated for the loss caused to them by the wrongful act of the *Argonaftis* by payment of US$200,000 and the Registrar's decision was correct.

But if the vessel has no market value, then the only alternative yardstick to estimate her value is her original cost, less proportionate depreciation. A ship lost through another's wrongdoing act might have a special value to her owners.

*Liesbosch, Dredger* v *SS Edison* [1933] AC 449, HL
The *Liesbosch* was lost after having been dragged from where she was moored in Patras harbour into the open sea. This happened by reason of the negligence of the vessel *Edison*. At the time, *Liesbosch* was performing harbour dredging work under a contract which provided for severe penalties for delay. The lost dredger could have been replaced by a newly-purchased one, but her owners were not in a sufficiently good financial position to

do so immediately. They were obliged at great expense to hire a replacement. In their claim for damages for the loss of their dredger they included the costs of hiring in addition.

*Held*: that although the damages in respect of the hiring of the replacement were not recoverable under the rule in *Re Polemis* (see page 305) since that was the direct result of the claimant's financial instability and not the defendant shipowner's negligence, nevertheless the claimant was entitled to the value of *Liesbosch as a going concern* and not merely her value as a somewhat old dredger.

If a vessel is earning freight at the time of her loss there is a right of recovery of it less the cost of earning it. What is or can be taken into account in favour of the wrongdoer is the admittedly indeterminate element of risk saved because it should always be borne in mind that a freight-earning voyage is an adventure in the true sense of the word and there is never a guarantee of a successful conclusion earning the shipowner his absolute right to freight. This element itself can be assessed as an allowance in favour of the wrongdoer when estimating damages in respect of loss of freight over and above the value of the ship itself. Reasonable certainty of gain, however, is the criterion.

Interest is recoverable. If the ship was in ballast only when lost the interest recoverable runs from the date of the collision to the date of payment of compensation due. Where freight was being earned, the interest runs from the date freight would have been duly paid.

## MEASURE OF DAMAGES WHERE SHIP IS DAMAGED BUT NOT LOST

The general principle for the assessment of damages is restitutio in integrum. But if this means that the value of the ship after repairs is increased, this is the wrongdoer's bad luck. The repairs must be satisfactory and carried out at reasonable cost under the circumstances. The wrongdoer has no right to choose the place of repair or to nominate the repairer; but, conversely, the innocent shipowner must act prudently and as if he was uninsured or unindemnified in making these choices.

*The Ferdinand Retzlaff* [1972] 2 Lloyd's Rep. 120
The *Cape Nelson* was in collision with the *Ferdinand Retzlaff* in the English Channel in April 1965. Blame was apportioned 60 per cent to *Cape Nelson* and 40 per cent to *Ferdinand Retzlaff*. At the time of the collision *Cape Nelson* was trading under a long-term charter and was currently on a voyage from Monrovia to a West German port. She was thereafter fixed to perform a further round voyage, after which she was scheduled to go for routine survey and owners' repairs. The ship was in fact sent direct to the designated repair yard where survey work, collision repairs and owners' repairs were carried out at the same time. Her owners claimed damages for detention on the grounds that they had acted reasonably in having the collision damages immediately repaired, that the carrying out of owners' repairs and survey work at the same time as the permanent collision repairs did not lengthen the total time taken in repair or increase the cost of collision repairs. They denied that they should have to give credit to the owners of *Ferdinand Retzlaff* on the grounds of a supposed advantage gained. The *Ferdinand Retzlaff's* owners counter-argued that the decision to effect permanent repairs immediately and at the previously chosen dry dock was unreasonable. Temporary repairs afloat would have been sufficient. At least, they

argued, credit should be given for the time saved in bringing forward the special survey and owners' repairs so as to be performed concurrently with the collision repairs.

*Held*: that the test to be applied to determine whether an innocent shipowner had acted reasonably was that of the prudent uninsured owner under the same circumstances. On these facts the *Cape Nelson's* owners had acted reasonably in effecting permanent repairs immediately. Furthermore, it was reasonable for such repairs to be done at the dry dock they had already selected. The other shipowner was not entitled to receive credit for the saving of time in bringing forward the survey and owners' repairs for there was no evidence to show that this had adversely affected either the cost of the collision repairs or the time occupied by them. Damages for detention for the full period (13 days) were awarded.

The wrongdoer is also liable for consequential losses, viz. delay due to the collision, i.e. loss of profit-making use (less the expenses of earning the profit) but (see *The Soya* [1956] 1 Lloyd's Rep. 557, CA) profit lost must not be too speculative or remote. The true measure of damages is the net rate of profit under the immediate charter, i.e. definite employment not speculative employment.

Out-of-pocket expenses are recoverable. This could include salvage and towage expenses (frequently the first expenses to be incurred), cost of surveys, dock dues, repair cost, adjusting charges, agency fees, to name but a few of the most common.

Detention expenses are recoverable with certain reservations. The basic rule when it is necessary to ascertain the damages due, if any, for the detention of the vessel following a collision is that actual consequential loss must have resulted and the amount claimed must be reasonably proved. In short, what, but for the collision and resulting detention and deprivation of her use, would her owner have earned from the use of her? Speculative, uncertain or exceptional profits will in the normal course be excluded from the calculation of damages. Clearly, where a commercially trading vessel is undergoing collision repairs at a time when she would otherwise be idle and earning no profit there has been no assessable loss to her owner and no damages for detention are payable.

Equally strongly it could be argued that where a damaged ship's owner had, prior to the collision, entered into arrangements to repair his ship and neither routine scheduled repairs nor collision repairs were urgent, no provable loss resulted from the collision.

Where both owners' repairs and collision repairs were necessary but the detention period was not lengthened by reason of the collision repairs, detention costs will be borne by her owners.

There is nothing to prevent an owner whose ship needs necessary repairs after a collision from taking the opportunity of repairing his ship (owners' repairs) whilst the ship is repairing collision damage and he is entitled to be reimbursed in full for detention costs provided the detention period is not increased due to his own repairs.

To sum up, it would be fair to say that if a vessel has to go out of commission in order to perform repair work following a collision, the owners are entitled to take the opportunity of performing non-collision work without prejudicing their claim for detention. If, however, the vessel was bound to go out of commission in any event, e.g. for annual drydocking or special survey, then the collision claim for detention fails, except in so far as the collision repairs may extend the period for which the vessel could otherwise have been at the repair yard.

It is up to any court assessing detention damages to take into consideration the actual number of days between the start of the deprivation of the vessel's use after a collision and the point of time when the owner recovers the use of her and to adjust the actual money figure by assessing at the same time the attendant circumstances, such as diligence and speed, with which the repair work is done, the existence of any impromptu or force majeure delays such as strikes, inclement weather and other circumstances affecting the merits of the claim generally. The rationale of this is that when someone claims in respect of lost time, such items as efficiency and quality of work and the degree of control of the plaintiff and defendant which naturally varies in degree from place to place must have a significant bearing on the final assessment. Loss of earnings generally can be the basis for a claim for general damages, viz. if a ship was definitely engaged to take a spot cargo (*The Argentino* (1888) 13 PD 191, CA; affirmed 14 App Cas 519, HL).

Where loss of contractual earnings is an item of damage, the innocent shipowner cannot also charge demurrage. This *would* be duplicating damages.

*The Pacific Concord* [1960] 2 Lloyd's Rep. 270

In September 1955 two ships collided in the River Thames. Essential repairs were effected at Falmouth. The other vessel then sailed. A charterparty was concluded in November 1956 with the cancelling date being 5 February 1957. In December 1956 the vessel arrived at Newcastle and, after part discharge, proceeded to London where she entered dry dock to complete repairs. She eventually arrived at the loading port nominated in the charterparty 10 days later than the cancelling date. The charterers agreed to accept the vessel in consideration of a slight freight reduction. The shipowner claimed from the other ship at fault, inter alia, loss of profit, detention, grounding damage and running costs during repairs.

*Held*: that the duty on the innocent shipowner was to make arrangements for repairs as if he were a prudent uninsured owner. Arrangements had been made to drydock in London without proper regard to the charterparty requirements. No particular urgency existed for final repairs. It was not possible to supplement the claim for loss of earnings through detention by proving an actual loss sustained by the non-performance of a charterparty. In this sort of case the question to be decided was: what have the owners lost by their inability to employ their ship as a profit-earning instrument by reason of her being laid up in consequence of collision repairs? The value of the charter was an accurate measure of the value of the ship to her owner during the time she was under repair.

Damages that are too remote and not directly consequential upon the original act of negligence must be excluded. An example of this would be that the plaintiff (innocent) shipowner might be forced owing to his present precarious financial situation to borrow money at unusually high rates of interest to replace his vessel. This would probably be regarded as too remote a consequence as to form a valid claim against the wrongdoing shipowner.

To sum up, the innocent shipowner is not obliged to give credit to the wrongdoer where (a) it was reasonably necessary for him to carry out repairs immediately; (b) the carrying out of owners' repairs does not add to the cost of or lengthen the time occupied; and (c) he takes advantage of the ship being in dock to repair collision damage to effect repairs which may be only advisable as opposed to essential. It follows from this that where by effecting his own repairs contemporaneously with collision repairs he incurs increased costs and increased detention time, he is debarred from claiming such additional costs from the wrongdoer and must limit his claim to the amount which he would have been permitted to recover if the repair of the collision damage had been performed separately at a reasonable cost and in a reasonable period of time.

## ASCERTAINING THE REMOTENESS OF DAMAGE

Damages that are far too remote from the negligent act are not recoverable from the wrongdoer but there has been uncertainty as to the true tests which should be applied to determine what is remote or not. The test which springs from the *Re Polemis* dispute (below) was that, provided that some damage could be foreseen, however slight, all loss and damage consequential upon and directly flowing from the original negligent act were recoverable by the innocent party.

Law students and practitioners alike will recall the facts in *Re Polemis.*

*Re Polemis & Furness Withy & Co* [1921] 3 KB 560, CA
A sling being swung by stevodores in the course of cargo operations struck a wooden board which fell into the ship's hold causing a spark which ignited petrol vapour resulting in immediate conflagration and the loss of the ship. The arbitrators studied the facts and in a special case stated found that no reasonable person could have foreseen that a spark would result from the mere falling of a board though very minor and routine damage might perhaps have been anticipated.

This left some measure of uncertainty in that it blurred to some extent what should have been the clear distinction between all foreseeable consequences and all direct consequences. The facts of the case perhaps unwittingly lend themselves to the somewhat unsatisfactory resulting rule. Criticism of the decision was voiced 40 years later in *The Wagon Mound* dispute (below) where it was emphatically stated that 'foreseeability' should be the key word and that any consequences not reasonably foreseeable, however directly or immediately resulting, should fall into the 'too remote' category.

*Overseas Tankship (UK) Ltd v Morts Dock & Engineering Co Ltd* [1961] AC 388, PC
The appellants were the charterers of the *Wagon Mound.* She was in the harbour at Sydney taking on board furnace oil. Servants of the charterers negligently permitted the escape of oil into the water. The spilt oil was carried over by the wind and the tide to a wharf belonging to the respondents at which they carried on the business of shipbuilding and repair. Some of their employees were at that particular time carrying out repairs to a ship which was moored alongside the wharf and in the course of the operations they were making use of welding equipment. One of the respondents' managers noticed the floating oil and stopped the welding operations in order to consult the wharf manager who assured him that it was quite safe to continue working since previous experience had shown that sparks were unlikely to set fire to floating oil. With due caution, therefore, work recommenced but a piece of molten metal fell from the wharf setting fire to a piece of cotton waste which happened to be floating on the oil. This, in turn, set the oil aflame and the respondents' wharf was extensively damaged.

The Supreme Court of New South Wales, following *Re Polemis,* held the appellant liable but when the matter came before the Judicial Committee of the

Privy Council on appeal, the appeal was allowed since the Privy Council considered that *Re Polemis* should no longer be reckoned good law. The proper test should be foreseeability of the actual harm resulting. The damage by fire was thus too remote whereas the fouling of the wharf by the oil itself, had there been such damage, would have been foreseeable and thus the subject of a successful claim for damages.

The decision in *The Wagon Mound* was, however, not without difficulties. Being a Privy Council decision it did not bind the English courts but was of persuasive value only. *Re Polemis* was a Court of Appeal decision which, though bound by its own previous decisions, would nevertheless be unlikely to survive long in the atmosphere of the extreme likelihood that the House of Lords would almost certainly overthrow a similar decision if one was put before them. The 'eggshell skull' doctrine must necessary stand out as surviving exception to *The Wagon Mound* doctrine and must continue for the present to be accepted as such. The 'eggshell skull' rule that a wrongdoer takes his victim as he finds him may, however, not necessarily apply in cases of financial or economic loss as opposed to physical harm or damage; and of this view the *Liesbosch Dredger* case (page 300) is an illustration. Indeed a judge in modern times has given a graphic example of how disproportionate compensation might become if one considered that through momentary inattention of a ship's officer on the bridge of a ship that ship collided with a bridge, as a result of which a large suburban area which included shops and factories was deprived of its main means of access, great loss might be suffered by tens of thousands of persons; it would be out of all proportion to the wrong done that the wrongdoer should be required to compensate all those who had suffered pecuniary loss. By the same token, the economic loss suffered by three railway companies because they had to reroute their trains because of damage to a railway bridge caused by a ship colliding with it was not a reasonably foreseeable direct result of the collision and therefore not a loss which the innocent railway companies could properly recover from the wrongdoing vessel owner.

The *Giacinto Motta* decision (page 286) has further strengthened the idea that foreseeability is the paramount test both for blameworthiness and as a fair basis for damages payable, and that this concept now firmly presents the correct statement of law.

Another dispute which well illustrates this concept is *The Daressa*, below.

*The Daressa* [1971] 1 Lloyd's Rep. 60
In November 1961 the vessel *President Arthur* collided with the *Daressa*. The *Daressa* was solely at fault. The *President Arthur* was detained for 23 days repairing. Her owners, during that period, would have earned a commercial profit of just over $30,000 and also could have received an operating differential subsidy of a little over $36,000 payable by the Federal Maritime board. The board refused payment on the ground that the sum was legally recoverable from the owners of *Daressa*. In the consequent dispute, *Daressa's* owners argued that the loss of the subsidy was caused not by the collision but by the decision of the board to refuse to pay and that in any event the loss was not reasonably foreseeable by them.

*Held:* that the loss of the subsidy was proximately caused by the collision, that as to foreseeability the foresight of *Daressa's* Master, not of her owners, was what mattered, and that her Master should reasonably have foreseen that any ship with which she collided might be operating with the assistance of a government subsidy which might be lost during detention of the vessel.

A common example would be an exceptionally profitable charterparty lost as a consequence of a collision.

*The Naxos* [1972] 2 Lloyd's Rep. 149
In January 1967 the Greek vessel *Aliartos* (on charter) collided with the Danish ship *Naxos* in Antwerp. The *Naxos* was found solely to blame. It was discovered that permanent repairs to the *Aliartos* could be postponed and temporary repairs were carried out in Piraeus some six weeks later. She completed her current charter and performed four more subsequent to that. In September of the same year she was fixed at a much higher rate than usual. Owing to a delay of five days during which she was undergoing permanent collision repairs, her owners claimed a trading loss, arguing that she had come on hire at the commencement of this very favourable charter five days late. The owners of *Naxos* counter-argued that the ship could have been repaired whilst she was actually trading and that her owners had chosen an unusual time to carry out the repairs. They contended also that the daily profit rate should be calculated on the mean average over several voyages.

*Held:* that the owners of *Aliartos* had not acted unreasonably so far as the mitigation question was concerned. Also that the charterparty rate which came into force immediately after the detention period was unusually high and to expect the wrongdoing shipowner to pay at that rate rather than on a broader more averaged basis would be unfair.

### *In what currency should a court or tribunal award damages?*

One very significant issue in the assessment of damages after a collision is that of deciding in what currency damages should be awarded in each individual circumstance. In 1976 litigation occurred on this point which altered the prevailing rule that damages could only be awarded in sterling. If it was a matter of breach of contract the conversion to sterling being made at the time of the breach and if, as in collision cases, it was a matter of tort, at the date when the loss or expenditure involved was incurred (*Miliangos* v *George Frank (Textiles) Ltd* [1976] 1 Lloyd's Rep. 201, HL, a non-maritime case). That case established a rule that the courts should have the power to give judgment in a foreign currency making conversion into sterling no longer relevant or necessary. Beyond this basic concept, however, the *Miliangos* case did not elaborate in detail what methods should be used to implement the rule. The facts of the *Miliangos* case involved a debt in a foreign currency. Since 1976 therefore there have been three equally arguable alternatives for solving the vexed question of how damages should be awarded. Firstly, the old idea of the sterling basis solution, whereby damages would be awarded in sterling only and if the claim was in a foreign currency it would be converted as at the time of the loss. Secondly, the awarding of damages in the currency of the expenditure or loss, meaning the currency in which the innocent party directly or immediately incurred it. Thirdly (a choice most likely to be put forward by the plaintiff claimant) the notion that damages should be awarded in the currency of the plaintiff, that is to say, the currency in which he actually effectively felt his loss and which would probably, though not necessarily, be normal operating or 'home-based' currency. Two factors affect this whole problem, the inescapable fact that the fluctuation from time to time in exchange rates can have a drastic effect on the eventual damages which the innocent party may receive and, bearing in mind the principle of restitutio in integrum, the final resulting figure could be somewhat unrealistic, and the other underlying concept of the law of tort that the wrongdoer must take his victim as he finds him (sometimes known as the 'eggshell skull' principle). This latter consideration lends support to the view that the preferred choice between sterling and the currency of loss solutions should be the latter.

### *Should losses following a breach of contract be treated differently from losses resulting from a tort?*

An additional complication comes from the Admiralty law concept of setting off liabilities between the colliding shipowners in both-to-blame situations. As has been explained, the theory as applied by the Admiralty Court is that there is only one judgment, that being for the difference between the amounts of the two respective liabilities. Therefore, where the two liabilities are expressed in differing currencies which currency should be the one selected to give effect to the set-off, and at what point of time should this reduction to a 'common denominator' take place? Recently it was decided that the answer to this question should be to convert the currency of the lesser liability into that of the greater liability and then give effect to the 'set-off' at the time when the two amounts concerned were mutually agreed.

*The Despina R* [1977] 2 Lloyd's Rep. 319, CA
In April 1974 two ships collided off Shanghai, both Greek-owned. The owners of one vessel, the *Eleftherotria*, took legal action against the *Despina*'s owners alleging negligence by the latter's employees. The matter was settled so far as liability was concerned in July 1976, *Despina* being found 85 per cent to blame. Both parties reserved to themselves the right to apply to the Admiralty Court for determination of the identity of the currency in which damages should be paid and how the computation should be done. The *Eleftherotria*'s owners exercised their option. The damages suffered by them consisted of expenses directly caused by the collision including temporary and permanent repairs, loss through detention and other additional expenses.

*Held:* that the plaintiff who had incurred a loss or expenditure directly in a certain foreign currency was entitled to recover the damages due to him in that same currency. Judgment was given for the appropriate amount in that currency or its sterling equivalent on the date of payment.

In this dispute it was necessary to determine whether an English court could enter judgment in the same foreign currency as that in which the loss or damage had been suffered by the injured party. The matter naturally had to be considered in the light of *Miliangos* v *George Frank (Textiles) Ltd* [1976] 1 Lloyd's Rep. 201, HL. The *Miliangos* doctrine strictly applied to damages for breach of contract and begged the question of the position when a tort had been committed. The old rule had been that judgment must be given in sterling and the relevant date for conversion in tort cases was the date of the loss (*The Volturno* (1921) 8 Ll.L.Rep. 449). The *Miliangos* doctrine was more in keeping with the changing economic climate and created a more just rule in the light of financial trends. What must really be examined in this type of dispute is in what currency was the loss *effectively* felt or borne by the injured party. If that was his own currency, then that should be the currency of judgment. The plaintiffs in the case were entitled to the amounts of reasonable expenditure and loss expressed in US dollars or sterling equivalents as at the date of payment. In other words, if the injured party's expenditure or loss was incurred directly in any currency other than his own (i.e. any currency other than US dollars) the relevant sums should be converted into his own at the rate ruling on the date of the incurring of the expense.

More recent cases concerning the currency of loss are *The Transoceanica Francesca and Nicos V*, and *The Lash Atlantico.*

*The Transoceanica Francesca and Nicos V* [1987] 2 Lloyd's Rep. 155
In 1974 a collision occurred off the coast of Portugal between the plaintiffs' Italian vessel, *Transoceanica Francesca* and the defendants' vessel, *Nicos V.* Following the commencement of Admiralty proceedings, the solicitors for the parties agreed that the plaintiffs and the defendants were equally to blame for the collision. It was further agreed that the damages should be referred to the Admiralty Registrar for assessment. In 1982 the plaintiffs' statement of damages was made in Italian lire. Three-and-a-half years later, they reamended their claim and sought to recover a substantial part of their claim in US dollars.

The Admiralty Registrar assessed the amount of damages suffered by each party and in particular decided that the plaintiffs' claim should be based in Italian lire. The plaintiffs are an Italian company carrying on business in Italy. The vessel at the time of the collision was on a long-term charterparty under which hire was paid in US$ dollars. Although the currency in which the plaintiffs first felt their loss was US currency in the sense that payments were made out of their US dollar account, that was not a decisive factor. The plaintiffs held a US dollar account as a convenient dollar float to avoid the necessity of repeated Exchange Control Applications to cover individual items of expenditure in currency other than lire. Had the plaintiffs really felt their loss in US currency it was strange that they initially presented their claim as a lire claim and persisted in that for several years.

The plaintiffs appealed against the decision of the Admiralty Registrar contending that the proper currency of their claim was US dollars on the basis that that was the currency in which the loss was effectively felt or borne by them. The issues for decision by the Admiralty Court were (1) in what currency should the plaintiffs' claim be assessed; (2) if this was Italian lire, then what was the correct method of setting off the amounts of the claim and counter-claim.

*Held*: the Admiralty Register was right in his decision that the plaintiffs' claim should be assessed in lire. A limited use was made of a dollar account, but in truth the plaintiffs' 'felt their loss' in their own currency, namely lire; their ships were insured against loss in lire; those ships were regarded as lire assets. There were frequent conversions from dollars into lire and, save for the balance in hand in the dollar account, the plaintiffs regarded lire as the currency of their accounts. (The earlier case of *The Despina R* was considered.) Secondly, where there was a claim and counterclaim, neither party was liable to pay until a balance had been struck. In 1986, the parties agreed the amount of the plaintiffs' claim: it was smaller than the amount of the defendants' claim which had already been agreed; since that was the date on which the amount of both liabilities was finally agreed, the plaintiffs' claim ought to be converted into dollars (being the currency of the defendants' claim) on that date and subtracted from the defendants' claim. The defendants were entitled to recover the balance from the plaintiffs.

*The Lash Atlantico* [1987] 2 Lloyd's Rep. 114
The vessel *Manina* was owned by a Panamanian company and managed by Greek managing agents. Following a collision, the question was what currency should damages be awarded to the owners.

*Held*: the owners had established that their loss fell to be measured in dollars. All the relevant operations, the trading of the ship generally and the alleviation of the consequences of this casualty fell to be measured in dollars alone. That was the currency with which the owners' investment in the vessel had its closest commercial connection. It was impossible and would be quite unreasonable to conclude that the owners did not feel this loss in dollars simply because they did not manage the vessel themselves but had it managed through their Greek managing agents. The reality was that the owners' trading venture, in the form of this vessel was conducted exclusively in US dollars. It was irrelevant in what currency the resulting accounts were drawn up. Everything pointed to US dollars as the appropriate currency.

Thus the rule in *Miliangos*, established as it was in the field of contract, is extended to tort by way of this collision dispute. The *Miliangos* decision is a significant milestone in the development of English law in the sphere of judgments in foreign currencies. It should certainly have an encouraging influence on foreign plaintiffs who will not so easily be deterred from enlisting the aid of British courts or resorting to London arbitration by the fear existing before *Miliangos* that they could only hope for a judgment in devalued sterling, a poor prospect!

The date of payment of a repair bill is usually the date from which interest may run.

It should be borne in mind that the costs of arrest are recoverable.

Public vessels which may not be able to prove special damages, i.e. loss of definite trading profits, can claim general damages.

*The Chikiang* [1926] AC 637, HL

The owners of the *Chikiang* appealed against the assessment of damages made against them after an Admiralty Court hearing in connection with a collision between their vessel and HMS *Cairo* in Chinese waters in August 1921. The *Chekiang*'s owners had admitted liability, but they objected to two items of damage, (1) in respect of loss of use of the other ship for a stipulated period, and (2) pay and allowances of the ship's officers and men. The former item was disputed on the grounds that the Crown had not been deprived of her use and because the Crown's vessel was due to go for extensive overhaul anyway and the collision repairs only occupied part of the time spent in general overhaul and neither delayed nor extended the period that the ship was in dock.

*Held:* that this being the claim of the owners of a non-profit-making vessel, there was nonetheless no reason why they should not be awarded damages. Where there may be no provable *special* damages, this did not debar the aggrieved shipowner from claiming general damages based on any actual loss which the facts themselves might show, and each case was to be treated on its merits. Vessels in continual public use must obviously be treated differently from those being used for private trading or commercial purposes. Regard must be had to the basic rule of English law that damages recoverable from a wrongdoer in a case of collision at sea must be measured accordingly to the ordinary principles of common law.

The question for decision was 'would the repairs carried out by the owner apart from the collision damage, even though necessary, have in fact been done quite so soon as they were?' There was no specific rule of law on this point and it was a question of degree. Even though the law did not specifically say that because repairs for owners' own account were effected sooner than they would have been but for the collision, the time occupied by such repairs must be taken into consideration and allowed against the award of damages, the courts had the power to exercise their discretion based on the courts' common sense and the merits of the case concerned. The idea that because a vessel earned no money for her owners but merely rendered general service her owners were not entitled to damages beyond actual loss as reflected in repairs or provable loss of wages etc., was buried once and for all at the outset of this century (*The Greta Holme* [1897] AC 596, HL, and *The Marpesa* [1907] AC 241, HL). Since then it has been established that general damages could be recovered by the injured vessel, including possibly the costs of procuring a replacement vessel. To put it shortly, what was the actual loss which the injured shipowner suffered as a direct result of his being deprived of the use of his chattel? If it can be shown that the period of collision damage enabled the owners to execute other repairs, the completion of which otherwise would with reasonable certainty have deprived the owners of some period of beneficial use, the time so saved, with all proper discounts for uncertainly etc. might properly be taken into account. In the present case it was clear that the plaintiffs did not lose the whole beneficial use of the ship during the 20 days in question. They occupied her with her officers and men during the whole period and during the same period were engaged in carrying out her usual annual refit.

A charterer of a vessel in collision, unless he has taken the vessel under demise terms, will have no direct cause of action against the wrongdoing vessel-owner. The reasoning behind this is that as he is someone who has a contractual relationship only with the injured shipowner and is not, as is a goods owner, the owner of property in the strict sense on board the ship, he falls outside the category of persons to whom the wrongdoing shipowner could be said to owe a duty of care. That a time charterer, for example, is unable to recover compensation direct from a third-party shipowner for losses suffered by reason of the latter's negligence causing a collision seems to be well established.

*Federal Commerce & Navigation* v *Marathonian* [1975] AMC 738
Federal Commerce & Navigation, time charterer of the vessel *Eolwi*, involved in a collision on Lake Michigan in October 1973 with the ship *Marathonian*, brought an action against the *Marathonian*'s owners.

*Held:* that a time charterer was barred from recovering losses sustained as a result of a third party's negligent interference with the performance of his charter.

CHAPTER 7

# SALVAGE

Towards the end of the last century a judge summed up the concept of salvage by saying that the jurisdiction which is exercised by the court in salvage cases is of a peculiarly equitable character. The right to salvage may, but does not necessarily, arise out of an actual contract. It is a legal liability arising out of the fact that property has been saved, that the owner of the property who had had the benefit of it should make remuneration to those who have conferred the benefit upon him notwithstanding that he had entered into any contract on the subject (*The Five Steel Barges* (1890) 15 PD 142). It is suggested therefore that it is misleading to refer to 'salvage contracts'. It implies that we are exclusively in the 'world of' the law of contract. We are not. We are into the law of salvage. A perhaps less misleading expression would be 'salvage agreements'. Lord Diplock in *The Tojo Maru* [1971] 1 Lloyd's Rep. 341 implied that the right to a reward sprang from an expressed or implied contractual obligation but it is here submitted that to regard this as a basis is moving perilously close to an eventual acknowledgement that salvors are not truly volunteers, whereas salvors most certainly are as this chapter will endeavour to explain.

It is the equitable principle of remunerating private and individual services, meritorious in their nature, which forms the foundation of salvage in accordance with the rules of simple justice. The protection of lives at sea and of maritime property is of paramount importance and is to be encouraged, not discouraged, by the courts. Without such encouragement the maritime industry could be one so fraught with such dangers and risks that few, if any, would reasonably engage in such day-to-day commercial ventures.

As early as the beginning of the 19th century, Lord Stowell in *The Neptune* (1824) 1 Hag Adm 227 described a salvor as:

> 'one who, without any particular relation to the ship in distress, proffers useful service and gives it as a volunteer adventurer without any pre-existing covenant that connected him with the duty of employing himself for the preservation of that ship'.

This concise definition effectively includes two of the essential ingredients of proper maritime salvage, namely, voluntariness and a degree of success.

The principles and rules of salvage bear, for obvious reasons, striking similarity to those applying to general average. Perhaps the shortest, most direct and simplest definition of salvage is 'the voluntary saving of maritime property from danger at sea'. The two words 'voluntary' and 'danger' would certainly remind one of general average, for there, too, it will be remembered that the general average act or sacrifice must be made voluntarily and the property saved must have been in real and not imagined danger. The guiding principles which go to confirm and validate a salvage service rendered are: (a) the service must be rendered to a legally recognized subject of salvage, that is to say, to vessels, their apparel, cargo and merchandise, bunkers, wreck and so-called freight at risk; (b) the service must be voluntary; (c) the subject of the salvage must be in danger and (d) the service must be successful.

## MARITIME PROPERTY

Until the enactment of legislation relating to salvage of aircraft or hovercraft the only property which could become the subject of salvage was a vessel, her apparel, cargo, or wreck and, so far as it may be called property, freight at risk. The saving of other types of property such as a buoy adrift from its moorings or goods in a house on fire does not give rise to any right to a salvage reward. Although it is not easy to categorically define what pieces of property may be subject to maritime salvage, it is unlikely that such non-moving or non-navigable things as a drilling rig would be so classed.

One of the many classes of salvage services is 'protection or rescue of a ship or her cargo or the lives of persons on board her from pirates or plunderers. . . .'.

*The Trelawny* (1801) Ch Rob 216n
A slave ship was rescued from insurgent slaves by another slave ship off the coast of Africa. Deliverance out of the hands of such persons was held to be equivalent to deliverance out of the hands of pirates.

Before we continue to study the four prerequisites necessary to enable a person to claim successfully a reward for saving property at sea let us look at:

### *Life salvage*

Life salvage independent of property is a rare occurrence and reported cases this century are almost, if not entirely, non-existent. The principle upon which life salvage is based is that there must be, first of all, actual danger to the persons whose lives have been saved or at least a substantial apprehension of danger. Without this, there is nothing to be saved from. It is, therefore, this factor, and this alone, which justifies a claim to life salvage. As, under the Admiralty doctrine, there must be a fund formed from the salved property out of which salvage is paid or payable, and as it is impossible to value human life in terms of 'hard cash', life cannot be a distinct and separate subject of salvage within the accepted sense of the word. A philosopher might counter-argue that you *can* value human life (e.g. the assessing of *death* damages in court). He in turn should be contradicted by the statement that you are thereby valuing not human life but the *consequences of a death*. A human's value to others as a 'dead and gone' person is assessable in monetary terms but this is a different 'slant' to valuing the life of somebody who has *not* died and is still living through the efforts of a salvor. Where, however, as is usually the case, life and property are saved in one and the same operation, it is the custom and practice to award a greater remuneration than if property alone had been saved. If there has been saving of life at some point of time in the salvage operation, then ship and/or cargo-owners as owners of the salved properties may find themselves liable to pay life salvage, but where life *only* is saved there is no binding legal obligation. Perhaps a secondary reason for there being no legal obligation is that the saving of human life should not need financial incentive. It should be instinctive in all human beings who behave reasonably.

That there is no remuneration legally payable for the saving of human life is confirmed by the International Convention on Salvage 1989 which has the force of law in the United Kingdom (see section 224 of the Merchant Shipping Act 1995). This does not apply legally to salvage operations before 1 January 1995. However, under Part II in certain circumstances the Secretary of State may pay for life salvage in UK waters. The Convention does countenance the enhancing of a reward made for saving property or for preserving the environment *if* life has been saved in the same overall operation.

The duty on Masters to render assistance to any person in danger of being lost at sea, within the limits of *not* endangering his own vessel and persons thereon, is, not surprisingly, preserved by Article 10 of the Convention.

## VOLUNTARINESS

The requirement that the service must be given voluntarily does not preclude the salvor, i.e. the one who performs the service, from making the service the subject of an agreement and this in practice is often done (see Lloyd's Standard Form of Salvage Agreement in the Appendix to this chapter, page 545, *post*). To avoid the requirement of voluntariness and thus defeat a claim for salvage it must be shown beyond doubt that there existed a duty to render the service wholly and completely and, secondly, that that duty was owed to the owners of the property saved, e.g. a pilot on board or the crew of the ship in distress are usually unable to claim salvage unless the services rendered are outside or beyond the scope and bounds of their duties under contract. It may happen, and indeed has happened, that a pilot contracted to perform a pilotage service has acted over and above the call of duty and voluntarily to the extent of bringing his actions within the realm of salvage services independently of his contractual duties as a pilot.

*The Sandefjord* [1953] 2 Lloyd's Rep. 557
The Master of a vessel stranded on the Goodwin Sands in charge of a pilot accepted the pilot's advice that offers of assistance by tugs should be rejected and that a kedge anchor should by laid by a lifeboat. The court found that the pilot's services were salvage services and upheld his claim for salvage. Not only did the pilot take a personal risk in giving this advice, because had his recommendations eventually proved disastrous he could have put his personal reputation and even job in jeopardy, but also he relieved the ship's owners of the almost certain alternative of a vast salvage award for tug assistance. The problem for any court in determining the right award in such circumstances is to make it big enough to compensate for the risk taken in that particular instance but at the same time not so big as actively to encourage pilots in future circumstances to take similar undue risks. Obviously, the basic, guiding and underlying reason for salvage awards is to encourage seafaring people to take reasonable risks for the purpose of saving maritime property in danger.

## INSTANCES WHERE THE CREW OF A SHIP IN DISTRESS CAN CLAIM SALVAGE

No right to salvage accrues to crewmen as such and claiming as individual salvors unless their contract of employment has been actually or constructively terminated before the salvage service commenced, since it is implied in the terms and conditions of their contract of service that they shall use their best endeavours and strive to the best of their ability to save and preserve their ship in time of peril.

Termination of their employment contract could be brought about by: (1) the authorized abandonment of ship under the Master's authority (see *The San Demetrio*, below); (2) the Master's discharge of the crewmen concerned (see *The Warrior*, below); or (3) the capture of the vessel in hostile encounter (see *The Two Friends*, below and *The Beaver*, below).

*The San Demetrio* (1941) 69 Ll.L.Rep. 5
A tanker was severely damaged in the North Atlantic by gunfire from a German warship. She was fully loaded with a cargo of petrol. The Master gave the order to abandon ship. The whole crew left in three lifeboats. Subsequently the tanker caught fire after being hit again. The following day the tanker, still on fire, was sighted again by one of the lifeboats. Under command of the second officer, the boats' crew reboarded the ship and, with great skill and courage, brought the vessel several hundred miles through bad weather to safety on the Clyde. The crew claimed salvage awards.

*Held*: that the vessel had been properly abandoned under the orders of her Master. Therefore under the circumstances the vessel's own crew were entitled to claim salvage.

*The Warrior* (1862) Lush 476
A steamship was disabled and drifted in calm weather onto a rocky shore in the Canary Islands. Subsequently she filled with water and some hours later the Master and crew left the vessel and went ashore. On the following day the Master formally discharged his entire crew in a written document. Subsequent to that discharge some crew members at the chief officer's request returned to the ship and after several days' effort were successful in saving stores and a substantial amount of the cargo.

*Held*: that the seamen concerned were entitled to a salvage reward since their contract of employment was validly terminated by the discharge given by the Master and, in the absence of any fraud in accepting such discharge, the crew who had returned to the vessel were truly salvors.

*The Two Friends* (1799) 1 Ch Rob 271
Seamen claimed a salvage reward for their successful efforts in recapturing their ship from the possession of French captors. That hostile capture such as this automatically brings about the dissolution of a seaman's contract of employment was emphatically affirmed even in those early days. It was said to be no part of the general and expected duties of a seaman to rescue or take his ship back from an enemy captor, and to refuse to attempt to do so would not amount to desertion from any such duty.

*The Beaver* (1800) 3 Ch Rob 92
The Master and a boy apprentice of a British merchant ship were awarded salvage remuneration for bravely regaining possession of their vessel from French privateers and, with a little outside assistance, navigating it safely back to an English port.

Regarding abandonment, there must, at the time of the order to abandon, be no hope or intention of returning to the stricken ship (expressed in the Latin phrase 'sine spe revertendi'). There is no suggestion that a mere temporary abandonment, as frequently takes place subsequent, for example, to a collision and as a result of sudden fear or panic and before the situation has been fully evaluated, would operate to dissolve the crew's contract of employment.

*The Albionic* (1941) 70 Ll.L.Rep. 257
A ship caught fire and her steering gear jammed on her way out of Avonmouth. The vessel's wireless operator claimed a salvage award for his part in saving the ship with 11 other members of its crew, including the chief officer. He was bringing the action as a test case and, if successful, the 11 others intended to make similar claims. The ship's Master, together with other crew members, had left the vessel in some of the ship's lifeboats which had broken away from the ship and drifted away.

*Held*: that as no express order had been given by the Master to abandon ship there was no abandonment either actual or constructive and that therefore the crew's contracts of service were not terminated at the time when they performed what they considered were salvage services. The claim was dismissed.

Such intentional abandonment by Master and crew was one of several issues which was material in a post-World War Two salvage dispute over property recovered from a sunken German submarine off the Malayan coast.

*Simon* v *Taylor, Leishman, Bastian, Dickie, Contract Services, Evermore Marine Technical Services Pte* [1975] 2 Lloyd's Rep. 338, Singapore High Court
During World War Two a German U-boat was sunk 25 miles north of Penang in international waters. In 1969 divers employed by X found the wreck. The following year Germany laid claim to it and agreed that X should raise it. In 1971 X went into liquidation. Later that year four divers financed by two firms, Y and Z, brought up 12 tons of mercury from the wreck, a part of which was handed over to one of the two firms, the balance to the Penang receiver of wrecks. Q, the plaintiff in the case, in 1972 negotiated with the four divers, all defendants in the suit, and assigned to himself and his company all rights and interests accrued to X under their earlier agreement with Germany. He then claimed ownership of that portion of the mercury not delivered to the receiver of wrecks. The defendants claimed, inter alia, that the wreck was a derelict and a res nullius since the Germany which existed during the war had ceased to exist.

*Held*: that the submarine was not a derelict because when she was sunk her commander and crew did not intend to abandon her, that the German State had not ceased to exist and that the ownership of the U-boat had never passed from Germany to X under the agreement. Further, the divers had not rendered salvage services since the mercury was not in danger and the divers' actions were entirely self-serving and not for the benefit of the owners of the mercury.

## THE POSITION OF A PASSENGER CLAIMING AS SALVOR

Self-interest is never a sound basis for claiming salvage and thus ordinarily a passenger, who is instinctively bound to have his own safety partly, if not wholly, in mind, is precluded from making a salvage claim. It is, of course, true that he is under no contractual duty to help preserve ship or cargo and there are exceptions to the general exclusion of passengers as properly recognized salvors. One type of situation where a passenger could justify his claim to reward is if he chose to remain with a stricken ship to assist in her preservation when an alternative means of safety for himself and his property was offered to him.

*Newman* v *Walters* (1804) 3 Bos & P 612
A sailing ship stranded on shoals off the English coast was abandoned by her Master and the bulk of the crew. The pilot was too intoxicated to be capable of any action. The ship was brought to safety by the efforts of a passenger who, as it happened, was a qualified merchant marine captain and who acceded to the request of the vessel's chief officer to take control.

*Held*: that in so acting he ceased to be a passenger altogether and certainly did more than was expected of him under the circumstances.

What assistance a passenger does provide, however, must be material and significantly contribute to ultimate success. These rules concern passengers on the stricken ship itself. A passenger travelling on another ship who renders assistance would be treated in the same way as would any other volunteer salvor.

Thus in *The American Farmer* (see page 352) five passengers on a salving vessel of their own free will went aboard the stricken ship and personally and meritoriously contributed to the eventual successful bringing to safety of the disabled ship.

## REAL DANGER

The requirement that the subject of salvage must be in danger means real, but not necessarily immediate, danger, provided that it is not so remote as to be a mere possibility. It is the task of the person claiming salvage to show that at the time when the performance of the service commenced such real danger existed. It is up to the court or arbitrator hearing the case to determine for itself or himself whether the property was really in danger, taking into consideration all the facts and circumstances. What is normally in dispute is not the existence of the danger but the degree of danger which does exist. A frightened, timid and perhaps incompetent ship's Master, although suffering from an illusion that there was a real danger when in fact there was not could, by his very attitude, constitute the existence of a danger himself under some circumstances. Naturally every situation has to be treated on its own merits and the tests must necessarily be both subjective and objective. One reasonably effective test is, would the Master of a vessel in distress, assuming him to be a reasonable man, have answered 'yes' or 'no' to the offer of assistance? Perhaps what is of importance to determine is, was there a real apprehension of danger even though that danger was not necessarily certain, absolute, and immediate? Or, on the other hand, was it mere whim, fancy or illusion or so remote as to be only a possibility? An overall picture can only be gained by studying the situations which have given rise to disputes over the years.

*The Helmsman* (1950) 84 Ll.L.Rep. 207
A tanker lay alongside a steamship which was in turn moored alongside a wharf on the Tyne. The former was transferring oil to the latter. The steamship's moorings broke and both ships drifted across the river at the mercy of the tide and a gale force wind. With the aid of tugs the ships were re-berthed. The steamship paid salvage but it was disputed that the tanker had ever been in danger.

*Held*: that the tanker, although adrift, could have used her engines and could have saved herself at any time. No salvage was payable in respect of any services to her.

An interesting case in the mid-1960s which illustrates admirably the definition of danger and what the law of salvage requires and also clearly brings out the idea of voluntariness in salvage is *The Cythera*, below.

*The Cythera* [1965] 2 Lloyd's Rep. 454, NSW Supreme Court
The auxiliary yacht *Cythera* was stolen off New South Wales with the intention on the part of the thieves to sail her to South America. Subsequently the *Cythera* was sighted off Norfolk Island by the Master of the *Colorado del Mar*. The island's administration was informed but refused to send out a government launch due to the adverse weather conditions. They did, however, give permission for a police officer to accompany the *Colorado del Mar* if she should attempt recovery. The *Colorado del Mar* went in pursuit of *Cythera* and when the yacht took avoiding action a collision occurred. The thieves were thrown into the water and later taken on board *Colorado del Mar* but attempts by *Colorado del Mar* to take possession of *Cythera* were unsuccessful. The yacht was then unmanned and without power. The administration was again informed and a government launch was dispatched, the *Cythera* boarded and brought into Cascade Bay. The plaintiffs, the owners of *Colorado del Mar*, claimed a salvage reward on the grounds that they had recovered the *Cythera* from pirates. The defendants denied such a right, alleging negligence and counter-claimed for damage caused by the collision.

*Held*: that the plaintiffs were entitled to a reward. The *Cythera* was in danger, even if not physical danger, within the requirements of the salvage law and also the plaintiffs' endeavours were voluntarily undertaken. The act of collision was not sufficient evidence of negligence. The defendants' defence and counter-claim failed.

*The Cythera* case should be borne in mind when the subject of a salvor's alleged negligence whilst performing salvage operations is discussed later in this chapter (see page 355, *post*).

*The Glaucus* (1948) 81 Ll.L.Rep. 262
*The Glaucus* was disabled because of trouble with its boilers in the Indian Ocean whilst en route from the Far East to the United Kingdom. The vessel *Rhesus* towed her to Aden. It was found impossible to repair the ship at Aden, so another ship (the *Antenor*) towed her to Suez where she was repaired. It was admitted that the services rendered by the *Rhesus* were in the nature of salvage but disputed that the *Antenor* performed a salvage service in that the *Glaucus* was no longer in danger when she reached Aden.

*Held*: that so long as her main boilers were still disabled, the *Glaucus* was potentially in a position of danger. It was meaningless to argue that valuable property such as this was safe if it could not be used. For example, if fire had broken out on board no steam in sufficient quantities would have been available. Both vessels had therefore performed salvage services and were awarded salvage.

*The Troilus* [1951] 1 Lloyd's Rep. 467, HL
A steamship bound for Liverpool from Australia carrying a cargo of food lost her propeller in the Indian Ocean. She was towed by a motor vessel to Aden. Salvage services were acknowledged. However, Aden had no repair facilities and a second vessel towed her to the United Kingdom, with the exception of through the Suez Canal when canal company tugs took over. Salvage was claimed by the second vessel. The defence to the claim was that the danger to the *Troilus* had finished at Aden and that therefore the service was merely in the nature of towage.

*Held*: that although the vessel and her tug were physically safe once they had reached Aden, both would have deteriorated if they had not been removed and the likelihood of expense and delay should be considered. The second towing vessel's services were therefore properly salvage services.

The consensus of case law on the subject in recent times seems to favour a liberal interpretation of the concept of danger. Perhaps it would be not too wide of the mark to say that if the ship and/or its cargo is beyond the point where it is able to save *itself* or bring *itself* to a place of refuge and *needs* outside assistance then it is in a situation of real danger. This interpretation covers the idea that the danger need not be immediate, e.g. a ship may be helplessly drifting but rocks may still be miles away.

The relevance of the *territorial* aspect of where the salvage service takes place to entitlement to a salvage reward was touched upon in the following case:

*The Goring* [1986] 1 Lloyd's Rep. 127
Five members of the Island Bohemian Club based near Reading rescued the passenger vessel *Goring* in the River Thames. The plaintiff issued a writ in the Admiralty Court claiming remuneration for salvage services rendered. The question arose as to whether the court had any jurisdiction to award salvage because the services were rendered in non-tidal waters.

The Admiralty Court decided that jurisdiction could be invoked by a writ in rem in respect of salvage services occurring anywhere in the world provided that a writ in rem could be served upon a ship liable to pay salvage. Article 1 of the Convention for the Unification of Certain Rules of Law relating to Assistance and Salvage at Sea recognized that assistance to vessels of inland navigation in whatever waters the services had been rendered might be salvage services and it would have been anomalous if that had not been recognised. There was no justification for an artificial rule which would differentiate between services rendered to a ship in tidal waters and identical services rendered to a ship in non-tidal waters. If a ship or her cargo was in danger in non-tidal waters it was highly desirable as a matter of public policy that other ships should be encouraged to go to their assistance without hesitation.

The Court of Appeal disagreed. They decided that there was nothing in the language used in section 6 of the Admiralty Court Act 1840 to indicate that it was intended to extend the jurisdiction of the Admiralty Court to non-tidal waters. Salvage services to a vessel earned a reward under section 546 of the Merchant Shipping Act 1894 only if rendered to a vessel in peril on tidal waters defined in section 742 to mean any part of the sea and any part of a river within the ebb and flow of the tide at ordinary spring tides and not being a harbour. It was impossible to suppose that when legislating in these terms Parliament envisaged that there was a right to reward for salvage services in non-tidal waters or that the High Court had Admiralty jurisdiction to entertain such claim. The plaintiffs then appealed.

The House of Lords [1988] 1 Lloyd's Rep. 397 affirmed this decision.

### *Part II*

Part II (Article 2) of Schedule 11 to the Merchant Shipping Act 1995 provides that the International Convention on Salvage 1989 does not apply to:

(a) a salvage operation which takes place in inland waters of the United Kingdom in which all the vessels involved are of inland navigation; and
(b) a salvage operation which takes place in inland waters of the United Kingdom and in which no vessel is involved.

'Inland waters' does not include any waters within the ebb and flow of the tide at ordinary spring tides or the waters of any dock which is directly or (by means of one or more other docks) indirectly, connected with such waters.

## THE SALVAGE SERVICE MUST BE SUCCESSFUL IF ONLY PARTIALLY

The requirement that service must be successful can be summed up in this often used expression, 'no cure—no pay'. Success need not, however, be total. Partial success, however small, that is to say provided there is some measure of preservation to the owners, is sufficient. Arising out of this concept is the allied rule that salvage can in certain circumstances still be payable where the service to be rewarded has not actually contributed to the final saving of the property, as, for example, where another vessel answers a call for assistance but her efforts produce no success and indeed worsen the situation because perhaps the two ships come into collision through the fault of the salving vessel. This, in itself, may cause the salvor's claim to fail but if that fault has not occurred, a court may admit that the owners of the salving ship would have been entitled to an award.

*The Rene* [1955] 1 Lloyd's Rep. 101
A vessel answered a call for assistance but her efforts produced no success and indeed worsened the situation since the two ships collided through the fault of the salving vessel. This in itself caused the salvor's claim to fail; but had that fault not occurred the court admitted that the owners of the salving ship would have been entitled to an award.

That the ultimate outcome must be successful in some degree before a reward can be paid is based on the simple idea that a reward is paid out of the fund preserved as a result of the property having been saved. The concept is epitomized in the world-famous title to the Lloyd's Open Form of Salvage Agreement—the 'No cure—no pay' document. Here is a good point to commence a study of that document.

The Master of a ship in distress has reasonably wide powers when faced with a case of urgency and necessity. As early as 1883 it was decided that he had the power to bind his owner by his actions in negotiating and fixing a salvage agreement, provided that he had no chance or means of communicating with them beforehand. This decision was made before the development of highly sophisticated and speedy means of communication when the Master was deemed to be acting in the capacity of what is sometimes called an 'agent of necessity' both for the shipowner and the cargo-owner. Clearly such authority recognized legally as binding on his principals would be bound to give weight to the terms and conditions negotiated when subsequently a court, sitting to consider a reasonable salvage award, began its deliberations. In any case the actual sum to be paid in salvage is seldom, if ever, fixed before the start of operations even under the popular Lloyd's form of salvage agreement, but is left for subsequent assessment by some independent arbitrator or tribunal.

## WHEN MAY A CHARTERER BE ENTITLED TO CLAIM SALVAGE?

A charterer may, under limited circumstances, claim salvage; those circumstances being: (a) if he is a charterer by demise and to all intents is thereby tantamount to the owner 'pro tem', so to speak, then logically he should be entitled to the salvage award due, particularly as under the terms of the customary demise (or bareboat charter) he, the charterer, is the employer and provider of the Master and crew; and (b) if by the express terms of the relevant charterparty it is stipulated that the charterer becomes owner in the context of and with reference to salvage only, then similarly, he, not the owner, may claim the salvage award if the vessel performs a salvage service.

There is no reason why a charterparty should not contain a provision in it stipulating for salvage to be shared between the shipowner and the charterer.

## WHEN MAY A CARGO OWNER BE ENTITLED TO CLAIM SALVAGE?

For the first time, cargo owners advanced a claim for salvage in the case of *The Sava Star* [1995] 2 Lloyd's Rep. 134. The plaintiffs were the owners of 2951 tons of complex fertilizer NPK in bulk which was being carried on board the vessel *Sava Star*. The cargo was found to be decomposing on board the vessel, and the plaintiffs initiated a crisis plan which included contacting the Humberside Fire Brigade, arranging a helicopter overflight to make an inspection, constructing fire lances and providing chemists. The plaintiffs' general manager also assisted the salvage contractors, which led to a successful salvage. The contractors who were engaged on the LOF 90 Form were awarded a salvage reward before the Salvage Arbitrator but the plaintiffs brought a separate claim in the High Court for salvage.

*Held*: on the authorities, a shipowner was not entitled to claim salvage against himself: where ship and cargo were salved by a vessel under the same ownership as the salved ship, the Master and crew of the salving ship were entitled to salvage against the owners of the salved ship and the owners of her cargo; and in such a case the shipowners were entitled to salvage against the owners of the cargo on the salved ship unless the casualty was caused by an actionable breach of contract on the part of the plaintiffs, in which case (subject to the possible effect of limitation of liability) the claim failed for circuity of action; the fact that the salving and the salved ships were in common ownership or common management was relevant to the quantum of the salvage award. The court should encourage, not discourage sister-ship salvage in an appropriate case.

There was no logical reason why, if a shipowner was entitled to claim salvage against the owner of cargo carried in his ship, a cargo owner should not be entitled to claim salvage against a ship carrying his cargo. There were no rigid categories of salvor. They included any volunteer who rendered service of a salvage nature: and there was no reason why they should not include cargo owners who personally rendered salvage services.

The defendants' argument that the cargo owners were not volunteers as they were under a duty to assist ship and cargo was rejected. The limiting criterion could not be solely that to be debarred from claiming salvage the person concerned must owe a duty to the particular owner of the salved vessel. The reason why the Master and crew could not ordinarily recover salvage was that they were performing services ordinarily to be expected of them in their capacity or capacities as Master and members of the crew respectively.

The cases on passengers claiming salvage established no more than that to be salvage services the services must be more than those ordinarily expected of the passenger and what might ordinarily be expected of a passenger might vary in different times would be accepted. The sole controlling factor could not be whether the passenger owed a legal duty to the owners of the salved property because it could not properly be held that such a duty was owed either to the shipowners or to the cargo owners to render any services at all. The position was essentially the same in a case of a passenger or crew member i.e. that he could not recover in respect of services which he could ordinarily be expected to carry out in his capacity as a passenger or crew member. The same principle ought to apply to a cargo owner.

There was no reason why services which went beyond those which would ordinarily be expected of a cargo owner should not be regarded as voluntary services in respect of which the cargo owner should be entitled to a salvage award. A typical example would be the provision of a tug or other salving vessel or the rendering of fire fighting services. Save in the restricted circumstances where the cargo owner does no more than is to be expected of him as a cargo owner, the cargo owner is a volunteer and as such, in principle, is entitled to salvage remuneration.

## LLOYD'S FORM OF SALVAGE AGREEMENT (LOF 80)

The Lloyd's Open Form (LOF) was originally published in 1908 and the LOF 80 was the eighth edition. Although there are also a LOF 90 and a LOF 95, the earlier LOF 80 remains in use.

The LOF 80 provides that the contractor (the salvor) shall use his best endeavours to salve the property and then take it or them to an agreed place or a place of safety. The Master's role as agent of necessity originally arose in the old days before sophisticated communications. Under the Lloyd's form, in his capacity as 'agent of necessity', the Master of the stricken vessel by his signature binds the owners of the vessel and the owners of cargo to the performance of the agreement. The Master does not bind himself personally. But the Master is as-agent of necessity was reviewed in the case of the *Choko Star.*

*The Choko Star* [1990] 1 Lloyd's Rep. 516 (CA)

The vessel grounded in the River Parana and was stranded. The Master was unable to refloat her without assistance and, by an agreement in writing made on 30 May 1986, he engaged the salvors to refloat the vessel on LOF terms. The salvors were successful in their efforts to refloat the vessel and claimed salvage remunation. An arbitrator was appointed. The claim of the salvors against the shipowners was settled by agreement between the parties. The cargo owners contended that the Master had no authority to engage salvors on their behalf. The cargo owners attended the arbitration under protest. Following the salvage award, the cargo owners paid their proportion of the salvage award.

In the High Court, the cargo owners argued that it was unreasonable for the Master or the shipowners to make a salvage contract with the salvors and it was not in the best interests of the cargo owners for such a contract to have been made. They claimed a refund of their contribution to the salvage award, alternatively all monies in excess of a reasonable sum. Various issues were put to the High Court for a decision, including:

(1) whether the shipowners had implied actual authority, and therefore ostensible authority, to make reasonable contracts with the salvors on behalf of the owners on the cargo on reasonable terms;
(2) whether the Master of a ship had implied actual authority, and therefore ostensible authority, to make reasonable contracts with salvors on behalf of the owners of cargo on reasonable terms.

The Court of Appeal decided that there was no basis on which a term that the Master was authorized to contract on behalf of cargo owners with third parties (whether with salvors or others) could be implied, save as agent of necessity. In the circumstances of the contracts of carriage the cargo owners would only be bound by the salvage contract if it could be established that there was a true agency of necessity. The questions as to implied actual and ostensible authority as presented to the court were unsatisfactory and too wide and in too general terms to be capable of a satisfactory answer. In the present case the cargo owners' appeal was allowed. It should be borne in mind that Article 6 of the International Convention on Salvage 1989 provides that the Master has a wide authority 'to conclude this contract on behalf of the owners of the property on board the vessel'. This provision was originally incorporated by the Merchant Shipping (Salvage and Pollution Act) 1994 which has now been repealed. The 1989 Convention has the force in law in the UK under section 224 of the Merchant Shipping Act 1995.

Another case is the *Pa Mar* (LMLN 461). The issue was whether cargo owners were bound by a salvage contract and it was common ground that the cargo owners were only bound by the LOF if the Master, managers and owners had made the contract on their behalf as agents of necessity in the light of the *Choko Star* case. The criteria of an agency of necessity were:

(i) it was necessary to take salvage assistance;
(ii) it was not reasonably practical to communicate with the cargo owners or to obtain their instructions (which was accepted by cargo owners);
(iii) the Master or shipowners acted bona fide in the interests of the cargo; and
(iv) it was reasonable for the Master or shipowner to enter into the particular contract.

The burden was on the salvors and the criteria had to be established as at the time the contract was made.

On the evidence, it was found that an oral agreement had been made between the Master of the *Pa Mar* and the salvors on 9 June which provided that the salvors should render towage services under the LOF and that further agreement (as to the place of delivery) was left until later. In the event, the provision 'Dubai/ Colombo owners' option' was subsequently agreed either later that day or on the next day. That was a variation of the original agreement. As to the question whether the *Choko Star* criteria were satisfied as at the date of the original LOF agreement, the position on any view of the evidence was that the vessel had been unable to proceed under her own power in the ordinary way for a considerable period of time before she accepted the services of the salvors' tug. Even if there were no problems with the tail shaft, the vessel could not safely get to port under her own power because of the problems with her generators. It did not necessarily follow that it was prudent to take salvage assistance, but the evidence showed that no towage assistance was available on commercial terms so that, unless the vessel and her cargo were to be left indefinitely immobilized, prudence dictated the engagement of the tugs under the LOF. The vessel was not in a place of safety and she was in an exposed position and indefinitely immobilized, which was a relevant danger for salvage purposes. The vessel had been in need of towage assistance and in the absence of this being available on commercial terms it was prudent for the Master to agree towage on LOF terms.

Accordingly it was necessary to take salvage assistance, and the Master and managers had acted reasonably in the interests of those shipping cargo when the original LOF agreement was made. Therefore, criteria (iii) and (iv) were satisfied, and the cargo owners were bound by the contract in the original form. However, a reasonable shipowner would have appreciated that the generators might have been the cause of the problem and would have investigated the situation before committing the cargo owners to tow at least as far as Dubai under the LOF. Accordingly the salvors had failed to discharge the burden of proving that the manager acted bona fide and reasonably in the interests of cargo in agreeing to a variation of the LOF by adding the Dubai/Colombo option.

Criteria (iii) and (iv) were not satisfied in the case of the variation. The court granted declarations that the LOF 90 was agreed between the Master of the *Pa Mar* and the salvors on 9 June and that the cargo owners were bound by that agreement. Furthermore, the agreement was subsequently varied by giving the owners an option to have the *Par Mar* and her cargo taken to Dubai/Colombo and that the cargo owners were not bound by that agreement.

The LOF is an established form of agreement which both the rescued party and the rescuer will find or agree to, and this agreement governs the right to remuneration determined by an arbitration award or by agreement. The signing of the LOF does not in any way change the nature of the rescue. The signing of this form does not constitute the passing of consideration and does not therefore affect the voluntary nature of the operation. Salvage law established over the centuries, recognized by the Brussels Convention 1910 (which has not been formally adopted by statute) a firm principle of 'no cure—no pay'. The basic principle behind the LOF 80 is 'no cure—no pay'.

Oil pollution disasters during the 1970s made it plain that salvors are still exposed to being unremunerated for performing a service which, although not successful in the sense of preserving maritime property and creating a fund out of which a salvage award may be paid, nevertheless such service does play a part in averting pollution or in avoiding likely pollution in coastal or harbour areas. Casualties such as the *Amoco Cadiz*, *Torre Canyon* and *Cristos Bitas* (which in 1978 was towed out into the Atlantic and deliberately sunk with her underwriters' blessing to avoid further risk) underlined the increasing need to have the then 1972 Lloyd's Form amended in this manner. More recently there have been incidents such as the *Braer* and *Exxon Valdez*.

Hull and cargo interests early in the 1970s argued in favour of the creation of a fourth piece of maritime property capable of being preserved and thus able to 'fund' a salvage reward. Basically it was called 'liability salvage'. It was supposed to be a fictional piece of property intended to be symbolic of attempts by volunteer salvors to avert danger to, to minimize damage to or generally preserve the marine environment arising from spillage from a laden and stricken tanker. This, they said, should be the fourth subject of salvage, additional to the existing and traditional three, ship, cargo and freight at risk. The P & I Clubs ('on' for third-party liability risks) became involved in discussions on which underwriters should be responsible for what. Agreement was eventually reached with the Hull and Cargo insurers regarding the appropriate responsibility for reward in respect of environmental damage prevention. The LOF 1980 broke new ground by departing from the 'no cure—no pay' principle to the limited extent when salvage services were rendered to tankers carrying cargoes of oil. It had long been recognized that the 'no cure—no pay' principle failed to meet the ecological needs of the twentieth century, particularly in respect of oil spills. The 'no cure—no pay' principle gave salvors little incentive to undertake a difficult and costly salvage operation (involving an incident and causing considerable risk of damage to the environment) where any success was unlikely.

The exception to the fundamental principle of 'no cure—no pay' was the introduction in the LOF 80 of a 'safety net' which was to encourage salvors to take on casualties which caused or threatened oil pollution. In limited circumstances, the salvors can claim against the shipowners their reasonably incurred expenses plus an increment of not more than 15 per cent of those expenses as the arbitrators consider fair. Any award under the 'safety net' provision was only to be made to the extent that the salvors' expenses together with the increment were greater than any amount otherwise recoverable under the salvage agreement. The limited circumstances in which the salvors can claim their expenses under the 'safety net' provision in the LOF 80 are:

(a) the property being salved is a tanker laden or partly laden with a cargo of potentially pollutant oil. In fact clause 1(a) of the LOF 90 provides that 'A contractor further agrees to use his best endeavours to prevent the escape of oil from the vessel while performing these services of salving the subject vessel and/or her cargo bunkers and stores;
(b) the salvor (contractor), his servants and agents are not negligent;
(c) the services are not successful or are only partially successful or the salvor is prevented from completing such services.

Within the meaning of the said exception to the principle of 'no cure—no pay' expenses shall in addition to actual out-of-profit expenses include a fair rate for all tugs, craft, personnel and other equipment used by the contractor in the services and oil shall mean crude oil, fuel oil, diesel oil and lubricating oil [see clause 1(a)]. As the provisions of the safety net relate solely to cargo, services which involve the salving of bunkers are not covered. Also, there are no provisions for salvage services involving vessels laden with chemical and other hazardous cargo. It appears that the safety net applies on a worldwide basis.

The 'safety net' award is made against the owners of the tanker alone. This departs from the normal 'no cure—no pay' situation where all the salved interests, shipowners, cargo and freight at risk bunkers should contribute rateably to the salvage award according to their respective values. Such liability of the shipowners is normally covered by their P & I Club. Clause 1 also provides that the amount of the salvor's remuneration shall be determined by arbitration in London in accordance with English law. It also allows the contracting parties to agree the appropriate currency in which security is to be provided failing which security will be given in pounds sterling (see below). Indeed, the *Amoco Cadiz* disaster is an ideal illustration of a wholly unsuccessful salvage attempt, and, being at the time a laden oil tanker bound to the terms of a Lloyd's Open Form, an equally admirable illustration of how Clause 1 of the LOF 80 would have applied to the facts and circumstances of that disaster if they had occurred after the LOF 80 had come into effect.

Clause 2 of the LOF 80 introduced afresh a new obligation that the owners of the stricken property co-operate generally with the contractor (salvor). This is of particular relevance in the matter of eventually obtaining access to the agreed place or a place of safety wherein the property may be formally redelivered to its owner. The owners must promptly accept redelivery at such place. It goes without saying that in practical terms a prerequisite for ultimate success in services of this nature is good co-operation between saviour and the party being saved.

Clause 4 deals with the provision of security. The salvor has to notify the Committee of Lloyd's and where practicable the owners of the amount of security required inclusive of costs, expenses and interest. Unless otherwise agreed by the parties such security shall be given to and in a form by the Committee of Lloyd's. The Committee is not responsible for the sufficiency of any security given. Under Clause 11 the Arbitrator has power to 'condemn the contractor in the whole or part of the expense of providing' excessive security. In the case of *The Tribels* [1985] 1 Lloyd's Rep. 128 the Admiralty Court restrained the salvors by injunction from seeking excessive security. Such injunction does not affect the owners' right to seek to have the salvors condemned if the security provided still turns out to be excessive.

In years past it was common that shipowners gave security not only on their own behalf, but also on behalf of the cargo they carried. However, as the years progressed they became less and less inclined to do this, since it was correspondingly popular for owners of cargo to refuse to contribute, on the grounds that the salvage services were necessitated in the first place by some unseaworthy condition of the vessel which carried the cargo, amounting to a fundamental breach of the contract of carriage. In modern times shipowners are reluctant to furnish security other than in respect of their own interests. Whilst the salvor during the negotiations leading up to the LOF 80 sought a provision imposing a duty on shipowners to give security on behalf of cargo this was not achieved.

However Clause 5 of the LOF 80 does provide that the shipowners, their servants and agents shall use their best endeavours to ensure that the cargo-owners provide security before the cargo is released. Certainly the salvor making use of the LOF is not without security. His very position as salvor entitles him to a maritime lien on the maritime property saved. Attaching as this lien does to the property (the 'res') the property may not be moved without the salvor's written agreement. In consideration of the property owner thus abiding by his agreement not to remove his property, the salvor will customarily undertake not to arrest the property to enforce his lien so long as adequate security is provided within 14 days after the termination of the salvage services (Clause 5). Only if the salvor has reasonable grounds for believing that the salved property would nevertheless be moved in breach of agreement will he resort to arrest procedure. If the salvor has to enforce his lien or arrest property the arbitrator is given power to include in his award the expenses incurred by the salvor including lien insurance. Clause 5 also provides for the provision of security by the shipowners where the 'safety net' provisions are likely to apply.

Much of the LOF 80 is devoted to the provisions for and the conduct of arbitration. Clause 6 is sub-divided into two subsections, (a) providing that where security within the provisions of the Agreement is given to the Committee of Lloyd's in whole or in part the Committee shall appoint an arbitrator in respect of the interests covered by such security, and (b) providing that whether or not security is given the Committee shall appoint the arbitrator upon receipt of a written or telex or telegraphic notice of a claim for arbitration from any of the parties entitled or authorized to make such a claim. Provisions for terminating the arbitration in the event of amicable resolution are found in Clause 7, which provides that where an arbitrator has been appointed by the Committee, and the parties do not wish to proceed, the parties shall jointly notify the Committee in writing or by telex or telegram and the committee may thereupon terminate the appointment of such arbitrator as they may have appointed under Clause 6. Clause 8 details the parties who are entitled to claim arbitration, namely the shipowners, cargo-owners, freight separately at risk, owners of bunkers and stores, salvor (contractor) and any other person who is the party to this Agreement.

Clause 10 empowers the arbitrator to fix the remuneration for the services rendered within the meaning of the agreement, and make an interim award for such payment on terms which seem fair and just. An arbitrator appointed by the Committee of Lloyd's has a reasonably wide measure of discretion. It is customary for an arbitrator to be a Queen's Counsel currently practising at the Admiralty Bar and with experience in maritime claims. The arbitrator may, according to the wording of the agreement, conduct the arbitration in a manner in which the arbitrator thinks fit (Clause 11). The provision for an interim award, or in other words a payment on account, is designed to meet the case where the salvor has incurred considerable expenses but may not obtain an arbitration award in his favour for some time. An appeal cannot be made from an interim award without the leave of the appeal arbitrator (Clause 13) but the salvor undertakes to repay the balance, if the final award is less than the interim award (Clause 15). Under Clause 11 the arbitrator can 'call for receive and act upon any such oral or documentary evidence or information (whether the same be strictly admissible as evidence or not) as he may think fit'. The parties are at liberty to adduce expert evidence at the arbitration unless the arbitrator shall otherwise direct. Expert evidence is particularly important in 'safety net' cases and assessing the risk to the salved property and the value of the salved property. Any award of the arbitrator (subject to appeal) is final and binding on all the parties concerned. The arbitrator and the Committee of Lloyd's may charge reasonable fees and expenses for their services in connexion with the arbitration, whether it proceeds to a hearing or not and all such fees and expenses shall be treated as part of the cost of the arbitration.

One piece of information normally withheld from the arbitrator is how much security has been demanded by the salvor. This is to enable him fairly to fix the reward with a mind uninfluenced by that particular factor. If, when the arbitrator is subsequently told, he considers the security demand excessive he has power to penalize the salvor (Clause 11). At the arbitration hearing, documentary evidence will be submitted and oral evidence is quite rare as statements/expert reports will already have been provided. Oral evidence may be necessary where there are allegations of negligence against the salvor. At the arbitration hearing, Counsel will usually be present—one on behalf of the salvors and one on behalf of the other parties to the agreement either separately or jointly. The arbitrator's award will be accompanied by his reasons for making the award which will not actually be part of the award itself.

Clause 12 provides for the payment of interest on the award after the expiration of 21 days from the date of publication of the award until payment. Interest is normally awarded also for the time prior to the salvage award.

In the case of the *Yolaine* [1995] 2 Lloyd's Rep. 7, common law salvage was rendered to a 35' cruising ketch in 1991. One of the questions raised was when interest should start to run. The plaintiffs' salvors argued that interest should be awarded as from 26 October 1991 which was the date of the termination of the services. The owner of the yacht argued that following the approach in the case of the *Rilland* [1971] 1 Lloyd's Rep. 455 interest should only be awarded from the date when it could fairly be said that persons in the position of the defendants, acting honestly and reasonably, would pay. He submitted that the appropriate date was July 1992 when the repairs were completed and when the salved value had been assessed.

The High Court mentioned that there had been a number of changes in the LOF, since the *Rilland* case, namely LOF 1980, LOF 1990 and LOF 1995. The judge referred to clause 10 of the LOF 90 whereby arbitrators award interest from the date of termination of the services, save in special circumstances. The High Court decided that they should not approach the exercise of the court's discretion with regard to interest in a way differently from the way in which arbitrators exercise their discretion in the vast majority of salvage disputes arising under the LOF resolved in London. Accordingly, interest should be awarded from the termination of the services save in special circumstances. However, some special circumstances were found in this somewhat unusual case, and it was decided that it would have taken the owner or, more accurately, his insurers, some time to assess the position. Therefore, interest was awarded from a little after termination of the services, namely from 1 January 1992. The judge decided that the appropriate course with regard to the rate of interest was to follow the practice of Lloyd's Arbitrators, which is 2 per cent over the appropriate base rate for sterling.

The LOF 80 also includes provisions for appeal (Clause 13) which in practice is heard by a single appeal arbitrator. Clause 14 contains provisions for the conduct of any appeal. There is a limited period of time within which an appeal may be lodged and the appeal arbitrator is also appointed by the Committee of Lloyd's. Unless the appeal arbitrator in his discretion otherwise allows, no new evidence shall be called. The appeal arbitrator has the power to increase, reduce or leave the original arbitration award unaltered and to condemn the salvor for the cost of providing excessive security and to award the costs of appeal. So far as the procedure is concerned on appeal, this is generally speaking the same as the procedure to be observed in the original arbitration. Specific time limits are set out in Clause 15 for the payment of sums due to the salvor.

Clause 17 importantly provides that the Master in entering into the LOF does so as 'Agent for the vessel, her cargo, freight, bunkers and stores and the respective owners thereof'. Clause 18 allows the arbitrator in making his award and considering the amount of the salvor's expenses to take account of currency fluctuations. In practical terms, this is known as 'downpush' and 'uplift'. Clause 20 permits the salvor to claim on behalf of sub-contractors where the sub-contractors have performed salvage services. In these circumstances the claiming salvors have to indemnify and hold harmless the owners of the property salved against all claims by or liabilities incurred by the sub-contractors, servants or agents including the Master and crew members. Quite often the main and sub-contractors (salvors) enter into a sub-contract (award-sharing) agreement. Clause 21 which also provides that the salvor can limit liability under the 1976 Limitation Convention.

However, it is quite clear that a Master has ostensible authority to accept an offer of salvage services on behalf of the shipowner from the case of *Unique Mariner* [1978] 1 Lloyd's Rep. 438. This case also illustrates the use of the LOF on 'no cure—no pay' terms. It was relied upon by the salvors in the case of the *Choko Star* (above) when arguing that the Master had implied authority to bind cargo owners to a salvage contract but the Court of Appeal decided that such term could only be implied if the Master acted as agent of necessity. It should be borne in mind that in the case of *Unique Mariner* the vessel was in ballast.

*Unique Mariner* [1978] 1 Lloyd's Rep. 438

In February 1977 the vessel ran aground about 30 miles south-west of Singapore whilst on a ballast voyage. Efforts to refloat her were unfruitful and her Master cabled his managers for assistance. He received a reply that a suitable tug would be despatched from Singapore. Meanwhile, the tug *Salvaliant* observed the stricken ship from its nearby position on another assignment and proceeded to her aid. This tug's Master boarded *Unique Mariner* and offered to salve her. The ship's Master under the mistaken impression that *Salvaliant* was the tug he was expecting from Singapore signed a Lloyd's form on a 'no cure—no pay' basis.

Subsequent cabled advice confirmed that the other tug was on its way. This prompted the ship's Master to tell the Master of *Salvaliant* to cease the arrangements he was putting in hand. He also asked for the return of the Lloyd's open form, which request was refused. The other tug eventually arrived and after several attempts successfully refloated the grounded ship. The owners of *Unique Mariner* disputed the binding effect of the Lloyd's salvage agreement and the ability of the owners of *Salvaliant* to claim remuneration and/or compensation for wrongful dismissal as salvors. They put forward for reasons for the agreement lacking validity: misrepresentation, want of authority, mistake and non-disclosure.

*Held*: On the issue of authority that the implied authority of the ship's Master was to accept the offer of suitable services on the terms of any reasonable contract. There was nothing unusual in the Master's accepting *Salvaliant's* offer and conversely no reason why the Master of *Salvaliant* should have doubted that he possessed the implied authority. On the question of mistake, even if, at the time of signing the Lloyd's form, the Master thought he was dealing with the Master of the tug expressly despatched from Singapore, the Master of *Salvaliant* did not know this nor could he reasonably have been deemed to know and in any case such a mistake would not go to the root of the contract.

Mr Justice Brandon said at page 449:

'The principles of law applicable to this issue can, I think, be stated in three propositions, as follows: first, the relevant authority of a Master, for the purpose of deciding whether his owners are bound, as against a third party, by an act which he has purported to do on their behalf, is his ostensible, rather than his actual, authority; secondly, the ostensible authority of a Master is the same as his implied actual authority, unless the latter has been restricted by express instructions from his owners or their representatives, and the third party concerned is, or should be taken to be, aware of such restriction; thirdly, the implied actual authority of a Master, unless restricted by such instructions lawfully given, extends to doing whatever is incidental to, or necessary for, the successful prosecution of the voyage and the safety and preservation of the ship.'

Parker LJ said in the Court of Appeal hearing of the *Choko Star* [1990] 1 Lloyd's Rep. at page 523:

'The principles there set out (above in the *Unique Mariner*) may well be correct when the matter under consideration is, as it was in that case, the authority of an admitted agent of the shipowner to bind his principals. In the instant case, however, we are concerned with the question whether the master, or shipowners, neither of whom is the agent of the cargo-owners, can bind them by a contract with salvage services purporting to be made on their behalf, otherwise in circumstances giving rise to an agency of necessity . . . Unless, therefore, it is possible in a particular case to imply a term into the contracts of carriage that, in circumstances falling short of those constituting the master an agent of necessity, the Master is authorized to contract on behalf of cargo-owners, the question of the master's or shipowners' authority must depend on all the circumstances of the case. There can be no preliminary question which could be answered in favour of salvors. It was, albeit without much enthusiasm, suggested that such a term could be implied in the contracts of carriage herein questioned. I have no hesitation in rejecting such suggestion. I can see no basis upon which any such term could be implied.'

Slade LJ also said at page 525:

'These three propositions (in the *Unique Mariner* above) do not, in my judgment, greatly assist the resolution of the issues before this court, which concern the actual and ostensible authority of the shipowner or the Master to bind the cargo-owners to a contract with salvors. Until an emergency arises, such as to give rise to an agent of necessity, there is no question of the shipowner or Master being an agent for the cargo owners. Accordingly, it is not possible to spell out authority for either of them to bind the cargo-owners to a salvage contract, as merely incidental to his pre-existing general authority as an agent'.

On the issue of non-disclosure, contracts of salvage services did not require uberrimae fides. Lastly there were no grounds for invalidating the agreement for misrepresentation. The matter proceeded through arbitration and appeal arbitration at which a special case for the court was stated. The Admiralty Court then held that under the common law salvors may be summarily dismissed by the Master of the salved ship at any time subject to payment only of sums (in the nature of salvage) to represent compensation for loss of opportunity. Further, that dispossessed salvors may only recover damages for breach of contract if there existed some salvage agreement (e.g. Lloyd's Open Form) which included some implied term, but if the salvor was willing to do the work, the party who engaged him under the agreement should not prevent him so doing. The Master of *The Unique Mariner* had repudiated the LOF agreement and the shipowners were liable to pay damages.

On the want of authority issue the court restated the principle of law as follows: for the purposes of deciding whether the owners of a stricken vessel are bound as against a third party, it is a Master's ostensible authority, not his actual authority, which counts. Qualifying this, the ostensible authority is the same as implied actual authority, unless the latter has been restricted by express instructions from his owners or their representatives and the third party concerned was, or should have been, aware of such restriction. Another principle to be applied is that the implied actual authority of a ship's Master, unless it is restricted by such instructions lawfully given, extends to doing whatever is incidental to, or necessary for, the successful prosecution of the voyage and the safety and preservation of the ship.

The very fact that a substantial part of the agreement is devoted to arbitration provisions gives the document a basically procedural flavour and it could be reasonably argued that the substantive law which it contains is somewhat superficial. The duty of care which is now clearly established (see *The Tojo Maru* [1971] 1 Lloyd's Rep. 341, HL) as existing, is however, firmly implied against a salvor when the LOF is used by the wording of the first three clauses of the document. The LOF has achieved a high and justified degree of popularity and it has separate advantages. The principle of 'no cure—no pay', one of the essential ingredients of salvage in any event, is specifically expressed. (Indeed the words are printed in large block capitals in the heading to the agreement.) This is an obvious advantage to the owner of the property being saved. Secondly, the agreement is couched in simple, fair and readily understandable terms, most of which are common knowledge to seafarers. When time is short due to the urgency of the situation, the Master of the vessel will know that he is safe to accept the terms and conditions of the agreement orally, even though he may not necessarily put his signature to it until the salvage has been successfully concluded. A third advantage is the 'safety-net' provisions (increased by the LOF 90) and the reference of disputes to London arbitration, the salvage arbitrator having much experience in these matters.

## THE INTERNATIONAL CONVENTION OF SALVAGE 1989

Much concern was expressed about the need for an adequate salvage response following the *Amoco Cadiz* oil pollution incident. A draft Salvage Convention was proposed in a meeting of the Comité Maritime International in Montreal in 1981. Following further discussions, the International Convention of Salvage was adopted on 28 April 1989 by a conference convened under the auspices of the International Maritime Organisation. Its intention was to come into force one year after 15 States had expressed their consent to be bound by it. This Convention came into force in the UK on 1 January 1995, being incorporated in the Merchant Shipping (Salvage and Pollution) Act 1994.

The whole of the 1994 Act has now been repealed. Section 224 of the Merchant Shipping Act 1995 provides that Part 1 of Schedule 11 (the 1989 Salvage Convention) has the force of law in the United Kingdom. However, this does not affect any rights or liabilities arising out of any salvage operations started or other acts done before 1 January 1995. The Convention and the 1995 Act deal with a number of matters. Its most important aims are to revise the law relating to the provision of salvage services so as to provide better protection to the environment and to encourage salvors to undertake salvage operations in respect of vessels and other property in danger.

Article 1 of the Convention opens with definitions. A salvage operation is defined as 'any act or activity undertaken to assist a vessel or other property in danger in navigable waters or in any other waters whatsoever'. This overturns the case of the *Goring* [1988] 1 Lloyd's Rep. 397 that a salvage operation must take place in tidal waters before the Admiralty Court has jurisdiction. A vessel, to be the proper subject of maritime salvage and rights arising from it, must be 'capable of navigation'.

Property is defined as 'any property not permanently and intentionally attached to the shoreline and including freight at risk'. Property can give rise to salvage independently of any vessel. Fixed or floating platforms are excluded from the operation of the Convention.

'Damage to the environment' is defined as 'substantial physical damage to human health or to marine life or resources in coastal or inland waters or areas adjacent thereto, caused by a pollution, contamination, fire, explosion or similar major events'. This acknowledges the reality on a vastly increased scale of a salvor's efforts being concentrated on averting or at least minimizing harm to the marine environment as a result of a spillage or potential spillage from, e.g. a laden and endangered ship. The scope of the word 'environment' in this context includes human health, marine life and resources in coastal areas or inland waters.

Contained in Articles 6 and 7 are explicit provisions about the exercising of undue influence by salvors hoping to extract unreasonably favourable terms out of a Master beset by worry about the danger confronting his vessel, crew, and cargo. Whilst the parties can contract out of the Convention, a salvage contract may be nullified or modified if it has been entered into under undue influence or if the terms are inequitable or if the payment under the contract is in an excessive degree too large or too small for the services actually rendered. The word 'inequitable' is particularly appropriate and in accord with the concept of maritime salvage being based on the idea of an equitable right to remuneration for volunteers who have saved the property of others at sea. The right was never based on a contract. The law of salvage is not part of the law of contract as emphasized at the beginning of this chapter. Importantly, Article 6(3) provides that no contract may exclude the salvor's duty to prevent or minimize damage to the environment.

The Convention provides that the Master (or the owners) has authority to 'conclude such contracts on behalf of the owners of the property on board the vessel'. The Master has clear authority in all cases to enter into a salvage contract on behalf of the owners of property on board the vessel. This is welcome because some disasters in the last 30-odd years, notable examples being the *Amoco Cadiz* and the *Union Star*, have tended to create the impression that the concept was rapidly vanishing into oblivion that the Master was exclusively in control of his own thoughts and judgment on the urgency of any given disaster situation and the need or otherwise to accept outside help.

Article 8 emphasizes the importance of co-operation between the owner of the property being saved and the saviour. The duties of a salvor are expressly to include the exercise of due care to prevent or minimize damage to the environment and one cannot contract out of this duty. Indeed the whole concept of preservation of the environment is an underlying theme of this Convention, emphasized the more so because both the saviour and saved have such a duty.

The principles contained in *The Tojo Maru* [1971] 1 Lloyd's Rep. 341, HL (also referred to at page 387 of Chapter 9) are underscored in Article 8, that the salvor is under a duty to carry out the operation with reasonable care and skill, the implication being that failure to do so will saddle him with legal liability for the consequences of such failure. As to the standard of care expected, this depends upon his status as salvor, whether a professional at the business, in which case the law will require him to use the skill expected of and the expertise available to a person of his calling, or merely an 'amateur', such as an ocean ship's Master, who will be deemed to be possessed of a lesser degree of skill and, therefore, not burdened with such a high degree of care.

There is also a duty of the salvor to seek assistance from other salvors when circumstances reasonably require this and to accept intervention in certain circumstances.

An example of salvors competing to obtain the same 'job' is the case of *The Pergo* [1987] 1 Lloyd's Rep. 582.

The vessel *Pergo* was abandoned by her Master and crew and ran aground on a rocky shore in East Lothian, Scotland. The salvors using three fishing vessels waited for the *Pergo* to refloat on the next high tide. Whilst waiting they switched off their navigation lights in order not to betray their presence to other vessels capable of effecting a rescue. On refloating they towed her to Leith. The salvors contended that the *Pergo* was a derelict and that but for the salvage services she would have become exposed to severe weather and would have been wrecked. The owners argued that the *Pergo* would have refloated, drifted into the Firth of Forth and have been rescued by a tug. The Scottish courts had to consider the appropriate amount of salvage.

It was decided that in the absence of an explanation from the Master and crew of the *Pergo* there was a prima facie inference that she was a derelict. The fact that she was a derelict did not itself increase the salvage award, but it was relevant to its bearing the degree of danger faced by the *Pergo*. The salvors displayed a high degree of skill and used intimate local knowledge of the area where the *Pergo* had grounded and if the salvors had not intervened the *Pergo* would have been in grave danger of becoming a total loss. The failure to display navigation lights while waiting for the *Pergo* to refloat revealed a degree of astuteness on the part of the salvors, but in the circumstances that called for no more than a modest discount on the special value which their local knowledge had brought to the salvage operation. The incident during the towage operation which endangered one of the salving vessels justified neither an increase nor decrease in the award. The appropriate award for the services rendered to the *Pergo* was £60,000.

The duty of the ship's Master to render assistance to those in danger of being lost at sea is, expectedly, preserved in the Convention although a shipowner will be under no liability for his Master's breach of such duty which presumably emasculates the imposing of the duty. If the Master fails in his duty he is liable for an offence in the UK (Article 3—Part II of Schedule 11 to the Merchant Shipping Act 1995). The owner of the property has to co-operate with the salvor and to accept delivery of the property at the termination of the services when reasonably requested.

Article 11 obliges a Contracting State party to take into account the need for co-operation between salvors, other interested parties and public authorities to ensure a successful salvage operation. This seems aimed at some problems experienced by salvors in persuading harbour authorities to allow entry of a stricken vessel into port for redelivery purposes.

Article 12 underlines 'no cure—no pay'. It provides that 'salvage operations which have had a useful result give right to a reward' and 'except as otherwise provided (ie special compensation) no payment is due under this Convention if the salvage operations have had no useful effect'. 'Useful result' is not defined. It seems that some of the property must have been preserved or in other words there is a salved fund.

Article 13 details the factors which must be taken into account in the fixing of a salvage reward. Salvage operations must be encouraged. The factors which are to be taken into account in assessing a salvage award include the salved value of the vessel and other property, measure of success, nature and degree of danger, skill and efforts of the salvors, time used and expenses and losses incurred by the salvors, the risk of liability and other risks run by the salvors or their equipment, the promptness of the services rendered, availability and use of vessels or other equipment intended for salvage operations, state of readiness and efficiency of the salvor's equipment and value.

One new factor is the skill and efforts of the salvors in preventing or minimizing damage to the environment. However this factor would have been taken into account by the arbitrators in fixing a salvage award such as preventing the escape of oil and the consequences of such escape is part of salvage by reason of Clause 1(a) of the LOF 80 and also by reason of clause 1(a)(ii) of the LOF 90. There is an equivalent provision in the LOF 95. Although the salvor's efforts in protecting the environment are to be taken into account in assessing his remuneration this is still subject to the 'no cure—no pay' principle set out in Article 12 and also subject to the provision in Article 13(3) that the reward shall not exceed the salved value of the vessel and other property, i.e. cargo, bunkers and freight at risk. Article 13(2) provides that payment of the reward is in proportion to the salved values. It only applies to rewards under Article 13. It is worth noting that the UK has not exercised its right under Article 13(2) to make the ship responsible for payment of all salvage with a right of recourse against cargo interests. Article 4 of Part II, Schedule 11 to the Merchant Shipping Act 1995 which has effect in the United Kingdom provides 'In fixing a reward under Article 13 and assessing special compensation under Article 14 the court or arbitrator (or, in Scotland, arbiter) is under no duty to fix a reward under Article 13 up to the maximum salved value of the vessel and other property before assessing the special compensation to be paid under Article 14'.

The saving of life is dealt with in Article 16. No-one is obliged to pay salvage for the saving of life but the Convention respects any national law which may contain contrary provisions. In the UK, in certain circumstances the Secretary of

State may, if he thinks fit, pay salvage for life salvage (Article 5 of Part II of Schedule 11 to the Merchant Shipping Act 1995). Where, however, property is successfully salved then an enhancement may be made in respect of the saving of life if life was saved during the same operation. Article 17 requires that the salvor must be a volunteer. Services performed under a pre-existing contract are not salvage.

*The Texaco Southampton* [1983] 1 Lloyd's Rep. 94 (Australia).
The vessel *Texaco Southampton* after being disabled was towed into Sydney Harbour under a towage contract. The crew of the tug claimed a salvage contract and the question was whether the crew were volunteers.

*Held*: Services rendered by a towing vessel to a distressed ship pursuant to a towage contract were not voluntary. They were not salvage services but towage services only, unless supervening events placed the service outside the scope of the contract and that exception was not fulfilled unless: (1) the tow was in danger by reason of circumstances which could not reasonably have been contemplated by the parties; and (2) risks were incurred or duties performed by the tug which could not reasonably be held to be within the scope of the contract. The work performed by the crew did not go outside the scope of their normal duties and exposed them to no risk which were not within the contemplation of their contract of employment. Even though the towage was performed under a sub-contract the crew were not volunteers and could not claim a salvage award.

Article 18 provides that the salvor may lose all or part of the salvage reward if the salvage operations have become necessary or more difficult because of the fault or neglect of the salvor or where the salvor has been guilty of fraud or other dishonest conduct. Article 19 provides that the salvor will not be entitled to a salvage reward where the shipowner and Master expressly and reasonably have refused salvage assistance. Article 20 preserves the salvors' right to a maritime lien under any international Convention or national law. The salvor may not enforce his maritime lien when satisfactory security for his claim, including interest has been tendered or provided.

Article 21 emphasizes that the salved property may not, without the salvor's consent, be removed from its place of safety to which it is initially brought without satisfactory security having first been furnished by its owner. A special duty is placed on the owner of a salved vessel to try his best to ensure that the salved cargo-owner provides security for the claims against him (cargo), including interest and costs. Security is provided separately by ship and cargo and other interests, i.e. bunkers. Furthermore the salved vessel and other property cannot be removed from the place of arrival after completion of the salvage services without the consent of the salvor until satisfactory security has been provided. Article 22 provides for the making of an interim payment as is 'just and fair'. Any claim for salvage under the Convention is time barred after two years commencing on the day when the salvage operation was terminated (Article 23).

## SPECIAL COMPENSATION FOR PREVENTING OR MINIMIZING DAMAGE TO THE ENVIRONMENT

A further incentive to the salvors to protect the environment is provided by Article 14 which gives the salvor extra compensation in the case of a salvage operation which protects the environment. Under Article 14(1) the salvor is entitled to special compensation where he has carried out salvage operations on a vessel which by itself or its cargo threaten damage to the environment and has failed to earn a reward under Article 13 which is 'at least equivalent to the special compensation assessable in accordance with this Article'. Such special compensation is obtainable from the owner of the vessel (usually the appropriate P & I Club) equivalent to his expenses. It is not necessary for the salvor to achieve any success in preventing or minimizing damage to the environment. If success is achieved, a greater amount of special compensation is payable [see Article 14(2)].

The expenses recoverable by the salvor are defined as 'out-of-pocket' expenses reasonably incurred by the salvor in the salvage operation and a fair rate for equipment and personnel actually and reasonably used in the salvage operation. In order for the salvor to obtain special compensation, it must be shown that the vessel by herself or her cargo threatened damage to the environment. This goes further than the safety net provisions in the LOF 80 which is limited to tankers laden with oil. Another requirement is that the salvor must have failed to earn a reward under Article 13, that is at least equivalent to the special compensation available. In practice, the salvage arbitrator will firstly have to consider what award would be payable under Article 13 and then consider the amount of special compensation and whether this compensation is greater than an Article 13 award (see the case of *Nagasaki Spirit* below). It is clear, however, that, if there is no salved fund, no reward under Article 13 is payable and the salvor may bring a claim under Article 14 if he complies with the requirements.

If the salvage operation actually prevents or minimizes damage to the environment, the salvor will be able to claim enhanced special compensation under Article 14(2). The amount of the salvage award may be increased up to a maximum of 30 per cent of the expenses incurred by the salvor. It goes on to say that the arbitrator may indeed increase the special compensation to 100 per cent of the expense incurred when it is deemed fair and just to do so, bearing in mind the relevant criteria set out in Article 13, paragraph 1. Therefore the Convention goes further than the 15 per cent increment allowed in LOF 80. The amount of special compensation, payable only by the owner of the vessel, can be more than the salved fund.

## LLOYD'S FORM OF SALVAGE AGREEMENT (LOF 90)

The LOF 90 was introduced following the International Convention of Salvage 1989 and incorporates some of the changes brought in by the 1989 Convention (which is now part of UK law by reason of the Merchant Shipping (Salvage and Pollution) Act 1994), mainly those relating to the provision for special compensation. Although there is now a LOF 95, the LOF 90 is still used. The intention of the LOF 90 was to bring into effect immediately the provisions of the 1989 Convention which significantly expanded the safety net concept. The duty upon the salvor under the LOF 80 to use his best endeavours to prevent the escape of oil is widened by LOF 90 so as to prevent or minimize damage to the environment. It basically is still 'no cure—no pay' apart from the special compensation. Some of the changes brought about by the LOF 90 are highlighted below.

Under clause 1(a)(ii) the salvor (contractor) undertakes an obligation to use his best endeavours (while performing the salvage services) to prevent or minimize damage to the environment. The LOF 90 reflects the 1989 Convention, as it allows salvage operations in navigable waters or in any other waters whatsoever so that a salvage award is obtainable for operations in non-tidal waters (contrast the case of the *Goring* [1986] 1 Lloyd's Rep. 127, see page 318 above). Clause 2 provides that Articles 1(a) to (e), 8, 13.1, 13.2 first sentence, 13.3 and 14 of the 1989 Convention are incorporated and these Articles are set out in detail at the end of the form after Clause 19. The amount of the salvor's remuneration is still determined by London arbitration and governed by English law including the English law of salvage.

Under Clause 3 the owners, their servants and agents are obliged to co-operate fully with the salvor not only in the salvage operation but also in the process of obtaining entry to the place named or the place of safety as defined in clause 1 which reflects the duty of co-operation provided by the 1989 Convention albeit differently worded. The salvor is entitled to make reasonable use of the vessel's machinery, equipment etc, for the services of the salvage operation free of expense but shall not necessarily damage, abandon or sacrifice this equipment or any property which is the subject of this agreement.

Clauses 4 and 5 deal with the provision of security. Under clause 4(d) the owners are obliged to use their best endeavours to ensure that the cargo owners provide their proportion of security before the cargo is released. Under clause 5 the salvor has a maritime lien on the property salved for his remuneration until security has been provided. The owners of the salved property are under an obligation not to remove their property from the place of safety without the consent in writing of the salvors and the salvors may not withhold such consent unreasonably. Also, under clause 4(b) where the exception to the principle of 'no cure—no pay' under Convention Article 14 becomes likely to be applicable, the owners shall on the demand of the salvors provide security for the salvor's special compensation. The salvage arbitrator has power to include in the salvage award expenses reasonably incurred by the salvor in (1) ascertaining, demanding and obtaining the amount of security reasonably required and (2) enforcing and/or protecting by insurance or otherwise or taking reasonable steps to enforce and/or protect his lien.

Clauses 6 and 7 deal with arbitration. Clause 6(c) provides that the Council of Lloyd's can recover their fees, costs and expenses where an arbitrator has been appointed and the parties do not proceed to arbitration. Clause 7 provides that the salvor's remuneration shall not be diminished by reason of the exception to the principle of 'no cure—no pay' under Article 14 of the 1989 Convention.

Clause 8 provides that any party to the salvage agreement who wishes to adduce evidence shall nominate a person in the UK to represent him, failing which the arbitrator shall proceed as if the party has renounced his right to be heard or to adduce evidence. Therefore parties who are not represented are still liable for any part of the salvage award, provided they have had reasonable notice of the arbitration.

Clause 9 details the conduct of the arbitration. In particular, the arbitrator has power to admit oral or documentary evidence or information as he thinks fit and conduct the arbitration as he thinks fit subject to the procedural rules of Lloyd's Council. Such rules provide that, within six weeks of the appointment of the salvage arbitrator, he shall call a preliminary meeting of the parties unless the parties agree a consent order which the arbitrator approves. At the meeting the arbitrator must give directions as may be fair and just such as fixing dates for proof of values, discovery, expert evidence. The aim of these procedural rules is to ensure that the salvage arbitration is heard as soon as practicably possible because the salvor who has incurred expenses should not experience cash flow problems pending the determination of the salvage reward.

Clause 10 deals with interest. It specifically provides that the salvage arbitrator has a discretion to award interest as from the date of the termination of the services until the publication of the award (as well as from 21 days after the award until payment). As interest can now be paid for the whole period of time, this is an incentive to resolve the arbitration speedily. Clauses 11 and 12 deal with the conduct of any appeal and Clause 13 with payment of any salvage award. Under Lloyd's procedural rules, a party challenging the arbitrator's findings on the salved value or that as to the person whose property was at risk must give grounds of appeal in the Notice of Appeal.

Clause 18 provides that where there is no longer any reasonable prospect of a useful result leading to the salvage reward under Article 13 the owners can terminate the services of the salvor by giving notice to the salvor in writing.

The LOF 90 also incorporates Articles 13.1, 13.2 first sentence, 13.3 and 14 of the 1989 Convention. Article 13.1 states 10 separate criteria which the arbitrator is obliged to take into account when fixing an award. These include the salved value of the vessel and other property, the skill and efforts of the salvor in preventing or minimizing damage to the environment, the measure of success obtained by the salvor, the nature and degree of the danger, the skill and efforts of the salvor, the time used and expenses and losses incurred by the salvor etc. Article 13.2 says that a salvage award is to be paid by the owners of the salved property in proportion to their respective salved values. Article 13.3 states the principle that a conventional salvage award, exclusive of any interest and recoverable legal costs, cannot exceed the salved value of the vessel and other property.

The incorporation of Article 14 of the 1989 Convention into the LOF 90 is of paramount importance although the Attachment 1 (which concerns the common understanding of Articles 13 and 14) is not incorporated. Normally an award under Article 13 is split rateably between all the interests saved by the salvage operation such as the vessel, cargo, freight at risk and bunkers, and any salvage award is paid by the hull and cargo underwriters. However, an award under Article 14 is only paid by the owners and, normally, by their P & I Club subject to any dispute on cover. Also, time charterer members of the Charterers' P & I Club have their salvage contributions in respect of bunkers and freight at risk paid out of Club funds. It is useful to consider the requirements of a salvor to obtain an award for special compensation (the widened safety net provisions) under Article 14.

Article 14(1) provides:

If the salvor has carried out salvage operations in respect of a vessel which by itself or its cargo threatened damage to the environment and has failed to earn a reward under Article 13 at least equivalent to the special compensation assessable in accordance with this Article, he shall be entitled to special compensation from the owner of that vessel equivalent to his expenses as herein defined.

A salvage operation is defined in Article 1(a) as 'any act or activity undertaken to assist a vessel or any other property in danger in navigable waters or in any waters whatsoever'. A vessel is defined in Article 1(b) as 'any ship or craft, or any structure capable of navigation'.

The entitlement to special compensation is triggered by the vessel by itself or its cargo having threatened damage to the environment. There is a distinction between the vessel and her cargo. Article 14 applies whatever the nature of the pollutant, oilcargo, hazardous chemical cargoes and other cargoes capable of pollution, bunkers, slops. It should be borne in mind that pollution damage is also relevant to an Article 13 normal 'no cure—no pay' reward. It only matters that damage to the environment is threatened. Under Article 14.1, the salvor can obtain an award of special compensation in circumstances where no actual services or benefits have been conferred and the award of special compensation consists only of expenses with no increment.

The question can arise as to what point in time is 'threatened damage to the environment' judged. Is it when the salvage operations commence, or after completion of the salvage operation when all the facts are known? What is the situation if a threat originally exists but is removed before the completion of the salvage services? What is the situation if a threat only becomes apparent to the salvor some time after the salvage operation was commenced? There is nothing in the 1989 Convention limiting the threat to the commencement of the salvage operations or at any other time. A situation can arise during the salvage operation causing a threat of damage to the environment. It would not be right that the salvor could not recover his expenses for preventing damage in view of the purpose of the Convention. It is thought that a threat should not be judged purely by hindsight, for instance, if a vessel with explosive cargo on board and a lot of bunkers is seen drifting ashore in bad weather, a reasonable man must take a view that there is a risk of substantial damage to the environment. If circumstances change, there is still a threat even though it did not exist at the outset. Whereas in assessing danger for the purposes of Article 13.1 which sets out the criteria for assessing a reward, one looks at the danger (and the degree of danger) to the salved property at the commencement of the salvage operations. On the other hand, speculation of a threat is insufficient.

'Threat of damage' seems to convey a wider meaning than danger of damage which is a common law requirement of salvage, and under Article 13. One way of approaching this question could be to ask whether there is a realistic possibility of damage to the environment. All the circumstances, facts surrounding the salvage operation should be considered and factors which could be taken into account are risk of pollution affecting the shoreline, risk of an explosion causing damage which is prevented by the salvage operation. Pure economic loss to the local population should not be taken into account, nor physical damage to an individual property unless there is potential damage to the environment as a whole. The salvor must prove that there is a real risk, not a remote risk, of damage to the environment.

What is meant by damage to the environment? This is defined in Article 1(d) of the 1989 Convention incorporated into the LOF 90, namely 'substantial physical damage to human health or to marine life or resources in coastal or inland waters or areas adjacent thereto, caused by pollution, contamination, fire, explosion or similar major incidents'. Article 1(a) is also interesting in that it defines a salvage operation as 'any act or activity undertaken to assist a vessel or any other property in danger in navigable waters or in any other waters whatsoever'. In order to understand the effect of Article 1(d), the salvage arbitrator may well look at the overall purpose of the 1989 Convention and the travaux préparatoires. In the CMI Report on the draft Convention in 1981, it was stated that:

> 'By using the words "substantial" and "major" as well as the reference to "pollution, explosion, contamination, fire", it is intended to make it clear that the definition does not include damage to any particular person or installation. There must be a risk of damage of a more general nature in the area concerned, and it must be a risk of substantial damage'.

So if a barrel of oil is lost, which causes localized damage, this is unlikely to be 'damage to the environment'; however, if a barrel of highly toxic material is lost, this is likely to have a much wider effect and cause major damage to the environment. If a ship runs aground and as a result of bottom damage, her bunkers escape into the sea causing damage to a tourist beach then this falls within Article 1(d). Such damage must occur 'in coastal or inland waters or areas adjacent thereto'. It should be borne in mind that the safety net provisions of the LOF 1980 had no territorial restrictions. So if a tanker is now towed out into the middle of the ocean and sunk causing pollution, it is unlikely that the salvors can claim special compensation under LOF 90 but the salvor might have been able to recover his expenses under the LOF 80.

There is no definition of 'substantial' physical damage or of a 'major' incident in Article 1(d) of the 1989 Convention. This involves questions of law and fact. The CMI Report to the IMO on the 1981 Draft Convention states:

> 'The *Amoco Cadiz* incident demonstrates the need for rules prescribing the duties on the owners and the Master of the vessel in danger as well as on the salvor, in similar situations. It also became clear that the existing rules of salvage did not offer sufficient incentives to induce the salvor to render salvage services in cases where there is very little prospect of succeeding in saving the property while, on the other hand, major salvage operations might be urgently needed to prevent or minimize damage to the environment. A general revision of the traditional rules of salvage as contained in the 1910 Convention (i.e. Brussels Convention on Salvage) was also needed in the light of the age of these rules and the substantial developments since they were formulated'.

The 1989 Convention does not define the degree of threat to the environment. Article 14.1 provides that the salvor can obtain his expenses irrespective of the degree of threat. It does not matter whether the threat is imminent, grave, long term or minimal. The degree of threat can be relevant with regard to assessing the increment under Article 14.2. It is thought that the threatened damage is not confined to major casualties such as the *Amoco Cadiz* but has a wider application.

The idea behind the Convention was to encourage salvors to undertake salvage operations and to protect the environment and in fact the preamble to the Convention states 'the increased concern for the environment' and is 'conscious of the major contribution which efficient and timely salvage operations can make to the protection of the environment'. It should be borne in mind that 'substantial physical damage' must be limited to the 'area concerned'. It may be that it is sufficient if a reasonable person considers that there is a realistic possibility of damage occurring at some stage during the salvage.

The salvor must also prove that he has failed to earn a reward under Article 13 that is at least equivalent to the special compensation available. Unless there is no salved fund available and no claim under Article 13 then the salvage arbitrator will have to take two steps before deciding whether any special compensation is payable. First he will have to assess any reward under Article 13 and secondly, assess the amount of special compensation under Article 14. Only if the latter is greater than the former will the salvor be entitled to special compensation. The balance is payable by the shipowner without any recovery from the cargo-owner in general average. Sometimes the determination of awards under Articles 13 and 14 are dealt with separately.

In fact, Attachment 1 to the 1989 Convention provides that 'The Tribunal is under no duty to fix a reward under Article 13 up to the maximum salved value of the vessel and other property before assessing the special compensation to be paid under Article 14'. This is implemented in the UK (Article 4 of Part II of Schedule 11 of the Merchant Shipping Act 1995). Therefore, it is unlikely that a very large Article 13 award will be made before special compensation is considered which will be paid by the owner and not cargo interests. In some circumstances Article 13 will not even be considered because there is no salved fund, the vessel and her cargo being lost or where the salved fund is so small or the salvor has achieved no success or very limited success and there is little point in bringing a claim under Article 13. The value of the salved fund and the degree of success is irrelevant to determining the amount of special compensation.

Article 14.2 provides that:

> 'If, in the circumstances set out in paragraph 1, the salvor by his salvage operations has prevented or minimised damage to the environment, the special compensation payable by the owner to the salvor under paragraph 1 may be increased up to a maximum of 30% of the expenses incurred by the salvor. However, the Tribunal, if it deems it fair and just to do so and bearing in mind the relevant criteria set out in Article 13, paragraph 1, may increase such special compensation further, but in no event shall the total increase be more than 100% of the expenses incurred by the salvor.'

This provides for a second tier of special compensation if the salvage operation has actually 'prevented or minimised the damage to the environment', i.e. a benefit. A claim cannot be brought under Article 14.2 unless the requirements of Article 14.1 are satisfied. The burden of proof is on the salvor. The salvage arbitrator will first decide whether any increment is due under Article 14.2 and then bear in mind the initial limit of 30 per cent but if he deems it fair and just he can award an increment up to a maximum of 100 per cent. It would be very rare for the increment to exceed 30 per cent. An important factor taken account by the arbitrator is the benefit occurred by the salvage operation. Other factors could be the expertise of the salvors, the nature of and the risks undertaken by them.

Article 14.3 provides:

'Salvor's expenses for the purpose of paragraphs 1 and 2 means the out-of-pocket expenses reasonably incurred by the salvor in the salvage operation and a fair rate for equipment and personnel actually and reasonably used in the salvage operation, taking into consideration the criteria set out in Article 13, paragraph 1(h), (i) and (j).'

The salvage 'out-of-pocket expenses' must be reasonably incurred. These are expenses incurred by the salvor in performing the whole of the salvage operation and not just that part relating to environmental protection. If there is no agreement between the parties to the salvage arbitration as the appropriate expenses the arbitrator must decide whether the out-of-pocket expenses were reasonably incurred in the salvage operation. Such expenses shall be distinguished from a 'fair rate' for equipment etc. In the absence of agreement between the parties the arbitrator will also have to determine a fair rate for equipment and personnel actually, and again, reasonably used in the salvage operation. The House of Lords decided in the case of *Nagasaki Spirit* (see below at page 343) that a 'fair rate' should not include any element of profit.

Article 14.4 re-confirms that special compensation is payable only if the amount assessed is greater than the conventional award of salvage remuneration. If the salvor has been negligent and failed to prevent or minimize damage to the environment he may be deprived of all or part of any special compensation due under Article 14 [see Article 14(5)]. Also, nothing in Article 14 affects the right of recourse on the part of the owner [see Article 14(6)]. For instance, if the casualty occurs due to the fault of the cargo-owner, the shipowner may be able to recover any special compensation payable to the salvor from the cargo-owner.

## LLOYD'S FORM OF SALVAGE AGREEMENT (LOF 95)

To coincide with the coming into force on 1 January 1995 of the International Salvage Convention 1989 by reason of the Merchant Shipping (Salvage and Pollution) Act 1994, the LOF 90 was updated and replaced by LOF 95. The 1994 Act has been repealed by the Merchant Shipping Act 1995. A copy of the LOF 95 can be found at Appendix 9. New procedural rules of Lloyd's were introduced in February 1997 and are attached at Appendix 9. As the 1989 Convention is now in force in the UK the full articles of this Convention are set out in the LOF 95 for information only. The main principle is still 'no cure—no pay', subject to the statutory provisions relating to special compensation. The reference to the Convention in the LOF 95 is a reference to the International Convention Salvage 1989. The LOF 95 is very similar to the LOF 90 in its intent, save in numbering. Some new pertinent points are as follows.

Clauses 5 and 6 deal with the provision for security. Clause 5(b) now provides that where a claim is made or may be made for special compensation the owners of the vessel shall on the demand of the contractor ('salvor') whenever made provide security for the contractor's claim for special compensation, provided always that such demand is made within two years of the date of termination of the services. It should be borne in mind that a claim for salvage cannot be brought after two years, see page 361.

Clause 6(b) has now been expanded to provide that when the salvor gives consent to the salved property being removed from the place to which it has been taken by the salvor on condition that the salvor is provided with temporary security pending completion of the voyage the contractor's maritime lien on the property salved shall remain in force to the extent necessary to enable the salvor to compel the provision of security in accordance with clause 5(c).

Clause 11 provides that interest is payable on the fees and expenses of the arbitrator and the Council of Lloyd's, as well as the salvage award. Clause 12 provides that the arbitrator can, in so far as it may be fair and just in all the circumstances, give effect to the consequences of any change or changes in the relevant rates of exchange which may have occurred between the date of the termination of the services and the date on which the award is made. The appeal arbitrator can also award interest on any fees and expenses charged under clause 14.

Clause 16 removes any ambiguity as to the scope of the Master's authority to bind cargo interests and provides that 'the Master or other person signing this agreement on behalf of the property to be salved enters into this agreement as agent for the vessel, her cargo, freight, bunkers, stores and any other property thereon and the respective owners thereof and binds each (but not the one for the other or himself personally) to the due performance thereof'. The owners' rights to terminate services upon giving reasonable notice to the salvor in writing when there is no longer any reasonable prospect of a useful result leading to a salvage reward in accordance with Convention Article 13 is now contained in Clause 4.

One should add that discussions are taking place as to whether a new LOF should be introduced and as to its wording. Also there is a BIMCO 'Salvhire' and 'Salvcon' form which is for use in salvage when engaging tugs and equipment on a daily or lump sum basis.

## CODE OF PRACTICE BETWEEN ISU (INTERNATIONAL SALVAGE UNION) AND INTERNATIONAL GROUP P & I CLUBS

According to a survey of ISU, salved values over the five-year period 1991–95 under all forms of 'no cure—no pay' contract amounted to US$7.4bn. Salvors received in the form of settlements and awards just under 5.2 per cent of the value of the property recovered. In the 1991–95 period, Article 14 awards which concerned owners and their P & I Club totalled US$18.5m. According to the data of the ISU during the period of 1994–96 the six member companies of ISU assisted 436 ship casualties and recovered oils, chemicals and bunkers totalling more than 5.3m tons. During the 1994–96 period ISU salvors responded to vessels carrying over 200,000 tons of chemicals. Therefore it is apparent that considerable efforts were made by the salvors to minimize damage to the environment which is encouraged by Article 14.

In order to assist the efficiency of the salvage response to environmental and pollution threats, new measures were agreed by the International Salvage Union and the International Group of P & I Clubs and a code of practice came into force in August 1996. This code of practice is to be found at Appendix 9. It does not have legal effect, although the ISU and P & I Clubs have said they will recommend to their respective members to apply the code where Article 14 is relevant.

The code provides that the salvor should advise the relevant P & I Club as soon as possible where he considers there is a possibility of an Article 14 special compensation claim arising. The P & I Club may then appoint an observer to attend the salvage operation but any decision on the conduct of the salvage services remains with the salvor. The P & I Club when reasonably requested by the salvor will immediately advise the salvor whether or not the particular member is covered for special compensation and liability.

The salvor will not call for security to be lodged with Lloyd's (as required under LOF 95) but will accept a Club letter of undertaking in relation to Article 14 claims. The provision of a Club letter of undertaking is not automatic and P & I Clubs will reply to any request by a salvor regarding security, as quickly as reasonably possible. A standard form of such letters of undertaking have been agreed between the ISU and the P & I Clubs. This code is part of a wider programme of co-operation with P & I Clubs and other parties represented on the Salvage Liaison Group, including shipowners and property insurers. It seems that some P & I Clubs are interested in taking a more 'hands on' approach to salvage and there is considerable debate about this.

### *Nagasaki Spirit*

A very important case concerning Articles 13 and 14 of the International Salvage Convention, incorporated in LOF 90 (now LOF 95) came before the House of Lords in the *Nagasaki Spirit* [1997] 1 Lloyd's Rep. 323. The analysis of this case which follows is lengthy but in view of the importance attached to its issues in Salvage and P & I circles the author considers it justified.

On 19 September 1992, *Nagasaki Spirit* collided with the container ship *Ocean Blessing* in the northern part of the Malacca Strait. At the time, she was part laden with a cargo of 40,154 tons of crude oil and, as a result of the collision, about 12,000 tons were released into the sea and caught fire. Both ships were engulfed by fire. Semco Salvage, the contractors, agreed to salve *Nagasaki Spirit* and her cargo on the terms of LOF 90. The contractors mobilized a number of tugs and extinguished the fire on *Nagasaki Spirit* on 22 September. The Malaysian police ordered the contractors to tow the vessel out to sea and at anchorage off Belawan in Indonesia the contractors transferred the cargo remaining on board to another vessel and the *Nagasaki Spirit* was redelivered to her owners subsequently in Singapore. The contractors' claim against the owners for salvage remuneration was referred to arbitration, their claim against the cargo owners being settled.

The arbitrator made an award against the shipowners and bunker owners of US$6,913,117 and assessed the special compensation under Article 14.3 in the sum of US$7,658,117. He held that a fair increment under Article 14.2 was 65 per cent of that sum and the total special compensation was S$12,635,893 and that as he would have made an award of S$9.5m had the shipowners, bunker owners and cargo owners all been before him he awarded the contractors S$3,135,893. The appeal arbitrator subsequently set aside the award. He held that, had the shipowners, cargo owners and bunker owners all been before him, he would have made an award of S$10,750,000. He made an award against the shipowners and bunker owners of S$7,322,737. He assessed the special compensation under Article 14.3 in the sum of S$5,216,404.20. He held that a fair increment under Article 14.2 was 65 per cent of that sum and the total special compensation was, in consequence, S$8,607,066.90. Since, under Article 14.4, that figure was less than the award for the salvage services, no special compensation was payable.

The contractors and the shipowners appealed to the High Court, some of the issues being:

(1) what was the meaning of 'fair rate' in Article 14.3 of the Convention?;
(2) in respect of what period was a salvor entitled to special compensation under Article 14.3?;
(3) was the appeal arbitrator's assessment of the fair rate correct in principle?

The High Court [1995] 2 Lloyd's Rep. 44 decided the following:

(1) With regard to the meaning of 'a fair rate' in Article 14.3, the ordinary natural meaning of the words 'a fair rate' imported the idea of a fair rate of remuneration which would ordinarily include an element of profit. However, if the words were construed in their context, it could be seen that the Convention drew a distinction between remuneration or reward on the one hand and compensation or expenses on the other; to be remunerated or rewarded was to receive some profit from the service concerned, whereas to be compensated was to receive recompense for expenditure; the notion of compensation or expense did not naturally encompass the idea of remuneration, reward or profit. What was being defined in Article 14.3 was expenses and not remuneration or reward and, if it was intended that the expenses referred to in Article 14.1 should include an element of profit, it would have been very simple to make that clear. The scheme of Article 14 was that the salvor was to be able to recover expenses and not remuneration if he satisfied Article 14.1 and that he was to be entitled not only to his expenses but also to remuneration if he satisfied Article 14.2. A fair rate including an element of profit could not fairly be regarded as part of expenses which had been 'reasonably incurred': A 'fair rate' meant fair rate of expense and not fair rate of remuneration and no element of profit was included.
(2) Article 14 was intended to deal primarily with the case where a ship sustained a casualty such that both she or her cargo needed salvage assistance and there was a threat of damage to the environment; Article 14.3 defined the expenses he was entitled to and there was nothing in the wording of Article 14.3 or indeed of Article 14.1 or Article 14.2

which suggested that those expenses were limited to a particular part of the salvage operation. The natural meaning of 'salvage operation' in Article 14.3 was the whole of the salvage operation performed by the salvor.

(3) The Appeal Arbitrator's assessment of the fair rate was not correct and the figures adopted by him could not be explained.

The salvors then appealed to the Court of Appeal [1996] 1 Lloyd's Rep. 449, the issues being:

(1) what would be the meaning of 'fair rate' in Article 14.3?;
(2) in respect of what period was a salvor entitled to special compensation under Article 14.3?

The Court of Appeal decided:

(1) What was meant by 'fair rate' was a fair rate of expense which is to be comprehensive of indirect or overhead expenses and was to take into account the additional cost of having resources instantly available. What was a fair rate was a matter for the tribunal of fact. Although Evans LJ dissented, the two other Court of Appeal judges decided that in the context of expenses a fair rate for equipment and personnel could not encompass remuneration or a concept of profit and the salvors' appeal failed.
(2) The natural meaning of 'salvage operation' in Article 14.3 was that special compensation was payable for the duration of the salvage operations once the vessel or its cargo threatened damage to the environment. The language of Article 14.3—equipment and personnel actually and reasonably used in the salvage operation—meant the whole operation from start to finish. The shipowners' cross-appeal failed.

The salvors appealed and shipowners cross-appealed to the House of Lords [1997] 1 Lloyd's Rep. 323. The principal issue in the appeal was concerned with the definition of expenses in Article 14.3 and in particular that which included in expenses 'a fair rate for equipment and personnel actually and reasonably used in the salvage operations'. The period of the salvage services was also considered.

The House of Lords decided that:

'A fair rate for equipment and personnel actually and reasonably used in the salvage operation' in Article 14.3 means a fair rate of expenditure and did not include any element of profit. This was clear from the context and in particular from the references to 'expenses' in Article 14.2 and the definition of 'salvors' expenses' in Article 14.3; the computation prescribed by Article 14.3 required the fair rate to be added to the 'out-of-pocket' expenses, as clear an instance as one could find of a quantification which contained no element of profit. The ascertainment of the fair rate had necessarily to be performed with a fairly broad brush. Article 14.3 is not concerned with the remuneration, but with a more restricted basis of recovery. In the context of Article 14, the word 'rate' simply denoted an account attributable to the equipment and personnel used. Resort to the travaux preparatoires was not strictly justified, as the meaning of Article 13 was clear enough. However, the analysis of the travaux reinforced the view formed on the words in Article 14 themselves read in their context.

Lord Mustill said at page 332:

'The promoters of the Convention did not choose, as they might have done, to create an entirely and distinct category of environmental salvage, which would finance the owners of vessels and gear to keep them in readiness simply for the purpose of preventing damage to the environment. Paragraphs 1, 2 and 3 of Article 14 all make it clear that the right of special compensation depends on the performance of 'salvage operations', which, as already seen, are defined by Article 1(a) as operations to assist a vessel in distress. Thus, although Article 14 is undoubtedly concerned to encourage professional salvors to keep vessels readily available, this is still for the purposes of a salvage, for which the primary incentive remains a traditional salvage award. The only structural change in the scheme is that the incentive is now made more attractive by the possibility of obtaining new financial recognition for conferring a new type of incidental benefit. Important as it is, the remedy under Article 14 is subordinate to the reward under Article 13, and its functions should not be confused by giving it a character too closely akin to salvage.'

The House of Lords agreed with the earlier decisions that it is to the entirety of the salvage operation that the expenses should be referred and adopted the reasons given by Mr Justice Clarke.

## WHO CONTRIBUTES TO A SALVAGE AWARD?

Basically, the owners of all property which has benefited from a salvage award must contribute to it unless the salvage award is under the 'safety net' provisions of the LOF 80 or Article 14 of LOF 90 and LOF 95. Exceptions to this rule in respect of property are: (a) the personal effects of the Master and crew; and (b) postal packets (Crown property). Also excepted from contributing are lenders on a bottomry bond.

However, it is *not* necessary that there should be legal ownership. For example, a time charterer may have benefited by the saving of the vessel. It could indeed be *anyone* who has an interest in the property saved.

*The Meandros* (1925) 132 LJ 750

A Greek ship was requisitioned by the Greek government and was salved during the requisition period. After de-requisition action was taken for a salvage award which the shipowner resisted.

*Held*: that he was bound to pay as he had had the benefit of the actual ship instead of the value of the ship and thus derived benefit from the services performed.

Shipowners can claim contribution from cargo interests unless the salvage operation is necessitated directly by actionable fault on their part. The shipowner has a possessory lien on the cargo for the cargo's proportion of salvage. Unless, however, there is a special salvage agreement, the owners of the ship and the cargo are liable independently of each other and severally to salvors who, if they sue the separate interests separately, will only obtain judgment against either for their own particular portion.

Where there is a salvage agreement signed by the Master this may, by its terms, bind the shipowner expressly to pay the whole sum due under the agreement, or to be assessed under the terms of the agreement, and not merely what would be contributed by ship and freight.

The shipowner's security lies in his ability to withhold delivery of the salved cargo eventually to its rightful owners until such time as he has received suitable security for any payments by way of salvage he may have made or may still have to make in respect of the cargo itself.

It is open to cargo interests to raise objections to contributing on the grounds, for example, that the agreed remuneration was unreasonable. Conversely, however, it also follows that cargo interests may not reap advantage from salvage agreements to which they are not direct parties. If a vessel-owner enters into a towage contract which stipulates that there shall be 'no salvage charges' owners of cargo on board the towed ship may not reap the benefits of this stipulation and cargo could remain liable to pay any remuneration for any services rendered by the contracted tug which are in the nature of purely salvage services.

## HOW ARE VALUES ASSESSED?

### *Ships*

The value of the ship is assessed according to circumstances. Either as her value to her owners as a going concern (and this could include the consideration of pending profitable engagements but does not mean simply just adding freight earnings to the market value because this could be duplicating values) or as her value to her owners in her damaged condition.

*The Queen Elizabeth* (1949) 82 Ll.L.Rep. 803
This case involved claims in respect of salvage performed by the owners, Masters and crews of various tugs to the *Queen Elizabeth* when she went aground just outside Southampton Water in April 1947. Her sound value was £6,000,000, her value as salved property £5,983,000 and the value of her cargo was £225,000, making a grand total of £6,208,000.

*Held*: that despite the value of the salved property being exceptionally high, the value must still be taken for account when assessing a fair and reasonable salvage award.

In the case of the *Yolaine* [1995] 2 Lloyd's Rep. 7, the value of a 35' cruising ketch in her damaged condition was assessed to be £10,500. However, the salved value of the vessel was found to be £15,000 i.e. deducting the cost of repairs, £12,500 from the sound value figure of £27,500. The High Court decided that, since the owner of a vessel like *Yolaine* could reasonably be expected not to sell the vessel but to arrange for repairs, the salved value of the vessel was likely to be more than the amount for which she could be sold in her damaged condition and that a salved value of £15,000 was not unreasonable and this included equipment which was removed such as VHF, depth sounder etc, during the salvage services.

### *Cargo*

In assessing the value of the cargo, regard will be had to the deduction of all customary expenses involved in the unloading, storage and sale. There will be no difficulty if the salvage services terminate at the port of destination or at a place where there is a market for the particular cargo concerned. Where, however, cargo is carried to a place where there is no market for it, then its value must be assessed by reference to the nearest convenient market, less an allowance for its transport there.

*Banca Agricola di Greci* v *Impresa Cesara Davanzali* [1975] ELD 686 (an Italian decision)

*Held*: by Ancona Court of Appeal: that, in assessing a salvage award, the value of the cargo was calculated as at the place were the salvage services where rendered, or if the cargo reached its destination, at its value there, at the c.i.f. price. The importers' profit was irrelevant. An arbitrator assessing a salvage award must apportion the value between the ship and cargo, an error in valuation of either would vitiate the award.

### Freight at risk

Whether or not the cargo-owner pays salvage on freight saved separately is in practice immaterial, but if he pays freight due by contract and thereafter pays the whole of the salvage award assessed against cargo he will be entitled to recover from the shipowner the portion which would have been assessed against the freight only.

If the salvors carry cargo to a port which is not the contractual destination, the question of freight being fully payable can become disputable. It should be noted that: (a) if the cargo is never eventually carried to its destination, no freight is earned; (b) if the cargo is not carried to its agreed destination because its owner prevents this, full freight is payable; and (c) if the cargo-owner elects to take delivery where it is, pro rata freight will be payable.

The common law idea that freight is not legally due until 'right and true delivery at the agreed destination' could produce injustice if strictly applied when salvage services terminate at an intermediate port. The Admiralty Court applies more equitable principles and will take into account that the performance of the voyage may be substantially if not wholly completed at the time of the rendering of salvage services and therefore the freight at least is 'partly' earned.

A case involving salvage under common law as opposed to under a LOF was the *Yolaine* [1995] 2 Lloyd's Rep. 7. The issue was what was a fair amount of salvage remuneration, which depended in part on the salved value of the *Yolaine*.

The *Yolaine* was a 35-foot cruising ketch which encountered difficulties off Porlock Weir and went aground. Salvage services were rendered by various plaintiffs who were not professional salvors, and their services were entirely successful. It was held that the salved value was to be assessed at the time when, and the place where, the services terminated i.e. at Porlock Weir on 26 October 1991 and one method of arriving at that value was to ascertain the sound value of the vessel and to deduct the reasonable costs of repairs. The yacht should be valued on the basis that it was about average for its size, type and age, and a fair figure to take for its sound value at the time was about £27,500, which included the equipment such as VHF, depth sounder, which was removed from the vessel during the salvage. On the evidence, the reasonable costs of repairs was £12,500 and the salved value of the vessel was £15,000 i.e. deducting the cost of repairs £12,500 from the sound value figure of £27,500. Since the owner of a vessel like *Yolaine* could reasonably be expected not to sell the vessel but to arrange for repairs, the salved value of the vessel was likely to be more than the amount for which she could be sold in her damaged condition and a salved value of £15,000 was not unreasonable and this included the equipment removed during the salvage. The cost of repairs included a deduction of £1,000 for betterment plus a deduction for repairs occasioned by a second incident plus an allowance for the repairs to the yacht by the owner himself. On the other hand, the value of the vessel in her damaged condition was assessed to be £10,500 whereas the court decided that the salved value should be taken as £15,000. Some of the plaintiffs rendered salvage assistance after the vessel's equipment such as the VHF had been taken off. The same salved value was applied in respect of all the plaintiffs' claims. When the vessel was lying aground with a hole in her starboard side, both the hull and equipment required salvage assistance. The assistance was provided in the first place by two plaintiffs and subsequently by other salvors. The effect of all the services was to salve the hull and equipment. Therefore it was appropriate to take the salved value of the hull and all the equipment at the termination of the services. A salvage award was granted in favour of all the plaintiffs together in the sum of £4,750 and interest was awarded at 2 per cent over the base rate for sterling as from 1 January 1992.

### *Pro rata payment of the salvage award*

The general rule is that any salvage award is paid by the property saved, i.e. ship, cargo, bunkers, freight at risk in proportion to their contribution to the total salved fund. In fact in the case of *The Vatan* (below) it was stated that various old cases showed the general principle that the liability of each salved interest is only for its pro rata share of the total salvage award applies:

(1) even though ship and cargo are salved from different risks;
(2) even though the claim against one party has been settled;
(3) even though the claim against one party has failed; and
(4) even though a claim is made only against one party.

*The m.v. Vatan* [1990] 1 Lloyd's Rep. 336
An ultra large crude oil tanker was struck by a missile in July 1985. The Master agreed to engage salvors on LOF terms noting however, that 'cargo owners are not authorising us to give instructions regarding cargo salvage'. The arbitrator found that the value of the salved property was US$77 million including ship bunkers and cargo. This included nearly 400,000 tons of crude oil worth US$73 million. A fair reward for the salvage was US$4.75 million. Applying the long established pro rata rule that shipowners would be liable to pay only their proportion of the total salvage award which the value of their ship related to the total value of all the property salved resulted in a figure of some US$221,350. However the arbitrator decided that the shipowners were liable to pay the salvors US$850,000 on the basis that in the exceptional circumstances of the case the salvors were unlikely to make any substantial recovery from the cargo owners. The appeal arbitrator decided that the original arbitrator had erred in principle in departing from the pro rata rule and in the assessment of a fair reward for the services as a whole. The appeal arbitrator decided that the salvage reward should have been assessed at US$7.7 million and that the shipowners were liable to pay 4.6 per cent of the total, i.e. US$350,000. The salvors appealed to the High Court and asked for the sum fixed by the original arbitrator as payable by the shipowners to be reinstated.

*Held*: There was no basis from departing from the pro rata rule. The fact that the salvors had not recovered a salvage award from the cargo owners could not be a good reason for ordering the shipowners to pay US$500,000 more than their pro rata share of the proper reward for the services rendered. In holding the balance between the salvors and the shipowners it could not be fair to both parties to impose on the shipowners the burden of making good to the salvors a part of the remuneration due to them from the cargo owners. It was clear from the authorities that the pro rata rule was recognised as a general rule. Having regard to the element of chance which played a large part in salvage and which affected the amount of salvage payable by the shipowners it was preferable as a matter of policy that there should be no exception to the general rule arising from the fact that the ship and cargo were exposed to different damages and different degrees of danger. Accordingly the appeal arbitrator's award was upheld.

## APPORTIONMENT AS BETWEEN OWNERS, MASTER AND CREW OF SALVING VESSEL

It is well established that Masters, individual officers or other members of the crew of an assisting vessel may successfully claim salvage rewards in their own right provided that they can individually (or jointly if they consolidate their claims) show that their claim(s) have merit and that the services they rendered personally contained all the necessary 'ingredients' of proper salvage. It should not be assumed that the existence of some form of salvage agreement between the respective owners of the salved and the salving vessels serves to deprive the prospective individual salvage claimants of their rights in this respect.

In the days of sail, the shipowner's share was comparatively small, but with the advent of steam, the 'principal salvor' is really now the ship itself. The shipowner's share is relatively much greater. However, the apportionment of a salvage award between members of the crew of the salving ship is really a domestic matter within the sphere of the ship itself and the governing law, if any, is the law of the ship's flag. It is customary these days for an ordinary apportionment to be that the shipowner takes about three-quarters, but each case is (as usual) considered on its merits. The ordinary apportionment to a ship's Master is about one-third of what remains. The ordinary calculation for the officers and members of the crew is that the lump sum remaining should be shared according to their rating.

On the many occasions when LOF is used the contracted salvor is empowered to claim also on behalf of his Master and crew and any sub-contractor he may have engaged in addition to claiming on his own behalf, but if he does so he must provide an acceptable indemnity against those parties subsequently claiming individually in their own right. Where these provisions are not fully implemented a court or arbitrator may be asked to state in his award an apportionment to individuals/parties who had meritoriously contributed to the ultimate success. It should be remembered that crews of *professional salvage tugs* are normally on *salvage* articles and therefore they would be under a pre-existing duty to render salvage services anyway.

Bonus payments to which crews may be entitled under their contracts of service are not normally taken into account in the apportionment.

*The Empire Gulf* (1948) 81 Ll.L.Rep. 255
It was decided that generally speaking only the crew's basic wages should be taken into

account when assessing or apportioning crew's reward. War bonus payments, for example, are *not* taken into consideration.

*The Southern Venturer* [1953] 1 Lloyd's Rep. 428, Court of Session
Bonus payments calculated in proportion to the success of a whaling expedition and paid to the crew were not taken into consideration in apportioning a salvage award amongst the crew as salvors. Basic wages only were the basis for calculation. The ship's wireless operator, although sharing in the award, was not given a special award.

Radio officers are in a special category as frequently they are not the employees of the shipowner, even though listed on the ship's articles. In this event, if they have performed salvage services in their personal capacity they would be entitled to sue separately for an award.

*The Elpenor* (1933) 47 Ll.L.Rep. 183
The court was requested to make a special award to the sole radio operator on board the salving ship who had remained on duty manning his radio for 24 consecutive hours.

*The Firethorn* (1948) 81 Ll.L.Rep. 178
The case illustrates how a court may grant liberal personal salvage awards to certain crew members for additional work, special gallantry or hardship. Apportionment was weighted in favour of the crew generally but a double share went to the ship's mate.

*The Oceanic Grandeur* [1972] 2 Lloyd's Rep. 396
In March 1970, the *Oceanic Grandeur*, fully loaded with oil, struck an uncharted rock in the Torres Straits and came to anchor in shallow water. She was holed in places and her tanks were damaged. Another tanker came and stood by but the Master of *Oceanic Grandeur* initially refused offers of help. Eventually, the respective ships' owners agreed that the assisting ship should take off some of *Oceanic Grandeur's* cargo under terms to be agreed later, except that it was agreed specifically that any loss sustained by the assisting vessel was to be indemnified by *Oceanic Grandeur's* owners. The transhipment of cargo was successful and the Master, chief and second officers of the assisting ship claimed salvage rewards in a joint action, with the remaining officers and crew claiming rewards also in a similar joint action.

Holding that the claims were justified, the court found that (a) the services rendered by the claimants were voluntary since, although they had acted on the orders of their owners, this did not affect the voluntary nature of their actions (see also *The National Defender* [1970] 1 Lloyd's Rep. 40 (United States District Court for the Southern District of New York)); (b) the services rendered were proper salvage services and not merely 'lightening services'; (c) the alleged salvage agreement did not operate to bar their claim since no term could be implied to that effect and in any case the assisting ship's owners had no authority to contract on the plaintiffs ' behalf and thus deprive them of their rights to a salvage reward; (d) the Master of the *Oceanic Grandeur* had accepted salvage services; (e) all the necessary ingredients of danger were present to fulfil the basic requirements of the law of salvage, particularly as the cargo itself was of a hazardous nature.

*The Geertje K* [1971] 1 Lloyd's Rep. 285
A salvage claim was brought by the coxswain and crew of the lifeboat *Charles Henry* for services rendered to the German vessel *Geertje K*, her cargo and freight. Evidence showed that the risk of the vessel, which was in distress off Selsey, becoming a total loss was practically nil though there was a distinct possibility that she would suffer serious bottom damage. If the lifeboat had not come to her rescue no doubt other would-be rescuers would have appeared. There was little danger or risk involved to the salvors or their boat and the claim was purely one for personal individual rewards as the Royal National Lifeboat Institution does not claim salvage itself. £1,000 was awarded for personal services rendered. The value of the vessel saved was proved to be £42,000.

*The Golden Sands* [1975] 2 Lloyd's Rep. 166
The yacht *Golden Sands* was used to bring illegal immigrants into the United Kingdom. She broke down in the English Channel and was without motive power or any means by which she could communicate. She was towed to a place of safety by the Dover lifeboat but the towage proved difficult, being over a distance of some 20 miles and it took four hours to accomplish. The weather at the time was unfavourable. The coxswain and crew of the lifeboat claimed rewards.

The court accepted that the value of the *Golden Sands* was £3,000 and that there had been a real risk that she would be damaged if not totally lost. They assessed a fair amount for salvage services as rendered as £300. These were personal services rendered and not services by the owners of the lifeboat. The services rendered by the claimants were not especially difficult but nevertheless were of a sufficiently meritorious nature to entitle them to their rewards.

There have been occasions, however, when members of a salving ship's crew who have not been members of a boarding party put on to the distressed vessel and therefore have not personally made any meritorious contribution to the eventual success have nevertheless been able to share in the reward.

*The St Paul Marine Transportation Corp* v *Cerro Sales Corp* [1975] AMC 503
In June 1968 the crew of the small tramp steamer, the *North America*, abandoned her when she caught fire about 600 miles east-south-east of Honolulu. The motorship *St Paul* was directed to the scene and after saving 22 lives put a boarding party onto the stricken ship which appeared likely to sink. They extinguished the fire, closed the portholes and doors and then the vessel was taken in tow until the tow line broke. The *St Paul* then left with the approval of the US Coast Guard and the disabled ship was towed by another ship to port and the cargo salved. The owners of the *St Paul* claimed a salvage reward.

*Held* (as to who had the right to a salvage award): that the owner of the salving ship who was not on board and crewmen who were not in the boarding party were entitled to a share in the award. Also that for saving the cargo valued at $1,850,000, $200,000 should be awarded as salvage of which 65 per cent should go to the owner of the *St Paul* and 35 per cent to the crew.

In any case, the court has wide discretionary powers in apportioning as well as in assessing aggregate salvage awards.

## APPORTIONMENT AMONGST VARIOUS SETS OF SALVORS OR SALVING SHIPS

The general principles of apportionment are that: (1) there is priority in time. The first salvors, in the absence of any fault on their part, tend to be treated with more generosity than later ones; but (2) if there is no question of wrongful dispossession of the first salvors by any subsequent salvors and if second or subsequent salvors have given more meritorious service, they will be treated with more generosity than the first salvors.

*The American Farmer* (1947) 80 Ll.L.Rep. 672
The US ship *American Farmer* was seriously damaged in collision in the Atlantic about 650 miles from Land's End. Her Master and crew were taken on board the other colliding ship and subsequently transferred to a third ship. The *American Farmer* was left derelict. At the time of the collision (31 July 1946) SOS signals were sent as a result of which two large ocean-going tugs sailed from England. Before they arrived, the British ship *Elisabete*

altered course and reached the *American Farmer*. She attempted to take her in tow and made fast a tow rope but could not turn her on to an easterly course. Five hours later the vessel *American Ranger* (sister ship of the *American Farmer*) arrived and put men on board. It was found that the 'derelict' ship's engines were undamaged. The *Elisabete* kept her rope attached and also retained her boarding party on the stricken ship. Neither boarding party attempted to interfere with the other. Eventually the *Elisabete* began towing and *American Farmer's* engines began to get underway. The tow ropes were cut and *American Farmer* finished its journey unaided. The two salvage tugs merely stood by and were not involved in the subsequent claims for salvage.

*Held*: that the dispossession of the *Elisabete* by the *American Ranger* was justified under the circumstances since there was no reasonable probability of the *Elisabete* (the first salvor) bringing the derelict to safety at the time of the dispossession by the second salvors. This, however, did not disentitle the first salvor to any award. On the contrary, they were entitled to a liberal award though not as liberal as the second salvors who were the principal cause of success.

## WRONGFUL DISPOSSESSION OF EARLIER SALVORS BY LATER SALVORS

Unless dispossession of earlier salvors by later salvors was due to some 'reasonable' cause, a claim based on wrongful dispossession may be brought successfully. If such reasonable cause is not actual, then it must at least be apparent. A salvor who is dismissed or superseded should not forcibly resist but should rely on the assistance of a court.

*The Loch Tulla* case, below, clearly illustrates how a superseded salvor is best advised not to resist forcibly but to rely rather on the court's recognition of his situation. The case also illustrates the court's view of the rights to compensation of a superseded salvor who has in good faith attempted, before being superseded, to refloat a stricken vessel, and failed, and who has nevertheless stood by in order to continue to render assistance if called upon.

*The Loch Tulla* (1950) 84 Ll.L.Rep. 62
A steam trawler of limited tonnage attempted to refloat the *Loch Tulla*, a similar type of vessel, in a Scandinavian harbour at a time of very adverse weather and when the *Loch Tulla* was unable to help herself. Her attempts were initially unsuccessful and she stood by to wait for another tide. Meanwhile, after consultation between the *Loch Tulla's* Master and an insurance representative, a larger vessel was engaged to assist which successfully refloated her.

The court took the view that the first assisting vessel's owners, Master and crew should not go unrewarded. The fact that she had stood by despite her initial lack of success and that she might (even if perhaps the likelihood was small) have ultimately succeeded, were both good grounds for entitling her owners, Master and crew to compensation by way of salvage reward. The court emphatically related the law of salvage to be interpreted in this particular set of circumstances to be that of an act of assistance, even if unproductive of benefit, should not go unrewarded if it has involved the expenditure of time, labour and/or risk. Also included in an award should be an element of compensation for the loss which a salvage claimant has sustained in being prevented from attempting to complete the service which he originally agreed to render. A small portion of the salvage fund was accordingly allocated to the superseded vessel.

The question of damages which may be awarded to a superseded salvor was dealt with in a second case which arose from *The Unique Mariner* incident ([1979] 1 Lloyd's Rep. 37). One basic point was the nature of the sum awarded. Was it damages or a reward for salvage services? The superseded salvors claimed damages for breach of contract and/or remuneration for services rendered under Lloyd's form. The arbitrator awarded $75,000. This was reduced by the appeal arbitrator to $35,000 but he sought the court's guidance on certain questions of law by way of special case: (a) were the salvors entitled to money in addition to salvage for services actually rendered? (b) were they entitled to 'restitutio in integrum' either as compensation or as damages for breach of contract or both? (c) were factors such as the fact that the stricken ship's owners had had to pay the tug expressly ordered from Singapore and the amount they had to pay or the fact that the superseded salvor had nevertheless still continued to stand by the casualty relevant to a fair and proper payment to them?

In addition to these questions the court considered the more generalized questions as to what are the rights of a salvor, not engaged under any express contract, who is superseded after having commenced upon his work and furthermore as to whether salvors engaged under terms such as Lloyd's Open Form have under these circumstances different or greater rights.

The Admiralty Court judge held (inter alia):

(a) Salvors engaged without any express agreement *are* entitled to salvage remuneration for services *actually* rendered before being superseded *and* compensation for lost opportunity to complete their services but not to the full extent comparative to damages for breach of contract or duty on a 'restitutio in integrum' basis.
(b) Parties to LOF were governed as to their rights and obligations by the express or implied terms of that agreement and by the general law of maritime salvage in so far as that might be expressly or impliedly incorporated into the agreement.
(c) The LOF *did* have a term implied into it that the owners of the property being saved should not act in such a way as to prevent the salvors from performing the services which they had undertaken so long as they were willing and able to do so; this should include not to dismiss or supersede.

Answering the arbitrator's questions of law the judge said: (a) the salvors were not entitled to money for services actually rendered but were entitled to damages for breach of contract; (b) the fact of payment and the amount of payment to the second salvor were both irrelevant; (c) the fact of continuing to stand-by *could* be relevant.

## POSSESSORY RIGHTS OF A SALVOR

A salvor's *possessory* rights can be protected by injunction.

*The Tubantia* (1924) 18 Ll.L.Rep. 158
This Dutch ship was sunk by a German warship in the North Sea in 1916. Salvage operations were commenced in 1922 after the wreck had been located 50 miles from the

English coast. Marker buoys were positioned and work continued for two seasons, weather permitting. Parts of the ship and cargo were eventually brought to the surface, but the salved property was of small value and the salvors' expenses alone amounted to £40,000 or more. During this period a well-equipped salvage vessel arrived to find and take possession of the wreck. They deliberately tried to prevent the existing salvors from carrying on further operations. The latter sued for damages for trespass or wrongful interference.

*Held*: that the first salvors were in possession of the wreck and entitled to prevent other potential salvors from interfering. An injunction was granted.

*Morris* v *Lyonesse Salvage Co Association* (The *Association* and the *Romney*) [1970] 2 Lloyd's Rep. 59
The Admiralty judge commented that in order to establish that salvors are in possession of a derelict, they must show, first, that they have animus possidendi, and, secondly, that they have exercised such use and occupation as is reasonably practicable having regard to the subject-matter of the derelict, the location, and the practice of the salvors.

*The Lusitania* [1986] 1 Lloyd's Rep. 132
As is common knowledge this passenger liner was sunk by a German U-boat in 1915. During salvage operations in 1982 a dispute arose as to whether certain items recovered were the property of the Crown or of those who recovered them. The wreck was extra-territorial and did not vest in the Crown. No one, therefore, had a better right than the claimant salvors.

## TO WHAT EXTENT MAY A SALVOR BE HELD LEGALLY RESPONSIBLE FOR THE CONSEQUENCES OF HIS NEGLIGENCE?

A few remarks would be of value on the attitude, sometimes lenient, of the courts generally towards errors which are made by salvors in their bona fide attempts to save life and/or property. The 'public policy' nature of salvage services which underlies the entire concept, assessment and calculation of a fair and reasonable salvage remuneration comes into sharp issue with the committing of negligent acts by salvors' employees when they are carrying out their meritorious 'rescue-type' work. Whatever may have been the attitude over the centuries, all doubt has now been dispelled that salvors who undertake, albeit voluntarily, to perform a salvage service shall become liable for loss or damage consequent upon the negligent performance of their operations. They have a duty of care either implied or expressly stated (see the Lloyd's form of agreement in the appendix to this chapter, page 357) to use reasonable care and skill, and to fall short of that exposes them to the consequences of actionable fault. A case prior to the recent LOFs may be of interest.

*Anglo-Saxon Petroleum Co Ltd* v *The Admiralty; Same* v *Damant* (1947) 80 Ll.L.Rep. 459, CA
The tanker *Delphinula* and the bulk of her cargo was lost by reason of fire off Alexandria in 1943. The salvage department of the Royal Navy were charged by the owners of the tanker and the owners of her cargo, suing jointly, with having caused the loss through negligence. It should be noted that the Navy salvage department stationed in that area was operating under the provisions of the Merchant Shipping (Salvage) Act 1940, which gave the Crown the same rights as any private salvor where salvage services are given by or with the aid of any ship. It is not intended to give the full facts which can be found in detail in

the relevant Lloyd's Law Report but the court's view was that everything which happened prior to the ship breaking her back and splitting in two places (she burned for nearly a month prior to that) was the direct or indirect result of the salvor's negligence and there was no new intervening cause. A salvor does come under some measure of duty according to the circumstances to use reasonable skill and care, the breach of which entails liability.

The special status of salvors does not entitle them to immunity or special privilege to any degree. For the present, let us consider the consequences of negligence in the course of the salvage operation. The 19th century idea was that the owner of salved maritime property would have his obligation to pay his salvor reduced to a varying degree according to the nature and extent of the error of judgment which constituted the negligence. The theory was one of a shield to the stricken property-owner rather than a sword in his hands. What the lessening of obligation could in effect amount to varied from the trivial (perhaps a denial of costs) to the extreme (very rarely), a forfeiture of the award.

In the course of the 20th century, the theory of the 'sword' gradually replaced that of the 'shield' and an independent right of the damaged-property owner to claim compensatory damages for the consequences of the salvors' negligence was eventually recognized. This principle was crystallized in *The Tojo Maru* case, below.

*The Tojo Maru* [1971] 1 Lloyd's Rep. 341
The salvors' employee negligently fired a bolt through the vessel's plating into a tank which had not been gas-freed, resulting in an explosion. The arbitrator appointed to consider the salvors' claim for remuneration and the *Tojo Maru's* owners' counter-claim for damages found that the *Tojo Maru's* damages amounted to £331,767 and that a proper remuneration to the salvors was £125,000. The matter found its way up to the Court of Appeal and eventually to the House of Lords. The Court of Appeal, having held that the shipowners were not entitled to counter-claim in respect of the damage caused by the salvors' employee, the House of Lords in pronouncing on the shipowners' appeal against that decision, held that the owners were entitled to counter-claim and furthermore that their claim was not restricted to the amount of the award which would be made. One of their Lordships in the course of his speech said that success in the salvage operation did not depend upon the salvors having done more good than harm but rather that the vessel had been brought to a place of safety. In rejecting the salvors' argument that the maritime law has a rule that the successful salvor cannot be liable in damages to the owner of the salved ship for the result of any negligence on his part their Lordships generally agreed that no such rule exists no matter how hard one tries to find it in the long history of English maritime law.

The long-term aim of the Admiralty Court is to encourage persons to perform salvage services rather than to discourage them.

*The St Blane* [1974] 1 Lloyd's Rep. 557
In July 1970 a steamship, the *St Blane,* went to the assistance of a yacht, the *Ariadne,* in dire distress in heavy weather in the Irish Sea. The yacht's owner, his wife and two boys were taken aboard the vessel and the yacht itself was eventually secured alongside the ship. However, the yacht began to sustain ranging damage and the *St Blane's* Master unsecured her for this reason whereupon the yacht promptly sank. The yacht owner sued the vessel's owner for the loss of his craft alleging negligence and contending that the Master of the *St Blane* performed the operation negligently in his handling of the yacht in that he collided with her whilst manoeuvering and in that he had secured her alongside longer

than he needed. That she sank was the direct consequence of such negligence. The *St Blane's* owners denied these allegations and counter-argued the yacht owner's own negligence.

*Held*: that the Master, employed by the defendant shipowner, had not acted unreasonably in his initial getting hold of the yacht; that it was not established that the collision with the yacht was due to negligent handling by the ship's Master and that the yacht owner plaintiff had not established that the sinking of his yacht was caused by the Master's negligence even though the Master may have failed to take all reasonable care to avoid damage to the yacht after he had rescued her crew. The Master was not a professional salvor and could only, in performing the operation, work on the time-honoured principle of 'trial and error'.

*The Eschersheim; The Jade* [1976] 2 Lloyd's Rep. 1, HL
In June 1974 the Admiralty Court considered some motions brought before it pursuant to actions in rem against the ship *Eschersheim* and others, the motions being brought by salvors who had performed salvage services after a vessel named the *Erkovit,* of Sudanese nationality, had been in collision with a West German vessel, the *Dortmund,* in the Bay of Biscay. As a result of the collision, the *Erkovit's* engine room was holed and flooded. The tug *Rotesand,* also West German and a sister ship of the *Eschersheim,* went to her assistance and an agreement on Lloyd's Open Form was signed. She took her in tow and later beached her already sinking off Corunna on the Spanish coast. Despite efforts by the salvors to save her, she became a total loss. Much of the cargo was lost or damaged and it included insecticide which polluted the coastal waters causing interference to fishing. This alone prompted the Spanish government to commence litigation against both the *Erkovit's* owners and the salvors.

Four further actions in rem were commenced: (a) by the owners of *Erkovit* against the owners of *Dortmund* for damage caused by the collision; (b) by the owners of *Erkovit*'s cargo against the owners of *Dortmund;* (c) by the owners of *Erkovit* against the salvors for damage caused by negligent salvage operations; and (d) by the owners of the *Erkovit*'s cargo against the salvors. The salvors applied to set aside or stay court proceedings caused by the collision for which the *Dortmund*'s owners should pay compensation. The *Dortmund*'s owners argued that the loss of the *Erkovit* and the pollution of Spanish waters was caused solely by the salvor's negligence and that their liability, if any, lay only in respect of the immediate collision damage. The salvors sought further to establish that the salvage agreement stipulated the settling of disputes by arbitration. They attempted to exclude the application of the Administration of Justice Act 1956, section 1 (1), which read as follows: 'The Admiralty jurisdiction of the High Court shall be as follows, that is to say, jurisdiction to hear and determine any of the following questions or claims . . . (d) any claim for damage done by a ship; (e) any claim for damage received by a ship; . . . (g) any claim for loss of or damage to goods carried in a ship; (h) any claim arising out of any agreement relating to the carriage of goods in a ship or to the use or hire of a ship; (j) any claim in the nature of salvage . . . '. The court ruled that the Lloyd's Open Form of agreement was, on this occasion, an agreement for the use of a ship within the meaning of section 1(h) and that the action for damages alleging negligent salvage by the *Erkovit*'s owners was sound, as also was the similar claim in the action by the cargo interests on the *Erkovit* against the salvors. The court's reasoning was also influenced by the desire generally to avoid duplication of proceedings in Spain and England. The salvors' motion seeking to stay or send to arbitration the shipowners' claims arising out of the collision and the subsequent loss of *Erkovit* was dismissed.

Regrettably, certainly from the point of view of a textbook author, these various cross disputes were subsequently settled out of court so that an opportunity was lost for further judicial views to be voiced on the question of salvorial negligence.

## A SALVOR'S ABILITY TO LIMIT LIABILITY

The potential exposure of a professional (or indeed any) salvor to unlimited liability was vividly underlined by the decision of the House of Lords in *The Tojo Maru* case (see page 356). The restrictions placed upon the right to limit under the Merchant Shipping (Liability of Shipowners and Others) Act 1958—viz. the requirement that the act, neglect or default must be in the course of the navigation or management of the ship—left salvors, in situations similar to the *Tojo Maru* salvage operations, powerless to limit liability after negligence resulting in damage or loss. Frequently there is no ship belonging to the salvors even near the scene of the salvage operation. This exposure to full legal liability caused much worry to salvors, whether professional or amateur, during the 1970s, but the introduction of the Merchant Shipping Act 1979 came to their rescue.

The 1979 Act, by section 17, brought into effect in the UK the provisions of the Convention on Limitation of Liability for Maritime Claims 1976 (the London Convention). However section 17 of the 1979 Act has been repealed by the Merchant Shipping Act 1995. The London Convention now has the force of law in the UK under section 185 of the Merchant Shipping Act 1995. Article 1 of the Convention provides that shipowners *and* salvors may limit and a salvor is defined as 'any person rendering services in direct connection with salvage operations'. Included in the definition of 'salvage operations' are operations in respect of wreck raising, removing, destroying or rendering harmless a vessel *or* its cargo (Article 2). On this basis it is irrelevant whether or not a tug is present at the scene of the operation. If the salvor is not at the material time operating from a tug or if he was operating solely on board the stricken vessel, his limitation will be based on a notional tonnage of 1,500 tons (Article 6).

However section 185(4) of the 1995 Act provides:

> The provisions having the force of law under this section shall not apply to any liability in respect of loss of life or personal injury caused to, or loss of or damage to any property of, a person who is on board the ship in question or employed in connection with that ship or with the salvage operations in question if—
>
> (a) he is so on board or employed under a contract of service governed by the law of any part of the United Kingdom; and
>
> (b) the liability arises from an occurrence which took place after the commencement of this Act.

As mentioned earlier in the chapter (page 328) the current LOF wording has incorporated the provisions of the 1976 London Convention on Limitation. Thus salvors under the agreement have been able to limit their liability, as per the Convention's terms, *in their own right* as salvors and not, as previously they have had to, with all the attendant adverse restrictions, under the 1957 Convention (UK's 1958 Merchant Shipping (Liability of Shipowners and Others) Act).

In summary, in salvage operations the negligence alleged must be something more substantial than a mere error of judgement, that is to say it must amount to such want of skill as first to lessen the achievement of salvage and also to provide an affirmative independent action for compensatory damages. It need not, however, amount necessarily to gross negligence. In assessing the want of care and skill which has been displayed in any given set of circumstances and in thus arriving at the extent of negligence, regard must be paid to the area where the operation took place, the degree of danger to both salvor and salved persons or property and the class or professional qualifications of the salvor, whether a person or company. This is particularly relevant in judging the navigation and manoeuvering of a salving ship (see *The Rene* [1955] 1 Lloyd's Rep. 101).

## WHAT HAPPENS IF AND WHEN A WRONGDOER 'TURNS SALVOR'?

The consequences of negligence can also be looked at from a very different viewpoint, that of the salvor who voluntarily takes on the role after an act of negligence has been committed by him or by someone with whom he has a close legal relationship. It is trite to say that he who does wrong, e.g. commits a tort, should reap no benefit from his wrongdoing. A leading mid-19th century case (*Cargo ex Capella* (1867) LR 1 A & E 356) established this rule clearly. In the field of salvage, for example, a ship which collides with another for which the former is to blame, wholly or partly, cannot thereafter 'turn salvor' and successfully claim a reward, however meritorious the subsequent salvage services may, in practice, be. The possible partial fault of the salved ship is irrelevant and does not affect this rule. The only significant departures from this legal concept are circumstances involving a situation where the delinquent vessel and the salving vessel, though two distinct vessels with two distinct crews, are nevertheless under common ownership or have a common proprietary interest. The courts have managed to achieve a measure of fairness on this point by introducing the fiction that the common owner of the two vessels is two separate legal entities, the one the 'dirty' hand which caused through its fault the original damage by collision, the other the 'clean'.

*The Beaverford* v *The Kafiristan* [1938] AC 136, HL
A collision occurred in June 1935 between the *Empress of Britain* and the *Kafiristan*. The *Kafiristan* was badly damaged and needed salvage assistance. The *Empress of Britain* stood by for six hours when the *Beaverford* (owned by the company which owned the *Empress of Britain*) arrived on the scene. At the request of her Master, *Kafiristan* was taken in tow by *Beaverford* to Nova Scotia and after 100 miles was taken in tow by a salvage vessel (the *Foundation Franklin*) which completed the voyage. The issue in the case was whether the owners of the *Beaverford* were entitled to a salvage award despite the fact that another vessel also owned by them was partly to blame for the collision (75 per cent).

*Held*: that the claim to salvage was not based on and did not have any connection with the fact that the *Empress of Britain* was guilty of negligent navigation. It was founded on a separate fact that *Beaverford* had performed a salvage service. They did not seek to profit from their own wrong. They paid for their blame in the original collision separately as a result of the apportionment of blame/damages in the collision action. The owners (and Master and crew) of the *Beaverford* were entitled to a salvage award.

## CIRCUITY OF ACTION IN THE CONTEXT OF SALVAGE ACTIONS

Circuity of action is the institution of legal action in respect of a claim against a third party who might have, or has, a counterclaim of as great a value which swallows up and renders abortive the original claim.

The avoidance of circuity of action is an alternative defence pleaded by the defendants to a salvage action when the wrongdoing ship in a collision and the salving ship which saves the 'innocent' ship are under the same ownership.

Salvage paid after a collision is merely one item in the damage claim that the ship saved makes against the other colliding ship which is wholly or partly to blame. Where the blame is partial only, the salvage award must be fixed in order to determine accurately the total damages which are to be set off on either side (two colliding ships) so as to arrive at the correct final balance of account. Where, however, one ship is entirely to blame, the innocent ship will add into the damage claim against the wrongdoer the entire sum paid in salvage. This is simple reasoning but may not be feasible for two reasons: (a) the apportionment of blame for the collision may not be determined until after the salvage award is made; and (b) there may be a right to limit liability.

In respect of reason (b), if the total damage claim of the innocent ship against the wholly-to-blame ship is £220,000, *excluding* salvage of £45,000, and the wrongdoing ship's limit is, say, £240,000, then the innocent ship would be £25,000 out of pocket. This would be the position after a collision where the salving and wrongdoing ships were in different ownership. But where they are in the *same* ownership some might argue that such a result was unjust. However, the incidence of joint ownership should not of itself have a bearing on, or detract in any way from, the meritorious nature of the services rendered by way of salvage.

The opportunity to plead circuity of action is only available where the respective rights of the parties to the whole litigation are such that the one would be entitled to recover from the other the same amount which the other sought from the one. In a situation where the salvage remuneration paid brings the total damage claim above the figure at which the other party is permitted to limit his liability, this is clearly not the case.

*The Susan V Luckenbach* (1950) 84 Ll.L.Rep. 538, CA
The American ship *Susan V Luckenbach* collided in the Gulf of Suez with the Danish ship *Nea Hellas.* In the subsequent collision action, the *Nea Hellas* was found solely to blame. The *Nea Hellas,* at the time of collision, was bare-boat chartered to the Crown and was manned by officers and crew appointed by the British government. Because of the collision, the *Susan V Luckenbach* required salvage assistance. This was rendered by a salvage tug (the *Confederate*) which was operated by the Admiralty and by HMS *Arpha.* The salvors claimed against the owners of the *Susan V Luckenbach* for a salvage remuneration.

*Held*: that salvage was rightly claimed by the owners of the salving vessels even though they also owned the vessel which was found solely to blame for the collision. It was held also that, owing to limitation of liability, the owners of the 'innocent' ship in the collision would not recover from the owners of the ship at fault, as part of the damages awarded to them, the same sum in respect of salvage services as they had paid out for the salvors, and therefore there was no circuity of action.

Logic would seem to indicate that the only situation where circuity of action could be successfully pleaded would be when a plaintiff shipowner claiming salvage was also the defendant in a collision action in which his ship was found wholly to blame and no question of limitation of liability enters into the reckoning. Then, perhaps, an award of salvage to him could be superfluous and therefore reasonably avoided.

## TIME LIMIT

Under Article 23 of the 1989 Convention, which has the force in law in the UK under the Merchant Shipping Act 1995 it is provided that any action relating to payment under this Convention shall be time-barred if judicial or arbitral proceedings have not been constituted within a period of two years. The limitation period commences on the day on which the salvage operations are terminated. During this period, it can be agreed by the parties to extend time. An action for indemnity by a person liable may be instituted after the expiration of the limitation period, provided that it is brought within the time allowed by the State in which proceedings are brought.

## WHEN DOES TOWAGE BECOME SALVAGE?

A suggested criterion for whether a towing vessel has become a salving vessel is: 'have there been supervening circumstances which would justify her in abandoning her contract?—*not* abandoning the tow, but abandoning the contract *to tow.*'

In other words, were the services that were to be rendered *eventually* by the tug such as to have been beyond the reasonable contemplation of the parties when they originally negotiated the towage contract? What must be beyond doubt is that towage *and* salvage services cannot be performed concurrently. One must finish before the other starts or one must supersede the other.

Nevertheless, definite guidelines have been established through cases to enable those concerned to determine where towage 'stops' and salvage 'starts', because one thing which is beyond dispute is that both cannot exist at the same time when one is contemplating one physical operation. In *The Homewood* (1928) 31 Ll.L.Rep. 336 it was established that for a tug-owner to consider rightly that he had taken on the role of salvor it was essential that (a) the services he performed were of such an extraordinary nature that they could not have been within the reasonable contemplation of the parties to the original towage contract, and (b) that the services in fact performed and the risks in fact run would not have been reasonably remunerated if the contractual remuneration only was paid. In short, mere difficulty in the performance of the towage does not automatically 'convert' towage into salvage.

The burden of proof is heavy and lies upon the party claiming the salvage reward. He must show that the nature of the service changed from mere towage to salvage through no fault or want of skill on his part and simply and solely by accident or fortuitous circumstance over which he had no control.

Equally it may fall for consideration when, where and why salvage services terminate and the situation reverts to one of towage or pilotage, or both.

*The Aldora* [1975] 1 Lloyd's Rep. 617
A 10,500-ton vessel loaded with full cargo of aluminum ore in bulk went aground on a sand bank in February 1972. She sustained damage to her bottom plates. Four tugs went to her assistance and a harbour pilot boarded. There was an agreement that attempts should be made to refloat her. With tug assistance and under the direction of the pilot, the vessel was quickly refloated and subsequently towed up channel to a buoy to await permission to enter Blyth harbour. Legal action was taken by the tug-owners and the pilot claiming salvage services. The questions for decision were: (1) where and when did salvage service terminate? (2) whether interest could be claimed?

*Held*: as to (1), that salvage services ceased when the ship was near the fairway buoy. From that point the pilot was entitled to a pilotage fee only and the tug-owners to a towage fee only. As to the salvage, the pilot had voluntarily undertaken serious responsibility in the refloating operation and the tugs had rendered skilful and prompt assistance. When the ship's Master found himself aground he would have been unwise not to have accepted their offer of help. Salvage was awarded, £4,500 to the owners, Master and crew of tug *A*; £4,000 to tug *B*; £3,750 to tugs *C* and *D*; and £1,000 to the pilot.

*Held:* as to (2), that salvage was like any other debt and the court had the power to award interest.

CHAPTER 8

# TOWAGE

Towage is in essence a service by one vessel to another for a fixed remuneration. The most common reason for one vessel to require such service is that, for one reason or another, it lacks its own motive power. The case which follows is cited purely as an illustration of an 'exclusively' towage situation. That a salvage element entered into it was eventually discredited. It was a dispute arising simply from an alleged breach of a towage contract.

*The Kismet* [1976] 2 Lloyd's Rep. 585

*The Kismet* was a steam tanker which left Aden for Durban on 20 November 1970. She was fully loaded with petroleum products. She also had 131 tons of distilled water and could produce distilled water from her own evaporators at the rate of 35 tons per day. On 25 November she developed engine trouble which involved the evaporators fracturing and the starboard boiler leaking. This caused her to use up an excessive quantity of distilled water. She anchored off the Mozambique coast and her owners (the defendants in the action) entered into negotiations by telephone with the operators of a salvage tug, the *Statesman*, who were the plaintiffs in the action. It was agreed that the *Statesman* should proceed from Durban to the *Kismet* and supply her with the required amount of water and that, if considered necessary, should escort or tow the *Kismet* to Durban. Later, disagreement arose as to how much water had been supplied. Thirty to 35 tons was lost as a result of valves on the *Kismet*'s tanks being inadvertently left open. There was also an allegation by the *Kismet*'s officers that the water was contaminated. It was agreed to recall the *Statesman*, which by that time had left, and that she should tow the *Kismet* to Durban. A towing connection was established on 2 December and the vessels reached Durban on 9 December.

The plaintiffs subsequently claimed £19,525.52 as remuneration for water supply and towage on a 'time occupied' basis under contract. The defendants disputed this on the grounds that the plaintiffs had breached their contract by failing to supply the right quantity of water and it was only as a result of this breach that towing to Durban had become necessary. Alternatively, they argued that if they were liable to pay for the towage they were at least entitled to counter-claim the whole amount as damages for breach of contract and they pleaded that the principle of circuity of action (see Chapter 7, page 353) applied to defeat that part of the plaintiff's claim. The defendants conceded that the plaintiffs were entitled to £10,416, which was the amount payable if the water had been properly supplied, but sought to set off against this another counter-claim for loss of charter hire.

*Held*: that the plaintiffs had contracted to use their best endeavours to supply 100 tons of water, but in any event 75 tons, and found as a fact that they had only supplied 65. Had the *Kismet* received the extra 35 tons she could safely have reached Durban under her own steam. Nevertheless, the decision to tow her to Durban would still likely have been taken since she lost 30 to 35 tons on board through carelessness. Judgment was given for the plaintiffs for the £19,525 and only £2 nominal damages was awarded against them for their breach of contract.

A vessel may emerge from a dockyard and be still without functioning engines. Alternatively, she may be manoeuvring in a restricted area of water where her very size could cause her to be a hazard to other waterway traffic if she relied on her own motive power entirely.

The terms and conditions under which towage is to be performed is customarily embodied in a written agreement, in printed form, the form in the United Kingdom being the UK Standard Conditions for Towage and Other Services as revised 1986. The main purpose of this agreement is to place most of the liability on the tow. A revision prior to 1986 had taken place in 1983. There are other forms for ocean towage such as Towhire (daily rate) and Towcon (lump sum).

Before examining the 1986 wording of the agreement, however, it would be of advantage to see how the courts dealt with the respective liabilities of tug-owner and tow-owner in the preceding years and the following are some cases reported in the last hundred years.

*The Niobe* (1888) 13 PD 55
The tug *Flying Serpent* was towing the vessel *Niobe* under towage contract terms. Both tug and tow collided with the ship *Valletta*. The *Niobe* was keeping a poor look-out. Had she observed the *Flying Serpent* the collision would not have occurred. The *Niobe*'s owners denied liability for the negligence of the *Flying Serpent* on the grounds that they were not their servants but independent contractors.

*Held*: that the *Niobe* was responsible for the *Flying Serpent*'s negligence on the basis that in law the tow had control over the tug.

This case well illustrates how tug-owners have always attempted to contract out of as much liability as possible and how the English courts have respected such freedom of contract.

The tug-owner purports to protect himself by writing into the contract the idea that the tug Master and crew, whilst carrying out the towage service thus defined as regards commencement and termination, are the servants of the tow (or its owner) and *not* of the tug-owner. This cuts across the general principle of vicarious liability which basically confines itself to the employer/employee relationship. Such a clause, therefore, amounts to what one might describe as an assignment of vicarious responsibility. It does, however, accord with the Admiralty concept of the tug and tow arrangement that the tug and tow during the performance of the contract service are deemed to be, as it were, 'one shipping unit' with the controlling mind (the brain) being the tow and the motive power (the brawn) being the tug. This basic transfer of responsibility paves the way for the 'punch' clause of a towage contract which purports to allow the tug-owner to escape responsibility for any damage or loss caused by his employees through any act, neglect or default either to his own craft or to the hirer's vessel (or indeed to any innocent third vessel) and additionally gives him the right to seek indemnity from the hirer wherever this may be applicable.

This principle is illustrated by the later case of *The President Van Buren*, below.

*The President Van Buren* (1924) 16 Asp MLC 444
The owners of the *President Van Buren* engaged the Port of London Authority's tug *Sirdar*

to tow her into the main dock at Tilbury. The terms of the contract included a stipulation that 'the Master and crew of the tug shall cease to be under the control of the port authority during . . . the towage and shall become subject to the orders and control of the Master of the vessel towed and are the servants of the owner thereof who thereby undertakes to pay for any damage caused to any of the port authority's property'. The tug and tow were in collision due to the negligence of the crew of the tug, both suffering damage. Each vessel's owner took legal action against the other to recover damages.

*Held*: that the tug-owner succeeded and the tow-owner's counter-claim failed. Although the blame lay entirely with the tug, the stipulations in the contract clearly indicated that the parties had intended that the Master and crew of the tug were to become the servants of the tow-owner during towage.

If the tug-owner contracts to supply a named tug of the tow-owner's choice, the tug-owner's responsibilities for the seaworthiness of the tug are lower on the grounds that the hirer has not relied so much on the contractor's skill. The following case illustrates this point but, as it is a salvage case, it is not conclusive as a precedent on this point in claims under a towage contract.

*The Maréchal Suchet* (1911) 80 LJP 51
The *Maréchal Suchet* was towed from Falmouth to London. The tug was not fit for the voyage and a strong south wind drove the tug and tow off course with the result that the tow grounded. The tug with extra assistance refloated the tow and subsequently they all claimed a salvage reward. The contracted tug's claim was denied, the reasons being that the contract of towage did not call for a *named* tug to be supplied (as the tug-owner argued) but for a tug to be supplied. There was, therefore, an implied warranty that the tug should be efficient. Nothing but force majeure would excuse them under the circumstances.

It is the duty of the owner of the tow to disclose all information relevant to the tug contractor. This principle bears some similarity to the principle of uberrima fides (utmost good faith) between an assured and an insurer under policies of marine insurance. However, it is thought that the English courts will only not enforce a towage contract where the non-disclosure makes the contract seriously inequitable (i.e. it should have been salvage).

*Elliott Steam Tug Co Ltd* v *New Medway Steam Packet Co Ltd* (1937) 59 Ll.L.Rep. 35
A employed the services of B's tug to tow a lighter from West Mersea to Chatham. When the tug reported for duty it was found to be impossible to reach the lighter owing to an insufficient depth of water except at high tide. The lighter's owners had made no effort to move the lighter to a position where she could conveniently be taken in tow. B claimed damages alleging that A had broken an implied contractual term that the lighter was in such a practicable position.

*Held*: that B's claim was good and the action was successful.

*The Unique Mariner* [1978] 1 Lloyd's Rep. 438. The vessel *Unique Mariner* ran aground and the owners notified the master that a tug was being despatched from Singapore. Another tug the *Salvaliant* was in the vicinity and the Master mistakenly thought that this tug was the one sent by the owners. He signed an LOF with the *Salvaliant* and when appreciating the mistake the Master ordered the vessel *Salvaliant* to stop work. The owners of the *Unique Mariner* disputed the validity of the agreement with the tug *Salvaliant*. They argued, inter alia, that the contract was uberrima fidei and the tug master should have disclosed all material facts, one of which being that the rendezvous had been made by chance. This argument was rejected by the High Court.

In August 1957 an incident happened which led to some interesting and significant litigation in towage rights and liabilities. It involved the scope and interpretation of the following two clauses of the relevant towage contract. Although the contract of towage was performed in Australia, the terms and conditions of the agreement were sufficiently similar to the stipulations contained in the UK agreement as to be worth describing here. The relevant clauses were:

'2. On the employment of a tug, the Master and crew thereof become the servants of and identified with the hirer and are under the control of the hirer or his servants or agents, and anyone on board the hirer's vessel who may be employed and/or paid by the tug-owner shall be considered the servants of the hirer.

'3. The tug-owner shall not, whilst towing, bear or be liable for . . . any personal injury . . . arising from any cause including negligence at any time of the tug-owner's servants or agents . . . and the hirer shall pay for all . . . personal injury . . . and shall also indemnify the tug-owner against all consequences thereof . . . '

The case in which these clauses were considered is described below.

*Taylor* v *Geelong Harbour Trust Commissioners and Howard Smith* [1962] 1 Lloyd's Rep. 143, Supreme Court of Victoria

The plaintiff, a crew member of a hired launch, was injured whilst assisting in the berthing of a vessel, attending by a dolphin to secure her by ropes to the pier. The plaintiff sued the vessel owner (the hirer) and the tug-owner (Geelong Harbour Trust) jointly and severally. There was a cross-claim by each defendant against the other for contributions to the damages, if awarded. The plaintiff alleged that his accident resulted from the negligence of the servants or agents of either defendant, or both. The hirer was exonerated from liability on the grounds that it had not been sufficiently established that he was, in law, the employer of the plaintiff and thus owed him a duty of care, nor was there a sufficient degree of control by the hirer over the berthing operation generally to imply that there was vicarious liability on the part of the hirer for the negligence of the tug Master who was instrumental in causing the plaintiff's injuries. Judgment was, however, given against the tug-owner. The issue of indemnity was then discussed and the tug-owner based his claim on contract, not on the liability of joint tortfeasors.

*Held* (on the issue of indemnity): that the tug Master was negligent, that his negligent act was the proximate cause of the plaintiff's injuries, that it was not the result of a defective system of work per se. The combination of indemnity clauses in the towage conditions adequately covered the tug-owner and, provided that where the cause of the accident was connected with the towing operation, as it was here, the wording was not too wide to allow this act of negligence and its resulting injury to be brought within the scope and intention of the indemnity clauses, thus allowing the tug contractor to be indemnified by the hirer.

The same conclusion was reached in *Great Western Railway Co* v *Royal Norwegian Government* (1945) 78 Ll.L.Rep. 152; the only difference being that the injured man there was a member of the tug's crew, not a member of the crew of an additionally hired launch.

English law as currently in force (i.e. since 1978) would treat the *Taylor* case very differently as will be seen later.

One recent case involving the tug-owners' duty to ensure the towage will be safely and successfully carried out and the fact that this can be delegated to independent contractors is:

*Goliath Transport & Shipping BV* v *The General Authority of the Port of Alexandria* (*The Salviva*) [1987] 2 Lloyd's Rep. 457
This case concerned a contract to tow a floating crane from Japan to Alexandria and the terms included a provision that the tow would be prepared for towage by the tug-owner and provided with the necessary documentation. Another clause provided that if the tug and tow en route met a typhoon or tropical storm, which was officially recognized as such, any deviation necessitated or delay occasioned by it to the tug would be indemnified by the tow-owner to the tug-owner at the rate of US$5,000 per day for extra steaming time. Another clause obliged the tug-owner to bear the expense of and pay for the lashing wire, lashing works and all preparations at the Japanese shipyard.

The towing seaworthy survey was to be carried out by Lloyd's Register but due to the time expected to be required for the examination, the Japanese firm was instructed to carry out the survey. The tug and tow duly left the Japanese shipyard in mid-October 1981 and their route to Alexandria took them via Singapore, the Bay of Bengal, around the south of Sri Lanka, up to Aden into the Red Sea and Suez. While still in the open sea south west of Japan the tug deviated to avoid the effect of a typhoon and incurred three days' extra steaming time. Whilst still on the periphery of the typhoon and due to continued rolling and pitching damage was caused to the sea fastening and the tug Master gave notice that he would have to put into Singapore for repairs. Surveyors there attributed the damage to the heavy weather, but considered that inadequate welding and insufficient lashing and securing of the crane jib, before leaving Japan, were contributory causes.

The tug-owners paid the repair bill. Later on in the Red Sea the tug was instructed to deviate to assist a stranded vessel and later still after encountering further rough weather, further damage was found to the sea fastening on arrival at Suez and there was another delay at Port Said whilst repairs were effected before the tow continued on to Alexandria.

At the end of all this the tug-owners claimed under various heads, extra steaming time, cost of repairs at Singapore, demurrage at Singapore, detention at Port Said and for the cost of putting a runner crew aboard the crane barge. This amounted in aggregate to approximately US$270,000. The owner of the tow denied liability. They said they had never agreed to the employment of Japanese surveyors rather than Lloyd's Register, that the deviation by the tug was unnecessary and dangerous, that the tug-owners should have been responsible for seeing that the sea fastening was properly performed and that they should have warranted the adequacy of it.

*Held*: by the Commercial Court Judge that there was sufficient evidence of the approval by the tow-owners' representative on the spot in Japan for a change of surveyor, secondly that the deviation was properly covered by the typhoon clause in the contract as being a deviational delay occasioned by an officially recognized tropical storm or typhoon and thirdly the tug-owner was entitled to rely on the expertise of the Japanese marine surveyors who had been engaged to approve of the fitness of the tow for the towage and that it was a failure in the surveyor's expertise which was the proximate cause of the sea-fastening work having degenerated to the point where it needed repairs at Singapore.

All in all, the tow-owner was responsible for the entire claim of the tug-owner and although the tow-owner appealed, the Court of Appeal dismissed the appeal and decided that on the true construction of the towage contract the tug-owner was entitled to recover all the disputed amounts.

One clause which has given rise to many disputes is that which purports to define the period of towage and to fix and pinpoint accurately the moment when the stipulations in the towage agreement are deemed to commence to be effective and the moment when they are deemed to cease to be effective. In short, there has always been the need to define and apply, in each individual set of circumstances, the expression 'whilst towing'. This is important as this is the period when the tow assumes great risks. Such definition is radically different from the common law position that the towage commences when the tow rope has passed to the tug.

There are two comparatively 'vintage' cases before 1974 on this particular issue.

*The Uranienborg* (1935) 53 L1.L.Rep. 165
The tug *Kenia* was contracted to tow the *Uranienborg*. The UK Standard Towage Conditions governed the contract. The tug collided with the ship causing her damage. The shipowner argued that at the material time nobody on the ship was preparing to give orders and when the tug arrived (although in hailing distance) she was not in a position to receive orders. The tug-owner argued that the collision occurred within the period of towing as contemplated by Clause 1 of the conditions.

*Held*: that the tug–owner could not succeed. The tug-owner, in order to be protected, had to be in a position to receive orders to pick up ropes or lines and not just general orders.

The particular rule emphasized in the above case, i.e. that it is not sufficient to receive general orders only but that they must be specific and the type of order contemplated in the 'definitions' clause, is worthy of special note.

*The Impetus* [1959]1 Lloyd's Rep. 269
The vessel *Blenheim* collided with the tug *Impetus*. At the time, the *Impetus* was under contract to tow the *Blenheim* under the terms of the UK Standard Towage Conditions. The collision occurred before a heaving line had been thrown. The *Blenheim* had given no order to this effect and, although the tug's crew were prepared, the tug was not properly positioned. The contract terms incorporated the phrase 'whilst towing', defined as 'the period beginning when the tug is in a position to receive orders from the hirer's vessel to pick up ropes or lines'. It was also stipulated that the tug-owner should not be responsible for damage done by the tug whilst towing.

*Held*: that the owners of the *Impetus* were protected. The vessel and tug were ready to give and receive orders respectively, even though the tug may not have been in a position immediately to carry out the order. The collision took place during the 'towing period'.

In *The Glenaffric* [1948] P 159, CA, it was decided that it is not necessary for the tow to be ready to give such specific orders so long as the tug is ready to receive the orders should they be given. Whether or not the tug could *immediately* comply with the order when given is irrelevant.

Even greater certainty and clarification was achieved by a 1971 decision in the courts when it was suggested that three conditions should be fulfilled if the tug-owner was to be able to establish his indemnity claim against the hirer (the tow-owner) under the provisions of Clause 1 of the Standard Towage Conditions.

*The Apollon* [1971] 1 Lloyd's Rep. 476
The motor vessel *Apollon* was lying in the south lock, Newport, waiting to enter dock and the Master signed a towage order for two tugs. The plaintiff's tug was made fast to the head and started towing. When the *Apollon* was only partially clear of the south lock, her pilot requested the other engaged tug, also owned by the plaintiffs, to take a line aft and act as stern tug. As this other tug manoeuvred to take up position astern of the tow she struck a moored dock gate and suffered damage to her propeller. The plaintiffs claimed indemnity under Clause 1 of the UK Standard Towage Conditions. The defendants argued that the tug which was damaged was not at the time 'towing' within the meaning of the stipulation of the agreement.

*Held*: for the plaintiffs, on the ground that for a tug to be in a position to receive orders direct from the hirer's vessel to pick up ropes or lines as required by Clause 1 of the Standard Towage Conditions: (a) those on board the tug must reasonably expect the ship to give the tug an order to pick up ropes or lines; (b) the tug must be ready to respond to such an order if given; and (c) the tug must be within hailing distance. All three conditions in this case were fulfilled. It is perfectly normal and to be expected that a tug might have to execute a manoeuvre after receiving an order.

An interesting case which concerned the Port of London Authority came before the courts as follows:

*Knapp* v *Port of London Authority and Cory Bros Shipping Ltd* (*Third Party*) [1977] 1 Lloyd's Rep. 662
K claimed damages for personal injuries suffered whilst employed by the Port of London Authority on their tug, *Plagal*, in February 1974 when the tug was towing the vessel *Neptune Topaz* belonging to Cory Bros. The authority admitted liability for its employee's injuries but sought to be indemnified by the third party, Cory Bros. They relied on clauses contained in their booklet under the heading 'Hire and Use of Tugs' which they maintained contained the terms and conditions upon which their tugs were supplied. The relevant clauses were: 'The PLA shall not whilst towing bear or be liable for damage of any description done by or to the tug or done by or to the hirer's vessel . . . or for any personal injury . . . arising from any cause including negligence at any time of the PLA's servants . . . and the hirer shall pay for all loss or damage and personal injury . . . and shall also indemnify the PLA against all consequences thereof and the PLA shall not, whilst at the request express or implied, of the hirer, rendering any other service than towing, be held responsible for any damage done to the hirer's vessel and the hirer shall indemnify the PLA against any claim by the third party . . . for personal injury . . . ' And ' . . . the hirer shall not bear or be liable for any loss or damage of any description done by or to the tug otherwise than whilst towing . . . or for loss of life or injury to the crew of the tug . . . ' A clear distinction is here drawn between the situation where the tug is actually towing and the situation where the tug is performing any service other than towing. In the case of the latter situation, the hirer is not bound to indemnify the tug-owner where a tug crew member has been injured.

*Held*: that the defendants were entitled to be indemnified by the third-party hirer as the accident happened 'whilst towing'.

That the law would treat this case differently under the law *now* in force will be seen later.

The scope of the period of the contract has been more clearly defined and it has been elaborated in more detail than in the standard terms and conditions which were in force prior to 1974. As it is probably true to say that as many accidents resulting in damage occur prior to the making fast of (or subsequent to the casting-off of) the connecting towing line, there has long been a pressing need for an unambiguous definition. Obviously it is unrealistic to regard the period of towage as being confined only to that period of time when both tug and tow are physically joined by the towing rope.

In the 'definitions' clause (Clause 1 of the United Kingdom Standard Conditions for Towage; see Appendix 10, page 553) the phrase 'whilst towing' received more comprehensive treatment under the 1974 revision than previously in that it provided for towage to commence from that point of time when the tug or tender is in a position to receive orders direct from the tow to commence *pushing*, *holding*, *moving*, *escorting* or *guiding* the vessel or to pick up ropes or lines (the italicized words being intended to ensure that the concept of towing includes the allied services of guiding and/or escorting). Those five italicized words were increased under the 1983 and 1986 revisions to include 'pulling' and 'standing by'. One area of doubt which remains concerns the determination of the party on which responsibility should fall. This extraordinarily difficult problem, which pervades the law of contract generally, may be stated as: was there a 'meeting of minds' in relation to the contract of towage? This may be stated in different terms: although the tug may have considered herself at the material time to be in a position to receive orders within the meaning of Clause 1, did those in charge of the tow take the same view in the absence of an express communication of intent between them?

The scope of the service of towing under the wording in the 1974, 1983 and 1986 revisions has been gradually enlarged to include the allied services of escorting and guiding performed by the contractor's vessel. 'Escort services' is the standard description of a service performed frequently by a tug contractor and featuring in his debit note for fees rendered to the hirer. This idea has in fact been in vogue for some considerable time and *The Leoborg* [1962] 2 Lloyd's Rep. 146 is illustrative of this.

Under the 1974 wording, the tug-owner appeared to have strengthened his position still further for at least two reasons. Firstly, whereas (before the revision of the wording) the tow-owner could not under the standard conditions be held responsible when loss of life or injury resulted to the tug crew, the hirer of the tug was now exposed to providing full indemnity in that event also. Secondly, the hirer's ability to exclude himself from the onerous stipulations of Clause 4 would be defeated by any element of contributory negligence on his part, however trivial or minor. In other words, however substantial the personal fault or privity or other failure of the tug-owner may be, the slightest element of negligence on the hirer's part which directly contributed to the causing of the loss or damage would debar the hirer from extricating himself from responsibility under the contract terms.

One purpose of the 1986 and 1983 revisions of the UK standard conditions for towage and other services was to comply with the provisions of the Unfair Contract Terms Act 1977 (effective from 1 February 1978) which is the legislative principal contribution towards a social development of fair trading in the UK. However it should be borne in mind that the Unfair Contract Terms Act 1977 mostly does not apply to salvage or towage except where a person is dealing as a consumer. However, section 2(1) applies to all towage contracts irrespective of whether a person is a consumer. Section 2(1) prohibits exclusion of liability for death or personal injury resulting from negligence. The contractual provisions for indemnity regarding death or personal injury have been modified in order to conform with section 2 of the 1977 statute. This has been done by the addition of sub-paragraph (e) to paragraph 4 which reads as follows:

'Notwithstanding anything contained in clauses 4(a) and (b) hereof the liability of the Tug owner for death or personal injury resulting from negligence is not excluded or restricted thereby.'

By these few words of modification the towage terms thus comply with the statutory requirement that no-one may contract out of his liability for death or injury caused by his negligence or the negligence of his servants or agents. Under section 12 of the 1977 statute a person is a consumer if he does not make a contract in the course of a business nor holds himself out as doing so and the other party does make the contract in the course of a business. Most towage contracts are made between commercial organizations although there are many cases where a pleasure yacht, owned by a consumer is towed to port. In the latter case it should be borne in mind that under the 1977 statute an exclusion of liability for negligence or breach of contract for loss or damage to property must satisfy the reasonableness test. It seems that Clauses 4(c)(i) and (ii) of the 1986 revision have been drafted to take account of the 1977 Act. The wording of these subsections may be studied in full in Appendix 10. Suffice it here to say that it relieves the hirer in cases, first, where the tug owner or his manager or anyone to whom he has specifically delegated the duty to use care to make the tug seaworthy has failed in that duty and, secondly, where the accident happens when the tug is not in a 'position of proximity or risk' to the vessel, unless the tug at that time is carrying at the hirer's request persons or property other than the tug's own crew or equipment and his presence contributes to the rising of the subsequent claim.

The actual operation of towing and the prior and subsequent manoeuvres are so closely identified under the current stipulations that, whereas the obsolete conditions gave the hirer scope to exclude his liability for that part of any service not expressly in the nature of physical towing, the hirer is no longer so protected.

Clause 5 also extends extra protection to the tug-owner. Its wording contemplates two situations. Firstly, that the tug contractor may wish to substitute one tug or tender for another and, secondly, that he may want totttsub-contract part of the work out to another contractor whom he may wish to have corresponding benefits, immunities, obligations and duties vis-à-vis the original hirer. The effect of the current wording under this clause is to make the tug-owner the agent of the hirer in respect of his role as negotiator of the sub-contract, or perhaps an intermediary generally between the original hirer and the sub-contractor. The concept of agency, if it is not expressed in writing, could easily be implied from the circumstances.

## TUG-OWNER'S RIGHT TO LIMIT LIABILITY

Clause 6 of the Standard Conditions for Towage 1986 expressly preserves the tug-owner's right to limit his liability in addition to reserving all rights in respect of salvage remuneration or compensation for any other 'extraordinary services rendered'. What extraordinary services are contemplated, other than those in the nature of salvage, is not clear.

Clause 7, which allows the tug-owner to except himself from liability for the consequences of certain extraneous circumstances, has been extended by the addition of 'acts of terrorism or sabotage' so as to give it a contemporary look. The words 'delays of any description, howsoever caused or arising' in Clause 7 ensure that the tug-owner's exemption from liability is comprehensive.

## Towage

The last clause of the Standard Conditions for Towage 1986 (Clause 8) was introduced for the first time into the 1974 revision. It purports to prevent the hirer from attempting to bring an action direct against individual employees (crew members, for example) of the tug-owner where circumstances would indicate such action would be logical, viz. in cases of negligence by members of the crew.

A clause in a towage contract which may be intended to provide wide protection to the tug-owner and may purport to exclude to the maximum possible extent his liability, may nevertheless have some restricting or qualifying sentence in it such as the frequently used wording in the standard indemnity clause which runs as follows: 'loss or damage of any kind whatsoever or howsoever or wheresoever arising in the course of *and* in connection with the towage'.

This tends to limit rather than enlarge the scope of the clause and to oppose rather than to favour the tug-owner's interests. It is possible that what may amount to 'loss or damage' arising in the course of the towage, may not necessarily, and at the same time, be 'in connection' with it. The word 'and' is, of course, the key word and is restrictive in this context. A case in point is *The Carlton* (1931) 40 Ll.L.Rep.101, which centred around the fault of a lock supervisor and a resulting accident which happened in the course of the towage but not 'in connection' with it.

During 1972 and 1973 two interesting towage cases appeared before the Admiralty Court involving Conoco vessels. It had been long argued that it was inappropriate to use an action in rem to obtain a decree of specific performance which is essentially an equitable remedy and should be enforced by action in personam.

*The Conoco Britannia* [1972] 1 Lloyd's Rep. 342
The court decided that in its capacity of an Admiralty Court it had jurisdiction, under section 1(1)(h) of the Administration of Justice Act 1956,[1] to entertain a claim arising out of a towage contract for such a claim arose out of an agreement relating to the use or hire of a ship within the meaning of that subsection. Thus the court had power in an action in rem to entertain a claim for the specific performance of a contract.

*The Conoco Arrow* [1973] 1 Lloyd's Rep. 86
A tug contractor agreed to supply tugs for a vessel under the UK Standard Conditions for Towage then in force. They included an express stipulation that the contractor could substitute one tug for another and sub-let the work to other tug-owners who should also have the benefits and be subject to the liabilities of the terms and conditions to the same extent as the principal parties. One tug sank after colliding with the towed vessel. That tug's owner instituted an action in rem against the hiring vessel and her owners alleging (a) negligent navigation by the *Conoco Arrow*, and (b) breach of contract. The registrar struck out the cause of action based on contract on the grounds that the plaintiff tug-owner was not a party to the contract. The plaintiff appealed.

*Held*: on appeal, that the Admiralty Registrar was correct in striking out the cause of action and that there was no reason to question the validity of the long-established legal principle that a party cannot succeed upon a claim brought under a contract to which he was not a party and if that was the principle of law then there was no point in allowing such a cause of action to go forward.

1. Supreme Court Act 1981.

It may have been with the second of the two above-quoted cases in mind that Clause 5 of the Standard Conditions for Towage 1986 (which was originally drafted into the 1974 and 1983 terms) was included.

The damages payable to a tug-owner arise essentially out of contract and indemnity.

*Furness Withy & Co Ltd* v *Duder* [1936] 2 KB 461
A claim was lodged under what are now the provisions of section 1(1)(h) of the Administration of Justice Act 1956. The circumstances produced a situation where the owner of the tow was obliged to indemnify the owner of a tug following a collision and resulting damage. The tow-owner was insured and his hull policy included a running-down clause. This was of no avail to him, however, in his bid to recover under that clause because the damage which he was bound to pay to the tug's owner were payable under an obligation springing from contract and a contractual relationship.

Two US cases arising out of towage disputes are worthy of mention.

*Mobile Towing Co* v *The Janita* [1975] AMC 1074, US District Court
Where the Master of a barge grain carrier ordered tugs to tow the ship from an elevator to an anchorage $1\frac{1}{2}$ miles downstream in the Mobile River despite a heavy early morning fog and one of the tugs capsized when the tow line became taut, the tug's failure to release the tow line was not the proximate cause of the accident, but the Master's decision to shift the vessel in those circumstances caused the casualty. The ship was not negligent in not having an axe at hand in order to cut the taut tow line.

*A/S Atlantica* v *Moran Towing & Transportation Co Inc* [1974] AMC 555, US Court of Appeals
The US Court of Appeals, Southern District of New York, will not follow the doctrine that an undocking pilot's failure to request adequate tug power breaches the workmanlike service warranty implied in the towage contract and is therefore outside the protection of a pilotage clause providing: 'When any licensed pilot or a Captain of any tug furnished to or engaged in the service of assisting a vessel making use of or having available her own propelling power, goes on board such vessel, it is understood and agreed that he becomes the borrowed servant of the vessel assisted and her owner or operator for all purposes and in every respect, his services while so on board being the work of the vessel assisted and not of the tugboat company and being subject to the exclusive provision and control of the ship's personnel'.

The pilotage clause excused a tug company from liability for the undocking pilot's negligent plan of operation where his final decision to turn a 570–foot vessel in a 600-foot-wide channel was made and the plan was implemented after the pilot had boarded the assisted vessel.

Also of interest is a Dutch case.

*Amsterdam London Verzekering Maats NV* v *NV Rederij V/H Gebr Goedkoop and Another* 27 November 1974, No 30 S & S 1975, Amsterdam District Court
An offer to transport two pneumatic grain towers from Haarlem to Rotterdam was made on 'usual standard condition' and incorporated by reference the Netherlands Tugboat Conditions 1951. The offeree confirmed the offer by letter, ending: 'our conditions for carriage by water apply to this order'. Due to negligent navigation by the first defendant's tug Master, one of the towers on the pontoon, belonging to the second defendant, struck the underside of Van Brienenoord bridge.

*Held*: that the Netherlands Tugboat Conditions 1951 and the offeree's own standard conditions were not incompatible. The tugboat conditions plainly applied since the offeree could not reasonably expect the tug-owner to carry out transportation of the towers without tug assistance, which in turn necessitated the employment of tugs, which meant that the standard tugboat conditions would apply. The tug Master's negligence would not be visited upon his owners; nor would the tug Master be deemed to be the employee of the owner of the pontoon since the latter craft was unmanned.

CHAPTER 9

# LIMITATION OF LIABILITY

## HISTORICAL DEVELOPMENT

The basic idea behind the right to limit liability was that every encouragement should be given to shipowners to carry on their business. Going to sea in ships was an adventurous pursuit to be encouraged rather than discouraged in the interests of the promotion and flourishing of international trade and if those who were prepared to gamble what capital they did have knew that they were faced with exposure to unlimited liability and often in situations over which they might have no personal control, their keen adventurous spirit might have been stifled before it had had time to blossom. Centuries ago a serious maritime disaster would very likely have resulted in the instant bankruptcy of the shipowner. The chances were that he might abandon the ship and her freight into the hands of those third parties with valid claims against him. This in itself produced in practical terms a form of limitation of liability. Recognition of the inescapable economic fact that aggrieved third-party claimants would not recover their losses where the shipowners' adjudged liability far exceeded his assets was the essence of the pro-limitation argument. Looking at it from a creditor's viewpoint, it is surely preferable to live in the certainty of obtaining a substantial percentage of the compensation due rather than face the uncertainty of not knowing whether or not they would ever receive the much larger sums to which they had a right.

Whereas it could be said to be fair and right that a person should be responsible without limit for loss or damage to others caused by his own fault, it is less obviously right and just that he should be liable *without limit* for loss or damage caused to other persons or other persons' property through the act, neglect or default of his servants, ie. his vicarious liability. Some maritime countries, including some on the continent of Europe, allow shipowners to limit their liability to the value of the ship and freight. England passed similar legislation by statute in 1733, a Responsibility of Shipowners' Act which had the effect of limiting a shipowners' liability for loss of cargo by theft by the Master or crew to the value of the ship and freight. It was not until well into the early 19th century that the idea of limiting liability for damages resulting from collisions began to temper the common law and the maritime law notion of unlimited liability. However, towards the close of the 19th century, the Merchant Shipping Act 1894 and its amendments on limitation, culminating in 1958, set a quite different standard: limitation to an amount calculated by reference to the ship's tonnage, which will be explained in detail later on, and which is described by some as an arbitrary method intended to reach a more certain basis than the more uncertain value of ship and freight alternative.

On the international scene, Conventions have formed the basis for much shipping legislation in the UK and on the subject of limitation it was the 1957 Convention on the Limitation of Liability of Owners of Sea-going Ships (itself based on earlier Conventions), which provided the basis of the UK legislation the following year, 1958, with the passing of the Merchant Shipping (Liability of Shipowners and Others) Act 1958 which established the then current rules by which limitation was controlled and governed. The 1957 Convention was acceded to by various countries, such as India, Algeria, Iceland, Iran, Singapore, Luxembourg. Another Convention on Limitation of Liability for maritime claims was adopted on 19 November 1976 and signed in London on 1 February 1977 (the 1976 (London) Convention). This Convention introduced some radical changes which will be the subject of commentary later in this chapter. The 1976 (London) Convention was originally incorporated into the law of the UK by section 17 of the Merchant Shipping Act 1979 and came into force on 1 December 1986. Section 17 of the Merchant Shipping Act 1979 was repealed by the Merchant Shipping Act 1995 which came into force on 1 January 1996. The 1976 (London) Convention has the force of law in the UK (see section 185 and Schedule 7 to the Merchant Shipping Act 1995). Other countries have acceded to the 1976 (London) Convention such as Australia, Spain, Norway. It can be important to know which country has implemented which Convention for the purposes of limitation when seeking agreement on the appropriate jurisdiction say, for a collision action. With this in mind we shall consider both the past and present law of limitation of liability in the UK.

The relevant section of the Merchant Shipping Act 1894 which dealt with limitation read as follows:

> '503.—(1) The owners of a ship, British or foreign, shall not, where all or any of the following occurrences take place without their actual fault or privity; (that is to say),
> (a) Where any loss of life or personal injury is caused to any person being carried in the ship;
> (b) Where any damage or loss is caused to any goods, merchandise, or other things whatsoever on board the ship; . . . '

*Moore* v *Metcalf Motor Coasters* [1958] 2 Lloyd's Rep. 179; [1959] 1 Lloyd's Rep. 264, CA

A ship's chief engineer drowned as a result of falling from an allegedly defective gangway. He was returning to the ship from shore. The question arose, inter alia, whether the seaman was 'being carried in the ship' within the meaning of section 503(1)(a). The court stressed the difference between the expression 'being carried in the ship' and the expression 'on board the ship'. The latter expression means physically on board the ship. The former expression has a wider meaning and must include the concept of the status of the person being carried, e.g. being carried under a contract of employment or as a result of some other contractual arrangement, e.g. a passenger contract. Such an interpretation should rightly be accepted as correct in order to avoid a most unwelcome possible legal nicety by which shipowners could avail themselves of the benefit of the section if the deceased (or injured person) was just stepping on to the ship's gangway to leave the ship but if he was two steps further down the gangway they would lose the benefit of the section. This, it is submitted, would be palpably nonsensical.

A significant amendment was made by the Merchant Shipping Act 1979 in respect of loss of life or injury and damage to property. The amendment contained in section 35(1) of the 1979 Act provided that where loss of life or injury has occurred to someone on board the ship *in question* or indeed there has been damage to property belonging to a person on board the ship *in question*, provided that the person was on board pursuant to a contract of employment governed by the law of the UK, there is no limitation of liability effective as against that person. However, this has been repealed by the Merchant Shipping Act 1995 (see Schedule 12).

The text of section 503(1) of the 1894 Act continued as follows, and thereafter the text of section 503(2) is quoted in full.

'(c) Where any loss of life or personal injury is caused to any person carried in any other vessel by reason of the improper navigation of the ship;

(d) Where any loss or damage is caused to any other vessel, or to any goods, merchandise, or other things whatsoever on board any other vessel, by reason of the improper navigation of the ship;

be liable to damages beyond the following amounts; (that is to say,)

(i) In respect of loss of life or personal injury, either alone or together with loss of or damage to vessels, goods, merchandise, or other things, an aggregate amount not exceeding fifteen pounds for each ton of their ship's tonnage; and

(ii) In respect of loss of, or damage to, vessels, goods, merchandise, or other things, whether there be in addition loss of life or personal injury or not, an aggregate amount not exceeding eight pounds for each ton of their ship's tonnage.

(2) For the purposes of this section—

(a) The tonnage of a steam ship shall be her gross tonnage without deduction on account of engine room; and the tonnage of a sailing ship shall be her registered tonnage;

Provided that there shall not be included in such tonnage any space occupied by seamen or apprentices and appropriated to their use which is certified under the regulations schedules to this Act with regard thereto.

(b) Where a foreign ship has been or can be measured according to British law, her tonnage, as ascertained by that measurement shall, for the purpose of this section, be deemed to be her tonnage.

(c) Where a foreign ship has not been and cannot be measured according to British law, the surveyor-general of ships in the United Kingdom, or the chief measuring officer of any British possession abroad, shall, on receiving from or by the direction of the court hearing the case, in which the tonnage of the ship is in question, such evidence concerning the dimensions of the ship as it may be practicable to furnish, give a certificate under his hand stating what would in his opinion have been the tonnage of the ship if she had been duly measured according to British law, and the tonnage so stated in that certificate shall, for the purposes of this section, be deemed to be the tonnage of the ship'.

Subsequent amendments to the provisions are referred to later in this chapter.

One of the first things to determine is what is meant by a 'ship'. The original legal definition of a ship included every ship, vessel or boat used in navigation and not propelled by oars. This was extended to include any structure, whether completed or in the course of completion, launched and intended for use in navigation as a ship or part of a ship (see the Merchant Shipping (Liability of Shipowners and Others) Act 1958, section 4(1)). Time also saw the inclusion of every description of lighter, barge or like vessel used in navigation, however propelled. It *did not*, however, include any lighter, barge or like vessel used *exclusively* in non-tidal waters other than harbours.

*Steedman* v *Scofield* [1992] 2 Lloyd's Rep. 163
The question was whether a jet ski was a vessel used in navigation and if so, a ship. The plaintiff, whilst riding a jet ski in the vicinity of Brighton Pier, was involved in a collision with a speedboat. He was injured and brought a claim against the owners of the speedboat for personal injuries.

*Held*: the jet ski was not a boat nor was it a vessel. A vessel was usually a hollow receptacle for carrying people and the word 'vessel' was used to refer to crafts larger than rowing boats and included every description of watercraft used or capable of being used as a means of transportation on water. Furthermore, a jet ski was not a vessel used in navigation. The phrase 'used in navigation' conveyed the concept of transporting persons or property to an intended destination; navigation was not synonymous with movement on water but was planned or ordered movement from one place to another. Whilst a jet ski was capable of movement on water at very high speed, its purpose was not to go from one place to another. Accordingly, the plaintiff's personal injury action was not time barred under section 8 Maritime Conventions Act 1911 (see below). The normal three-year limitation period applied.

The definition of a ship now is 'every description of vessel used in navigation' (see section 313 of the Merchant Shipping Act 1995).

The words 'without their actual fault or privity' which appeared in section 503 were possibly the most significant and meaningful words in the entire scope and structure of shipping law. As has been hinted in the introduction to this section, it is logical and reasonable, and indeed perhaps equitable, that whereas a man should be allowed to limit his liability in respect of acts, neglects or defaults of his servants resulting in loss or damage to third persons or their property, it is not necessarily so reasonable that if he is personally at fault or has some form of knowledge or constructive knowledge which, because he did not use it, resulted in the calamity in question, he should similarly be allowed to limit his liability. The right to limit which featured in section 503 was only available provided that the occurrence which resulted in the loss or damage happened without the actual personal fault or privity of the person entitled to limit. The actual fault or privity rule has, however, been replaced as of December 1986 (which was when the 1976 London Convention became effective in the UK) by a different set of standards. The provisions of the London Convention are discussed later in this chapter (pages 395–412). It is at that point of time that historical development merges into current ruling law.

In the days when the owner of a ship was often also the Master of his ship, the problem of deciding whether or not there had been actual fault or privity was very simple. However, in the modern-day complexities of large shipping organizations, subsidiary companies, consortia, etc., it can be, and very frequently is, extremely difficult to pinpoint whether or not the actual fault is that of the shipowner himself or somebody so closely identified with the company owning the ship as to be said to be a person who spoke and acted as the shipowning company itself or whether it is the neglect or default or act of a servant of the shipowner.

The word 'fault' needs no further explanation. The word 'privity', on the other hand, needs a little further definition. If one is 'privy' to something this means, generally speaking, that one has a certain knowledge, either confidential or otherwise, of some relationship or agreement or situation existing between two or more other people. In other words, one could virtually but perhaps not entirely describe the word 'privity' as being equivalent to the word 'knowledge'.

*The Eurysthenes* [1976] 2 Lloyd's Rep. 171, CA
The vessel *Eurysthenes* stranded during a cargo-carrying voyage from the USA to the Philippines. Her cargo was substantially lost or damaged. The cargo interests claimed against the shipowner, alleging that the ship had sailed without her full complement of certificated deck officers, without proper charts, with an unserviceable echo-sounder and with a boiler which would not work. The vessel was consequently alleged to be unseaworthy through lack of due diligence. There was an independent question whether the shipowner, after settling cargo claims, had the right to be reimbursed by his protecting and indemnity underwriter. The crucial issue was whether the shipowner was privy to the condition in which his ship had put to sea and, following on that, whether he was entitled to the right to limit his liability under section 503 of the Merchant Shipping Act 1894. Should the criterion which decides whether there has been 'actual fault or privity' be wilful misconduct or reckless deliberate action by the shipowner personally or merely his personal negligence?

The Court of Appeal, referring to privity, commented that privity did not mean that there was any wilful misconduct by the shipowner but only that he knew of the act beforehand and concurred in its being done; that 'privity' did not mean that he himself personally did the act but only that someone else did it and that he knowingly concurred. In other words, 'without [his] privity' is equivalent in meaning to 'without his knowledge or concurrence'.

However, it need not necessarily be actual knowledge, it can be 'constructive knowledge' which means something which that person ought to have known, even if he did not in fact know it. English law is perhaps not quite so liberal as US law in this respect. Privity or knowledge in respect of defective design or breach of required standards in a vessel can operate to defeat a shipowner's right to limit as was the issue in a United States case.

*The Marine Sulphur Queen* [1973] 1 Lloyd's Rep. 88, US Court of Appeals
The demise charterers and the owners (who were a wholly-owned subsidiary of the demise charterers) were unable to limit their liability in respect of wrongful death claims against them. They were unable to show that proved unseaworthiness was not the cause of the loss of the ship with the resultant loss of life and since they were considered to be personally 'statutorily' at fault in that the reconstruction of the vessel, a molten sulphur carrier, had not complied with American Bureau standards they were liable in full to the death claimants.

The tests which are used to describe whether the 'actual fault or privity' rule comes into play and in trying to determine whether the person was or could be said to be the directing mind of the company are, firstly, one of determining whether or not that particular person was or could be said to have been to all intents and purposes 'in control' of the particular situation. Purely as illustrations the following United States cases deal with this point.

*Re Liberty Shipping* (*Owners of the Don Jose Figueras*) [1973] AMC 2241, US District Court
The neglect of the shipowners' managerial and supervisory personnel in failing to see that officers and crew were reasonably competent and trained to control and extinguish a fire

renders the shipowners liable for cargo damage. After detecting smoke from the cargo hold ventilator, the ship's officers attempted to extinguish a fire with $CO_2$ but faulty vent-closing devices prevented sealing of the cargo holds and the ship was eventually abandoned after three cargo holds filled with water and caused a 38° list. A marine engineering firm had periodically advised the shipowners that the vent-closing devices were faulty and that the officers and crew were not properly trained. Limitation of liability was denied by the US District Court.

*The Petition of Meljoy Transportation Co Inc* [1974] AMC 1293, US District Court
On 7 January 1972 the motor ship *Martin* down-bound on the River Ohio with a tow of two unladen petroleum barges, was passing beneath the Baltimore and Ohio Railway Co bridge. While the tow was passing beneath the bridge, the barges exploded, killing two crew members, injuring others aboard the *Martin* and causing physical damage to the bridge and to structures ashore. A number of separate actions against the owner and operator of the tow were consolidated for trial of the limitation of liability issues.

*Held* (by District Court, Northern District of West Virginia): (1) that the explosion was caused by the ignition of fumes during the negligent stripping and venting of the unladen petroleum barges. (2) That the railroad bridge, with a 326.5 ft channel between the piers, did not constitute an unreasonable hazard to a 100 ft wide tow. (3) That where the transportation company's offices and directors delegated all operational responsibilities to the port captain, the latter's negligent order to vent the petroleum barges empty tanks while under tow precluded the company from limiting its liability for the resulting explosion.

*United States* v *Standard Oil Co of California (Limitation)* [1974] AMC 580, US Court of Appeals
On 26 September 1966 the barge No 18, owned by the Standard Oil Co of California, and loaded with 989,730 gallons of gasoline, grounded in San Francisco Bay. One of her tanks was punctured and gasoline leaked into the waters of the bay. The duty officer representing the captain of the port ordered Coast Guard Patrol Boat CG40427 to go into the area to investigate. The patrol boat was later ordered to return to the gasoline-covered waters for the purpose of obtaining information needed for an oil pollution form. During the operation of the patrol boat in the area a fire was started either by a back-fire or by the sparking of an exposed electrical contact in the patrol boat's electrical system.

*Held*: that because it was often difficult to determine the actual cause of fire damage, causal connection might be shown by circumstantial rather than direct evidence. The District Court's finding that the duty officer had been negligent in ordering the patrol boat to return was affirmed. It was further held that whether an employee's acts are within the privity or knowledge of the owner depends not on the title or rank of the employee but rather on the 'largeness' of his authority. It was also held that the Coast Guard chief petty officer standing duty watch as captain of the port had sufficient supervisory authority to charge the United States with privity and knowledge of his negligence.

The second criterion to determine whether or not there is 'actual fault or privity' is to determine whether or not it was reasonably likely that if a particular person had performed and carried out his obligations properly the happening which resulted in the loss or damage would not have occurred.

*The Lady Gwendolen* [1965] 1 Lloyd's Rep. 335, CA
The *Lady Gwendolen*, owned by the plaintiff, collided with and sank the *Freshfield*, owned by the defendant. The *Freshfield* was at anchor in the Mersey. Despite thick fog, the *Lady Gwendolen* was proceeding at full speed with her radar operating but not continuously manned, and the Master only occasionally looked at it. The Master had been in the habit of sailing at excessive speed for some time and if the shipowner's superintendent had

examined the ship's log, as he should have done, he would have discovered that this was the case and it would have been his duty to have reprimanded the ship's Master. The facts and circumstances demonstrated that the shipowner's agents were involved in addition to the ship's Master.

*Held*: that the plaintiffs were not entitled to limit their liability since their 'actual fault or privity' had contributed to the accident. A reasonably prudent shipowner would appreciate the navigational problems involved in the use of radar in fog and would emphasize the vital nature of these problems to their ships' Masters. The shipowner had failed to do this and thus had personally contributed to the collision.

It was in its consideration of *The Lady Gwendolen* case that the court devised a two-part test to determine who in a corporate personality was the 'alter-ego', the 'mirror-image' individually of the company itself. The two-part test was:

(a) Who is or was the directing mind behind the voyage in question?
(b) If that person had acted as a person in his position should reasonably have done, would the accident still have happened?

On *The Lady Gwendolen* facts/evidence the answer to (a) was clearly 'the superintendent', and the answer to (b)—'No'.

*The Alletta* [1973] 1 Lloyd's Rep. 375, CA
The plaintiffs applied to limit their liability after a collision between their ship the *Alletta*, and the defendants' ship the *England* in the River Thames. The defendants argued that the collision was caused or contributed to by actual fault or privity of the *Alletta*'s managing owner in failing to ensure that the *Alletta*'s Master did not navigate in the Thames without a pilot; and also that the Master had sufficient knowledge to navigate in the Thames (in particular failing to supply him with copies of the relevant river by-laws).

*Held*: that the managing owner ought to have foreseen that without specific instructions the Master, however competent he might be, might have failed to have the by-laws available or might have failed to study them. The managing owner should at least have given specific instructions to the Master regarding the by-laws and the evidence did not establish the existence of any practice that owners expected their Master to obtain for himself copies of regulations for foreign ports. Lastly, the plaintiffs had failed to disprove that the absence of the by-laws was a contributory cause of the disaster and, as a result, their application to limit liability was denied.

The 'actual fault or privity' issue was frequently in dispute as the following cases illustrate.

*The Norman* [1960] 1 Lloyd's Rep. 1, HL
The trawler *Norman* sank with loss of life when she struck an uncharted rock at night in fog. Her owners sought to limit their liability. It was proved that the owners had received fresh information as to dangers in the area in which the ship was likely to be sailing but they did not pass this information on to the ship's Master.

*Held*: that the shipowners should have foreseen the possibility of the ship being in the area in which she foundered and it was their duty to pass on fresh information. Thus they had failed to prove that the loss occurred wholly without their actual fault or privity.

*The Chugaway 2* [1973] 2 Lloyd's Rep. 159, Exchequer Court (Admiralty) of Canada
A tug, owned by the plaintiff, was towing an empty barge up a river. The height of the barge was 26 ft and a chart showed that the clearance of the river bridge was 24 ft above high water. Whilst passing under the bridge, the barge struck the bridge and caused personal injury to those on it and also damage to the bridge and surrounding property. The plaintiffs applied to limit liability in respect of the damage to the bridge. The counter-

argument was that the collision happened owing to the actual fault and privity of the tug-owner in that he had failed to instruct his Master to use the chart and had failed to explain to him an alternative channel.

*Held*: the plaintiff was entitled to limit liability since the tug Master was responsible to act under the circumstances and the tug-owner could not have foreseen how he would act in such a way as to give him instructions.

*The Dayspring* [1968] 2 Lloyd's Rep. 204
The *Dayspring*, a motor trawler, collided with a motor tanker off the Isle of Man. The mate of the *Dayspring* saw the other vessel ahead but left the wheelhouse without giving instructions to the helmsman. The *Dayspring* altered course to port until she was across the bows of the tanker and then the collision occurred. The helmsman did not see the other ship because the forecastle blocked his view, because he had poor eyesight anyway and because he was not keeping look-out since he did not consider it was his duty to do so. The owners of the *Dayspring* kept standing orders displayed in the wheelhouse providing, inter alia, that at least two men should be in the wheelhouse at all times and that a log-book should be kept. The *Dayspring*'s owners, being partly to blame, sought to limit their liability.

*Held*: that the Master and chief officer knew that, generally speaking, the ship should not be underway in charge of the helmsman alone but what was not clear was whether it was their intention that this rule should be strictly adhered to. Fault lay with the plaintiffs for failing to insist that log-books were properly kept and for failing to ensure that much more positive action was taken than the mere posting of a notice in the wheelhouse. The plaintiffs had not proved to the satisfaction of the court that the incident took place without their actual fault or privity.

*The Truculent* [1951] 2 Lloyd's Rep. 308
The Admiralty tried to limit liability for damage and loss of life when HM submarine *Truculent* collided with a ship and sank. The Third Sea Lord admitted that he knew that the steering light did not conform with the regulations.

*Held*: that there was 'fault' in connection with the lights exhibited by the *Truculent* and also that this contributed to the loss and damage. It was also held that the fault being that of the Third Sea Lord, a member of the Board of Admiralty, meant that the Crown, as owner of the submarine, was unable to limit liability.

*The Kathy K* [1972] 2 Lloyd's Rep. 36 and [1976] 1 Lloyd's Rep. 153, Supreme Court of Canada
The crew of a yacht were killed after a collision with a tug towing an unmanned barge. The tug was held 75 per cent and the yacht 25 per cent to blame. Since the president and managing director of the tug and barge was the same individual and was personally at fault, the tug-owners were unable to show absence of actual fault or privity and therefore were unable to limit liability.

That an unsafe system of work could bring the 'actual fault or privity' into operation against a vessel's owners was illustrated in *Hook* v *Consolidated Fisheries*, below.

*Hook* v *Consolidated Fisheries* [1953] 2 Lloyd's Rep. 647 CA
A deckhand on board a steam trawler claimed damages after having his leg crushed between the vessel and a dolphin when the Master told him to jump on to it in Lowestoft harbour to assist in securing the vessel. The court recognized that this system was common practice but that it involved risks and that failure to adopt a safer system was indicative of the vessel owner's actual or privity in regard to the deckhand's accident.

One of the more recent cases, and certainly the most controversial, came before the House of Lords and, as it turned out, probably formed the end of the line of disputes to receive top-level judicial review and which were governed by the 1957 Convention and the 'actual fault or privity' rule contained in it. It was:

*Grand Champion Tankers Ltd* v *Norpipe A/S and others (The Marion)* [1984] 2 Lloyd's Rep. 1
The Master of a Liberian tanker anchored at Hartlepool to wait for a berth and when he dropped the ship's anchor it fouled an undersea pipeline. Oil companies who had an interest in the pipeline sued the ship's owners, claiming $25 million damages (direct and consequential losses). The owners admitted liability but sought to limit under the existing law (i.e. as *presently* being described in this chapter). They claimed that the Master had negligently used an out-of-date chart which did not have the pipeline marked on it.

The owners had long since delegated the operation and management of the vessel to English ship managers who had supplied charts to the ship. The Admiralty judge hearing the application to limit initially granted limitation on the ground that the provision and maintenance of the charts was the sole responsibility of the Master and it was *his* negligence in using an out-of-date chart which was the sole cause of the damage/losses.

The Court of Appeal reversed this decision on the ground that it was the ship managers' duty to ensure that there was an *effective* and properly supervised system of chart provision *and* maintenance and such a system was absent in this case. This lack of adequate system was emphasized by the fact that a Liberian inspectorate report, issued over a year before the pipeline incident and which drew particular attention to the lack of correct updating of charts, had gone unheeded and unacted upon. This failing upon the part of the ship's managers was considered by the House of Lords to be directly causative of the oil companies' losses, and, furthermore, the owners in turn were to be held legally responsible for the negligence of their managers. Thus the owners *were* personally at fault and were denied the right to limit.

This very significant case seems to emphasize the shift towards the view that *effective* management control is essential if a shipowner is to successfully limit and also seems to imply that the Master, especially of a large sophisticated ship, is becoming less and less the 'Master of his own little world'.

Another interesting case involving the role of managers and whether their actions/inactions debars them from limiting liability is illustrated by the following case.

*The Ert Stefanie* [1989] 1 Lloyd's Rep. 349
The vessel *Ert Stefanie* was owned by a Panamanian company whose sole proprietor was Mr Sorensen. It was managed by Sorek Shipping Limited which was also under the control of Mr Sorensen. Mr Baker, a director of Sorek, ran the technical side of the business, which included responsibility for the maintenance of the vessel. The Charterers' cargo claim succeeded against the Shipowners in arbitration because thetttvessel was unseaworthy. One issue raised in the Court of Appeal, was whether the Shipowners could limit liability under section 503 of the Merchant Shipping Act 1894. The Shipowners argued that the 'alter ego' of the managers and shipowners was Mr Sorensen alone and since he was not to blame, there was no actual fault or privity. The faults of Mr Baker had to do with functions which, if the company had been larger, would have fallen to employees at a comparatively subordinate level such as that of a marine superintendent.

*Held* (Court of Appeal): that the constitution of Sorek entrusted the management and control of the company to the board of directors en bloc. The board of directors of a corporation might not always comprise the whole of the group of people who together constitute the governing mind and will of the corporation. Nevertheless any director must necessarily be a member of the group unless he is dis-seized of responsibility. Mr Baker was a director and was responsible for operational matters. He was in charge of the aspects of the company's business which went wrong. He was personally at fault and the shipowners had no right to limit liability.

## CIRCUMSTANCES WHERE MASTER OR CREW MEMBER MAY WISH TO LIMIT

That a ship's Master or crew member should similarly be allowed the benefits of being able to limit his liability is also logical since they, of course, are just as liable to be sued for damages resulting from their acts or neglect as the shipowner, although in a case where the Master or a crew member is either the owner or at least a part owner of the vessel it will become necessary to decide whether the 'fault or privity' was that of the 'shipowner' or the ship's Master or crew member. It then becomes a simple matter of deciding which 'hat' that person was said to be wearing at the time. In fact Article 6(3) of the 1957 Convention provides that where the Master or member of the crew is at the same time the owner, charterer manager or operator of the vessel, such person will only be entitled to limit his liability if he commits the act, neglect or default in his capacity as Master or as a member of the crew.

*The Annie Hay* [1968] 1 Lloyd's Rep. 141
Due to negligent navigation by a ship's Master, who also happened to be the owner of the vessel, a collision occurred.

*Held*: that the Master was entitled to limit his liability. Under the provisions of the Merchant Shipping Act such a privilege is allowed in respect of an act or omission of any person in his capacity as the Master or a member of the crew and the relevant wording of the relevant section of the Act was broad enough in scope to cover a ship's Master who happens also to be the owner of the ship. It should be noted, however, that such a person would lose his right to limit liability if his fault had been committed in his capacity as shipowner, for example, in that perhaps he had failed to pass on or indeed to observe instructions provided by the Admiralty or Department of Trade or indeed to fit into his ship proper and required or recommended navigational equipment.

*The Hans Hoth* [1952] 2 Lloyd's Rep. 341
The collision took place in broad daylight and in fine weather between a British ship and the vessel *Hans Hoth* at the entrance to Dover harbour. Blame was attributed to the *Hans Hoth* in that the Master should have followed the signals which were given by the port authority. The particular issue in the case was that the Master was part owner of the vessel and the point for decision was whether he was personally at fault in regard to the limiting of his own liability.

*Held*: that in the special circumstances, the Master's duty did not extend to the knowledge of the local signals and that he could thus limit his liability.

In the case of *Ert Stefanie* (at page 383), section 3 of the 1958 Act was raised as Mr Baker a director of the management company was at fault in failing to appreciate the defective character and inadequacy of the vessel and in not checking and advising the management company of the special requirements for the carriage of ferrosilicon, or ensuring that the Master had the necessary data on board the vessel. However, as the action by charterers was against the shipowners of the vessel as opposed to Mr Baker personally, section 3 did not apply. In particular, there was no need to enquire whether the claim arose because of a mistake made by Mr Baker in his capacity as Master or member of the crew. Mr Baker a director of the management company in charge of running the ship was at fault. These were the mistakes of the management company and the shipowners had no right to limit liability.

When the Merchant Shipping Act 1894 was passed it was intended that only the actual owner of a ship (or the charterer by demise) should be able to benefit from that part of the Act (Part VIII), but over the years the benefits have been granted to a wider group than merely shipowners. At present, the word 'owner' in the context of the limitation of liability under the Merchant Shipping Act 1894 is deemed to include the following: the shipowner, the charterer of the ship (whether he be a charterer by demise or a time charterer), the manager or operator of a ship, any person having an interest in or actually possessing a ship, i.e. possibly a shipbuilder or a ship repairer if relevant. This was provided by section 3(1) of the Merchant Shipping (Liability of Shipowners and Others) Act 1958. Additionally, under certain circumstances, others entitled to these benefits are (a) a ship's Master, (b) a member of the ship's crew (section 3(2)), and (c) the Crown.

The 1958 Act followed on the 1957 Convention and it was designed to amend Part VIII of the 1894 Act and section 2 of the Merchant Shipping (Liability of Shipowners and Others) Act 1900. Section 1(1) brought about the transformation from sterling basic figures to the gold franc basis with this wording:

'1.—(1) In ascertaining the limits set to the liability of any persons by section five hundred and three of the Merchant Shipping Act 1894, or section two of the Merchant Shipping (Liability of Shipowners and Others) Act 1900, there shall be substituted—

(a) for the amount of fifteen pounds mentioned in the said section five hundred and three, an amount equivalent to three thousand one hundred gold francs;

(b) for each of the amounts of eight pounds mentioned in the said sections, an amount equivalent to one thousand gold francs;

and the number by which the amount substituted by paragraph (a) of this subsection is to be multiplied shall be three hundred in any case where the tonnage concerned is less than three hundred tons.'

Section 1(1)(a) lays down a minimum figure of 300 tons even if the limiting ship's tonnage is less. This applies only to the high gold franc figure (i.e. the 'life' fund figure). It does *not* apply to the lower (1,000 franc) figure. Section 1(2) defines what is meant by a gold franc:

(2) For the purposes of this section a gold franc shall be taken to be a unit consisting of sixty-five and a half milligrams of gold of millesimal fineness nine hundred.'

Up until October 1984 sterling equivalent orders were promulgated from time to time and this was statutorily provided by section 1(3).

These orders quoted sterling equivalents calculated by reference to the special drawing rights value of a gold franc converted into sterling at the current market rates. However, by a Merchant Shipping Act of 1981, effect was given in the UK to a 1979 Protocol to the 1957 Convention. The Protocol replaced the 3,100 and 1,000 gold francs by 206.67 SDRs and 66.67 SDRs respectively. The effective date for this in the UK was 29 November 1984. As from that date the calculation was to be by way of direct reference to the SDR/sterling exchange rate as calculated *daily* by the International Monetary Fund (to be found published each day in the financial press and/or *Lloyd's List*). The relevant date is to be, if a limitation action is brought, that on which the limitation fund is constituted and, in any other case, the date of the judgment in question.

The tendency is for courts now to be more flexible in assessing fair rates of interest in limitation actions. An out-of-date fixed rate is rejected in favour of modern rates; furthermore, considerations of public policy are not necessarily considered relevant.

*The Funabashi* [1972] 1 Lloyd's Rep. 371
The *Funabashi* (owned by the plaintiffs) and the *White Mountain* (owned by the defendants) collided on 16 February 1966 and the latter sank with her rice cargo. The *Funabashi* was considered 75 per cent to blame. The plaintiffs commenced limitation proceedings and a decree was subsequently issued by the Admiralty Registrar limiting their liability to £173,248 with interest at $5\frac{1}{2}$ per cent, to be applied from the date of the collision to the date of payment into court or payment. The defendants contested the rate of interest which they said should be $6\frac{1}{2}$ per cent.

*Held*: that interest rates should be based on the idea that the party seeking limitation has kept the claimants from their money and had the use of it himself. Also in principle there should be no distinction between interest on a limitation fund and interest, for example, on damages for personal injury. There was no particular merit in stabilization of interest rates and English rates were appropriate even for foreigners. The rate of interest was a matter for the discretion of the court.

Section 2(1) was perhaps the 'meat' of the Merchant Shipping (Liability of Shipowners and Others) Act 1958 and significantly amended the nature of the limited liability available under section 503 of the Merchant Shipping Act 1894 (see page 376, *ante*). It provided:

'2.—(1) In subsection (1) of section five hundred and three of the Merchant Shipping Act 1894, the following paragraphs shall be substituted for paragraphs (c) and (d)—

'(c) where any loss of life or personal injury is caused to any person not carried in the ship through the act or omission of any person (whether on board the ship or not) in the navigation or management of the ship or in the loading, carriage or discharge of its cargo or in the embarkation, carriage or disembarkation of its passengers, or through any other act or omission of any person on board the ship;

(d) where any loss or damage is caused to any property (other than any property mentioned in paragraph (b) of this subsection) or any rights are infringed through the act or omission of any person (whether on board the ship or not) in the navigation or management of the ship, or in the loading, carriage or discharge of its cargo or in the embarkation, carriage or disembarkation of its passengers, or through any other act or omission of any person on board the ship;'

and for the words "loss of or damage to vessels, goods, merchandise or other things", both where they occur in paragraph (i) and where they occur in paragraph (ii), there shall be substituted the words "such loss, damage or infringement as is mentioned in paragraphs (b) and (d) of this subsection".'

One phrase in the wording of this section required particular explanation and that was 'the navigation or management of a ship'. This requirement restricted the scope of the type of act which causes the loss or damage and it was essential for the purposes of the operation of section 503 that the person whose act it was was at the time engaged exclusively in the process of navigating or managing the ship, the offending ship, so to speak. Thus, for example, a servant of the shipowner who caused loss or damage to other persons or property but who was not himself so engaged at the time (he might, for example, be engaged in underwater operations) did not entitle the shipowner to the benefits of section 503.

*The Tojo Maru* [1971] 1 Lloyd's Rep. 341, HL
Salvage services were given to the *Tojo Maru* and in the course of the performance of the services a diver employed by the salvage company whilst performing underwater work fired a bolt through the shell plating into a tank which had not in fact been gas-freed. There was a resulting explosion and £330,000-worth of additional damage was done to the *Tojo Maru*. There were resulting cross-actions, one by the owners of the *Tojo Maru* against the salvors alleging negligence and seeking damages, and the other a claim for salvage reward by the salvors against the owners of the *Tojo Maru*. The salvors attempted to limit their liability in accordance with the provisions of the Merchant Shipping (Liability of Shipowners and Others) Act 1958.

*Held*: that the negligent act of the diver was not an act of a person in the course of the management of the vessel and that therefore the salvors could not limit their liability.

It should be noted that now that the 1976 Convention has become effective, situations such as the *Tojo Maru* and the seeming injustice done to the salvor on that occasion will not arise again (as will be seen later) and already in salvage operations performed pursuant to the 1995, 1990 (and the earlier 1980) versions of Lloyd's Open Form it cannot happen since the Lloyd's Open Form in its current wording incorporates the provisions of the London Convention and thus, in a sense, has foreshadowed it.

It is worth noting that the *management* of the ship in the context of section 503 (as amended) was intended to cover a wider variety of situations than the equivalent expression in, for example, Carriage of Goods by Sea Act 1924 or 1971, which specifically exclude acts directly referable to cargo. The interpretation of the phrase in the Merchant Shipping Act 1894 *does* include acts referable to cargo as the following two cases illustrate.

*The Teal* (1949) 82 Ll.L.Rep. 414
An explosion occurred on board the plaintiffs' barge which at the time was loaded with chemicals and damage was caused to the defendant's property. The reason for the explosion was that drums which had been loaded were in a leaky condition.

*Held*: the fact that the servants of the plaintiffs had accepted the drums in their leaky state and had stowed them on board was 'improper' management and as a result the plaintiffs were allowed to limit their liability.

*The Athelvictor* (1945) 78 Ll.L.Rep. 529
Three sea valves had been negligently left open to the tanker *Athelvictor* after cargo discharge. On the next voyage the ship sailed to Lagos and, as a result of the negligence, approximately 60 tons of petrol escaped from the ship and a fire occurred. In turn, as a result of the fire, there were explosions which caused damage to trawlers and other shore-side property. People were killed or died ashore or were less seriously injured. The owners of the *Athelvictor* sought to limit their liability, arguing that the losses and damages were directly caused by the improper navigation of the ship within the meaning of section 503 of the Merchant Shipping Act 1894. They argued, alternatively, that if such losses were not caused by negligent navigation they were caused by improper management of the ship within the meaning of the Act. The counter-argument was that the losses were caused by the improper management of the cargo.

*Held*: that (1) liability could not be limited because the failure to close the valves could certainly not be deemed improper navigation. (2) Under the provisions of the Merchant Shipping Act 1900, where appliances are fitted which cover both the management of the ship and the management of the cargo, the party applying to limit liability may be entitled to regard the appliances as being ship-managing rather than 'cargo-managing'. They were therefore entitled to limit liability.

It is not necessary for the person whose act causes the damage or loss to be on board the vessel provided that his act is within the scope of management or navigation of the ship.

Additional contingencies were provided for in section 2(2) of the Merchant Shipping (Liability of Shipowners and Others) Act 1958, but were never brought into force, probably so as to conform with the UK's policy of keeping liability for wreck removal expenses unlimited.

'(2) For the purposes of the said subsection (1), where any obligation or liability arises—

(a) in connection with the raising, removal or destruction of any ship which is sunk, stranded or abandoned or of anything on board such a ship; or

(b) in respect of any damage (however caused) to harbour works, basins or navigable waterways, the occurrence giving rise to the obligation or liability shall be treated as one of the occurrences mentioned in paragraphs (b) and (d) of that subsection, and the obligation or liability as a liability to damages.'

Limitation in respect of wreck-raising expenses also became an issue in *The Berwyn*, below.

*The Berwyn* [1977] 2 Lloyd's Rep. 99, CA

The *Berwyn* sank in Liverpool Bay having been holed as a result of striking land near Taylor's Spit at the entrance to Crosby Channel. In the exercise of powers granted to them under the local statute, the Mersey Docks and Harbour Board raised the wreck and for the purpose of recovering at least part of the costs of so doing they sold certain items from the vessel for a modest amount. There was, however, remaining a heavy balance of over £25,000 and the authority instituted suit under two separate and distinct causes of action, namely to recover damages based on negligence of the vessel in striking land and to recover the balance of the removal expenses.

The Merchant Shipping Acts since 1894 and those amendments which have been concerned with limitation of liability have provided that where damage results from acts, neglects, or defaults of the servants of the vessel owner in the navigation or management of the ship the benefits of limitation may be available provided there was no actual fault or privity. This meant that the concept of fault was underlying, but it is not quite so clear whether the position was the same where there is a concept of 'no fault' in the claim against the vessel. Although, admittedly, nobody doubts that the *Berwyn* would not have sunk unless there had been some previous negligent act in her navigation there did also eventually arise, because of the statutory raising of the wreck, a debt which in itself was in no way connected with the concept of fault. Thus there would appear to be in *The Berwyn* case two separate and distinct causes of action: one based on the principle of fault, the other based on a 'no fault' concept which springs from the statutory debt. The owners of the *Berwyn* made no effort to contest the Mersey Docks and Harbour Board's ability to bring the action under two causes of action, but they counter-argued that the right to limitation under the Act, and particularly under the 1958 amendment, applied overall in one limitation figure to both sums claimed under the two actions, the action for damages and the statutory debt.

Based on previous legal decisions, the right to limit did not appear to extend to liabilities in the nature of statutory debts not based on actionable fault. This, however, does not take into account the 'then future' ideas which section 2(2)(a) of the 1958 amendment introduced. The court in *The Berwyn* case took the view that the local harbour authority statute provided exclusively for the matter in respect of the statutory debt cause of action and the Merchant Shipping Act provided exclusively for the situation in respect of the action for damages. Whatever interpretation the court placed on the facts, there was no doubt that the harbour authority could not recover more than the total amount of the deficiency claimed; namely just in excess of £25,000. This could be achieved by aggregating the two figures obtained by limiting liability under both causes of action separately and it was in this manner that the court felt that the matter should be resolved. As it happened, it would seem that section 2(2) of the Merchant Shipping (Liability of Shipowners and Others) Act 1958 only applied to wreck-raising expenses incurred through exercise of statutory powers which take the form of a simple debt and not a claim for damages.

## THE LIMITATION FUND

Whether under the 1957 Convention or under the current 1976 Convention, the distribution of the fund (once calculated according to the method laid down and paid into court) is not based on the principle of 'first come, first served', that is, the earlier the claimant lodges his claim the more likely he is to be paid in full. The procedure is very much fairer than that. If the fund is insufficient to meet all claims in full, the system is applied pro rata and the court will ensure that each individual claimant will be paid a proportion of his claim, such proportion being based on how the amount available in the fund relates to the total aggregated amount of all claims arising from the incident.

*The World Mermaid/Giacinto Motta* collision case (see page 286) also clarified a point in limitation. The Admiralty judge decided that the *World Mermaid* in limiting her own liability could not set off the whole of her 100 per cent payment to the *Giacinto Motta*'s cargo-owners against her limitation fund. This would be doing better than she should under the existing English law whereunder the cargo claimant would only have received 50 per cent from her. Therefore, only 50 per cent of her actual payments in the US could be counted into the limitation calculations made under English law.

*Stoomvart Maatschappij Nederland* v *P & O Steam Navigation Co* (1882) 7 App Cas 876, HL

Two ships collided and the owner of one brought an action in rem against the owner of the other who in turn counter-claimed. Both ships were to blame. The owners of one ship limited their liability and paid the requisite amount into court. The damage to the other ship was greater and the fund deposited in court was insufficient to satisfy all the claims for which the owners of the other ship were responsible.

*Held*: that the owners of the other ship (i.e. the one which did not pay the fund into court) were entitled to show cause against the fund for a moiety of their damages less a moiety of the damage sustained by the other ship and to be paid in respect of the balance due to them after the requisite deduction pari passu with the other claimants.

Loss of life and personal injury claims enjoy priority. If the 'life' fund, as it is called, is insufficient to meet all life or injury claims, the claimants receive a pro rata payment and the unsatisfied part of their claims rank alongside (or pari passu with) the 'property' claims to be paid out of the 'property' fund.

Under the 1957 provisions the 'life' fund was formed by taking the first 2,100 gold francs (equivalent under the 1979 Protocol now to 140 SDRs) multiplied by the ship's tonnage in accordance with the Merchant Shipping Act provisions (where English jurisdiction applied), leaving the remaining 1,000 francs (equivalent to 66.67 SDRs) to form the property fund out of which the property damage and unsatisfied balance of life and injury claims were to be satisfied.

The principle of priority for life and injury claimants is only relevant when the shipowner succeeds in effectively limiting his liability. If he cannot, or does not even apply to limit, all claimants rank equally and, in the event of the vessel being sold to satisfy claims and the proceeds are insufficient, unsatisfied or partly unsatisfied claimants would only have further recourse against whatever other separate assets the defendant shipowners might have.

It is established that the courts may grant limitation even when there is only one claim lodged against a shipowner. Authority for this may be found in *The Kathleen* (1925) 22 Ll.L.Rep. 80 and *The Penelope* [1979] 2 Lloyd's Rep. 42.

When assessing damages generally, a court is not influenced by the likelihood that the defendant shipowner may succeed in his application to limit liability.

*Glaholm* v *Barker* (1866) LR 2 Eq 598

This case concerned the death of several crew members of one ship caused by the fault of the owners of another vessel. Proceedings were instituted under the provisions of the Merchant Shipping Act by the vessel at fault to limit her liability.

*Held:* that in determining the amount to which the liability can be limited, the damages which have been suffered by the deceased seamen's families are to be calculated in the same manner as if the liability were unlimited, and if the amount so arrived at is greater than the liability of the owner of the ship, is calculated by reference to the tonnage of the ship, then the total amount of his liability is to be distributed pro rata amongst the various claimants.

Where a foreign (i.e. a non-British) ship was concerned in an action to limit, her tonnage for the purpose of limitation was measured according to British law. If this was physically impossible, a certificate issued by the UK Surveyor General of Ships stating his opinion as to the relevant figure was sufficient to satisfy a court. Vessels belonging to the British Crown may, when limitation is sought, be measured by the Chief Surveyor as if they were commercial vessels.

Limitation actions are usually, but not necessarily, heard *after* the liability issue is determined but *before* damages are assessed. The defendant to the suit would be one named party chosen from the claimants seeking restitution of their claims arising from the incident. He would be the representative of the others who would remain unnamed. He who sought to limit, i.e. the plaintiff in the limitation action, had to prove his right to claim the privilege. The named defendant had the right to show why he considered the shipowner should be denied his application to limit. One should note the difference in emphasis and the shift in the burden of proof under the 1976 provisions (page 402). Interesting opposing arguments were put forward in *The Empire Jamaica* below.

*The Empire Jamaica* [1955] 1 Lloyd's Rep. 50
This ship was found to be at fault in a collision and it was discovered that the ship's second officer, who happened to be the officer on the bridge at the time of the collision, was not in possession of a second officer's certificate in accordance with the relevant Hong Kong ordinance. In an application to limit liability, the defendant interests argued that the shipowner had knowingly sent the vessel to sea with an uncertificated second officer and was therefore not entitled to limit his liability.

*Held*: that the second officer, despite his lack of certificate, was a fully competent seaman and his lack of certificate was not causally connected to the negligent navigation which resulted in the collision. The shipowner was thus entitled to limit his liability.

If there is only one claim then the shipowner can plead limitation of liability as a defence. In fact it may be that the shipowner should plead limitation as a defence in view of the comments of the then Admiralty Judge, Sheen J in the case of *The Mekhanik Evgrafov* which concerned section 503 of the Merchant Shipping Act 1984.

*The Mekhanik Evgrafov* [1988] 1 Lloyd's Rep. 330
Cargo interests brought a claim for damage to a cargo of newsprint. The shipowners admitted liability for the claim without prejudice to their right to limit liability under the Merchant Shipping Acts. Cargo interests replied that the appropriate course of action was for the shipowners to plead limitation of liability by way of defence and/or immediately to apply for a declaration as to their rights to limit their liability. Judgment was entered in favour of cargo interests. The shipowners then issued a writ claiming limitation of liability. The cargo interests applied to strike out the action on the grounds that it was an abuse of the process of the court since the matter was res judicata.

*Held*: Both parties took the view that it was permissible even if unnecessary costs would be incurred to raise the question of limitation after judgment had been given and cargo interests were aware before the action came to trial that the shipowners would rely upon limitation of liabiliy. There were special circumstances which would prevent the cargo interests from relying successfully upon the plea of res judicata. Cargo interests application to strike out the writ claiming limitation of liability was dismissed. The Admiralty Judge commented that where there is only one claim section 503 ought to be pleaded as a defence and that after this case there may not be any special circumstances which would prevent a plea of res judicata from being successful.

A limitation action is commenced by shipowners in the Admiralty Court. Under English law it is not necessary to constitute a limitation fund prior to seeking a decree of limitation of liability. However it is common that a limitation fund is constituted by paying into court the sterling equivalent of the appropriate limit together with interest from the date of the occurrence until payment into court. If the shipowners obtain a decree of limitation then the court will distribute the limitation fund amongst the various claimants.

In view of the likelihood that the claimants could be many, varied and widespread, the court has to be satisfied that due notice and publicity had been given before it made an order for any payments to be made out of the fund paid into court. Jurisdiction to postpone or delay payments, if necessary, was given by the 1958 Act (s. 7(1)). The process and principle of pro rata settlement of claims was not affected by the fact that any particular claim might have originally conferred a lien on the claimant. Section 7(2) required *all* claimants to proceed against the fund once formed and to bar them from going against any other property of the shipowner. In other words the 'res' was the fund. Normally the court will advertise so that any other potential claimants against the limitation fund can have an opportunity to file a claim against this fund or to take steps to set aside the decree of limitation. But if the benefits of limitation were not granted, all claims ranked equally; and, if the proceeds available from the sale of the ship were insufficient, the only other recourse available for an unsatisfied claimant was to proceed against any other assets which the shipowner might have.

There was no right to limit in relation to: (a) a salvage award: or (b) a bottomry bond (by definition, as this calls for repayment of the entire loan).

A limitation fund can be constituted in the shipowners place of domicile of his choice. This could be relevant to the question of the appropriate jurisdiction to determine claims against a shipowner. In fact the Court of Appeal commented in the case of *The Volvox Hollandia* that the settled practice was that a shipowner was at liberty to set up a limitation fund in his own country's court and that the English court should be slow to interfere with this practice in the absence of any claim for an injunction staying foreign proceedings.

*The Volvox Hollandia* [1988] 2 Lloyd's Rep. 361
A dredger owned and operated by the sub-contractors VO2, a Dutch corporation, damaged a pipeline in the North Sea. VO2 commenced limitation proceedings in the Rotterdam court. Writs were then issued in England and served on VO2 in which declarations were sought that VO2 were not entitled to limit their liability.

The Court of Appeal decided that such claims for negative declarations were improper and could not be allowed in the writ. It was not necessarily unjust or inconvenient for liability and limitation to be tried separately. To interfere with the settled practice that the shipowner was at liberty to choose his domiciliary court as the forum in which to set up his limitation fund would be out of step with the principles underlying the Brussels Convention 1968.

## APPLICATION OF LIMITATION AFTER MARITIME COLLISION BETWEEN TWO VESSELS AT FAULT

On the basis of single liability adjustment—that is to say where cross-claims are off-set, the one against the other leaving the fair balance of liabilities to be restored by the one party paying the other in a single payment—limitation of liability is applied at *that* point and *not* earlier. Thus, to take the very simplest of examples: X collides with Y and both are equally to blame. X has suffered damages totalling £1,000,000; Y, £500,000. To redress the correct balance by a *single* payment, Y pays £250,000. If he, Y, is able to limit to, say, £300,000 he gains nothing from limiting and must pay the full £250,000. However, had he been able to limit against X's gross claim *before* offsetting his own he would eventually have only had to pay £50,000, i.e.£500,000 limited to £300,000 less his own claim of £250,000 leaves £50,000.

A little more elaborate example, introducing loss of life/injury claims and cargo/property claims. Supposing there had been an aggregate of life claims on ship X of £1,000,000 and of cargo damage on ship X of £400,000. The 'property' fund stands, as we have already seen, at £300,000, the 'life' fund is, say, £700,000. The residual (unsatisfied) life claims (£300,000) rank equally (pari passu) with the property claims (i.e. £250,000—ship damage; £400,000—cargo damage), making a grand total of £950,000 to be paid pro rata out of the property fund.

(The single liability theory does not, generally speaking, apply to the obligations of the hull insurer to his assured where the former, in paying out to the latter under the provisions of the running-down clause, moneys which the assured has had to pay out to the other ship after a collision for damages sustained by that other ship or its cargo, will pay out only on the basis of cross-liabilities. That is to say, the insurance claim ignores the set-off of the assured's own claim against the other ship. In the first simple example above, hull underwriters and the assured's Protecting and Indemnity Club (who cover the one-quarter *not* covered by the running-down clause) will pay out £500,000, seemingly £250,000 too much, viewed from the single liability angle. The underwriters, however, take credit for the notional recovery and set this against the costs of repaying the assured's vessel for which, of course, they are responsible.

This could, in the case of a very small-tonnage insured vessel, produce a situation where its owners could even make a considerable profit out of their insurance, particularly where they have the advantage of limitation also. Thus the single liability principle is used where either vessel successfully invokes limitation. It will be realized that there will be 'borderline' cases where there may be, as it were, a 'switch' from the cross-liability to the single liability principle in insurance recoveries.

## TUG AND TOW SITUATIONS

Where tug and tow collide with a third vessel and the tug and tow are in common ownership the limitation position seems to be as stated in *The Sir Joseph Rawlinson*, below.

*The Sir Joseph Rawlinson* [1972] 2 Lloyd's Rep. 437
A tug towing a dumb barge collided with a sludge carrier, the *Sir Joseph Rawlinson*, which sank with loss of life. The collision was the joint fault of the Master of the tug and the second officer of the sludge carrier. There was no causative negligence on the part of the tow. The plaintiffs, the demise charterers of both tug and tow, applied to limit liability and as there was no 'actual fault or privity' they were successful. The only further issue was whether they were entitled to limit to an amount based on the tonnage of the tug alone or an aggregated amount based on the combined tonnages of tug and tow.

*Held:* that in circumstances where the tug alone is negligent the owners (or, in this case, the demise charterers) of tug and tow are entitled to limit their liability for negligence by taking into account the tug's tonnage only and disregarding the tonnage of the tow.

*The Sir Joseph Rawlinson* case was decided with a previous decision in mind, *The Bramley Moore*, below.

*The Bramley Moore* [1963] 2 Lloyd's Rep. 429, CA
The *Bramley Moore* was a tug towing the barge *Millet*. The *Millet* collided with a motor vessel, the *Egret*. The collision was partly the fault of those on board the *Bramley Moore*. The barge had a crew of three, one of whom was drowned in the accident.

*Held:* that the owners of the *Bramley Moore*, who were not also the owners of the barge, could limit their liability according to the tug's tonnage alone.

In *The Smjeli* [1982] 2 Lloyd's Rep. 74 the owners of certain groynes situated on the south-east coast of England damaged by a dumb barge loaded with steel sections of an oil rig which had been driven by winds after its towing hawser had snapped claimed damages from the defendant owners of the towing tug and the barge (who happened to be the same party). The towing hawser, the tug, and the load had received the approval of an independent technical expert engaged by the load's owner but subsequent evidence revealed that both the tug Master and the technical expert should have known that it was not good practice to use a towing wire with as low a breaking strain as was in fact used.

The defendants sought to limit their liability under the Merchant Shipping Act (which they were granted because of their lack of personal fault or privity) *and* to limit to the tonnage of their tug *only*. This was denied on the ground that the plaintiffs had more than one cause of action (a) arising from faults amounting to negligence before the tug and tow had left its loading port of Rotterdam, and (b) for acts of negligence at sea. Each cause of action gave rise to one (limited) liability. Thus the barge's limitation tonnage was also relevant and the defendants were obliged to limit to the combined tonnages of tug *and* barge.

As a result of the judgments delivered in *The Bramley Moore* and *The Sir Joseph Rawlinson* cases, the rule on this issue may fairly be summarized as: where only the negligence of those on board the tug is involved, the tug's owner is entitled to limit in accordance with the tonnage of his tug. Similarly, where only the negligence of those on board the tow in involved, the owner of the tow may limit in accordance with the tonnage of the tow. Where the negligence of those on board the tug and on the tow is involved, the tug-owner may limit to the tonnage of the tug and the tow-owner to the tonnage of the tow. This principle would seem to be in accord with the basic idea that the benefits of limitation, which should be remembered are conferred by statute, are only available to those owners whose own servants were exclusively negligent in the actual situation which gave rise to the seeking of limitation.

As Lord Denning pointed out in the *The Bramley Moore* case, 'a small tug has comparatively small value and should have a correspondingly low measure of liability even though it may be engaged in towing a great liner and does great damage. I agree that there is not much room for justice in this rule; but limitation of liability is not a matter of justice. It is a rule of public policy which has its origin in history and its justification in convenience'. Convenient indeed it may be to he who benefits by it but not so convenient to those who stand to gain less, and possibly very much less, than full satisfaction of their claims.

Strangely perhaps, the 1976 Convention (described hereafter) does not clarify, any more than does the existing Convention, what is the rule when accidents involving tug and tow occur. One is left to assume that causative fault on the part of whichever vessel will continue to be the governing criterion for purposes of calculating limitation.

# THE CONVENTION ON LIMITATION OF LIABILITY FOR MARITIME CLAIMS 1976

By 1985 the requisite 12 states (minimum to allow the Convention to become effective) had ratified or somehow in the equivalent adopted its provisions. Thus 12 months after the 12th ratification, to be exact on 1 December 1986, the Convention became effectively part of English law.

The present position is that the Convention on Limitation of Liability for Maritime Claims 1976 as set out in Part 1 of Schedule 7 (in this section and Part II of that Schedule) referred to as 'the Convention' has the force of law in the UK (see section 185 of the Merchant Shipping Act 1995 which came into force on 1 January 1996). These provisions apply to Her Majesty's ships as well as other ships.

Article 1 reads as follows:

### *Article 1: Persons entitled to limit liability*

'1. Shipowners and salvors, as hereinafter defined, may limit their liability in accordance with the rules of this Convention for claims set out in Article 2.

2. The term 'shipowner' shall mean the owner, charterer, manager or operator of a seagoing ship.

3. Salvor shall mean any person rendering services in direct connexion with salvage operations. Salvage operations shall also include operations referred to in Article 2, paragraph 1(d), (e) and (f).

4. If any claims set out in Article 2 are made against any person for whose act, neglect or default the shipowner or salvor is responsible, such person shall be entitled to avail himself of the limitation of liability provided for in this Convention.

5. In this Convention the liability of a shipowner shall include liability in an action brought against the vessel herself.

6. An insurer of liability for claims subject to limitation in accordance with the rules of this Convention shall be entitled to the benefits of this Convention to the same extent as the assured himself.

7. The act of invoking limitation of liability shall not constitute an admission of liability.'

Probably the most significant of the newly introduced items in Article 1 is that *salvors* have been added to the list of persons or parties who may limit their liability in accordance with the rules of the Convention. We have seen that salvors up to the introduction of the 1976 Convention, or possibly more accurately certainly until the introduction of the more recent revisions of the Lloyd's Open Form of Salvage Agreement, have been rather hard done by and their legal situation was strongly epitomized in *The Tojo Maru* case (see page 387) simply because under the 1957 Convention they were merged in with shipowners and were not recognized as a separate category of individuals pursuing a specialized type of operation. Under Article 1 of the 1976 Convention they are given a category in their own right and may limit their liability totally independently of shipowners and in respect of acts, neglects or defaults arising in direct connexion with the conduct of salvage operations. How they may limit, i.e. the method of limitation is dealt with in a separate Article, namely, Article 6(4). Reference should also be made to section 185(4) of the Merchant Shipping Act 1995.

Article 1.2 redefines the basic persons who are entitled to limit and enlarges the term 'shipowner' to include charterer, manager or operator of a sea-going ship and this reflects the previous enlargement of the type of persons who could limit which featured in the 1957 Convention. It seems that it no longer matters whether an owner/Master does an act in his capacity as Master or owner.

Article 1.4 casts the net even wider by making it possible for any person for whose act, neglect or default the shipowner or salvor is responsible to be entitled to avail himself of the right of limitation given in the Convention. The wording of this paragraph would seem to afford the right of limitation even to an independent contractor, such as a firm of stevedores engaged by a shipowner provided that the shipowner could show that he was responsible in law for their actions. Thus, this paragraph provides a wider circle of persons able to limit than the 1957 Convention which did not include independent contractors employed by the traditional parties able to limit, but rather only their servants.

Article 1.6 introduced another class of person hitherto unable to limit, namely an insurer of liability for claims subject to limitation. The party which most springs to mind here is a P & I Club who act as underwriters in respect of a wide range of P & I risks. The wording of the paragraph makes it plain that such insurers shall be entitled to the benefits of this Convention only to the same extent as the assured himself. It is well known that insurers are subject to direct action from third parties in situations where the assured has become bankrupt or gone into liquidation. It is therefore quite logical that this development in the law should have taken place, so that insurers when they find themselves thus in the shoes of their assured, should have the same limitations and defences as he had available to him. It is not the place of this book to describe in detail the operation of the Third Parties (Rights against Insurers) Act of 1930 which is the statute under which third parties may take legal action direct against insurers, but it has been made plain by various recent judicial decisions that the third party cannot and should not have greater rights against the insurer than he originally would have had against the assured had the assured remained viable and capable of satisfying a judgment. It is not clear from the words of Article 1.6 as to whether the words 'to the same extent' implied that the insurer may not be entitled to limit his liability and may have to pay the claim of the suing third party in full if the assured had been denied his own right to limit. The true interpretation must necessarily at this stage be conjecture only since there has not been a test case on this point since the introduction of the 1976 Convention into English law.

### *Article 2.1: Claims subject to limitation*

'1. Subject to Articles 3 and 4 the following claims, whatever the basis of liability may be, shall be subject to limitation of liability:

(a) claims in respect of loss of life or personal injury or loss of or damage to property (including damage to harbour works, basins and waterways and aids to navigation), occurring on board or in direct connexion with the operation of the ship or with salvage operations, and consequential loss resulting therefrom;

(b) claims in respect of loss resulting from delay in the carriage by sea of cargo, passengers or their luggage;

(c) claims in respect of other loss resulting from infringement of rights other than

contractual rights, occurring in direct connexion with the operation of the ship or salvage operations;
(d) claims in respect of the raising, removal, destruction or the rendering harmless of a ship which is sunk, wrecked, stranded or abandoned, including anything that is or has been on board such ship;
(e) claims in respect of the removal destruction or the rendering harmless of the cargo of the ship;
(f) claims of a person other than the person liable in respect of measures taken in order to avert or minimize loss for which the person liable may limit his liability in accordance with this Convention, and further loss caused by such measures.'

Claims which are subject to limitation under this Convention are redefined and the language of Article 2 differs from that of the equivalent provision in the 1957 Convention in that the latter restricted claims to those arising from acts, faults or neglects of those on board the ship, or, if not on board, committed in the course of the navigation or management of the ship. This necessarily restricted the types of claim for which limitation could be sought and/or granted. The particular phrase which seems to liberalize the scope and to 'throw off the shackles' of the restrictions by which persons were restricted in the 1957 Convention is 'occurring in direct connexion with the operation of the ship or with salvage operations'. This adequately covers the *Tojo Maru*-type factual situation which, under the 1957 Convention, was excluded from the ability to limit for the reason described above. For example, limitation under the current wording could possibly apply where a ship is actually 'out of navigation' in dock, e.g. undergoing repairs, and somebody for whom the shipowner is responsible commits a negligent act in connection with the operation of the ship, which is quite likely, that person perhaps not even being on board the ship himself such as a bunker supplier. It is, however, early days in the life of the Convention and test cases of this sort will no doubt be coming before the courts in due course. This article also allows limitation in respect of consequential damages. (See now *Caspian Basin* v *Bouygues* (*No. 4*) [1997] 2 Lloyd's Rep. 507.)

Article 2.1(b) appears to introduce the element of loss resulting from delay in the carriage not only of passengers or their luggage, but also of cargo by sea. This, however, may not be new in that damages for delay has for long since now entitled the sufferer to recover his provable financial loss and would also have been included with the wider definition of the word 'damages'. In fact it may be arguable that the claim need not sound in damages because the opening sentence provides 'whatever the basis of liability may be.'

Article 2.1(d) deals specifically with claims in respect of removal of wreck expenses except where the claim relates to remuneration under a contract with the person liable (Article 2.2). It should be remembered that the removal of a wreck can be done pursuant to a contractual right/duty or pursuant to a statutory requirement. The P & I Clubs, for example, cover the risk of wreck removal expenses, but only if the removal is compulsorily required by order of a national or local authority. Some doubt is cast upon exactly what is meant in this paragraph since at the commencement of Article 2, in the opening two lines, the words 'whatever the basis of liability may be' apply to all the claims listed in the article generally and which are to be subject to limitation.

As has been seen earlier in the chapter, the 1957 Convention (as enacted by the

Merchant Shipping Act 1958) excluded claims in respect of raising, removal or destruction of a ship which is sunk, wrecked, stranded or abandoned, since the British Government never in fact brought that particular paragraph into statutory effect. The same thing has happened with the British version of the 1976 Convention where a reservation has been made in respect of this particular paragraph (see paragraph 3 of Part II of Schedule 7 to the Merchant Shipping Act 1995). There would appear to be a conflict between the opening words of Article 2.1 and the reservation made in paragraph 3 of Part II in that the latter appears, by implication, to apply only to instances where a wreck is removed under statutory authority or at the order of a government or local authority of some sort. Whereas if one takes the opening words of Article 2 at their face value it is irrelevant as to what the basis of liability is when claims in respect of the raising, removal, destruction or rendering harmless of a ship form the basis of an application for limitation.

Article 2.1(e) appears to conflict with the previous sub-paragraph (d) in that cargo is just as much 'anything that is or has been on board such ship' as anything else. Therefore if sub-paragraph (d) is still an excluded sub-paragraph until such time as it is given statutory effect, how can it be said that sub-paragraph (e) can be an included claim unless possibly it is referring to the removal or destruction of cargo which may have been on board the ship before the moment when the ship has become sunk, wrecked, stranded or abandoned. Unless such an interpretation is put on sub-paragraph (e) then there does appear to be a conflict.

The final sub-paragraph (f) of Article 2.1 deals with claims of third parties in respect of measures taken to avert or minimize the loss. Clearly such loss should be in respect of which the right to limit liability has accrued in the person liable. Also the expenses which have been incurred must have been incurred by persons other than the person who is liable/potentially able to limit. Thirdly, where there is a contractual relationship existing between the person liable/potentially able to limit and the third party who has taken the measures to avert the loss and thus incurred expenses such a claim may not be subject to limitation.

### *Article 2.2*

'2. Claims set out in paragraph 1 shall be subject to limitation of liability even if brought by way of recourse or for indemnity under a contract or otherwise. However, claims set out under paragraph 1(d), (e) and (f) shall not be subject to limitation of liability to the extent that they relate to remuneration under a contract with the person liable.'

The purpose of this small paragraph is to make clear that any claim which has arisen by way of liability by X to Y and where X has a right to be indemnified or seek recourse from Z limitation may lie in respect of what appears to be an indemnity claim just as much as it can lie under the primary claim itself. The most obvious type of circumstances where the situation can arise is where there is a collision between a ship steaming under its own power with another vessel proceeding under the control of a tug. The tug and tow may have, and very probably will have, a contract of towage existing between them with indemnity clauses in it. The tug may have a primary liability to the third ship in the collision, but may also have a full right of indemnity from the vessel which it is towing at the time.

### *Article 3: Claims excepted from limitation*

'The rules of this Convention shall not apply to:
(a) claims for salvage or contribution in general average;
(b) claims for oil pollution damage within the meaning of the International Convention on Civil Liability for Oil Pollution Damage dated 29th November 1969 or of any amendment or Protocol thereto which is in force;
(c) claims subject to any international convention or national legislation governing or prohibiting limitation of liability for nuclear damage;
(d) claims against the shipowner of a nuclear ship for nuclear damage;
(e) claims by servants of the shipowner or salvor whose duties are connected with the ship or the salvage operations, including claims of their heirs, dependents or other persons entitled to make such claims, if under the law governing the contract of service between the shipowner or salvor and such servants the shipowner or salvor is not entitled to limit his liability in respect of such claims, or if he is by such law only permitted to limit his liability to an amount greater than that provided for in Article 6.'

Article 3 sets out these claims which are excepted from limitation. The first sub-paragraph deals with claims for salvage or contribution in general average. This quite clearly applies only to direct claims for a salvage award or for a contribution in general average and would not apply, for example, where cargo interests have paid their salvage or general average contributions, but subsequently have tried to claim back what they have paid from the shipowner on the basis that the vessel has been found unseaworthy and there has been a fundamental breach of the contract of carriage by the shipowner. This would, so far as the cargo interests' claim against the shipowners is concerned, be a claim in damages and would be subject to limitation. This is illustrated by the case of *The Breydon Merchant*, below.

*The Breydon Merchant* [1992] 1 Lloyd's Rep. 373
The vessel *Breydon Merchant* suffered a serious fire in her engine room and salvors were engaged. The shipowners sought a decree limiting their liability under the 1976 Convention. Cargo owners argued that the vessel was unseaworthy and their claim for damages, including a salvage contribution, was not subject to limitation because salvage claims were excluded by Article 3.

*Held*: that cargo owners' claim was not one for salvage but for damages for breach of contract. One element in the assessment of damages would be cargo's contribution to salvage. Article 2 of the Convention provides that shipowners can limit their liability for various claims, including loss of or damage to property occurring on board, and consequential loss 'whatever the basis of liability may be'. It did not matter whether shipowners' liability arose in contract, tort or by statute. The shipowners could limit liability for the claim by cargo-owners arising from their breach of contract.

Sub-paragraph (b) deals with oil pollution damage and thus any commentary on this particular head of claim may be found in Chapter 10 later on in this book.

Sub-paragraph (c) nuclear damage has long been considered a serious enough type of damage to justify its being dealt with separately by separate international Convention and/or national legislation. In this respect it has 'special category' status as much as oil pollution. In as much as any limitation is allowed as a result of nuclear damage provisions may be found in the Nuclear Installations Act 1965, as far as the right to limit is concerned.

Sub-paragraph (d) specifically refers to nuclear damage caused by a nuclear ship. The relevant Convention which covers damage of this nature is the Convention on Liability of Operators of Nuclear Ships 1962 where provisions for limitation may be found.

Sub-paragraph (e) deals with claims arising in connection with contracts of service. Reference should also be made to section 185(4) of the Merchant Shipping Act 1995. Thus claims in respect of this type of cause of action carry unlimited liability.

### *Article 4: Conduct barring limitation*

> 'A person liable shall not be entitled to limit his liability if it is proved that the loss resulted from his personal act or omission, committed with the intent to cause such loss, or recklessly and with knowledge that such loss would probably result.'

Ironically this Article, though only just under four lines in length possibly produces the most significant alteration from its equivalent Article in the 1957 Convention. The 'actual fault or privity rule' has disappeared in favour of a more drastic type of conduct which is vividly described in the brief Article itself. It is a sobering thought that anybody, particulary the owner of a ship, could have in mind to act with 'the intent to cause loss' though it is not so difficult to imagine that conduct can be and is reckless and even with knowledge that loss would probably result. One only has to consider the number of fatal accidents on the roads to see tragic examples of reckless driving heedless as to whether anybody will get injured or killed as a result. As previously, it will still be required to operate the test for determining who is the 'alter ego' of the corporate person seeking to limit, i.e. the so-called *Lady Gwendolen* test, since we are still looking to find the 'personal' acts or omissions of the party liable. Personal actions of personal individuals are easy to determine since they either do or do not exist, but personal acts of corporate persons need to be investigated to determine whether they were the very action of the company itself. The concept of deliberate and reckless conduct is becoming accepted by and in other Conventions and is particularly to be noticed in the Athens Convention relating to the Carriage of Passengers and their Luggage by Sea 1974 and in the 1955 Protocol of the Warsaw Convention on Carriage by Air.

The meaning of 'person liable' in the opening words of Article 4 presumably has to be set against Article 1 where the persons entitled to limit liability are defined and set out. But whose 'personal act' will it be that can break the right to limit? Undoubtedly if it is the personal act of the person liable, then he will be prevented from limiting his own liability, but would the personal act of one category of person able to limit prevent another category of person being able to limit if the liability arose from the same incident? The answer to this question must to some extent lie in the concept of the 'alter ego'. An analysis of this concept has been gradually pieced together over the years between 1957 and the present day by various court cases, probably the most influential of which have been *The Lady Gwendolen* (page 380) and *The Marion* (page 383) which have both spot-lighted the thinking which must go into the determination of who in the corporate structure of an owning company is that person who can be identified with and be regarded as the 'mirror image' of the shipowner for the purposes of limitation. If such a person is the person who has committed the personal act, then his identity as the 'alter ego' will prevent the principal shipowner enjoying the benefit of limitation on that particular occasion. If, however, he is not such an 'alter ego', then his act or omission would prevent him himself successfully limiting, but would not prevent his principal, the shipowner or other party attempting to limit, who would still be free to do so.

The words which probably capture the imagination most in the brief wording of Article 4 are the words 'intent to cause such loss' and the words 'or recklessly and with knowledge that such loss would probably result'. The former phrase is, to say the least, harsh. Can we really imagine that people go around, other than criminals or potential criminals, with the actual intent to cause loss or harm to other people? But nevertheless that is what the words say and it would be incumbent upon those trying to deny limitation to prove that the 'person liable' definitely intended to cause the loss complained of. It is difficult to imagine how anybody could prove this because to do so it would almost seem to be necessary to explore the mind of the party who had committed the act or expose that person to truth drugs or some equally infallible method of exposing the true intentions of the person concerned. The alternative is contained in the latter phrase where the word 'recklessly' is to be found. 'Recklessness' or 'reckless' are forms of a word which also does not submit easily to definition. Recklessness has to be coupled with knowledge that such loss would probably result. Guidance may be sought in the case of *Goldman* v *Thai Airways International Ltd* [1983] 3 All ER 693 concerning the Warsaw Convention. The Court of Appeal said that the word 'recklessly' had to be construed in Article 25 of the Warsaw Convention along with the words 'and with knowledge that damage would probably result'. Eveleigh LJ stated at page 700 that:

> 'An act may be reckless when it involves a risk, even though it cannot be said that the danger envisaged is a probable consequence. It is enough that it is a possible consequence, although there comes a point when the risk is so remote that it would not be considered reckless to take it. We look for an element of recklessness which is perhaps more clearly indicated in the French term "temerairement". Article 25 however, refers not to possibility, but to the probability of resulting damage. Thus something more than a possibility is required. The word "probable" is a common enough word. I understand that to mean something is likely to happen. I think that that is what is meant in Article 25. In other words, one anticipates damage from the act or omission.'

The requirement of proof that there has been reckless behaviour and with knowledge that loss would probably result is capable of being satisfied by a more objective test. The burden of proving intent, however, must be by its very nature a subjective test.

Whatever the nature of the test, objective or subjective, quite clearly it is going to be far harder under the 1976 Convention to 'break' limitation because the instances of recklessness or intention to cause loss must by their very nature be more scarce than the old idea of personal fault, negligence or privity.

As the 1976 Convention has not long been in force in English law, the courts have only considered one case brought under it, but what does make an interesting speculative study is what the English court would have made of the facts and circumstances of the *Herald of Free Enterprise* disaster if the matter had been allowed to get to court on the subject of limitation of liability, which did not in fact happen. It would perhaps be wrong to speculate in detail in these pages, but it does bear interesting thinking as to whether the leaving open of the bow doors of a cross-channel ferry, even in the fairest of weather, when the ship left harbour, was recklessness or mere negligence. Could it have been foreseen by the owners (the persons liable) that loss would *probably* result. We do not know, we did not have to know and we shall never know and thus one ideally constructed precedent has been lost to the catalogue of case law precedents on this particular issue.

Another interesting contrast between the 1957 and the 1976 Convention is as to where lies the burden of proof for the entitlement of limitation benefits. Under the 1957 regime it was clearly placed upon the party who was seeking to limit liability. He had to show that he personally had no fault or privity directly resulting in or contributing to the incident giving rise to the liability. Under the 1976 Convention the point is left vague and has to be determined by way of construction from the wording of the Articles concerned. Article 2(1) says quite definitively that claims *shall* be subject to limitation of liability and this gives the natural impression that if limitation is to be broken or denied then it is up to the party in opposition, i.e. the plaintiff, to introduce evidence sufficient to prove to the satisfaction of the court that the party who is claiming limitation was guilty of the particular type of conduct defined in Article 4 as denying limitation rights. So it is safe to assume that the onus of proof has shifted from what it was under the 1957 Convention to entirely the opposite way under the 1976 Convention, i.e. that the party seeking to deny limitation has the burden of proof in showing that the conduct displayed by the person liable fell within the definition laid down in Article 4. In fact in the case of *The Bowbelle* [1990] 1 Lloyd's Rep 532 Sheen J stated that the effect of Articles 2 and 4 was that specified claims were subject to limitation of liability unless the person making the claim proved that the loss resulted from a personal act or omission of the shipowner committed with intent to cause such loss or recklessly and with knowledge that such loss would probably result. That imposes upon the claimant a very heavy burden.

We refer also to section 186 of the Merchant Shipping Act 1995 which provides:

*Exclusion of liability*

**186.**—(1) Subject to subsection (3) below, the owner of a United Kingdom ship shall not be liable for any loss or damage in the following cases, namely—

(a) where any property on board the ship is lost or damaged by reason of fire on board the ship; or

(b) where any gold, silver, watches, jewels or precious stones on board the ship are lost or damaged by reason of theft, robbery or other dishonest conduct and their nature and value were not at the time of shipment declared by their owner or shipper to the owner or master of the ship in the bill of lading or otherwise in writing.

(2) Subject to subsection (3) below, where the loss or damage arises from anything done or omitted by any person in his capacity of master or member of the crew or (otherwise than in that capacity) in the course of his employment as a servant of the owner of the ship, subsection (1) above shall also exclude the liability of—

(a) the master, member of the crew or servant; and
(b) in a case where the master or member of the crew is the servant of a person whose liability would not be excluded by that subsection apart from this paragraph, the person whose servant he is.

(3) This section does not exclude the liability of any person for any loss or damage resulting from any such personal act or omission of his as is mentioned in Article 4 of the Convention set out in Part I of Schedule 7.

(4) This section shall apply in relation to Her Majesty's ships as it applies in relation to other ships.

(5) In this section "owner", in relation to a ship, includes any part owner and any charterer, manager or operator of the ship.

### *Article 5: Counterclaims*

'Where a person entitled to limitation of liability under the rules of this Convention has a claim against the claimant arising out of the same occurrence, their respective claims shall be set off against each other and the provisions of this Convention shall only apply to the balance, if any.'

The question of counterclaims raises the controversial issue of set-off of one claim against another and the fact that limitation is applied after set-off. This Article provides that claims and counterclaims arising out of the same occurrence must be set-off against each other and limitation is to be applied only to the balance if any, payable. Persons entitled to limit liability under the 1976 Convention include salvors as well as charterers, managers and operators of the ship. As the text of the Article states, all persons entitled to limitation of liability are entitled to the set-off facility if they have a counterclaim. A question could be whether salvors can set off a claim for salvage against a shipowner's counterclaim for negligence in the performance of salvage services before applying his right to limit liability to any balance due to the shipowner.

The 1971 case of *The Tojo Maru* involved a salvage claim and a counterclaim by the owners of the *Tojo Maru* for damages to their vessel caused by the negligent act of a servant of the salvage company. The Court of Appeal decided that limitation would have to be applied before set-off if it had been available. The House of Lords did not express an opinion on this issue but comment was made that the Courts below may not have reached a correct conclusion on this matter. If this case had involved the 1976 Convention it is suggested that the question of set-off would not apply as the salvor's claim for salvage remuneration did not arise out of the same occurrence as that which gave rise to the shipowner's claim for negligence. It may well be that Article 5 does not apply in similar circumstances to that of *The Tojo Maru.*

### *Article 6: The general limits*

'1. The limits of liability for claims other than those mentioned in Article 7, arising on any distinct occasion shall be calculated as follows:

(a) in respect of claims for loss of life or personal injury,

(i) 333,000 Units of Account for a ship with a tonnage not exceeding 500 tons,
(ii) for a ship with a tonnage in excess thereof, the following amount in addition to that mentioned in (i):
for each ton from 501 to 3,000 tons, 500 Units of Account;
for each ton from 3,001 to 30,000 tons, 333 Units of Account;
for each ton from 30,001 to 70,000 tonns, 250 Units of Account; and
for each ton in excess of 70,000 tons, 167 Units of Account,

(b) In respect of any other claims.
(i) 167,000 Units of Account for a ship with a tonnage not exceeding 500 tons,
(ii) for a ship with a tonnage in excess thereof the following amount in addition to that mentioned in (i):
for each ton from 501 to 30,000 tons, 167 Units of Account;
for each ton from 30,001 to 70,000 tons, 125 Units of Account; and
for each ton in excess of 70,000 tons, 83 Units of Account.

2. Where the amount calculated in accordance with paragraph 1(a) is insufficient to pay the claims mentioned therein in full, the amount calculated in accordance with paragraph 1(b) shall be available for payment of the unpaid balance of claims under paragraph 1(a) and such unpaid balance shall rank rateably with claims mentioned under paragraph 1(b).

3. However, without prejudice to the right of claims for loss of life or personal injury according to paragraph 2, a State Party may provide in its national law that claims in respect of damage to harbour works, basins and waterways and aids to navigation shall have such priority over other claims under paragraph 1(b) as is provided by that law.

4. The limits of liability for any salvor not operating from any ship or for any salvor operating solely on the ship to, or in respect of which he is rendering salvage services, shall be calculated according to a tonnage of 1,500 tons.

5. For the purpose of this Convention the ship's tonnage shall be the gross tonnage calculated in accordance with the tonnage measurement rules contained in Annex 1 of the International Convention on Tonnage Measurement of Ships, 1969.'

Article 6 deals with the general limits of liability and this Article also has differences from the equivalent Article in the 1957 Convention, the most obvious being that whereas in the 1957 Convention there was a flat rate of Poincaré gold francs (3,100) multiplied by the ship's tonnage, under Article 6 of the 1976 Convention there is a sliding scale with the amount of currency getting less in proportion to the greater amount of tonnage. Another noticeable difference is that the gold franc has disappeared in favour of the units of account which, by Article 8, is to be defined as the special drawing right (SDR) as defined by the International Monetary Fund the value of which may be found as against the various national currencies in the daily editions of the *Financial Times* or *Lloyd's List*. The appropriate value date is when the limitation fund is constituted, payment is made or security is given. A quick glance at the scales provided in sub-paragraphs (a) and (b) of paragraph 1 of Article 6 will show that the fund formed for loss of life or personal injury claim is exactly twice the size of the fund formed (sub-paragraph (b)) in respect of 'any other claims'.

Paragraph 2 of Article 6 creates a slight dilemma since it does not make clear exactly how these funds are to be used. Under the old regime (1957) it was quite clear that where both loss of life and injury and property (other) claims arose from the same incident, the total limitation fund was calculated and the first 2,100 gold francs part of it was set aside in order to satisfy the life and injury claims and if the fund was not sufficient then the unsatisfied balance would rank alongside (pari passu) with the property claims, these to be satisfied, if possible, out of the lesser fund which was the remaining balance of 1,000 Poincaré gold francs multiplied by the ship's tonnage.

The wording of paragraph 2 of Article 6 is unclear. The ranking of the unsatisfied balance of claims against the 'lesser' fund could equally well be allowed *whether or not* there *are* 'other' claims. Where, in the final line of Article 6.2 it speaks of 'such unpaid balance shall rank rateably with claims mentioned under paragraph 1 (b)' this could easily be construed as meaning if there *are* any such other claims. This would not be distorting the wording too greatly.

Paragraph 4 of Article 6 caters for the situation in which salvors find themselves not operating from any ship. It will be remembered that under the old Convention salvors had a very 'rough' time, since they could very rarely, if ever, bring themselves within the restrictive requirement that only those acts, neglects or defaults which were committed within the course of the navigation or management of the ship could rank for an application for limitation. Now that salvors have been allowed to limit in their own right as salvors, it is necessary to provide a notional calculation upon which they can base their limitation fund and it is in this paragraph where it can be found, namely, that salvors not operating from any ship or operating entirely on board the ship which they are trying to save, shall be entitled to calculate their limits of liability according to a notional tonnage of 1,500 tonnes. The burden of proof of showing that one of those two alternative circumstances were indeed true and correct presumably falls upon the salvor seeking to limit.

### *Article 7: The limit for passenger claims*

'1. In respect of claims arising on any distinct occasion for loss of life or personal injury to passengers of a ship, the limit of liability of the shipowner thereof shall be an amount of 46,666 Units of Account multiplied by the number of passengers which the ship is authorised to carry according to the ship's certificate, but not exceeding 25 million Units of Account.

2. For the purpose of this Article "claims for loss of life or personal injury to passengers of a ship" shall mean any such claims brought by or on behalf of any person carried in that ship:

(a) under a contract of passenger carriage, or
(b) who, with the consent of the carrier, is accompanying a vehicle or live animals which are covered by a contract for the carriage of goods.'

This Article deals especially with claims in respect of loss of life or personal injury to passengers. The Article appears on the surface to be in direct conflict with Article 7(1) of the Athens Convention. It is pure coincidence that the number of the Article in each Convention should be the same. In order to see exactly where and how the conflict lies, it is best to compare the areas of difference in these two contrasting Articles.

## Limitation of liability

| *The Athens Convention* | *1976 (London) Convention* |
|---|---|
| The limit is 46,666 SDR, this to passengers claiming. The limit established applies per 'carriage' which is interpreted as being the whole period over which the passenger is being carried. | The limit shall be 46,666 units of account multiplied by the number of passengers which the ship is authorized to carry etc., with an overall limit of 25 million units of account. This fund applies *on any distinct occasion.* |

Thus, although the actual limitation figure (46,666 SDR or units of account) is the same in each Convention, the limit under the Athens Convention is calculated by multiplying that figure by the number of passengers who are actually on board and are travelling and are injured/killed. Under the 1976 (London) Convention, the limit is fixed, on the contrary, at an amount reached by multiplying that same figure (46,666 SDR) by the number of passengers which the ship is allowed by its certificate to carry. This means that the limitation fund under the 1976 Convention is not in the least influenced by the actual number of passengers on board and travelling and/or claiming. There is a different figure under the Athens Convention where the carrier has his principal place of business in the UK.

How can these two separate Articles in separate Conventions dealing with exactly the same subject-matter be reconciled? There is no ready answer to this as there has not as yet been a test case before the English courts on this particular point since the 1976 Convention came into effect in Britain, the Athens Convention having come into effect prior to that. The nearest approach to what might have become a test case was the tragic accident of the *Herald of Free Enterprise* but the matter did not come before the court on the subject of limitation of liability.

Article 19 of the Athens Convention does provide that 'this Convention shall not modify the rights or duties of the carrier, the performing carrier, and their servants or agents provided for in the International Conventions relating to the limitation of liability of owners of seagoing ships'. Also Article 12 of Schedule 6 to the Merchant Shipping Act 1995 provides that nothing in the Athens Convention affects the operation of section 185 of the 1995 Act. Article 13 says that nothing in section 186 shall relieve a person of any liability imposed on him by the Convention. It seems that the carrier may be able to rely on the lower limitation figure in the 1976 Convention.

### *Article 9: Aggregation of claims*

'1. The limits of liability determined in accordance with Article 6 shall apply to the aggregate of all claims which arise on any distinct occasion:

(a) against the person or persons mentioned in paragraph 2 of Article 1 and any person for whose act, neglect or default he or they are responsible; or

(b) against the shipowner of a ship rendering salvage services from that ship and the salvor or salvors operating from such ship and any person for whose act, neglect or default he or they are responsible: or

(c) against the salvor or salvors who are not operating from a ship or who are operating solely on the ship to, or in respect of which, the salvage services are rendered and any person for whose act, neglect or default he or they are responsible.

2. The limits of liability determined in accordance with Article 7 shall apply to the aggregate of all claims subject thereto which may arise on any distinct occasion against the person or persons mentioned in paragraph 2 of Article 1 in respect of the ship referred to in Article 7 and any person for whose act, neglect or default he or they are responsible.'

The only point worthy of comment in the above Article is the expression 'on any distinct occasion' which is a matter for determination, as it were, on 'each distinct occasion' by the relevant court. Borderline examples are not difficult to conjure up, particularly where two ships are in collision and then one ship, in the course of withdrawing from contact, strikes another vessel and causes further damage. As to whether that is two separate collisions and thus damage caused on two distinct occasions would be a matter for court interpretation.

### *Article 10: Limitation of liability without constitution of a limitation fund*

'1. Limitation of liability may be invoked notwithstanding that a limitation fund as mentioned in Article 11 has not been constituted.
2. If limitation of liability is invoked without the constitution of a limitation fund, the provisions of Article 12 shall apply correspondingly.
3. Questions of procedure arising under the rules of this Article shall be decided in accordance with the national law of the State Party in which action is brought.'

This Article provides for a situation where liability is limited without a limitation fund being constituted. English law has always recognized that the invoking of limitation may be pursued by one of two methods. First, a person can plead limitation as a form of defence in an action against him. This basically means that if damages which would ordinarily be assessed in fact exceed the amount to which the person could limit, then judgment will be given only for the limit. Under this method there is no obligation to constitute a limitation fund prior to judgment being given. The disadvantage of using limitation merely as a defence to an ordinary liability action is that it does not concentrate all claims against that same person arising from that same incident into one jurisdiction, but rather is merely a defence to that one particular claim in that one particular action. Thus, if some other claimant brings another action in respect of loss or damage in particular to him arising out of the same incident, the defendant might be found liable to pay the limitation figure over again, assuming that the loss or damage was in excess of the limitation figure. The second method of using the right of limitation is to institute a limitation action and such method entitles the person who takes such action to limit his liability as against all persons whoever they may be who are claiming or who are entitled to claim in respect of the loss or damage which has arisen from that one particular incident. English law does not seem to lay down an obligation to constitute a fund until the limitation proceedings are well under way, although for the protection of the person seeking to limit himself it is advisable to pay the amount into court at an early date so as to avoid the risk that the quantum of the fund will increase if he were to delay longer. There has been nothing under English law to prevent a person instituting a limitation action before admitting liability, but, from a common sense point of view if for no other reason, it is necessary for liability to be admitted before any pronouncement in respect of limitation could be made. Although there is nothing to be lost by the invoking of limitation at an early stage, since it does not constitute an admission of liability, logic alone decrees that liability must at some stage be admitted since the pronouncement will eventually be that *liability* is limited and not that the 'likelihood' of liability is limited.

### *Article 11: Constitution of the fund*

'1. Any person alleged to be liable may constitute a fund with the Court or other competent authority in any State Party in which legal proceedings are instituted in respect of claims subject to limitation. The fund shall be constituted in the sum of such of the amounts set out in Articles 6 and 7 as are applicable to claims for which that person may be liable, together with interest thereon from the date of the occurrence giving rise to the liability until the date of the constitution of the fund. Any fund thus constituted shall be available only for the payment of claims in respect of which limitation of liability can be invoked.

2. A fund may be constituted, either by depositing the sum, or by producing a guarantee acceptable under the legislation of the State Party where the fund is constituted and considered to be adequate by the Court or other competent authority.

3. A fund constituted by one of the persons mentioned in paragraph 1(a), (b) or (c) or paragraph 2 of Article 9 or his insurer shall be deemed constituted by all persons mentioned in paragraph 1(a), (b) or (c) or paragraph 2, respectively.'

This Article is concerned with the constitution of the limitation fund. Paragraph 1 provides for the fund to be constituted with a court or other competent authority and states, what some might say was the obvious, that it should be constituted in the sum of the amounts set out in Articles 6 and 7, thus including the relevant types of claim—loss of life, injury and property claims and also passenger claims where applicable. Under the law of England (and Wales) interest is to be included in the calculation of the fund running from the date of the incident which gives rise to the liability through until the date when the fund is constituted. As to what rate that interest should be is left entirely up to the law of that country where the fund is constituted. The final sentence of subparagraph 1 provides that only those claims in respect of which limitation can be invoked shall be paid out of the constituted fund and, although this too is probably stating the obvious, any claim against which it is not possible for the defendant to limit his liability will receive entirely separate treatment and will not rank against the fund and, if it needs enforcing, it will have to be enforced, not against the fund, but against any other assets which the person who is liable may have.

Paragraph 2 provides for the fund being constituted not only by way of depositing a cash sum, but also alternatively by way of production of an acceptable guarantee. English law has always fought against the formation of a limitation fund by any other method than a cash deposit, but it may be that, eventually, although there is nothing in the 1979 Merchant Shipping Act specifically referring to this, the UK will have to bow to the internationally accepted idea that the deposit of a limitation fund by way of a guarantee acceptable to the court or other competent authority of the State party is the equivalent of a deposit by cash.

Paragraph 3 of this Article only deserves comment in respect of the three words 'or his insurer' in the second line, the insurer not being, on the face of it, a person mentioned in the relevant sub-paragraph of Article 9 as being 'any person alleged to be liable'. It is curious, therefore, that a fund set up by an insurer on behalf of his assured should satisfy the provisions of this Convention in regard to the constituting of the fund.

An interesting case is that of *The Waltraud*, below.

*The Waltraud* [1991] 1 Lloyd's Rep. 389
Following the capsize of the vessel *Waltraud* two separate actions were commenced by various cargo interests claiming summary judgment for damages to be assessed and for an order that an interim payment be made by shipowners in respect of their claims. The Admiralty Court granted summary judgment in favour of the cargo interests on the ground that the vessel was unseaworthy. The Admiralty Court commented that if the shipowners are entitled to limit their liability they can constitute a limitation fund with the Court. When a limitation fund has been constituted in accordance with Article 11 of the 1976 Convention any person having made a claim against the fund shall be barred from exercising any right in respect of such claim against any other assets of the shipowner. Although the shipowners had not set up a fund they could plead limitation of liability if the claim exceeds their limit of liability. However that was not normally a sensible course of action if there is more than one claim. Cargo interests argued that until a limitation fund has been constituted there was no reason why shipowners should have the benefit of the 1976 Convention. Whilst the Admiralty Court saw the force in that argument it decided that in exercising their discretion to make an order for an interim payment such payment should not exceed a reasonable proportion of the damages which, in the opinion of the court, are likely to be recovered by cargo interests. It would not be just to make an order for interim payment which exceeded the limit of the shipowners' liability. The Admiralty Court ordered that interim payments be made in both actions by shipowners to cargo interests not exceeding the global tonnage limitation of the vessel.

### *Article 12: Distribution of the fund*

'1. Subject to the provisions of paragraphs 1 and 2 of Article 6 and of Article 7, the fund shall be distributed among the claimants in proportion to their established claims against the fund.

2. If, before the fund is distributed, the person liable, or his insurer, has settled a claim against the fund such person shall, up to the amount he has paid, acquire by subrogation the rights which the person so compensated would have enjoyed under this Convention.

3. The right of subrogation provided for in paragraph 2 may also be exercised by persons other than those therein mentioned in respect of any amount of compensation which they may have paid, but only to the extent that such subrogation is permitted under the applicable national law.

4. Where the person liable or any other person establishes that he may be compelled to pay, at a later date, in whole or in part any such amount of compensation with regard to which such person would have enjoyed a right of subrogation pursuant to paragraphs 2 and 3 had the compensation been paid before the fund was distributed, the Court or other competent authority of the State where the fund has been constituted may order that a sufficient sum shall be provisionally set aside to enable such person at such later date to enforce his claim against the fund.'

Under this Article, the fund shall be distributed against established claims. The word 'established' in this context does not merely mean calculated and submitted, but recognized by the court (in the case of England and Wales that is taken to mean the High Court). The fund referred to must mean the fund as properly constituted and defined in Article 11 and this would include interest from the date of occurrence to the date of constitution. Whether interest earned *after* that amount of time is to be distributed with the rest is not specifically mentioned. Presumably this would have to be dealt with in accordance with the law of the State in which the fund is constituted (see Article 14). It is likely that interest earned after the constitution of the fund will be distributed amongst established claims.

The text of paragraph 2 merely confirms the law as it stood prior to the 1976 Convention, namely, that if the person liable or his insurer settles a claim direct with the plaintiff, the claim being one which would be allowed to be made against the fund when distributed, he may be subrogated to rights against the fund, but only up to and not exceeding the amount which that claim could have recovered from the distributed fund had it been proved direct against it.

Article 12.3 speaks for itself. It is difficult to see who else other than the liable person or his insurer would be such a person entitled to the right of subrogation but the laws of various countries may well find this subsection convenient to accommodate.

Article 12.4 provides for those who wish to 'hedge their future bets' (or more appropriately, liabilities). An appropriate portion of the fund can be set aside for use at a future time to cope with claims for which the liable person or his insurer knows he will have a liability arising out of the same occurrence but which have not, at the time of the distributing of the fund, yet been presented or proved against him. To put it briefly, this subsection protects a liable person by preserving his subrogated rights for a future time. A question can arise as to how interest is dealt with when striking a balance. This question arose in the case of *The Botany Triad and Lu Shan*, below.

*The Botany Triad and Lu Shan* [1993] 2 Lloyd's Rep. 259
Following a collision between two vessels it was agreed that each party was 50 per cent to blame and damages were agreed. The question arose as to the appropriate method of dealing with interest on the respective claims.

*Held*: that interest should be added to each claim before a balance was struck as opposed to afterwards. The correct course was to strike a balance when agreement was reached between the parties as opposed to the date of the collision. Then one converted the currency of the smaller claim into the currency of the larger on that date and calculated interest on both claims up to that date. The balance between the two sums would, therefore, be struck inclusive of interest. This approach reflected both the capital loss caused by the collision and the inevitable fact that time would have passed between the collision and assessment of damages.

The question arose in the case of *The Capitan San Luis* as to who should pay the costs of limitation proceedings under the 1976 Convention.

*The Capitan San Luis* [1993] 2 Lloyd's Rep. 573
Following a collision off the coast of Cuba it was agreed that the vessel *Celebration* was 25 per cent to blame and the vessel *Capitan San Luis* was 75 per cent to blame. One question was who should pay the costs of the owners of the *Capitan San Luis* seeking a declaration of limitation under the 1976 Convention.

*Held*: that the claimants were obliged to pay the owners' costs on the issue of limitation other than those costs which were incurred by owners in order to prove (as they must) that the claim fell within Article 2. If after investigation the claimants were unable to break limitation, then they would be liable for the owners' costs in contesting the claimants' arguments. The just result would be that costs followed the event.

### *Article 13: Bar to other actions*

'1. Where a limitation fund has been constituted in accordance with Article 11, any person having made a claim against the fund shall be barred from exercising any right in respect of such a claim against any other assets of a person by or on behalf of whom the fund has been constituted.

2. After a limitation fund has been constituted in accordance with Article 11, any ship or other property, belonging to a person on behalf of whom the fund has been constituted, which has been arrested or attached within the jurisdiction of a State Party for a claim which may be raised against the fund, or any security given, may be released by order of the Court or other competent authority of such State. However, such release shall always be ordered if the limitation fund has been constituted:

(a) at the port where the occurrence took place, or, if it took place out of port, at the first port of call thereafter; or
(b) at the port of disembarkation in respect of claims for loss of life or personal injury; or
(c) at the port of discharge in respect of damage to cargo; or
(d) in the State where the arrest is made.

3. The rules of paragraphs 1 and 2 shall apply only if the claimant may bring a claim against the limitation fund before the Court administering that fund and the fund is actually available and freely transferable in respect of that claim.'

Article 13 basically provides that no other assets of the liable person are to be exposed to legal action and the claimant's rights can be exercised solely against the constituted fund. Under paragraph 2, although so far as the English law view of this Article is concerned the position roughly re-establishes the aim of the 1957 Convention, there is a difference in that under Britain's enactment of the 1957 Convention, an English court would not permit the release of a ship arrested in the UK, even if a *foreign* limitation fund has been established, unless such a reliable person was clear of any serious question of actual (personal) fault or privity. The position previously in England concerning section 5 of the Merchant Shipping (Liability of Shipowners and Others) Act 1958 is shown by the case of the *Wladyslaw Lokietek*, below.

*The Wladyslaw Lokietek* [1978] 2 Lloyd's Rep. 520
Following a collision in the Baltic Sea the plaintiffs arrested a sistership of the defendants, *Wladyslaw Lokietek* in England on 30 May. The defendants brought proceedings in the Polish court for the purpose of limiting their liability and constituted a limitation fund on 1 June. One day later the defendants gave security to the plaintiffs in the form of a guarantee by their P & I Club and the *Wladyslaw Lokietek* was released from arrest in England. The defendants applied for the release of the guarantee under section 5 of the 1958 Act.

The Admiralty Court decided that even if a limitation fund was established in another court (here Poland) the vessel would not be released from arrest in England unless the defendant could prove that there was no serious question to be tried in relation to absence of actual fault or privity on his part under section 503 of the 1894 Act. The defendant failed to discharge this burden of proof. Furthermore the defendant having only made their payment into court in Poland after the *Wladyslaw Lokietek* had been arrested had not previously given security within section 5 of the 1958 Act.

This requirement, however, under the 1976 Convention seems to have been effectively disposed of because, as has been said earlier in this chapter, the burden of proof of being barred or not barred from the right to limit, as the case may be, lies not with the person seeking to limit (as under the 1957 Convention) but with the claimants against him.

The paragraph clearly distinguishes between circumstances where the court *must* release and those where it has a discretion to release.

In the case of *The Bowbelle* [1990] 1 Lloyd's Rep. 533 the then Admiralty Judge, Sheen J stated that the 1976 Convention was intended to overcome the effect of the decision of *The Wladyslaw Lokietek* and to ensure that shipowners would only be compelled to provide one limitation fund.

*The Bowbelle* [1990] 1 Lloyd's Rep. 532
Following the tragic collision between the ships *Bowbelle* and *Marchioness* in the River Thames involving loss of life, the owners of the *Bowbelle* set up a limitation fund under the 1976 Convention. They applied to file a praecipe requesting that a caveat against the issue of a warrant to arrest any of 14 named ships in the praecipe be entered in the caveat book of the Admiralty and Commercial Registry.

*Held*: that the owners could only be compelled to constitute one fund in court under Article 11. Any claimant might bring a claim against the limitation fund in court and Article 13(1) made it clear that any person who had not made a claim against the fund in court was not entitled to arrest any ship in the same ownership as *Bowbelle*.

Common sense dictates that the owners should file a praecipe signed by their solicitor who must acknowledge service of any writ against owners and state that a limitation fund had been constituted. If a claimant then arrests one of the ships named in the praecipe the court will be bound to order its release.

The Rules of Supreme Court (RSC Order 75, Rule 6(1A)) now provides that a person seeking to limit liability must file a praecipe in the Admiralty and Commercial Registry. This praecipe should state that a limitation fund has been constituted and undertake to acknowledge service of any writ issued against owners as a result of which a caveat against the arrest of the vessels named in the praecipe is issued. It is unlikely that a claimant will now seek to arrest a vessel when a limitation fund has been constituted by her owners because they will be aware of the fund due to the caveat.

### *Article 14: Governing law*

Article 14 is self-explanatory and reads as follows:-

> 'Subject to the provisions of this Chapter the rules relating to the constitution and distribution of a limitation fund, and all rules of procedure in connection therewith, shall be governed by the law of the State Party in which the fund is constituted.'

The remaining Articles of the Convention which are contained in Chapters 4 and 5 are not receiving individual comment in this chapter due to an overall aim not to allow the book to get over long, but the test of the Articles (Articles 15 to 22 inclusive) is contained in Appendix 11 (page 557).

## TIME LIMITATIONS

Various limitations by time are placed upon legal actions against shipowners and they may be able so to avoid liability.

We do not intend to address these in any detail except to say that the Maritime Conventions Act 1911 used to provide a two-year period in which a shipowner must bring legal action against the other ship after a collision. It also stipulated a similar two-year period in respect of salvage claims.

*The Niceto De Larrinaga* [1965] 2 Lloyd's Rep. 134
The mother of a man killed in a collision between two ships on 23 September 1961 issued a writ on 18 September 1964 against the owner of the ship in which her son was. The shipowner contended that the action was time-barred because the two-year limit under the Maritime Conventions Act 1911 applied.

*Held*: That the two-year limit did not apply to third-party claims against the *carrying vessel*. The woman had brought her action within three years which was within time under the Fatal Accidents Act 1976.

The judge in this case emphasized most firmly that the wording of section 8 categorizes distinctly the types of claims contemplated, namely, claims in respect of damage or loss to cargo or property or loss of life or personal injury which lie against the *other* vessel. It does not deal with nor does it apply to *all* claims.

The court used to have a discretionary power to extend the period of two years which is illustrated by the following cases—

*The Alnwick* [1965] 1 Lloyd's Rep. 69
A male passenger was killed as a result of a collision between the carrying passenger ship and a tug (the *Alnwick*) in April 1962. The collision was caused by the negligence of a third vessel not concerned in the actual collision. A writ was issued against the tug's owners in December 1963, but not against the third vessel's owners until July 1964. The third vessel's owners argued that the issue of the writ against them was 'out of time' (Maritime Conventions Act 1911, s. 8).

*Held*: that the court's discretionary powers should be exercised to allow the action to continue.

*The Gaz Fountain* [1987] 2 Lloyd's Rep. 151
A collision occurred between two vessels on 2 January 1982 and negotiations took place between the respective P & I Clubs. Extentions of time were given for the plaintiffs' claim until 30 December 1986, nearly some five years after the collision. On 14 January 1987 the plaintiffs issued a writ claiming damages as a result of the collision and the defendants contended that as the extension of time had not been renewed the writ ought to be struck out because the claim was time-barred. The plaintiffs applied for an order that the period of limitation provided by section 8 of the 1911 Act be extended for such period as would enable the action commenced by the writ issued on 14 January to be maintained.

*Held*: that the delay in issuing the writ was devoid of excuse. The court's discretion to extend time should only be exercised when the plaintiffs show special circumstances. There were no special circumstances and there were no grounds which justified extending the period of limitation. The plaintiffs' claim was time-barred.

*The Zirje* [1989] 1 Lloyd's Rep. 493
A collision between the plaintiffs' vessel and the defendants' vessel arose in the Kiel Canal. There were negotiations between the parties' representatives and the defendants confirmed that they had no claim to pursue against the plaintiffs. The only question outstanding was the quantum of the plaintiffs' damages. A time extension for commencing

proceedings was not agreed and the plaintiff issued a writ three days out of time and asked the court for the limitation to be extended by three days under section 8.

*Held*: that a time extension should be granted if, in all the circumstances of the case, it appeared that there was good reason for doing so. The exercise of this discretion should not be confined only to those cases where there appear to be exceptional or special circumstances. The defendants had agreed not to contest liability: they were at the material time willing to grant an extension of time for one year but wished to impose a term for which there was no justification. The extension for which the plaintiffs applied was only three days. Although there was no direct cause or link between the conduct of the defendants and the oversight of the plaintiffs in failing to issue a writ in time, it was clear that if the system operated by the defendants for ensuring that important telexes reached the named addressee had not been defective a writ would have been issued in time. All these factors were taken into account and in the circumstances of the case the court extended the limitation period for three days which enabled the plaintiffs' writ, issued three days late, to be in time.

*The Seaspeed America* [1990] 1 Lloyd's Rep. 150
A collision occurred in Lagos as a result of which the defendants admitted liability. Negotiations took place as to the costs of repair of the plaintiffs' vessel. The plaintiffs allowed time for issuing the writ to pass because of an oversight and applied for an extension of 13 days, after the two-year limit had passed, to bring a claim against the defendants.

*Held*: that the court would only extend the two-year time limit if in all the circumstances of the case there was good reason for doing so. There was good reason for extending the time limit by 13 days in that liability was admitted, the parties were negotiating about the cost of repairs and the P & I Club's representative was not concerned with the time limit. Accordingly the time limit for commencing the action of the plaintiffs was extended for such time as was necessary for the action to be brought.

*The Al Tabith and Alanfushi* [1993] 2 Lloyd's Rep. 214
Following a collision negotiations took place between the owners' P & I Clubs. The plaintiffs' P & I Club obtained a six-month time extension but only issued a writ some 17 days after the time extension had expired. The plaintiffs applied for an order that the period of limitation under section 8 of the 1911 Act be extended.

*Held*: The defendants' conduct did not cause or contribute to the plaintiffs missing the time-bar. The fact that the parties were negotiating in order to achieve a settlement was not by itself a good reason for extending the normal two-year limitation period. The plaintiffs had to show that their failure to comply with the time limit was not merely due to their own mistake; it could not be a good reason for extending the time limit that the defendants are unable to show that there would be any specific prejudice to them in conducting their defence. Here the plaintiffs' P & I Club failed to give instructions to solicitors to issue a writ in time and there was no good reason to extend the time limit.

The two-year time limit for salvage claims is now contained in the International Convention on Salvage 1989 which has the force of law in the United Kingdom under the Merchant Shipping Act 1995. Also section 190 of the Merchant Shipping Act 1995 has replaced section 8 of the Merchant Shipping Act 1911 (below) but the reasoning of the courts before may still apply when seeking an extension of time. Section 190 of the 1995 Act provides:

*Time limit for proceedings against owners or ship*

**190.**—(1) This section applies to any proceedings to enforce any claim or lien against a ship or her owners—

(a) in respect of damage or loss caused by the fault of that ship to another ship, its cargo or freight or any property on board it; or
(b) for damages for loss of life or personal injury caused by the fault of that ship to any person on board another ship.

(2) The extent of the fault is immaterial for the purposes of this section.

(3) Subject to subsections (5) and (6) below, no proceedings to which this section applies shall be brought after the period of two years from the date when—
(a) the damage or loss was caused; or
(b) the loss of life or injury was suffered.

(4) Subject to subsections (5) and (6) below, no proceedings under any of sections 187 to 189 to enforce any contribution in respect of any overpaid proportion of any damages for loss of life or personal injury shall be brought after the period of one year from the date of payment.

(5) Any court having jurisdiction in such proceedings may, in accordance with rules of court, extend the period allowed for bringing proceedings to such extent and on such conditions as it thinks fit.

(6) Any such court, if satisfied that there has not been during any period allowed for bringing proceedings any reasonable opportunity of arresting the defendant ship within—
(a) the jurisdiction of the court, or
(b) the territorial sea of the country to which the plaintiff's ship belongs or in which the plaintiff resides or has his principal place of business,

shall extend the period allowed for bringing proceedings to an extent sufficient to give a reasonable opportunity of so arresting the ship.

CHAPTER 10

# OIL POLLUTION

Oil pollution is, from the practitioner's point of view, perhaps even more than from the student's viewpoint, of paramount importance in the maritime world. Oil pollution as a problem was not seriously discussed internationally until the mid-1950s when an international conference (1954) was held to discuss prevention of pollution of the sea by oil. But a sense of urgency for international action did not arise until the *Torrey Canyon* catastrophe in 1967. Ever since that disaster the problem of oil pollution has been a major headache throughout the world. That incident illuminated the immense range of damage which one oil spill from one vessel is able to do. Every available method known at the time of coping with the spill and confining the damage was used, ranging from spraying polluted beaches with detergent to using RAF bombers to burn up the cargo. It was said in discussion preparatory to the 1969 conference which led to the Convention alluded to later in this chapter that Britain had waited a whole week before resorting to the tactics of bombing the wreck because she was unsure of her legal right to take such action.

Just 11 years after that accident, the supertanker *Amoco Cadiz* (in March 1978) spilled its load of crude oil onto the beaches of Brittany after encountering problems with her steering gear 13 miles off the French coast just before entering, north-east-bound, the traffic routeing system in the English Channel. Despite tug assistance she ended up a twisted and battered wreck on a rock, as it happened uncharted, adjacent to the French coast. Ironically, as the RAF had bombed the wreck of the *Torrey Canyon*, so French military helicopters dropped explosive devices on to the wreck to try to speed up the flow of oil from the tanker's ruptured tanks and so hope to mitigate to some extent the widespread effects of the pollution.

A few weeks later again, the tanker *Eleni V* was split in two as a result of a collision with another vessel off the east coast of England. A considerable amount of her oil cargo polluted the English coastline which was estimated to cost the British government in the region of £3,000,000. There was again inordinate delay before the decision was taken by Britain to blow up the wrecked tanker's remaining bow section.

The major spill (more than 10 million gallons of crude oil) from the *Exxon Valdes* in Alaskan waters in 1989 was almost certainly the factor which precipitated the US Congress into enacting legislation totally independent from the International Conventions, all of which this chapter is committed to describing. If the *Torrey Canyon* and the *Amoco Cadiz* took the world by surprise because of the enormity of those spills and of their consequences, the *Exxon Valdes* emphasized the aggressive way in which responsible parties and victims could react to each others' attitude, indifference, lack of response, etc. Also noticeable was the urge to quantify even the most abstract and nebulous losses in terms of money, e.g. loss of holiday possibilities. The *Exxon Valdes* spill also high-lighted the instinct for revenge on and punishment of those presumed to be guilty. A jury in Anchorage, Alaska, found that Exxon had been reckless in permitting the Master of the *The Exxon Valdes* with a history of alcohol abuse, to take command of one of its super tankers. This jury verdict completed the first phase of the trial of the whole matter and also paved the way for a possible eventual award of punitive damages, of which US$15 billion was being sought in addition to compensatory damages of US$1.5 billion. Exxon paid out US$3.5 billion in promptly cleaning up the oil spill and eventually reached a US$900 million settlement in the State of Alaska. Subsequently a punitive damage award was made against Exxon of US$5 billion. The beneficiaries were to be local fishermen, natives, and any other individuals who suffered as a result of the spill. Exxon are currently appealing this on the ground that they have 'been punished enough already'.

By comparison, *The Braer* which was buffeted by heavy weather and spilled its oil cargo on the shores of the Shetland Islands in 1993 'hit the headlines' for a short period and caused initial consternation to the islanders. However, the action of wind and waves eventually caused a dispersal of the oil so that the aftermath was relatively speaking quieter than the preceding disasters.

Of all the many types of maritime claims, those arising from pollution must be the most international in flavour, if only because the very substance which causes the third-party loss of suffering can actually drift from jurisdiction to jurisdiction.

The shipping industry is naturally the primary butt for the emotional wrath of governments and other innocent third-party sufferers from oil pollution although, despite what surveys might show, it is doubtful whether more than 50 per cent of the oceans' pollution is caused by ship-based sources, the remaining 50 per cent being caused by land-based sources. Regardless of this, however, the principle of unlimited liability and, in many cases the absolute liability, of an offending shipowner has been frequently alluded to by many of the world's governments and such principles if they were to become crystallized in law would provide insurance problems of insuperable magnitude to shipowners.

It is intended within the scope of this chapter to touch on the insurance aspects of the problems whilst dealing in the main with the legal liabilities of vessel owners who pollute the seas and the international Conventions and national legislation which has been enacted to cope with this complex problem. So rapid is the development of maritime law in this field in particular that much of what was current in a preceding edition of this book has become history in the process of updating. What is history, however, should not simply be omitted since what has gone before plays a very important part in understanding what rules now. We will look at the law first.

What perhaps should not be forgotten in the volumes of international agreements and consequential legislation is that there can well be liability for pollution under the common law and this point seems to be chronologically the most suitable one to allude to it. Pollution in simple terms is interference, presumably unjustifiable, with acquired possession and/or enjoyment of property, be it land or sea. Routine discharge of the contents of bilges, slops from tankers, etc., are obvious examples and liability for such under the common law can come under one or more of the following torts: trespass, public nuisance, private nuisance, or just plain negligence.

## TRESPASS

Whether the floating of oil on the surface of the sea could reasonably be described as direct interference so as to constitute trespass if it eventually drifts in or on to specific harbour property is at least arguable. There have been differing views (see *Esso Petroleum Co* v *Southport Corporation* [1953] 2 Lloyd's Rep. 414; [1954] 1 Lloyd's Rep. 446, CA; [1955] 2 Lloyd's Rep. 655, HL). At most, interference with property resulting from the drifting of oil on the surface could be described as consequential interference. Similarly, pollution as a result of fire or explosion on board would be indirect or consequential. Therefore not only do the legal authorities indicate, but common sense also, that pollution of this nature could not be classed properly as pure trespass. If trespass was thus alleged, two defences might be available. The first might be that the discharge of oil was necessary in the interests of saving human life and possibly, if such was necessary, to save the ship herself. But even this defence could fail if the lives or property had been placed in jeopardy by the fault of the vessel or her owners in the first place.

As Lord Blackburn said in 1877 in the *River Wear Commissioners* v *Adamson* (1877) 2 App Cas 743, HL:

> 'the common law is, I think, as follows:—property adjoining to a spot on which the public has a right to carry on traffic is liable to be injured by that traffic. In this respect there is no difference between a shop, the railings or windows of which may be broken by a carriage on the road and a pier adjoining a harbour in a navigable river by the sea which is liable to be injured by a ship. In either case the owner of the injured property must bear his own loss unless he can establish that some other person is at fault and liable to make it good.'

His principle was reiterated in *Esso Petroleum Co* v *Southport Corporation*, below.

The second possible defence to a claim in trespass would be that the weight of legal authority tended to show that negligence must be proved for liability to be established in this type of situation (see *Rylands* v *Fletcher* (1868) LR 3 HL 330).

*Esso Petroleum Co* v *Southport Corporation* [1955] 2 Lloyd's Rep. 655, HL
This was an action brought by the Southport Corporation against the owners of the *Inverpool* and her Master, seeking damages as a result of oil discharged into an estuary and subsequently fouling the foreshore, etc. Allegations of negligence, nuisance and trespass were made. The case rose through various stages of appeal to the House of Lords where the shipowner was the appellant and the corporation the respondent. It was considered sufficient answer to the charges of trespass and nuisance that the discharge of oil was necessary under the circumstances in the interests of the crew's safety and to lighten the ship. For some initially inexplicable reason the ship's steering had become erratic and the

Master continued regardless to his destination at Preston despite the necessity of having to negotiate a comparatively narrow and shallow channel. He considered this the lesser of two evils, the only other alternative being to turn back into what was extremely adverse weather. The nuisance allegation included a charge that the Master was guilty of negligent navigation and grounding on a revetment wall and instead of seeking assistance of a pilot and/or tugs had unreasonably ordered the discharge of oil.

The House dismissed these allegations as unfounded. The fracture of the stern frame, which was subsequently found to have been the cause of the erratic steering although it might have constituted unseaworthiness, could not be attributed to negligence. The appeal was allowed.

## PUBLIC NUISANCE

The tort of public nuisance must affect a sufficient number of persons to justify the description 'public' (*Attorney-General* v *PYA Quarries* [1957] 2 QB 169, CA). Under this heading, the interference need not be direct but it should be foreseeable (note the principle enunciated in *The Wagon Mound* [1961] 1 Lloyd's Rep. 1, PC).[1] An individual claimant can succeed in his claim under this cause of action provided that he can show satisfactorily that he personally has suffered special damages peculiar to himself.

## PRIVATE NUISANCE

Private nuisance is a wrongful interference with a person's use or enjoyment of his land or some right connected with it. Hence it must be a prerequisite to success in a claim that the claimant shows that he has a proprietory interest in the land. He need not prove special damages but what he has suffered must have been foreseeable by the wrongdoer. Nuisance having been thus established, the torteasor is left with little recourse other than to show that under the circumstances the interference was reasonable, a virtual impossibility in the sphere of oil pollution.

## CIVIL LIABILITY BASED ON INTERNATIONAL CONVENTION

Now is a good moment to commence looking at the early beginnings of the International Conventions. These were based upon two separate concepts: one being that of the civil liability of merchant ships for pollution by oil which has its origins in the Civil Liability Convention 1969, the other being the intention of the law to prevent pollution and to establish criminal liability for the prohibited discharge of oil. The former contained and provided for an oil carrier's liabilities to third parties, the latter contained preventive and punitive provisions. We will concentrate upon the civil liabilities in this Chapter.

The agreement arrived at in 1969 was born of a consciousness of four things:

1. See page 306.

first, the dangers of oil pollution inherent in the world-wide carriage of oil in bulk by sea; secondly, the need to ensure that adequate compensation was available to persons who suffer damage caused by pollution resulting from the escape or discharge of oil from ships; thirdly, the paramount desire for the adoption of uniform rules and procedures for determining questions of liability and providing adequate compensation; and, fourthly, the desire of governments to feel more confidence in taking early, decisive action, viz. the lesson of the *Torrey Canyon* disaster mentioned at the beginning of the chapter.

## INTERNATIONAL CONVENTION ON CIVIL LIABILITY FOR OIL POLLUTION 1969

The International Convention on Civil Liability for Oil Pollution 1969 concluded at Brussels imposed liabilities on the shipowner which, although comprehensive enough to reflect the gravity of the world-wide pollution situation, were not so drastic and onerous as to defeat their own objects by making the risks to which shipowners can be exposed virtually uninsurable. It defined liability as strict where persistent oil is discharged into coastal waters causing damage to third parties' property. A limit of liability was laid down (Article V) which was available to shipowners who could prove that there had been no actual fault or privity on their part. The limit was 2,000 gold francs per limitation ton (net tonnage plus the engine room space) with a maximum of 210,000,000 gold francs. This limit applied only to claims falling within the scope of the Convention. Any claims falling outside its ambit were covered by the standard limit of liability provisions set out under conventional limitation rules. It was a principle of the 1969 Convention that tanker owners may invoke a limitation of their responsibilities to a certain amount, provided that they constituted a fund for that amount with the court in which the action was brought. Further conferences on the law of the sea were held subsequently to consider whether still more stringent measures should be adopted against shipping interests.

Indeed, the devastating experience of the *Amoco Cadiz* disaster sharply emphasized the need to increase the level of compensation available for innocent victims. The *Amoco Cadiz* litigation (described later on page 446) terminated in a judgment on liability by the Chicago court with damages awarded to French interests of approximately US$250 million.

The 1992 Protocol to the Convention has provided for increases in limitation as can be seen later on (page 438).

It was perhaps a defect in the machinery of the 1969 Civil Liability Convention that no easy, flexible provision was made to increase the limitation figures to suit subsequent trends without the maximum of bureaucratic formalities. This has been remedied for the future by a lessening of the requirements for the effecting of increases, two of which are:

(a) the support of only one-quarter of the contracting States to any proposals for increase;
(b) no increase is to be greater than 6 per cent per annum (compound) as from 1984 with the proviso that the total cannot rise to an amount

greater than three times the original increase brought into effect in 1984.

There have been constant moves (which have eventually proved sucessful) to amend the 1969 Civil Liability Convention provisions also so as to cover oil in unladen tankers and perhaps also to widen the definition of the word 'oil' to include 'non-persistent' mineral oils.[1]

The necessity to link the level of liability to that of the available insurance market was carefully considered and accepted in the 1969 Convention. Under it (Article VII) a tanker owner is only required to maintain insurance in the sums fixed for determination of the limitation of liability, and he is free to choose the type of guarantee subject only to certain administrative criteria. For the Convention's provisions to become effective ratification by no less than eight States represented at Brussels was a prerequisite. At least five of these States must each have no less than one million tons gross of registered tanker tonnage. By June 1975 enough signatory States had ratified it to bring it into force. The UK, by enacting the Merchant Shipping (Oil Pollution) Act 1971 gave it limited application to British ships from January 1973. By 1992 75 States had acceded to the Convention.

It takes little imagination to realize that pollution gives rise to a type of claim which can involve several different jurisdictions and brings against the offending shipowner claims from parties of differing nationalities. Despite major spills from tankers which have occurred in more recent times the best example is probably still the *Amoco Cadiz*. The main claimants clearly were the French, their government in respect of clean-up costs, other claimants for loss of tourist revenue and local fishermen for their livelihood, etc. The British government also assisted in cleaning up, and ranked as a claimant; and the governments of the Channel Islands also incurred expenses in connexion with its protective measures for their own coastlines. In the context of the times there could, in the final analysis, foreseeably have been a judgment in sums so vast that full satisfaction of it could be prevented from being enforced by conventional limits of liability or alternatively by a simple inability to marshal enough assets to meet the full liabilities. (For a fuller account of this casualty, see the end of this chapter.)

The seven main purposes of the Convention were: (a) to make the shipowner strictly liable for the escape or discharge of oil, unless he could bring himself within one of four main exceptions; (b) to exclude the liability of his employees or agents; (c) to exclude him from any other legal liability; (d) to allow for owners whose ships carried more than 2,000 tons of persistent oil in bulk as cargo to be sufficiently insured or, alternatively, to be capable of producing sufficient security; (e) to allow for direct action against the insurer or person providing the security; (f) to provide a limitation period of three years from the date of the damage or six years from the date of the incident causing the damage; and (g) to introduce procedures for limiting liability, now, as explained, undergoing increases.

The Convention did *not* allow for dealing with any costs incurred or damage

1. The UK, by s. 154 of its Merchant Shipping Act 1995 has extended to other ships the same strict liability for oil pollution as is imposed on tankers.

suffered in excess of the limitation fund. Having laid down clearly and adequately the principle of strict liability and provided for a system of compulsory insurance or suitable alternative financial guarantees, it left unattended the problems of *full* protection for all victims in all situations. However, a subsequent conference, known as the Conference on the Establishment of an International Fund for the Compensation for Oil Pollution Damage 1971, was held and resulted in a related international Convention, to which also the UK was a signatory.

There is little doubt that the Civil Liability Convention provided the basic structure for international law on oil pollution even though by no means all States ratified or openly accepted its provisions into their domestic legal systems. However a sufficient number of States did ratify it so as to cause it to be effective as between contracting States; but a question which at the time arose in every practitioner's mind is the practical applicability of it to each slightly varying situation. That the polluting substance must be persistent oil, or some oil mixture, seemed universally accepted and thus pollution by chemical products necessarily fell outside the Convention's provisions. Also it was virtually accepted that the pollution should be geographically situated in the territorial waters of a State. But should it be a contracting State? This must be assumed. The flag of the ship or the respective nationalities of the offender or victims was quite irrelevant. If oil is the polluting substance and if the area polluted is within the territorial waters of a contracting State, the Convention applied but was this fully embracing as a test? Here we could look to the judgment of the Chicago District judge in *The Amoco Cadiz* case for guidance and relevant comment. He was quoted as having said that the fact that the law of France (the territorial scene of the pollution) contained the Civil Liability Convention was immaterial to the ability or otherwise of the victims to sue the alleged wrongdoers (US subjects) in the USA. The Civil Liability Convention was not the *exclusive* remedy available to victims and did not control the bringing of legal action against a party who was neither registered owner nor his servant nor agent (i.e. in this instance the US 'parent' of the vessel owners). There can be, and indeed have been, incidents where literally everyone and everything concerned belongs to one particular State; admittedly possibly a contracting State (see *The Urquiola*, below). Why should an internationally recommended Convention apply, albeit that it has been integrated into a domestic legal system?

*The Urquiola* (unreported)
In May 1976 a Spanish tanker owned by a Spanish company was en route to Corunna. As she was proceeding up the narrow channel of Corunna Bay she went aground on rocks submerged beneath the surface. Her Master ordered his crew of 37 to abandon ship. Subsequently fire broke out on board and some of her cargo of 110,000 tons of crude oil escaped into the sea. There was considerable fear and speculation at the time that this casualty could become a major local disaster and cause severe havoc to the local tourist and fishing industries. The ship's Master lost his life in the disaster.

The total damages and clean-up costs combined were estimated to be in excess of US$60 million.

Here was pollution damage involving a ship with a Spanish flag, Spanish waters, a Spanish shipowner, oil owned by Spaniards, Spanish victims and even Spanish insurance in the background. A very different situation from the disaster which originally sparked off the Convention where the original spill was on the high seas, the offending vessel American, the ship's flag Liberian and the eventual territorial victims the UK and France (i.e. the *Torrey Canyon*). What logical basis is there for a thoroughly all-round national domestic disaster to be governed by an international Convention? Spain admittedly, by a 1976 official degree, accepted into its legal system the Convention's rulings, which was a prerequisite to individual States' recognition of it since it is widely accepted to be a non-selfexecuting treaty. Spain had no pre-existing internal law on oil pollution liability so that in her case the Convention's recommendations filled a void. The same could be said of the UK and it is doubtful whether, prior to 1959, any single sovereign State with territorial waters had any effective legislation on the subject. The fact that the accent was on pollution of *territorial* waters seemed to underline the intention of the Convention that it should achieve integration eventually into the municipal legal systems of the maximum number of States. If any previous legislation had existed, the Convention would either replace or at the least modify or complement whatever existed. Every international Convention is intended basically to achieve uniformity among States and this one is no exception to that principle.

However domestic any individual oil pollution disaster might be, the Convention added an international flavour to it by providing that behind every ship of whatever registry there should be suitable insurance and sufficient financial guarantee. Such guarantees in the vast majority of cases are supplied by the vessel-owner's protecting and indemnity underwriter, (i.e. a 'P & I Club').

As the 1969 Convention is slipping back into the pages of history reference to its provisions in this edition has been appropriately abbreviated. Its main provisions were:

> '1. A ship means any sea-going vessel and any seaborne craft of any type whatsoever, actually carrying oil in bulk as cargo.
>
> 'Oil' meant any persistent oil such as crude oil, fuel oil, heavy diesel oil, lubricating oil and whale oil, whether carried on board a ship as cargo or in the bunkers of such a ship.'

Perhaps the one word in the definitions provided in the 1969 Convention which emphasizes more than any other the menace of oil pollution is 'persistent'. The tenacity and lingering nature of oil as a polluting substance is well known. How often do we hear of oil slicks drifting for lengthy periods undispersed despite the effects of winds, wave, currents, etc? The *Argo Merchant* disaster is an apt reminder of this, and is quoted here purely to illustrate this point and not as a legal precedent. This vessel grounded off Cape Cod and spilled over a reported 7,500,000 gallons of oil. The slick drifted resolutely over intensely rich fishing grounds. Three thousand orange markers were dropped on it to monitor it and to plot currents and its drift was computer-recorded. The destruction to marine life and environment could be incalculable. The vessel eventually broke in two and her entire cargo escaped into the Atlantic, spreading over thousands of square miles. Fears arose that the spill could eventually reach the shores of Great Britain. The effects of the Gulf Stream deposited some on the shores of Iceland, according to some reports. Fishermen of Cape Cod and local environmentalists filed lawsuits in the multi-million dollar range. The *Argo Merchant*, flying a flag of convenience, was said to have had a long history of breakdowns and oil leakages and this news further inflamed the wrath of the world and the public outcry for stricter laws to control, prevent or curb the escape of oil from vessels. In fact, the huge claims feared to be likely to arise from this casualty miraculously did not materialize.

'2. Strict liability for any pollution damage caused by oil which has escaped or discharged from the ship. To this regime of strict liability there were three exceptions which a tanker owner could invoke if he could prove that one or other of them was the whole cause:

(a) an act of war, hostilities, civil war, insurrection or a natural phenomenon of an exceptional, inevitable and irresistible character, or
(b) an act or omission done with intent to cause damage by a third party,[1] or
(c) the negligence or other wrongful act of any government or other authority responsible for the maintenance of lights or other navigational aids in the exercise of that function.'

A possible inadequacy in the wording of this particular exception was highlighted by the Swedish pollution incident involving the vessel *Tsesis*, a Soviet tanker which in 1977 struck a submerged rock whilst in charge of a pilot within Swedish territorial waters. This ripped a length of its bottom out with resultant spilling of oil and pollution. The rock was not marked on the relevant chart. Sweden has adopted the Civil Liability Convention by way of an Oil Liability Act which provides that a shipowner shall be free of liability if he can show that the damage was caused by the fault or neglect of any Swedish or foreign authority in the fulfillment of a duty to maintain lights *or other aids of navigation*. The question of where fault lay—on the Swedish State or on the ship—found its way up on appeal to the Swedish Supreme Court who finally found the State to be at fault, not the ship, thus allowing the ship's owners to bring the matter within this exception. But the further question was—was a chart an 'other aid to navigation' within the wording of the exception and was failure to maintain a chart thus caught by this exception. (Had an English court or English law been interpretive of the provision the 'ejusdem generis' rule would probably have applied so as to include only those aids to navigation of 'like nature' to lights, thus *ex*cluding charts. The Supreme Court seemed to manage to 'side-step' the question by finding fault not only in chart maintenance but also in sectionizing of the light at a certain lighthouse in the vicinity of the accident.)

Arguably one of the most significant provisions of the Civil Liability Convention 1969 is the limitation provision which makes the Convention as much a Limitation Convention as a Liability Convention. Summarized these are: the owner (and it is emphasized this is the registered owner and does not include any form of disponent owner or demise charterer) may limit to 2,000 (gold) francs per ship's tonne with a maximum of 210 million francs. Limitation may be defeated by actual (personal) fault or privity of the owner.

Additional provisions on limitation of liability will be discussed later on in the chapter when equivalent provisions of the Civil Liability Convention 1992 are examined.

1. Sabotage springs to mind as an obvious example.

So far as English law is concerned, by ship's tonnage in paragraph 1 of Article V is meant the registered tonnage with the addition of the engine room space deduction. This would equally well apply in respect of the tonnage of a registered ship measured for length in accordance with the Merchant Shipping Act 1983 and/or registered in the separate 'small ships registry' introduced by section 5 of that same Act (section 9 of the 1983 Act). However, under the 1992 Protocol the ship's tonnage is the *gross* tonnage calculated in accordance with the tonnage measurement regulations contained in Annex 1 to the International Convention on Tonnage Measurement of Ships 1969.

At the end of the 1970s the gold franc was statutorily replaced in the United Kingdom with the Special Drawing Right (effective from 1984); since then 2,000 gold francs equalled 133 SDRs and 210 million francs became 14 million SDRs. Special drawings rights are treated as 'equal to such a sum in sterling as the International Monetary Fund have fixed as being the equivalent of one SDR for the day on which the determination is made or, if no sum has been fixed for that day, the last day before that day for which a sum has been so fixed' (section 38(2) of the Merchant Shipping Act 1979).

### *Compulsory Insurance*

In view of the potential for loss or damage on an immense scale which it was quickly realized could be caused by oil spills from vessels, the question of demanding evidence from tanker vessels that they were adequately covered by current insurance for oil pollution risks was addressed square-on and the Civil Liability Convention 1969 contained the following words in Article 7: 'the owner of a ship registered in a Contracting State and carrying more than 2,000 tonnes of oil in bulk as cargo, shall be required to maintain insurance or other financial security, such as the guarantee of a bank or a certificate delivered by an international compensation fund, in the sums fixed by applying the limits of liability prescribed in Article 5 (paragraph 1) to cover his liability for pollution damage under this Convention'.

There were other sub-paragraphs but their updated equivalents will be reviewed when the 1992 wording is examined.

## INTERNATIONAL CONVENTION ON THE ESTABLISHMENT OF AN INTERNATIONAL FUND FOR COMPENSATION 1971

The following commentary on the 1971 Fund Convention is being retained in this edition despite the emergence onto the international scene of the 1992 Fund Convention, a fuller commentary upon which will be found below (page 441).

The Fund Convention, as it is called by way of abbreviated reference, was introduced to provide substantial supplementary compensation to victims of major oil pollution disasters where full or even adequate compensation was not possible out of the sums to which a tanker could limit its own liability under the CLC. 'Fund' was an internationally motivated attempt to make the oil industry itself a substantial contributor towards making good the vast losses which could result from a major spill. Indeed the Convention itself acknowledged that:

> 'The economical consequences of oil pollution damage resulting from the escape or discharge of oil carried in bulk at sea by ship should not exclusively be borne by the shipping industry, but should in part be borne by the oil cargo interests.'

The Fund Convention came into force in 1978 and by 1992 50 States had acceded to it. Its primary purpose was the establishment of an international fund for compensation for pollution damage, the name of which was to be: The International Oil Pollution Compensation Fund. The fund was intended to provide (a) compensation for damage resulting from pollution in cases where the constituted fund under CLC was insufficient to cope (b) to provide relief to tanker owners from the 'additional financial burden' (to use the Convention's own words—(Article (2)(1)(b)) imposed upon them by CLC.

The fund is a legal entity and is capable of suing and being sued in its own right. It is financed by levies made upon receivers of crude/heavy oil whose places of business are within States which are contracting parties to the Convention. Any person (or party) who in any one calendar year received in aggregate 150,000 tonnes of contributing oil is liable to contribute. The definition of 'contributing oil' given in Article 1 is:

> '. . . crude oil and fuel oil as defined in sub-para (a) and (b) below:
>
> (a) Crude oil means any liquid hydro carbon mixture occurring naturally in the earth whether or not treated to render it suitable for transportation. It also includes crude oils from which certain distillate fractions have been removed (sometimes referred to as "top crudes") or to which certain distillate fractions have been added (sometimes referred to as "spiked" or "reconstituted" crudes).
>
> (b) "fuel oil" means heavy distillates or residues from crude oil or blends of such materials intended to use as a fuel for the production of heat or power of a quality equivalent to "American society for testing materials specification for number four fuel oil" (designation D 396–69) or heavier.'

The circumstances in which the fund will be used to compensate sufferers are the following alternatives:

(1) where no liability arises under CLC;
(2) where a tanker owner is incapable of meeting his CLC obligations or where his insurance cover and/or financial security is itself inadequate;
(3) where the value of the damage exceeds the vessel-owner's liability under CLC.

### *Where does fund incur no obligation?*

(1) Damage resulting from act of war, hostilities, civil war or insurrection or where oil is spilled from a warship or a ship owned by a government on non-commercial service.
(2) Where the claimant fails to prove the damage resulted from an incident involving one or more ships.

Moreover, the fund will get exoneration from responsibility if it can show that the person who suffered the damage himself was a contributing cause of the damage because of a positive act or omission with intent to cause damage.

### *How much in total is the fund obliged to pay out?*

The text of the original Convention provided for a sum not exceeding 450 million Francs (Article 4(4)(a)). This included any sum which the fund is obliged to pay out by way of indemnity to the vessel-owner (known in the trade as 'roll-back relief').

Machinery was laid down to increase this total amount if future circumstances justified it, provided that the amended total did not exceed 900 million Francs.

### *'Roll-Back relief' (Article 5)*

This is amounts in excess of the equivalent of 1,500 Francs for each tonne of the ship's tonnage or 125 million Francs, whichever is the less *and* which do not exceed the equivalent of 2,000 Francs for each tonne of the ship's tonnage or 210 million Francs whichever is the less. The fund will not be bound to pay relief if the damage is caused by the wilful misconduct of the tanker owner found to be contributing to the damage.

Roll-back relief may, however, soon be of historical interest only and serve only as a reminder of the relationship between the oil and the sea transport industries with a view to providing overall the maximum compensation which can reasonably be collected together. This is because the 1992 Convention makes provision for the abolition of 'roll-back relief'.

It is worthy of additional note when considering the British attitude towards this Convention that the Merchant Shipping Act 1974 gives recognition to the advantages of reciprocal enforcement of awards. Thus section 6 deals with the jurisdiction of the courts of the UK and also with the enforcement of judgments and, in the latter respect, subsection (4) provides that Part I of the Foreign Judgments (Reciprocal Enforcement) Act 1933 shall be applicable to any judgment given by a court in a Fund Convention country to enforce a claim in respect of liability incurred under any provision corresponding to section 4 or section 5 of that Act. Section 8 is concerned with subrogation and the rights of recourse of the fund against the owner or guarantor, which rights would be acquired from the recipient of the funds by process of subrogation.[1]

### *How pollution damage is variously defined*

The way oil pollution damage is defined varies according to which of the Conventions or voluntary agreements is applicable to a particular situation. Taking the four different categories in turn:

1. Section 169 of the Merchant Shipping Act 1995 provides that nothing in the pollution section of the Act shall prejudice any claim, or the enforcement of any claim, a person incurring any liability may have against another person in respect of that liability.

(1) Under CLC, pollution damage includes the following:
loss or damage resulting from the escape or discharge of oil from the ship including the cost of preventive measures and any escalation of loss or damage caused by such preventive measures.

(2) The Fund Convention follows this same definition but takes a different view from CLC as to the definition of 'oil' itself. This is restricted to persistent hydro carbon mineral oils.

(3) Under the Tovalop (see page 431) standing Agreement the phrase is intended to cover loss or damage resulting from the escape or discharge of oil from the tanker vessel provided that it is caused on the territory of any State (including its territorial sea). The phrase includes the costs of any preventive measures and also extra loss or damage caused by the implementation of preventive measures but excludes any loss or damage that is too remote or speculative or which is not the direct result of escape or discharge.

Under the Tovalop supplement the phrase is defined as meaning physical loss or damage caused as a result of the escape or discharge of oil from the vessel wherever it may occur including any loss or damage caused by preventive measures taken. Secondly, any economic loss which can be proved as having actually been sustained whether or not it has resulted from original physical damage provided it can be shown to be the direct result of the contamination by oil which has spilled from the involved tanker. Thirdly, it includes costs incurred in taking reasonable and necessary measures to restore or replace natural resources damaged as a direct result of an 'applicable' incident. (See page 432.)

(4) The text of Cristal defines pollution damage in a wholly similar way to the Tovalop supplement and thus allows for recovery of proved economic loss whether or not there is any accompanying physical damage. It also allows for recovery of costs actually incurred in restoring or replacing damaged natural resources.

### *Difference between preventive measures and threat removal measures*

Threat removal measures are, by the very sound of the phrase, those measures which would be taken in the very first instances before there has been a natural escape or discharge of oil but where there is apparently a grave and immediate danger of there being such an escape. Preventive measures are measures taken *after* an incident has occurred and there has been an escape of oil. The main purpose of preventive measures would be with a view to preventing any further pollution damage or any further escape or discharge of oil from the ship. The distinguishing between what are preventive measures on these lines and what is in fact a salvage operation could be difficult and in order to make that distinction it will be necessary to determine whether the measures taken were directed towards the prevention of further pollution damage or further escape or discharge of oil and not taken for the wider reasons of ensuring the safety of the tanker itself, its crew and/or its cargo. Measures taken with the latter and wider purposes in mind would be classed as salvage services and would therefore be outside the scope of the oil pollution treaties or agreements.

### *Environmental damage*

How far the offending tanker owner and/or his insurers should be made accountable for damage of this nature has been deeply discussed in the jurisdictions of various different countries. Damage under this title implies damage to forms of natural resources. The expression 'natural resources as contemplated by US OPA 90 includes land, fish, wild life, biota, air, water, ground water, drinking water, drinking water supplies and other such resources belonging to, managed by, held in trust, appertaining to, or otherwise controlled by the USA (including the resources of the Exclusive Economic Zone) any state or local government or Indian tribe or any foreign government'. The same definition is given in the provisions of CERCLA (Comprehensive Environmental Response, Compensation and Liability Act). Details of CERCLA have no place in this book as it is dedicated to pollution by hazardous circumstances and not by oil. One of the main difficulties in coming to any reasonable definition or defining the perimeters of this type of damage is that the environment is not, strictly speaking owned by any individuals whether persons or corporate and thus it is impossible to put any specific economic value on damage. The group Clubs, throughout the history of major oil pollution disasters, have heavily resisted paying out damages on the basis of harm done to natural resources.

Jurisdictions in which the matter has been extensively discussed are the United States in the (1981) case of the *Zoe Colocotroni* where the Appeal Court ruled that the determination of recoverable damages should be based on the tests as to whether the cost was reasonably incurred by the sovereign agency to restore or rehabilitate the environment to its pre-existing condition or as closely thereto as was possible without grossly disproportionate expenditure. Four years later in the *Patmos* disaster, the Italian Court of first instance decided that only real rights over individual possessions and not rights of territorial sovereignty can be the subject of a claim for damages pursued in a civil legal action. In the *Patmos* matter the Italian ministry of Merchant Marine claimed an indemnity for ecological damage to marine flora and fauna. This claim, said the Italian court of first instance could not be allowed. Territorial waters were not State-owned property, but rather a 'communis omnium' and there can be no injury claim by any private persons for this reason. However, this was appealed by the Italian Government who strongly argued that the claim related not only to actual damage to the environment, but also to actual economic loss suffered by the tourist industry and by fishermen. Thus, they argued, the definition of pollution damage under CLC should include their claim. The Italian appellate court dealt with the Italian Government's appeal in March of 1989 and held that the damage was in principle recoverable subject to it being quantified by experts.

Traditionally, the general maritime law or common law had been reluctant to recognize that States, as opposed to private individuals, have a right to recover damages for injury or harm to natural resources. But as the 20th century progressed, individual States began to assert their rights to maintain such actions and by the 1970s federal courts were accepting such pleas. A case of note (1973) was (the State of) *Maine* v *M/V Tamarno*, during the course of which the judge stated his clear view that Maine (or presumably any other coastal State) has an interest in its coastal waters which is distinct from the rights of any individual citizen of that State. *Zoe* went a step further and decreed that a State may create its own rights and liabilities within its borders, provided that these do not run counter to federal laws.

At the end of the 1980s, an item hit the international headlines when the State of Florida tried to obtain damages for the loss of 214 birds which they had claimed were 'natural resources' and had been destroyed as a result of an oil spill. The claim was quantified at US$176,000 for the deaths of these birds. The attorney for the offending tanker owner did not deny that the birds had died but contested the ability of Florida to estimate the worth of the birds since there was no fair market value as they were not a species that was normally traded in any sale and purchase market. Thus the quantum was speculative and therefore outside the range of recoverable claims.

It is a provision of the OPA 1990 (see page 443) that in determining recoverable damages for harm to the environment, account should be taken of 'all reliably calculated use values'. This means that the person assessing the values is required to put a price on the loss to each individual citizen of damaged flora or fauna by reference to his deprived right for future enjoyment of the injured resource.

Particularly in regard to the United States, the attitude appears to be that merely because damage to the environment is difficult to quantify, it does not mean that an attempt should not be made to do so. Just as the 'green' political parties are gaining advances in Europe and elsewhere around the world, so a consciousness of the importance of the preservation of the environment is growing and in the same proportion as that consciousness grows, so wherever there has been pollution resulting in damage to the environment, there will be an increasingly greater effort made by whoever are the persons claiming to make a realistic quantification of the damage under that heading and ensure that there is some court which will look favourably upon their arguments that this head of damage should be recoverable from the offending tanker owner and whoever else may be the responsible party and/or their respective insurers.

## TOVALOP

As of February 1997 Tovalop passed from the current practical world into the pages of maritime history, together with its industrial 'cousin' Cristal. In its twenty-eight year life it played a major part in the general scheme of compensation/assistance to be provided to victims of spills. For this reason alone, both it and Cristal continue to deserve more than a passing reference in this edition and thus the commentary to be found in the 4th edition is retained here, pausing only to convert it from present to past tense.

Because at the time of the *Torrey Canyon* disaster there was no effective international law in existence to provide comprehensive relief for victims or compensation for clean-up costs, tanker owners entered into a voluntary agreement to reimburse national governments for expenses of preventing or cleaning up spills affecting their coastlines. The term 'tanker owner' included a bareboat charterer. Those owners had to ensure their capability to cope financially and on this basis had the backing and cover of their Protecting and Indemnity Clubs (P & I Clubs).

The agreement was known as the 'Tanker Owners Voluntary Agreement concerning Liability for Oil Pollution', or, more familiarly, 'Tovalop'. The agreement was legally binding. Tovalop was administered by the International Tanker Owners Pollution Federation Ltd. The idea was to reimburse national governments only and not private individuals, except in circumstances where a privately owned coastline was cleaned up by a national government or, alternatively, to find the costs of preventing or removing oil pollution. Any owner or bareboat charterer of a tank vessel was free to participate in the agreement. Under the agreement, a claimant did not have to show legal liability on the owner or bareboat charterer. The idea was to speed up payment of compensation irrespective of who was ultimately liable or why. A government was not obliged to take proceedings under Tovalop. If it did so, however, and obtained reimbursement, it had subsequently to give up any further rights of claim it might have under any local law in force in the area. The enforcing of a claim was achieved, if necessary, by arbitration, there being a two-year period within which arbitration proceedings could be instituted.

A tanker owner could, under Tovalop as originally framed, limit his liability to US$100 per gross registered ton, or US$10,000,000 per vessel, per incident, whichever was the less. The right to limit was sacred and could not be broken by a showing of actual fault or privity, as could be done under CLC provisions. Tovalop was originally intended to encourage tanker owners to take measures themselves voluntarily to clean up spills regardless of the need for establishing where legal liability lay. The scheme, in turn, caused the creation of a special mutual 'Club' known as the International Tanker Owners Insurance Association. In practice, however, its member vessels were oil company-owned and it became heavily integrated into the overall cover provided to tanker-owners by their individual P & I Clubs. Tovalop also operated where there was a serious threat of spill and costs were incurred in an attempt to prevent it.

Tovalop came into being in late 1968/early 1969, nearly two years after the *Torrey Canyon* disaster. At its inception some 50 per cent of owners of tanker tonnage were parties to the agreement. This soon rose to 99 per cent. It was that disaster which so starkly spotlighted the gaps and inadequacies in the existing maritime law in this particular field and provided the impetus for fashioning such an agreement. The very inadequacies of the Tovalop limit, however, soon became apparent. How could the limitation fund of a 10,000 gross registered ton vessel meet a three million dollar government claim? Indeed it was in the matter of voluntary clean-up that things became confused. There was a very real likelihood that if a tanker owner knew that his limits were fixed by, e.g. Tovalop, he would 'offer his fist' to that extent financially but walk away from further responsibility. Prompt and effective clean-up measures were to be heavily *en*couraged not *dis*couraged and the major oil companies themselves were the chief advocates of such a policy. Proof of their keenness was the introduction in earlier years of the so-called 'Tovalop' clauses giving them, as charterers, carte blanche to carry out clean-up operations for the tanker-owners' eventual account. Potentially, millions of dollars could be spent on clean-up costs alone, far in excess of the (by oil pollution standards) relatively modest Tovalop limits. The zeal of affluent oil company charterers in performing clean-up operations without considering costs worried the vessel's owners' P & I Clubs who saw themselves, even though protected by reinsurance pooling arrangements exposed to massive reimbursement. Hence the coming into being of—

## THE CRISTAL AGREEMENT

The acronym stands for 'contract regarding an interim supplement to tanker liability for oil pollution'. Its date of birth was 1 April 1971. Its membership was composed of oil companies whose business is the production of oil or who were engaged in refining, marketing or distribution. The application of the Cristal agreement to an incident was contingent upon the cargo being owned by a party who was a participant in the Cristal scheme and the incident of the spillage being one where liability would arise under the provisions of the Civil Liability Convention or the tanker involved was a vessel participating in Tovalop. Initially 50 per cent of the world's oil company receivers/importers were signatories. Eventually more like 90 per cent of crude or fuel oil importers subscribed to it. Like Tovalop it was a voluntary scheme and was designed originally to be interim only, as the name implies. Cristal applied only when a tanker was carrying a cargo of persistent oil. It did not, as did Tovalop, apply to a ballast voyage. Nevertheless, the spill could be from the ship's bunkers provided that the tanker was loaded with a cargo of the covered description.

The aim of the scheme was to furnish supplemental compensation to governments and other third parties who had suffered from damage by pollution in cases where the limited funds from Tovalop or CLC were insufficient to provide full compensation and where 'Fund' had no application. An additional aim was to provide supplemental finance and so encourage the voluntary cleaning up of spilt oil. The costs of so doing, which ran in excess of $125 per gross registered ton of the vessel or $10,000,000, whichever was the less, would be reimbursed to the owner concerned or his P & I underwriter under the scheme's provisions. Where a government and the defending vessel's owners spent money on removal or clean-up, the expenses incurred were pro-rated against the Tovalop calculated limits if the total expenses exceeded such limits. The overall aggregate cover for any one incident was $30,000,000.

Cristal had, however, considerable restrictions, magnanimous though the scheme may have sounded. Payment from the Cristal fund whether to a government 'victim' or a private party 'victim' could be up to, but not exceeding, $30,000,000 per accident, but this was only after the following deductions had been made:

(1) Clean up costs incurred by the offending tanker owners, not yet reimbursed, up to an amount of $125 per gross registered tonne or $10,000,000, whichever was the less.
(2) Any previous payments made to the tanker's owners for clean-up expenses.

(3) The amount of the tanker owner's liability to the government under Tovalop.
(4) Any amount reasonably recoverable by the claimant from any other source.

Those who subscribed to the Cristal scheme never intended that they should assume the guise of shipowners' underwriters. But nevertheless the combined effect of the Tovalop and Cristal schemes would seem in practice to have been little different to the combined effect of the two related international treaties, the 1969 and 1971 Conventions. Perhaps this thought is reflected in the word 'interim' in the very wording of the title 'Cristal'—the 'stop-gap' nature of its function to bridge an otherwise ugly gap before all or substantially all nations fully implemented the treaties. The likelihood of this happening as we progressed through the 1980s diminished and was eclipsed temporarily at any rate at the outset of the 90s by the United States, which had traditionally been a trendsetter for International Legislation in the maritime field, firmly turning its back on the International Conventions (even despite the protocols) by enacting its own domestic and heavily anti-vessel owner legislation in the form of OPA 1990 which in turn leaves each coastal State to enact its own statutes.

Under the Cristal scheme, the courts of the UK had jurisdiction. England was probably chosen for this role because of her longstanding familiarity with maritime problems.

### *Revisions to Tovalop*

These took place in 1978 and 1987, the earlier of the two being intended to refashion Tovalop to be more reflective of CLC 1969, but still to retain the features which were 'extra' to CLC e.g. covering demise (or bareboat) charterers, of applicability to tankers, whether or not loaded with oil cargo and its cover of a threat situation where there has been no actual escape. The aim was still to let it be seen as a short term voluntary scheme, so that sovereign States should continue to be encouraged to accept the imposed regime of CLC. The limits were raised to be in line with CLC limits.

The 1987 revision caused a split of Tovalop into two parts which would operate side by side. The existing agreement (that was the 1978) should exist apart from the 1987, or as it became known, the Standing Agreement and was to be used where the oil cargo which spilled was not owned by a Cristal member and the part newly forged in 1987 was to be used when the oil was owned by a Cristal member. It was to be known as the supplementary agreement and had inflated limits up to a maximum of US$70 million, at which cut off point Cristal took over.

### *Cristal revision*

The revised Cristal agreement included in it substantive provisions for the providing of what is called 'roll-back' relief which would be paid regardless of whether the incident did or did not give rise to liability under the Liability Convention or the revised Tovalop agreement or any other relevant law. For a definition of 'roll-back' relief the reader should refer to the text of the Fund Convention, Article 5(1). By the middle of 1983 some of the members of the agreement were questioning whether the agreement should continue at all beyond mid-1984 on the two grounds that (a) that it was becoming too much of a self-imposed financial burden to the oil companies, and (b) it, if anything, removed the real incentive to governments to ratify the two Conventions (particularly their revised (1984) versions). The Cristal agreement did implement one threat (as from June 1984) by deleting the provision which allows tanker owners to obtain indemnity from Cristal funds in respect of their liabilities for pollution damage and threat removal measures to the extent that the aggregate exceeds US$160 per ton (or $16,800,000) whichever is the less by reason of the application to the incident of a legal regime other than the Liability Convention. This blow to tanker-owning interests caused a rift between the oil and tanker industries the result of which was that the tanker-owners announced that they were no longer happy to accept a small ship minimum of US$1,000,000 which was originally given in consideration of Cristal's concessions to them and below which Cristal was not required to be involved.

Wrangling such as this in the mid-1980s may well have been the beginnings of the end of the Tovalop and Cristal schemes and of the realization that all industrial schemes which have as their declared aim and purpose the gathering of funds to adequately compensate victims of their commercial profit-making activities, have an eye in the end to their own successful conducting of business and thus an element of self-serving and self-preservation, particularly from the view point of how the two schemes relate to each other.

The Tovalop and Cristal schemes concluded finally on 20 February 1997. Students and concerned professionals should nevertheless continue to be aware of the schemes for two reasons:

(a) that they have played a great part in the development and shaping of the international mechanism for compensation of victims of oil escape incidents from ships and
(b) that the author believes that in presenting the state of the law on any subject as it stands now, it is of considerable value to describe the history of the law as it stood in the immediate past and sometimes in the distant past.

Now that the USA has totally rejected backing the 1984 Protocol to the CLC with the virtually inevitable practical consequence that the 1984 Protocol would never achieve international effect, the 1992 Protocol, which has a coming into force mechanism which does not mean that the USA's acceptance is vital, has been given international effect and is now known as the International Convention on Civil Liability for Oil Pollution Damage 1992. In substance the 1992 Convention provides the same as the 1984 Protocol.

The closing years of the millennium will see a transitional period with many countries in the world left with CLC 1969 as their only primary (ship-based) source of compensation. With the Tovalop and Cristal schemes no longer available, victims in those countries will have only restricted scope for compensation namely when oil, as cargo, is actually discharged from a laden tanker. They will be uncompensated when pollution occurs from a tanker in ballast or where measures are taken to avoid or minimize the threat of pollution. Victims in those countries who have given recognition to the 1992 Convention already will benefit from those extended bases of liability and it will be interesting to observe how rapid is the acceleration of acceptances of the 1992 Convention from this point on.

Throughout the 1970 decade inflation was eroding the value of funds whether it was limitation under CLC or aggregate funds under the Fund Convention, i.e. what might have been adequate funds to cope with the *Torrey Canyon* disaster would, if reproduced in 1978 to cope with the *Amoco Cadiz* crisis, have proved far from adequate as the French government shrewdly realized and consequently contrived to ease the litigation out of their own jurisdiction and into the more lucrative judicial pastures of the United States. Thus amendments to both the Conventions were drawn up under the auspices of IMO and were crystallized into two Protocols both listed under the year 1984. Clearly the outstanding feature of each was the upgrading of limits.

In a previous edition, the 1984 Protocol to CLC was summarized and its full text formed an appendix to the chapter. However, to achieve international recognition and thus international effect, six States with not less than 1 million tonnes gross tanker tonnage had to ratify or accept it, one of which would have had to be the United States. In the few years which have now intervened, however, it has become clear that the USA has 'travelled its own road' and has no intention of accepting this or any other International Convention on the subject. Thus the 1992 Protocol has taken the place of the 1984 and although the substantive provisions are the same, the machinary for implementing acceptance by individual States is such that the United States' acceptance is unnecessary and the 1992 Protocol has now become the 1992 Convention. Its full text is therefore appended to this chapter in place of the 1984.

Here follows a commentary on the significant sections of the 1992 CLC.

## 1992 CIVIL LIABILITY CONVENTION

The broad aim (and indeed effect) of the Convention is to additionally embrace those areas of compensation which were traditionally provided by the ship and which were covered by Tovalop, but were *un*covered by CLC 1969. This was believed essential if 'life after Tovalop' (RIP 20 February 1997) was, from a victim's point of view, to be as full of compensation as it was when Tovalop was alive and well.

Thus CLC 1992 includes the following significant changes:

1. Where CLC 1969 was *territorial* in its definition of where pollution damage occurred, meaning that it should be the (solid) territory, plus the extension of the territorial waters to the limit prescribed by a particular Contracting State, the area which can trigger the application of the 1992 Convention is widened to include the Exclusive Economic Zone up to a limit not exceeding 200 miles (Article II).

   If any particular state has not established such a zone it should be taken to be an area beyond and adjacent to the territorial sea of that State, determined by that State in accordance with international law and extending not more than 200 nautical miles from the baselines from which the breadth of its territorial sea is measured.

2. Pollution damage is given a widened meaning. The Convention will apply not only where damage is physically caused by an actual escape of oil, but also where
   (a) damage is caused as a result of measures taken by way of an attempt to prevent or minimize the damage caused by an actual oil escape, or
   (b) expense has been incurred by way of the cost of measures reasonably taken as described in (a) above (Article I(6)).
3. Additional even to that considerably broadened definition, liability under the Convention shall lie for
   (a) the cost of any measures reasonably taken to avert or minimize a *grave or imminent threat* of any damage which *might* be caused *if* there was an escape or discharge of oil and
   (b) any damage caused by the implementation of such measures (Article I(6), (7)).
4. Widened also is the definition of a ship from which a spill (or the threat of a spill) might occur. For a ship to be caught by the Convention's liability provisions it needs to be constructed or adapted for the carrying of oil in bulk. If it is *capable* of carrying cargoes other than oil, then provided that at the time of the spill (or threat of a spill) it is carrying oil in bulk as cargo or even if it is performing a voyage subsequent to one carrying oil, unless the owner can prove (and the onus is on him) that there were no residues remaining on board when that following voyage was performed, the provisions of the Convention will be invoked (Article I(2)).
5. Oil is also more broadly defined. Article I(5) defines it as 'any persistent hydrocarbon mineral oil such as crude oil, fuel oil heavy diesel oil and lubricating oil, whether carried on board a ship as cargo or in the bunkers of such a ship'. A spill of bunkers is now covered by the Convention provisions, thus preserving a feature of the now defunct Tovalop agreement.

Thus in the definitions of area, ship and pollution damage, the 1992 CLC has greatly improved the victims' chances of a meaningful restitution.

Now to liability and limitation of liability:

### *Liability*

This has been left intact from 1969. Liability continues to be strict with specific and named exceptions. The onus is upon the owner of the involved ship to show that the loss/damage was caused wholly and solely by one or other of them. Strict liability and any exceptions from it applies to any ship, whether purpose built or constructed oil carrier, adapted for oil carriage i.e. as defined in Article I(2).

### *Limitation of liability*

Yet again this has received extensive treatment. Limitation has been raised to a level considerably above 1969 CLC, on the current US$ exchange rates possibly more than four times as high. However, balanced against these higher limits, the standards by which limitation can be 'broken' and the owner deprived of this valuable right has also been changed, making it far more difficult (and indeed probably very rare) for a claimant to rob an owner of his limitation rights. It will be recalled that the test under 1969 CLC was actual fault or privity, whereas 1992 uses the test (also to be found in the 1976 Convention on limitation in maritime claims, other than pollution) of personal act or omission of the owner committed either deliberately or recklessly and with knowledge that pollution damage would probably result (Article V(2)). Under the 1992 Convention the burden of proof is on the plaintiff to show that the tanker owner should be deprived of his right to limit.

The calculation of limitation in 1992 CLC is as follows:

(a) in relation to a ship not exceeding 5,000 tonnes—3 million units of account,
(b) in relation to a ship exceeding 5,000 tonnes—3 million units of account together with an additional 420 SDRs for each tonne of its tonnage in excess of 5,000 tonnes up to a maximum amount of 59.7 million units of account (Article V(1)).

Article V(3) provides that an owner who has successfully exercised his limitation rights under this same Article (V(1)) shall 'constitute a fund' with the court or other competent authority of the Contracting State by an actual deposit of the calculated amount or by establishing a bank guarantee or other guarantee both acceptable to and considered adequate by the court concerned. It shall be distributed upon a strictly pro rata basis proportionate to the individual established claims, that is in the same ratio as the total limitation fund bears to the aggregate of claims registered against it (Article V(4)).

Other provisions of Article V are that any claim by the owner himself or expenses outlayed or sacrifices reasonably made with a view to prevention or minimizing of pollution shall rank alongside others against the constituted fund. If, for example, an owner (or his servant or agent) has paid a claim prior to that owner constituting his limitation fund, he may be subrogated for that amount as against the constituted fund (Article V(6)).

Units of account being the Special Drawing Right, as defined by the International Monetary Fund are no longer an innovation to the shipping community. They are firmly entrenched in this and other Limitation Conventions currently in force. Suffice it to be mentioned here that where a Contracting State is not a member of the IMF, a calculation shall be made in the manner determined by that State. Indeed, as a separate sub-paragraph (9(b)) such a non-member Contracting State is permitted to equate a unit of account 15 gold francs (the unit previously used in the sixties and seventies).

The ship's tonnage referred to in the Convention is the gross tonnage calculated in accordance with the tonnage measurement regulations contained in

Annex 1 of the International Convention on Tonnage Measurement of Ships 1969.

The insurer is entitled to constitute its own fund notwithstanding that the owner is not entitled to form his own, but if this happens it must not prejudice a claimant's rights against the owner.

Article 6 provides very importantly for the fund of an owner if and when constituted to be the sole source of satisfaction for claims. No other asset of the owner may be approached or interfered with. Any ship or other property to which that owner has title and which may already have been arrested, must be released by order of the competent court as authority of the relevant Contracting State, as must also be any alternative security already placed.

More than ever before restrictions are placed upon the attaching of liability for oil pollution. Whatever the type of ship, the owner of it shall not be liable otherwise than under the designated liability sections (i.e. Article III, sections 1, 2 and 3). Furthermore, CLC 1992 expressly lists those categories of persons who shall not be liable for any damages, costs or expenses enumerated under the liability sections, unless such damages, costs or expenses, have resulted or were incurred as a result of his positive acts or omission committed with intent to cause harm or damage or incur costs/expenses or recklessly and in the knowledge that any such damage or costs would probably result.

The list of such exempt persons is to be found in Article III section 4. They are:

(a) servants or agents of the owner or a member of the crew;
(b) the pilot or any other person, who without being a member of the crew, performed services for the ship;
(c) any charterer (including a bareboat (demise) charterer, manager or operator of the ship);
(d) any person performing salvage operations with the consent of the owner or on the instructions of a competent authority;
(e) any person taking preventive measures, and
(f) all servants or agents of persons mentioned in paragraphs c, d and e, unless the damage resulted from their personal act or omission, committed with the intent to cause such damage, or recklessly and with knowledge that such damage would probably result.

These people are the sort of persons who one might expect could be connected or somehow involved with the vessel when an incident involving an oil spill, or the threat of one might occur. In the case of charterers it stands in sharp contrast to the US OPA 90 which expressly includes demise (bareboat charterers and operators of ships as parties who can and will be directly responsible for the consequences of an escape of oil from a vessel.

As to those who perform salvage operations, it can only be right and just that they should not be held legally accountable under 1992. Salvors are, as the chapter on salvage in this book extensively emphasizes, volunteers, called in in times of real danger in emergency to attempt to avert catastrophe. The law admittedly says that salvors can be answerable for damage caused by their negligence, but short of the more extreme conduct described in this section, salvors are rightly cloaked with immunity from liability from pollution.

### *Compulsory insurance*

It was a feature of the 1969 CLC that every ship registered in a Contracting State and carrying more than 2,000 tonnes of oil in bulk as cargo, shall maintain insurance or other form of security to cover the sum arrived at by applying the limitation of liability calculations provided for elsewhere in the Convention's text. This requirement is retained in the same form in the 1992 Convention and can be found in Article VII.

The requirement is in practice attested to by a certificate issued to the vessel by the appropriate authority of the Contracting State once that authority has satisfied itself that adequate insurance or alternative security is in place. Such insurance will normally be provided by a P & I which includes within its ordinary third party risk cover, oil pollution to the extent and limit of the Convention's provisions.

It is specially provided (Article VII, section 8) that any claim for compensation for damage caused by oil pollution may be brought directly against the insurer or whoever provides the security and means that the insurer thus becomes guarantor and is exposed to direct action. He may, however, in *his own right*, limit his liability regardless of whether the shipowner himself has lost or retained his own right to limit.

The limitation fund may only be used for the satisfaction of claims allowed under the Convention.

A measure of uniformity and flexibility is introduced by Article VII, section 7 whereby certificates which are issued or certified under the authority of a particular Contracting State will be accepted by other Contracting States and shall be regarded by other Contracting States as having the same force as certificates issued or certified by them, even if issued or certified in respect of a ship not registered in a Contracting State. This section also allows a Contracting State to consult with the issuing or certifying State if it considers that the insurer or guarantor named in the certificate is not in fact financially capable of meeting the obligations which are imposed by the Convention.

Article VII, section 10 makes the strict provision that a Contracting State shall not permit a ship under its flag to which Article VII applies to trade, unless a certificate has been issued in pursuance of Article VII and futhermore, section 11 requires each Contracting State to ensure that insurance or some other form of security required by Article VII is in force in respect of any ship, wherever it may be registered, when it enters or leaves a port in its territory or arrives at or leaves an off-shore terminal in its territorial sea provided, of course, that that ship actually carries more than two thousand tonnes of oil in bulk as cargo.

By the close of 1996 some 19 countries including the UK, had signified adoption of 1992 CLC but to obtain details of current ratifications and the names of the countries, those interested should contact the Institute of Maritime Law which publishes such statistics.

## THE FUND CONVENTION 1992

The declared aim of this Convention which is born out of the Protocol to the 1971 Convention is on a par with the aims of the latter earlier Convention. These are inter alia:

(a) a conviction that there is a need to ensure that adequate compensation to persons (commonly referred to as victims) who suffer damage caused by pollution resulting from oil escaping or discharging from ships;
(b) a recognition that the CLC is inadequate to provide full compensation, and
(c) an awareness that shipowners should not have to bear an overload of responsibility and that the oil industry itself should at least bear part of it.

The fund is to be recognized in each Contracting State as a legal entity capable of suing and being sued, having rights and liabilities, the director of the fund being its legal representative (Article 2(2)). The application of the Convention follows the same lines as CLC in 1992, i.e. pollution damage caused:

(a) in the territory of a Contracting State (including its territorial waters);
(b) in the Exclusive Economic Zone of a Contracting State and if a State does not have a specific zone, it describes an area seaward from the territorial water boundary extending not more than 200 miles.

The fund may be used also to compensate those who may have taken preventive measures or measures to minimize pollution damage.

Compensation under Fund 1992 is to be paid where the 1992 CLC has proved inadequate because either:

(a) no liability (upon the vessel) has arisen under 1992 CLC or
(b) the offending owner cannot meet his obligations in full or any financial security given on his behalf is insufficient, thus depriving the innocent victim of his chances of obtaining full redress for the damage/losses he has suffered or
(c) because the total value of the damage exceeded the owners liability as limited by the 1992 CLC.

### *What are the exceptions to the obligations of the fund to pay compensation?*

1. Proof that (the onus is upon the Fund) the damage was proximately caused by an act of war, hostilities, civil war or insurrection, or that the oil had escaped from a warship or other ship owned/operated by a State and used at the material time on government and/or non-commercial service.
2. Where the claimant cannot show that the damage resulted in an incident involving one or more ships.
3. If the fund can prove that the pollution was the result either entirely or partially of an act or omission committed by the person who has suffered

with intent to cause damage, the Fund may be absolved from honouring its obligation to compensate such person either in whole or in part.

### *What is the maximum amount of compensation the fund must pay out?*

The limit of liability arising from any one incident shall be 135 million units of account, this to be *inclusive* of any amount payable under the 1992 CLC (Article 4(4)(a)). This amount may rise to 200 million when an incident which gives rise to fund liability occurs in any period when there are three parties to the Convention in respect of which the combined relevant quantity of contributing oil received by persons in the territories of such parties, during the preceding calendar year, equalled or exceeded 600 million tonnes (the wording of this subsection needs two or three readings before its meaning can be properly absorbed).

### *Conversion of units of account*

As customary in the CLC and Fund Conventions the conversion of units of account into any particular national currency is effected by reference to the Special Drawing Right on the date of the decision of the Assembly of the Fund as to the first date of payment of compensation.

### *There should be a fair distribution of compensation*

When the aggregate of claims against the fund which have arisen from any one incident exceeds the maximum amount payable, there shall be a pro rata distribution of the amount so that no one single claimant gets less than his correct proportional share.

### *Who contributes to the fund?*

Any person who in a designated calendar year has received more than 150,000 tonnes of oil. For oil to be considered 'contributing' oil for the purposes of this obligation, it should be either crude or fuel, these two oil types being defined in detail in Article 1(3)(a) and (c) (see Appendix 13). Finer details of the obligation to contribute to the fund are contained in subsections (a) and (b) to sections 1 and 2 of Article 10, the full text of which is available in the appendix.

By the end of 1996, 16 countries had signified adoption of Fund 1992. The United Kingdom was one of them.

### *Can complete uniformity and reciprocity ever be truly achieved?*

To change to a more philosophical note, it may be wondered whether there *can* be complete uniformity and full reciprocity between nations even under Conventions such as the 1992 Conventions. States which are prepared, perhaps reluctantly, to give up some of their sovereign rights in consideration of the expectation of some greater protection of their own interests in some other State's jurisdiction may find that adherence to such Conventions does not provide a certain remedy to the consequences of pollution in their own territory which originated elsewhere. Quite apart from that thought, it has been the aim of the oil industry right from the inception of international legislation on compensation for oil pollution that it should only be 'on call' in the event of spills of catastrophic size and consequence. The shipping industry, it is argued, should bear the brunt of spills, small or large. The oil industry has always campaigned in favour of fixing a ship's limitation without reference to the ship's size. This proposal met with powerful opposition from tanker interests, particularly the Clubs, who are the offending ships' indemnity underwriters for CLC and/or Tovalop liabilities. They were adamantly against parting from the traditional method of global limitation in maritime claims—i.e. linking the calculation to the ship's tonnage. Limitation of liability is the fundamental issue in this subject and all, whether tanker-owners, their underwriters or the oil men, have an interest in keeping maximum to a minimum.

## US OIL POLLUTION LEGISLATION

Through the 1980s and particularly so long as the 1984 Protocols to the two Conventions were an option, it was thought the US Congress would be persuaded to adopt the International Conventions, but in 1990 they declared their intention to 'go it alone' by introducing the (Federal) Oil Pollution Act of that year. The US decision has divided the world into two camps—the USA and the 'bloc' of Convention adherents. Regrettably it has caused the bringing in of a double standard and has put vessels trading to or from the United States with full cargoes of oil in danger of becoming uninsurable in so far as their liabilities are concerned.

### *Who can be liable?*

The Act names three 'responsible' parties who are exposed to direct liability, these being (a) a vessel owner, (b) a demise charterer and (c) an operator. (a) and (b) need no defining. An operator, so it appears from a consensus of legal opinion, does *not* include a charterer who is not in possession or control (i.e. not a time or voyage charterer). It would, however, include whoever has responsibility for the execution of voyages and for other duties which might normally be associated with the role of manager or managing agent, e.g. victualling and manning.

Each of these responsible parties is jointly, severally and *strictly* liable.

Time and voyage charterers, though exempt from direct liability under the statute, are or can be exposed under possible indemnity terms incorporated in the charterparty, the most likely of which would be a possible breach of the safe port or safe berth warranty a consequence of which could be a spill of oil within US waters.

*Cargo*-owners are not exposed to liability under OPA 1990, despite initial efforts in the draft stages of this Bill to have them at least share liability with the vessels' interests.

## Oil pollution

### *Circumstances creating liability*

Actual discharge of oil from the vessel or a reasonably serious threat of an escape. The oil need not be cargo. It could be fuel and the offending vessel may be of any type.

### *Are there any exceptions to liability?*

Only act of God, act of war or act of a third party (other than an agent, employee or person in a contractual relationship with a 'responsible' party).

### *Can a responsible party limit his liability?*

For tankers exceeding 3,000 gross tonnes US$1,200 per gross tonne or US$10 million whichever is the greater. For tankers of 3,000 tonnes or less whichever is the greater of US$1,200 per gross tonne and US$2 million. For dry cargo vessels, either US$600 per gross tonne or US$500,000, whichever is the greater. An additional provision of OPA 1990 is that in respect of oil pollution claims a responsible party cannot have the benefit of the 1851 (Federal) Limitation of Liability Act which has applicability to other maritime claims generally.

### *What will 'break' limitation?*

If the incident giving rise to the liability was caused by the gross negligence or wilful misconduct of the liable party, limitation will be denied. Gross negligence in this context is defined as a deliberate failure to perform a duty coupled with a reckless disregard for what may be the consequences. Wilful misconduct is a slightly different viewpoint implying a form of conduct which manifests a reckless lack of care for the safety of other people.

Other ways in which a responsible party will forfeit limitation are violation of a Federal safety regulation failure, either deliberate or through neglect, to report a spill of oil, refusal to co-operate in removal operations or to obey an order by an official legally authorized to act in response to a spill. The 1990 OPA offers limitation 'like a carrot on a string' to owners who are prepared to conduct their vessels with good practice and comply with safety rules. Taking into account the willingness of the US Court to 'break limitation' wherever and whenever it is reasonably possible, this layout of the right of limitation does not in practical terms fall far inside the border of unlimited liability.

One of the most onerous provisions, from a tanker owner's point of view, or of his liability insurer (P & I Club), is that the OPA allows individual States to enact their own domestic legislation even on terms more onerous and imposing greater liability on responsible parties than the Federal law itself even permitting them to provide for unlimited liability. Probably the most drastic of the State laws is the Californian statute. This requires that as from 1 January 1991 any vessel wishing to transport oil across the waters of the State either in or out or to load or discharge from any terminal within the jurisdiction of the State, must have a certificate of financial capability to pay at least US$500 million. The statute also requires for the future that this amount be raised to US$750 million as from 1 July 1995 and further up to US$1 billion on 1 January 2000. The statute also requires that virtually parties who have an interest in the vessel and this will include the tanker owner, an operator, a demise charterer, a time or voyage charterer and a manager will all be jointly and severally required to produce such a certificate.

### *Financial responsibility under OPA 1990*

The responsible party for any vessel over 300 tonnes gross is required to establish evidence of financial capability of meeting the maximum amount of his liability under the limitation provisions set down in the OPA 1990 of the largest vessel which that party owns or operates. If he fails to provide the necessary certificate, his vessel may be denied entry into the US port or it may even be detained or seized and forfeited. Any guarantor who provides the required evidence of financial responsibility (and that would include an insurer) is entitled to the same defences and limitation rights as the responsible party himself. An absolute defence to such a guarantor is that the incident which resulted in the loss/damage was caused by the wilful misconduct of that responsible party.

### *Do victims fare better under OPA 90 or 1992 Convention?*

OPA 90 is able to offer more substantial compensation to victims in cases of catastrophic spills than can the 1992 Convention. This coupled with the tying of the granting of limitation to the responsible party to the latter's strict observance of safety rules and good conduct generally, shows that victims would look upon OPA 90 as a 'better bet' than the 1992 Convention. For minor spills, however, the difference will be of no significance.

### *Insurance for oil pollution liabilities*

Ninety-five per cent or more of the world's ships are covered as to their third-party liabilities in mutual insurance associations known as Protecting and Indemnity Clubs. The cover provided by these clubs used to be unlimited though now, after much discussion amongst the management companies of the International Group of P & I Clubs, a limit has been placed upon cover.

One exception to the formerly unlimited cover provided is the risk of oil pollution upon which a limit of US$500 million is placed. This highlights the gravity with which the Clubs regard this particular risk.

Ordinary Club cover includes CLC liabilities and used also to provide funding for Tovalop (both standing and supplemental) liabilities. The financial requirements of CLC, namely that tanker owners should produce evidence of capability to meet their CLC liabilities, can be provided by the Clubs in the form of appropriate certificates as required by CLC and also as required under the US Federal Water Pollution Control Act. The Clubs, however, are not prepared to provide any form of certificate evidencing financial responsibility required under any other National or State legislation. This refusal includes even the provision of a certificate required under the OPA 1990 for the amount of limitation allowed under that statute. The Clubs refused to provide even this certificate despite the fact that they give cover up to US$500 million. The reason for this is that a line has to be drawn somewhere and that line is drawn at the International (Convention) Legislation and the US Federal Water Pollution Control Act only. The attitude of the Clubs is entirely reasonable when one considers that what these certificates contain means that they are a form of anticipatory guarantee meaning that the guarantee is in place before there has ever been a spill of oil likely to result in a claim and before it is known what the circumstances would be and whether there would be any defences to liability anyway. This refusal or, at the most reluctance, to provide guarantees of an anticipatory nature is not restricted to claims in respect of oil pollution; it has been traditional for the Clubs to provide guarantees to assist their Members whose ships and/or other assets have been arrested or threatened with arrest *after* an incident has arisen resulting in a claim and where the bare details of the claim and the rough estimate of value is at least known before the Club concerned provides its guarantee.

However, since the draconian legislation introduced at the beginning of this decade in the United States and in particular the domestic legislation of California, the Clubs have expressed a reluctance to cover their members' ships which trade in and out of the US with oil and expose themselves to the responsibilities imposed by the US legislation. The Clubs take the view that the anticipatory guarantees required and the possible liabilities to be faced (even limited liabilities) are so heavy as to make the risk one which is too exceptional to be regarded as mutual. Any tanker owner who wishes to make sure that he has sufficient cover for his US liabilities is free to purchase an extra US$200 million additional cover, either through his Club or direct in the insurance market at an additional premium to be assessed. Wary charterers of tankers intended to be traded to the United States are seeking warranties from tanker owners that cover is in place up to US$700 million and the Clubs are currently warning tanker owners that they should be careful before warranting any such figures, particularly in a long-term charterparty, because of the obvious inability of a tanker owner to foresee that he will be able to maintain that warranty over a lengthy charter which might extend beyond the current period of Club cover.

## THE AMOCO CADIZ

In concluding this chapter, a brief description of the facts and circumstances of the *Amoco Cadiz* casualty and of the financial liabilities arising from it will not only be of interest, but will also, as being one of the worst disasters to date involving an oil spill from an oil carrier, serve well to illustrate the operation of the Civil Liability Convention 1969 and the Cristal fund—a neat combination of international law and a voluntary scheme.

On 16 March 1978 the fully-laden tanker suffered steering failure in heavy weather off the North Brittany coast. In answer to a radio call for assistance, when the tanker's Master realized he was beyond self-help, the tug *Pacific*, owned by Bugsier, proceeded to assist. After agreeing the terms and conditions on which the tug should take the vessel in tow, the tanker's Master signed a Lloyd's Open Form of Salvage Agreement. Much difficulty and delay was encountered in securing a tow line. It broke and had to be resecured. It soon became apparent, as ship and tug were being swept dangerously close to the shore, that the tug could not hold the ship. Anchors were dropped but these too failed to hold the ship and she struck rocks about 12 hours after the initial steering gear failure.

The tanker quickly broke up, spilling its entire cargo of 221,000 tons of light crude oil and polluting the Brittany coast over a 60-mile stretch. Arrangements for clean-up operations were laid on by the French government with assistance from the British government, and the ship's owners themselves helped by providing special clean-up equipment.

France has implemented the 1969 Convention and under its provisions a limitation fund of the French currency equivalent of US$16.35 million was formed and provided. The fund was deposited in two banks within the jurisdiction of the Court of Brest (France). The cargo was owned by a Cristal member (the Shell Co) and thus the fund was increased (bearing in mind that the spill occurred before the latest amendments (described above) to the Cristal scheme) up to the maximum Cristal figure of US$30,000,000, subject to the ship's owners being permitted to limit in accordance with the 1969 Convention.

Proceedings were later instituted in Illinois (USA) on behalf, inter alios, of French hoteliers and fishermen for loss of business/livelihood, followed very soon by the French government itself instituting proceedings in the New York courts for pollution damages. The ship's owners commenced counter-proceedings to limit their liability. The registered owners of the ship were, however, only one of the defendants named in the US litigation, two others being Standard Oil (the parent) and Amoco International Oil Co (another wholly owned subsidiary of Standard). The US litigation seemed on the face of it to be in defiance of the 1969 Convention which provides that the courts of the country where the fund is constituted should have sole jurisdiction and that other, possibly exposed defendants, viz. ship's managers, should not be independently pursued. During the revising of this book a judgment on liability has been given in Illinois. Liability was found against the ship's registered owner, against Standard *and* against AIOC; Standard because of its overall responsibility for its subsidiaries and AIOC because of the special responsibility it bore for the maintenance, repair and crewing of the vessel. The basis of liability was the negligence of AIOC, Standard's vicarious responsibility for the negligence of its subsidiaries (which amounted under the circumstances to its *personal* liability) and the registered owner's privity to this negligence which of itself deprived them of any limitation rights they might have had under US law.

An award of damages was deferred to a future date but has now been made and is said to be in excess of US$250 million.

Other examples of major spills (some of which have already received a mention earlier in the chapter) in recent years have been:

In 1989 the *Exxon Valdes* devastated the coast of Alaska with a spill of 37,000 tonnes of oil inflicting severe damage to the environment and causing havoc to lucrative fishing grounds. There is reported to have been a final settlement at US$1.1 billion.

In 1993 the *Braer* polluted the waters around the Shetland Islands (UK) having suffered an engine failure and having consequently been driven ashore in severe weather. Oil cargo and bunkers spilt totalling about 84,000 tonnes. The eventual effect of this spill was mitigated by the action of the wind and waves which caused the oil largely to be dispersed by natural means, though substantial claims were still presented in respect of contamination to farmland (sheep) by oily spray blown ashore and quite widespread damage to fishing grounds, not to mention also clean-up costs.

In February 1996 the tanker *Sea Empress* spilt about half of its cargo of 130,000 tonnes of light crude affecting a substantial stretch of the coast of Wales. Light crude can, fortunately, be dispersed more easily than heavy oils which meant that this spill was less of a disaster than it might have been.

CHAPTER 11

# SEAFARERS AND THE SHIP'S MASTER

The shipping industry is of such importance to international trade and so vital to the economy of maritime nations, that the law has developed very much on protective lines regarding seamen whose daily work is to man the ships. In past centuries seamen were unhappily exploited. What few rights they possessed were not clearly expressed to, or understood by, them and once the vessel had put to sea their welfare, health and working conditions were very much in the hands of and at the personal whim of the ship's Master. Masters were often unscrupulous, bullying or even of a drunken nature and seamen themselves were prone to drunkenness, indiscipline, insubordination and desertion.

The early, established method of ensuring that no undue hardship or exploitation of seamen took place was the procedure of signing articles of agreement by each individual. The seaman would be read his rights, thus ensuring that his possible illiteracy would not prejudice his interests. The articles of agreement would initially be opened by the Master's signature and then each seaman would sign in turn, the whole being witnessed by an official of the Mercantile Marine Department of the Department of Transport. However, we are not so much concerned with what used to be, but with what the situation is today.

The Merchant Shipping Act 1970 now consolidated as the Merchant Shipping Act 1995 confirmed the improvement of conditions and the welfare of seamen with a clearer delineation of their rights, duties, responsibilities and immunities. Since 1850 national legislation has always had a part to play in seamen's contracts of service but it can only reasonably be said that seamen have as 'fair a deal' as (and arguably fairer than) any shore-based employee since the Merchant Shipping Act 1970 came into force. The main body of the 1970 Act came into force on 1 January 1973 and was amended in 1974. Further sections of the Act, with amendments, came into force with the passing of the Merchant Shipping Act 1979. The 1995 Act came into force on 19 July 1995. Before this, the main Act was the Merchant Shipping Act 1894, as amended in 1906 and 1970.

The Secretary of State for Trade is authorized to supervise all matters concerning merchant shipping and seaman.

## THE CONTRACT OF EMPLOYMENT

This now goes under the slightly less formal title of 'crew agreement'. A crew agreement must be in writing but gone is the formal process of reading out and signing as described above.

Perhaps the most basic change enshrined in the recent legislation is that the crew is now not so much a 'collective unit' signing articles of agreement but a number of individuals, each in his own right, entering into a contract of employment with his employer. Each individual seaman agrees to serve in accordance with the terms of his contract of employment.

The shift and emphasis is away from the notion of the Master employing the crew; he never did, but the old ideas of the Master and seamen respectively signing the articles gave this false impression. Even in the past the Master was signing as agent of his owners.

The Merchant Shipping Act 1995 stipulates that there is to be an agreement in writing, unless exempted by the Secretary of State, between the employer and the seaman employed in the ship. A 'contract of employment' between the employer and employee. The agreement is to be contained 'in one document'—the crew agreement. Only with the approval of the Secretary of State may the agreement be contained in more than one document or indeed an agreement relate to more than one ship. 'Multiple ship agreements', as such arrangements constitute, are applicable to contracts of service on board, for example, cross-Channel ferries. The legislation clearly states that the Secretary of State must approve all terms and conditions of employment. They specify the contractual provisions to be inserted in the crew agreement, the limitations on the use of voyage and notice clauses and categorically state that no additional clause must be inserted into the crew agreement without their approval. The requirements are currently set out in the Merchant Shipping (Crew Agreement, Lists of Crew and Discharge of Seamen) Regulations 1991.

Any conditions of employment outside the scope of the crew agreement are to be included in a separate non-statutory contract. With the effective disappearance of exploitation, so also has the formal signing-on ceremony been dispensed with. It is no longer necessary for a Mercantile Marine Superintendent to be present at the time a seaman is 'signed on' the crew agreement. There is no longer a requirement for the employer to give prior notice to the Secretary of State of opening a new agreement, nor need he be furnished with a copy of the agreement. A copy must be kept prominently displayed on board and the seaman who is party to it has a right to demand a copy of the contractual clauses and any other document to which these clauses refer. A 'multiple ship agreement' by its very nature must be kept at an establishment ashore, though certified copies of such agreement must be posted on board.

There being only one copy of the crew agreement, this is carried in the ship, and on request must be produced on demand to a seaman who is a party to the agreement, or to an official of customs and excise, a superintendent appointed by the Secretary of State or the Registrar General of Shipping and Seamen. If the crew agreement covers an indefinite period, a copy shall be delivered within seven days of being opened to a superintendent or proper officer for the place where the ship was when the agreement was opened. As every agreement has a commencement so also must it have a termination. The process of 'signing off' used to be as traditional a ceremony as 'signing on'. In the normal course of events a seaman's discharge from his contractual obligations takes place before the employer, Master or some person authorized by the employer.

On closure of the crew agreement it is to be deposited with the employer and to be retained for a period of five years.

Elsewhere in this book (see Chapter 7, Salvage) automatic dissolution of a seaman's contract of employment is described as being effected by a formal order to abandon ship by the Master. This terminates a voyage before its natural end and relieves the seamen from their contractual obligations.

## CREW LISTS

In addition to the crew agreement, the Merchant Shipping Act 1995 and the Merchant Shipping (Crew Agreements Lists of Crew and Discharge of Seamen) Regulations 1991 require the Master of every ship registered in the United Kingdom to make and maintain a crew list. The particulars to be specified in the crew list are laid down by the Regulations.

A crew list must be maintained by the managing owner, ship's husband or manager, or if there is no such person, the owner of the ship, at an address in the UK.

Should the ship be lost or abandoned the owner must immediately deliver the copy of the crew list to a superintendent appointed by the Secretary of State.

A copy of the crew list must be delivered to a superintendent appointed by the Secretary of State by the employer as soon as it is received at his premises in the UK. Closed crew lists will remain deposited with the employer and, as with the crew agreement, be retained for a period of five years from the date of closure. The Regulations now provide for the Registrar General of Shipping and Seamen to have the right to demand from the owners the list of crew on board the vessel on a given date. A crew list must also be provided to a superintendent appointed by the Secretary of State or the Registrar-General every six months showing changes when the crew Agreement is for an indefinite period.

When the crew list ceases to be in force it must be delivered to a superintendent or proper officer for the place where the ship is when the crew list ceases to be in force.

## SEAMEN'S DOCUMENTS

Regulations have been made with respect to both British seamen's cards and discharge books. The regulations detail the entries which must be made in the discharge book for all members of the crew. Present discharge books no longer require entries with respect to conduct and ability. A seaman requesting a report on his conduct and ability may request such information to be given on the appropriate form (DIS 4).

## NUMAST (NATIONAL UNION OF MARINE AVIATION AND SHIPPING TRANSPORT)

There is no longer a national organization set up to negotiate crew employment contracts (the Merchant Navy Establishment Administration). Negotiation is, however, carried out on behalf of its members by NUMAST where there is in place a negotiating agreement with the owner.

## RIGHTS AND DUTIES OF THE SEAMAN

The word 'seaman' is defined in the Merchant Shipping Act 1995 (section 313), as including every person employed or engaged in any capacity on board any ship except the Master and pilots. The Master is employed by written agreement and must appear in the crew list, but is not a seaman within the statutory definition.

Rights and duties imposed by any contract are either expressed or implied and the crew agreement is no exception to this general rule. It could be strongly argued that the traditional role of a seaman calls for a higher devotion to duty than the work of an employee in any other industry or occupation. Seamen and their ships are exposed to the perils of the sea for long periods of their working lives; the long history of maritime disasters is proof enough of this. Therefore one of the implied duties of a seaman is to endeavour at all times to save his ship in time of trouble or danger. It is expected of him as a duty and he can never, unless his employment contract has already been dissolved, claim reward for helping to save his own ship.

It is also inherent in his terms of employment that he must carry out the lawful orders of the Master providing such orders relate to the ship, or things pertaining to her, including the cargo she is carrying. A seaman must be able to perform his designated task with reasonable care and skill. Contracts of service or employment, being inextricably bound by codes of conduct, are essentially based on trust. What has been the custom and practice over the years, and has become a recognized and established method of performing employment contracts can give rise, by implication, to binding contractual obligations on either party to the contract.

## WAGES

### *Historical theory*

The basic consideration given by the shipowner or employer in exchange for all the duties expressed or implied which the seaman agrees to carry out is the payment of wages. Under the old common law a seaman was only due his wages at the successful termination of the voyage. He was, as it were, a joint venturer in the risk. If the voyage never terminated he lost his right to wages. The idea sprang from the notion that wages were paid out of freight earned and, under common law, freight was not earned until right and true delivery of the cargo. The injustice of this is not difficult to see. For a long time wages have been paid in consideration of services rendered and in accordance with the length of period of service. Successful completion of the voyage is irrelevant. This change is of particular importance where a ship has been wrecked or lost.

### *Circumstances where ship is wrecked or lost*

When a ship registered in the UK is wrecked or lost, a seaman's employment in the ship is thereby terminated before the date contemplated in the crew agreement under which he is employed. He becomes entitled to continuance of wages for every day on which he is unemployed in the two months following the date of the wreck or loss, unless it can be shown that he did not make reasonable efforts to save the ship, persons and property in her. However, he is not entitled to wages if it is proved that he was able to obtain suitable employment but unreasonably refused or failed to take it.

'Wreck', for these purposes, implies physical damage to the ship, such that she is unseaworthy so as to make the continuance of the voyage as a commercial venture useless. This is an expression of the doctrine of frustration which, under the law of contract, calls for the dissolving of a contract where there has been a supervening event which destroys the original commercial purpose of the contract and frustrates the original intentions of the parties to the contract.

*Barras* v *Aberdeen Steam Trawling Co* (1933) 45 Ll.L.Rep. 199
A trawler engineer brought an action against the trawler's owners claiming wages during the two weeks in which his vessel was laid up undergoing repairs after being in collision. The case revolved around the interpretation of section 1(1) of the Merchant Shipping (International Labour Conventions) Act 1925, and particularly the meaning of the words 'wreck or loss'. The rule laid down in *The Olympic* [1913] P 92, CA, had been that the words 'wreck or loss' included any accident occasioned by a peril of the sea which rendered the ship unfit or unable to proceed on her voyage. The facts in this case did not indicate that the interruption caused by the collision had frustrated the whole adventure which was the sum and substance of the seaman's contract. The seaman's appeal against the reversal of the original judgment in his favour was dismissed by the House of Lords.

The facts in *The Olympic* dispute were that the vessel collided with a Royal Naval vessel shortly after leaving Southampton bound for New York. She returned to Southampton and subsequently proceeded under her own steam to Belfast where she was fully repaired and nine weeks later resumed her service on the Atlantic route.

The Court of Appeal decided that the vessel was a 'wreck' within the meaning of section 158 of the Merchant Shipping Act 1894, the then current legislation on this issue. The wreck of the ship, in the context of the crew's employment contract, was said to be anything happening to the ship which rendered her incapable of carrying out the maritime adventure in respect of which the seaman's contract was entered into.

Many now believe *The Olympic* was wrongly decided.

As wreck or loss means physical loss it does not include capture, confiscation or detention through hostile action.

The date from which the two months runs for the purposes of remuneration is the date of the wreck or loss. This has been held to be the date of the final abandonment of the maritime adventure and not the date of the actual accident which caused the loss or wreck. (See *The Terneuzen* (1938) 60 Ll.L.Rep. 368.) Present legislation infers that he is entitled to wages following the date on which his employment is terminated due to the loss. This statutory protection is available to all seamen.

### *A seamen's remedies if wages unpaid*

If, due to a shortage of time, the wages due to a seaman have been estimated, any further amount due to him must be paid within seven days of the time of discharge. If the balance of wages shown in the account delivered to the seaman exceeds £50 and it is not practicable to pay the whole amount at the time of discharge, not less than £50 nor less than one-quarter of the amount due must be paid at that time. Any remaining balance is payable within seven days of the time of discharge. Failure to pay wages can expose an employer to liability to pay, at the contract rate, for up to 56 days in the absence of some innocent mistake or reasonable dispute as to the liability being the cause of such failure.

Entitlement to full payment on discharge can in certain circumstances be a very valuable safeguard to a seafarer. This entitlement to full payment on discharge can only be qualified subject to the seaman receiving regular payments throughout the period of the crew agreement.

A seaman who has not been paid should be in a strong position since he has a maritime lien for his unpaid wages (*The Halcyon Skies* [1976] 1 Lloyd's Rep. 461). Such lien travels with the vessel through changes of ownership and can be enforced through the courts by an action in rem. This valuable right is preserved and protected by current legislation and cannot be renounced by any agreement. It does not, however, apply to severance payments which are made to compensate a seaman for the termination of his employment and not in relation to services rendered in and to a particular ship (*The Tacoma City* [1991] 1 Lloyd's Rep. 330).

Incidental disputes as to wages can be resolved by an appeal to a superintendent or proper officer. Such officer or superintendent is at liberty to refuse to entertain the matter referred to him, but if he does accept, his decision is both binding and final.

Although wages, by statute, must be paid on discharge from the ship, certain agreements approved by the Secretary of State allow wages to be paid directly into an account. However, the seaman must agree to settle all outstanding debts monthly, or as required by the clauses in the crew agreement.

### *Payment of wages*

The statutory provisions relating to wages including those of the Master, may be found in sections 30–41 of the Merchant Shipping Act 1995.

The wages due to a seaman under a crew agreement shall be paid to him either at the time of his discharge from the ship or no later than the date when the next payment would fall due. When a seaman is discharged from a ship outside the UK but returns to the UK under arrangements made for him by his employers, he is entitled to payment of wages until the time of his return. A seaman is entitled to have an account showing any deductions that have been made from his wages up to the time of his discharge. These deductions are clearly defined in the appropriate regulations.

The Master is required to deliver an account of wages to every seaman employed under a crew agreement not later than 24 hours before the time of discharge. If a seaman is discharged without notice, or with less than 24 hours' notice, the account should be delivered at the time of discharge.

### *Allotment of wages*

Since a seaman's work necessarily removes him from his habitual place of residence for lengthy periods he is entitled, under statute, to make an allotment of his wages. The Master or employer (shipowner) is required to enquire as to the wishes of the seaman in this respect at the time of his engagement on the crew agreement. The amount which a seaman may leave may be limited by regulations made by the Secretary of State.

The system of allotment available to seamen is another indication of the importance attached to their work. In land employment it is not a customary practice and employment law makes no provision for same. What is of interest is that the law forbids a seaman's wages to be attached by creditors. Subject to voluntary allotment arrangements and the deductions which the seaman's employer may make by contract or statute the wages due to him must be paid and no interference by creditors is permitted.

### *Claims against a seaman's wages*

A responsible authority has the power to seek an order of a magistrates' court to recover from a seaman's wage expenses incurred for the maintenance of his dependents. This is, for the maintenance of his spouse and any person under the age of 18 for whom he is liable.

The Merchant Shipping Act 1995 section 40, makes the earnings of merchant seamen attachable for the purpose of defraying expenses incurred by a responsible authority for the benefit of a dependant of the seaman. The provisions of the Attachment of Earnings Act 1971, also apply under the Merchant Shipping Act 1995, section 34(4) The amount which may be attached is limited to one-half of the seaman's wages if the notice relates to one dependant and two-thirds if it relates to two or more dependants.

## CERTIFICATES OF COMPETENCY AND MANNING

Ever since the middle of the 19th century the British government, now through the Secretary of State for Trade, has had the authority to supervise and examine prospective Masters and officers of UK registered ships. The importance of certification cannot be over-emphasized in terms of the need to maintain high standards of efficiency, competence and vessel safety. UK registered ships fell into two main categories in this respect: foreign-going and home-trade. Present-day legislation refers to 'limited European', 'Extended European' and 'unlimited' trading areas.

Present legislation, with respect to the certification of officers is contained in various statutory instruments i.e. Merchant Shipping (Certificate of Deck Officers) Regulations 1985; Merchant Shipping (Certification of Marine Engineer Officers and Licensing of Marine Engine Operators) Regulations, and the

Merchant Shipping (Certification of Deck and Marine Engineer Officers) (Amendment) Regulations 1995. To obtain a thorough understanding of these provisions, the reader is advised to consult the appropriate regulations.

Classes of certificate originally designated under the Merchant Shipping Act 1984 have been redefined and, in the case of deck officers, examples of the revised equivalents are as follows:

Master foreign-going—Class 1 (Master Mariner)
First mate foreign-going—Class 2

A system of 'command endorsements' has been introduced for deck officers such that a deck officer holding a certificate below the grade Class 1 (Master Mariner) may, with the addition of an appropriate command endorsement and subject to the certificate held, command a ship within limited European or Extended European. The number and class of certificates to be carried on board each and every ship, in respect of both deck and engineering departments, is laid down in the appropriate legislation. The 1995 Regulations provide for the recognition of foreign certificates of equivalent standard to UK certificates.

### *Other specialists' positions*

Radio officers are required to be certificated to serve on board ships equipped with radio telegraphy. The number of officers required to be carried depends on the extent of the radio equipment, class of ship and duration of voyage. Ship's cooks must hold a certificate of competency if serving in a UK registered ship, in unlimited trading areas exceeding 1,000 tons gross registered tonnage.

### *Other ranks*

As the expression 'able seaman' implies, non-officer ranks are also required to exhibit a measure of competency for the task to which they are assigned under their contract of employment. Current Merchant Shipping Regulations (SI 1996/3243) provide: (a) an able seaman must hold a certificate showing him to be such; and (b) a boatswain is required to be duly certificated as an able seaman, be at least 20 years of age, and prove that he has had at least four years' service at sea on deck.

There is a complete prohibition against employing a child in a ship, i.e. a person who is under the age of 16 years, except on the rare occasion that the ship is staffed exclusively by members of one family.

### *Safe manning scales*

The Merchant Shipping Act 1995, section 47 gives power to the Secretary of State to make regulations on the manning of UK registered ships to the extent that it appears necessary in the interests of safety. These powers relate not only to certificated officers, doctors and cooks but also to other seamen of any description. A great deal of study was given to the way in which the regulations could be framed so as to provide the flexibility required by modern conditions. This study showed that the required degree of flexibility could only be achieved by considering ships individually, having regard to their construction, equipment and the nature of the service intended.

A Merchant Shipping notice sets out the way in which the Secretary of State is prepared to give the industry the necessary guidance on deck manning. This notice applies to all sea-going merchant ships registered in the UK with the exception of the following: (a) oil rig supply vessels; (b) small coasting vessels.

The above categories are in some respect dealt with under their own regulations. The latest provisions are based on the principle that the crew of any ship shall be composed of enough seamen with appropriate skills and experience to ensure that the following factors can be fulfilled: (a) the vessel can maintain a safe bridge watch whilst at sea, this to include general surveillance of the vessel; (b) the vessel can operate and effectively maintain watertight systems, including the setting into motion of effective damage control procedures; (c) the vessel can maintain and operate effectively fire-fighting and life-saving equipment and is capable of mustering and disembarking passengers where relevant; (d) the vessel, in general, can perform satisfactorily any function connected with her safety at sea; (e) the capability to maintain a safe engineering watch at sea; (f) provision of medical care; and (g) the capability to maintain a safe radio watch.

In conformity with these principles the requirements of each ship will be examined on its merits and on application of the shipowners to the Secretary of State the manning requirement will be expressed in terms of the minimum number of categorized seamen which, in the opinion of the Secretary of State, is required in the interests of the safe manning of that particular ship. This introduces flexibility in place of the previous rigid generalization.

Three new categories are now in existence in the deck department, i.e. Categories I, II and III, which effectively replace those of an able seaman, efficient deck hand and an ordinary seaman. The category descriptions and grading structure relate to seamen of any nationality subject to the existing statutory requirement of a knowledge of the English language. (See the Merchant Shipping Act 1995, section 51.)

Whatever the Secretary of State decides should be the manning requirements for a particular ship will be stated in a safe manning certificate issued to the ship's owners who are required to display it on board the vessel. With these revised provisions both in connection with the crew and officer requirements it is clearly the ultimate aim that every ship will carry a comprehensive statement of her crew carefully selected to suit her individual needs in respect of safety according to her construction, equipment and the employment to which the ship is put.

## THE EMPLOYMENT OF ALIENS IN UNITED KINGDOM—REGISTERED SHIPS

Under the Aliens Restriction (Amendment) Act 1919, no alien can act as Master of a British ship unless that ship was habitually employed on voyages between ports outside the UK. There is one exception to this rule: any alien who had acted as Master during World War One and who was certificated by the Admiralty to have performed good and faithful service, was allowed to continue to act.

The law has developed much since those days and so have race relations. So also have the rules as to who is, or is not, a citizen of the UK. However, it is still a fact that no alien may act as Master, chief officer or chief engineer of a UK registered ship unless the ship habitually trades outside the UK. Interestingly, but logically, in connection with the foregoing, it is not a breach of the current race relations laws to discriminate when appointing seamen for employment on board a UK registered ship when recruited abroad, even if they are brought to the UK to sign the crew agreement. This is, of course, subject to the applicable law in the place of recruitment. Generally, it is not permitted to employ an alien in whatever capacity he may be engaged at a rate of pay less than the ruling rate for his British counterpart.

## WELFARE, SAFETY AND ACCOMMODATION

In the old days once a ship was at sea a seaman's welfare, safety and accommodation were very much left in the control of the Master. In modern times very clearly defined statutory requirements are laid down in respect of accommodation, provisions and water. An essential prerequisite to a seaman's health in addition to his personal comfort, dignity and welfare, is that he has adequate accommodation.

## HEALTH

A shipowner is responsible for ensuring that if a crew member contracts an illness or suffers an injury in the course of his employment, adequate medical attention is provided. The requirement to carry a doctor on board is limited to vessels having 100 persons or more on board which are engaged on an International voyage of more than three days or on a voyage during which it is more than one and a half days' sailing time from a port with adequate medical equipment. Where it is not required that a doctor be carried on board there must be a member of the crew who is sufficiently capable of providing first aid and medical treatment to a sick or injured seaman. Vessels must carry medical supplies of an approved standard.

Reasonable expenses of medical or surgical treatment incurred by a seaman must be paid for by his employer. The same applies to dental or optical treatment which cannot reasonably be postponed without prejudicing the seaman's capacity to work.

## REPATRIATION

The statutory provisions relating to the relief and repatriation of seamen left behind may be found in sections 73 to 76 of the Merchant Shipping Act 1995. There is now provision in section 76 for the Secretary of State to provide grants or loans to assist shipowners with travel expenses for seamen joining or leaving a ship outside European waters.

A seaman's employer has prima facie responsibility for caring for and arranging the repatriation of a seaman who has been left abroad or landed abroad after a shipwreck. The employer's liabilities in this respect are to bear the costs of maintaining and repatriating; to arrange any essential medical, dental or optical treatment as stated above; to provide suitable accommodation ashore; to be liable for reasonable legal costs for the defence of the seaman in criminal proceedings in respect of any act or omission within the scope of his employment; and to arrange for his repatriation (including applying to the appropriate official for a suitable conveyance order) where necessary. This obligation is limited where a seaman goes absent without leave or where the seaman has been absent for a period in excess of three months during which time his employer was not aware of his whereabouts. In all other cases the employer's liability commences as soon as the seaman is left behind and is available for return.

A seaman should be returned to his home or to any other mutually agreed place. It is the duty of the ship's Master to ensure that immigration laws permit the repatriated seaman to re-enter the country concerned. If the ship's Masters are requested by a proper officer to carry seamen back to their home countries under a conveyance order, they are not obliged to do so if to obey such an order would break the law, would require a Master to deviate from his customary voyage, or would cause his ship to be unreasonably delayed. He must, if he does carry such a seaman or seamen, make the appropriate entries in the official log book. The Master may receive a sum, not exceeding £2 per day, for each day that a seaman is on board in compliance of a conveyance order. The provisions of this Part of the Act are applicable to Masters as well as seamen.

## DECEASED SEAMEN

The Merchant Shipping Act 1995, section 271, requires an inquiry to be held whenever a member of the crew, including the Master, dies on board or in a place outside the UK. The inquiry must be held by a proper officer or superintendent and their findings reported to the Secretary of State. A copy should be made available to interested parties, i.e. the deceased's next of kin. No inquiry should be held where the matter is to be investigated by a coroner in England, Wales or Northern Ireland, or is the subject of a public inquiry under the provisions of Scottish law. It is the duty of the Master of the ship, in any event, to notify the deceased person's next of kin within three days of the death.

The Merchant Shipping Act 1979, section 29, extends the Merchant Shipping Act 1970 and empowers the Secretary of State to institute an inquiry if the Master or a seaman, after being discharged due to injury or illness, subsequently dies outside the UK and the death occurs within one year of the cessation of his employment. Where there is any uncertainty as to the cause of death, e.g. lost from a ship, an inquiry must be held.

The property and wages of a deceased seaman will be taken care of by the Master who will enter full details in the official log book.

## INDUSTRIAL DISPUTES

Labour law, as such, has no place in this book other than in a passing reference. Mention is required here nevertheless in respect of industrial disputes involving seamen, which are covered by section 42 of the Merchant Shipping Act 1970. The section provides that despite what may be contained in the crew agreement, a seaman employed in a ship registered in the UK may terminate his employment by leaving the ship in pursuance of an industrial dispute. He must, however, give the ship's Master at least 48 hours' notice of his intention to do so, and may not be compelled (unless such notice is withdrawn) to go to sea in the 48 hours following the giving of such notice. *But*, one proviso is that such a notice will be of no effect unless the ship is in the UK and securely moored in a safe berth.

The fact that the ship must be securely moored in port clearly indicates and emphasizes that the law takes a very different view of anything in the nature of a strike or dispute taking place whilst the seaman and ship are at sea. It should be noted that before a seaman involves himself in an industrial dispute he must have terminated his employment with the ship, i.e. he must have signed off the crew agreement.

In the past, the application of the criminal law was generally removed from the scene of industrial disputes between employers and employees. The years 1979 and 1980 saw the rights and liabilities of parties to industrial disputes, particularly the right of picketing, whether primary or secondary, fall into the ambit of reform. The right to strike is generally well entrenched and hallowed in the UK and the merchant seaman is expressly, though in the limited way described, included with his shore-based counterparts.

## DISCIPLINE

Disciplinary offences committed by a seaman are the subject of the Merchant Shipping Acts 1970, 1974 and 1979, and the disciplinary regulations made and amended in pursuance of these Acts. In particular, reference should be made to sections 27 to 41 of the 1970 Act and (when they are brought into operation) sections 23 to 25 of the 1979 Act.

It is in this sphere that the role of the Master becomes especially relevant. He is primarily responsible for maintaining discipline and in the confined space of a ship this is no easy task. Discipline is a prerequisite to safety. The common law has for centuries provided wide powers to the Master but statute has confined these powers to reasonable limits. The Master has the power of arrest which, in the interests of safety and the preservation of good order, allows him to place any person 'under restraint' so long as it is necessary to achieve these ends.

*Hook* v *Cunard Steamship Co* [1953] 1 Lloyd's Rep. 413
A lounge steward in the *Queen Elizabeth* claimed damages for false imprisonment and for breach of contract of employment and wrongful dismissal. The arrest and imprisonment of Hook on board was action taken by the Master's authority as the result of a strong complaint lodged by a passenger that Hook had indecently assaulted and behaved obscenely towards his ten-year-old daughter. The Master contended that he had reasonable cause to believe the arrest and imprisonment of Hook was necessary in the interests of preserving order in the ship and the safety of child passengers.

*Held*: that the defendant shipowners had not discharged their obligations of showing that the plaintiff's arrest and confinement was necessary for the preservation of order in the ship. Rather, the evidence showed that the Master took the action he did purely to placate an irate passenger and to avoid unwanted publicity. The plaintiff was awarded £250 damages for false imprisonment.

It should be mentioned here that this action was brought under common law and not under any statutory provision, but nevertheless the case is illustrative of how the law treats this type of situation.

The assize court judge, in commenting on the common law position as opposed to any statutory right of a ship's Master, said that 'the Master of a merchant ship is justified at common law in arresting and confining in a reasonable manner and for a reasonable time any sailor *or other person* on board his ship, if he has reasonable cause to believe that such arrest or confinement is necessary for the preservation of order and discipline, or for the safety of the vessel or the persons or property on board'.

It is significant that the word 'reasonable' appears three times in one sentence in the above quotation. Just as significant is the word 'necessary'. It is equally vital in the interests of justice that the Master should believe in the necessity of his actions. No one expects a Master, however, to wait for a mutiny to break out before he takes reasonable measures. Nevertheless he must use his powers discreetly and be careful not to abuse them.

The Merchant Shipping Acts recognize that employment on board a ship must be treated a little—but not totally—differently from employment ashore. Because of the need for discipline and safety at sea, there must be specially created penalties for offences relating to the preservation and safety of ship, crew, property and (where relevant) passengers. This does not make, nor was it ever intended to make, a seaman into a 'criminal' within the general meaning of that expression and with all the allied stigma which it implies.

The Acts make provision for the imposition of fines or imprisonment where a seaman is brought before the appropriate court as a consequence of a breach of the law. Such offences are of a far more serious nature than those which can be dealt with on board the ship under the disciplinary regulations or disciplinary procedures. The serious offences for which a seaman may be convicted on indictment to imprisonment for a term not exceeding two years and a fine, and, on summary conviction, to a fine not exceeding £2,000, are:

(1) Misconduct endangering the ship or persons on board. This statutory provision includes the Master of, or any seaman employed in, a ship registered in the UK or in territorial waters and proceeding to or from such a port: Merchant Shipping Act 1970 (Unregistered Ships) Regulations 1991 (SI 1991/1366). The provisions now appear in the Merchant Shipping Act 1995, section 58(1). The Master of, or any seaman employed in, a ship registered in the UK or the Master of, or seaman employed in, a ship which is registered outside the UK, but which is at the time in a UK port shall be guilty of an offence if he does any act which causes or is likely to cause: (a) loss or destruction of or serious damage to a ship or its machinery etc.; (b) loss or destruction or serious damage to any other ship or structure; or (c) the death of or serious injury to any person. Equally he will be guilty of an offence if he omits to do anything to either preserve his ship or its machinery etc. or to preserve any person on board his ship from death or serious

injury or (d) to prevent his ship from causing loss or destruction or damage to any other ship or structure or the death or serious injury to any person not on his ship. Found guilty of an offence, the penalty upon conviction on indictment could be either imprisonment for not exceeding two years or a fine or both. On summary conviction that person is liable to a fine not exceeding the statutory maximum. The 1995 Act retains the broader concept of conduct 'likely to cause' introduced by the 1979 Act to enable prosecutions to take place for misconduct which is likely to cause destruction of, or serious damage to, a ship's machinery, navigational equipment or safety equipment.

(2) Drunkenness on duty. This section of the 1970 Act which provided for prosecution for drunkenness etc., on duty was amended by the 1979 Act (now 1995 Act section 53) to apply to a seaman while employed on board a fishing vessel registered in the United Kingdom.

(3) Continued or concerted disobedience, neglect of duty, etc.

Where any person, i.e. a stowaway, goes to sea in a ship without permission, then the above offences apply in general as if that person were a seaman employed in the ship.

One of the most important statutory steps taken towards the aim of preserving safety at sea was sections 30–31 of the Merchant Shipping Act 1988 (now the Merchant Shipping Act 1995, sections 94–100). This firmly imposes burdens on both the shipowner and the ship's Master, if any ship either (a) registered in the UK and in any port wheresoever or (b) in a UK port, is found unfit to go to sea without putting human life at serious risk. Both owner and *Master* shall each be guilty of an offence. Subsection (3) lists those conditions which would render a ship thus unfit:

(1) condition or unsuitability for its purpose, of the ship, its machinery or its equipment, or any part of the ship or its machinery or equipment;
(2) undermanning;
(3) overloading or unsafe or improper loading;
(4) anything else relevant to the ship's safety.

The statute allows for a fine on summary conviction up to £50,000 to be imposed.

In *The Safe Carrier* [1994] 1 Lloyd's Rep. 589) the managers were charged under section 31 of the Act where the vessel had put to sea after a new chief engineer had only two hours 50 minutes to familiarize himself with the engines and the vessel broke down within two hours. On a case stated the House of Lords held that the putting to sea of the vessel in these circumstances was not attributable to the failure of the manager to take all reasonable steps to secure that the ship was operated in a safe manner and that the Divisional Court had correctly quashed the conviction.

### *Disciplinary procedures for the Merchant Navy*

The subject of discipline in the Merchant Navy has been a matter of review in recent times by a working party of shipowners, seafarers' organizations and the Department of Transport. The working party was set up by the Secretary of State and the result of their work was published in November 1975. The principal recommendations of the working party or 'group' called for a new disciplinary system, including a code of conduct and a disciplinary structure ashore to deal with serious or persistent offenders.

The principal recommendations were: (a) offences prejudicial to safety to remain the subject of criminal prosecution and the scope of such prosecutions to be widened (see above); (b) a stringent code of conduct to replace the short list of offences contained in the disciplinary regulations; (c) the Master's powers of investigation, decision and logging to remain unchanged; (d) the Master's power to levy fines to be abolished, i.e. the disciplinary regulations to be repealed, and the following penalties to be available to him: (i) warning; (ii) reprimand; (iii) adverse report to a shore-based committee; and (iv) dismissal from the ship; (e) the Master's powers at ports abroad to be enlarged. Repatriation would be at the employer's expense but the offender would be liable to contribute up to one week's wages towards the costs; and (f) joint disciplinary committees, with statutory backing, to deal ashore with seafarers dismissed from their ships for indiscipline, with powers to exclude from the industry and to remove an offender's discharge book in the most serious cases.

The cornerstone of the new disciplinary arrangements was to be the code of conduct, which would be applicable to all officers and ratings serving in UK registered ships. The code was to contain a list of offences which would warrant dismissal or lesser disciplinary action and was to lay down detailed procedures for the maintenance of discipline on board ship. The code was to be designed to embrace the fundamental principles in the ACAS Code of Practice and Procedures in Employment.

It was hoped that early in the 1980s a code of conduct would be published with the approval of the Secretary of State for Transport and incorporated into all crew agreements; this however has not been possible. As mentioned above, the code relates to the need and importance of disciplined behaviour and the conduct required on board in emergencies and in situations other than emergencies. It details a range of offences, breaches of the code and explains the correct procedure to be used on board for dealing with such breaches.

On 1 January 1979 a code of conduct for the Merchant Navy, published by the National Maritime Board for use on board ships subject to NMB conditions, was incorporated into the contractual clauses of the crew agreement and each seaman on signing on thereby agrees to comply with the code of conduct for the Merchant Navy for the time being in force. An additional clause in the crew agreement stipulates that the provisions of the Merchant Shipping (Disciplinary Offences) Regulations 1972 (since repealed), including the Master's power to impose fines, shall not be applied to any seaman employed under such an agreement.

The NMB ceased to function in 1990 and since then many shipping companies have incorporated similar codes into their crew agreements and company service contracts.

The Master's power to fine a seaman when in breach of the crew agreement is of long standing and, prior to 1 January 1973, six offences were specified in the articles of agreement for which seamen could be fined one day's pay, for the first occasion on which such offence was committed during the currency of the agreement, and two day's pay for the second or any subsequent occasion. It should be noted that the Master's power to fine a seaman does not apply to certified officers whereas the code of conduct applies to *all* seamen, including certified officers.

## STOWAWAYS; UNAUTHORIZED PRESENCE ON BOARD SHIP

The distinction between a stowaway and a person who is on board without authority is that the former is going or attempting to go to sea whereas the latter merely goes on board without consent or remains on board when requested to leave. The fines on summary conviction differ in value—not exceeding £500 for stowaways and not exceeding £200 for unauthorized presence on board. See the Merchant Shipping Act 1995, sections 103 and 104.

Ship's Masters are expected to be on their guard for stowaways and to make regular searches of their ships. Stowaways are notoriously difficult to land due to strict immigration laws in most countries and the cost of maintaining them until their eventual return to their country of origin, in the event that countries of ports of call en route refuse to take them, is for the owner's account. It is a problem of increasing concern to the maritime community. There are ever increasing numbers of stowaways, principally from third world countries whose presence on board causes considerable inconvenience and expense for shipowners and their P & I Clubs.

The presence of stowaways, when discovered, must be reported in the official log book so that there is a written record of the incident available for study by the police or other investigating officers at the arrival port. Where a stowaway is landed abroad for repatriation to the UK, the log book copies of the appropriate entries must be produced to a proper officer since that officer must certify that the copies are a true extract from the official log book. No court of law will accept uncertified copies as evidence and without such evidence the stowaway cannot be prosecuted.

## UNFAIR DISMISSAL

It has been a common law right of any employee to seek damages in the courts if he considers that he has been dismissed without justification. In recent years there has been created, in the UK, a statutory concept of unfair dismissal. This has not displaced any common law right but it has superimposed itself and provided for defined circumstances in which remedies are available to an employee who is found to have been unfairly dismissed. Legislation in this respect developed through the 1970s, the most recent statute on the subject being the Employment Protection (Consolidation) Act 1978.

The law on unfair dismissal is as applicable to seafarers serving in UK registered ships as it is to their shore-based counterparts. It is indisputable that Masters, officers and seamen are employees within the meaning of the Act and that there is a contract of employment between the employee and employer whether it be a company service contract or the crew agreement. The problem, should there be one, is to include seafarers within the scope of the legislation which applies basically to the relationship of employer and employee within the UK. Seamen spend a large, if not major, part of their working life outside the jurisdiction of their home country. The position of a seaman serving in a UK registered ship is that unless his employment is *wholly* outside Great Britain or he is not *ordinarily resident* in Great Britain he is entitled to the protection of the legislation on unfair dismissal. This is logical because his home base, even if he rarely sees it, is in the UK. If it is not his normal place of residence, he is not protected by the UK legislation.

If there is any doubt as to his entitlement to the protection of the unfair dismissal legislation, then the base test should be applied. In the absence of special factors, the country which contains the seafarer's base is likely to be regarded as where he is ordinarily working under his contract of employment. Other contractual factors which will be examined are whether he is obliged to pay UK national insurance contributions, the currency in which he is paid, where his home is or is expected to be, and any terms defining his operational base or which indicate where the voyages in his employment begin and end.

## LIABILITY FOR INJURY

At common law an employer is responsible if his negligence results in an injury to his employee and, by the extension of this principle, is also vicariously responsible for the negligent acts or defaults of his servants which similarly cause injury. By the terms and conditions of the contract of employment, expressed or implied, it is the duty of the shipowner to provide a safe vessel and equipment and to ensure that his employees (seamen) are reasonably competent to perform the tasks for which they have been employed. Furthermore, an employer may be in breach of a statutory duty.

*Foulder* v *Canadian Pacific Steamship Co* [1968] 2 Lloyd's Rep. 366

Foulder, a steward, claimed damages from his employers for injuries received when he was badly scalded under a hot shower in the *Empress of England*. He alleged negligence and/or breach of statutory duty under the Merchant Shipping (Crew Accommodation) Regulations 1953. The defendant employers argued that at the time Foulder was under the influence of drink and that he was personally to blame for his own misfortune as he failed to test the temperature of the water first.

*Held*: that the water was dangerously hot and, if normal precautions had been taken by those responsible for the equipment, the dangerous situation would not have existed. The defendants were in breach of the regulations. They had not proved that Foulder was under the influence of alcohol and they could not validly criticize him for not testing the temperature of the water which he had a right to expect should be reasonable. Foulder was awarded £8,400 damages.

It is no defence for a shipowner to say that the injured seaman was contributorily negligent, i.e. personally contributed to his injuries by his own fault. Where a seaman is at fault, then his degree will be assessed and taken into account in the awarding of damages. The duties imposed by the Merchant Shipping Acts on a shipowner to provide safe working conditions may make it extremely difficult for a shipowner to defend himself against an action for damages for personal injury.

The personal representatives of any crew member killed in the course of sea duties may bring an action under the Fatal Accidents Act 1976, alleging that his death resulted directly from the negligence of the shipowner or his servants.

*Waddy* v *Boyd Line* [1966] 1 Lloyd's Rep. 335
The plaintiff's husband, a boatswain, was drowned when his trawler, the *Arctic Viking*, owned by the defendants, capsized and sank in heavy weather in the North Sea. His widow brought an action under the Fatal Accidents Acts and the Law Reform (Miscellaneous Provisions) Act 1934. She alleged that the trawler's skipper was negligent in that he failed to take precautions to prevent the boat from capsizing.

Although evidence emerged that the wind was force 8 and the ship was listing to port and taking water over the port side, the Admiralty judge found that the signs of danger were neither severe nor frequent enough to warn the seaman that what did happen was likely to happen. The skipper was not negligent and the widow's claim failed.

Under the Merchant Shipping Act 1995, a shipowner is no longer able to limit his liability with respect to claims for loss of life or personal injury, or loss of, or damage to any property of a person (the seaman) who is employed on board under a contract of service (the crew agreement). (Section 35(1).) The Health and Safety at Work etc. Act 1974, provides that every employer has the duty to ensure, so far as is reasonably practicable, the health, safety and welfare at work of his employees (see section 2). The Act applies to all persons, including seamen, whilst at work in Great Britain. Employees must take reasonable care to avoid injury to themselves or to others by their work activities, and must co-operate with their employers and others to meet the statutory requirements (see section 7).

The ultimate responsibility for accident prevention at sea rests with the Master. Employers should provide all available information about matters affecting health and safety at work. The Code of Safe Working Practices for the Safety of Merchant Seamen and the various codes of safe practice for ships carrying different types of cargo provide a sound basis upon which those concerned can maintain safe working conditions on board ship and in port, and they are designed to reduce the number of accidents.

Merchant Shipping notices, 'M' notices, are another important source of information about health and safety matters which are freely available to Masters, officers and seaman.

The Merchant Shipping Act 1995 contains specific provisions relating to the safety and health of seafarers, which apply to seamen on board UK registered ships throughout the world. These provisions enable regulations to be made as appropriate by the Secretary of State for the purposes of securing the safety of seafarers and protecting their health.

Recent regulations made under the above Acts bring UK ships into line with their counterparts in industry ashore. Such legislation is similar to that under the Health and Safety at Work etc, Act 1974.

The Merchant Shipping Act 1995 makes provision for the serving of improvement notices and prohibition notices in connection with statutory provisions relating to the safety of ships.

Research is continuously being carried out with a view to improving safety and health standards on board ship and the legislation is being continuously updated under powers afforded under the Merchant Shipping Acts.

## THE ROLE OF THE SHIP'S MASTER

The Master of a ship is a man of many parts. He needs to be part disciplinarian, part accountant, part lawyer and more than part seaman/navigator. Above all, perhaps he needs to command the respect of his fellow men. He needs to have more than a fair measure of self-confidence and an ability to make a cool and rational judgment, sometimes at very short notice, in times of crisis. He is a servant in law, an agent both for his principal, the shipowner, and to some extent the owner of the goods he is carrying. If his ship is under charter and the charterparty so stipulates, he must obey the instructions of the charterer in respect of the employment of the vessel. He is also a commander of men, his crew, and he occupies a position of special trust, a fiduciary relationship with his owners. He is absolutely responsible for the safety of his ship and remains in command regardless of whether or not his ship is in charge of a pilot at any given time.

A Master needs to have at least a basic knowledge, preferably more than basic, of the various clauses/provisions of printed charterparties (either general or, if his ship operates in specialized trades, special forms) and any additional typed provisions which are customarily added in as riders. He, as agent for his owners, is responsible for seeing that charter provisions are complied with in so far as it may fall within the scope of his duties to do so, e.g. the giving of proper notices of readiness to load or discharge, the notifying of estimated times of arrival (ETA), etc. He will be required to check and endorse statements of fact, time sheets, etc. Additionally, when under time charter, he will be required to obey any directions lawfully given to him by the charterer under and pursuant to his, the charterer's, right to use and employ the ship. Put simply, and in elaboration of this last sentence, a charterer may direct a Master to which port to sail to load or discharge or to await orders but he may not tell him *when* to sail because if he does he would be improperly encroaching upon the Master's exclusive right to decide and rule upon matters affecting the safety and navigation of his ship.

It is not the role of this chapter, nor indeed of this book, to enlarge upon the various rights or obligations of a Master and/or his owners arising from the clauses of this or that charterparty. It is simply here sufficient to emphasize that the Master, being the 'man on the spot' and legally the owners' servant or agent, is responsible to his owners for the day-to-day compliance with his owners' responsibilities under a charter, bearing in mind that he also 'wears another hat' which obliges him to obey the orders or directions of a charterer within the limits imposed on the charterer by the charterparty itself.

He has the authority to bind his principals, the owners, provided that he acts within the scope of his authority, whether it be expressed or implied. This includes entering into contracts such as stevedoring agreements, salvage agreements (see also *The Unique Mariner* (page 328)), and contracts of carriage evidenced by bills of lading. He has no authority to sign a bill of lading for cargo which has never been physically placed on board. This was held, as early as 1851, to be acting beyond the scope of his authority.

*Grant* v *Norway* (1851) 20 LJPC 93
Twelve bales of silk were arranged for shipment in an ocean carrier and the ship's Master signed a bill of lading evidencing the receipt of these 12 bales on board. Subsequently the

original bill of lading was acquired by a third party for value and subsequent to that it was found that the 12 bales had never been physically placed on board the ship named in the bill of lading.

The Master's act of signing the bill of lading for goods which were never in fact on board was an act outside the scope of his implied authority and as such did not bind the ship's owner in obligation towards the rightful and innocent holder of the original bill of lading.

The effect of this decision, which caused some Victorian raised eyebrows at the time, but which lasted nevertheless for a century or more, has been rendered virtually sterile by Article 3, paragraph 4, of the Hague-Visby rules (the amendment to the 1924 Hague rules). Article 3, paragraph, 4 reads as follows:

'such a Bill of Lading shall be prima facie evidence of the receipt by the carrier of the goods as therein described in accordance with paragraph 3 (a), (b) and (c). However, proof to the contrary shall not be admissible when the Bill of Lading has been transferred to the third party acting in good faith'.

It is the last sentence of the above quoted text which puts the nail in the coffin of *Grant* v *Norway.*

A Master who signs, or upon whose express authority someone else signs, a bill of lading, binds his owners to the contractual terms and conditions which are contained in that bill of lading printed form. The awareness that this is so takes on an especial significance when it is remembered that the Carriage of Goods by Sea Act 1992, causes or can cause rights and liabilities embodied in the bill of lading to be transferred to an innocent rightful transferee of the document, despite the fact that that holder of the document was not an original party to the contract evidenced by the bill of lading and eventually contained in it. By reason of the negotiable nature with which the bill of lading as a document is endowed the eventual holder of the bill could, in a free market, be anyone. Thus a Master needs to be particularly careful in the signing of a bill or in the determining of the party to whom he may delegate his authority to sign, since in so doing he is creating a contractual relationship between his owners and Mr X, the innocent endorsee and/or purchaser of the document.

If the ship is at the material time operating under a *demise* charter, which form of charter gives the *charterer* beneficial possession and control of the ship which he effectively demonstrates by exercising his contractual right to engage, employ and pay the Master and crew, then, as would be expected, the Master's signature binds the charterer as being the Master's employer and as being the party who controls the ship and takes on the role of carrier vis-à-vis the cargo of some third party carried on board.

In short, unless there is a clear expression to the contrary, a Master's signature binds the owners when the ship is under charter unless the terms of the charter are such as to amount to a charter by demise. Authority for the foregoing may be found in *The Berkshire* [1974] 1 Lloyd's Rep. 185 where the then Admiralty judge, Brandon J, said that whether the Master signs himself or the charterers 'short-circuit' and sign themselves on his behalf, the effect is the same, i.e. that it is the owners of the ship who, as principals to the contract contained in or evidenced by the bill of lading, are bound to its terms. The Master cannot, however, be obliged (by the charterer) to sign bills (of lading) 'manifestly inconsistent' with the charterparty or which have extraordinary terms contained in them.

There is a long established commercial practice, still commonly used in sea trade, whereby a shipper of goods or charterer who is anxious to obtain 'clean' bills of lading (that is to say bills which testify to the cargo concerned being in apparent good order and condition at the time of shipment) in order to conform to the terms of a letter of credit which may have been arranged pursuant to the international sale of those same goods, may, if the goods *are* noted to be damaged at the time of shipment, offer a letter of indemnity to the Master, in his capacity as the owners' representative on the spot, to induce him to leave off any notation in the bill of lading which might refer to such discrepant condition of the goods. This practice, though frequently followed in international sea carriage, is fraudulent since it involves an inducement by one party to another party to issue a fraudulent document likely to result in eventual detriment to some innocent third party.

A Master's legal duty is to properly state and accurately note in the bill of lading (which is, amongst its other roles, a document of title to the goods carried) the condition of the goods at the time of shipment and in accepting such a letter of indemnity for commercial or business reasons he is deviating from that duty. He and his owners must also realize that although the acceptance of such indemnity may be common commercial practice they will be unable to enforce the terms of the letter (should they ever wish to do so) by invoking the aid of a court of law. The courts, for obvious reasons, will not come to their assistance. Furthermore, owners who allow their Masters to accept such letters or actually instruct them to do so put themselves outside the scope of ordinary P & I Club (third-party liability insurance) cover since they have voluntarily assumed a deliberate risk for commercial reasons.

In respect of dangerous goods, the Master is given the power, whilst on the carrying voyage, to dispose of goods which are a danger, or are in the process of becoming a danger, to persons or other property carried in the same ship. The right of disposal is granted by statute. The Carriage of Goods by Sea Act 1971 (which incorporates the Hague Rules as amended by the Brussels Protocol 1968 into English law), Schedule, Article IV, rule 6, reads:

'Goods of an inflammable, explosive or dangerous nature to the shipment whereof the carrier, Master or agent of the carrier has not consented, with knowledge of their nature and character, may at any time before discharge be landed at any place, or destroyed or rendered innocuous by the carrier without compensation and the shipper of such goods shall be liable for all damages and expenses directly or indirectly arising out of or resulting from such shipment. If any such goods shipped without such knowledge and consent shall become a danger to the ship or cargo, they may in like manner be landed at any place, or destroyed or rendered innocuous by the carrier without liability on the part of the carrier except to general average, if any.'

He can give a bottomry bond (very rare nowadays) or a respondentia bond (also rare) and so bind his owners or the cargo owners in cases of dire necessity when he finds himself left with no alternative other than to raise money by pledging the ship and/or freight and/or cargo in a situation (such as a foreign port) where his owners have no financial credit. His ultimate obligation is to complete the contract voyage and his basic duty is to prosecute the voyage with reasonable dispatch.

The word frequently used to describe the needs of this type of situation is 'necessaries', and persons who supply the needs of the ship on these occasions are often described as 'necessaries men', be they ship chandlers or suppliers of any items essential to the successful prosecution of the voyage. The Master is often described in such situations as 'the agent of necessity'.

Other examples of a Master's power to act without prior express authority in exceptional or extraordinary circumstances are: (a) in times of danger he may perform what is known as a general average act or sacrifice, or incur a general average expense in the common interest for the purpose of saving or safely prosecuting the common venture to its ultimate conclusion; or (b) he may enter into salvage agreements with third parties for the latter's assistance in time of real danger, provided that such agreements are on reasonable terms (e.g. Lloyd's Open Form, the terms of which are generally agreed world-wide to be reasonable). In *The Choko Star* [1990] 1 Lloyd's Rep. 516 the question of whether the Master could bind cargo interests where he entered into a salvage contract was considered. The Court of Appeal, reversing the decision at first instance, held that there was no basis on which a term that the Master was authorised to contract on behalf of cargo owners with third parties (whether with salvors or others) could be implied, save as an agent of necessity.

Modern instant and sophisticated communication systems have made urgent contact between ship and shore control a great deal easier but this does not mean that the Master in law may not be regarded as an agent of necessity, in times of real emergency at sea, for those whose property has been entrusted to his care on a maritime venture. Either a lack of realization of his role as an agent of necessity or a natural human hesitation arising from a fear of ultimate repercussions (after the event) from his owners may, though only may, have been, if not the root cause, at least a contributing factor of some maritime disasters which perhaps might not have occurred if a Master had acted promptly and on his own initiative without allowing precious minutes to slip away attempting to seek his owners' prior instructions to, e.g. accept outside help. These last comments are necessarily speculative only since 'dead men in disasters cannot be cross-examined afterwards'. That in fact such delay was a contributing factor to the *Amoco Cadiz* disaster in 1978 seems now to have been ruled out (see the Illinois court judgment in April 1984). Whether or not it was a part cause of the *Union Star*'s tragic loss in December 1981 can only be guessed at.

In practical terms, though perhaps this point has very little relevance in a law textbook, the Master acts as a 'safety officer' in his ship. Compliance with safety regulations on board and the ensuring that his crew and anyone else lawfully on board, whether passengers, harbour workers or merely visitors, comply or at least are appropriately warned, hardly needs emphasizing. An owner is heavily exposed to liability for death or injury occurring on board to whatever category of person, especially under US jurisdiction where exposure to liability exists both under Federal statute (viz. the Jones Act *re* crew and the Longshoremen and Harbourworkers' Compensation Act *re* maritime shoreworkers) and under the general maritime law. There is also increasing regulation of the hours which Masters can work. The Merchant Shipping (Local Passenger Vessels) (Masters' licences and Hours, Manning and Training) Regulations 1993 provide not only for the Master's competence to be certified by the Secretary of State, but also regulate the hours which a Master can work. No more than 16 hours in a working day can be worked. This is still a considerable increase over shore-based employees c.f. drivers of goods vehicles on international journeys who are limited to four-hour continuous periods and eight hours per day.

A Master frequently has the unenviable task of reconciling his concurrent responsibilities of ensuring the continued safety of his ship and her human occupants and indeed of her cargo and equipment carried, and ensuring also that the economic interests of his owners are served to the fullest extent. This difficulty of reconciliation is probably at its greatest in times of turbulent weather on a cargo- or passenger-carrying voyage.

CHAPTER 12

# PASSENGERS

Contracts to carry passengers at sea are subject to the ordinary rules governing contracts generally and are not in any sense specialized or out of the ordinary so far as the rights and liabilities of the two parties to the contract are concerned. However, as in many types of contract, one party (i.e. the shipowner or carrier) is far more conversant with the terms and conditions of the agreement because it is in the course of his business to be so than is the other party to the contract. It has been common, in fact almost universal, to include in all contracts of passage an exclusion clause which excludes liability for any personal injury suffered during the course of the contract of passage, howsoever caused. Many will regard this as a very onerous clause and indeed some exclusion clauses have in the past been regarded by the courts of some countries as too onerous and biased in favour of one party to have validity. However, it has always been the tradition in the UK that freedom of contract should, wherever possible, be cherished and it is one of the basic principles upon which our law is founded. For that reason, two parties have always been permitted to enter freely into an agreement on whatever terms and conditions they mutually agree. However, in regard to contracts of passage (passenger tickets usually, but not always, contain the full terms and conditions of the agreement somewhere upon them, albeit in very small print), one of the most significant points to be determined in coming to the decision as to whether there is liability for injury or not is whether sufficient notice was given to the passenger in advance of the contract so as to enable the shipowner (i.e. the putative defendant to an action for breach of contract) to say that all the terms and conditions of the passenger contract were made sufficiently known to the passenger (including the exclusion clause) and that he entered into the contact fully aware of the risks involved and the circumstances in which a shipowner or carrier could escape liability even if he had (from a point of view of wrongdoing or negligence) caused either personally or through the acts, neglect or default of his employees injury to the passenger concerned.

Previously in the UK, passengers have been met often with a good defence under the exclusion clause which would allow them only a cause of action against the particular member of the crew, or the Master himself, who might have been personally responsible for the injury or accident which the passenger suffered. In that event an action against the individual member of the crew would lie under the law of tort and it is almost certain that the shipowner (i.e. the employer) would ultimately support his employee in his troubles and in practice would bear the financial burden himself.

A leading case on this was *Adler* v *Dickson*, below.

## Passengers

*Adler* v *Dickson* [1954] 2 Lloyd's Rep. 267, CA
A female passenger suffered injury during a voyage in the *Himalaya* as a result of the negligence of a member of the ship's crew. Her ticket contained an exclusion clause, freeing the ship's owner from liability for death or injury howsoever caused. The court found that the shipowner could escape liability by reason of the terms of carriage but that the passenger had a valid case in tort against the negligent crew member direct. (It is of interest to note that it was this case and this vessel which gave rise to the now well-known *Himalaya* clause in cargo carriage contracts contained in bills of lading.)

Since the early 1960s, however, there have been signs that the courts are tending to look with less favour on the apparently impregnable position in which carriers of passengers for value seek to place themselves by contract. Up until that time the courts had refused to be deflected from the basic doctrine that a contract of passage is only concluded with the delivery of the passage ticket into the passenger's hands. In *Cockerton* v *Naviera Aznar SA* [1960] 2 Lloyd's Rep. 450, which also concerned injury of a passenger at sea, the judge ruled that the contract of passage was not perfected until the delivery of the ticket to the passenger. 'When' said the judge, 'a person enters into such a contact he is buying a "chose in action" of which the ticket is the evidence'. He is, in effect, buying a series of rights, the right to be conveyed, the right to occupy specified accommodation, the right to enjoy amenities, food, etc. (Compare the 'buying' of a bill of lading which buys, inter alia, the right to claim possession of the specified goods.) Up until that time the ticket itself was considered to be the contractual document and the ticket holder or passenger was bound by the terms and conditions. (This is borne out by the long line of so-called 'ticket' cases (e.g. *Parker* v *South Eastern Railway Co* (1877) 2 CPD 416, CA; *Thompson* v *London, Midland & Scottish Railway Co Ltd* [1930] 1 KB 41, CA; *Olley* v *Marlborough Court Ltd* [1949] 1 KB 532, CA) which admittedly are not sea-carriage disputes; Parker and Thompson being railway passengers and Olley being a guest in a hotel, but nevertheless the principle is the same.)

In sharp contrast to the *Cockerton* case is *The Hollingsworth* case below.

*The Eagle* [1977] 2 Lloyd's Rep. 70
A 71-year old woman passenger suffered severe injuries when her chair tilted in the ship's restaurant during a heavy swell in the Bay of Biscay and she fell, striking her head. Her passage had been booked by a friend and the passage ticket, which the friend eventually gave to her, contained a customary exclusion of liability clause. The attention of prospective passengers to the fact that there were terms and conditions of carriage was drawn in the brochure. The most serious of the allegations supporting the lady's claim for damages were (a) that the chair was not attached to the floor; and (b) that it did not have splayed legs to give it a greater degree of stability. The defendant shipowners denied liability and relied on the exclusion clause in the ticket.

*Held:* that the shipowners were negligent in providing a chair of the 'vertical-leg' type. They were also in breach of their statutory duties under the Occupiers' Liability Act 1957. The contract of passage was concluded before delivery of the ticket to the passenger and the shipowners could not regard the ticket itself as the contractual document. The fact that the passenger's friend had read the brochure which drew his attention to the existence of certain terms and conditions was not sufficient reason to allow the shipowners to escape liability. The lady was awarded £600 as agreed special damages and £5,000 general damages.

Clearly the conclusion must be drawn from the court's more recent attitude that the delivery of the ticket to the passenger is not the point at which the contract is deemed to be perfected. The contract, on the contrary, is concluded before that, at the time of the reserving of the passage or the signing (if it is signed) of the booking form in the travel agent's office. Colonel Bowley who arranged and booked Mrs Hollingsworth's passage in the *Eagle* was said by the court to be a reasonable man (the 'legal' man on the Clapham omnibus) and he admitted to being 'horrified' when he had time to sit down and quietly study the terms of the purported passage contract printed in the passage ticket. Even a reasonable man who has been actually made aware, through reading a travel brochure in the course of inquiries prior to the acceptance of the booking, that a passenger is carried on certain stipulated terms and conditions, would not reasonably contemplate that the terms were as onerous or 'exclusive' as were actually printed in the ticket eventually handed to him at which time, of course, a reasonably minded passenger is hardly likely to want to cancel his booking. (See also *McCutcheon* v *David MacBrayne Ltd* [1964] 1 Lloyd's Rep. 16.)

A relatively recent interesting case regarding the incorporation of terms and conditions came before the Australian court.

*The Mikhail Lermontov* [1991] 2 Lloyd's Rep. 155
A passenger received a booking form on paying a deposit for a cruise which stated 'Contract of Carriage for travel as set out . . . will be made only at the time of issuing of tickets and will be subject to the conditions and regulations printed on the tickets'. The passenger then paid the balance of the fare and received a ticket containing terms and conditions limiting the shipowners' liability for personal injury and personal effects. One question was whether the ticket terms and conditions were part of the contract.

The Court of Appeal of New South Wales of Australia decided that the contract of carriage came into force at the time appointed and notified in the booking form. At that time the passenger had not had a reasonable opportunity to see and agree to the terms and conditions which the shipowners sought subsequently to impose on her by the delivery of the ticket. Once the contract was made it was not open, without fresh agreement for further terms and conditions to be imposed by the unilateral action of one contracting party. The passenger was entitled to take the view that she would be issued with a ticket which would contain no unusual provisions, specifically no provisions of which she was not on notice limiting the shipowners liability for claims in respect of the luggage. The shipowners were not entitled to rely on the conditions under which they limited liability.

The Unfair Contract Terms Act 1977, which came into effect in England on 1 February 1978, has effectively deprived shipowners of their ability to insert such unreasonable exclusion clauses in their contracts and rely on them being held valid. It is likely that there will be more successful claims lodged by passengers against the shipowners carrying them than there were before 1978.

Also contained in many passage contracts and/or tickets is a limitation clause which limits the liability of the carrying shipowner to a certain maximum amount of money in the event of a claim for damages for personal injury or illness brought by the passenger against him under the terms and conditions of the passage contract. The US courts tend to disregard such a limitation clause as being against public policy and their courts have, in the past, tended in individual cases to disregard the law of contract generally in determining disputes between passengers and shipowners and have applied the general principles of the law of negligence and determined a shipowner's liability on that basis rather than on the basis of an alleged breach of contract.

What is applicable in contracts of this nature, and indeed in many other contracts as well, is the idea that there must be no misdescription by the shipowner when he advertises for business and attracts passengers upon his ship. Misrepresentation may lead to a passenger's entering into a contract that he would not have entered into had he known the true facts and circumstances and, as in every other contract, there must initially be an offer and acceptance and the minds of the two parties to the contract must be ad idem. It must, however, be remembered that it is always possible for a party to contract out of his common law obligations and, as the principles of common law apply to a passenger's rights, then (within reason) a shipowner is quite within his rights in contracting as far as may be possible for him out of his common law obligations.

Bearing in mind that lack of care and negligence plays a great part in the practical relationship between a carrying shipowner and his employees and the carried passenger, the idea of personal carelessness and fault on the part of the passenger himself is relevant and a passenger, like any crewman or shore-worker on board a vessel, can be accused of contributory negligence causing his own injuries and this, under the law of contributory negligence in the UK (see the Law Reform (Contributory Negligence) Act 1945), can operate to reduce substantially the damages which can be claimed by a passenger or possibly even to have the case dismissed altogether against the shipowner. It is said frequently that a claimant is entirely the 'author of his own misfortune'. Most frequently, of course, it is the case that both parties are to blame, passenger and shipowner, and it is for the court in that event to decide and apportion the relative degrees of fault on each side.

The Merchant Shipping Acts, ever since the main Act in 1894, have always made special provisions for the safeguarding of the conditions and lives generally of all classes of passengers, particularly in the old emigrant-type ships where persons of small financial means were obliged to travel from one country to another and in a class of accommodation which would not normally be enjoyed by the average person travelling for pleasure; for example, steerage passages. Over the years the various amendments to the Merchant Shipping Acts, culminating in the major amendments of 1949 and 1964 which enacted two international safety Conventions held just prior to those respective years, have developed relatively strict rules which govern and regulate the construction and maintenance of ships and their equipment. Passenger ships, so far as the safety Conventions and the safety laws are concerned, are said to be ships which are constructed to carry more than 12 passengers. It will be recalled that one of the most tragic maritime accidents of all time was the disaster involving the *Titanic* in 1912 where a very large number of people drowned in the North Atlantic. One of the main causes of this tragic loss of life was the fact that the *Titanic* was not equipped with water-tight bulk-heads and it was impossible to isolate the inrush of sea water into the ship and confine it to certain parts of the ship, thus possibly preventing the sinking of the ship altogether. In those days the stringent laws regarding construction of passenger ships were not in force and it is, of course, necessary now for a passenger ship to be constructed with water-tight bulk-heads as one of the many requirements of improved safety conditions in ships carrying in excess of 12 passengers. Further more stringent safety regulations have been introduced since the tragic ferry disasters of the *Herald of Free Enterprise* and *Estonia*. Under the Merchant Shipping Act 1995 which came into force on 1 January 1996 the Secretary of State can make safety regulations and specific offences exist for passenger ships.

Frequently it happens that a passenger ship is in collision with another vessel and there is blame on both sides. In that event the passenger in the carrying ship would be perfectly free to bring his action in negligence against the owner of the non-carrying ship to recover full damages. In fact, he is free to sue the owner of either ship, but of course his relationship with the carrying shipowner would be a contractual relationship and the contract of passage in past years could, as has been said, have had sufficiently clear and sufficiently clearly advertised exclusion clauses in it to allow the carrying shipowner to escape responsibility. However, the owner of the non-carrying ship is not allowed to plead the contributory negligence of the carrying vessel so as to reduce the damages which he, the non-carrying shipowner, would be condemned to pay the passenger who had suffered injury.

The time limitation period within which claims for personal injury of this nature should be brought is customarily three years from the date of the accident. It is possible to obtain extensions of time as in other types of claim provided that it is done with the leave of the court concerned.

The Unfair Contract Terms Act 1977, briefly referred to earlier, has now imposed further limitations on the extent of liability for breach of contract or for negligence under the laws of the UK. The Act affects, among other types of contract, the contract of passage contained in passage tickets and, as a result, onerous exclusion clauses must necessarily disappear. The accent of the Act is on 'reasonableness'; and any contract term must satisfy a strictly defined test of reasonableness. However, the test of reasonableness has no application to any clause which deals specifically with death and personal injury and avoidance of liability therefor (section 2). In the first subsection of section 2 the simple statement is made that a person cannot by reference to any contract term or notice exclude or restrict his liability for death or personal injury resulting from negligence. Subsection (3) of the same section would appear to emphasize that the awareness of any such clause purporting to so exclude or restrict liability does not of itself imply voluntary acceptance of its validity by the other party.

## ATHENS CONVENTION

The Athens Convention relating to the Carriage of Passengers and their Luggage by Sea 1974 came into force internationally on 28 April 1987. It was originally brought into effect in the UK by section 14 of the Merchant Shipping Act 1979 which came into force on 30 April 1987 (by S.I. 1987 No. 635). It applies to any contract made on or after 1 January 1981 for the carriage of passengers for reward with or without their luggage where either:

(a) the contract is for international carriage and is made in the UK;

(b) the contract is for international carriage where either the place of departure or of destination is in the U.K. or
(c) any contract where the places of departure and destination are in the geographical area consisting of the UK, the Channel Islands and the Isle of Man and whereunder there is no intermediate port of call outside that area (the latter maintains the interim provision of SI 1980 No 1092).

However, section 14 of the Merchant Shipping Act 1979 has now been repealed by the Merchant Shipping Act 1995, which states that the Convention relating to the carriage of passengers and their luggage by sea shall have the force of law in the United Kingdom (see sections 183, 184 and Schedule 6).

Amongst the definitions contained in Article 1 is that of a carrier (a person who concludes a contract of passenger carriage, or on whose behalf such a contract is concluded, *whether or not* he actually performs the carriage). This could include tour operators, ferry companies and cruise companies. A distinction is drawn between a performing carrier who is someone *other* than the carrier who wholly or partly performs the carriage: he could be shipowner, charterer or operator. So if the vessel Sea is owned by company X and chartered to company Y who issues his own passenger ticket, company Y will be the carrier and company X will be the performing carrier. The carrier and performing carrier are jointly and severally liable and both can rely on the terms of the Athens Convention.

### *Basis of liability*

Under Article 3 the carrier is liable for damage suffered as a result of the death of or personal injury to a passenger and the loss of or damage to luggage if the incident was due to the fault or neglect of the carrier or of his servants or agents acting within the scope of their employment. The claimant passenger has to prove such fault on the part of the carrier or his employees or agents, unless the passenger's death or injury or loss of or damage to his cabin luggage results directly from shipwreck by collision, stranding, explosion or fire, or defect in the ship, in which case the burden of proof will be reversed. Fault or neglect is presumed unless the contrary is proved in the case of claims for loss or damage to 'other luggage' (as opposed to 'cabin luggage').

Under Article 1 'luggage' is defined as any article or vehicle carried under a contract of carriage excluding articles or vehicles carried under a charterparty, bill of lading or other contract primarily concerned with the carriage of goods. Live animals are also excluded. 'Cabin luggage' is defined as the passenger's personal effects in his cabin or in his possession, custody or control. This also includes luggage in the passenger's vehicle except for the application of limitation of liability under Article 8.

Article 4 states that the carrier remains liable for the entire carriage even though the performance of the carriage or part thereof has been entrusted to a performing carrier. The carrier is liable for the acts and omissions of his own servants and agents acting within the scope of their employment and for the acts and omissions of the performing carrier. The performing carrier is also liable for incidents occurring during the part of the carriage performed by him. The liability of the carrier and performing carrier is joint and several but any right of recourse as between them is not prejudiced by the provisions of Article 4. Article 5 provides that the carrier is not liable for the loss of or damage to monies, negotiable securities, gold, silverware, jewellery, ornaments, works of art or other valuables except where such valuables have been deposited with the carrier for the agreed purpose of safekeeping in which case unless a higher limit is agreed, the carrier shall not be liable beyond the limits contained in Article 8. Under Article 6 the court may relieve the carrier wholly or partly from his liability if he establishes that the death of or personal injury or loss of or damage to luggage was caused or contributed to by the passenger, i.e. contributory negligence of the passenger.

### *Limit of liability*

Originally the limit of liability under Articles 7 and 8 was expressed in gold francs as follows:

| | *Poincaré gold francs* |
|---|---|
| For death or personal injury | PGF 700,000 |
| For cabin luggage (excluding luggage in or on a vehicle) | PGF 12,500 |
| For a vehicle and luggage in it or on it | PGF 50,000 |
| For other luggage | PGF 18,000 |

The limits for the first, second and fourth of the above items are per passenger and for the third per vehicle.

Item 3 leaves open the question of how the limited compensation should be appointed where several individuals (e.g. passengers in a bus) make a claim. Only when the Convention's provisions are finally tested will this doubt be resolved. However gold francs have been substitued by special drawing rights (units of account) as defined by the International Monetary Fund due to the 1976 Protocol to the Athens Convention which came into force on 30 April 1989. For the purpose of converting from special drawing rights to sterling the amounts stated in Articles 7 and 8 in respect of which judgment is given, one special drawing right shall be treated as equal to such a sum in sterling as the International Monetary Fund have fixed as being the equivalent of one special drawing right for (a) the day on which the judgment is given; or (b) if no sum has been fixed for that day, the last day before that day for which the sum has been fixed. Furthermore, a certificate given by or on behalf of the Treasury stating certain facts shall be conclusive evidence for the purposes of Articles 7–9 of the Convention. This is now contained in Article 5 of Part II of Schedule 6 to the Merchant Shipping Act 1995.

Therefore the limits of liability under the Athens Convention are:

**Passengers**

| | |
|---|---|
| For death or personal injury | 46,666 units of account |
| For cabin luggage (excluding luggage in or on a vehicle) | 833 units of account |
| For a vehicle and luggage in it or on it | 3,333 units of account |
| For other luggage | 1,200 units of account. |

Article 8(4) states the carrier and passenger may agree that the liabilty of the carrier shall be subject to a deductible not exceeding 117 special drawing rights for damages to a vehicle and 13 special drawing rights per passenger for loss of or damage to luggage. The carrier cannot stipulate lower limits than that provided in the Convention. However the carrier can agree to higher limits with the passenger provided that any agreement is express and in writing (Article 10). Any higher limit will not bind the performing carrier unless the latter agrees to this expressly and in writing (Article 4(3)). Interest on damages and legal costs are not included in the limits of liability contained in Articles 7 and 8.

The Secretary of State can increase the limit of liability for personal injury claims in relation to a carrier whose principal place of business is in the United Kingdom (see Article 4 of Part II of Schedule 6 to the Merchant Shipping Act 1995).

Following the *Herald of Free Enterprise* disaster the Secretary of State increased the limit of liability for death or personal injury to a passenger to 1,525,000 gold francs where the carrier has his principal place of business in the UK. This came into force on the 1 June 1987 by the Carriage of Passengers and their Luggage by Sea (United Kingdom Carriers) Order 1987, SI 1987 No. 855. References to 1,525,000 gold francs were substituted by references to 100,000 units of account as of 10 November 1989 by virtue of the Carriage of Passengers and their Luggage by Sea (United Kingdom Carriers) (Amendment) Order 1989, SI 1989/1880.

A new Protocol was approved by an IMO conference in London in March 1990 to enhance compensation and to establish a simplified procedure for updating the amounts of limitation. Once this comes into force the limit of liability mentioned above will be increased to 175,000, 1,800, 10,000 and 1,200 units of account.

The servant or agent of the carrier or of the performing carrier can limit his liability for death of or personal injury to a passenger, or for loss of or damage to luggage or vehicles incurred whilst acting within the scope of his employment (Article 11). The performing carrier can also limit his liability.

### *Loss of right to limit*

A significant feature of the Athens Convention limitation provisions is that the right to limit will be lost if the loss or damage is proved to have resulted from an act or omission of the carrier done with the intent to cause such damage or recklessly and with knowledge that such loss or damage would probably result (Article 13, paragraph 1). The employees or agents of the carrier, who by the provisions of Article 11 can avail themselves generally of the benefits and defences available to the carrier, similarly are denied the right to limit if it is proved that they are guilty of such reckless or deliberate conduct (Article 13, paragraph 2). A proposal, before the Convention was finally drafted, that the carrier himself should be denied the right to limit if his employees or agents were guilty of reckless conduct, was rejected. Also rejected was a proposal that a carrier should be liable for any delay to a passenger. The conduct of the carrier alone is relevant in determining whether or not he can limit liability. The conduct of his servant or agent is irrelevant unless that servant is the alter ego of the carrier.

*The Lion* [1990] 2 Lloyd's Rep. 144
The plaintiffs' coach was driven on to the defendants' ferry, *Lion* at Boulogne for a crossing to Dover. The coach was not secured. During the crossing the vessel took a violent roll to starboard and the coach was badly damaged. The plaintiffs claimed that the damage was caused by the reckless conduct of the defendants' servants, the crew of the ferry. The defendants denied that there was any fault and even so they were entitled to limit their liability.

*Held*: that the word 'carrier' in the Athens Convention did not include the servant or agents of the carrier. The defendants were entitled to limit their liability under Article 8 of the Athens Convention and that was not affected by any question of whether any servant or agent of theirs who was not an alter ego of the defendants was guilty of an act of omission of the kind referred to in Article 13.

Article 14 provides that no claim for damages for death or personal injury to a passenger or for loss or damage to luggage may be brought against the carrier or performing carrier otherwise than in accordance with the Athens Convention. As mentioned previously in Chapter 9, Article 19 of the Athens Convention provides that such Convention does not modify the rights or duties of the carrier, the performing carrier and their servants or agents under other Conventions such as the 1976 London Convention. The effect of both these Conventions has not been tested in the English courts to determine which Convention would have precedence if both were applicable to the same incident. *The Herald of Free Enterprise* case was settled short of court proceedings and the *Bowbelle/Marchioness* tragedy in the River Thames is another example of both Conventions applying. In the latter case the Shipowners paid the limitation fund into court under the 1976 London Convention.

In fact article 12 of Part II of Schedule 6 to the Merchant Shipping Act 1995 provides: 'It is hereby declared that nothing in the Convention affects the operation of section 185 of this Act (which limits a shipowner's liability in certain cases of loss of life, injury or damage)'. Article 13 provides 'Nothing in section 186 of this Act (which among other things limits a shipowner's liability for the loss or damage of goods in certain cases) shall relieve a person of any liability imposed on him by the Convention'.

### *Time bar for legal action*

The time bar period for the beginning of actions for damages is two years, and the period starts running from the date of disembarkation of the passenger in the event of personal injury, or in the case of death occuring during carriage, from the date when the passengers should have disembarked. When death results later from an injury incurred during carriage, the time is to run from the date of death with the proviso that this period shall not exceed three years from the date of disembarkation (Article 16).

In the case of luggage claims, the time shall run from the date of disembarkation or the date when disembarkation should have taken place, whichever is the later. The period of limitation may be extended by a declaration of the carrier or by agreement of the parties, in writing, after the cause of action has arisen. Article 15 provides that unless written notice of damage to luggage is given to the carrier or his agent within certain periods of time then it is presumed that the passenger received the luggage undamaged unless the contrary is proved. A recent case on the question of time limit is *Higham* v. *Stena Sealink* [1996] 2 Lloyd's Rep. 26. The plaintiff, while a passenger on the defendant's ferry sailing between Holyhead and Dunlaoghrie in the Republic of Ireland, suffered injury when she slipped on some broken glass on the deck and fell. Over two years later she issued proceedings in the Liverpool county court claiming damages for negligence and/or breach of statutory duty on the part of the defendant. At the time, the Athens Convention had the force of law in the United Kingdom pursuant to section 14 of and Schedule 3 to the Merchant Shipping Act 1979 albeit this has now been replaced by section 183 of and Schedule 6 to the Merchant Shipping Act 1995. Article 16 of the Athens Convention provides for a two-year time limit for bringing claims for personal injury from the date of the passenger's disembarkation. The defendants applied to the Liverpool county court to strike out the plaintiff's claim on the basis that the proceedings were issued outside the time limit laid down in Article 16 of the Athens Convention. This application was dismissed on the basis that section 33 of the Limitation Act 1980 applied to this action for personal injury, and the judge in the exercise of her discretion disapplied the time limit. On appeal, the action was struck out. The basis of the judge's decision, in a nutshell, was that the words 'suspension' and 'interruption' as contained in Article 16(3) of the Athens Convention were inapplicable to section 33 of the Limitation Act 1980 so that the two-year time bar was effective. The plaintiff then appealed to the Court of Appeal which rejected the defendants' argument that section 39 of the Limitation Act excluded altogether the application of the 1980 Act to the Athens Convention. The whole of Part II of the 1980 Act was potentially applicable to the Merchant Shipping Act. Section 33 of the Limitation Act (which is headed *Discretionary Exclusion of Time Limits for Actions in Respect of Personal Injuries or Death*) empowered the court to exclude altogether a period which already had run its course and could not possibly be treated as a ground for suspension or interruption eligible under Article 16(3). Even if it was so eligible, section 33(1) which expressly referred to 'Provisions of section 11 or 11A or 12 of the Act' (which set down time limits) would not be construed as embracing the Athens Convention. The plaintiff's appeal was dismissed and her was claim time barred.

Prior to section 14 of the Merchant Shipping Act 1979, which has now been replaced by the Merchant Shipping Act 1995, coming into force the Athens Convention was implemented in the UK by virtue of SI 1980 No 1092. By another statutory instrument (SI 1980 No 1125) a carrier was required to give notice to passengers of specific provisions of the Athens Convention. Such provisions are those relating to (a) valuables, (b) the limit of the carrier's liabilty for death or personal injury and for loss or damage to his luggage. Notice of these specific provisions is to be given before departure and it is further provided that where a ticket is issued, and it is practicable to do so, the ticket itself shall contain a statement specifying these points. Failure to comply with these requirements rendered the carrier guilty of an offence and liable on summary conviction to a fine (SI 1987 No 703). In the case of *The Lion* [1990] 2 Lloyd's Rep. 144 it was decided that the carrier could limit liability under the Athens Convention even though they had failed to give notice to the passenger as required by SI 1980 No 1125.

# CHAPTER 13

# PILOTAGE

It is not intended within the confines of this book to cover the administration aspects of pilotage in the UK, except only in brief detail.[1] This chapter concentrates on the rights and liabilities of, and the general legal relationships between, ship's Masters, shipowners, pilots and third parties with whom they come into contact.

Where safety of life or property is concerned, whether at sea or otherwise, it is almost essential that there should be some degree of government control. Such control has for years been exercised in the UK by central government under powers granted by statute and by local government authorities who from time to time pass by-laws fashioned to suit the needs and individual requirements of the local area concerned. The Secretary of State for Transport has responsibility for the promulgating of 'pilotage orders'. The guidelines for these orders are laid down at the beginning of Part 2 of the Pilotage Act 1913. What distinguishes the Pilotage Act from other general statutes which confer powers to make subordinate legislation is that not all the pilotage orders promulgated by the Secretary of State require confirmation by statutory instrument.

The Pilotage Act 1987 came into force on 1 October 1988. The Act is divided into four parts subheaded:

1. Pilotage functions of competent harbour authorities.
2. General provisions governing pilotage.
3. Winding up of existing pilotage organization.
4. Supplementary.

A definition of a 'pilotage authority' may be found in the Pilotage Authorities (Limitation of Liability) Act 1936:

'. . . a body of persons or authority incorporated, constituted or established as a pilotage authority by a pilotage order made under the Pilotage Act, 1913, and where any existing body of persons or authority constituted or established for other purposes and with other duties or any committee of any such existing body of persons or authority are constituted or established a pilotage authority by any such order includes that body of persons, authority or committee.'

## WHAT IS A PILOT?

Any person not belonging to a ship who has the conduct of her is a pilot. This statutory definition was adopted as early as 1854 by the Merchant Shipping Act

1. The reader is recommended to refer to *The Law of Harbours Coasts and Pilotage* (4th ed) by Douglas & Geen (Lloyd's of London Press Ltd, 1997).

of that year. A consequential amendment to the Pilotage Act 1987 made by the Merchant Shipping Act 1995 is the definition of a pilot 'means any person not belonging to a ship who has the conduct thereof'. A Master is defined in the Merchant Shipping Act 1995 as 'includes every person (except a pilot) having command or charge of a ship and, in relation to a fishing vessel, means the skipper' (see section 313). Such 'conduct' is confined to the process of navigation. Unless a ship requires to be navigated (or 'conducted', if the statutory term is used), there is no need for a pilot. He is in charge of a vessel only to the extent that he is in sole control of the navigation.

How then does the Master's practical role and legal position relate to the pilot when a pilot is taken on board?

The question of the legal relationship between a ship's Master and a pilot is another matter. There is no doubt that the scope of a pilot's duties have over the years been clearly defined. That he has exclusive control and conduct of the ship is seldom disputed, but this is very different from having command of the ship. No reasonable person could suppose that the pilot has any disciplinary power in the vessel or any authoritative personal command over the ship's crew. The Master is never in this sense superseded. Delegation of power even in the navigation of the vessel should never be confused with a total abrogation of authority. Following on from this, the Master has the ability with impunity and without prejudicing the shipowner's legal position to interfere legally with the pilot's actions so long as he acts reasonably and with good motive under the circumstances. Conversely, if he fails to interfere where his own instincts based on his own skill and knowledge tell him not to remain silent and this would be detrimental to the interests of safe navigation and the safety of the ship and the property of others generally, he could be adjudged eventually to have contributed to any resulting accident.

Interference, however, is not a matter of half-measures, vague suggestions or mere tentative advice. It is based on whether or not there has been a positive order by the Master either directly revoking an existing instruction by the pilot given earlier or filling in a gap left by the absence of any firm order from the pilot.

Divided authority has traditionally been the cause of disaster. Conflict would seem to be inevitable. We know how dangerous a car becomes when driven at the same time by husband *and* wife (sitting beside him). One theory of the pilot's role is that he is perhaps the ship's Master's most expert navigational aid; unique because he is a human being not a machine such as a radar set or echo sounder. However, accidents resulting from hostility, mistrust or antagonism between Master and pilot are happily rare. A qualified pilot has every right to be proud of his specialized knowledge and ability and to expect to be given carte blanche to make instantaneous decisions when required and where there is no time to consult the Master. Conversely, however, he has the right to expect co-operation from the Master and crew and assistance if the ship which he is conducting has special or awkward handling characteristics with which he would be unfamiliar. What a pilot is *not*, purely and simply, is an adviser. This would be almost an insult to his role on board. Such a description is absolutely inconsistent not only with the statutory definition but also with the practical concept of a pilot; he who, being a 'stranger' to the ship, has 'conduct' of her. As will be seen there are several passages of the current and foregoing pilotage statutes which would have little, if any, significance if the pilot was merely an adviser. Indeed, the statutory expressions used on several occasions are 'he takes charge of', 'obtains charge of', 'has charge of'.

A view of the courts in the early 1950s was expressed during the hearing of the limitation action by the Master and part-owner of the vessel *Hans Hoth*, below.

*The Hans Hoth* [1952] 2 Lloyd's Rep. 341
This case concerned a collision in broad daylight between a British and German ship at the entrance to Dover harbour. The *Hans Hoth* was solely to blame. There was a compulsory pilot on board who had disregarded the signal displayed by the harbour authority prohibiting vessels entering while another vessel was leaving. The Master was in control of the engines and was on the bridge. The shipowners instituted limitation proceedings. There were three part-owners of the vessel, one of whom was the Master himself. The question was whether the Master was personally at fault so as to defeat the motion to limit.

*Held*: that the Master should not be blamed for failing to post a special look-out forward. Although the Master was under a duty to assist in navigation when a compulsory pilot was on board, this duty did not extend to matters of local significance. In rejecting an argument that the Master had by his own actions or lack of care directly contributed to the collision which occurred the court said that 'it would be too much to expect him to question each of the pilot's actions in regard to his interpretation of local port signals. A reasonably prudent Master is entitled to rely on a pilot's guidance.'

Although the issue in the above case which was of particular importance was the right to limit liability and the possibly 'two-hatted' role of the Master, the incident also emphasizes the particular personal value of a pilot and the services he renders to the vessel and her Master in matters of purely local significance where, clearly, specialized knowledge of local rules and customs is vital to safe navigation.

Many lucid comments have been made by learned judges through the years on the respective duties of pilot and ship's Master. To pick one at random. Lord Alverstone in *The Tactician* (1907) 10 Asp MLC 534, 537, said:

'I think the cardinal principle to be borne in mind in these cases is that the pilot is in sole charge of the ship and that all directions as to speed, course, stopping and reversing and everything of that kind are for the pilot. But side by side with that principle is the other principle that the pilot is entitled to the fullest assistance of a competent crew, of a competent look-out and a well-found ship.'

To comment historically for a moment, the UK's laws regarding pilotage were codified in the original Merchant Shipping Act 1894 (Part X), the relevant sections being sections 572 to 632. However, significant changes in the law were enacted by the Pilotage Act 1913, which was designed to some extent to enact into the legal system in the UK certain provisions of the Brussels Convention 1910 to unify certain rules pertaining to Collisions at Sea and which, as a result, virtually replaced Part X of the 1894 Act. In particular, section 633 of the 1894 Act was entirely replaced by section 15 of the 1913 Pilotage Act which laid down that—'the owner or Master of a vessel navigating under circumstances in which pilotage is compulsory shall be answerable for any loss or damage caused by the vessel or by any fault of the navigation of the vessel in the same manner as he would if pilotage were not compulsory'. This section did not take effect until

January 1918, the last year of World War One. By this amendment, law in the UK was brought into line with that of the other maritime countries. Where the law had previously indicated that a shipowner was *not* vicariously liable for the acts, neglects or defaults of a compulsory pilot, from 1918 onwards he was so vicariously liable.

*Clark* v *Hutchinson* (1924) 18 Ll.L.Rep. 27
This case involved a claim by the widow of a chief engineer for the death of her husband who had been drowned as a result of a collision due to the fault of the compulsory pilot on board. The Liverpool district was involved and the relevant section of the Pilotage Act 1913 was section 15. As a pilot (even a compulsory pilot) is considered the servant of the shipowner, the defence of common employment succeeded.

Section 15 of the 1913 Act was 'transplanted' into section 35 of the 1983 Act without variation in the wording, and, by the most recent amendment of all, the wording of section 16 of the 1987 Act reads:

'The fact that a ship is being navigated in an area and in circumstances in which pilotage is compulsory for it shall not affect any liability of the owner or Master of the ship for any loss or damage caused by the ship or by the manner in which it is navigated'.

This, in even simpler words effectively preserves the principle that, even if a ship is under command of a compulsory pilot at the time when the ship may cause harm, loss or damage to third persons or the property of third persons, the legal liability for such harm, loss or damage lies with the ship and/or her Master and/or her owners.

*Towerfield (Owners)* v *Workington Harbour & Dock Board* (1950) 84 Ll.L.Rep. 233, HL
The ship had taken ground on entering port, had broken her back and had become a constructive total loss. The shipowner sued the harbour board alleging breach of duty, warranty and negligence in that it had failed to keep the port approaches free from obstruction. The harbour board denied the charges and counter-claimed for the damage to its property which, it argued, was due to the negligence of those in the vessel. The issue centred around the interpretation of the word 'answerable' and its meaning in the context of section 15(1). The case found its way eventually to the House of Lords where their Lordships took the view that the word was intended to include responsibility for actionable errors of navigation resulting not only in damage to the property of others but also in damage to the ship in which the pilot is carrying out his duties.

Damage was done to the ship and to harbour dock property through the fault of a compulsory pilot. The effect of section 15 of the Pilotage Act 1913 (temporarily re-enacted in the 1983 Act and how enshrined in section 16 of the 1987 Act) was to: (*a*) debar the shipowner from claiming damage to his ship either in tort or in contract; and (*b*) make him liable for the damage done to the harbour authority's property. It should, however, be borne in mind that the circumstances from which this litigation arose occurred before the introduction of the Law Reform (Contributory Negligence) Act 1945 when the existing rule was that one party was debarred from claiming damages from another party when the plaintiff was partly to blame for his own loss of damage. It was *The Towerfield* case as much as any which established that the word 'answerable' in section 15 of the Pilotage Act 1913 (whose sense is preserved by section 16 of the 1987 Act) means 'responsible' and the liability of the ship's owners is involved both where the damage is sustained by their own ship and where damage is done to the property of others. It is the role of a pilot basically to give the benefit of his specialized local knowledge in an area which will naturally be strange and unfamiliar to the ship's Master and crew, but nevertheless the Master still bears ultimate responsibility. It is still incumbent on the Master and his crew to be alert and to give such assistance to the pilot as may be required. They do not, when the ship is in charge of a pilot, become as it were 'mere passengers' on board their ship (see *SS Alexander Shukoff* v *SS Gothland* [1921] AC 216, 223, HL).

A Canadian case serves to illustrate the operation of section 15 of the Pilotage Act 1913 (although the case of course was decided under the equivalent Canadian Act), and presumably is equally illustrative of the effect of section 16 of the 1987 Act.

*The Irish Stardust* [1977] 1 Lloyd's Rep. 195, Federal Court of Canada
The vessel *Irish Stardust*, owned by the plaintiffs, sailed from Kitimat to Port Mellon, a compulsory pilotage area, in charge of a pilot. Although the pilot felt inclined to take the ship along the traditional route, he decided, being a new pilot, to follow the traffic separation scheme and thus comply with the Department of Transport's recommendations. Also his decision was influenced by the presence of an oncoming ship the *Island Princess*. Shortly before midnight the *Irish Stardust* grounded and sustained damage. The owners of the *Irish Stardust* claimed damages from the Crown, alleging that the Department of Transport had been negligent in putting into operation and recommending the use of a scheme which was dangerous and unsafe for navigation. They contended that the vessel's grounding was the result of the sea passage being inadequately lit and because a particular sector light had not been installed. It was argued by the Crown in defence that the grounding was directly caused by the failure of those in charge of the vessel, including her Master and the pilot.

*Held*: for the Crown for these reasons: (a) the ship was off course when she grounded; (b) if the pilot had suspected there might be difficulties he still had the choice of taking the alternative northern route and to so advise the oncoming vessel of his intentions; (c) those on board were never misled by any navigational aids provided by the scheme which were all in due position and duly published on notices and charts; (d) those on board were not entitled to look for navigational aids which were not there and which they knew were not there; and (e) it was the plaintiff's burden to establish the cause of the accident and merely to suggest that the placing of an additional light would have prevented the accident was insufficient. The plaintiff shipowner was accordingly responsible under the Pilotage Act for the pilot's negligence.

## WHAT IS COMPULSORY PILOTAGE?

Two of the four parts of which the Pilotage Act 1987 consists contains provisions relating to compulsory pilotage. Section 7 of Part 1 allows a competent harbour authority (and that is defined in section 1 as requiring it to have two features: (a) possessing statutory powers in relation to the regulation of shipping movements and the safety of navigation within its harbour *and* (b) whose harbour falls wholly or partly within an active former pilotage district), if it considers it should do so in the interest of safety to direct (by way of what is to be known as a 'pilotage direction') that pilotage shall be compulsory for ships navigating in that area, or any part of that area. Such a direction shall not apply to ships less than 20 metres long or to fishing vessels having a registered length of less than 47.5 metres. So as presumably not to spring such directions 'over night' on unsuspecting vessels customarily using the area, the authority is obliged to consult owners of such ships beforehand and anyone else carrying on harbour operations (section 7(4)). Section 8 provides for the authority to grant pilotage exception certificates to any applicant, Master or mate, whose skill, competence or experience it considers to be sufficient for navigating in the area without a pilot's assistance. Sufficient knowledge of English could also be a prerequirement for an exception certificate.

Historically, the idea of compulsory pilotage was based on the need for national security and the protection of life and property in harbour and port areas. This is the rationale of compulsory pilotage generally in those countries where it exists by law. Some say though that this in nothing more than a possible additional reason, that compulsory pilotage is justified as a means of raising revenue. What is clear is that its purpose is defeated if the law is observed merely by a compulsory pilot being taken on board but his services not being used. Only the most illogical of persons would argue that a law which requires a compulsory pilot to be taken on board should not also require that such a pilot should also take charge of and 'conduct' the ship. From this it follows that if a Master without justification interferes with the actions, orders or instructions of a compulsory pilot he might expose himself to liability under the pilotage legislation.

In *The Prinses Juliana* (1936) 18 Asp MLC 614, 619 the judge remarked that:

> '. . . if the Master takes upon himself to take the navigation of his ship out of the hands of the pilot and countermands the latter's orders, he must show to the court's satisfaction that he was justified in so doing . . . .'

Section 11 of the Pilotage Act 1913 provided that a vessel navigating in a compulsory pilotage district for the purpose of entering, leaving or making use of any port in the district and any ship (unless it is an 'expected' ship) carrying passengers navigating in such a compulsory district must be under the pilotage of a licensed pilot of that same district or a bona fide Master or mate possessing a pilotage certificate for that district.

Section 11 expressly stipulated that every ship *carrying* passengers (unless an 'excepted' ship) shall comply with the section: but a passenger ship *not* carrying passengers did not come within the provision. The material distinction to be drawn in each case is *not* 'was the ship a passenger ship?' but 'was or was not the ship carrying passengers?' The payment of a fare is not necessary to class a person as a passenger.

The equivalent section in the 1983 Act was section 31 and, although it was similar to section 11 of the 1913 Act, was only very limited in duration as the 1987 Act followed hard on its heels and contained section 15, which is now current, which provides that a ship navigating where pilotage is designated as compulsory shall be under either the pilotage of an authorized pilot, accompanied by an assistant if so required under the pilotage direction, or of a Master or mate holding an exemption certificate (section 15(1)). If any ship is not under such pilotage care after having been offered the required facilities, the Master shall be liable on summary conviction to a fine (section 15(2)).

*Clayton* v *Albertson* [1972] 2 Lloyd's Rep. 457

In September 1971 information was proffered against the Master of the vessel *Somerset* that he had failed to be under pilotage and failed to display a pilotage flag in circumstances where pilotage was compulsory in the Tyne District in respect of the entering and using of the Port of Tyne and that the ship at the time was carrying passengers. This was alleged to be in breach of sections 11 and 43 of the Pilotage Act 1913. The issue before the court was whether certain lorry drivers carried on board were 'passengers' within the meaning of the word as used in the Act. The *Somerset* was a 'roll-on/roll-off' ship. No fare was paid by the lorry drivers. Food was provided for them and they were given accommodation separately from the crew in the ship. They performed no duties with respect of the ship itself but did carry out routine maintenance to their vehicles whilst carried on board the ship.

The trial court ruled that the drivers were not passengers but that finding was reversed on appeal, i.e. they were held to be passengers; they were expected to be there and they were accommodated on board for the express purpose of performing their duty to drive their lorries on and off the ship. The case was referred back to the justices who were directed to convict.

In *The Alletta* [1965] 2 Lloyd's Rep. 479 (affirmed [1966] 1 Lloyd's Rep. 573, CA) the wife and child of the Master who were travelling on board were held not to be passengers within the meaning of the Pilotage Act 1913.

Under the 1983 Act there were certain classes of vessel which were exempted from the requirements of compulsory pilotage, these being known as 'excepted vessels'. They were: (a) Her Majesty's ships; (b) ferry boats plying as such exclusively within the limits of the harbour authority; (c) fishing vessels of which the registered length is less than 47.5 metres; (d) ferries exclusively operating within harbours; (e) ships of less than 50 gross registered tonnage; and (f) any other ship exempted by a by-law. Under the 1987 Act (section 7(3)) most of these categories have lost their privilege of being exempted vessels. Section 7(3) reads:

'A pilotage direction shall not apply to ships of less than 20 metres in length or for fishing boats of which the registered length is less than 47.5 metres.'

The obvious assumption from this is that in the intervening four years it has been decided that in order to tighten up on safety of navigation in harbour areas, the categories of excepted vessels should be considerably cut down. Indeed it might be said that not only has the Pilotage Act 1987 cut down these categories of excepted vessels, but it has even given facility for a competent harbour authority, if it considers that pilotage should be compulsory for ships navigating in any area *outside* its harbour, to apply for a harbour revision order to extend the limits over which it, as an authority, has jurisdiction for the purposes of pilotage. This is contained in section 7(5) of the 1987 Act and underlines even more the basic purpose of the Act which is to preserve the highest standard that is reasonably possible in regard to the safety of navigation in ports of the UK over which the Act has jurisdiction.

Under the 1987 Act (section 7), the operative word defining the geographical extent of a pilotage direction is *area*. The statute does not use words like 'port', 'district' nor does it get involved with expressions such as 'entering or leaving' (port). It is therefore to be assumed that problems of former years such as does a ship merely 'passing through' or calling for orders require to take on a pilot, need tax a Master's mind no longer. He needs to answer simply the question 'am I in or about to enter an area covered by a pilotage direction?' Bearing in mind that compulsory pilotage was the aim of raising to the highest possible level standards of navigational safety on or around a country's coastline, the approach of a ship close to a port for a specific purpose can constitute potentially as much a hazard in a compulsory pilotage area as one actually entering or leaving or navigating within the port. Thus it is naturally desirable that such a ship should take a compulsory pilot.

By section 32(1) exemption from compulsory pilotage is granted to craft such as tugs, dredgers, sludge-vessels, barges and other similar craft if belonging or hired to certain public authorities (e.g. a water authority) and being used in exercise of the authority's statutory powers or duties and navigating within a particular pilotage district, etc.

There are in hand new proposals for compulsory pilotage *which are not yet in force* but which are presently contained in section 30 of the 1983 Act. It is a simpler provision because it excludes the words 'for the purpose of entering, leaving or making use of any port in the district' and the consequent need of judicial interpretation of those phrases. The new proposals place emphasis on safety since they require the licensed pilot concerned to be accompanied by a qualified assistant.

Home trade limits within the meaning of this legislation mean the UK, the Channel Islands, the Isle of Man and the continent of Europe between the River Elbe and Brest inclusive (Merchant Shipping Act 1894, section 742). The interpretation is strict in this regard and a ship that was merely on one voyage outside the home trade limits, but which otherwise was habitually a 'home limit trader', was not exempt from the requirement if on that 'extra-limits' voyage she called at a port within the limits (*Smith* v *Veen* [1955] 1 Lloyd's Rep. 438.

Section 8 of the 1979 Merchant Shipping Act has been superseded by the 1983 Act. The position of by-laws (contemplated by subsection 2 of section 8 of the 1979 Act) is preserved by virtue of paragraph 1 of Schedule 2 of the 1983 Act which allows for the continuing in force of by-laws already in force and for the revoking of them in the same manner as could be done if the original 1913 Act was still in force.

The significant changes brought in by the 'gap-bridging' effect of section 8 of the 1979 Act were: (a) a ship's Master shall be liable *on summary* conviction; (b) the nature and extent of the dues demanded (section 8(1)(a)); (c) pleasure yachts are no longer classed as excepted ships; (d) fishing vessels only to be excepted if less than 47.5 metres in registered length ; (e) ships which could be classed 'excepted' (viz. ships trading coastwise etc.) by operation of by-laws may not be; and (f) recognition of assistants to pilots if required by by-law.

The absence of specific reference to 'ships carrying passengers', which in the 1913 Act (section 11) received specific mention, leaves no alternative than to assume it is not so much that the carrying of passengers has become irrelevant to the need to take a licensed pilot but, on the contrary, it goes without saying that it is necessary.

The law also remains unaffected that a Master of a vessel is under no obligation to engage a pilot in order to enter a *non*-compulsory pilotage area unless the ship is carrying passengers and is over 50 gross registered tonnage (see *The Alletta* case [1965] 2 Lloyd's Rep. 479; affirmed [1966] 1 Lloyd's Rep. 573, CA).

## DEFENCE OF COMPULSORY PILOTAGE

What has become known as the 'defence of compulsory pilotage' (i.e. the ability of a shipowner and/or the ship's Master to avoid liability where loss or damage occurred as a result of a compulsory pilot's fault) was abolished by the Pilotage Act 1913 which repealed section 633 of the Merchant Shipping Act 1894. There is one special exception to the current rule that shipowners are responsible whether a pilot is voluntarily or compulsorily engaged, and that is under the Defence of the Realm Act 1914, which is, as its title implies, applicable in time of war or national emergency when the government is empowered to put ships in full charge of a pilot whether or not the ship is navigating in a compulsory pilotage district.

## GEOGRAPHICAL APPLICATION OF PILOTAGE ACT

The application of the Pilotage Act is restricted geographically to the UK and the Isle of Man with the consequent effect that where loss or damage occurs outside this area when the vessel is in charge of a compulsory pilot the courts of the UK will recognize the 'defence' of compulsory pilotage since it is a general rule of law that a shipowner in such a situation must be liable in tort under the law of the country where the wrong was committed and not under the law of the UK.

*The Waziristan* [1953] 2 Lloyd's Rep. 361
A vessel grounded in the Shatt-Al-Arab (Iraq). It was alleged that a contributing cause was the fault of the Master and/or the pilot continuing passage down the river, thus disregarding the advice of the shore radio to return. The pilot was a compulsory pilot.

*Held*: that there was no negligence but, even assuming that the vessel had been negligently navigated, she had discharged the onus of showing that negligence was entirely the negligence of the compulsory pilot. In any case, the shipowner was not responsible for a compulsory pilot's negligence under Iraqi law.

One practical effect which resulted from the change was the discarding of costly and possibly protected litigation and the confining of issues arising under pilotage law largely to courts of summary jurisdiction.

As to the matter of deciding over the years whether pilotage was compulsory in any given area the tests applied were: (a) was the pilotage charge recoverable whether a pilot was engaged or not? and (b) could the employment of a qualified pilot be enforced by penalty?

## OBLIGATIONS UNDER THE COMPULSORY PILOTAGE PROVISIONS

Obligations of ships navigating where there is a pilotage direction for compulsory pilotage are contained in the three subsections under section 15 of the 1987 Pilotage Act. The section reads in full as follows:

'**15.**—(1) A ship which is being navigated in an area and in circumstances in which pilotage is compulsory for it by virtue of a pilotage direction shall be—

(a) under the pilotage of an authorised pilot accompanied by such an assistant, if any, as is required by virtue of the direction; or
(b) under the pilotage of a master or first mate possessing a pilotage exemption certificate in respect of that area and ship.

(2) If any ship is not under pilotage as required by subsection (1) above after an authorised pilot has offered to take charge of the ship, the master of the ship shall be guilty of an offence and liable on summary conviction to a fine not exceeding level 5 on the standard scale.

(3) If the master of a ship navigates the ship in an area and in circumstances in which pilotage is compulsory for it by virtue of a pilotage direction without notifying the competent harbour authority which gave the direction that he proposes to do so, he shall be guilty of an offence and liable on summary conviction to a fine not exceeding level 2 on the standard scale.'

Generally speaking a pilot whilst acting within the scope of his authority is considered to be an agent of the shipowner, and must be obeyed by the crew. The pilot does *not*, however, supersede the Master. Any failure of the crew to render assistance to the pilot will be regarded as shipowner's negligence.

A question is whether a pilot employed by the Harbour Authority is the servant of the shipowner or of the Harbour Authority. This issue arose in the following cases:

*Esso Petroleum Co Ltd* v *Hall Russell & Co Ltd* [1989] 1 Lloyd's Rep. 8, HL.
In 1978 an incident occurred at Sullom Voe when the vessel *Esso Bernicia* was under the control of a compulsory pilot, the Pilotage Act 1913 being the governing statute. One question was whether the Shetland Islands Council, as employers of the pilot were vicariously liable for the negligence of a pilot.

*Held*: It had long been established that a shipowner was liable to third parties for the negligent navigation of a voluntary pilot and since 1 January 1918 (the Pilotage Act 1913) he had been similarly liable for the negligent acts of compulsory pilots. As a general rule the employer of a qualified licensed pilot was not vicariously liable to the owner of a ship damaged by his negligence while under pilotage; the basis of the rule was that a pilot was an independent person who navigated the ship as a principal and not as a servant of his general employer. Section 15(1) of the Pilotage Act 1913 made him the servant of the shipowner for all purposes connected with navigation. The Shetland Islands Council was not liable.

The fact that section 16 of the 1987 Act did not intend to alter the meaning of section 15 of the 1913 Act was stated in the case of *The Cavendish*.

*The Cavendish* [1993] 2 Lloyd's Rep. 292
The vessel *Cavendish* whilst in charge of a compulsory pilot employed by the Port of London authority ('PLA') struck a buoy in the approaches to the River Thames causing damage to the vessel. The shipowners contended that:

(1) the PLA was vicariously liable for the assumed negligence of the pilot in that by the Pilotage Act 1987 they owed a positive duty to provide pilotage services;
(2) the PLA was liable to the shipowners in contract which was subject to a common law implied term that the pilotage services would be performed with reasonable skill and care; and
(3) their claim was not precluded by section 16 of the 1987 Act.

*Held*: the PLA was not vicariously liable in tort for the negligence of the pilot on board the vessel *Cavendish*. The arrangement made between the PLA and the shipowners was no more than an arrangement to discharge the shipowners' statutory obligation by taking a compulsory pilot and paying for his services. There was no basis for holding a contract to exist between the parties. Section 16 of the 1987 Act imposed a liability for negligence of a compulsory pilot on shipowners in respect of claims by third parties. Section 16 created the relationship of Master and servant between the compulsory pilot and the shipowner so as to make the shipowner liable to third parties. The pilot was not the servant of the port authority.

### *Right of authorized pilot to supersede unauthorized pilot*

Section 17 of the 1987 Act has replaced section 36 of the 1983 Act and under subsection (1) an authorized pilot has the right to supersede an unauthorized person who may have been employed to pilot the ship in question. Section 17(2) places guilt on the Master of any ship who navigates it in any part of the harbour under the pilotage of an unauthorized person without first notifying the competent harbour authority that he proposes to do so. Subsection (3) of the same section provides that if an unauthorized person pilots a ship within a harbour knowing that an authorized pilot has offered pilotage, he shall be guilty of an offence and subsection (4) places guilt on the Master of a ship who navigates within a harbour and knowingly employs or continues to employ an unauthorized person after an authorized pilot has offered to pilot it.

Cases quoted hereunder do not admittedly derive from incidents arising after the introduction of the 1987 Act nor even the 1983 Act, but nevertheless they illustrate similar incidents which did take place during the currency of earlier legislation.

*Smith* v *Cocking* [1959] 1 Lloyd's Rep. 88
A pilot not licensed for Dover piloted a ship into harbour. During this performance a *licensed* pilot offered his services but the Master refused them. The unlicensed pilot knew of this refusal but still continued to pilot the ship.

*Held*: that this was an offence under section 30(3) of the Pilotage Act 1913, exposing the pilot to the statutory fine. (The equivalent provision in the 1983 Act is section 36(3)).

For being a party to this contravention, the ship's Master may find himself liable for a similar fine and it is his burden to prove himself innocent.

*Montague* v *Babbs* [1972] 1 Lloyd's Rep. 65
A licensed waterman, who was not a licensed pilot, piloted the *Minster* from Erith Buoys to Fords Jetty at Dagenham (less than two miles) within the London Pilotage District. He was charged with an offence under section 30(3) of the Pilotage Act 1913. The waterman claimed that section 30(3) of the Pilotage Act 1913 did not apply in view of an existing London Pilotage District by-law which, inter alia, exempted the movements of ships between moorings within a defined area and over a lesser distance than two nautical miles. It was established that at all material times the Trinity House Pilot Station at Gravesend (nine miles distant) had displayed a pilot flag constituting an offer of licensed pilotage available.

*Held*: that a movement within the by-law was a movement to which section 30 did not apply and also that the universal offer of pilotage was not an offer within the meaning of section 30(3) of the Pilotage Act 1913.

Section 17(3) makes it an offence only at the point 'when the unlicensed pilot *knew*' that a licensed pilot for the district had offered to pilot the ship.

*McMillan* v *Crouch* [1972] 2 Lloyd's Rep. 325, HL
By application of a local by-law a vessel which would otherwise have been navigating in a pilotage district was held not to be so navigating and there was consequently no liability under section 11(1) of the Pilotage Act 1913. On the facts, the ship's Master was not bound to display a pilot flag as normally required by section 43 of the Act, nor did a licensed pilot have any right to supersede an unlicensed person, as he might have had under different circumstances under section 30 of the 1913 Act.

*Buck* v *Tyrrel* (1922) 10 Ll.L.Rep. 74
There was no custom of the port in the River Thames area below Gravesend justifying the employment of an unlicensed pilot so as to take the facts in the dispute outside the operation of section 30 of the Pilotage Act 1913.

## WHAT CONSTITUTES AN OFFER OF PILOTAGE SERVICES?

Mere display of a pilot flag at a pilot station may not be sufficient to constitute an offer of pilotage services. There must be a clearer communication of the offer in the light of the particular movement of the vessel which is intended to be piloted. Conversely, section 50 obliges a ship's Master to display a pilot signal when navigating in a compulsory area and to keep it displayed until a suitably licensed pilot boards the ship. Furthermore, whether the area is one of compulsory pilotage or not, if the ship is in charge of a pilot *not* licensed for that particular district the pilot signal must nevertheless still be displayed.

(In accordance with the obvious intention of the draftsmen of the revised pilotage laws to temper the law somewhat, section 50(3) which penalizes a Master who fails to display a pilot signal has added to it after the word 'fails' the qualifying extra words 'without reasonable excuse'.

*Rindby* v *Brewis* (1926) 25 Ll.L.Rep. 26
The Master of a Danish vessel failed to take a pilot in a compulsory pilotage area (Harwich) and so breached section 11(2) of the Pilotage Act 1913 and also section 44 which requires a Master to keep a reasonable look-out for the offer of pilotage services and, if offered, to facilitate the boarding of the pilot. The facts showed that there had been a deliberate disregard by the Master of a pilotage offer. (The equivalent section to section 44 is section 51 of the 1983 Act).

The law as interpreted then was that it was not absolutely prohibited to navigate without a pilot in a compulsory pilot area but that there was a continuing obligation to fly a pilot flag and to take the pilot on board if he offered. A reasonable look-out must also be kept.

*Muller (WH) & Co* v *Trinity House* (1924) 20 Ll.L.Rep. 56
Navigation without a pilot in a compulsory pilotage area is not absolutely prohibited but there is a continuing obligation to fly the pilot flag and to keep a reasonable look-out.

Sections 18, 19 and 20 of the 1987 Act lay down specific obligations on the Master of a ship, some of them reproductions of statutory obligations in former statutes and some not. First, in section 18, the Master must declare, if so required by the pilot, the ship's draught of water, length and beam and any other information which the pilot might require in order to enable him to carry out his duties as a pilot. Also the Master is bound to bring to the notice of any authorized person piloting the ship any defects in the machinery or equipment of the ship of which he knows and which could materially affect the navigating of the ship. Section 19 expressly forbids a Master without reasonable excuse to take an authorized pilot, without his consent, beyond that point up to which he has been engaged to pilot the ship (19(1)). Section 19(2) provides for a fine or summary conviction for any person who contravenes the requirement in subsection (1). Section 20 requires the Master of the ship when he is accepting the services offered to him of an authorized pilot to facilitate the pilot boarding his ship and subsequently leaving it. Any contravention of this requirement lays the Master open to an offence and being liable on summary conviction to a fine.

## MISCONDUCT OF PILOT

Pilots may be guilty of an offence if they do anything to cause loss, destruction or serious damage to the ship, her machinery, navigation or safety equipment or the death or serious injury of anyone on board. They may be guilty if they omit to do anything required to preserve the ship etc, or any person from death or serious injury.

The act or omission resulting in the above must either (a) be deliberate or (b) be one amounting to a breach or neglect of duty or (c) be one committed or omitted under the influence of drink or drugs (section 21(1)(a)(b), 1987 Pilotage Act). The punishment shall be not exceeding six months' imprisonment on summary conviction or a fine or both or not exceeding two years in prison on conviction on indictment or a fine or both (section 21(2)).

## LIMITATION OF A PILOT'S LIABILITY

The Pilotage Act 1987 introduces revised provisions regarding the limitation of liability in respect of pilots and these are to be found in section 22 which contains nine subsections. In the previous Pilotage Act, the statute of 1983, the pilot's liability is limited to £100 together with the amount payable to him as remuneration for the pilotage services he was at the time rendering. Under subsection (1) of section 22 of the 1987 Act, the liability of an authorized pilot for any loss or damage caused by any act or omission of his whilst acting as such a pilot shall not exceed £1,000 and the amount of the pilotage charges in respect of the voyage during which the liability arose. Thus the limitation figure would seem to have been increased by 10 times. Under subsection (2) the definition of the word 'authorized' is that such a pilot should be piloting the ship to that area from a place where pilots authorized for that harbour regularly board ships navigating to it or, alternatively, that he is piloting the ship from that harbour to a place where such pilots regularly leave ships navigating from it.

Subsections (3) and (4) govern the limitation of a pilotage authority and will be dealt with under the next sub-heading. Subsection (5) provides that the limit of liability shall apply to the whole of any losses and damages which may arise upon any one distinct occasion, although such losses and damages may be sustained by more than one person. This subsection echoes a principle already well symbolized by the limitation laws contained in the Limitation Convention of

1976 (and sections 185 and 186 of the Merchant Shipping Act 1995) described in detail in Chapter 9. Subsection (6) provides for the jurisdiction of the court in which proceedings in connection with limitation are taken and such court is empowered to (a) determine the amount of the liability and (b) distribute that amount rateably among the *defendants* once the amount has been paid by the *defendant* into the court, (c) to stay any proceedings pending in any other court in relation to the same matter, (d) proceed in such a manner and subject to such requirements as the court thinks just in connection with (1) making interested persons parties to the proceedings, (2) excluding any claimants whose claims are not made within a certain time, (3) obtaining security from the defendant and (4) payment of any costs.

## A PILOT AUTHORITY'S RIGHT TO LIMIT

A pilot authority's right to limit, which in the old days was governed by the Pilotage Authorities (Limitation of Liability) Act 1936, is now contained in section 22(3) and (4) of the 1987 Act. Under subsection (3) where, without any such personal act or omission by a competent harbour authority (these words are reflected by Article 4 of the 1976 Convention on Limitation of Liability and Maritime Claims contained in Schedule 7 to the Merchant Shipping Act 1995), any loss or damage to any ship, to any property on board any ship or to any property or rights of any kind, is caused by an authorized pilot employed by it, the authority shall not be liable to damages beyond the amount of £1,000 multiplied by the number of authorized pilots employed by it at the date when the loss or damage occurs. Subsection (4) provides similarly for the provision of piloting services by an agent on behalf of a competent harbour authority and lays down that the agent, assuming that he is not guilty of any such personal act or omission within the meaning of Article 4 of the Limitation Convention of 1976, shall not be liable to damages beyond the amount of £1,000 multiplied by the number of authorized pilots employed by him, providing piloting services for that authority, at the date when the loss or damage occurs.

A licensed pilot may not refuse to pilot a vessel unless he has a reasonable ground for his refusal. This in practice will probably be restricted to occasions where he is requested to pilot a damaged vessel for only the normal pilotage dues remuneration. Under such circumstances his services would probably be regarded by a court as services 'in the nature of salvage'. The other possible circumstances in which a pilot's refusal could be justified is when to follow the instruction of a ship's Master might, of itself, lead the ship into danger.

## PILOTAGE CHARGES

As was provided in the previous Pilotage Act (1983) the 1987 Act by its section 10 provides for the charges which may be made by a competent harbour authority. The section is self-explanatory and subsections (1)–(5) and (7) are given below in full.

'**10.**—(1) A competent harbour authority may make reasonable charges in respect of the pilotage services provided by it.

(2) Without prejudice to the generality of subsection (1) above, the charges to be made under that subsection may include—

(a) charges for the services of a pilot authorised by the authority;

(b) charges in respect of any expenses reasonably incurred by such a pilot in connection with the provision of his services as a pilot;

(c) charges by way of penalties payable in cases where the estimated time of arrival or departure of a ship is not notified as required by the authority or the ship does not arrive or depart at the notified time;

(d) charges in respect of the cost of providing, maintaining and operating pilot boats for the area; and

(e) charges in respect of any other costs involved in providing and maintaining the pilotage organisation provided by the authority.

(3) A competent harbour authority which has given a pilotage direction may also make reasonable charges in respect of any ship navigating within the area to which the direction applies under the pilotage of a master or first mate who is the holder of a pilotage exemption certificate in respect of the area and ship in question.

(4) Different charges may be made under this section in different circumstances.

(5) A competent harbour authority shall arrange for the charges to be made by it under this section to be published in such manner as to bring them to the notice of those persons likely to be interested.

(7) Charges imposed by a competent harbour authority under this section shall be recoverable as a civil debt or in any other manner in which ship, passenger and goods dues are recoverable by the authority.

Although subsection (7) does not specifically say in what manner pilotage charges could be recovered in the event of default in payment, it is assumed that the previous system of application to a magistrates' court would be the proper method. Although summary proceedings are the normal procedure, section 20(2)(e) of the Supreme Court Act 1981 would suggest that proceedings for recovery could also be brought in the Admiralty Court.

APPENDIX 1

# MERCHANT SHIPPING ACT 1995

## PART II REGISTRATION

### General

*8. Central register of British ships*

(1) There shall continue to be a register of British ships for all registrations of ships in the United Kingdom.

(2) The register shall be maintained by the Registrar General of Shipping and Seamen as registrar.

(3) The Secretary of State may designate any person to discharge, on behalf of the registrar, all his functions or such of them as the Secretary of State may direct.

(4) The Secretary of State may give to the registrar directions of a general nature as to the discharge of any of his functions.

(5) The register shall be so constituted as to distinguish, in a separate part, registrations of fishing vessels and may be otherwise divided into parts so as to distinguish between classes or descriptions of ships.

(6) The register shall be maintained in accordance with registration regulations and the private law provisions for registered ships and any directions given by the Secretary of State under subsection (4) above.

(7) The register shall be available for public inspection.

*9. Registration of ships: basic provisions*

(1) A ship is entitled to be registered if—

- (a) it is owned, to the prescribed extent, by persons qualified to own British ships; and
- (b) such other conditions are satisfied as are prescribed under subsection (2)(b) below;

(and any application for registration is duly made).

(2) It shall be for registration regulations—

- (a) to determine the persons who are qualified to be owners of British ships, or British ships of any class or description, and to prescribe the extent of the ownership required for compliance with subsection (1)(a) above;
- (b) to prescribe other requirements designed to secure that, taken in conjunction with the requisite ownership, only ships having a British connection are registered.

(3) The registrar may, nevertheless, if registration regulations so provide, refuse to register or terminate the registration of a ship if, having regard to any relevant requirements of this Act, he considers it would be inappropriate for the ship to be or, as the case may be, to remain registered.

(4) The registrar may, if registration regulations so provide, register a fishing vessel notwithstanding that the requirement of subsection (1)(a) above is not satisfied in relation

to a particular owner of a share in the vessel if the vessel otherwise has a British connection.

(5) Where a ship becomes registered at a time when it is already registered under the law of a country other than the United Kingdom, the owner of the ship shall take all reasonable steps to secure the termination of the ship's registration under the law of that country.

(6) Subsection (5) above does not apply to a ship which becomes registered on a transfer of registration to the register from a relevant British possession.

(7) Any person who contravenes subsection (5) above shall be liable on summary conviction to a fine not exceeding level 3 on the standard scale.

(8) In this section 'the relevant requirements of this Act' means the requirements of this Act (including requirements falling to be complied with after registration) relating to—

(a) the condition of ships or their equipment so far as relevant to their safety or any risk of pollution; and

(b) the safety, health and welfare of persons employed or engaged in them.

(9) In this Part references to a ship's having a British connection are references to compliance with the conditions of entitlement imposed by subsection (1)(a) and (b) above and 'declaration of British connection' is to be construed accordingly.

*10. Registration regulations*

(1) The Secretary of State shall by regulations (to be known as registration regulations) make provision for and in connection with the registration of ships as British ships.

(2) Without prejudice to the generality of subsection (1) above, registration regulations may, in particular, make provision with respect to any of the following matters—

(a) the persons by whom and the manner in which applications in connection with registration are to be made;

(b) the information and evidence (including declarations of British connection) to be provided in connection with such applications and such supplementary information or evidence as may be required by any specified authority;

(c) the shares in the property in, and the numbers of owners (including joint owners) of, a ship permitted for the purposes of registration and the persons required or permitted to be registered in respect of a ship or to be so registered in specified circumstances;

(d) the issue of certificates (including provisional certificates) of registration, their production and surrender;

(e) restricting and regulating the names of ships registered or to be registered;

(f) the marking of ships registered or to be registered, including marks for identifying the port to which a ship is to be treated as belonging;

(g) the period for which registration is to remain effective without renewal;

(h) the production to the registrar of declarations of British connection or other information relating thereto, as respects registered ships, at specified intervals or at his request;

(i) the survey and inspection of ships registered or to be registered and the recording of their tonnage as ascertained (or re-ascertained) under the tonnage regulations;

(j) the refusal, suspension and termination of registration in specified circumstances;

(k) matters arising out of the expiration, suspension or termination of registration (including the removal of marks and the cancellation of certificates);

(l) the charging of fees in connection with registration or registered ships;

(m) the transfer of the registration of ships to and from the register from and to registers or corresponding records in countries other than the United Kingdom;

(n) inspection of the register;

(o) any other matter which is authorised or required by this Part to be prescribed in registration regulations;

but no provision determining, or providing for determining, the fees to be charged or prescribing any arrangements for their determination by other persons shall be made without the approval of the Treasury.

(3) Registration regulations may—

(a) make different provision for different classes or descriptions of ships and for different circumstances;

(b) without prejudice to paragraph (a) above, make provision for the granting of exemptions or dispensations by the Secretary of State from specified requirements of the regulations, subject to such conditions (if any) as he thinks fit to impose; and

(c) make such transitional, incidental or supplementary provision as appears to the Secretary of State to be necessary or expedient, including provision authorising investigations and conferring powers of inspection for verifying the British connection of a ship.

(4) Registration regulations—

(a) may make provision for the registration of any class or description of ships to be such as to exclude the application of the private law provisions for registered ships and, if they do, may regulate the transfer, transmission or mortgaging of ships of the class or description so excluded;

(b) may make provision for any matter which is authorised or required by those provisions to be prescribed by registration regulations; and

(c) shall make provision precluding notice of any trust being entered in the register or being receivable by the registrar except as respects specified classes or descriptions of ships or in specified circumstances.

(5) Registration regulations may create offences subject to the limitation that no offence shall be punishable with imprisonment or punishable on summary conviction with a fine exceeding level 5 on the standard scale.

(6) Registration regulations may provide for—

(a) the approval of forms by the Secretary of State; and

(b) the discharge of specified functions by specified authorities or persons.

(7) Registration regulations may provide for any of their provisions to extend to places outside the United Kingdom.

(8) Any document purporting to be a copy of any information contained in an entry in the register and to be certified as a true copy by the registrar shall be evidence (and, in Scotland, sufficient evidence) of the matters stated in the document.

(9) Registration regulations may provide that any reference in any other Act or in any instrument made under any other Act to the port of registry or the port to which a ship belongs shall be construed as a reference to the port identified by the marks required for the purpose by registration regulations.

APPENDIX 2

# BILL OF SALE (BODIES CORPORATE AND INDIVIDUALS)

*Note*: This form is reproduced by kind permission of the Commissioners of Customs and Excise. Crown copyright is reproduced with the permission of the Controller of Her Majesty's Stationery Office.

Department of Transport
Merchant Shipping Act 1995

# Bill of Sale

- **Warning: A purchaser of a British registered ship does not obtain complete title until the appropriate Bill(s) of Sale has been recorded with the Registry, and a new Certificate issued.**
- Registered owners who are mortgagees *must* inform the Registry of any change of address.
- Where one owner is selling to two or more owners, separate forms are required unless they are buying as joint owners.
- Applications to change ownership received within 30 days of the change attract a 'transfer fee' rather than the more expensive 'full registration' fees.
- Please write in black ink using BLOCK CAPITALS, and tick boxes where appropriate

## SECTION 1: DETAILS OF THE SHIP

Name of ship

Official number (if any) | Length (metres)

## SECTION 2: DETAILS OF THE SALE

| Body Corporate please give | Company name | Principal place of business[1] | |
|---|---|---|---|
| Individuals please give | Full name(s) | Address(es) | Occupation(s) |
| ***I/we the transferor(s)**<br>☐ as joint owners<br>*(Please tick box if you are joint owners)* | | | |

**in consideration of (*the sum of)**

***paid/given to *me/us by:**

| Body Corporate please give | Company name | Principal place of business[1] | |
|---|---|---|---|
| Individuals please give | Full name(s) | Address(es) | Occupation(s) |
| **The transferee(s)**<br>☐ as joint owners<br>*(Please tick box if you are joint owners)* | | | |

[1]Companies incorporated other than in the UK or British Dependant Territories - enter place of business
*Delete as necessary

## SECTION 2: DETAILS OF THE SALE (continued)

**the receipt of which is acknowledged, transfer** [ ]

**shares in the above ship and its appurtenances to the transferee(s).** **(figures & words)**

**Further, *I/we the said transferor(s) for *myself/ourselves, hereby declare that *I/we have the power to transfer in the manner aforesaid the above-mentioned shares, and that they are free from encumbrances **save as appears by the registry of the above ship.**

** Delete (and initial the deletion) if there are no outstanding registered mortgages.

**If any registered mortgage is outstanding please tick this box** ☐

## SECTION 3: FOR COMPLETION WHEN SALE IS BY A COMPANY

**Executed by the transferor as a deed on this**

*COMPANY SEAL*

________**day of**____________________**19** ______**by:-**

* **(a) the affixing of the common seal of the transferor in the presence of the following persons signing;** *or*
* **(b) signing by the following persons;**

Director ____________________

Director or Secretary ____________________

Authorised Signatory ____________________

**Witnessed by ____________________

Name ____________________

Address ____________________

____________________

* Delete as appropriate

Note: IN ENGLAND, WALES & NORTHERN IRELAND - signature may be by two directors; or by a director and the secretary of the company. No witness is required. If the common seal is affixed any special requirement of the company's articles about signing must be complied with.

IN SCOTLAND - signature may be a director or the secretary of the company; or by a person authorised to sign the document on behalf of the company.

** The signature must be witnessed and the name and address of the witness must be given.

## SECTION 4: FOR COMPLETION WHEN SALE IS BY INDIVIDUAL(S)

* **Executed as a deed** (in England or Wales)
* **Signed** (in Scotland)
* **Signed, sealed and delivered** (in Northern Ireland)

* Delete as appropriate

Seal(s) if executed in Northern Ireland

**on this** ____________**day of** ________________**19**_______

**by the following person(s) signing as transferor(s)**

| Signature(s) of transferor(s) | | |
|---|---|---|
| In the presence of: | | |
| Name(s) of witness(es) | | |
| Address(es) | | |
| Occupation(s) of witness(es) | | |

NOTE: Every signature must have one witness

When completed you should send this form, together with the appropriate fee and supporting documents (if required) to:
REGISTRY OF SHIPPING AND SEAMEN
PO BOX 165, CARDIFF CF4 5FU

**OFFICIAL USE ONLY**

**Entry in Register made on** ____________________**(date)**

**at**____________________**(time)**

**Officer's Initials** [ ]

APPENDIX 3

# BILLS OF SALE (INDIVIDUALS AND JOINT OWNERS AND BODY CORPORATE)

These forms are now replaced by that in Appendix 1. The forms are, however, still in regular use in sales of vessels registered under foreign flags.

*Note:* This form is reproduced by kind permission of the Commissioners of Customs and Excise. Crown copyright is reproduced with the permission of the Controller of Her Majesty's Stationery Office.

Prescribed by the Commissioners of Customs & Excise with the consent of the Secretary of State for Trade

*Form No. 10*

X.S.79

# BILL OF SALE (Individuals or Joint Owners)

| Official number | Name of Ship | Number, year and port of registry | Whether a sailing, steam or motor ship | Horse power of engines (if any) |
|---|---|---|---|---|
| 1234 | LUCKY STREAK | 1974 LONDON | MOTOR | 3050 B H P |

| | Feet | Tenths | Number of Tons (*Where dual tonnages are assigned the higher of these should be stated*) Gross | Register |
|---|---|---|---|---|
| Length from fore part of stem, to the aft side of the head of the stern post/fore side of the rudder stock | 390 | 2.5 | | |
| Main breadth to outside of plating | 62 | 1.0 | | |
| Depth in hold from tonnage deck to ceiling amidships | 23 | 0.5 | 5353.40 | 3308.51 |

and as described in more detail in the Register Book.

(a) I the undersigned (b) Earnest Carefree, Playboy, of 6 Idleness Place, London (hereinafter called "the transferor(s)") in consideration of the sum of Six hundred and Sixty thousand pounds paid to (c) Me by (d) John Soxup and James Neesup, Merchants of 2 Prosperous Row London as Joint Owners (hereinafter called "the transferee(s)") the receipt whereof is hereby acknowledged, transfer all the shares in the Ship above particularly described, and in her boats and appurtenances, to the said transferee(s).

Further (a) I the said transferor(s) for (e) Myself and My heirs covenant with the said transferee(s) and (f) Their assigns, that (a) I have power to transfer in manner aforesaid the premises hereinbefore expressed to be transferred, and that the same are free from encumbrances (g) Save as appears by the Registry of the Said Ship

In witness whereof (a) I have hereunto subscribed (h) My name(s) and affixed (h) My seal on 20th April 19 79

Executed by the above named transferor(s)
In the presence of (i) I. Eavesdrop
Secretary of 10 Routine Road, London

(j) ..........

Seal

(a) "I" or "we". (b) Full name(s), address(es) and description of transferor(s). (c) "me" or "us". (d) Full name(s) and address(es) of transferee(s) with their description in the case of individuals, and adding "as joint owners" where such is the case. (e) "myself and my" or "ourselves and our". (f) "his", "their" or "its". (g) If any subsisting encumbrance add "save as appears by the registry of the said ship". (h) "my" or "our".
(i) Name, address and description of witness. If the ship is registered in Scotland two witnesses are required (j) Signature of transferor(s).

*NOTE—A purchaser of a registered British Vessel does not obtain a complete title until the Bill of Sale has been recorded at the Port of Registry of the ship; and neglect of this precaution may entail serious consequences.*

*NOTE—Registered Owners or Mortgagees are reminded of the importance of keeping the Registrar of British Ships informed of any change of residence on their part.*

Prescribed by the Commissioners of Customs & Excise with the consent of the Secretary of State for Trade

*Form No. 10A*

X.S. 79 A

# BILL OF SALE (Body Corporate)

| Official number | Name of Ship | Number, year and port of registry | | | Whether a sailing, steam or motor ship | Horse power of engines (if any) |
|---|---|---|---|---|---|---|
| 4321 | LUCKY STREAK | 1975 LONDON | | | MOTOR | 3000 B H P |
| | | | Feet | Tenths | Number of Tons *(Where dual tonnages are assigned the higher of these should be stated)* | |
| Length from fore part of stem, to the aft side of the head of the stern post/fore side of the rudder stock | | | 440 | 1.5 | Gross | Register |
| Main breadth to outside of plating | | | 83 | 2.0 | | |
| Depth in hold from tonnage deck to ceiling amidships | | | 27 | 0.5 | 6565.70 | 4407.68 |
| and as described in more detail in the Register Book. | | | | | | |

We, (a) Lucky Shipping Company Limited (hereinafter called "the transferors") having our principal place of business at 90 Paradise Street London in consideration of the sum of Seven Hundred and Forty Thousand Pounds (£740,000) paid to us by (b) Unfortunate Transportation Company Limited, 8 Stormy Crescent, Bristol (hereinafter called "the transferee(s)") the receipt whereof is hereby acknowledged, transfer All the shares in the Ship above particularly described, and in her boats and appurtenances, to the said transferee(s).

Further, we, the said transferors for ourselves and our successors covenant with the said transferee(s) and (c) Its assigns, that we have power to transfer in manner aforesaid the premises hereinbefore expressed to be transferred, and that the same are free from encumbrances (d) And Maritime Liens

In witness whereof we have hereunto affixed our common seal on 20th April 1980

The Common Seal of the transferors was affixed hereunto in the presence of (e)

Mark Well

Director of 19 Ocean Drive, London

(a) Name in full of Body Corporate. (b) Full name(s) and address(es) of transferee(s) with their description in the case of individuals, and adding "as joint owners" where such is the case. (c) "his", "their" or "its". (d) If any subsisting encumbrance add "save as appears by the registry of the said ship". (e) Signatures and description of witnesses, i.e. Director, Secretary, etc. (as the case may be).

***NOTE –*** *A purchaser of a registered British Vessel does not obtain a complete title until the Bill of Sale has been recorded at the Port of Registry of the ship; and neglect of this precaution may entail serious consequences.*

***NOTE –*** *Registered Owners or Mortgagees are reminded of the importance of keeping the Registrar of British Ships informed of any change of residence on their part.*

APPENDIX 4

# MEMORANDUM OF AGREEMENT (NORWEGIAN SALEFORM 1987)

*Note*: This agreement is reproduced by kind permission of the Norwegian Shipbrokers' Association.

# MEMORANDUM OF AGREEMENT

Norwegian Shipbrokers' Association's Memorandum of Agreement for sale and purchase of ships. Adopted by The Baltic and International Maritime Council (BIMCO) in 1956.

Code-name

**SALEFORM 1987**

Revised 1966, 1983 and 1986

Dated:

hereinafter called the Sellers, have today sold, and 1

hereinafter called the Buyers, have today bought 2

Classification: 3

Built: by: 4

Flag: Place of Registration: 5

Call sign: Register tonnage: 6

Register number: 7

on the following conditions: 8

**1. Price** 9

Price: 10

**2. Deposit** 11

As a security for the correct fulfillment of this contract, the Buyers shall pay a deposit of 10% — 12
ten per cent — of the Purchase Money within banking days from the date of this 13
agreement. This amount shall be deposited with 14

and held by them in a joint account for the Sellers and the Buyers. Interest, if any, to be credited the 15
Buyers. Any fee charged for holding said deposit shall be borne equally by the Sellers and the Buyers. 16

**3. Payment** 17

The said Purchase Money shall be paid free of bank charges to 18

on delivery of the vessel, but not later than three banking days after the vessel is ready for delivery 19
and written or telexed notice thereof has been given to the Buyers by the Sellers. 20

**4. Inspections** 21

The Buyers shall have the right to inspect the vessel's classification records and declare whether 22
same are accepted or not within 23

The Sellers shall provide for inspection of the vessel at/in 24

The Buyers shall undertake the inspection without undue delay to the vessel. Should the Buyers 25
cause such delay, they shall compensate the Sellers for the losses thereby incurred. 26

The Buyers shall inspect the vessel afloat without opening up and without cost to the Sellers. Du- 27
ring the inspection, the vessel's log books for engine and deck shall be made available for the Buyers' 28
examination. If the vessel is accepted after such afloat inspection, the purchase shall become definite 29
— except for other possible subjects in this contract — provided the Sellers receive written or telexed 30
notice from the Buyers within 48 hours after completion of such afloat inspection. Should notice of 31
acceptance of the vessel's classification records and of the vessel not be received by the Sellers as 32

aforesaid, the deposit shall immediately be released, whereafter this contract shall be considered null and void. 33 34

**5. Place and time of delivery** 35

The vessel shall be delivered and taken over at/in 36

Expected time of delivery: 37

Date of cancelling (see clause 14): 38

The Sellers shall keep the Buyers well posted about the vessel's itinerary and estimated time and place of drydocking. 39 40

Should the vessel become a total or constructive total loss before delivery the deposit shall immediately be released to the Buyers and the contract thereafter considered null and void. 41 42

**6. Drydocking** 43

In connection with the delivery the Sellers shall place the vessel in drydock at the port of delivery for inspection by the Classification Society of the bottom and other underwater parts below the Summer Load Line. If the rudder, propeller, bottom or other underwater parts below the Summer Load Line be found broken, damaged or defective, so as to affect the vessel's clean certificate of class, such defects shall be made good at the Sellers' expense to[1] 44 45 46 47 48

satisfaction without qualification on such underwater parts.[2] 49

Whilst the vessel is in drydock, and if required by the Buyers or the representative of the Classification Society, the Sellers shall arrange to have the tail-end shaft drawn. Should same be condemned or found defective so as to affect the vessel's clean certificate of class, it shall be renewed or made good at the Sellers' expense to the Classification Society's satisfaction without qualification. 50 51 52 53

The expenses of drawing and replacing the tail-end shaft shall be borne by the Buyers unless the Classification Society requires the tail-end shaft to be drawn (whether damaged or not), renewed or made good in which event the Sellers shall pay these expenses. 54 55 56

The expenses in connection with putting the vessel in and taking her out of drydock, including drydock dues and the Classification Surveyor's fees shall be paid by the Sellers if the rudder, propeller, bottom, other underwater parts below the Summer Load Line or the tail-end shaft be found broken, damaged or defective as aforesaid or if the Classification Society requires the tail-end shaft to be drawn (whether damaged or not). In all other cases the Buyers shall pay the aforesaid expenses, dues and fees. 57 58 59 60 61 62

During the above mentioned inspections by the Classification Society the Buyers' representative shall have the right to be present in the drydock but without interfering with the Classification Surveyor's decisions. 63 64 65

The Sellers shall bring the vessel to the drydock and from the drydock to the place of delivery at their own expense. 66 67

**7. Spares/bunkers etc.** 68

The Sellers shall deliver the vessel to the Buyers with everything belonging to her on board and on shore. All spare parts and spare equipment including spare tail-end shaft(s) and/or spare propeller(s), if any, belonging to the vessel at the time of inspection, used or unused, whether on board or not shall become the Buyers' property, but spares on order to be excluded. Forwarding charges, if any, shall be for the Buyers' account. The Sellers are not required to replace spare parts including spare tail-end shaft(s) and spare propeller(s) which are taken out of spare and used as replacement prior to delivery, but the replaced items shall be the property of the Buyers. The radio installation and navigational equipment shall be included in the sale without extra payment, if same is the property of the Sellers. 69 70 71 72 73 74 75 76

The Sellers have the right to take ashore crockery, plate, cutlery, linen and other articles bearing the Sellers' flag or name, provided they replace same with similar unmarked items. Library, forms, etc., exclusively for use in the Sellers' vessels, shall be excluded without compensation. Captain's, Officers' and Crew's personal belongings including slop chest to be excluded from the sale, as well as the following additional items: 77 78 79 80 81

The Buyers shall take over remaining bunkers, unused lubricating oils and unused stores and provisions and pay the current market price at the port and date of delivery of the vessel. 82 83

Payment under this clause shall be made at the same time and place and in the same currency as the Purchase Money. 84 85

**8. Documentation** 86

In exchange for payment of the Purchase Money the Sellers shall furnish the Buyers with legal Bill of Sale of the said vessel free from all encumbrances and maritime liens or any other debts whatsoever, duly notarially attested and legalised by the                                        consul together with a certificate stating that the vessel is free from registered encumbrances. On delivery of the vessel the Sellers shall provide for the deletion of the vessel from the Registry of Vessels and deliver a certificate of deletion to the Buyers. The deposit shall be placed at the disposal of the Sellers as well as the balance of the Purchase Money, which shall be paid as agreed together with payment for items mentioned in clause 7 above. 87 88 89 90 91 92 93 94

The Sellers shall, at the time of delivery, hand to the Buyers all classification certificates as well as all plans etc. which are onboard the vessel. Other technical documentation which may be in the Sellers' possession shall promptly upon the Buyers' instructions be forwarded to the Buyers. The Sellers may keep the log books, but the Buyers to have the right to take copies of same. 95 96 97 98

**9. Encumbrances** 99

The Sellers warrant that the vessel, at the time of delivery, is free from all encumbrances and maritime liens or any other debts whatsoever. Should any claims which have been incurred prior to the time of delivery be made against the vessel, the Sellers hereby undertake to indemnify the Buyers against all consequences of such claims. 100 101 102 103

**10. Taxes etc.** 104

Any taxes, fees and expenses connected with the purchase and registration under the Buyers' flag shall be for the Buyers' account, whereas similar charges connected with the closing of the Sellers' register shall be for the Sellers' account. 105 106 107

**11. Condition on delivery** 108

The vessel with everything belonging to her shall be at the Sellers' risk and expense until she is delivered to the Buyers, but subject to the conditions of this contract, she shall be delivered and taken over as she is at the time of inspection, fair wear and tear excepted. 109 110 111

However, the vessel shall be delivered with present class free of recommendations. The Sellers shall notify the Classification Society of any matters coming to their knowledge prior to delivery which upon being reported to the Classification Society would lead to the withdrawal of the vessel's class or to the imposition of a recommendation relating to her class. 112 113 114 115

**12. Name/markings** 116

Upon delivery the Buyers undertake to change the name of the vessel and alter funnel markings. 117

**13. Buyers' default** 118

Should the deposit not be paid as aforesaid, the Sellers have the right to cancel this contract, and they shall be entitled to claim compensation for their losses and for all expenses incurred together 119 120 with interest at the rate of 12% per annum. 121

Should the Purchase Money not be paid as aforesaid, the Sellers have the right to cancel this con- 122
tract, in which case the amount deposited together with interest earned, if any, shall be forfeited to 123
the Sellers. If the deposit does not cover the Sellers' losses, they shall be entitled to claim further com- 124
pensation for their losses and for all expenses together with interest at the rate of 12% per annum. 125

**14. Sellers' default** 126

If the Sellers fail to execute a legal transfer or to deliver the vessel with everything belonging to her 127
in the manner and within the time specified in line 38, the Buyers shall have the right to cancel this contract 128
in which case the deposit in full shall be returned to the Buyers together with interest at the rate of 12 % per 129
annum. The Sellers shall make due compensation for the losses caused to the Buyers by failure to execute a 130
legal transfer or to deliver the vessel in the manner and within the time specified in line 38, if such are due to 131
the proven negligence of the Sellers. 132

**15. Arbitration** 133

If any dispute should arise in connection with the interpretation and fulfilment of this contract, 134
same shall be decided by arbitration in the city of[3] 135
and shall be referred to a single Arbitrator to be appointed by the parties hereto. If the parties cannot 136
agree upon the appointment of the single Arbitrator, the dispute shall be settled by three Arbitrators, 137
each party appointing one Arbitrator, the third being appointed by[4] 138
139

If either of the appointed Arbitrators refuses or is incapable of acting, the party who appointed 140
him, shall appoint a new Arbitrator in his place. 141

If one of the parties fails to appoint an Arbitrator — either originally or by way of substitution — 142
for two weeks after the other party having appointed his Arbitrator has sent the party making default 143
notice by mail, cable or telex to make the appointment, the party appointing the third Arbitrator 144
shall, after application from the party having appointed his Arbitrator, also appoint an Arbitrator on 145
behalf of the party making default. 146

The award rendered by the Arbitration Court shall be final and binding upon the parties and may 147
if necessary be enforced by the Court or any other competent authority in the same manner as a 148
judgement in the Court of Justice. 149

This contract shall be subject to the law of the country agreed as place of arbitration. 150



*1) The name of the Classification Society to be inserted.*
*2) Notes, if any, in the Surveyor's report which are accepted by the Classification Society without qualification are not to be taken into account.*
*3) The place of arbitration to be inserted. If this line is not filled in, it is understood that arbitration will take place in London in accordance with English law.*
*4) If this line is not filled in it is understood that the third Arbitrator shall be appointed by the London Maritime Arbitrators Association in London.*

APPENDIX 5

# MEMORANDUM OF AGREEMENT (NORWEGIAN SALEFORM 1993)

*Note*: This agreement is reproduced by kind permission of the Norwegian Shipbrokers' Association.

# MEMORANDUM OF AGREEMENT

Norwegian Shipbrokers' Association's Memorandum of Agreement for sale and purchase of ships. Adopted by The Baltic and International Maritime Council (BIMCO) in 1956.
Code-name
**SALEFORM 1993**
Revised 1966, 1983 and 1986/87.

Dated:

hereinafter called the Sellers, have agreed to sell, and 1

hereinafter called the Buyers, have agreed to buy 2

Name: 3

Classification Society/Class: 4

Built: By: 5

Flag: Place of Registration: 6

Call Sign: Grt/Nrt: 7

Register Number: 8

hereinafter called the Vessel, on the following terms and conditions: 9

**Definitions** 10

"Banking days" are days on which banks are open both in the country of the currency 11
stipulated for the Purchase Price in Clause 1 and in the place of closing stipulated in Clause 8. 12

"In writing" or "written" means a letter handed over from the Sellers to the Buyers or vice versa, 13
a registered letter, telex, telefax or other modern form of written communication. 14

"Classification Society" or "Class" means the Society referred to in line 4. 15

**1. Purchase Price** 16

**2. Deposit** 17

As security for the correct fulfilment of this Agreement the Buyers shall pay a deposit of 10 % 18
(ten per cent) of the Purchase Price within banking days from the date of this 19
Agreement. This deposit shall be placed with 20

and held by them in a joint account for the Sellers and the Buyers, to be released in accordance 21
with joint written instructions of the Sellers and the Buyers. Interest, if any, to be credited to the 22
Buyers. Any fee charged for holding the said deposit shall be borne equally by the Sellers and the 23
Buyers. 24

**3. Payment** 25

The said Purchase Price shall be paid in full free of bank charges to 26

on delivery of the Vessel, but not later than 3 banking days after the Vessel is in every respect 27
physically ready for delivery in accordance with the terms and conditions of this Agreement and 28
Notice of Readiness has been given in accordance with Clause 5. 29

**4. Inspections** 30

a)* The Buyers have inspected and accepted the Vessel's classification records. The Buyers have also inspected the Vessel at/in on and have accepted the Vessel following this inspection and the sale is outright and definite, subject only to the terms and conditions of this Agreement. 31 32 33 34

b)* The Buyers shall have the right to inspect the Vessel's classification records and declare whether same are accepted or not within 35 36

The Sellers shall provide for inspection of the Vessel at/in 37

The Buyers shall undertake the inspection without undue delay to the Vessel. Should the Buyers cause undue delay they shall compensate the Sellers for the losses thereby incurred. The Buyers shall inspect the Vessel without opening up and without cost to the Sellers. During the inspection, the Vessel's deck and engine log books shall be made available for examination by the Buyers. If the Vessel is accepted after such inspection, the sale shall become outright and definite, subject only to the terms and conditions of this Agreement, provided the Sellers receive written notice of acceptance from the Buyers within 72 hours after completion of such inspection. 38 39 40 41 42 43 44 45
Should notice of acceptance of the Vessel's classification records and of the Vessel not be received by the Sellers as aforesaid, the deposit together with interest earned shall be released immediately to the Buyers, whereafter this Agreement shall be null and void. 46 47 48

* *4 a) and 4b) are alternatives; delete whichever is not applicable. In the absence of deletions, alternative 4a) to apply.* 49 50

**5. Notices, time and place of delivery** 51

a) The Sellers shall keep the Buyers well informed of the Vessel's itinerary and shall provide the Buyers with , , and days notice of the estimated time of arrival at the intended place of drydocking/underwater inspection/delivery. When the Vessel is at the place of delivery and in every respect physically ready for delivery in accordance with this Agreement, the Sellers shall give the Buyers a written Notice of Readiness for delivery. 52 53 54 55 56

b) The Vessel shall be delivered and taken over safely afloat at a safe and accessible berth or anchorage at/in 57 58

in the Sellers' option. 59

Expected time of delivery: 60

Date of cancelling (see Clauses 5 c), 6 b) (iii) and 14): 61

c) If the Sellers anticipate that, notwithstanding the exercise of due diligence by them, the Vessel will not be ready for delivery by the cancelling date they may notify the Buyers in writing stating the date when they anticipate that the Vessel will be ready for delivery and propose a new cancelling date. Upon receipt of such notification the Buyers shall have the option of either cancelling this Agreement in accordance with Clause 14 within 7 running days of receipt of the notice or of accepting the new date as the new cancelling date. If the Buyers have not declared their option within 7 running days of receipt of the Sellers' notification or if the Buyers accept the new date, the date proposed in the Sellers' notification shall be deemed to be the new cancelling date and shall be substituted for the cancelling date stipulated in line 61. 62 63 64 65 66 67 68 69 70 71

If this Agreement is maintained with the new cancelling date all other terms and conditions hereof including those contained in Clauses 5 a) and 5 c) shall remain unaltered and in full force and effect. Cancellation or failure to cancel shall be entirely without prejudice to any claim for damages the Buyers may have under Clause 14 for the Vessel not being ready by the original cancelling date. 72 73 74 75 76

d) Should the Vessel become an actual, constructive or compromised total loss before delivery the deposit together with interest earned shall be released immediately to the Buyers whereafter this Agreement shall be null and void. 77 78 79

**6. Drydocking/Divers Inspection** 80

a)** The Sellers shall place the Vessel in drydock at the port of delivery for inspection by the Classification Society of the Vessel's underwater parts below the deepest load line, the extent of the inspection being in accordance with the Classification Society's rules. If the rudder, propeller, bottom or other underwater parts below the deepest load line are found broken, damaged or defective so as to affect the Vessel's class, such defects shall be made good at the Sellers' expense to the satisfaction of the Classification Society without condition/recommendation*. 81 82 83 84 85 86 87

b)** (i) The Vessel is to be delivered without drydocking. However, the Buyers shall have the right at their expense to arrange for an underwater inspection by a diver approved by the Classification Society prior to the delivery of the Vessel. The Sellers shall at their cost make the Vessel available for such inspection. The extent of the inspection and the conditions under which it is performed shall be to the satisfaction of the Classification Society. If the conditions at the port of delivery are unsuitable for such inspection, the Sellers shall make the Vessel available at a suitable alternative place near to the delivery port. 88 89 90 91 92 93 94 95

(ii) If the rudder, propeller, bottom or other underwater parts below the deepest load line are found broken, damaged or defective so as to affect the Vessel's class, then unless repairs can be carried out afloat to the satisfaction of the Classification Society, the Sellers shall arrange for the Vessel to be drydocked at their expense for inspection by the Classification Society of the Vessel's underwater parts below the deepest load line, the extent of the inspection being in accordance with the Classification Society's rules. If the rudder, propeller, bottom or other underwater parts below the deepest load line are found broken, damaged or defective so as to affect the Vessel's class, such defects shall be made good by the Sellers at their expense to the satisfaction of the Classification Society without condition/recommendation*. In such event the Sellers are to pay also for the cost of the underwater inspection and the Classification Society's attendance. 96 97 98 99 100 101 102 103 104 105 106

(iii) If the Vessel is to be drydocked pursuant to Clause 6 b) (ii) and no suitable dry-docking facilities are available at the port of delivery, the Sellers shall take the Vessel to a port where suitable drydocking facilities are available, whether within or outside the delivery range as per Clause 5 b). Once drydocking has taken place the Sellers shall deliver the Vessel at a port within the delivery range as per Clause 5 b) which shall, for the purpose of this Clause, become the new port of delivery. In such event the cancelling date provided for in Clause 5 b) shall be extended by the additional time required for the drydocking and extra steaming, but limited to a maximum of 14 running days. 107 108 109 110 111 112 113 114

c) If the Vessel is drydocked pursuant to Clause 6 a) or 6 b) above 115

(i) the Classification Society may require survey of the tailshaft system, the extent of the survey being to the satisfaction of the Classification surveyor. If such survey is not required by the Classification Society, the Buyers shall have the right to require the tailshaft to be drawn and surveyed by the Classification Society, the extent of the survey being in accordance with the Classification Society's rules for tailshaft survey and consistent with the current stage of the Vessel's survey cycle. The Buyers shall declare whether they require the tailshaft to be drawn and surveyed not later than by the completion of the inspection by the Classification Society. The drawing and refitting of the tailshaft shall be arranged by the Sellers. Should any parts of the tailshaft system be condemned or found defective so as to affect the Vessel's class, those parts shall be renewed or made good at the Sellers' expense to the satisfaction of the Classification Society without condition/recommendation*. 116 117 118 119 120 121 122 123 124 125 126 127

(ii) the expenses relating to the survey of the tailshaft system shall be borne by the Buyers unless the Classification Society requires such survey to be carried out, in which case the Sellers shall pay these expenses. The Sellers shall also pay the expenses if the Buyers require the survey and parts of the system are condemned or found defective or broken so as to affect the Vessel's class*. 128 129 130 131 132

(iii) the expenses in connection with putting the Vessel in and taking her out of drydock, including the drydock dues and the Classification Society's fees shall be paid by the Sellers if the Classification Society issues any condition/recommendation* as a result of the survey or if it requires survey of the tailshaft system. In all other cases the Buyers shall pay the aforesaid expenses, dues and fees. 133 134 135 136 137

(iv) the Buyers' representative shall have the right to be present in the drydock, but without interfering with the work or decisions of the Classification surveyor. 138 139

(v) the Buyers shall have the right to have the underwater parts of the Vessel cleaned and painted at their risk and expense without interfering with the Sellers' or the Classification surveyor's work, if any, and without affecting the Vessel's timely delivery. If, however, the Buyers' work in drydock is still in progress when the Sellers have completed the work which the Sellers are required to do, the additional docking time needed to complete the Buyers' work shall be for the Buyers' risk and expense. In the event that the Buyers' work requires such additional time, the Sellers may upon completion of the Sellers' work tender Notice of Readiness for delivery whilst the Vessel is still in drydock and the Buyers shall be obliged to take delivery in accordance with Clause 3, whether the Vessel is in drydock or not and irrespective of Clause 5 b). 140 141 142 143 144 145 146 147 148 149

* Notes, if any, in the surveyor's report which are accepted by the Classification Society without condition/recommendation are not to be taken into account. 150 151

** *6 a) and 6 b) are alternatives; delete whichever is not applicable. In the absence of deletions, alternative 6 a) to apply.* 152 153

### 7. Spares/bunkers, etc. 154

The Sellers shall deliver the Vessel to the Buyers with everything belonging to her on board and on shore. All spare parts and spare equipment including spare tail-end shaft(s) and/or spare propeller(s)/propeller blade(s), if any, belonging to the Vessel at the time of inspection used or unused, whether on board or not shall become the Buyers' property, but spares on order are to be excluded. Forwarding charges, if any, shall be for the Buyers' account. The Sellers are not required to replace spare parts including spare tail-end shaft(s) and spare propeller(s)/propeller blade(s) which are taken out of spare and used as replacement prior to delivery, but the replaced items shall be the property of the Buyers. The radio installation and navigational equipment shall be included in the sale without extra payment if they are the property of the Sellers. Unused stores and provisions shall be included in the sale and be taken over by the Buyers without extra payment. 155 156 157 158 159 160 161 162 163 164

The Sellers have the right to take ashore crockery, plates, cutlery, linen and other articles bearing the Sellers' flag or name, provided they replace same with similar unmarked items. Library, forms, etc., exclusively for use in the Sellers' vessel(s), shall be excluded without compensation. Captain's, Officers' and Crew's personal belongings including the slop chest are to be excluded from the sale, as well as the following additional items (including items on hire): 165 166 167 168 169

The Buyers shall take over the remaining bunkers and unused lubricating oils in storage tanks and sealed drums and pay the current net market price (excluding barging expenses) at the port and date of delivery of the Vessel. 170 171 172
Payment under this Clause shall be made at the same time and place and in the same currency as the Purchase Price. 173 174

**8. Documentation** 175

The place of closing: 176

In exchange for payment of the Purchase Price the Sellers shall furnish the Buyers with delivery documents, namely: 177 178

a) Legal Bill of Sale in a form recordable in (the country in which the Buyers are to register the Vessel), warranting that the Vessel is free from all encumbrances, mortgages and maritime liens or any other debts or claims whatsoever, duly notarially attested and legalized by the consul of such country or other competent authority. 179 180 181 182

b) Current Certificate of Ownership issued by the competent authorities of the flag state of the Vessel. 183 184

c) Confirmation of Class issued within 72 hours prior to delivery. 185

d) Current Certificate issued by the competent authorities stating that the Vessel is free from registered encumbrances. 186 187

e) Certificate of Deletion of the Vessel from the Vessel's registry or other official evidence of deletion appropriate to the Vessel's registry at the time of delivery, or, in the event that the registry does not as a matter of practice issue such documentation immediately, a written undertaking by the Sellers to effect deletion from the Vessel's registry forthwith and furnish a Certificate or other official evidence of deletion to the Buyers promptly and latest within 4 (four) weeks after the Purchase Price has been paid and the Vessel has been delivered. 188 189 190 191 192 193

f) Any such additional documents as may reasonably be required by the competent authorities for the purpose of registering the Vessel, provided the Buyers notify the Sellers of any such documents as soon as possible after the date of this Agreement. 194 195 196

At the time of delivery the Buyers and Sellers shall sign and deliver to each other a Protocol of Delivery and Acceptance confirming the date and time of delivery of the Vessel from the Sellers to the Buyers. 197 198 199

At the time of delivery the Sellers shall hand to the Buyers the classification certificate(s) as well as all plans etc., which are on board the Vessel. Other certificates which are on board the Vessel shall also be handed over to the Buyers unless the Sellers are required to retain same, in which case the Buyers to have the right to take copies. Other technical documentation which may be in the Sellers' possession shall be promptly forwarded to the Buyers at their expense, if they so request. The Sellers may keep the Vessel's log books but the Buyers to have the right to take copies of same. 200 201 202 203 204 205 206

**9. Encumbrances** 207

The Sellers warrant that the Vessel, at the time of delivery, is free from all charters, encumbrances, mortgages and maritime liens or any other debts whatsoever. The Sellers hereby undertake to indemnify the Buyers against all consequences of claims made against the Vessel which have been incurred prior to the time of delivery. 208 209 210 211

**10. Taxes, etc.** 212

Any taxes, fees and expenses in connection with the purchase and registration under the Buyers' flag shall be for the Buyers' account, whereas similar charges in connection with the closing of the Sellers' register shall be for the Sellers' account. 213 214 215

**11. Condition on delivery** 216

The Vessel with everything belonging to her shall be at the Sellers' risk and expense until she is delivered to the Buyers, but subject to the terms and conditions of this Agreement she shall be delivered and taken over as she was at the time of inspection, fair wear and tear excepted. 217 218 219
However, the Vessel shall be delivered with her class maintained without condition/recommendation*, free of average damage affecting the Vessel's class, and with her classification certificates and national certificates, as well as all other certificates the Vessel had at the time of inspection, valid and unextended without condition/recommendation* by Class or the relevant authorities at the time of delivery. 220 221 222 223 224
"Inspection" in this Clause 11, shall mean the Buyers' inspection according to Clause 4 a) or 4 b), if applicable, or the Buyers' inspection prior to the signing of this Agreement. If the Vessel is taken over without inspection, the date of this Agreement shall be the relevant date. 225 226 227

* Notes, if any, in the surveyor's report which are accepted by the Classification Society without condition/recommendation are not to be taken into account. 228 229

**12. Name/markings** 230

Upon delivery the Buyers undertake to change the name of the Vessel and alter funnel markings. 231

**13. Buyers' default** 232

Should the deposit not be paid in accordance with Clause 2, the Sellers have the right to cancel this Agreement, and they shall be entitled to claim compensation for their losses and for all expenses incurred together with interest. 233 234 235
Should the Purchase Price not be paid in accordance with Clause 3, the Sellers have the right to cancel the Agreement, in which case the deposit together with interest earned shall be released to the Sellers. If the deposit does not cover their loss, the Sellers shall be entitled to claim further compensation for their losses and for all expenses incurred together with interest. 236 237 238 239

**14. Sellers' default** 240

Should the Sellers fail to give Notice of Readiness in accordance with Clause 5 a) or fail to be ready to validly complete a legal transfer by the date stipulated in line 61 the Buyers shall have the option of cancelling this Agreement provided always that the Sellers shall be granted a maximum of 3 banking days after Notice of Readiness has been given to make arrangements for the documentation set out in Clause 8. If after Notice of Readiness has been given but before the Buyers have taken delivery, the Vessel ceases to be physically ready for delivery and is not made physically ready again in every respect by the date stipulated in line 61 and new Notice of Readiness given, the Buyers shall retain their option to cancel. In the event that the Buyers elect to cancel this Agreement the deposit together with interest earned shall be released to them immediately . 241 242 243 244 245 246 247 248 249 250
Should the Sellers fail to give Notice of Readiness by the date stipulated in line 61 or fail to be ready to validly complete a legal transfer as aforesaid they shall make due compensation to the Buyers for their loss and for all expenses together with interest if their failure is due to proven negligence and whether or not the Buyers cancel this Agreement. 251 252 253 254

**15. Buyers' representatives** 255

After this Agreement has been signed by both parties and the deposit has been lodged, the Buyers have the right to place two representatives on board the Vessel at their sole risk and expense upon arrival at on or about 256 257 258
These representatives are on board for the purpose of familiarisation and in the capacity of observers only, and they shall not interfere in any respect with the operation of the Vessel. The Buyers' representatives shall sign the Sellers' letter of indemnity prior to their embarkation. 259 260 261

**16. Arbitration** 262

a)* This Agreement shall be governed by and construed in accordance with English law and any dispute arising out of this Agreement shall be referred to arbitration in London in accordance with the Arbitration Acts 1950 and 1979 or any statutory modification or re-enactment thereof for the time being in force, one arbitrator being appointed by each party. On the receipt by one party of the nomination in writing of the other party's arbitrator, that party shall appoint their arbitrator within fourteen days, failing which the decision of the single arbitrator appointed shall apply. If two arbitrators properly appointed shall not agree they shall appoint an umpire whose decision shall be final. 263 264 265 266 267 268 269 270

b)* This Agreement shall be governed by and construed in accordance with Title 9 of the United States Code and the Law of the State of New York and should any dispute arise out of this Agreement, the matter in dispute shall be referred to three persons at New York, one to be appointed by each of the parties hereto, and the third by the two so chosen; their decision or that of any two of them shall be final, and for purpose of enforcing any award, this Agreement may be made a rule of the Court.
The proceedings shall be conducted in accordance with the rules of the Society of Maritime Arbitrators, Inc. New York. 271 272 273 274 275 276 277 278

c)* Any dispute arising out of this Agreement shall be referred to arbitration at 279
, subject to the procedures applicable there. 280
The laws of shall govern this Agreement. 281

* *16 a), 16 b) and 16 c) are alternatives; delete whichever is not applicable. In the absence of deletions, alternative 16 a) to apply.* 282 283

APPENDIX 6

# NEW YORK PRODUCE EXCHANGE FORM 1946

*Note:* This form is reproduced with the kind permission of the Association of Ship Brokers and Agents.

## New York Produce Exchange Form 1946

# Time Charter

GOVERNMENT FORM

*Approved by the New York Produce Exchange*

November 6th, 1913—Amended October 20th, 1921; August 6th, 1931; October 3rd, 1946

1 **This Charter Party,** made and concluded in ........................................ day of .................... 19.....
2 Between ........................................
3 Owners of the good .................... { Steamship / Motorship } .................... of ....................
4 of .................... tons gross register, and .................... tons net register, having engines of .................... indicated horse power
5 and with hull, machinery and equipment in a thoroughly efficient state, and classed ....................
6 at .................... of about .................... cubic feet bale capacity, and about .................... tons of 2240 lbs.
7 deadweight capacity (cargo and bunkers, including fresh water and stores not exceeding one and one-half percent of ship's deadweight capacity,
8 allowing a minimum of fifty tons) on a draft of .................... feet .................... inches on .................... Summer freeboard, inclusive of permanent bunkers,
9 which are of the capacity of about .................... tons of fuel, and capable of steaming, fully laden, under good weather
10 conditions about .................... knots on a consumption of about .................... tons of best Welsh coal—best grade fuel oil—best grade Diesel oil,
11 now ........................................
12 .................... and .................... Charterers of the City of ....................

13 **Witnesseth,** That the said Owners agree to let, and the said Charterers agree to hire the said vessel, from the time of delivery, for
14 about ........................................
15 .................... within below mentioned trading limits.
16 Charterers to have liberty to sublet the vessel for all or any part of the time covered by this Charter, but Charterers remaining responsible for
17 the fulfillment of this Charter Party.
18 Vessel to be placed at the disposal of the Charterers, at ....................
19 ........................................
20 in such dock or at such wharf or place (where she may safely lie, always afloat, at all times of tide, except as otherwise provided in clause No. 6), as
21 the Charterers may direct. If such dock, wharf or place be not available time to count as provided for in clause No. 5. Vessel on her delivery to be
22 ready to receive cargo with clean-swept holds and tight, staunch, strong and in every way fitted for the service, having water ballast, winches and
23 donkey boiler with sufficient steam power, or if not equipped with donkey boiler, then other power sufficient to run all the winches at one and the same
24 time (and with full complement of officers, seamen, engineers and firemen for a vessel of her tonnage), to be employed, in carrying lawful merchan-
25 dise, including petroleum or its products, in proper containers, excluding ....................
26 (vessel is not to be employed in the carriage of Live Stock, but Charterers are to have the privilege of shipping a small number on deck at their risk,
27 all necessary fittings and other requirements to be for account of Charterers), in such lawful trades, between safe port and/or ports in British North
28 America, and/or United States of America, and/or West Indies, and/or Central America, and/or Caribbean Sea, and/or Gulf of Mexico, and/or
29 Mexico, and/or South America .................... and/or Europe
30 and/or Africa, and/or Asia, and/or Australia, and/or Tasmania, and/or New Zealand, but excluding Magdalena River, River St. Lawrence between
31 October 31st and May 15th, Hudson Bay and all unsafe ports; also excluding, when out of season, White Sea, Black Sea and the Baltic,
32 ........................................
33 ........................................
34 ........................................
35 as the Charterers or their Agents shall direct, on the following conditions:
36 1. That the Owners shall provide and pay for all provisions, wages and consular shipping and discharging fees of the Crew; shall pay for the
37 insurance of the vessel, also for all the cabin, deck, engine-room and other necessary stores, including boiler water and maintain her class and keep
38 the vessel in a thoroughly efficient state in hull, machinery and equipment for and during the service.
39 2. That the Charterers shall provide and pay for all the fuel except as otherwise agreed, Port Charges, Pilotages, Agencies, Commissions,
40 Consular Charges (except those pertaining to the Crew) and all other usual expenses except those before stated, but when the vessel puts into
41 a port for causes for which vessel is responsible, then all such charges incurred shall be paid by the Owners. Fumigations ordered because of
42 illness of the crew to be for Owners account. Fumigations ordered because of cargoes carried or ports visited while vessel is employed under this
43 charter to be for Charterers account. All other fumigations to be for Charterers account after vessel has been on charter for a continuous period
44 of six months or more.
45 Charterers are to provide necessary dunnage and shifting boards, also any extra fittings requisite for a special trade or unusual cargo, but
46 Owners to allow them the use of any dunnage and shifting boards already aboard vessel. Charterers to have the privilege of using shifting boards
47 for dunnage, they making good any damage thereto.
48 3. That the Charterers, at the port of delivery, and the Owners, at the port of re-delivery, shall take over and pay for all fuel remaining on
49 board the vessel at the current prices in the respective ports, the vessel to be delivered with not less than .................... tons and not more than
50 .................... tons and to be re-delivered with not less than .................... tons and not more than .................... tons.
51 4. That the Charterers shall pay for the use and hire of the said Vessel at the rate of ....................
52 .................... United States Currency per ton on vessel's total deadweight carrying capacity, including bunkers and
53 stores, on .................... summer freeboard, per Calendar Month, commencing on and from the day of her delivery, as aforesaid, and at
54 and after the same rate for any part of a month; hire to continue until the hour of the day of her re-delivery in like good order and condition, ordinary
55 wear and tear excepted, to the Owners (unless lost) at ....................
56 .................... unless otherwise mutually agreed. Charterers are to give Owners not less than .................... days
57 notice of vessel's expected date of re-delivery, and probable port.
58 5. Payment of said hire to be made in New York in cash in United States Currency, semi-monthly in advance, and for the last half month or
59 part of same the approximate amount of hire, and should same not cover the actual time, hire is to be paid for the balance day by day, as it becomes
60 due, if so required by Owners, unless bank guarantee or deposit is made by the Charterers, otherwise failing the punctual and regular payment of the
61 hire, or bank guarantee, or on any breach of this Charter Party, the Owners shall be at liberty to withdraw the vessel from the service of the Char-
62 terers, without prejudice to any claim they (the Owners) may otherwise have on the Charterers. Time to count from 7 a.m. on the working day
63 following that on which written notice of readiness has been given to Charterers or their Agents before 4 p.m., but if required by Charterers, they
64 to have the privilege of using vessel at once, such time used to count as hire.
65 Cash for vessel's ordinary disbursements at any port may be advanced as required by the Captain, by the Charterers or their Agents, subject
66 to 2½% commission and such advances shall be deducted from the hire. The Charterers, however, shall in no way be responsible for the application
67 of such advances.
68 6. That the cargo or cargoes be laden and/or discharged in any dock or at any wharf or place that Charterers or their Agents may
69 direct, provided the vessel can safely lie always afloat at any time of tide, except at such places where it is customary for similar size vessels to safely
70 lie aground.
71 7. That the whole reach of the Vessel's Hold, Decks, and usual places of loading (not more than she can reasonably stow and carry), also
72 accommodations for Supercargo, if carried, shall be at the Charterers' disposal, reserving only proper and sufficient space for Ship's officers, crew,
73 tackle, apparel, furniture, provisions, stores and fuel. Charterers have the privilege of passengers as far as accommodations allow, Charterers
74 paying Owners .................... per day per passenger for accommodations and meals. However, it is agreed that in case any fines or extra expenses are
75 incurred in the consequence of the carriage of passengers, Charterers are to bear such risk and expense.
76 8. That the Captain shall prosecute his voyages with the utmost despatch, and shall render all customary assistance with ship's crew and
77 boats. The Captain (although appointed by the Owners), shall be under the orders and directions of the Charterers as regards employment and
78 agency; and Charterers are to load, stow, and trim the cargo at their expense under the supervision of the Captain, who is to sign Bills of Lading for
79 cargo as presented, in conformity with Mate's or Tally Clerk's receipts.
80 9. That if the Charterers shall have reason to be dissatisfied with the conduct of the Captain, Officers, or Engineers, the Owners shall on
81 receiving particulars of the complaint, investigate the same, and, if necessary, make a change in the appointments.
82 10. That the Charterers shall have permission to appoint a Supercargo, who shall accompany the vessel and see that voyages are prosecuted
83 with the utmost despatch. He is to be furnished with free accommodation, and same fare as provided for Captain's table, Charterers paying at the
84 rate of $1.00 per day. Owners to victual Pilots and Customs Officers, and also, when authorized by Charterers or their Agents, to victual Tally
85 Clerks, Stevedore's Foreman, etc., Charterers paying at the current rate per meal, for all such victualling.
86 11. That the Charterers shall furnish the Captain from time to time with all requisite instructions and sailing directions, in writing, and the
87 Captain shall keep a full and correct Log of the voyage or voyages, which are to be patent to the Charterers or their Agents, and furnish the Char-
88 terers, their Agents or Supercargo, when required, with a true copy of daily Logs, showing the course of the vessel and distance run and the con-
89 sumption of fuel.
90 12. That the Captain shall use diligence in caring for the ventilation of the cargo.
91 13. That the Charterers shall have the option of continuing this charter for a further period of ....................
92 ........................................

93 on giving written notice thereof to the Owners or their Agents ........................days previous to the expiration of the first-named term, or any declared option.
94 14. That if required by Charterers, time not to commence before ........................................................................................ ......and should vessel
95 not have given written notice of readiness on or before ........................................................................................ but not later than 4 p.m. Charterers or
96 their Agents to have the option of cancelling this Charter at any time not later than the day of vessel's readiness.
97 15. That in the event of the loss of time from deficiency of men or stores, fire, breakdown or damages to hull, machinery or equipment,
98 grounding, detention by average accidents to ship or cargo, drydocking for the purpose of examination or painting bottom, or by any other cause
99 preventing the full working of the vessel, the payment of hire shall cease for the time thereby lost; and if upon the voyage the speed be reduced by
100 defect in or breakdown of any part of her hull, machinery or equipment, the time so lost, and the cost of any extra fuel consumed in consequence
101 thereof, and all extra expenses shall be deducted from the hire.
102 16. That should the Vessel be lost, money paid in advance and not earned (reckoning from the date of loss or being last heard of) shall be
103 returned to the Charterers at once. The act of God, enemies, fire, restraint of Princes, Rulers and People, and all dangers and accidents of the Seas,
104 Rivers, Machinery, Boilers and Steam Navigation, and errors of Navigation throughout this Charter Party, always mutually excepted.
105 The vessel shall have the liberty to sail with or without pilots, to tow and to be towed, to assist vessels in distress, and to deviate for the
106 purpose of saving life and property.
107 17. That should any dispute arise between Owners and the Charterers, the matter in dispute shall be referred to three persons at New York,
108 one to be appointed by each of the parties hereto, and the third by the two so chosen; their decision or that of any two of them, shall be final, and for
109 the purpose of enforcing any award, this agreement may be made a rule of the Court. The Arbitrators shall be commercial men.
110 18. That the Owners shall have a lien upon all cargoes, and all sub-freights for any amounts due under this Charter, including General Aver-
111 age contributions, and the Charterers to have a lien on the Ship for all monies paid in advance and not earned, and any overpaid hire or excess
112 deposit to be returned at once. Charterers will not suffer, nor permit to be continued, any lien or encumbrance incurred by them or their agents, which
113 might have priority over the title and interest of the owners in the vessel.
114 19. That all derelicts and salvage shall be for Owners' and Charterers' equal benefit after deducting Owners' and Charterers' expenses and
115 Crew's proportion. General Average shall be adjusted, stated and settled, according to Rules 1 to 15, inclusive, 17 to 22, inclusive, and Rule F of
116 York-Antwerp Rules 1924, at such port or place in the United States as may be selected by the carrier, and as to matters not provided for by these
117 Rules, according to the laws and usages at the port of New York. In such adjustment disbursements in foreign currencies shall be exchanged into
118 United States money at the rate prevailing on the dates made and allowances for damage to cargo claimed in foreign currency shall be converted at
119 the rate prevailing on the last day of discharge at the port or place of final discharge of such damaged cargo from the ship. Average agreement or
120 bond and such additional security, as may be required by the carrier, must be furnished before delivery of the goods. Such cash deposit as the carrier
121 or his agents may deem sufficient as additional security for the contribution of the goods and for any salvage and special charges thereon, shall, if
122 required, be made by the goods, shippers, consignees or owners of the goods to the carrier before delivery. Such deposit shall, at the option of the
123 carrier, be payable in United States money and be remitted to the adjuster. When so remitted the deposit shall be held in a special account at the
124 place of adjustment in the name of the adjuster pending settlement of the General Average and refunds or credit balances, if any, shall be paid in
125 United States money.
126 In the event of accident, danger, damage, or disaster, before or after commencement of the voyage resulting from any cause whatsoever,
127 whether due to negligence or not, for which, or for the consequence of which, the carrier is not responsible, by statute, contract, or otherwise, the
128 goods, the shipper and the consignee, jointly and severally, shall contribute with the carrier in general average to the payment of any sacrifices,
129 losses, or expenses of a general average nature that may be made or incurred, and shall pay salvage and special charges incurred in respect of the
130 goods. If a salving ship is owned or operated by the carrier, salvage shall be paid for as fully and in the same manner as if such salving ship or
131 ships belonged to strangers.
132 Provisions as to General Average in accordance with the above are to be included in all bills of lading issued hereunder.
133 20. Fuel used by the vessel while off hire, also for cooking, condensing water, or for grates and stoves to be agreed to as to quantity, and the
134 cost of replacing same, to be allowed by Owners.
135 21. That as the vessel may be from time to time employed in tropical waters during the term of this Charter, Vessel is to be docked at a
136 convenient place, bottom cleaned and painted whenever Charterers and Captain think necessary, at least once in every six months, reckoning from
137 time of last painting, and payment of the hire to be suspended until she is again in proper state for the service.
138 ........................................................................................................................................................................................................
139 ........................................................................................................................................................................................................
140 22. Owners shall maintain the gear of the ship as fitted, providing gear (for all derricks) capable of handling lifts up to three tons, also
141 providing ropes, falls, slings and blocks. If vessel is fitted with derricks capable of handling heavier lifts, Owners are to provide necessary gear for
142 same, otherwise equipment and gear for heavier lifts shall be for Charterers' account. Owners also to provide on the vessel lanterns and oil for
143 night work, and vessel to give use of electric light when so fitted, but any additional lights over those on board to be at Charterers' expense. The
144 Charterers to have the use of any gear on board the vessel.
145 23. Vessel to work night and day, if required by Charterers, and all winches to be at Charterers' disposal during loading and discharging;
146 steamer to provide one winchman per hatch to work winches day and night, as required, Charterers agreeing to pay officers, engineers, winchmen,
147 deck hands and donkeymen for overtime work done in accordance with the working hours and rates stated in the ship's articles. If the rules of the
148 port, or labor unions, prevent crew from driving winches, shore Winchmen to be paid by Charterers. In the event of a disabled winch or winches, or
149 insufficient power to operate winches, Owners to pay for shore engine, or engines, in lieu thereof, if required, and pay any loss of time occasioned
150 thereby.
151 24. It is also mutually agreed that this Charter is subject to all the terms and provisions of and all the exemptions from liability contained
152 in the Act of Congress of the United States approved on the 13th day of February, 1893, and entitled "An Act relating to Navigation of Vessels,
153 etc.," in respect of all cargo shipped under this charter to or from the United States of America. It is further subject to the following clauses, both
154 of which are to be included in all bills of lading issued hereunder:
155 U.S.A. Clause Paramount
156 This bill of lading shall have effect subject to the provisions of the Carriage of Goods by Sea Act of the United States, approved April
157 16, 1936, which shall be deemed to be incorporated herein, and nothing herein contained shall be deemed a surrender by the carrier of
158 any of its rights or immunities or an increase of any of its responsibilities or liabilities under said Act. If any term of this bill of lading
159 be repugnant to said Act to any extent, such term shall be void to that extent, but no further.
160 Both-to-Blame Collision Clause
161 If the ship comes into collision with another ship as a result of the negligence of the other ship and any act, neglect or default of the
162 Master, mariner, pilot or the servants of the Carrier in the navigation or in the management of the ship, the owners of the goods carried
163 hereunder will indemnify the Carrier against all loss or liability to the other or non-carrying ship or her owners in so far as such loss
164 or liability represents loss of, or damage to, or any claim whatsoever of the owners of said goods, paid or payable by the other or non-
165 carrying ship or her owners to the owners of said goods and set off, recouped or recovered by the other or non-carrying ship or her
166 owners as part of their claim against the carrying ship or carrier.
167 25. The vessel shall not be required to enter any ice-bound port, or any port where lights or light-ships have been or are about to be with-
168 drawn by reason of ice, or where there is risk that in the ordinary course of things the vessel will not be able on account of ice to safely enter the
169 port or to get out after having completed loading or discharging.
170 26. Nothing herein stated is to be construed as a demise of the vessel to the Time Charterers. The owners to remain responsible for the
171 navigation of the vessel, insurance, crew, and all other matters, same as when trading for their own account.
172 27. A commission of 2½ per cent is payable by the Vessel and Owners to
173 ........................................................................................................................................................................................................
174 on hire earned and paid under this Charter, and also upon any continuation or extension of this Charter.
175 28. An address commission of 2½ per cent payable to ........................................................................ on the hire earned and paid under this Charter.

By cable authority from

The original Charter Party in our possession. As..........................................For Owners

**BROKERS.**

APPENDIX 7

# INTER-CLUB NEW YORK PRODUCE EXCHANGE AGREEMENT 1996

*Note:* The Inter-Club New York Produce Exchange Agreement (1996) is reproduced by permission from the International Group of P & I Clubs.

This Agreement is made on the 1 of September 1996 between the P & I Clubs being members of The International Group of P & I Associations listed below (hereafter referred to as 'the Clubs').

This Agreement replaces the Inter Club Agreement 1984 in respect of all charterparties specified in clause (1) hereof and shall continue in force until varied or terminated. Any variation to be effective must be approved in writing by all Clubs but it is open to any Club to withdraw from the Agreement on giving to all the other Clubs not less than three months' written notice thereof, such withdrawal to take effect at the expiration of that period. After the expiry of such notice the Agreement shall nevertheless continue as between all the Clubs, other than the Club giving such notice who shall remain bound by and be entitled to the benefit of this Agreement in respect of all cargo claims arising out of charterparties commenced prior to the expiration of such notice.

The Clubs will recommend to their Members without qualification that their Members adopt this Agreement for the purpose of apportioning liability for claims in respect of cargo which arise under, out of or in connection with all charterparties on the New York Produce Exchange Form 1946 or 1993 or Asbatime Form 1981 (or any subsequent amendment of such Forms), whether or not this Agreement has been incorporated into such charterparties.

## Scope of application

(1) This Agreement applies to any charterparty which is entered into after the date hereof on the New York Produce Exchange Form 1946 or 1993 or Asbatime Form 1981 (or any subsequent amendment of such Forms).

(2) The terms of this Agreement shall apply notwithstanding anything to the contrary in any other provision of the charterparty; in particular the provisions of clause (6) (time bar) shall apply notwithstanding any provision of the charterparty or rule of law to the contrary.

(3) For the purposes of this Agreement, cargo claim(s) mean claims for loss, damage, shortage (including slackage, ullage or pilferage), overcarriage of or delay to cargo including customs dues or fines in respect of such loss, damage, shortage, overcarriage or delay and include
   (a) any legal costs claimed by the original person making any such claim;
   (b) any interest claimed by the original person making any such claim;
   (c) all legal, Club correspondents' and experts' costs reasonably incurred in the defence of or in the settlement of the claim made by the original person, but shall not include any costs of whatsoever nature incurred in making a claim under this Agreement or in seeking an indemnity under the charterparty.

(4) Apportionment under this Agreement shall only be applied to cargo claims where:

(a) the claim was made under a contract of carriage, whatever its form,

(i) which was authorised under the charterparty; or

(ii) which would have been authorised under the charterparty but for the inclusion in that contract of carriage of Through Transport or Combined Transport provisions,

provided that

1. in the case of contracts of carriage containing Through Transport or Combined Transport provisions (whether falling within (i) or (ii) above) the loss, damage, shortage, overcarriage or delay occurred after commencement of the loading of the cargo onto the chartered vessel and prior to completion of its discharge from that vessel (the burden of proof being on the charterer to establish that the loss, damage, shortage, overcarriage or delay did or did not so occur); and

2. the contract of carriage (or that part of the transit that comprised carriage on the chartered vessel) incorporated terms no less favourable to the carrier than the Hague or Hague Visby Rules, or, when compulsorily applicable by operation of law to the contract of carriage, the Hamburg Rules or any national law giving effect thereto

and

(b) the cargo responsibility clauses in the charterparty have not been materially amended. A material amendment is one which makes the liability, as between owners and charterers, for cargo claims clear. In particular, it is agreed solely for the purposes of this Agreement:

(i) that the addition of the words 'and responsibility' in clause 8 of the New York Produce Exchange Form 1946 or 1993 or clause 8 of the Asbatime Form 1981, or similar amendment of the charterparty making the Master responsible for cargo handling, is not a material amendment; and

(ii) that if the words 'cargo claims' are added to the second sentence of clause 26 of the New York Produce Exchange Form 1946 or 1993 or clause 25 of the Asbatime Form 1981, apportionment under this Agreement shall not be applied under any circumstances even if the charterparty is made subject to the terms of this Agreement;

and

(c) the claim has been properly settled or compromised and paid.

(5) This Agreement applies regardless of legal forum or place of arbitration specified in the charterparty and regardless of any incorporation of the Hague, Hague Visby Rules or Hamburg Rules therein.

## Time Bar

(6) Recovery under this Agreement by an owner or charterer shall be deemed to be waived and absolutely barred unless written notification of the cargo claim has been given to the other party to the charterparty within 24 months of the date of delivery of the cargo or the date the cargo should have been delivered, save that, where the Hamburg Rules or any national legislation giving effect thereto are compulsorily applicable by operation of law to the contract of carriage or to that part of the transit that comprised carriage on the chartered vessel, the period shall be 36 months. Such notification shall if possible include details of the contract of carriage, the nature of the claim and the amount claimed.

## The apportionment

(7) The amount of any cargo claim to be apportioned under this Agreement shall be the amount in fact borne by the party to the charterparty seeking apportionment, regardless of whether that claim may be or has been apportioned by application of this Agreement to another charterparty.

(8) Cargo claims shall be apportioned as follows:

(a) Claims in fact arising out of unseaworthiness and/or error or fault in navigation or management of the vessel:

100% Owners

save where the owner proves that the unseaworthiness was caused by the loading, stowage, lashing, discharge or other handling of the cargo, in which case the claim shall be apportioned under sub-clause (b).

(b) Claims in fact arising out of the loading, stowage, lashing, discharge, storage or other handling of cargo:

100% Charterers

unless the words 'and responsibility' are added in clause 8 or there is a similar amendment making the master responsible for cargo handling in which case:

50% Charterers
50% Owners

save where the charterer proves that the failure properly to load, stow, lash, discharge or handle the cargo was caused by the unseaworthiness of the vessel in which case:

100% Owners

(c) Subject to (a) and (b) above, claims for shortage or overcarriage:

50% Charterers
50% Owners

unless there is clear and irrefutable evidence that the claim arose out of pilferage or act or neglect by one or the other (including their servants or sub-contractors) in which case that party shall then bear 100% of the claim.

(d) All other cargo claims whatsoever (including claims for delay to cargo):

50% Charterers
50% Owners

unless there is clear and irrefutable evidence that the claim arose out of the act or neglect of the one or the other (including their servants or sub-contractors) in which case that party shall then bear 100% of the claim.

## Governing Law

(9) This Agreement shall be subject to English Law and Jurisdiction, unless it is incorporated into the charterparty (or the settlement of claims in respect of cargo under the charterparty is made subject to this Agreement), in which case it shall be subject to the law and jurisdiction provisions governing the charterparty.

APPENDIX 8

# GENCON

*Note:* GENCON is reproduced by permission of The Baltic and International Maritime Council.

# GENCON

| 1. Shipbroker | **RECOMMENDED**<br>**THE BALTIC AND INTERNATIONAL MARITIME COUNCIL**<br>**UNIFORM GENERAL CHARTER (AS REVISED 1922, 1976 and 1994)**<br>**(To be used for trades for which no specially approved form is in force)**<br>**CODE NAME: "GENCON"** Part I<br>2. Place and date |
|---|---|
| 3. Owners/Place of business (Cl. 1) | 4. Charterers/Place of business (Cl. 1) |
| 5. Vessel's name (Cl. 1) | 6. GT/NT (Cl. 1) |
| 7. DWT all told on summer load line in metric tons (abt.) (Cl. 1) | 8. Present position (Cl. 1) |
| 9. Expected ready to load (abt.) (Cl. 1) | |
| 10. Loading port or place (Cl. 1) | 11. Discharging port or place (Cl. 1) |
| 12. Cargo (also state quantity and margin in Owners' option, if agreed; if full and complete cargo not agreed state "part cargo" (Cl. 1) | |
| 13. Freight rate (also state whether freight prepaid or payable on delivery) (Cl. 4) | 14. Freight payment (state currency and method of payment; also beneficiary and bank account) (Cl. 4) |
| 15. State if vessel's cargo handling gear shall not be used (Cl. 5) | 16. Laytime (if separate laytime for load. and disch. is agreed, fill in a) and b). If total laytime for load. and disch., fill in c) only) (Cl. 6) |
| 17. Shippers/Place of business (Cl. 6) | (a) Laytime for loading |
| 18. Agents (loading) (Cl. 6) | (b) Laytime for discharging |
| 19. Agents (discharging) (Cl. 6) | (c) Total laytime for loading and discharging |
| 20. Demurrage rate and manner payable (loading and discharging) (Cl. 7) | 21. Cancelling date (Cl. 9) |
| | 22. General Average to be adjusted at (Cl. 12) |
| 23. Freight Tax (state if for the Owners' account (Cl .13 (c)) | 24. Brokerage commission and to whom payable (Cl. 15) |
| 25. Law and Arbitration (state 19 (a), 19 (b) or 19 (c) of Cl. 19; if 19 (c) agreed also state Place of Arbitration) (if not filled in 19 (a) shall apply) (Cl. 19) | |
| (a) State maximum amount for small claims/shortened arbitration (Cl. 19) | 26. Additional clauses covering special provisions, if agreed |



It is mutually agreed that this Contract shall be performed subject to the conditions contained in this Charter Party which shall include Part I as well as Part II. In the event of a conflict of conditions, the provisions of Part I shall prevail over those of Part II to the extent of such conflict.

| Signature (Owners) | Signature (Charterers) |
|---|---|
| | |

Printed and sold by Fr. G. Knudtzon Ltd., 55 Toldbodgade, DK-1253 Copenhagen K. Telefax +45 33 93 11 84
by authority of The Baltic and International Maritime Council (BIMCO), Copenhagen

# Appendix 8

## PART II
## "Gencon" Charter (As Revised 1922, 1976 and 1994)

1. It is agreed between the party mentioned in Box 3 as the Owners of the Vessel named in Box 5, of the GT/NT indicated in Box 6 and carrying about the number of metric tons of deadweight capacity all told on summer loadline stated in Box 7, now in position as stated in Box 8 and expected ready to load under this Charter Party about the date indicated in Box 9, and the party mentioned as the Charterers in Box 4 that:

   The said Vessel shall, as soon as her prior commitments have been completed, proceed to the loading port(s) or place(s) stated in Box 10 or so near thereto as she may safely get and lie always afloat, and there load a full and complete cargo (if shipment of deck cargo agreed same to be at the Charterers' risk and responsibility) as stated in Box 12, which the Charterers bind themselves to ship, and being so loaded the Vessel shall proceed to the discharging port(s) or place(s) stated in Box 11 as ordered on signing Bills of Lading, or so near thereto as she may safely get and lie always afloat, and there deliver the cargo.

2. **Owners' Responsibility Clause**

   The Owners are to be responsible for loss of or damage to the goods or for delay in delivery of the goods only in case the loss, damage or delay has been caused by personal want of due diligence on the part of the Owners or their Manager to make the Vessel in all respects seaworthy and to secure that she is properly manned, equipped and supplied, or by the personal act or default of the Owners or their Manager.

   And the Owners are not responsible for loss, damage or delay arising from any other cause whatsoever, even from the neglect or default of the Master or crew or some other person employed by the Owners on board or ashore for whose acts they would, but for this Clause, be responsible, or from unseaworthiness of the Vessel on loading or commencement of the voyage or at any time whatsoever.

3. **Deviation Clause**

   The Vessel has liberty to call at any port or ports in any order, for any purpose, to sail without pilots, to tow and/or assist Vessels in all situations, and also to deviate for the purpose of saving life and/or property.

4. **Payment of Freight**

   (a) The freight at the rate stated in Box 13 shall be paid in cash calculated on the intaken quantity of cargo.

   (b) Prepaid. If according to Box 13 freight is to be paid on shipment, it shall be deemed earned and non-returnable, Vessel and/or cargo lost or not lost.

   Neither the Owners nor their agents shall be required to sign or endorse bills of lading showing freight prepaid unless the freight due to the Owners has actually been paid.

   (c) On delivery. If according to Box 13 freight, or part thereof, is payable at destination it shall not be deemed earned until the cargo is thus delivered. Notwithstanding the provisions under (a), if freight or part thereof is payable on delivery of the cargo the Charterers shall have the option of paying the freight on delivered weight/quantity provided such option is declared before breaking bulk and the weight/quantity can be ascertained by official weighing machine, joint draft survey or tally.

   Cash for Vessel's ordinary disbursements at the port of loading to be advanced by the Charterers, if required, at highest current rate of exchange, subject to two (2) per cent to cover insurance and other expenses.

5. **Loading/Discharging**

   *(a) Costs/Risks*

   The cargo shall be brought into the holds, loaded, stowed and/or trimmed, tallied, lashed and/or secured and taken from the holds and discharged by the Charterers, free of any risk, liability and expense whatsoever to the Owners. The Charterers shall provide and lay all dunnage material as required for the proper stowage and protection of the cargo on board, the Owners allowing the use of all dunnage available on board. The Charterers shall be responsible for and pay the cost of removing their dunnage after discharge of the cargo under this Charter Party and time to count until dunnage has been removed.

   *(b) Cargo Handling Gear*

   Unless the Vessel is gearless or unless it has been agreed between the parties that the Vessel's gear shall not be used and stated as such in Box 15, the Owners shall throughout the duration of loading/discharging give free use of the Vessel's cargo handling gear and of sufficient motive power to operate all such cargo handling gear. All such equipment to be in good working order. Unless caused by negligence of the stevedores, time lost by breakdown of the Vessel's cargo handling gear or motive power – pro rata the total number of cranes/winches required at that time for the loading/discharging of cargo under this Charter Party – shall not count as laytime or time on demurrage.

   On request the Owners shall provide free of charge cranemen/winchmen from the crew to operate the Vessel's cargo handling gear, unless local regulations prohibit this, in which latter event shore labourers shall be for the account of the Charterers. Cranemen/winchmen shall be under the Charterers' risk and responsibility and as stevedores to be deemed as their servants but shall always work under the supervision of the Master.

   *(c) Stevedore Damage*

   The Charterers shall be responsible for damage (beyond ordinary wear and tear) to any part of the Vessel caused by Stevedores. Such damage shall be notified as soon as reasonably possible by the Master to the Charterers or their agents and to their Stevedores, failing which the Charterers shall not be held responsible. The Master shall endeavour to obtain the Stevedores' written acknowledgement of liability.

   The Charterers are obliged to repair any stevedore damage prior to completion of the voyage, but must repair stevedore damage affecting the Vessel's seaworthiness or class before the Vessel sails from the port where such damage was caused or found. All additional expenses incurred shall be for the account of the Charterers and any time lost shall be for the account of and shall be paid to the Owners by the Charterers at the demurrage rate.

6. **Laytime**

   * *(a) Separate laytime for loading and discharging*

   The cargo shall be loaded within the number of running days/hours as indicated in Box 16, weather permitting, Sundays and holidays excepted, unless used, in which event time used shall count.

   The cargo shall be discharged within the number of running days/hours as indicated in Box 16, weather permitting, Sundays and holidays excepted, unless used, in which event time used shall count.

   * *(b) Total laytime for loading and discharging*

   The cargo shall be loaded and discharged within the number of total running days/hours as indicated in Box 16, weather permitting, Sundays and holidays excepted, unless used, in which event time used shall count.

   *(c) Commencement of laytime (loading and discharging)*

   Laytime for loading and discharging shall commence at 13.00 hours, if notice of readiness is given up to and including 12.00 hours, and at 06.00 hours next working day if notice given during office hours after 12.00 hours. Notice of readiness at loading port to be given to the Shippers named in Box 17 or if not named, to the Charterers or their agents named in Box 18. Notice of readiness at the discharging port to be given to the Receivers or, if not known, to the Charterers or their agents named in Box 19.

   If the loading/discharging berth is not available on the Vessel's arrival at or off the port of loading/discharging, the Vessel shall be entitled to give notice of readiness within ordinary office hours on arrival there, whether in free pratique or not, whether customs cleared or not. Laytime or time on demurrage shall then count as if she were in berth and in all respects ready for loading/discharging provided that the Master warrants that she is in fact ready in all respects. Time used in moving from the place of waiting to the loading/discharging berth shall not count as laytime.

   If, after inspection, the Vessel is found not to be ready in all respects to load/discharge time lost after the discovery thereof until the Vessel is again ready to load/discharge shall not count as laytime.

   Time used before commencement of laytime shall count.

   * *Indicate alternative (a) or (b) as agreed, in Box 16.*

7. **Demurrage**

   Demurrage at the loading and discharging port is payable by the Charterers at the rate stated in Box 20 in the manner stated in Box 20 per day or pro rata for any part of a day. Demurrage shall fall due day by day and shall be payable upon receipt of the Owners' invoice.

   In the event the demurrage is not paid in accordance with the above, the Owners shall give the Charterers 96 running hours written notice to rectify the failure. If the demurrage is not paid at the expiration of this time limit and if the vessel is in or at the loading port, the Owners are entitled at any time to terminate the Charter Party and claim damages for any losses caused thereby.

8. **Lien Clause**

   The Owners shall have a lien on the cargo and on all sub-freights payable in respect of the cargo, for freight, deadfreight, demurrage, claims for damages and for all other amounts due under this Charter Party including costs of recovering same.

9. **Cancelling Clause**

   (a) Should the Vessel not be ready to load (whether in berth or not) on the cancelling date indicated in Box 21, the Charterers shall have the option of cancelling this Charter Party.

   (b) Should the Owners anticipate that, despite the exercise of due diligence, the Vessel will not be ready to load by the cancelling date, they shall notify the Charterers thereof without delay stating the expected date of the Vessel's readiness to load and asking whether the Charterers will exercise their option of cancelling the Charter Party, or agree to a new cancelling date.

   Such option must be declared by the Charterers within 48 running hours after the receipt of the Owners' notice. If the Charterers do not exercise their option of cancelling, then this Charter Party shall be deemed to be amended such that the seventh day after the new readiness date stated in the Owners' notification to the Charterers shall be the new cancelling date.

   The provisions of sub-clause (b) of this Clause shall operate only once, and in case of the Vessel's further delay, the Charterers shall have the option of cancelling the Charter Party as per sub-clause (a) of this Clause.

10. **Bills of Lading**

    Bills of Lading shall be presented and signed by the Master as per the "Congenbill" Bill of Lading form, Edition 1994, without prejudice to this Charter Party, or by the Owners' agents provided written authority has been given by Owners to the agents, a copy of which is to be furnished to the Charterers. The Charterers shall indemnify the Owners against all consequences or liabilities that may arise from the signing of bills of lading as presented to the extent that the terms or contents of such bills of lading impose or result in the imposition of more onerous liabilities upon the Owners than those assumed by the Owners under this Charter Party.

11. **Both-to-Blame Collision Clause**

    If the Vessel comes into collision with another vessel as a result of the negligence of the other vessel and any act, neglect or default of the Master, Mariner, Pilot or the servants of the Owners in the navigation or in the management of the Vessel, the owners of the cargo carried hereunder will indemnify the Owners against all loss or liability to the other or non-carrying vessel or her owners in so far as such loss or liability represents loss of, or damage to, or any claim whatsoever of the owners of said cargo, paid or payable by the other or non-carrying vessel or her owners to the owners of said cargo and set-off, recouped or recovered by the other or non-carrying vessel or her owners as part of their claim against the carrying Vessel or the Owners.

    The foregoing provisions shall also apply where the owners, operators or those in charge of any vessel or vessels or objects other than, or in addition to, the colliding vessels or objects are at fault in respect of a collision or contact.

12. **General Average and New Jason Clause**

    General Average shall be adjusted in London unless otherwise agreed in Box 22 according to York-Antwerp Rules 1994 and any subsequent modification thereof. Proprietors of cargo to pay the cargo's share in the general expenses even if same have been necessitated through neglect or default of the Owners' servants (see Clause 2).

    If General Average is to be adjusted in accordance with the law and practice of the United States of America, the following Clause shall apply: "In the event of accident, danger, damage or disaster before or after the commencement of the voyage, resulting from any cause whatsoever, whether due to negligence or not, for which, or for the consequence of which, the Owners are not responsible, by statute, contract or otherwise, the cargo shippers, consignees or the owners of the cargo shall contribute with the Owners in General Average to the payment of any sacrifices, losses or expenses of a General Average nature that may be made or incurred and shall pay salvage and special charges incurred in respect of the cargo. If a salving vessel is owned or operated by the Owners, salvage shall be paid for as fully as if the said salving vessel or vessels belonged to strangers. Such deposit as the Owners, or their agents, may deem sufficient to cover the estimated contribution of the goods and any salvage and special charges thereon shall, if required, be made by the cargo, shippers, consignees or owners of the goods to the Owners before delivery.".

13. **Taxes and Dues Clause**

    (a) On Vessel -The Owners shall pay all dues, charges and taxes customarily levied on the Vessel, howsoever the amount thereof may be assessed.

    (b) On cargo -The Charterers shall pay all dues, charges, duties and taxes customarily levied on the cargo, howsoever the amount thereof may be assessed.

    (c) On freight -Unless otherwise agreed in Box 23, taxes levied on the freight shall be for the Charterers' account.

# PART II

## "Gencon" Charter (As Revised 1922, 1976 and 1994)

**14. Agency**

In every case the Owners shall appoint their own Agent both at the port of loading and the port of discharge.

**15. Brokerage**

A brokerage commission at the rate stated in Box 24 on the freight, dead-freight and demurrage earned is due to the party mentioned in Box 24.

In case of non-execution 1/3 of the brokerage on the estimated amount of freight to be paid by the party responsible for such non-execution to the Brokers as indemnity for the latter's expenses and work. In case of more voyages the amount of indemnity to be agreed.

**16. General Strike Clause**

(a) If there is a strike or lock-out affecting or preventing the actual loading of the cargo, or any part of it, when the Vessel is ready to proceed from her last port or at any time during the voyage to the port or ports of loading or after her arrival there, the Master or the Owners may ask the Charterers to declare, that they agree to reckon the laydays as if there were no strike or lock-out. Unless the Charterers have given such declaration in writing (by telegram, if necessary) within 24 hours, the Owners shall have the option of cancelling this Charter Party. If part cargo has already been loaded, the Owners must proceed with same, (freight payable on loaded quantity only) having liberty to complete with other cargo on the way for their own account.

(b) If there is a strike or lock-out affecting or preventing the actual discharging of the cargo on or after the Vessel's arrival at or off port of discharge and same has not been settled within 48 hours, the Charterers shall have the option of keeping the Vessel waiting until such strike or lock-out is at an end against paying half demurrage after expiration of the time provided for discharging until the strike or lock-out terminates and thereafter full demurrage shall be payable until the completion of discharging, or of ordering the Vessel to a safe port where she can safely discharge without risk of being detained by strike or lock-out. Such orders to be given within 48 hours after the Master or the Owners have given notice to the Charterers of the strike or lock-out affecting the discharge. On delivery of the cargo at such port, all conditions of this Charter Party and of the Bill of Lading shall apply and the Vessel shall receive the same freight as if she had discharged at the original port of destination, except that if the distance to the substituted port exceeds 100 nautical miles, the freight on the cargo delivered at the substituted port to be increased in proportion.

(c) Except for the obligations described above, neither the Charterers nor the Owners shall be responsible for the consequences of any strikes or lock-outs preventing or affecting the actual loading or discharging of the cargo.

**17. War Risks ("Voywar 1993")**

(1) For the purpose of this Clause, the words:

(a) The "Owners" shall include the shipowners, bareboat charterers, disponent owners, managers or other operators who are charged with the management of the Vessel, and the Master; and

(b) "War Risks" shall include any war (whether actual or threatened), act of war, civil war, hostilities, revolution, rebellion, civil commotion, warlike operations, the laying of mines (whether actual or reported), acts of piracy, acts of terrorists, acts of hostility or malicious damage, blockades (whether imposed against all Vessels or imposed selectively against Vessels of certain flags or ownership, or against certain cargoes or crews or otherwise howsoever), by any person, body, terrorist or political group, or the Government of any state whatsoever, which, in the reasonable judgement of the Master and/or the Owners, may be dangerous or are likely to be or to become dangerous to the Vessel, her cargo, crew or other persons on board the Vessel.

(2) If at any time before the Vessel commences loading, it appears that, in the reasonable judgement of the Master and/or the Owners, performance of the Contract of Carriage, or any part of it, may expose, or is likely to expose, the Vessel, her cargo, crew or other persons on board the Vessel to War Risks, the Owners may give notice to the Charterers cancelling this Contract of Carriage, or may refuse to perform such part of it as may expose, or may be likely to expose, the Vessel, her cargo, crew or other persons on board the Vessel to War Risks; provided always that if this Contract of Carriage provides that loading or discharging is to take place within a range of ports, and at the port or ports nominated by the Charterers the Vessel, her cargo, crew, or other persons onboard the Vessel may be exposed, or may be likely to be exposed, to War Risks, the Owners shall first require the Charterers to nominate any other safe port which lies within the range for loading or discharging, and may only cancel this Contract of Carriage if the Charterers shall not have nominated such safe port or ports within 48 hours of receipt of notice of such requirement.

(3) The Owners shall not be required to continue to load cargo for any voyage, or to sign Bills of Lading for any port or place, or to proceed or continue on any voyage, or on any part thereof, or to proceed through any canal or waterway, or to proceed to or remain at any port or place whatsoever, where it appears, either after the loading of the cargo commences, or at any stage of the voyage thereafter before the discharge of the cargo is completed, that, in the reasonable judgement of the Master and/or the Owners, the Vessel, her cargo (or any part thereof), crew or other persons on board the Vessel (or any one or more of them) may be, or are likely to be, exposed to War Risks. If it should so appear, the Owners may by notice request the Charterers to nominate a safe port for the discharge of the cargo or any part thereof, and if within 48 hours of the receipt of such notice, the Charterers shall not have nominated such a port, the Owners may discharge the cargo at any safe port of their choice (including the port of loading) in complete fulfilment of the Contract of Carriage. The Owners shall be entitled to recover from the Charterers the extra expenses of such discharge and, if the discharge takes place at any port other than the loading port, to receive the full freight as though the cargo had been carried to the discharging port and if the extra distance exceeds 100 miles, to additional freight which shall be the same percentage of the freight contracted for as the percentage which the extra distance represents to the distance of the normal and customary route, the Owners having a lien on the cargo for such expenses and freight.

(4) If at any stage of the voyage after the loading of the cargo commences, it appears that, in the reasonable judgement of the Master and/or the Owners, the Vessel, her cargo, crew or other persons on board the Vessel may be, or are likely to be, exposed to War Risks on any part of the route (including any canal or waterway) which is normally and customarily used in a voyage of the nature contracted for, and there is another longer route to the discharging port, the Owners shall give notice to the Charterers that this route will be taken. In this event the Owners shall be entitled, if the total extra distance exceeds 100 miles, to additional freight which shall be the same percentage of the freight contracted for as the percentage which the extra distance represents to the distance of the normal and customary route.

(5) The Vessel shall have liberty:-

(a) to comply with all orders, directions, recommendations or advice as to departure, arrival, routes, sailing in convoy, ports of call, stoppages, destinations, discharge of cargo, delivery or in any way whatsoever which are given by the Government of the Nation under whose flag the Vessel sails, or other Government to whose laws the Owners are subject, or any other Government which so requires, or any body or group acting with the power to compel compliance with their orders or directions;

(b) to comply with the orders, directions or recommendations of any war risks underwriters who have the authority to give the same under the terms of the war risks insurance;

(c) to comply with the terms of any resolution of the Security Council of the United Nations, any directives of the European Community, the effective orders of any other Supranational body which has the right to issue and give the same, and with national laws aimed at enforcing the same to which the Owners are subject, and to obey the orders and directions of those who are charged with their enforcement;

(d) to discharge at any other port any cargo or part thereof which may render the Vessel liable to confiscation as a contraband carrier;

(e) to call at any other port to change the crew or any part thereof or other persons on board the Vessel when there is reason to believe that they may be subject to internment, imprisonment or other sanctions;

(f) where cargo has not been loaded or has been discharged by the Owners under any provisions of this Clause, to load other cargo for the Owners' own benefit and carry it to any other port or ports whatsoever, whether backwards or forwards or in a contrary direction to the ordinary or customary route.

(6) If in compliance with any of the provisions of sub-clauses (2) to (5) of this Clause anything is done or not done, such shall not be deemed to be a deviation, but shall be considered as due fulfilment of the Contract of Carriage.

**18. General Ice Clause**

*Port of loading*

(a) In the event of the loading port being inaccessible by reason of ice when the Vessel is ready to proceed from her last port or at any time during the voyage or on the Vessel's arrival or in case frost sets in after the Vessel's arrival, the Master for fear of being frozen in is at liberty to leave without cargo, and this Charter Party shall be null and void.

(b) If during loading the Master, for fear of the Vessel being frozen in, deems it advisable to leave, he has liberty to do so with what cargo he has on board and to proceed to any other port or ports with option of completing cargo for the Owners' benefit for any port or ports including port of discharge. Any part cargo thus loaded under this Charter Party to be forwarded to destination at the Vessel's expense but against payment of freight, provided that no extra expenses be thereby caused to the Charterers, freight being paid on quantity delivered (in proportion if lumpsum), all other conditions as per this Charter Party.

(c) In case of more than one loading port, and if one or more of the ports are closed by ice, the Master or the Owners to be at liberty either to load the part cargo at the open port and fill up elsewhere for their own account as under section (b) or to declare the Charter Party null and void unless the Charterers agree to load full cargo at the open port.

*Port of discharge*

(a) Should ice prevent the Vessel from reaching port of discharge the Charterers shall have the option of keeping the Vessel waiting until the re-opening of navigation and paying demurrage or of ordering the Vessel to a safe and immediately accessible port where she can safely discharge without risk of detention by ice. Such orders to be given within 48 hours after the Master or the Owners have given notice to the Charterers of the impossibility of reaching port of destination.

(b) If during discharging the Master for fear of the Vessel being frozen in deems it advisable to leave, he has liberty to do so with what cargo he has on board and to proceed to the nearest accessible port where she can safely discharge.

(c) On delivery of the cargo at such port, all conditions of the Bill of Lading shall apply and the Vessel shall receive the same freight as if she had discharged at the original port of destination, except that if the distance of the substituted port exceeds 100 nautical miles, the freight on the cargo delivered at the substituted port to be increased in proportion.

**19. Law and Arbitration**

* (a) This Charter Party shall be governed by and construed in accordance with English law and any dispute arising out of this Charter Party shall be referred to arbitration in London in accordance with the Arbitration Acts 1950 and 1979 or any statutory modification or re-enactment thereof for the time being in force. Unless the parties agree upon a sole arbitrator, one arbitrator shall be appointed by each party and the arbitrators so appointed shall appoint a third arbitrator, the decision of the three-man tribunal thus constituted or any two of them, shall be final. On the receipt by one party of the nomination in writing of the other party's arbitrator, that party shall appoint their arbitrator within fourteen days, failing which the decision of the single arbitrator appointed shall be final.

For disputes where the total amount claimed by either party does not exceed the amount stated in Box 25** the arbitration shall be conducted in accordance with the Small Claims Procedure of the London Maritime Arbitrators Association.

* (b) This Charter Party shall be governed by and construed in accordance with Title 9 of the United States Code and the Maritime Law of the United States and should any dispute arise out of this Charter Party, the matter in dispute shall be referred to three persons at New York, one to be appointed by each of the parties hereto, and the third by the two so chosen; their decision or that of any two of them shall be final, and for purpose of enforcing any award, this agreement may be made a rule of the Court. The proceedings shall be conducted in accordance with the rules of the Society of Maritime Arbitrators, Inc..

For disputes where the total amount claimed by either party does not exceed the amount stated in Box 25** the arbitration shall be conducted in accordance with the Shortened Arbitration Procedure of the Society of Maritime Arbitrators, Inc..

* (c) Any dispute arising out of this Charter Party shall be referred to arbitration at the place indicated in Box 25, subject to the procedures applicable there. The laws of the place indicated in Box 25 shall govern this Charter Party.

(d) If Box 25 in Part I is not filled in, sub-clause (a) of this Clause shall apply.

* *(a), (b) and (c) are alternatives; indicate alternative agreed in Box 25.*

** *Where no figure is supplied in Box 25 in Part I, this provision only shall be void but the other provisions of this Clause shall have full force and remain in effect.*

APPENDIX 9

# LLOYD'S STANDARD FORM OF SALVAGE AGREEMENT (1995 REVISION) AND SALVAGE AGREEMENT PROCEDURAL RULES

*Note:* Lloyd's Standard Form of Salvage Agreement (1995) and the Salvage Procedural Rules are reproduced by permission of Lloyd's.

# LLOYD'S STANDARD FORM OF SALVAGE AGREEMENT — LOF 1995

**LOF 1995**

LLOYD'S

*NOTES*

*1 Insert name of person signing on behalf of Owners of property to be salved. The Master should sign wherever possible.*

*2 The Contractor's name should always be inserted in line 4 and whenever the Agreement is signed by the Master of the Salving vessel or other person on behalf of the Contractor the name of the Master or other person must also be inserted in line 4 before the words "for and on behalf of". The words "for and on behalf of" should be deleted where a Contractor signs personally.*

*3 Insert place if agreed in clause 1(a)(i) and currency if agreed in clause 1(e)*

STANDARD FORM OF

**SALVAGE AGREEMENT**

(APPROVED AND PUBLISHED BY THE COUNCIL OF LLOYD'S)

---

NO CURE - NO PAY

---

On board the..............................................................

Dated..................................

*+ See Note 1 above*

IT IS HEREBY AGREED between Captain +...................................................................................... for and on behalf of the Owners of the "..........................................................................................." her cargo freight bunkers stores and any other property thereon (hereinafter collectively called "the Owners") and.........................................................................for and on behalf of .................................................................... ..........................................................(hereinafter called "the Contractor"*) that:-

** See Note 2 above*

1. (a) The Contractor shall use his best endeavours:-

(i) to salve the "........................................................................."and/or her cargo freight bunkers stores and any other property thereon and take them to #.................................................................. or to such other place as may hereafter be agreed either place to be deemed a place of safety or if no such place is named or agreed to a place of safety and

*# See Note 3 above*

(ii) while performing the salvage services to prevent or minimize damage to the environment.

(b) Subject to the statutory provisions relating to special compensation the services shall be rendered and accepted as salvage services upon the principle of "no cure - no pay."

(c) The Contractor's remuneration shall be fixed by Arbitration in London in the manner hereinafter prescribed and any other difference arising out of this Agreement or the operations thereunder shall be referred to Arbitration in the same way.

(d) In the event of the services referred to in this Agreement or any part of such services having been already rendered at the date of this Agreement by the Contractor to the said vessel and/or her cargo freight bunkers stores and any other property thereon the provisions of this Agreement shall apply to such services.

(e) The security to be provided to the Council of Lloyd's (hereinafter called "the Council") the Salved Value(s) the Award and/or any Interim Award(s) and/or any Award on Appeal shall be in #............................................................ currency.

*# See Note 3 above*

(f) If clause 1(e) is not completed then the security to be provided and the Salved Value(s) the Award and/or Interim Award(s) and/or Award on Appeal shall be in Pounds Sterling.

(g) This Agreement and Arbitration thereunder shall except as otherwise expressly provided be governed by the law of England, including the English law of salvage.

*15.1.08*
*3.12.24*
*13.10.26*
*12.4.50*
*10.6.53*
*20.12.67*
*23.2.72*
*21.5.80*
*5.9.90*
*1.1.95*

**PROVISIONS AS TO THE SERVICES**

2. *Definitions*: In this Agreement any reference to "Convention" is a reference to the International Convention on Salvage 1989 as incorporated in the Merchant Shipping (Salvage and Pollution) Act 1994 (and any amendment thereto). The terms "Contractor" and "services"/"salvage services" in this Agreement shall have the same meanings as the terms "salvor(s)" and "salvage operation(s)" in the Convention.

3. *Owners Cooperation*: The Owners their Servants and Agents shall co-operate fully with the Contractor in and about the salvage including obtaining entry to the place named or the place of safety as defined in clause 1. The Contractor may make reasonable use of the vessel's machinery gear equipment anchors chains stores and other appurtenances during and for the purpose of the salvage services free of expense but shall not unnecessarily damage abandon or sacrifice the same or any property the subject of this Agreement.

4. *Vessel Owners Right to Terminate*: When there is no longer any reasonable prospect of a useful result leading to a salvage reward in accordance with Convention Article 13 the owners of the vessel shall be entitled to terminate the services of the Contractor by giving reasonable notice to the Contractor in writing.

**PROVISIONS AS TO SECURITY**

5. (a) The Contractor shall immediately after the termination of the services or sooner notify the Council and where practicable the Owners of the amount for which he demands salvage security (inclusive of costs expenses and interest) from each of the respective Owners.

(b) Where a claim is made or may be made for special compensation, the owners of the vessel shall on the demand of the Contractor whenever made provide security for the Contractor's claim for special compensation provided always that such demand is made within two years of the date of termination of the services.

(c) The amount of any such security shall be reasonable in the light of the knowledge available to the Contractor at the time when the demand is made. Unless otherwise agreed such security shall be provided (i) to the Council (ii) in a form approved by the Council and (iii) by persons firms or corporations either acceptable to the Contractor or resident in the United Kingdom and acceptable to the Council. The Council shall not be responsible for the sufficiency (whether in amount or otherwise) of any security which shall be provided nor the default or insolvency of any person firm or corporation providing the same.

(d) The owners of the vessel their Servants and Agents shall use their best endeavours to ensure that the cargo owners provide their proportion of salvage security before the cargo is released.

6. (a) Until security has been provided as aforesaid the Contractor shall have a maritime lien on the property salved for his remuneration.

(b) The property salved shall not without the consent in writing of the Contractor (which shall not be unreasonably withheld) be removed from the place to which it has been taken by the Contractor under clause 1(a). Where such consent is given by the Contractor on condition that the Contractor is provided with temporary security pending completion of the voyage the Contractor's maritime lien on the property salved shall remain in force to the extent necessary to enable the Contractor to compel the provision of security in accordance with clause 5(c).

(c) The Contractor shall not arrest or detain the property salved unless:-

(i) security is not provided within 14 days (exclusive of Saturdays and Sundays or other days observed as general holidays at Lloyd's) after the date of the termination of the services or
(ii) he has reason to believe that the removal of the property salved is contemplated contrary to clause 6(b) or
(iii) any attempt is made to remove the property salved contrary to clause 6(b).

(d) The Arbitrator appointed under clause 7 or the Appeal Arbitrator(s) appointed under clause 13(d) shall have power in their absolute discretion to include in the amount awarded to the Contractor the whole or part of any expenses reasonably incurred by the Contractor in:-

(i) ascertaining demanding and obtaining the amount of security reasonably required in accordance with clause 5.
(ii) enforcing and/or protecting by insurance or otherwise or taking reasonable steps to enforce and/or protect his lien.

**PROVISIONS AS TO ARBITRATION**

7. (a) Whether security has been provided or not the Council shall appoint an Arbitrator upon receipt of a written request made by letter telex facsimile or in any other permanent form provided that any party requesting such appointment shall if required by the Council undertake to pay the reasonable fees and expenses of the Council and/or any Arbitrator or Appeal Arbitrator(s).

(b) Where an Arbitrator has been appointed and the parties do not proceed to arbitration the Council may recover any fees costs and/or expenses which are outstanding.

8. The Contractor's remuneration and/or special compensation shall be fixed by the Arbitrator appointed under clause 7. Such remuneration shall not be diminished by reason of the exception to the principle of "no cure - no pay" in the form of special compensation.

**REPRESENTATION**

9. Any party to this Agreement who wishes to be heard or to adduce evidence shall nominate a person in the United Kingdom to represent him failing which the Arbitrator or Appeal Arbitrator(s) may proceed as if such party had renounced his right to be heard or adduce evidence.

**CONDUCT OF THE ARBITRATION**

10. (a) The Arbitrator shall have power to:-

(i) admit such oral or documentary evidence or information as he may think fit
(ii) conduct the Arbitration in such manner in all respects as he may think fit subject to such procedural rules as the Council may approve
(iii) order the Contractor in his absolute discretion to pay the whole or part of the expense of providing excessive security or security which has been unreasonably demanded under Clause 5(b) and to deduct such sum from the remuneration and/or special compensation
(iv) make Interim Award(s) including payment(s) on account on such terms as may be fair and just
(v) make such orders as to costs fees and expenses including those of the Council charged under clauses 10(b) and 14(b) as may be fair and just.

(b) The Arbitrator and the Council may charge reasonable fees and expenses for their services whether the Arbitration proceeds to a hearing or not and all such fees and expenses shall be treated as part of the costs of the Arbitration.

(c) Any Award shall (subject to Appeal as provided in this Agreement) be final and binding on all the parties concerned whether they were represented at the Arbitration or not.

**INTEREST & RATES OF EXCHANGE**

11. *Interest*: Interest at rates per annum to be fixed by the Arbitrator shall (subject to Appeal as provided in this Agreement) be payable on any sum awarded taking into account any sums already paid:-

(i) from the date of termination of the services unless the Arbitrator shall in his absolute discretion otherwise decide until the date of publication by the Council of the Award and/or Interim Award(s) and
(ii) from the expiration of 21 days (exclusive of Saturdays and Sundays or other days observed as general holidays at Lloyd's) after the date of publication by the Council of the Award and/or Interim Award(s) until the date payment is received by the Contractor or the Council both dates inclusive.

For the purpose of sub-clause (ii) the expression "sum awarded" shall include the fees and expenses referred to in clause 10(b).

12. *Currency Correction*: In considering what sums of money have been expended by the Contractor in rendering the services and/or in fixing the amount of the Award and/or Interim Award(s) and/or Award on Appeal the Arbitrator or Appeal Arbitrator(s) shall to such an extent and in so far as it may be fair and just in all the circumstances give effect to the consequences of any change or changes in the relevant rates of exchange which may have occurred between the date of termination of the services and the date on which the Award and/or Interim Award(s) and/or Award on Appeal is made.

**PROVISIONS AS TO APPEAL**

13. (a) Notice of Appeal if any shall be given to the Council within 14 days (exclusive of Saturdays and Sundays or other days observed as general holidays at Lloyd's) after the date of the publication by the Council of the Award and/or Interim Award(s).

(b) Notice of Cross-Appeal if any shall be given to the Council within 14 days (exclusive of Saturdays and Sundays or other days observed as general holidays at Lloyd's) after notification by the Council to the parties of any Notice of Appeal. Such notification if sent by post shall be deemed received on the working day following the day of posting.

(c) Notice of Appeal or Cross-Appeal shall be given to the Council by letter telex facsimile or in any other permanent form.

(d) Upon receipt of Notice of Appeal the Council shall refer the Appeal to the hearing and determination of the Appeal Arbitrator(s) selected by it.

(e) If any Notice of Appeal or Cross-Appeal is withdrawn the Appeal hearing shall nevertheless proceed in respect of such Notice of Appeal or Cross-Appeal as may remain.

(f) Any Award on Appeal shall be final and binding on all the parties to that Appeal Arbitration whether they were represented either at the Arbitration or at the Appeal Arbitration or not.

**CONDUCT OF THE APPEAL**

**14.** (a) The Appeal Arbitrator(s) in addition to the powers of the Arbitrator under clauses 10(a) and 11 shall have power to:-

(i) admit the evidence which was before the Arbitrator together with the Arbitrator's notes and reasons for his Award and/or Interim Award(s) and any transcript of evidence and such additional evidence as he or they may think fit.
(ii) confirm increase or reduce the sum awarded by the Arbitrator and to make such order as to the payment of interest on such sum as he or they may think fit.
(iii) confirm revoke or vary any order and/or Declaratory Award made by the Arbitrator.
(iv) award interest on any fees and expenses charged under paragraph (b) of this clause from the expiration of 21 days (exclusive of Saturdays and Sundays or other days observed as general holidays at Lloyd's) after the date of publication by the Council of the Award on Appeal and/or Interim Award(s) on Appeal until the date payment is received by the Council both dates inclusive.

(b) The Appeal Arbitrator(s) and the Council may charge reasonable fees and expenses for their services in connection with the Appeal Arbitration whether it proceeds to a hearing or not and all such fees and expenses shall be treated as part of the costs of the Appeal Arbitration.

**PROVISIONS AS TO PAYMENT**

**15.** (a) In case of Arbitration if no Notice of Appeal be received by the Council in accordance with clause 13(a) the Council shall call upon the party or parties concerned to pay the amount awarded and in the event of non-payment shall subject to the Contractor first providing to the Council a satisfactory Undertaking to pay all the costs thereof realize or enforce the security and pay therefrom to the Contractor (whose receipt shall be a good discharge to it) the amount awarded to him together with interest if any. The Contractor shall reimburse the parties concerned to such extent as the Award is less than any sums paid on account or in respect of Interim Award(s).

(b) If Notice of Appeal be received by the Council in accordance with clause 13 it shall as soon as the Award on Appeal has been published by it call upon the party or parties concerned to pay the amount awarded and in the event of non-payment shall subject to the Contractor first providing to the Council a satisfactory Undertaking to pay all the costs thereof realize or enforce the security and pay therefrom to the Contractor (whose receipt shall be a good discharge to it) the amount awarded to him together with interest if any. The Contractor shall reimburse the parties concerned to such extent as the Award on Appeal is less than any sums paid on account or in respect of the Award or Interim Award(s).

(c) If any sum shall become payable to the Contractor as remuneration for his services and/or interest and/or costs as the result of an agreement made between the Contractor and the Owners or any of them the Council in the event of non-payment shall subject to the Contractor first providing to the Council a satisfactory Undertaking to pay all the costs thereof realize or enforce the security and pay therefrom to the Contractor (whose receipt shall be a good discharge to it) the said sum.

(d) If the Award and/or Interim Award(s) and/or Award on Appeal provides or provide that the costs of the Arbitration and/or of the Appeal Arbitration or any part of such costs shall be borne by the Contractor such costs may be deducted from the amount awarded or agreed before payment is made to the Contractor unless satisfactory security is provided by the Contractor for the payment of such costs.

(e) Without prejudice to the provisions of clause 5(c) the liability of the Council shall be limited in any event to the amount of security provided to it.

## GENERAL PROVISIONS

**16.** *Scope of Authority*: The Master or other person signing this Agreement on behalf of the property to be salved enters into this Agreement as agent for the vessel her cargo freight bunkers stores and any other property thereon and the respective Owners thereof and binds each (but not the one for the other or himself personally) to the due performance thereof.

**17.** *Notices*: Any Award notice authority order or other document signed by the Chairman of Lloyd's or any person authorised by the Council for the purpose shall be deemed to have been duly made or given by the Council and shall have the same force and effect in all respects as if it had been signed by every member of the Council.

**18.** *Sub-Contractor(s)*: The Contractor may claim salvage and enforce any Award or agreement made between the Contractor and the Owners against security provided under clause 5 or otherwise if any on behalf of any Sub-Contractors his or their Servants or Agents including Masters and members of the crews of vessels employed by him or by any Sub-Contractors in the services provided that he first provides a reasonably satisfactory indemnity to the Owners against all claims by or liabilities to the said persons.

**19.** *Inducements prohibited*: No person signing this Agreement or any party on whose behalf it is signed shall at any time or in any manner whatsoever offer provide make give or promise to provide demand or take any form of inducement for entering into this Agreement.

| **For and on behalf of the Contractor** | **For and on behalf of the Owners of property to be salved.** |
|---|---|
| ................................................................................ (To be signed by the Contractor personally or by the Master of the salving vessel or other person whose name is inserted in line 4 of this Agreement) | ................................................................................ (To be signed by the Master or other person whose name is inserted in line 1 of this Agreement) |

## INTERNATIONAL CONVENTION ON SALVAGE 1989

The following provisions of the Convention are set out below for information only.

### Article 1

**Definitions**

(a) *Salvage operation* means any act or activity undertaken to assist a vessel or any other property in danger in navigable waters or in any other waters whatsoever

(b) *Vessel* means any ship or craft, or any structure capable of navigation

(c) *Property* means any property not permanently and intentionally attached to the shoreline and includes freight at risk

(d) *Damage to the environment* means substantial physical damage to human health or to marine life or resources in coastal or inland waters or areas adjacent thereto, caused by pollution, contamination, fire, explosion or similar major incidents

(e) *Payment* means any reward, remuneration or compensation due under this Convention

### Article 6

**Salvage Contracts**

1. This Convention shall apply to any salvage operations save to the extent that a contract otherwise provides expressly or by implication

2. The master shall have the authority to conclude contracts for salvage operations on behalf of the owner of the vessel. The master or the owner of the vessel shall have the authority to conclude such contracts on behalf of the owner of the property on board the vessel

## Article 8

**Duties of the Salvor and of the Owner and Master**

1. The salvor shall owe a duty to the owner of the vessel or other property in danger:

(a) to carry out the salvage operations with due care;
(b) in performing the duty specified in subparagraph (a), to exercise due care to prevent or minimize damage to the environment;
(c) whenever circumstances reasonably require, to seek assistance from other salvors; and
(d) to accept the intervention of other salvors when reasonably requested to do so by the owner or master of the vessel or other property in danger; provided however that the amount of his reward shall not be prejudiced should it be found that such a request was unreasonable

2. The owner and master of the vessel or the owner of other property in danger shall owe a duty to the salvor:
(a) to co-operate fully with him during the course of the salvage operations;
(b) in so doing, to exercise due care to prevent or minimize damage to the environment; and
(c) when the vessel or other property has been brought to a place of safety, to accept redelivery when reasonably requested by the salvor to do so

## Article 13

**Criteria for fixing the reward**

1. The reward shall be fixed with a view to encouraging salvage operations, taking into account the following criteria without regard to the order in which they are presented below:

(a) the salved value of the vessel and other property;
(b) the skill and efforts of the salvors in preventing or minimizing damage to the environment;
(c) the measure of success obtained by the salvor;
(d) the nature and degree of the danger;
(e) the skill and efforts of the salvors in salving the vessel, other property and life;
(f) the time used and expenses and losses incurred by the salvors;
(g) the risk of liability and other risks run by the salvors or their equipment;
(h) the promptness of the services rendered;
(i) the availability and use of vessels or other equipment intended for salvage operations;
(j) the state of readiness and efficiency of the salvor's equipment and the value thereof

2. Payment of a reward fixed according to paragraph 1 shall be made by all of the vessel and other property interests in proportion to their respective salved values

3. The rewards, exclusive of any interest and recoverable legal costs that may be payable thereon, shall not exceed the salved value of the vessel and other property

## Article 14

**Special Compensation**

1. If the salvor has carried out salvage operations in respect of a vessel which by itself or its cargo threatened damage to the environment and has failed to earn a reward under Article 13 at least equivalent to the special compensation assessable in accordance with this Article, he shall be entitled to special compensation from the owner of that vessel equivalent to his expenses as herein defined

2. If, in the circumstances set out in paragraph 1, the salvor by his salvage operations has prevented or minimized damage to the environment, the special compensation payable by the owner to the salvor under paragraph 1 may be increased up to a maximum of 30% of the expenses incurred by the salvor. However, the Tribunal, if it deems it fair and just to do so and bearing in mind the relevant criteria set out in Article 13, paragraph 1, may increase such special compensation further, but in no event shall the total increase be more than 100% of the expenses incurred by the salvor

3. Salvor's expenses for the purpose of paragraphs 1 and 2 means the out-of-pocket expenses reasonably incurred by the salvor in the salvage operation and a fair rate for equipment and personnel actually and reasonably used in the salvage operation, taking into consideration the criteria set out in Article 13, paragraph 1(h), (i) and (j)

4. The total special compensation under this Article shall be paid only if and to the extent that such compensation is greater than any reward recoverable by the salvor under Article 13

5. If the salvor has been negligent and has thereby failed to prevent or minimize damage to the environment, he may be deprived of the whole or part of any special compensation due under this Article

6. Nothing in this Article shall affect any right of recourse on the part of the owner of the vessel

# STANDARD FORM OF SALVAGE AGREEMENT

## *Procedural Rules made by the Council of Lloyd's (pursuant to clause 10(a)(ii) of LOF 1995)*

1. (a) The Arbitrator appointed by the Council under clause 7 of LOF 95 shall within six weeks of his appointment or so soon thereafter as is reasonable or can reasonably be arranged hold a meeting unless a consent order shall have been agreed previously between the parties and approved by him/her.
   (b) When agreed by the Arbitrator and the parties the meeting may take the form of a conference telephone call.
   (c) When such a consent order is sought the Arbitrator must be provided with a brief summary in the form of a check list of the case prepared by the Contractor, any other party providing such comments as they deem appropriate, so that the Arbitrator is placed in a position to decide whether to make the order sought.
2. Unless there are special reasons, every initial order shall include:
   (a) a date for discovery,
   (b) a date for proof of values,
   (c) a date by which any party wishing to adduce expert evidence shall state the type of evidence deemed necessary together with briefly stated reasons, unless the Arbitrator has been informed that all represented parties are agreed,
   (d) a date by which any party applying for pleadings shall state the issue to which pleadings should be directed, unless the Arbitrator has been informed of agreement as in (c) above,
   (e) a date for a progress meeting or additional progress meetings unless all represented parties with reasonable notice agree that the same is unnecessary,
   (f) unless agreed by all represented parties to be premature, a date for the hearing and estimates for the likely time required by the Arbitrator to read in advance and for the length of the hearing,
   (g) any other matters deemed by the Arbitrator or any party to be appropriate to be included in the initial order.
3. In determining the terms of the initial order regard shall be had to:
   (a) the interests of unrepresented parties,
   (b) whether some form of shortened and/or simplified procedure is appropriate.

4. The date for the hearing shall be maintained unless application to the contrary is made to the Arbitrator within 14 days of the completion of discovery or unless the Arbitrator in the exercise of his discretion determines at a later time that an adjournment is necessary or desirable in the interests of justice or fairness.

5. In fixing or agreeing to a date for the hearing of an arbitration or arbitration on appeal, the Arbitrator or Arbitrator on Appeal shall not, unless agreed by all represented parties, fix or accept a date unless he/she can allow time to read the principal evidence in advance, hear the arbitration and produce his/her award to Lloyd's in not more than one month from the conclusion of the hearing.

6. If a hearing date cannot be agreed, fixed or maintained in accordance with Rules 4 and/or 5 due to the commitments of the Arbitrator or Arbitrator on Appeal such Arbitrator shall relinquish his/her appointment and the Council of Lloyd's shall appoint in his/her stead another Arbitrator who is able to accommodate the requirements of Rules 4 and/or 5.

7. The Arbitrator and/or Arbitrator on Appeal shall call for and/or hear such further preliminary meetings or consider such further consent orders as he/she or the parties consider necessary.

8. In case of non-compliance and/or late compliance with any such order the Arbitrator shall fix such terms as may be fair and just.

9. Nothing in the foregoing shall restrict or curtail the existing power of the Arbitrator or restrict the rights of the parties to apply to the Arbitrator for additional orders as to directions or payments on account.

10. Appeals

(a) In any case in which a party giving notice of appeal intends to contend that the Arbitrator's findings on the salved value of all or any of the salved property were erroneous or that the Arbitrator has erred in any finding as to the person whose property was at risk, a statement of such grounds of appeal shall be given in or accompanying the notice of appeal.

(b) In all cases grounds of appeal or cross-appeal will be lodged within 21 days of the notice of appeal or cross-appeal unless an extension of time is agreed.

(c) Any Respondent to an appeal who intends to contend that the award of the original Arbitrator should be affirmed on grounds other than those relied upon by the original Arbitrator shall give notice to that effect specifying the grounds of his contention within 14 days of receipt of the grounds of appeal mentioned in (b) above unless an extension of time is agreed.

APPENDIX 10

# UNITED KINGDOM STANDARD CONDITIONS FOR TOWAGE AND OTHER SERVICES (REVISED 1986)

*Note:* United Kingdom Standard Conditions for Towage and Other Services (revised 1986) is reproduced by permission of The British Tugowners Association.

1.(a) The agreement between the Tugowner and the Hirer is and shall at all times be subject to and include each and all of the conditions herein-after set out.

(b) for the purpose of these conditions

(i) 'towing' is any operation in connexion with the holding, pushing, pulling, moving, escorting or guiding of or standing by the Hirer's vessel, and the expressions 'to tow', 'being towed' and 'towage' shall be defined likewise.

(ii) 'vessel' shall include any vessel, craft or object of whatsoever nature (whether or not coming within the usual meaning of the word 'vessel') which the Tugowner agrees to tow or to which the Tugowner agrees at the request, express or implied, of the Hirer, to render any service of whatsoever nature other than towing.

(iii) 'tender' shall include any vessel, craft or object of whatsoever nature which is not a tug but which is provided by the Tugowner for the performance of any towage or other service.

(iv) The expression 'whilst towing' shall cover the period commencing when the tug or tender is in position to receive orders direct from the Hirer's vessel to commence holding, pushing, pulling, moving, escorting, guiding or standing by the vessel or to pick up ropes, wires or lines, or when the towing line has been passed to or by the tug or tender, whichever is the sooner, and ending when the final orders from the Hirer's vessel to cease holding, pushing, pulling, moving, escorting, guiding or standing by the vessel or to cast off ropes, wires or lines has been carried out, or the towing line has been finally slipped, whichever is the later, and the tug or tender is safely clear of the vessel.

(v) Any service of whatsoever nature to be performed by the Tugowner other than towing shall be deemed to cover the period commencing when the tug or tender is placed physically at the disposal of the Hirer at the place designated by the Hirer, or, if such be at a vessel, when the tug or tender is in a position to receive and forthwith carry out orders to come alongside and shall continue until the employment for which the tug or tender has been engaged is ended. If the service is to be ended at or off a vessel the period of service shall end when the tug or tender is safely clear of the vessel or, if it is to be ended elsewhere, then when any persons or property of whatsoever description have been landed or discharged from the tug or tender and/or the service for which the tug or tender has been required is ended.

(vi) The word 'tug' shall include 'tugs', the word 'tender' shall include 'tenders', the word 'vessel' will include 'vessels', the word 'Tugowner' shall include 'Tugowners', and the word 'Hirer' shall include 'Hirers'.

(vii) The expression 'Tugowner' shall include any person or body (other than the Hirer or the owner of the vessel on whose behalf the Hirer contracts as provided in Clause 2 hereof) who is a party to this agreement whether or not he in fact owns any tug or tender, and the expression 'other Tugowner' contained in Clause 5 hereof shall be construed likewise.

2. If at the time of making this agreement or of performing the towage or of rendering any service other than towing at the request, express or implied, of the Hirer, the Hirer is not the Owner of the vessel referred to herein as 'the Hirer's vessel', the Hirer expressly represents that he is authorized to make and does make this agreement for and on behalf of the owner of the said vessel subject to each and all of these conditions and agrees that both the Hirer and the Owner are bound jointly and severally by these conditions.

3. Whilst towing or whilst at the request, express or implied, of the Hirer, rendering any service other than towing, the master and crew of the tug or tender shall be deemed to be the servants of the Hirer and under the control of the Hirer and/or his servants and/or his agents, and anyone on board the Hirer's vessel who may be employed and/or paid by the Tugowner shall likewise be deemed to be the servant of the Hirer and the Hirer shall accordingly be vicariously liable for any act or omission by any such person so deemed to be the servant of the Hirer.

4. Whilst towing, or whilst at the request, either expressed or implied, of the Hirer rendering any service of whatsoever nature other than towing:

(a) The Tugowner shall not (except as provided in Clauses 4(c) and (e) hereof) be responsible for or be liable for:

(i) damage of any description done by or to the tug or tender; or done by or to the Hirer's vessel or done by or to any cargo or other thing on board or being loaded on board or intended to be loaded on board the Hirer's vessel or the tug or tender or to any other object or property; or

(ii) loss of the tug or tender or the Hirer's vessel or of any cargo or other thing on board or being loaded on board or intended to be loaded on board the Hirer's vessel or the tug or tender or any other object or property; or

(iii) any claim by a person not a party to this agreement for loss or damage of any description whatsoever;

arising from any cause whatsoever, including (without prejudice to the generality of the foregoing) negligence at any time of the Tugowner his servants or agents, unseaworthiness, unfitness or breakdown of the tug or tender, its machinery, boilers, towing gear, equipment, lines, ropes or wires, lack of fuel, stores, speed or otherwise and

(b) The Hirer shall (except as provided in Clauses 4(c) and (e)) be responsible for, pay for and indemnify the Tugowner against and in respect of any loss or damage and any claims of whatsoever nature or howsoever arising or caused, whether covered by the provision of Clause 4(a) hereof or not, suffered by or made against the Tugowner and which shall include, without prejudice to the generality of the foregoing, any loss of or damage to the tug or tender or any property of the Tugowner even if the same arises from or is caused by the negligence of the Tugowner his servants or agents.

(c) The provisions of Clauses 4(a) and 4(b) hereof shall not be applicable in respect of any claims which arise in any of the following circumstances:

(i) All claims which the Hirer shall prove to have resulted directly and solely from the personal failure of the Tugowner to exercise reasonable care to make the tug or tender seaworthy for navigation at the commencement of the towing or other service. For the purpose of this Clause the Tugowner's personal responsibility for exercising reasonable care shall be construed as relating only to the person or persons having the ultimate control and chief management of the Tugowner's business and to any servant (excluding the officers and crew of any tug or tender) to whom the Tugowner has specifically delegated the particular duty of exercising reasonable care and shall not include any other servant of the Tugowner or any agent or independent contractor employed by the Tugowner.

(ii) All claims which arise when the tug or tender, although towing or rendering some service other than towing, is not in a position of proximity or risk to or from the Hirer's vessel or any other craft attending the Hirer's vessel and is detached from and safely clear of any ropes, lines, wire cables or moorings associated with the Hirer's vessel. Provided always that, notwithstanding the foregoing, the provisions of Clauses 4(a) and 4(b) shall be fully applicable in respect of all claims which arise at any time when the tug or tender is at the request, whether express or implied, of the Hirer, his servants or his agents, carrying persons or property of whatsoever description (in addition to the Officers and crew and usual equipment of the tug or tender) and which are wholly or partly caused by, or arise out of the presence on board of such persons or property or which arise at anytime when the tug or tender is proceeding to or from the Hirer's vessel in hazardous conditions or circumstances.

(d) Notwithstanding anything hereinbefore contained, the Tugowner shall under no circumstances whatsoever be responsible for or be liable for any loss or damage caused by or contributed to or arising out of any delay or detention of the Hirer's vessel or of the cargo on board or being loaded on board or intended to be loaded on board the Hirer's vessel or of any other object or property or of any person, or any consequence thereof, whether or not the same shall be caused or arise whilst towing or whilst at the request, either express or implied, of the Hirer rendering any service of whatsoever nature other than towing or at any other time whether being during or after the making of this agreement.

(e) Notwithstanding anything contained in Clauses 4(a) and (b) hereof the liability of the Tugowner for death or personal injury resulting from negligence is not excluded or restricted thereby.

5. The Tugowner shall at any time be entitled to substitute one or more tugs or tenders for any other tug or tender or tugs or tenders. The Tugowner shall at any time (whether before or after the making of this agreement between him and the Hirer) be entitled to contract with any other Tugowner (hereinafter referred to as 'the other Tugowner') to hire the other Tugowner's tug or tender and in any such event it is hereby agreed that the Tugowner is acting (or is deemed to have acted) as the agent for the Hirer, notwithstanding that the Tugowner may in addition, if authorized whether expressly or impliedly by or on behalf of the other Tugowner, act as agent for the other Tugowner at any time and for any purpose including the making of any agreement with the Hirer. In any event should the Tugowner as agent for the Hirer contract with the other Tugowner for any purpose as aforesaid it is hereby agreed that such contract is and shall at all times be subject to the provisions of these conditions so that the other Tugowner is bound by the same and may as a principal sue the Hirer thereon and shall have the full benefit of these conditions in every respect expressed or implied herein.

6. Nothing contained in those conditions shall limit, prejudice or preclude in any way any legal rights which the Tugowner may have against the Hirer including, but not limited to, any rights which the Tugowner or his servants or agents may have to claim salvage remuneration or special compensation for any extraordinary services rendered to vessels or anything aboard the vessels by any tug or tender. Furthermore, nothing contained in these conditions shall limit, prejudice or preclude in any way any right which the Tugowner may have to limit his liability.

7. The Tugowner will not in any event be responsible or liable for the consequences of war, riots, civil commotions, acts of terrorism or sabotage, strikes, lockouts, disputes, stoppages or labour disturbances (whether he be a party thereto or not) or anything done in contemplation of furtherance thereof or delays of any description, howsoever caused or arising, including by the negligence of the Tugowner or his servants or agents.

8. The Hirer of the tug or tender engaged subject to these conditions undertakes not to take or cause to be taken any proceedings against any servant or agent of the Tugowner or other Tugowner, whether or not the tug or tender substituted or hired or the contract or any part thereof has been sublet to the owner of the tug or tender, in respect of any negligence or breach of duty or other wrongful act on the part of such servant or agent which, but for this present provision, it would be competent for the Hirer so to do and the owners of such tug or tender shall hold this undertaking for the benefit of their servants and agent.

9.(a) The agreement between the Tugowner and the Hirer is and shall be governed by English Law and the Tugowner and the Hirer hereby accept, subject to the proviso contained in sub-clause (b) hereof, the exclusive jurisdiction of the English Courts (save where the registered office of the Tugowner is situated in Scotland when the agreement is and shall be governed by Scottish Law and the Tugowner and the Hirer hereby shall accept the exclusive jurisdiction of the Scottish Courts).

(b) No suit shall be brought in any jurisdiction other than that provided in sub-clause (a) hereof save that either the Tugowner or the Hirer shall have the option to bring proceedings in rem to obtain the arrest of or other similar remedy against any vessel or property owned by the other party hereto in any jurisdiction where such vessel or property may be found.

APPENDIX 11

# CONVENTION ON LIMITATION OF LIABILITY FOR MARITIME CLAIMS 1976, ARTICLES 15–22

## Article 15

1. This Convention shall apply whenever any person referred to in Article 1 seeks to limit his liability before the Court of a State Party or seeks to procure the release of a ship or other property or the discharge of any security given within the jurisdiction of any such State. Nevertheless, each State Party may exclude wholly or partially from the application of this Convention any person referred to in Article 1, who at the time when the rules of this Convention are invoked before the Courts of that State does not have his habitual residence in a State Party, or does not have his principal place of business in a State Party, or any ship in relation to which the right of limitation is invoked or whose release is sought and which does not at the time specified above fly the flag of a State Party.

2. A State Party may regulate by specific provisions of national law the system of limitation of liability to be applied to vessels which are:

(a) according to the law of that State, ships intended for navigation on inland waterways;

(b) ships of less than 300 tons.

A State Party which makes use of the option provided for in this paragraph shall inform the depositary of the limits of liability adopted in its national legislation or the fact that there are none.

3. A State Party may regulate by specific provisions of national law the system of limitation of liability to be applied to claims arising in cases in which interests of persons who are nationals of other State Parties are no way involved.

4. The Courts of a State Party shall not apply this Convention to ships constructed for or adapted to, and engaged in, drilling:

(a) when that State has established under its national legislation a higher limit of liability than that otherwise provided for in Article 6; or

(b) when the State has become party to an international Convention regulating the system of liability in respect of such ships.

In a case to which sub-paragraph (a) applies that State Party shall inform the depositary accordingly.

5. This convention shall not apply to:

(a) aircushion vehicles;

(b) floating platforms constructed for the purpose of exploring or exploiting the natural resources of the seabed or the subsoil thereof.

## Article 16: Signature, Ratification and Accession

1. This Convention shall be open for signature by all States at the headquarters of the Inter Governmental Maritime Consultative Organisation (hereinafter referred to as 'the Organisation') from February 1st 1977 until December 31st 1977, and shall thereafter remain open for accession.

2. All States may become parties to this Convention by:
   (a) signature without reservation as to ratification, acceptance or approval; or
   (b) signature, subject to ratification, acceptance or approval followed by ratification, acceptance or approval: or
   (c) accession.

3. Ratification, acceptance, approval or accession shall be effected by the deposit of a formal instrument to that effect with the Secretary-General of the Organisation (hereinafter referred to as 'the Secretary-General').

## Article 17: Entry into force

1. This Convention shall enter into force on the first day of the month following one year after the date on which 12 States have either signed it without reservation as to ratification, acceptance or approval or have deposited the requisite instruments of ratification, acceptance, approval or accession.

2. For a State which deposits an instrument of ratification, acceptance, approval or accession, or signs without reservation as to ratification, acceptance or approval, in respect of this Convention after the requirements for entry into force have been met but prior to the date of entry into force, the ratification, acceptance, approval or accession or the signature without reservation as to ratification, acceptance or approval, shall take effect on the date of entry into force of the Convention or on the first day of the month following the 90th day after the date of signature or the deposit of the instrument, whichever is the later date.

3. For any State which subsequently becomes a Party to this Convention, the Convention shall enter into force on the first day of the month following the expiration of 90 days after the date when such State deposited its instrument.

4. In respect of the relations between States which ratify, accept, or approve this Convention or accede to it, this Convention shall replace and abrogate the International Convention relating to the Limitation of the Liability of Owners of Seagoing Ships, done at Brussels on October 10th 1957, and the International Convention for the Unification of certain Rules relating to the Limitation of Liability of the Owners of Seagoing Vessels, signed at Brussels on August 25th 1924.

## Article 18: Reservations

1. Any State may, at the time of signature, ratification, acceptance, approval or accession, reserve the right to exclude the application of Article 2, paragraph 1(d) and (e). No other reservations shall be admissible to the substantive provisions of this Convention.

2. Reservations made at the time of signature are subject to confirmation upon ratification, acceptance or approval.

3. Any State which has made a reservation to this Convention may withdraw it at any time by means of a notification addressed to the Secretary-General. Such withdrawal shall take effect on the date the notification is received. If the notification states that the withdrawal of a reservation is to take effect on a date specified therein, and such date is later than the date the notification is received by the Secretary-General, the withdrawal shall take effect on such later date.

## Article 19: Denunciation

1. This Convention may be denounced by a State Party at any time after one year from the date on which the Convention entered into force for that Party.

2. Denunciation shall be effected by the deposit of an instrument with the Secretary-General.

3. Denunciation shall take effect on the first day of the month following the expiration of one year after the date of deposit of the instrument, or after such longer period as may be specified in the instrument.

### Article 20: Revision and Amendment

1. A Conference for the purpose of revising or amending this Convention may be convened by the Organisation.

2. The Organisation shall convene a Conference of the States Parties to this Convention for revising or amending it at the request of not less than one-third of the Parties.

3. After the date of the entry into force of an amendment to this Convention, any instrument of ratification, acceptance, approval or accession deposited shall be deemed to apply to the Convention as amended, unless a contrary intention is expressed in the instrument.

### Article 21: Revision of the limitation amount and of Unit of Account or Monetary Unit

1. Notwithstanding the provisions of Article 20 a Conference only for the purposes of altering the amounts specified in Article 6 and 7 and in Article 8 paragraph 2, or of substituting either or both of the units defined in Article 8, paragraphs 1 and 2, by other units shall be convened by the Organisation in accordance with paragraphs 2 and 3 of this Article. An alteration of the amounts shall be made only because of a significant change in their real value.

2. The Organisation shall convene such a Conference at the request of not less than one-fourth of the States Parties.

3. A decision to alter the amounts or to substitute the units by other Units of Account shall be taken by a two-thirds majority of the States Parties present and voting in such Conference.

4. Any State depositing its instrument of ratification, acceptance, approval or accession to the Convention, after entry into force of an amendment, shall apply to the Convention as amended.

### Article 22: Depositary

1. This Convention shall be deposited with the Secretary-General.

2. The Secretary-General shall:

(a) transmit certified true copies of this Convention to all States which were invited to attend the Conference on Limitation of Liability for Maritime Claims and to any other States which accede to this Convention;

(b) inform all States which have signed or acceded to this Convention of:

(i) each new signature and each deposit of an instrument and any reservation thereto together with the date thereof;

(ii) The date of entry into force of this Convention or any amendment thereto;

(iii) any denunciation of this Convention and the date on which it takes effect;

(iv) any amendment adopted in conformity with Articles 20 or 21;

(v) any communication called for by any Article of the Convention.

3. Upon entry into force of this Convention, a certified true copy thereof shall be transmitted by the Secretary-General to the Secretariat of the United Nations for registration and publication in accordance with Article 102 of the Charter of the United Nations.

APPENDIX 12

# INTERNATIONAL CONVENTION ON CIVIL LIABILITY FOR OIL POLLUTION DAMAGE 1992

## Article I

For the purposes of this Convention:

1. 'Ship' means any sea-going vessel and seaborne craft of any type whatsoever constructed or adapted for the carriage of oil in bulk as cargo, provided that a ship capable of carrying oil and other cargoes shall be regarded as a ship only when it is actually carrying oil in bulk as cargo and during any voyage following such carriage unless it is proved that it has no residues of such carriage of oil in bulk aboard.

2. 'Person' means any individual or partnership or any public or private body, whether corporate or not, including a State or any of its constituent subdivisions.

3. 'Owner' means the person or persons registered as the owner of the ship or, in the absence of registration, the person or persons owning the ship. However in the case of a ship owned by a State and operated by a company which in that State is registered as the ship's operator, 'owner' shall mean such company.

4. 'State of the ship's registry' means in relation to registered ships the State of registration of the ship, and in relation to unregistered ships the State whose flag the ship is flying.

5. 'Oil' means any persistent hydrocarbon mineral oil such as crude oil, fuel oil, heavy diesel oil and lubricating oil, whether carried on board a ship as cargo or in the bunkers of such a ship.

6. 'Pollution damage' means:
   - (a) loss or damage caused outside the ship by contamination resulting from the escape or discharge of oil from the ship, wherever such escape or discharge may occur, provided that compensation for impairment of the environment other than loss of profit from such impairment shall be limited to costs of reasonable measures of reinstatement actually undertaken or to be undertaken;
   - (b) the costs of preventive measures and further loss or damage caused by preventive measures.

7. 'Preventive measures' means any reasonable measures taken by any person after an incident has occurred to prevent or minimize pollution damage.

8. 'Incident' means any occurrence, or series of occurrences having the same origin, which causes pollution damage or creates a grave and imminent threat of causing such damage.

9. 'Organisation' means the International Maritime Organisation.

10. '1969 Liability Convention' means the International Convention on Civil Liability for Oil Pollution Damage, 1969. For States Parties to the Protocol of 1976 to that Convention, the term shall be deemed to include the 1969 Liability Convention as amended by that Protocol.

## Article II

This Convention shall apply exclusively:
(a) to pollution damage caused:
(i) in the territory, including the territorial sea, of a Contracting State, and
(ii) in the exclusive economic zone of a Contracting State, established in accordance with international law, or, if a Contracting State has not established such a zone, in an area beyond and adjacent to the territorial sea of that State determined by that State in accordance with international law and extending not more than 200 nautical miles from the baselines from which the breadth of its territorial sea is measured;
(b) to preventive measures, wherever taken, to prevent or minimize such damage.

## Article III

1. Except as provided in paragraphs 2 and 3 of this Article, the owner of a ship at the time of an incident, or, where the incident consists of a series of occurrences, at the time of the first such occurrence, shall be liable for any pollution damage caused by the ship as a result of the incident.
2. No liability for pollution damage shall attach to the owner if he proves that the damage:
(a) resulted from an act of war, hostilities, civil war, insurrection or a natural phenomenon of an exceptional, inevitable and irresistible character, or
(b) was wholly caused by an act or omission done with intent to cause damage by a third party, or
(c) was wholly caused by the negligence or other wrongful act of any Government or other authority responsible for the maintenance of lights or other navigational aids in the exercise of that function.
3. If the owner proves that the pollution damage resulted wholly or partially either from an act or omission done with intent to cause damage by the person who suffered the damage or from the negligence of that person, the owner may be exonerated wholly or partially from his liability to such person.
4. No claim for compensation for pollution damage may be made against the owner otherwise than in accordance with this Convention. Subject to paragraph 5 of this Article, no claim for compensation for pollution damage under this Convention or otherwise may be made against:
(a) the servants or agents of the owner or the member of the crew;
(b) the pilot or any other person who, without being a member of the crew, performs services for the ship;
(c) any charterer (howsoever described, including a bareboat charterer), manager or operator of the ship;
(d) any person performing salvage operations with the consent of the owner or on the instructions of a competent public authority;
(e) any person taking preventive measures;
(f) all servants or agents of persons mentioned in subparagraphs (c), (d) and (e);
unless the damage resulted from their personal act or omission, committed with the intent to cause such damage, or recklessly and with knowledge that such damage would probably result.
5. Nothing in this Convention shall prejudice any right of recourse of the owner against third parties.

## Article IV

When an incident involving two or more ships occurs and pollution damage results therefrom, the owners of all the ships concerned, unless exonerated under Article III, shall be jointly and severally liable for all such damage which is not reasonably separable.

## Article V

1. The owner of a ship shall be entitled to limit his liability under this Convention in respect of any one incident to an aggregate amount calculated as follows:
   (a) 3 million units of account for a ship not exceeding 5,000 units of tonnage;
   (b) for a ship with a tonnage in excess thereof, for each additional unit of tonnage, 420 units of account in addition to the amount mentioned in sub-paragraph (a);

provided, however, that this aggregate amount shall not in any event exceed 59.7 million units of account.

2. The owner shall not be entitled to limit his liability under this Convention if it is proved that the pollution damage resulted from his personal act or omission, committed with the intent to cause such damage, or recklessly and with knowledge that such damage would probably result.

3. For the purpose of availing himself of the benefit of limitation provided for in paragraph 1 of this Article the owner shall constitute a fund for the total sum representing the limit of his liability with the Court or other competent authority of any one of the Contracting States in which action is brought under Article IX or, if no action is brought, with any Court or other competent authority in any one of the Contracting States in which an action can be brought under Article IX. The fund can be constituted either by depositing the sum or by producing a bank guarantee or other guarantee, acceptable under the legislation of the Contracting State where the fund is constituted, and considered to be adequate by the Court or other competent authority.

4. The fund shall be distributed among the claimants in proportion to the amounts of their established claims.

5. If before the fund is distributed the owner or any of his servants or agents or any person providing him insurance or other financial security has as a result of the incident in question, paid compensation for pollution damage, such person shall, up to the amount he has paid, acquire by subrogation the rights which the person so compensated would have enjoyed under this Convention.

6. The right of subrogation provided for in paragraph 5 of this Article may also be exercised by a person other than those mentioned therein in respect of any amount of compensation for pollution damage which he may have paid but only to the extent that such subrogation is permitted under the applicable national law.

7. Where the owner or any other person establishes that he may be compelled to pay at a later date in whole or in part any such amount of compensation, with regard to which such person would have enjoyed a right of subrogation under paragraphs 5 or 6 of this Article, had the compensation been paid before the fund was distributed, the Court or other competent authority of the State where the fund has been constituted may order that a sufficient sum shall be provisionally set aside to enable such person at such later date to enforce his claim against the fund.

8. Claims in respect of expenses reasonably incurred or sacrifices reasonably made by the owner voluntarily to prevent or minimize pollution damage shall rank equally with other claims against the fund.

9(a). The 'unit of account' referred to in paragraph 1 of this Article is the Special Drawing Right as defined by the International Monetary Fund. The amounts mentioned in paragraph 1 shall be converted into national currency on the basis of the value of that currency by reference to the Special Drawing Right on the date of the constitution of the fund referred to in paragraph 3. The value of the national currency, in terms of the Special Drawing Right, of a Contracting State which is a member of the International Monetary Fund shall be calculated in accordance with the method of valuation applied by the International Monetary Fund in effect on the date in question for its operations and transactions. The value of the national currency, in terms of the Special Drawing Right, of a Contracting State which is not a member of the International Monetary Fund shall be calculated in a manner determined by that State.

9(b). Nevertheless, a Contracting State which is not a member of the International Monetary Fund and whose law does not permit the application of the provisions of paragraph 9(a) may, at the time of ratification, acceptance, approval of or accession to this Convention or at any time thereafter, declare that the unit of account referred to in paragraph 9(a) shall be equal to 15 gold francs. The gold franc referred to in this paragraph corresponds to sixty-five and a half milligrammes of gold of millesimal fineness nine hundred. The conversion of the gold franc into the national currency shall be made according to the law of the State concerned.

9(c). The calculation mentioned in the last sentence of paragraph 9(a) and the conversion mentioned in paragraph 9(b) shall be made in such manner as to express in the national currency of the Contracting State as far as possible the same real value for the amounts in paragraph 1 as would result from the application of the first three sentences of paragraph 9(a). Contracting States shall communicate to the depositary the manner of calculation pursuant to paragraph 9(a), or the result of the conversion in paragraph 9(b) as the case may be, when depositing an instrument of ratification, acceptance, approval of or accession to this Convention and whenever there is a change in either.

10. For the purpose of this Article the ship's tonnage shall be the gross tonnage calculated in accordance with the tonnage measurement regulations contained in Annex I of the International Convention on Tonnage Measurement of Ships, 1969.

11. The insurer or other person providing financial security shall be entitled to constitute a fund in accordance with this Article on the same conditions and having the same effect as if it were constituted by the owner. Such a fund may be constituted even if, under the provisions of paragraph 2, the owner is not entitled to limit his liability, but its constitution shall in that case not prejudice the rights of any claimant against the owner.

## Article VI

1. Where the owner, after an incident, has constituted a fund in accordance with Article V, and is entitled to limit his liability:
    (a) no person having a claim for pollution damage arising out of that incident shall be entitled to exercise any right against any other assets of the owner in respect of such claim;
    (b) the Court or other competent authority of any Contracting State shall order the release of any ship or other property belonging to the owner which has been arrested in respect of a claim for pollution damage arising out of that incident, and shall similarly release any bail or other security furnished to avoid such arrest.

2. The foregoing shall, however, only apply if the claimant has access to the Court administering the fund and the fund is actually available in respect of his claim.

## Article VII

1. The owner of a ship registered in a Contracting State and carrying more than 2,000 tons of oil in bulk as cargo shall be required to maintain insurance or other financial

security, such as the guarantee of a bank or a certificate delivered by an international compensation fund, in the sums fixed by applying the limits of liability prescribed in Article V, paragraph 1 to cover his liability for pollution damage under this Convention.

2. A certificate attesting that insurance or other financial security is in force in accordance with the provisions of this Convention shall be issued to each ship after the appropriate authority of a Contracting State has determined that the requirements of paragraph 1 have been complied with. With respect to a ship registered in a Contracting State such certificate shall be issued or certified by the appropriate authority of the State of the ship's registry; with respect to a ship not registered in a Contracting State it may be issued or certified by the appropriate authority of any Contracting State. This certificate shall be in the form of the annexed model and shall contain the following particulars:

(a) name of ship and port of registration;
(b) name and principal place of business of owner;
(c) type of security;
(d) name and principal place of business of insurer or other person giving security and, where appropriate, place of business where the insurance or security is established;
(e) period of validity of certificate which shall not be longer than the period of validity of the insurance or other security.

3. The certificate shall be in the official language or languages of the issuing State. If the language used is neither English nor French, the text shall include a translation into one of these languages.

4. The certificate shall be carried on board the ship and a copy shall be deposited with the authorities who keep the record of the ship's registry or, if the ship is not registered in a Contracting State, with the authorities of the State issuing or certifying the certificate.

5. An insurance or other financial security shall not satisfy the requirements of this Article if it can cease, for reasons other than the expiry of the period of validity of the insurance or security specified in the certificate under paragraph 2 of this Article, before three months have elapsed from the date on which notice of its termination is given to the authorities referred to in paragraph 4 of this Article, unless the certificate has been surrendered to these authorities or a new certificate has been issued within the said period. The foregoing provisions shall similarly apply to any modification which results in the insurance or security no longer satisfying the requirements of this Article.

6. The State of registry shall, subject to the provisions of this Article, determine the conditions of issue and validity of the certificate.

7. Certificates issued or certified under the authority of a Contracting State in accordance with paragraph 2 shall be accepted by other Contracting States for the purposes of this Convention and shall be regarded by other Contracting States as having the same force as certificates issued or certified by them even if issued or certified in respect of a ship not registered in a Contracting State. A Contracting State may at any time request consultation with the issuing or certifying State should it believe that the insurer or guarantor named in the certificate is not financially capable of meeting the obligations imposed by this Convention.

8. Any claim for compensation for pollution damage may be brought directly against the insurer or other person providing financial security for the owner's liability for pollution damage. In such case the defendant may, even if the owner is not entitled to limit his liability according to Article V, paragraph 2, avail himself of the limits of liability prescribed in Article V, paragraph 1. He may further avail himself of the defences (other than the bankruptcy or winding up of the owner) which the owner himself would have been entitled to invoke. Furthermore, the defendant may avail himself of the defence that

the pollution damage resulted from the wilful misconduct of the owner himself, but the defendant shall not avail himself of any other defence which he might have been entitled to invoke in proceedings brought by the owner against him. The defendant shall in any event have the right to require the owner to be joined in the proceedings.

9. Any sums provided by insurance or by other financial security maintained in accordance with paragraph 1 of this Article shall be available exclusively for the satisfaction of claims under this Convention.

10. A Contracting State shall not permit a ship under its flag to which this Article applies to trade unless a certificate has been issued under paragraph 2 or 12 of this Article.

11. Subject to the provisions of this Article, each Contracting State shall ensure, under its national legislation, that insurance or other security to the extent specified in paragraph 1 of this Article is in force in respect of any ship, wherever registered, entering or leaving a port in its territory, or arriving at or leaving an off-shore terminal in its territorial sea, if the ship actually carries more than 2,000 tons of oil in bulk as cargo.

12. If insurance or other financial security is not maintained in respect of a ship owned by a Contracting State, the provisions of this Article relating thereto shall not be applicable to such a ship, but the ship shall carry a certificate issued by the appropriate authorities of the State of the ship's registry stating that the ship is owned by that State and that the ship's liability is covered within the limits prescribed by Article V, paragraph 1. Such a certificate shall follow as closely as practicable the model prescribed by paragraph 2 of this Article.

## Article VIII

Rights of compensation under this Convention shall be extinguished unless an action is brought thereunder within three years from the date when the damage occurred. However, in no case shall an action be brought after six years from the date of the incident which caused the damage. Where this incident consists of a series of occurrences, the six years' period shall run from the date of the first such occurrence.

## Article IX

1. Where an incident has caused pollution damage in the territory, including the territorial sea or an area referred to in Article II, of one or more Contracting States or preventive measures have been taken to prevent or minimize pollution damage in such territory including the territorial sea or area, actions for compensation may only be brought in the Courts of any such Contracting State or States. Reasonable notice of any such action shall be given to the defendant.

2. Each Contracting State shall ensure that its Courts possess the necessary jurisdiction to entertain such actions for compensation.

3. After the fund has been constituted in accordance with Article V the Courts of the State in which the fund is constituted shall be exclusively competent to determine all matters relating to the apportionment and distribution of the fund.

## Article X

1. Any judgment given by a Court with jurisdiction in accordance with Article IX which is enforceable in the State of origin where it is no longer subject to ordinary forms of review, shall be recognized in any Contracting State, except:

(a) where the judgment was obtained by fraud; or

(b) where the defendant was not given reasonable notice and a fair opportunity to present his case.

2. A judgment recognized under paragraph 1 of this Article shall be enforceable in each Contracting State as soon as the formalities required in that State have been complied with. The formalities shall not permit the merits of the case to be re-opened.

## Article XI

1. The provisions of this Convention shall not apply to warships or other ships owned or operated by a State and used, for the time being, only on government non-commercial service.

2. With respect to ships owned by a Contracting State and used for commercial purposes, each State shall be subject to suit in the jurisdictions set forth in Article IX and shall waive all defences based on its status as a sovereign State.

## Article XII

This Convention shall supersede any International Conventions in force or open for signature, ratification or accession at the date on which the Convention is opened for signature, but only to the extent that such Conventions would be in conflict with it; however, nothing in this Article shall affect the obligations of Contracting States to non-Contracting States arising under such International Conventions.

## Article XII bis

*Transitional provisions*

The following transitional provisions shall apply in the case of a State which at the time of an incident is a Party both to this Convention and to the 1969 Liability Convention:

(a) where an incident has caused pollution damage within the scope of this Convention, liability under this Convention shall be deemed to be discharged if, and to the extent that, it also arises under the 1969 Liability Convention;

(b) where an incident has caused pollution damage within the scope of this Convention, and the State is a Party both to this Convention and to the International Convention on the Establishment of an International Fund for Compensation for Oil Pollution Damage, 1971, liability remaining to be discharged after the application of sub-paragraph (a) of this Article shall arise under this Convention only to the extent that pollution damage remains uncompensated after application of the said 1971 Convention;

(c) in the application of Article III, paragraph 4, of this Convention the expression 'this Convention' shall be interpreted as referring to this Convention or the 1969 Liability Convention, as appropriate;

(d) in the application of Article V, paragraph 3, of this Convention the total sum of the fund to be constituted shall be reduced by the amount by which liability has been deemed to be discharged in accordance with sub-paragraph (a) of this Article.

## Article XII ter

*Final clauses*

The final clauses of this Convention shall be Articles 12 to 18 of the Protocol of 1992 to amend the 1969 Liability Convention. References in this Convention to Contracting States shall be taken to mean references to the Contracting States of that Protocol.

## Appendix 12

NOTE:
The following are the Articles 12 to 18 referred to in Article XII ter:

### Article 12

*Signature, ratification, acceptance, approval and accession*

1. This Protocol shall be open for signature at London from 15 January 1993 to 14 January 1994 by all States.

2. Subject to paragraph 4, any State may become a Party to this Protocol by:
   (a) signature subject to ratification, acceptance or approval followed by ratification, acceptance or approval; or
   (b) accession.

3. Ratification, acceptance, approval or accession shall be effected by the deposit of a formal instrument to that effect with the Secretary-General of the Organization.

4. Any Contracting State to the International Convention on the Establishment of an International Fund for Compensation for Oil Pollution Damage, 1971, hereinafter referred to as the 1971 Fund Convention, may ratify, accept, approve or accede to this Protocol only if it ratifies, accepts, approves or accedes to the Protocol of 1992 to amend that Convention at the same time, unless it denounces the 1971 Fund Convention to take effect on the date when this Protocol enters into force for that State.

5. A State which is a Party to this Protocol but not a Party to the 1969 Liability Convention shall be bound by the provisions of the 1969 Liability Convention as amended by this Protocol in relation to other States Parties hereto, but shall not be bound by the provisions of the 1969 Liability Convention in relation to States Parties thereto.

6. Any instrument of ratification, acceptance, approval or accession deposited after the entry into force of an amendment to the 1969 Liability Convention as amended by this Protocol shall be deemed to apply to the Convention so amended, as modified by such amendment.

### Article 13

*Entry into force*

1. This Protocol shall enter into force twelve months following the date on which ten States including four States each with not less than one million units of gross tanker tonnage have deposited instruments of ratification, acceptance, approval or accession with the Secretary-General of the Organization.

2. However, any Contracting State to the 1971 Fund Convention may, at the time of the deposit of its instrument of ratification, acceptance, approval or accession in respect of this Protocol, declare that such instrument shall be deemed not to be effective for the purposes of this Article until the end of the six-month period in Article 31 of the Protocol of 1992 to amend the 1971 Fund Convention. A State which is not a Contracting State to the 1971 Fund Convention but which deposits an instrument of ratification, acceptance, approval or accession in respect of the Protocol of 1992 to amend the 1971 Fund Convention may also make a declaration in accordance with this paragraph at the same time.

3. Any State which has made a declaration in accordance with the preceding paragraph may withdraw it at any time by means of a notification addressed to the Secretary-General of the Organization. Any such withdrawal shall take effect on the date the notification is received, provided that such State shall be deemed to have deposited its instrument of ratification, acceptance, approval or accession in respect of this Protocol on that date.

4. For any State which ratifies, accepts, approves or accedes to it after the conditions in

paragraph 1 for entry into force have been met, this Protocol shall enter into force twelve months following the date of deposit by such State of the appropriate instrument.

## Article 14

*Revision and amendment*

1. A Conference for the purpose of revising or amending the 1992 Liability Convention may be convened by the Organization.
2. The Organization shall convene a Conference of Contracting States for the purpose of revising or amending the 1992 Liability Convention at the request of not less than one third of the Contracting States.

## Article 15

*Amendments of limitation amounts*

1. Upon the request of at least one quarter of the Contracting States any proposal to amend the limits of liability laid down in Article V, paragraph 1, of the 1969 Liability Convention as amended by this Protocol shall be circulated by the Secretary-General to all Members of the Organization and to all Contracting States.
2. Any amendment proposed and circulated as above shall be submitted to the Legal Committee of the Organization for consideration at a date at least six months after the date of its circulation.
3. All Contracting States to the 1969 Liability Convention as amended by this Protocol, whether or not Members of the Organization, shall be entitled to participate in the proceedings of the Legal Committee for the consideration and adoption of amendments.
4. Amendments shall be adopted by a two-thirds majority of the Contracting States present and voting in the Legal Committee, expanded as provided for in paragraph 3, on condition that at least one half of the Contracting States shall be present at the time of voting.
5. When acting on a proposal to amend the limits, the Legal Committee shall take into account the experience of incidents and in particular the amount of damage resulting therefrom, changes in the monetary values and the effect of the proposed amendment on the cost of insurance. It shall also take into account the relationship between the limits in Article V, paragraph 1, of the 1969 Liability Convention as amended by this Protocol and those in Article 4, paragraph 4, of the International Convention on the Establishment of an International Fund for Compensation for Oil Pollution Damage, 1992.

6(a). No amendment of the limits of liability under this Article may be considered before 15 January 1998 nor less than five years from the date of entry into force of a previous amendment under this Article. No amendment under this Article shall be considered before this Protocol has entered into force.

(b) No limit may be increased so as to exceed an amount which corresponds to the limit laid down in the 1969 Liability Convention as amended by this Protocol increased by 6 per cent per year calculated on a compound basis from 15 January 1993.

(c) No limit may be increased so as to exceed an amount which corresponds to the limit laid down in the 1969 Liability Convention as amended by this Protocol multiplied by 3.

7. Any amendment adopted in accordance with paragraph 4 shall be notified by the Organization to all Contracting States. The amendment shall be deemed to have been accepted at the end of a period of eighteen months after the date of notification, unless within that period not less than one-quarter of the States that were Contracting States at

the time of the adoption of the amendment by the Legal Committee have communicated to the Organization that they do not accept the amendment in which case the amendment is rejected and shall have no effect.

8. An amendment deemed to have been accepted in accordance with paragraph 7 shall enter into force eighteen months after its acceptance.

9. All Contracting States shall be bound by the amendment, unless they denounce this Protocol in accordance with Article 16, paragraphs 1 and 2, at least six months before the amendment enters into force. Such denunciation shall take effect when the amendment enters into force.

10. When an amendment has been adopted by the Legal Committee but the eighteen-month period for its acceptance has not yet expired, a State which becomes a Contracting State during that period shall be bound by the amendment if it enters into force. A State which becomes a Contracting State after that period shall be bound by an amendment which has been accepted in accordance with paragraph 7. In the cases referred to in this paragraph, a State becomes bound by an amendment when that amendment enters into force, or when this Protocol enters into force for that State, if later.

## Article 16

*Denunciation*

1. This Protocol may be denounced by any Party at any time after the date on which it enters into force for that Party.

2. Denunciation shall be effected by the deposit of an instrument with the Secretary-General of the Organization.

3. A denunciation shall take effect twelve months, or such longer period as may be specified in the instrument of denunciation, after its deposit with the Secretary-General of the Organization.

4. As between the Parties to this Protocol, denunciation by any of them of the 1969 Liability Convention in accordance with Article XVI thereof shall not be construed in any way as a denunciation of the 1969 Liability Convention as amended by this Protocol.

5. Denunciation of the Protocol of 1992 to amend the 1971 Fund Convention by a State which remains a Party to the 1971 Fund Convention shall be deemed to be a denunciation of this Protocol. Such denunciation shall take effect on the date on which denunciation of the Protocol of 1992 to amend the 1971 Fund Convention takes effect according to Article 34 of that Protocol.

## Article 17

*Depositary*

1. This Protocol and any amendments accepted under Article 15 shall be deposited with the Secretary-General of the Organization.

2. The Secretary-General of the Organization shall:

(a) inform all States which have signed or acceded to this Protocol of:

(i) each new signature or deposit of an instrument together with the date thereof;

(ii) each declaration and notification under Article 13 and each declaration and communication under Article V, paragraph 9, of the 1992 Liability Convention;

(iii) the date of entry into force of this Protocol;

(iv) any proposal to amend limits of liability which has been made in accordance with Article 15, paragraph 1;

(v) any amendment which has been adopted in accordance with Article 15, paragraph 4;
(vi) any amendment deemed to have been accepted under Article 15, paragraph 7, together with the date on which that amendment shall enter into force in accordance with paragraphs 8 and 9 of that Article;
(vii) the deposit of any instrument of denunciation of this Protocol together with the date of the deposit and the date on which it takes effect;
(viii) any denunciation deemed to have been made under Article 16, paragraph 5;
(ix) any communication called for by any Article of this Protocol;

(b) transmit certified true copies of this Protocol to all Signatory States and to all States which accede to this Protocol.

3. As soon as this Protocol enters into force, the text shall be transmitted by the Secretary-General of the Organization to the Secretariat of the United Nations for registration and publication in accordance with Article 102 of the Charter of the United Nations.

## Article 18

*Languages*

This Protocol is established in a single original in the Arabic, Chinese, English, Russian and Spanish languages, each text being equally authentic.

# ANNEX. CERTIFICATE OF INSURANCE OR OTHER FINANCIAL SECURITY IN RESPECT OF CIVIL LIABILITY FOR OIL POLLUTION DAMAGE

Issued in accordance with the provisions of Article VII of the International Convention on Civil Liability for Oil Pollution Damage, 1992.

| Name of Ship | Distinctive Number or Letters | Port of Registry | Name and Address of Owner |
|---|---|---|---|
| | | | |

This is to certify that there is in force in respect of the above-named ship a policy of insurance or other financial security satisfying the requirements of Article VII of the International Convention on Civil Liability for Oil Pollution Damage, 1992.

## Appendix 12

Type of Security ..........................................................................................

..........................................................................................................

Duration of Security ....................................................................................

..........................................................................................................

Name and Address of the Insurer(s) and/or Guarantor(s)

Name ..........................................................................................................

Address .......................................................................................................

..........................................................................................................

This certificate is valid until .........................................................................

Issued or certified by the Government of ...................................................

..........................................................................................................

(Full designation of the State)

At ....................................................... On .......................................................

(Place) (Date)

..........................................................................................................

Signature and Title of issuing or certifying official.

## Explanatory Notes:

1. If desired, the designation of the State may include a reference to the competent public authority of the country where the certificate is issued.
2. If the total amount of security has been furnished by more than one source, the amount of each of them should be indicated.
3. If security is furnished in several forms, these should be enumerated.
4. The entry 'Duration of Security' must stipulate the date on which such security takes effect.

APPENDIX 13

# INTERNATIONAL CONVENTION ON THE ESTABLISHMENT OF AN INTERNATIONAL FUND FOR COMPENSATION FOR OIL POLLUTION DAMAGE 1992

## GENERAL PROVISIONS

### Article 1

For the purposes of this Convention:

1. '1992 Liability Convention' means the International Convention on Civil Liability for Oil Pollution Damage, 1992.

1 bis. '1971 Fund Convention' means the International Convention on the Establishment of an International Fund for Compensation for Oil Pollution Damage, 1971. For States Parties to the Protocol of 1976 to that Convention, the term shall be deemed to include the 1971 Fund Convention as amended by that Protocol.

2. 'Ship', 'Person', 'Owner', 'Oil', 'Pollution Damage', 'Preventive Measures', 'Incident', and 'Organization' have the same meaning as in Article 1 of the 1992 Liability Convention.

3. 'Contributing Oil' means crude oil and fuel oil as defined in sub-paragraphs (a) and (b) below:

(a) 'Crude Oil' means any liquid hydrocarbon mixture occurring naturally in the earth whether or not treated to render it suitable for transportation. It also includes crude oils from which certain distillate fractions have been removed (sometimes referred to as 'topped crudes') or to which certain distillate fractions have been added (sometimes referred to as 'spiked' or 'reconstituted' crudes).

(b) 'Fuel Oil' means heavy distillates or residues from crude oil or blends of such materials intended for use as a fuel for the production of heat or power of a quality equivalent to the 'American Society for Testing and Materials' Specification for Number Four Fuel Oil (Designation D 396–69)', or heavier.

4. 'Unit of account' has the same meaning as in Article V, paragraph 9, of the 1992 Liability Convention.

5. 'Ship's tonnage' has the same meaning as in Article V, paragraph 10, of the 1992 Liability Conventions.

6. 'Ton', in relation to oil, means a metric ton.

7. 'Guarantor' means any person providing insurance or other financial security to cover an owner's liability in pursuance of Article VII, paragraph 1, of the 1992 Liability Convention.

8. 'Terminal Installation' means any site for the storage of oil in bulk which is capable of receiving oil from waterborne transportation, including any facility situated off-shore and linked to such site.

9. Where an incident consists of a series of occurrences, it shall be treated as having occurred on the date of the first such occurrence.

## Article 2

1. An International Fund for compensation for pollution damage, to be named 'The International Oil Pollution Compensation Fund 1992' and hereinafter referred to as 'the Fund', is hereby established with the following aims:

(a) to provide compensation for pollution damage to the extent that the protection afforded by the 1992 Liability Convention is inadequate;

(b) to give effect to the related purposes set out in this Convention.

2. The Fund shall in each Contracting State be recognized as a legal person capable under the laws of that State of assuming rights and obligations and of being a party in legal proceedings before the courts of that State. Each Contracting State shall recognize the Director of the Fund (hereinafter referred to as 'The Director') as the legal representative of the Fund.

## Article 3

This Convention shall apply exclusively:

(a) to pollution damage caused:

(i) in the territory, including the territorial sea, of a Contracting State, and

(ii) in the exclusive economic zone of a Contracting State, established in accordance with international law, or, if a Contracting State has not established such a zone, in an area beyond and adjacent to the territorial sea of that State determined by that State in accordance with international law and extending not more than 200 nautical miles from the baselines from which the breadth of its territorial sea is measured;

(b) to preventive measures, wherever taken, to prevent or minimize such damage.

# COMPENSATION

## Article 4

1. For the purpose of fulfilling its function under Article 2, paragraph 1(a), the Fund shall pay compensation to any person suffering pollution damage if such person has been unable to obtain full and adequate compensation for the damage under the terms of the 1992 Liability Convention,

(a) because no liability for the damage arises under the 1992 Liability Convention;

(b) because the owner liable for the damage under the 1992 Liability Convention is financially incapable of meeting his obligations in full and any financial security that may be provided under Article VII of that Convention does not cover or is insufficient to satisfy the claims for compensation for the damage; an owner being treated as financially incapable of meeting his obligations and a financial security being treated as insufficient if the person suffering the damage has been unable to obtain full satisfaction of the amount of compensation due under the 1992 Liability Convention after having taken all reasonable steps to pursue the legal remedies available to him;

(c) because the damage exceeds the owner's liability under the 1992 Liability Convention as limited pursuant to Article V, paragraph 1, of that Convention or under the terms of any other international Convention in force or open for signature, ratification or accession at the date of this Convention.

Expenses reasonably incurred or sacrifices reasonably made by the owner voluntarily to prevent or minimize pollution damage shall be treated as pollution damage for the purposes of this Article.

2. The Fund shall incur no obligation under the preceding paragraph if:

(a) it proves that the pollution damage resulted from an act of war, hostilities, civil war or insurrection or was caused by oil which has escaped or been discharged from a warship or other ship owned or operated by a State and used, at the time of the incident, only on Government non-commercial service; or

(b) the claimant cannot prove that the damage resulted from an incident involving one or more ships.

3. If the Fund proves that the pollution damage resulted wholly or partially either from an act or omission done with the intent to cause damage by the person who suffered the damage or from the negligence of that person, the Fund may be exonerated wholly or partially from its obligation to pay compensation to such person. The Fund shall in any event be exonerated to the extent that the shipowner may have been exonerated under Article III, paragraph 3, of the 1992 Liability Convention. However, there shall be no such exoneration of the Fund with regard to preventive measures.

4. (a) Except as otherwise provided in sub-paragraphs (b) and (c) of this paragraph, the aggregate amount of compensation payable by the Fund under this Article shall in respect of any one incident be limited, so that the total sum of that amount and the amount of compensation actually paid under the 1992 Liability Convention for pollution damage within the scope of application of this Convention as defined in Article 3 shall not exceed 135 million units of account.

(b) Except as otherwise provided in sub-paragraph (c), the aggregate amount of compensation payable by the Fund under this Article for pollution damage resulting from a natural phenomenon of an exceptional, inevitable and irresistible character shall not exceed 135 million units of account.

(c) The maximum amount of compensation referred to in sub-paragraphs (a) and (b) shall be 200 million units of account with respect to any incident occurring during any period when there are three Parties to this Convention in respect of which the combined relevant quantity of contributing oil received by persons in the territories of such Parties, during the preceding calendar year, equalled or exceeded 600 million tons.

(d) Interest accrued on a fund constituted in accordance with Article V, paragraph 3, of the 1992 Liability Convention, if any, shall not be taken into account for the computation of the maximum compensation payable by the Fund under this Article.

(e) The amounts mentioned in this Article shall be converted into national currency on the basis of the value of that currency by reference to the Special Drawing Right on the date of the decision of the Assembly of the Fund as to the first date of payment of compensation.

5. Where the amount of established claims against the Fund exceeds the aggregate amount of compensation payable under paragraph 4, the amount available shall be distributed in such a manner that the proportion between any established claim and the amount of compensation actually recovered by the claimant under this Convention shall be the same for all claimants.

6. The Assembly of the Fund may decide that, in exceptional cases, compensation in accordance with this Convention can be paid even if the owner of the ship has not constituted a fund in accordance with Article V, paragraph 3, of the 1992 Liability Convention. In such case paragraph 4(e) of this Article applies accordingly.

7. The Fund shall, at the request of a Contracting State, use its good offices as necessary to assist that State to secure promptly such personnel, material and services as are necessary to enable the State to take measures to prevent or mitigate pollution damage

arising from an incident in respect of which the Fund may be called upon to pay compensation under this Convention.

8. The Fund may on conditions to be laid down in the Internal Regulations provide credit facilities with a view to the taking of preventive measures against pollution damage arising from a particular incident in respect of which the Fund may be called upon to pay compensation under this Convention.

## Article 5

*(Deleted by the 1992 Protocol, Art 7.)*

## Article 6

Rights to compensation under Article 4 shall be extinguished unless an action is brought thereunder or a notification has been made pursuant to Article 7, paragraph 6, within three years from the date when the damage occurred. However, in no case shall an action be brought after six years from the date of the incident which caused the damage.

*(Article 6(2) deleted by the 1992 Protocol, Art 8.)*

## Article 7

1. Subject to the subsequent provisions of this Article, any action against the Fund for compensation under Article 4 of this Convention shall be brought only before a court competent under Article IX of the 1992 Liability Convention in respect of actions against the owner who is or who would, but for the provisions of Article III, paragraph 2, of that Convention, have been liable for pollution damage caused by the relevant incident.

2. Each Contracting State shall ensure that its courts possess the necessary jurisdiction to entertain such actions against the Fund as are referred to in paragraph 1.

3. Where an action for compensation for pollution damage has been brought before a court competent under Article IX of the 1992 Liability Convention against the owner of a ship or his guarantor, such court shall have exclusive jurisdictional competence over any action against the Fund for compensation under the provisions of Article 4 of this Convention in respect of the same damage. However, where an action for compensation for pollution damage under the 1992 Liability Convention has been brought before a court in a State Party to the 1992 Liability Convention but not to this Convention, any action against the Fund under Article 4 of this Convention shall at the option of the claimant be brought either before a court of the State where the Fund has its headquarters or before any court of a State Party to this Convention competent under Article IX of the 1992 Liability Convention.

4. Each Contracting State shall ensure that the Fund shall have the right to intervene as a party to any legal proceedings instituted in accordance with Article IX of the 1992 Liability Convention before a competent court of that State against the owner of a ship or his guarantor.

5. Except as otherwise provided in paragraph 6, the Fund shall not be bound by any judgement or decision in proceedings to which it has not been a party or by any settlement to which it is not a party.

6. Without prejudice to the provisions of paragraph 4, where an action under the 1992 Liability Convention for compensation for pollution damage has been brought against an owner or his guarantor before a competent court in a Contracting State, each party to the proceedings shall be entitled under the national law of that State to notify the Fund of the proceedings. Where such notification has been made in accordance with the formalities required by the law of the court seized and in such time and in such a manner that the Fund has in fact been in a position effectively to intervene as a party to the proceedings,

any judgement rendered by the court in such proceedings shall, after it has become final and enforceable in the State where the judgement was given, become binding upon the Fund in the sense that the facts and findings in that judgement may not be disputed by the Fund even if the Fund has not actually intervened in the proceedings.

## Article 8

Subject to any decision concerning the distribution referred to in Article 4, paragraph 5, any judgement given against the Fund by a court having jurisdiction in accordance with Article 7, paragraphs 1 and 3, shall, when it has become enforceable in the State of origin and is in that State no longer subject to ordinary forms of review, be recognized and enforceable in each Contracting State on the same conditions as are prescribed in Article X of the 1992 Liability Convention.

## Article 9

1. The Fund shall, in respect of any amount of compensation for pollution damage paid by the Fund in accordance with Article 4, paragraph 1, of this Convention, acquire by subrogation the rights that the person so compensated may enjoy under the 1992 Liability Convention against the owner or his guarantor.
2. Nothing in this Convention shall prejudice any right of recourse or subrogation of the Fund against persons other than those referred to in the preceding paragraph. In any event the right of the Fund to subrogation against such person shall not be less favourable than that of an insurer of the person to whom compensation has been paid.
3. Without prejudice to any other rights of subrogation or recourse against the Fund which may exist, a Contracting State or agency thereof which has paid compensation for pollution damage in accordance with provisions of national law shall acquire by subrogation the rights which the person so compensated would have enjoyed under this Convention.

# CONTRIBUTIONS

## Article 10

1. Annual contributions to the Fund shall be made in respect of each Contracting State by any person who, in the calendar year referred to in Article 12, paragraph 2(a) or (b), has received in total quantities exceeding 150,000 tons:
   (a) in the ports or terminal installations in the territory of that State contributing oil carried by sea to such ports or terminal installations; and
   (b) in any installations situated in the territory of that Contracting State contributing oil which has been carried by sea and discharged in a port or terminal installation of a non-Contracting State, provided that contributing oil shall only be taken into account by virtue of this sub-paragraph on first receipt in a Contracting State after its discharge in that non-Contracting State.
2. (a) For the purposes of paragraph 1, where the quantity of contributing oil received in the territory of a Contracting State by any person in a calendar year when aggregated with the quantity of contributing oil received in the same Contracting State in that year by any associated person or persons exceeds 150,000 tons, such person shall pay contributions in respect of the actual quantity received by him notwithstanding that that quantity did not exceed 150,000 tons.

(b) 'Associated person' means any subsidiary or commonly controlled entity. The question whether a person comes within this definition shall be determined by the national law of the State concerned.

## Article 11

(*Deleted by the 1992 Protocol, Art 13.*)

## Article 12

1. With a view to assessing the amount of annual contributions due, if any, and taking account of the necessity to maintain sufficient liquid funds, the Assembly shall for each calendar year make an estimate in the form of a budget of:

(i) *Expenditure*

(a) costs and expenses of the administration of the Fund in the relevant year and any deficit from operations in preceding years;

(b) payments to be made by the Fund in the relevant year for the satisfaction of claims against the Fund due under Article 4, including repayment on loans previously taken by the Fund for the satisfaction of such claims, to the extent that the aggregate amount of such claims in respect of any one incident does not exceed four million units of account;

(c) payments to be made by the Fund in the relevant year for the satisfaction of claims against the Fund due under Article 4, including repayments on loans previously taken by the Fund for the satisfaction of such claims, to the extent that the aggregate amount of such claims in respect of any one incident is in excess of four million units of account;

(ii) *Income*

(a) surplus funds from operations in preceding years, including any interest;

(b) annual contributions, if required to balance the budget;

(c) any other income.

2. The Assembly shall decide the total amount of contributions to be levied. On the basis of that decision, the Director shall, in respect of each Contracting State, calculate for each person referred to in Article 10 the amount of his annual contribution;

(a) in so far as the contribution is for the satisfaction of payments referred to in paragraph 1(i)(a) and (b) on the basis of a fixed sum for each ton of contributing oil received in the relevant State by such persons during the preceding calendar year; and

(b) in so far as the contribution is for the satisfaction of payments referred to in paragraph 1(i)(c) of this Article on the basis of a fixed sum for each ton of contributing oil received by such person during the calendar year preceding that in which the incident in question occurred, provided that State was a Party to this Convention at the date of the incident.

3. The sums referred to in paragraph 2 above shall be arrived at by dividing the relevant total amount of contributions required by the total amount of contributing oil received in all Contracting States in the relevant year.

4. The annual contributions shall be due on the date to be laid down in the Internal Regulations of the Fund. The Assembly may decide on a different date of payment.

5. The Assembly may decide, under conditions to be laid down in the Financial Regulations of the Fund, to make transfers between funds received in accordance with Article 12.2(a) and funds received in accordance with Article 12.2(b).

### Article 13

1. The amount of any contribution due under Article 12 and which is in arrears shall bear interest at a rate which shall be determined in accordance with the Internal Regulations of the Fund, provided that different rates may be fixed for different circumstances.

2. Each Contracting State shall ensure that any obligation to contribute to the Fund arising under this Convention in respect of oil received within the territory of that State is fulfilled and shall take any appropriate measures under its law, including the imposing of such sanctions as it may deem necessary, with a view to the effective execution of any such obligation; provided, however, that such measures shall only be directed against those persons who are under an obligation to contribute to the Fund.

3. Where a person who is liable in accordance with the provisions of Articles 10 and 12 to make contributions to the Fund does not fulfil his obligations in respect of any such contribution or any part thereof and is in arrear, the Director shall take all appropriate action against such person on behalf of the Fund with a view to the recovery of the amount due. However, where the defaulting contributor is manifestly insolvent or the circumstances otherwise so warrant, the Assembly may, upon recommendation of the Director, decide that no action shall be taken or continued against the contributor.

### Article 14

1. Each Contracting State may at the time when it deposits its instrument of ratification or accession or at any time thereafter declare that it assumes itself obligations that are incumbent under this Convention on any person who is liable to contribute to the Fund in accordance with Article 10, paragraph 1, in respect of oil received within the territory of that State. Such declaration shall be made in writing and shall specify which obligations are assumed.

2. Where a declaration under paragraph 1 is made prior to the entry into force of this Convention in accordance with Article 40, it shall be deposited with the Secretary-General of the Organization who shall after the entry into force of the Convention communicate the declaration to the Director.

3. A declaration under paragraph 1 which is made after the entry into force of this Convention shall be deposited with the Director.

4. A declaration made in accordance with this Article may be withdrawn by the relevant State giving notice thereof in writing to the Director. Such notification shall take effect three months after the Director's receipt thereof.

5. Any State which is bound by a declaration made under this Article shall, in any proceedings brought against it before a competent court in respect of any obligation specified in the declaration, waive any immunity that it would otherwise be entitled to invoke.

### Article 15

1. Each Contracting State shall ensure that any person who receives contributing oil within its territory in such quantities that he is liable to contribute to the Fund appears on a list to be established and kept up to date by the Director in accordance with the subsequent provisions of this Article.

2. For the purposes set out in paragraph 1, each Contracting State shall communicate, at a time and in the manner to be prescribed in the Internal Regulations, to the Director the name and address of any person who in respect of that State is liable to contribute to the Fund pursuant to Article 10, as well as data on the relevant quantities of contributing oil received by any such person during the preceding calendar year.

3. For the purposes of ascertaining who are, at any given time, the persons liable to contribute to the Fund in accordance with Article 10, paragraph 1, and of establishing, where applicable, the quantities of oil to be taken into account for any such person when determining the amount of his contribution, the list shall be *prima facie* evidence of the facts stated therein.

4. Where a Contracting State does not fulfil its obligations to submit to the Director the communication referred to in paragraph 2 and this results in a financial loss for the Fund, that Contracting State shall be liable to compensate the Fund for such loss. The Assembly shall, on the recommendation of the Director, decide whether such compensation shall be payable by that Contracting State.

## ORGANIZATION AND ADMINISTRATION

### Article 16

The Fund shall have an Assembly and a Secretariat headed by a Director.

## ASSEMBLY

### Article 17

The Assembly shall consist of all Contracting States to this Convention.

### Article 18

The functions of the Assembly shall be:

1. to elect at each regular session its Chairman and two Vice-Chairmen who shall hold office until the next regular session;
2. to determine its own rules of procedure, subject to the provisions of this Convention;
3. to adopt Internal Regulations necessary for the proper functioning of the Fund;
4. to appoint the Director and make provisions for the appointment of such other personnel as may be necessary and determine the terms and conditions of service of the Director and other personnel;
5. to adopt the annual budget and fix the annual contributions;
6. to appoint auditors and approve the accounts of the Fund;
7. to approve settlements of claims against the Fund, to take decisions in respect of the distribution among claimants of the available amount of compensation in accordance with Article 4, paragraph 5, and to determine the terms and conditions according to which provisional payments in respect of claims shall be made with a view to ensuring that victims of pollution damage are compensated as promptly as possible;
8. (*Deleted by the 1992 Protocol, Art 18(2).*)
9. to establish any temporary or permanent subsidiary body it may consider to be necessary, to define its terms of reference and to give it the authority needed to perform the functions entrusted to it; when appointing the members of such body, the Assembly shall endeavour to secure an equitable geographical distribution of members and to ensure that the Contracting States, in respect of which the largest quantities of contributing oil are being received, are appropriately represented; the

Rules of Procedure of the Assembly may be applied, *mutatis mutandis*, for the work of such subsidiary body;

10. to determine which non-Contracting State and which inter-governmental and international non-governmental organizations shall be admitted to take part, without voting rights, in meetings of the Assembly and subsidiary bodies;

11. to give instructions concerning the administration of the Fund to the Director and subsidiary bodies;

12. (*Deleted by the 1992 Protocol, Art 18(6).*)

13. to supervise the proper execution of the Convention and of its own decisions;

14. to perform such other functions as are allocated to it under the Convention or are otherwise necessary for the proper operation of the Fund.

### Article 19

1. Regular sessions of the Assembly shall take place once every calendar year upon convocation by the Director.

2. Extraordinary sessions of the Assembly shall be convened by the Director at the request of at least one-third of the members of the Assembly and may be convened on the Director's own initiative after consultation with the Chairman of the Assembly. The Director shall give members at least thirty days' notice of such sessions.

### Article 20

A majority of the members of the Assembly shall constitute a quorum for its meetings.

### Articles 21–27

(*Deleted by the 1992 Protocol, Art 20.*)

## SECRETARIAT

### Article 28

1. The Secretariat shall comprise the Director and such staff as the administration of the Fund may require.

2. The Director shall be the legal representative of the Fund.

### Article 29

1. The Director shall be the chief administrative officer of the Fund. Subject to the instructions given to him by the Assembly, he shall perform those functions which are assigned to him by this Convention, the Internal Regulations of the Fund and the Assembly.

2. The Director shall in particular:
   (a) appoint the personnel required for the administration of the Fund;
   (b) take all appropriate measures with a view to the proper administration of the Fund's assets;
   (c) collect the contributions due under this Convention while observing in particular the provisions of Article 13, paragraph 3;

(d) to the extent necessary to deal with claims against the Fund and carry out the other functions of the Fund, employ the services of legal, financial and other experts;
(e) take all appropriate measures for dealing with claims against the Fund within the limits and on conditions to be laid down in the Internal Regulations, including the final settlement of claims without the prior approval of the Assembly where these Regulations so provide;
(f) prepare and submit to the Assembly the financial statements and budget estimates for each calendar year;
(g) prepare, in consultation with the Chairman of the Assembly, and publish a report of the activities of the Fund during the previous calendar year;
(h) prepare, collect and circulate the papers, documents, agenda, minutes and information that may be required for the work of the Assembly and subsidiary bodies.

### Article 30

In the performance of their duties the Director and the staff and experts appointed by him shall not seek or receive instructions from any Government or from any authority external to the Fund. They shall refrain from any action which might reflect on their position as international officials. Each Contracting State on its part undertakes to respect the exclusively international character of the responsibilities of the Director and the staff and experts appointed by him, and not to seek to influence them in the discharge of their duties.

## FINANCES

### Article 31

1. Each Contracting State shall bear the salary, travel and other expenses of its own delegation to the Assembly and of its representatives on subsidiary bodies.
2. Any other expenses incurred in the operation of the Fund shall be borne by the Fund.

## VOTING

### Article 32

The following provisions shall apply to voting in the Assembly:
(a) each member shall have one vote;
(b) except as otherwise provided in Article 33, decisions of the Assembly shall be by a majority vote of the members present and voting;
(c) decisions where a three-fourths or a two-thirds majority is required shall be by a three-fourths or two-thirds majority vote, as the case may be, of those present;
(d) for the purpose of this Article the phrase 'members present' means 'members present at the meeting at the time of the vote', and the phrase 'members present and voting' means 'members present and casting an affirmative or negative vote'. Members who abstain from voting shall be considered as not voting.

## Article 33

The following decisions of the Assembly shall require a two-thirds majority:

(a) a decision under Article 13, paragraph 3, not to take or continue action against a contributor;
(b) the appointment of the Director under Article 18, paragraph 4;
(c) the establishment of subsidiary bodies, under Article 18, paragraph 9, and matters relating to such establishment.

## Article 34

1. The Fund, its assets, income, including contributions, and other property shall enjoy in all Contracting States exemption from all direct taxation.
2. When the Fund makes substantial purchases of movable or immovable property, or has important work carried out which is necessary for the exercise of its official activities and the cost of which includes indirect taxes or sales taxes, the Governments of Member States shall take, whenever possible, appropriate measures for the remission or refund of the amount of such duties and taxes.
3. No exemption shall be accorded in the case of duties, taxes or dues which merely constitute payment for public utility services.
4. The Fund shall enjoy exemption from all customs duties, taxes and other related taxes on articles imported or exported by it or on its behalf for its official use. Articles thus imported shall not be transferred either for consideration or gratis on the territory of the country into which they have been imported except on conditions agreed by the Government of that country.
5. Persons contributing to the Fund and victims and owners of ships receiving compensation from the Fund shall be subject to the fiscal legislation of the State where they are taxable, no special exemption or other benefit being conferred on them in this respect.
6. Information relating to individual contributors supplied for the purpose of this Convention shall not be divulged outside the Fund except in so far as it may be strictly necessary to enable the Fund to carry out its functions including the bringing and defending of legal proceedings.
7. Independently of existing or future regulations concerning currency or transfers, Contracting States shall authorize the transfer and payment of any contribution to the Fund and of any compensation paid by the Fund without any restriction.

# TRANSITIONAL PROVISIONS

## Article 35

Claims for compensation under Article 4 arising from incidents occurring after the date of entry into force of this Convention may not be brought against the Fund earlier than the one hundred and twentieth day after that date.

## Article 36

The Secretary-General of the Organization shall convene the first session of the Assembly. This session shall take place as soon as possible after entry into force of this Convention and, in any case, not more than thirty days after such entry into force.

## Article 36 bis

The following transitional provisions shall apply in the period, hereinafter referred to as the transitional period, commencing with the date of entry into force of this Convention and ending with the date on which the denunciations provided for in Article 31 of the 1992 Protocol to amend the 1971 Fund Convention take effect:

(a) In the application of paragraph 1(a) of Article 2 of this Convention, the reference to the 1992 Liability Convention shall include reference to the International Convention on Civil Liability for Oil Pollution Damage, 1969, either in its original version or as amended by the Protocol thereto of 1976 (referred to in this Article as 'the 1969 Liability Convention'), and also the 1971 Fund Convention.

(b) Where an incident has caused pollution damage within the scope of this Convention, the Fund shall pay compensation to any person suffering pollution damage only if, and to the extent that, such person has been unable to obtain full and adequate compensation for the damage under the terms of the 1969 Liability Convention, the 1971 Fund Convention and the 1992 Liability Convention, provided that, in respect of pollution damage within the scope of this Convention in respect of a Party to this Convention but not a Party to the 1971 Fund Convention, the Fund shall pay compensation to any person suffering pollution damage only if, and to the extent that, such person would have been unable to obtain full and adequate compensation had that State been party to each of the above-mentioned Conventions.

(c) In the application of Article 4 of this Convention, the amount to be taken into account in determining the aggregate amount of compensation payable by the Fund shall also include the amount of compensation actually paid under the 1969 Liability Convention, if any, and the amount of compensation actually paid or deemed to have been paid under the 1971 Fund Convention.

(d) Paragraph 1 of Article 9 of this Convention shall also apply to the rights enjoyed under the 1969 Liability Convention.

## Article 36 ter

1. Subject to paragraph 4 of this Article, the aggregate amount of the annual contributions payable in respect of contributing oil received in a single Contracting State during a calendar year shall not exceed 27.5% of the total amount of annual contributions pursuant to the 1992 Protocol to amend the 1971 Fund Convention, in respect of that calendar year.

2. If the application of the provisions in paragraphs 2 and 3 of Article 12 would result in the aggregate amount of the contributions payable by contributors in a single Contracting State in respect of a given calendar year exceeding 27.5% of the total annual contributions, the contributions payable by all contributors in that State shall be reduced *pro rata* so that their aggregate contributions equal 27.5% of the total annual contributions to the Fund in respect of that year.

3. If the contributions payable by persons in a given Contracting State shall be reduced pursuant to paragraph 2 of this Article, the contributions payable by persons in all other Contracting States shall be increased *pro rata* so as to ensure that the total amount of contributions payable by all persons liable to contribute to the Fund in respect of the calendar year in question will reach the total amount of contributions decided by the Assembly.

4. The provisions in paragraphs 1 to 3 of this Article shall operate until the total quantity of contributing oil received in all Contracting States in a calendar year has

reached 750 million tons or until a period of 5 years after the date of entry into force of the said 1992 Protocol has elapsed, whichever occurs earlier.

## Article 36 quater

Notwithstanding the provisions of this Convention, the following provisions shall apply to the administration of the Fund during the period in which both the 1971 Fund Convention and this Convention are in force:

(a) The Secretariat of the Fund, established by the 1971 Fund Convention (hereinafter referred to as 'the 1971 Fund'), headed by the Director, may also function as the Secretariat and the Director of the Fund.

(b) If, in accordance with sub-paragraph (a), the Secretariat and the Director of the 1971 Fund also perform the function of Secretariat and Director of the Fund, the Fund shall be represented, in cases of conflict of interests between the 1971 Fund and the Fund, by the Chairman of the Assembly of the Fund.

(c) The Director and the staff and experts appointed by him, performing their duties under this Convention and the 1971 Fund Convention, shall not be regarded as contravening the provisions of Article 30 of this Convention in so far as they discharge their duties in accordance with this Article.

(d) The Assembly of the Fund shall endeavour not to take decisions which are incompatible with decisions taken by the Assembly of the 1971 Fund. If differences of opinion with respect to common administrative issues arise, the Assembly of the Fund shall try to reach a consensus with the Assembly of the 1971 Fund, in a spirit of mutual co-operation and with the common aims of both organizations in mind.

(e) The Fund may succeed to the rights, obligations and assets of the 1971 Fund if the Assembly of the 1971 Fund so decides, in accordance with Article 44, paragraph 2, of the 1971 Fund Convention.

(f) The Fund shall reimburse to the 1971 Fund all costs and expenses arising from administrative services performed by the 1971 Fund on behalf of the Fund.

# FINAL CLAUSES

## Article 36 quinquies

The final clauses of this Convention shall be Articles 28 to 39 of the Protocol of 1992 to amend the 1971 Fund Convention. References in this Convention to Contracting States shall be taken to mean references to the Contracting States of that Protocol.

NOTE:
The following are the Arts 28 to 39 referred to in Art 36 quinquies:

## Article 28

*Signature, ratification, acceptance, approval and accession*

1. This Protocol shall be open for signature at London from 15 January 1993 to 14 January 1994 by any State which has signed the 1992 Liability Convention.

2. Subject to paragraph 4, this Protocol shall be ratified, accepted or approved by States which have signed it.

3. Subject to paragraph 4, this Protocol is open for accession by States which did not sign it.

4. This Protocol may be ratified, accepted, approved or acceded to only by States which have ratified, accepted, approved or acceded to the 1992 Liability Convention.

5. Ratification, acceptance, approval or accession shall be effected by the deposit of a formal instrument to that effect with the Secretary-General of the Organization.

6. A State which is a Party to this Protocol but is not a Party to the 1971 Fund Convention shall be bound by the provisions of the 1971 Fund Convention as amended by this Protocol in relation to other Parties hereto, but shall not be bound by the provisions of the 1971 Fund Convention in relation to Parties thereto.

7. Any instrument of ratification, acceptance, approval or accession deposited after the entry into force of an amendment to the 1971 Fund Convention as amended by this Protocol shall be deemed to apply to the Convention so amended, as modified by such amendment.

## Article 29

*Information on contributing oil*

1. Before this Protocol comes into force for a State, that State shall, when depositing an instrument referred to in Article 28, paragraph 5, and annually thereafter at a date to be determined by the Secretary-General of the Organization, communicate to him the name and address of any person who in respect of that State would be liable to contribute to the Fund pursuant to Article 10 of the 1971 Fund Convention as amended by this Protocol as well as data on the relevant quantities of contributing oil received by any such person in the territory of that State during the preceding calendar year.

2. During the transitional period, the Director shall, for Parties, communicate annually to the Secretary-General of the Organization data on quantities of contributing oil received by persons liable to contribute to the Fund pursuant to Article 10 of the 1971 Fund Convention as amended by this Protocol.

## Article 30

*Entry into force*

1. This Protocol shall enter into force twelve months following the date on which the following requirements are fulfilled:

(a) at least eight States have deposited instruments of ratification, acceptance, approval or accession with the Secretary-General of the Organization; and

(b) the Secretary-General of the Organization has received information in accordance with Article 29 that those persons who would be liable to contribute pursuant to Article 10 of the 1971 Fund Convention as amended by this Protocol have received during the preceding calendar year a total quantity of at least 450 million tons of contributing oil.

2. However, this Protocol shall not enter into force before the 1992 Liability Convention has entered into force.

3. For each State which ratifies, accepts, approves or accedes to this Protocol after the conditions in paragraph 1 for entry into force have been met, the Protocol shall enter into force twelve months following the date of the deposit by such State of the appropriate instrument.

4. Any State may, at the time of the deposit of its instrument of ratification, acceptance, approval or accession in respect of this Protocol declare that such instrument shall not take effect for the purpose of this Article until the end of the six-month period in Article 31.

5. Any State which has made a declaration in accordance with the preceding paragraph

may withdraw it at any time by means of a notification addressed to the Secretary-General of the Organization. Any such withdrawal shall take effect on the date the notification is received, and any State making such a withdrawal shall be deemed to have deposited its instrument of ratification, acceptance, approval or accession in respect of this Protocol on that date.

6. Any State which has made a declaration under Article 13, paragraph 2, of the Protocol of 1992 to amend the 1969 Liability Convention shall be deemed to have also made a declaration under paragraph 4 of this Article. Withdrawal of a declaration under the said Article 13, paragraph 2, shall be deemed to constitute withdrawal also under paragraph 5 of this Article.

## Article 31

*Denunciation of the 1969 and 1971 Conventions*

Subject to Article 30, within six months following the date on which the following requirements are fulfilled:

(a) at least eight States have become Parties to this Protocol or have deposited instruments of ratification, acceptance, approval or accession with the Secretary-General of the Organization, whether or not subject to Article 30, paragraph 4, and

(b) the Secretary-General of the Organization has received information in accordance with Article 29 that those persons who are or would be liable to contribute pursuant to Article 10 of the 1971 Fund Convention as amended by this Protocol have received during the preceding calendar year a total quantity of at least 750 million tons of contributing oil;

each Party to this Protocol and each State which has deposited an instrument of ratification, acceptance, approval or accession, whether or not subject to Article 30, paragraph 4, shall, if party thereto, denounce the 1971 Fund Convention and the 1969 Liability Convention with effect twelve months after the expiry of the above-mentioned six-month period.

## Article 32

*Revision and amendment*

1. A conference for the purpose of revising or amending the 1992 Fund Convention may be convened by the Organization.

2. The Organization shall convene a Conference of Contracting States for the purpose of revising or amending the 1992 Fund Convention at the request of not less than one third of all Contracting States.

## Article 33

*Amendment of compensation limits*

1. Upon the request of at least one quarter of the Contracting States, any proposal to amend the limits of amounts of compensation laid down in Article 4, paragraph 4, of the 1971 Fund Convention as amended by this Protocol shall be circulated by the Secretary-General to all Members of the Organization and to all Contracting States.

2. Any amendment proposed and circulated as above shall be submitted to the Legal Committee of the Organization for consideration at a date at least six months after the date of its circulation.

3. All Contracting States to the 1971 Fund Convention as amended by this Protocol, whether or not Members of the Organization, shall be entitled to participate in the proceedings of the Legal Committee for the consideration and adoption of amendments.

4. Amendments shall be adopted by a two-thirds majority of the Contracting States present and voting in the Legal Committee, expanded as provided for in paragraph 3, on condition that at least one-half of the Contracting States shall be present at the time of voting.

5. When acting on a proposal to amend the limits, the Legal Committee shall take into account the experience of incidents and in particular the amount of damage resulting therefrom and changes in the monetary values. It shall also take into account the relationship between the limits in Article 4, paragraph 4, of the 1971 Fund Convention as amended by this Protocol and those in Article V, paragraph 1 of the International Convention on Civil Liability for Oil Pollution Damage, 1992.

6. (a) No amendment of the limits under this Article may be considered before 15 January 1998 nor less than five years from the date of entry into force of a previous amendment under this Article. No amendment under this Article shall be considered before this Protocol has entered into force.

(b) No limit may be increased so as to exceed an amount which corresponds to the limit laid down in the 1971 Fund Convention as amended by this Protocol increased by six per cent per year calculated on a compound basis from 15 January 1993.

(c) No limit may be increased so as to exceed an amount which corresponds to the limit laid down in the 1971 Fund Convention as amended by this Protocol multiplied by three.

7. Any amendment adopted in accordance with paragraph 4 shall be notified by the Organization to all Contracting States. The amendment shall be deemed to have been accepted at the end of a period of eighteen months after the date of notification unless within that period not less than one-quarter of the States that were Contracting States at the time of the adoption of the amendment by the Legal Committee have communicated to the Organization that they do not accept the amendment in which case the amendment is rejected and shall have no effect.

8. An amendment deemed to have been accepted in accordance with paragraph 7 shall enter into force eighteen months after its acceptance.

9. All Contracting States shall be bound by the amendment, unless they denounce this Protocol in accordance with Article 34, paragraphs 1 and 2, at least six months before the amendment enters into force. Such denunciation shall take effect when the amendment enters into force.

10. When an amendment has been adopted by the Legal Committee but the eighteen-month period for its acceptance has not yet expired, a State which becomes a Contracting State during that period shall be bound by the amendment if it enters into force. A State which becomes a Contracting State after that period shall be bound by an amendment which has been accepted in accordance with paragraph 7. In the cases referred to in this paragraph, a State becomes bound by an amendment when that amendment enters into force, or when this Protocol enters into force for that State, if later.

## Article 34

*Denunciation*

1. This Protocol may be denounced by any Party at any time after the date on which it enters into force for that Party.

2. Denunciation shall be effected by the deposit of an instrument with the Secretary-General of the Organization.

3. A denunciation shall take effect twelve months, or such longer period as may be specified in the instrument of denunciation, after its deposit with the Secretary-General of the Organization.

4. Denunciation of the 1992 Liability Convention shall be deemed to be a denunciation of this Protocol. Such denunciation shall take effect on the date on which denunciation of the Protocol of 1992 to amend the 1969 Liability Convention takes effect according to Article 16 of that Protocol.

5. Any Contracting State to this Protocol which has not denounced the 1971 Fund Convention and the 1969 Liability Convention as required by Article 31 shall be deemed to have denounced this Protocol with effect twelve months after the expiry of the six-month period mentioned in that Article. As from the date on which the denunciations provided for in Article 31 take effect, any Party to this Protocol which deposits an instrument of ratification, acceptance, approval or accession to the 1969 Liability Convention shall be deemed to have denounced this Protocol with effect from the date on which such instrument takes effect.

6. As between the Parties to this Protocol, denunciation by any of them of the 1971 Fund Convention in accordance with Article 41 thereof shall not be construed in any way as a denunciation of the 1971 Fund Convention as amended by this Protocol.

7. Notwithstanding a denunciation of this Protocol by a Party pursuant to this Article, any provisions of this Protocol relating to the obligations to make contributions under Article 10 of the 1971 Fund Convention as amended by this Protocol with respect to an incident referred to in Article 12, paragraph 2(b), of that amended Convention and occurring before the denunciation takes effect shall continue to apply.

## Article 35

*Extraordinary sessions of the Assembly*

1. Any Contracting State may, within ninety days after the deposit of an instrument of denunciation the result of which it considers will significantly increase the level of contributions for the remaining Contracting States, request the Director to convene an extraordinary session of the Assembly. The Director shall convene the Assembly to meet not later than sixty days after receipt of the request.

2. The Director may convene, on his own initiative, an extraordinary session of the Assembly to meet within sixty days after the deposit of any instrument of denunciation, if he considers that such denunciation will result in a significant increase in the level of contributions of the remaining Contracting States.

3. If the Assembly at an extraordinary session convened in accordance with paragraph 1 or 2 decides that the denunciation will result in a significant increase in the level of contributions for the remaining Contracting States, any such State may, not later than one hundred and twenty days before the date on which the denunciation takes effect, denounce this protocol with effect from the same date.

## Article 36

*Termination*

1. This Protocol shall cease to be in force on the date when the number of Contracting States falls below three.

2. States which are bound by this Protocol on the day before the date it ceases to be in force shall enable the Fund to exercise its functions as described under Article 37 of this Protocol and shall, for that purpose only, remain bound by this Protocol.

## Article 37

*Winding up of the Fund*

1. If this Protocol ceases to be in force, the Fund shall nevertheless:
   (a) meet its obligations in respect of any incident occurring before the Protocol ceased to be in force;
   (b) be entitled to exercise its rights to contributions to the extent that these contributions are necessary to meet the obligations under sub-paragraph (a), including expenses for the administration of the Fund necessary for this purpose.
2. The Assembly shall take all appropriate measures to complete the winding up of the Fund including the distribution in an equitable manner of any remaining assets among those persons who have contributed to the Fund.
3. For the purposes of this Article the Fund shall remain a legal person.

## Article 38

*Depositary*

1. This Protocol and any amendments accepted under Article 33 shall be deposited with the Secretary-General of the Organization.
2. The Secretary-General of the Organization shall:
   (a) inform all States which have signed or acceded to this Protocol of:
      (i) each new signature or deposit of an instrument together with the date thereof;
      (ii) each declaration and notification under Article 30 including declarations and withdrawals deemed to have been made in accordance with that Article;
      (iii) the date of entry into force of this Protocol;
      (iv) the date by which denunciations provided for in Article 31 are required to be made;
      (v) any proposal to amend limits of amounts of compensation which has been made in accordance with Article 33, paragraph 1;
      (vi) any amendment which has been adopted in accordance with Article 33, paragraph 4;
      (vii) any amendment deemed to have been accepted under Article 33, paragraph 7, together with the date on which that amendment shall enter into force in accordance with paragraphs 8 and 9 of that Article;
      (viii) the deposit of an instrument of denunciation of this Protocol together with the date of the deposit and the date on which it takes effect;
      (ix) any denunciation deemed to have been made under Article 34, paragraph 5;
      (x) any communication called for by any Article in this Protocol;
   (b) transmit certified true copies of this Protocol to all Signatory States and to all States which accede to the Protocol.
3. As soon as this Protocol enters into force, the text shall be transmitted by the Secretary-General of the Organization to the Secretariat of the United Nations for registration and publication in accordance with Article 102 of the Charter of the United Nations.

## Article 39

*Languages*

This Protocol is established in a single original in the Arabic, Chinese, English, French, Russian and Spanish languages, each text being equally authentic.

APPENDIX 14

# PARTIES TO: (1) THE INTERNATIONAL CONVENTION ON CIVIL LIABILITY FOR OIL POLLUTION DAMAGE, BRUSSELS, 1969 (2) THE SDR PROTOCOL 1976 TO THE CLC 1969 (3) THE 1992 PROTOCOL TO THE CLC 1969 (4) THE INTERNATIONAL CONVENTION ON THE ESTABLISHMENT OF AN INTERNATIONAL FUND FOR COMPENSATION FOR OIL POLLUTION DAMAGE, BRUSSELS, 1971 (5) THE SDR PROTOCOL 1976 TO THE FUND CONVENTION 1971 (6) THE 1992 PROTOCOL TO THE FUND CONVENTION 1971

| | | |
|---|---|---|
| Albania | CLC/SDR | Fund/SDR |
| Algeria | CLC | Fund |
| Australia | CLC/SDR/1992 | Fund/SDR/1992 |
| Bahamas | CLC/SDR | Fund/SDR |
| Bahrain | CLC/SDR/1992 | Fund/SDR/1992 |
| Barbados | CLC/SDR | Fund/SDR |
| Belgium | CLC/SDR | Fund/SDR |
| Belize | CLC/SDR | |
| Benin | CLC | Fund |
| Botswana | CLC | |
| Brazil | CLC | |
| Brunei Darussalam | CLC/SDR | Fund |
| Cambodia | CLC | |
| Cameroon | CLC/SDR | Fund |
| Canada | CLC/SDR | Fund/SDR |
| Chile | CLC | |
| China | CLC/SDR | |

| | | |
|---|---|---|
| Colombia | CLC/SDR | |
| Croatia | CLC | Fund |
| Cyprus | CLC/SDR | Fund/SDR |
| Denmark | CLC/SDR/1992 | Fund/SDR/1992 |
| Dominican Republic | CLC | |
| Djibouti | CLC | Fund |
| Ecuador | CLC | |
| Egypt | CLC/SDR/1992 | |
| Equatorial Guinea | CLC | |
| Estonia | CLC | Fund |
| Fiji | CLC | Fund |
| Finland | CLC/SDR/1992 | Fund/SDR/1992 |
| France | CLC/SDR/1992 | Fund/SDR/1992 |
| Gabon | CLC | Fund |
| Gambia | CLC | Fund |
| Georgia | CLC/SDR | |
| Germany | CLC/SDR/1992 | Fund/SDR/1992 |
| Ghana | CLC | Fund |
| Greece | CLC/SDR/1992 | Fund/SDR/1992 |
| Guatemala | CLC | |
| Iceland | CLC/SDR | Fund/SDR |
| India | CLC/SDR | Fund/SDR |
| Indonesia | CLC | Fund |
| Iraq | CLC/SDR | Fund/SDR |
| Ireland | CLC/SDR | Fund/SDR |
| Israel | CLC/SDR | Fund/SDR |
| Italy | CLC/SDR | Fund/SDR |
| Ivory Coast | CLC | Fund |
| Japan | CLC/SDR/1992 | Fund/SDR/1992 |
| Kazakhstan | CLC | |
| Kenya | CLC | Fund |
| Kiribati | CLC (provisional) | |
| Korea, Republic of | CLC/SDR | Fund |
| Kuwait | CLC/SDR | Fund |
| Latvia | CLC | |
| Lebanon | CLC | |
| Liberia | CLC/SDR/1992 | Fund/SDR/1992 |
| Luxembourg | CLC/SDR | |
| Malaysia | CLC | Fund |
| Maldives | CLC/SDR | Fund |
| Malta | CLC/SDR | Fund/SDR |
| Marshall Islands | CLC/SDR/1992 | Fund/SDR/1992 |
| Mauritania | CLC/SDR | Fund |
| Mauritius | CLC/SDR | Fund/SDR |
| Mexico | CLC/SDR/1992 | Fund/SDR/1992 |
| Monaco | CLC/1992 (from 8/11/97) | Fund/1992 (from 8/11/97) |
| Morocco | CLC | Fund/SDR |
| Netherlands | CLC/SDR/1992 (from 15/11/97) | Fund/SDR/1992 (from 15/11/97) |
| New Zealand | CLC | |
| Nicaragua | CLC/SDR | |

| | | |
|---|---|---|
| Nigeria | CLC | Fund |
| Norway | CLC/SDR/1992 | Fund/SDR/1992 |
| Oman | CLC/SDR/1992 | Fund/1992 |
| Panama | CLC | |
| Papua New Guinea | CLC | Fund |
| Peru | CLC/SDR | |
| Poland | CLC/SDR | Fund/SDR |
| Portugal | CLC/SDR | Fund/SDR |
| Qatar | CLC/SDR | Fund |
| Russian Federation | CLC/SDR | Fund/SDR |
| Saudi Arabia | CLC/SDR | |
| Senegal | CLC | |
| Seychelles | CLC | Fund |
| Sierra Leone | CLC | Fund |
| Singapore | CLC/SDR | |
| Slovenia | CLC | Fund |
| Solomon Islands | CLC (provisional) | |
| South Africa | CLC | |
| Spain | CLC/SDR/1992 | Fund/SDR/1992 |
| Sri Lanka | CLC | Fund |
| St Kitts and Nevis | CLC | Fund |
| St Vincent and Grenadines | CLC | |
| Sweden | CLC/SDR/1992 | Fund/SDR/1992 |
| Switzerland | CLC/SDR/1992 (from 4/7/97) | Fund/1992 (from 4/7/97) |
| Syrian Arab Republic | CLC | Fund |
| Tonga | CLC | Fund |
| Tunisia | CLC | Fund |
| Tuvalu | CLC | Fund |
| United Arab Emirates | CLC/SDR | Fund |
| United Kingdom | CLC/SDR/1992 | Fund/SDR/1992 |
| Vanuatu | CLC/SDR | Fund/SDR |
| Venezuela | CLC/SDR | Fund/SDR |
| Yemen | CLC/SDR | |
| Yugoslavia | CLC | Fund |

NOTES:

1. Parties as at December 1996. Details of current parties held by International Maritime Organization, London. For further information concerning the parties to this Convention, including reservations, see *The Ratification of Maritime Conventions*, produced by the Institute of Maritime Law.

2. The 1976 SDR Protocol to the Fund Convention came into force on 22 November 1994. Prior to that the Fund Assembly, by a resolution of November 1978, laid down a conversion rate of 15 francs to 1 SDR and, by a resolution of November 1987, amended the Fund limitation figures to show both gold francs and SDR.

3. United Kingdom ratification extended to Anguilla, Belize, Bermuda, British Indian Ocean Territory, British Virgin Islands, Cayman Islands, Falkland Islands and Dependencies, Gibraltar, Gilbert Islands, Guernsey, Hong Kong, Isle of Man, Jersey, Montserrat, Pitcairn, St Helena and Dependencies, Soloman Islands, Turks and Caicos Islands, Tuvalu and the UK Sovereign Base Areas of Akrotiri and Dhekelia in Cyprus.

4. The 1992 Protocols to the CLC and the Fund Convention came into force on 30 May 1996.

# INDEX

## Index